Diversity-Sensitive Personality Assessment

Diversity-Sensitive Personality Assessment is a comprehensive guide for clinicians to consider how various aspects of client diversity—ethnicity, gender, sexual orientation, age, nationality, religion, regionalism, socioeconomic status, and disability status—can impact assessment results, interpretation, and feedback. Chapters co-written by leading experts in the fields of diversity and personality assessment examine the influence of clinician, client, interpersonal, and professional factors within the assessment context. This richly informed and clinically useful volume encourages clinicians to delve into the complex ways in which individuals' personal characteristics, backgrounds, and viewpoints intersect. This book fills an important gap in the personality assessment literature and is an essential resource for clinicians looking to move beyond surface-level understandings of diversity in assessment.

Steven R. Smith, Ph.D., is Associate Professor in the Department of Counseling, Clinical, and School Psychology at the University of California, Santa Barbara. His clinical, research, and teaching interests include personality assessment, the psychology of men and boys, and the psychological needs of athletes.

Radhika Krishnamurthy, Psy.D., ABAP, is Professor of Clinical Psychology at the Florida Institute of Technology. She has co-authored two books on assessment using the MMPI-A, as well as several book chapters and journal articles on psychological assessment.

Diversity-Sensitive Personality Assessment

Edited by
Steven R. Smith and
Radhika Krishnamurthy

NEW YORK AND LONDON

First published 2018
by Routledge
711 Third Avenue, New York, NY 10017

and by Routledge
2 Park Square, Milton Park, Abingdon, Oxon, OX14 4RN

Routledge is an imprint of the Taylor & Francis Group, an informa business

Library of Congress Cataloging-in-Publication Data
Names: Smith, Steven R., 1972- editor. | Krishnamurthy, Radhika, editor.
Title: Diversity-sensitive personality assessment / Steven R. Smith and Radhika Krishnamurthy, editors.
Description: New York, NY : Routledge, 2018.
Identifiers: LCCN 2017055779 (print) | LCCN 2017058640 (ebook) | ISBN 9780203551578 (eBook) | ISBN 9780415823401 (hardback) | ISBN 9780415823418 (pbk.)
Subjects: LCSH: Personality assessment. | Personality and culture. | Ethnopsychology.
Classification: LCC BF698.4 (ebook) | LCC BF698.4 .D58 2018 (print) | DDC 155.2/8—dc23
LC record available at https://lccn.loc.gov/2017055779

ISBN: 978-0-415-82340-1 (hbk)
ISBN: 978-0-415-82341-8 (pbk)
ISBN: 978-0-203-55157-8 (ebk)

Typeset in Minion
by Keystroke, Neville Lodge, Tettenhall, Wolverhampton

Dedication

For my awesome graduate students, from whom I have learned much. –SRS

To the diverse people who enrich my personal and professional life. –RK

Contents

Contributors

Tania Abouezzeddine, Ph.D. is a member of the Rosemead School of Psychology Faculty at Biola University. Her research interests are in the areas of trauma and resilience as well as cultural differences in the areas of coping, social support, and identity. In addition, Dr. Abouezzeddine is a practicing pediatric clinical neuropsychologist and is interested in studying the administrative integrity and diagnostic accuracy of cognitive assessment among culturally diverse populations.

Vedant Agrawal is a third year student in the clinical psychology Ph.D. program at Palo Alto University. His clinical and research interests include ethnic minority issues, depression, trauma, and mechanisms of change in clinical psychotherapy.

Louise Baca, Ph.D. is a Professor of Clinical Psychology and the Associate Director of Clinical Training at the Arizona School of Professional Psychology. Her clinical work, consultation, and research work have all been approached with a focus on diversity and social justice.

Matthew R. Baity, Ph.D. is a Professor and Program Director of the Clinical Psychology Psy.D. Program in the California School of Professional Psychology at Alliant International University's Sacramento Campus. His clinical and research interests are in psychological assessment, doctoral clinical training issues, and severe mental illness.

Virginia Brabender, Ph.D., ABPP, is a member of the faculty of Widener University's Institute for Graduate Clinical Psychology. Her clinical and scholarly interests include personality assessment, group psychotherapy, and professional ethics.

Susan Broyles, M.A. is a doctoral candidate in Counseling Psychology at the University of Texas at Austin. Her research interests include perceptions of domestic violence survivors, racial attitudes, victim-blaming attitudes, and the belief in a just world.

Theodore R. Burnes, Ph.D. is a psychologist in the Division of Student Affairs at the University of California, Irvine. His professional interests include LGBTQI mental health and wellness, teaching and education in health service psychology, sex-positivity and sexual expression, and young adult development.

Clark D. Campbell, Ph.D. is the Dean of Rosemead School of Psychology at Biola University. His clinical and research interests are in integrative psychotherapy and the integration of psychology and theology.

Collette Chapman-Hilliard, Ph.D. is a member of the faculty in Counseling and Human Development Services at the University of Georgia. Her research and clinical interests are related to racial and ethnic minority psychology, culture-centered measurement, and social justice issues.

Joyce Chu, Ph.D. is an Associate Professor in Clinical Psychology at Palo Alto University. Her professional interests are in ethnic minority mental health, community mental health, and suicide in diverse underserved populations.

David M. Cimbora, Ph.D. is the Associate Dean of Doctoral Programs at Rosemead School of Psychology at Biola University. He has served on faculty at Biola since 1997. His research interests involve clinical training, forensic populations, and multicultural issues.

Sarah Comunale, Ph.D. is a clinical psychologist in private practice in Denver, Colorado. Her clinical interests include learning disabilities, ADHD, psychological assessment, parenting issues, and social-emotional issues. She also does clinical consultation for the Denver District Attorney's Office Juvenile Diversion Program.

Merith Cosden, Ph.D. is Professor Emeritus from the Department of Counseling, Clinical, and School Psychology at the University of California Santa Barbara. For over 30 years she served as a faculty member, Chair of the Department, and Acting Dean of the Gevirtz Graduate School of Education. She has studied the social and psychological impact of learning disabilities, and the impact of trauma on clients with substance abuse problems and their treatment providers.

Aaron Estrada, Ph.D. is a member of the faculties of the Psychology and Child Development Department at California Polytechnic State University, San Luis Obispo. His clinical and research interests are in personality assessment, diversity considerations in applied psychology, affective disorders, and clinical training and supervision.

Peter C. Hill, Ph.D. is Professor of Psychology at Rosemead School of Psychology, Biola University. Dr. Hill's research interests focus on four major areas in the psychology of religion and spirituality: (1) positive psychological virtues such as humility and forgiveness, (2) religious/spiritual measurement, (3) religious fundamentalism, and (4) the role of affect in religious and spiritual experience.

Alexander L. Hsieh, Ph.D. is a member of the faculties of the California School of Professional Psychology, and the Couple and Family Therapy Department at Alliant International University in Sacramento. His clinical and research interests are in cultural competency, minority issues, couples and families in therapy, and adolescent internalized issues.

Stacey Jackson, Ph.D. is an Assistant Professor of Psychology at the University of Wisconsin-Eau Claire. Her scholarship falls within the broad category of African American well-being. More specifically, she is interested in the relationship between racism on African American mental health and functioning within academic institutions.

Radhika Krishnamurthy, Psy.D., ABAP is a Professor of Clinical Psychology at Florida Institute of Technology and a licensed psychologist in Florida. She is a diplomate of the American Board of Assessment Psychology and fellow of the Society for Personality Assessment and the American Psychological Association. She was 2011–2013 President of the Society for Personality Assessment and 2008 President of Section IX, Assessment Psychology, of the American Psychological Association's Division 12. She serves on the editorial boards of the journals *Assessment*, *Journal of Personality Assessment*, *Psychological Assessment*, and

European Journal of Psychological Assessment. She has co-authored two MMPI-A books and several book chapters and journal articles on psychological assessment.

Lindsey Liles, M.A. is a doctoral candidate in the Department of Counseling, Clinical, and School Psychology at UC-Santa Barbara. She is currently fulfilling her internship requirement at the Carl T. Haden VA Medical Center in Phoenix, AZ. Her clinical and research interests include military identity, post-deployment reintegration, combat trauma, PTSD, and psychological flexibility.

Kathleen A. Malloy, Ph.D. was a faculty member at the School of Professional Psychology at Wright State University for 27 years and is currently Professor Emeritus. Her areas of scholarship include intimate partner violence and diversity training.

Hale Martin, Ph.D. is Clinical Professor in the Graduate School of Professional Psychology at the University of Denver. He is also a member of the Therapeutic Assessment Institute. He has a private practice where he practices therapeutic assessment.

Shannon McClain, Ph.D. is an Assistant Professor of Counseling Psychology at Towson University. Her research examines psychosocial factors impacting the academic achievement and mental health of racial-ethnic minority students.

Lamisha Syeda Muquit, M.S. is a doctoral candidate in the Diversity and Community Mental Health emphasis in Palo Alto University's Clinical Psychology Ph.D. program. Her clinical and research interests are in stigma related to mental health, ethnic minorities, addiction, and serious mental illness.

Hadas Pade, Psy.D. is a core faculty member of the Department of Clinical Psychology at CSPP-Alliant SF. Her clinical and research interests are in psychological assessment, developmental pathways to juvenile delinquency, and assessment teaching and supervision.

Claudia Porras Pyland, Ph.D. is an Assistant Professor at Texas Woman's University. Her clinical and research interests are in objective and projective personality assessment, intimate partner violence, and diverse college student development.

Verónica Portillo Reyes, Ph.D. is a Professor of Psychology at Universidad Autónoma de Ciudad Juárez. Her focus is on neuropsychological assessment of children and health psychology. She also has a clinical practice where she sees mostly children with developmental disorders.

Antonio E. Puente, Ph.D. is Professor of Psychology at the University of North Carolina Wilmington and has a private practice in clinical neuropsychology. He was the 2017 President of the American Psychological Association.

Gargi Roysircar, Ed.D., is the Founding Director of the Antioch Multicultural Center for Research and Practice at Antioch University New England and Professor of Clinical Psychology. She conducts research on disaster mental health in national and international settings, the effects of acculturation and enculturation on immigrant adjustments, multicultural competencies in practice and assessment, and training graduate students in culturally informed practice. She has authored 100 journal articles and chapters on these topics. Roysircar served on the APA Task Force for Re-envisioning the Multicultural Guidelines for the 21st Century, adopted by APA in August 2017.

Alissa Sherry, Ph.D. is the CEO of Legal Consensus, PLLC and past Associate Professor at the University of Texas at Austin. Her clinical and research interests are in forensic assessment, social justice, and attachment.

Steven R. Smith, Ph.D. is a member of the faculties of the Department of Counseling, Clinical, and School Psychology and the College of Creative Studies at UC-Santa Barbara. His clinical and research interests are in personality assessment, clinical sport psychology, and masculinity issues.

Sally D. Stabb is a Professor of Counseling Psychology and doctoral Training Director in the Department of Psychology and Philosophy at Texas Woman's University. Her scholarly, clinical, and teaching interests are in multiculturalism, training, qualitative research methods, gender and emotion, and context-sensitive approaches to psychotherapy.

Samantha M. Swanson, M.A. is a student at Alliant International University-California School of Professional Psychology in Sacramento, CA. Her research interests are in various domains of psychological assessment and her clinical interests lie in working with severe mental illness.

Jed Yalof, Psy.D. is Professor and Chair of the Department of Psychology and Counseling at Immaculata University, and Director of the Psy.D. program in Clinical Psychology. He is board certified in school neuropsychology, clinical psychology, assessment psychology, and adult psychoanalysis, and is a Training and Supervising Analyst at the Psychoanalytic Center of Philadelphia.

Foreword

As psychologists and psychology students, we are aware that the field of psychology is grappling with shifting demographics, increasing globalization, and an acknowledgment of the importance of human diversity. Countless books and articles have been written that explore the importance of diversity factors in psychotherapy and counseling, education, and even problem-solving and cognitive processing. We would argue, however, that the field of personality assessment has lagged somewhat behind. We give credit to Dr. Richard Dana (1992, 2005) for starting the dialogue about diversity in personality assessment, but with this volume we hope to take the discussion even further.

At the outset, we wanted to approach human diversity in as broad a manner as possible. Too often, discussions of diversity are limited only to race and ethnicity and may not attend to differences in age, nationality, disability status, or religion, for example. Also, many texts provide somewhat cookie-cutter and stereotypical perspectives of different groups. We hoped to sidestep both of these issues by covering a wide array of human factors and do so in as broad a way as possible so that assessment clinicians can integrate and consider all aspects of their client's identity.

We choose to present this work in four sections: Clinician Contexts, Client Contexts, Interpersonal Contexts, and Professional Contexts. In the opening chapter in Clinician Contexts, Baca and Smith call upon clinicians to examine their self-identifiers, their biases, and their worldviews as they might impact the clinical exchange. All assessment work begins with the clinician and clinical competency is an ongoing goal that should be central to the work. It is for this reason that we began the text there.

In the section on Client Contexts, we explore many of the ways that clients can define aspects of their identity. We introduce this section through two chapters by Cimbora and Krishnamurthy on ways to address client definitions and contexts through careful inquiry. This is followed by chapters on ethnicity (Chu, Muquit, Agrawal, & Krishnamurthy), gender (Malloy & Krishnamurthy), sexual and gender orientation (Burnes & Smith), religion (Abouezzeddine, Hill, Campbell, & Smith), disability (Cosden, Comunale, Liles, & Smith), nationality (Roysircar & Krishnamurthy), regionalism (McClain, Chapman-Hilliard, & Smith), age (Portillo Reyes, Krishnamurthy, & Puente), and socioeconomic status (Porras Pyland, Stabb, & Smith). Inherent in this work is the idea of intersectionality. That is, for all of us and all of our clients, we have aspects of our identity that may be more or less salient depending on our setting and life circumstances. For example, a homosexual Asian-American woman may find herself in a setting where her ethnicity is shared with others, but her sexual orientation sets her apart. Or she may find herself in a community that is supportive of her sexual orientation, but she is the only ethnic minority. Context matters, and the circumstances of our lives help determine which aspects of our identity feel the most relevant. We hope that this text can be used in an additive way to provide clinicians with the tools to examine all aspects of a client's identity and life experiences as reflected in test scores.

Recalling that psychological assessment is an interpersonal process, in the section on Interpersonal Contexts, we explore the contextual and situational variables that are salient during the assessment exchange. Chapter authors explore issues of setting, and power dynamics (Baity, Hsieh, & Swanson; Estrada), therapeutic models of assessment (Martin), and models of culturally-responsive assessment (Pade). Our authors remind us of the Gestalt of the assessment that is more than merely the interplay between a clinician and a client.

Finally, we examine Professional Contexts that might be relevant to your professional activities, growth, and development. From report writing (Chapman-Hilliard, McClain, Sherry, Broyles, & Jackson), to ethics (Brabender), and supervision (Yalof), these chapters will provide you tools, means of exploration, and knowledge about growing as a professional and providing the most competent care. Our concluding chapter on evidence-based practice discusses how diversity-sensitive assessment can and should be guided by a confluence of research evidence and professional experience.

The most important aspect of this book are the wonderful authors who have contributed their time and expertise. Rather than limiting the authorship to experts in personality assessment, we sought authors who were experts in diversity factors. We wanted each chapter to be a deep dive into the clinical and social research on each topic so that you can fully appreciate the complexity of these issues. For many of the chapters, we contributed information on how personality assessment administration, scoring, and even feedback might be impacted by a client's unique presentation. We hope that the melding of experts in diversity with experts in personality assessment allows for a more complex and informed analysis.

We have several people to thank for their assistance with this project. Our thanks to graduate students Jovany Avendano at Florida Institute of Technology and John W. Capps at the University of Texas, El Paso for their timely aid with the finishing touches. We appreciate the support from our academic department heads in bringing this work to fruition. Most of all, we are grateful for the help and patience of our Routledge editors, George Zimmar and Lillian Rand, and editorial assistant Jamie Magyar, as none of this would have been possible without their support. This project has taken longer than any of us would have predicted, and they have stood by us through this long journey. We think that the product is worth the wait.

References

Dana, R.H. (2005). *Multicultural assessment: Principles, applications, and examples*. New York: Routledge.

Dana, R.H. (1992). *Multicultural assessment: Perspectives for professional psychology*. San Antonio: Pearson.

PART I

Clinician Contexts

CHAPTER 1

The Role of Self-Reflection and Self-Assessment in the Psychological Assessment Process

Louise Baca and Steven R. Smith

No matter the reason, we are often uncomfortable when we make ourselves vulnerable to self-examination. This is particularly true for issues related to diversity because of the historical, personal, and social taboos around these topics. Treading into these waters takes courage, and an ability to tolerate both discomfort and ignorance. However, if we wish to be competent clinicians who are sensitive to the needs of the clients we serve, self-evaluation must be our first (and often-repeated) step. The importance of examining one's own value structure, biases, and social/cultural contexts cannot be overstated (Liang, Tummala-Narra, & West, 2011). Sensitivity to diversity issues requires that we, as clinicians, promote and embody the principles of life-long learning and reflective practice. This chapter asks you to be open to a process of challenging assumptions, to be open to a process of deliberate self-monitoring, and open to a process of asking for feedback from a trusted colleague or professional consultant. These exercises will allow you to carefully consider your challenges, strengths, and "gray areas" in assessing those who might be different from you or from the cultural norm.

There is guidance from the American Psychological Association's *Guidelines on Multicultural Education, Training, Research, Practice and Organizational Change* (APA, 2003) and *Guidelines for Providers of Psychological Services to Ethnic, Linguistic, and Culturally Diverse Clients* (APA, 1990) that implores psychologists to recognize that they might hold detrimental attitudes and beliefs that can influence their perceptions of, and interactions with, individuals who differ from them culturally, racially, and ethnically. As psychologists, we are also asked to strive to apply culturally appropriate skills in clinical and other applied psychological practices (APA, 2003). Effective clinical or counseling work with diverse individuals requires an understanding of the client's life experiences and historical oppression *before* selecting culturally appropriate assessment tools and recommending a course of treatment. In order to be ethical and competent, psychologists' personal self-reflection is an integral part of the assessment process.

Metacognition, or thinking about thinking, is daunting but necessary if we are to challenge our personal assumptions and biases so as to inform decisions or actions related to assessment. The monitoring of thoughts and feelings actively with persistent and careful consideration is the basis for self-reflection (Sheikh, Milne, & MacGregor, 2007). The dominant culture has the power and privilege to prioritize "action" over "reflection." In clinical work and training, we focus on conceptualization, treatment planning, and administration of assessment batteries and evaluation of treatment progress as the usual grist for the mill of our psychological work. However, few studies have examined the role of self-exploration and self-reflection on assessment-related decisions as part of the psychological tool kit. "If I only have a hammer then everything looks like a nail" is an unfortunate, but common metaphor that should direct us to move toward a broader and deeper understanding of the role of self-reflection in performing psychological assessment.

Challenging Assumptions

Traditional forms of psychological assessment are filled with assumptions that might be inappropriate or antagonistic to many culturally diverse groups (Sue & Sue, 2013). Awareness of biases and assumptions related to attitudes that are class-bound or culture-bound are often the "blind spots" that are associated with the "assumptive worlds" of both trainees and supervisors. Many supervisors often assume that trainees are as ignorant as they are in relation to multicultural competency. Trainees are then put in a difficult position of recognizing when the "worldview" of the supervisor is being imposed upon them as well as their clients. Should trainees risk upsetting the delicate power imbalance that leads to letters for internship by informing their supervisor that there are other perspectives to consider when approaching psychological assessment? Who is responsible for advocating for both trainees and their diverse clients?

As Fontes (2008) cautions, "We must also practice cultural humility, striving for habits of self-reflection and self-critique that safeguard us from imposing our values on others" (p. 306). But assumptions related to interpreting the meaning of both verbal and non-verbal communication styles of diverse groups are often unchallenged due to a hierarchical system of authority that expects conformity within the workplace or training environment. Assumptions related to the appropriateness of standardized testing or interpretation of performance-based measures or "spikes" on certain scales must all be explored to understand the diversity context of all parties involved in the assessment process. Students and their clients are hesitant to counter stereotypes by those who use their preconceived notions related to *social rhythms* as a basis for diagnosis and treatment. The complexity related to ethnicity alone is staggering as we talk with beautiful brown children who are a blend of several ethnicities and family lifestyles. Thus, assumptions and stereotypes must be challenged constantly and we have to remind each other that we will not be of service to each other unless we can be honest about how often our assumptions are wrong. We must value honesty and openness above "being right" in order to achieve this first step of self-reflection, which is acknowledging that the more we assume we know, the more we know we have a lot to learn.

Creating a flexible structure for *always* examining our assumptions about our work might be possible if we agree that we must acknowledge that our assumptions often get us into trouble because our assumptions about each other and about our clients are often wrong. *Who* is this person and who are her people? *Where* does she come from? *What* are the historical, transgenerational *soulwounds* of trauma that her people have endured (Duran & Duran, 1995)? *Why* is she here with me now? *How* can I truly listen so as to hear what matters? How can *we* work together to be open to our unique relationship with each other? These questions structure the kind of relationship that, when built on trust and authenticity, often allows us to explore our assumptions together and correct one another as we proceed in the assessment process. Can we listen *stereophonically*, on at least two levels of meaning (one manifest and the other more symbolic or metaphorical)? Can we see both the verbal and the non-verbal communication (the dance) that we do together? Are we checking with our client to make sure that we have truly achieved understanding? Rubin (2008) suggests that excellent listening involves listening deeply with concentration (not wandering into criticisms of you, anticipation of the future, regrets of the past) and equanimity (total acceptance). Why is it easier to achieve this deep listening with some clients rather than others?

When a psychologist experiences great doubt or when counter-transference is an obstruction to the assessment process then, supervision and consultation are the most ethical and practical ways to back up and challenge our initial assumptions. Distortions and illusions are commonplace among mere mortals, which includes those of us who are aware that we are somehow "not getting it" or if we feel "distant and dismissive" with some clients in need of a thorough assessment. The help from a trusted colleague, supervisor, or professional consultant is critical (Falender & Shafranske, 2008). Often the process of sharing assumptions and having these assumptions challenged by a different perspective is the best way to gain clarity and some insight regarding our patterns of connection with others. The critical questions might be the following: "Who do I typically connect with easily?" and "Who are the individuals that I struggle most to understand?" These questions ideally are those we ask ourselves and our trusted colleagues to help us with, in order to discern patterns in our clinical and other interpersonal relationships. Sometimes, we learn that it is *similarity* rather than *difference* that leads us to make assumptions and make mistakes in our assessment work. These similarities could be a function of all the diversity variables we can think of or unique interactions of diversity variables that are not easily discerned. Ethnicity can be obscured by names taken in marriage, level of acculturation, phenotype, and English dominance. Factors such as socioeconomic status can be subtle but conveyed by the type of shoes worn, level of education, and location of residence (Liu, Soleck, Hopps, Dunston, & Pickett, 2004).

Avoidant behavior in a clinical assessment can be due to an unexamined degree of homophobia or discomfort with sexuality. Personal discomfort can be ignored by the clinician and can create the environment for unexamined assumptions regarding affectional or sexual orientation. We might still dichotomize sexuality along with gender and make assumptions based upon dress, speech patterns or haircuts and yet, we might continue to be reluctant to check out what could be wrong assumptions. Are we relying on demographic information on forms to inform our clinical assessment rather than being actively engaged in understanding our clients and the bio-psycho-social contexts of their lives? Who is close and trusted enough for us to say, "What am I missing here?" or "Why am I struggling with understanding this person?" It is hard to self-reflect and realize that we might have internalized some socialization that is truly misogynous and derogatory with regard to feminine mannerisms, voice inflection, and worldviews.

Probably our greatest challenge regarding assumptions is taking the time to challenge our routine patterns of assessment and working with one another. The role of self-reflection might never be given the time it deserves to keep us honest with ourselves and others. We have research that leads us to begin to prioritize the self-reflection and self-correction needed to meet supervision and diversity competencies throughout the developmental stages of professional development (Rings, Genuchi, Hall, Angelo, & Cornish, 2009; Yabusaki, 2010). However, even the scholarly literature in psychology is sparse when we look for models of diversity-informed health, resilience, growth, and development (Reich, Zautra, & Hall, 2010). Are we taught how to see each other's strengths? Are we taught methods of extending compassion toward ourselves and in our work with the colleagues and clients we work with regularly? We can pathologize our clients, ourselves, and our co-workers in a manner that creates reticence to consult and receive feedback. We can feel guilty and be chastised for taking time to self-reflect. We are thus reluctant to ask for help in challenging our assumptions about each other and the clients we need to assess. Do the theories we use to guide our clinical work encourage us to self-reflect and self-correct? What theories guide us toward consultation and careful consideration of use of the power inherent in our role in the assessment process? Do we understand why we choose the theoretical conceptualizations we use to understand ourselves and our clients?

Wachtel (2010) discusses problematic assumptions in the pursuit of evidence-based practice. Tummala-Narra (2013) has argued that certain theoretical perspectives have privileged certain contexts of individual and social change with differences noted in the assumptions of community psychology. This is in contrast to traditional psychoanalysis (e.g. Kaufmann, 2003) with its tendency to focus primarily on internal, rather than community-level change. Such divergence in theoretical assumptions regarding change and the process of change obviously impacts our own personal assumptions and professional choices. How often do we explore the interaction of the personal assumptive base with that of what might be cherished theoretical assumptions? How does an interaction of such assumptions influence professional identity? Does social mirroring between ourselves, our professors, supervisors, and colleagues interact with our own methods of self-reflection or lack thereof?

Asking for Feedback

It always feels risky to ask for feedback. We open ourselves to hearing ideas or judgments that at first appear wrong or invalid, or even hurtful. That is why the relationship of the person from whom we seek feedback should ideally be safe, nurturing, and honest. We must be vulnerable and open when we ask for feedback. This process should not be an intellectual critique alone, but an opportunity to humbly feel the emotions that can range from mild confusion to outright sorrow and rage. Trusting the person or people whom we ask for feedback is a necessary precondition for learning more about our personal "blind spots." The emotional competency for clinical work demands that we balance our awareness of our own worldview with that of our client(s) and the cost of *not* doing this delicate balancing act can be costly (Pope & Vasquez, 2011). A recent review of studies on interpersonal bias and interracial distrust reveals that contemporary racism might be outside of individual awareness, yet nevertheless, be a subtle, unintentional factor in creating a race-based, self-fulfilling prophecy (Dovidio, Gaertner, Kakakamin, & Hodson, 2002).

Microaggressions or microinvalidations can stem from unexplored or uninformed reactions to a client's historical and current oppression. We should not be hesitant to ask for help understanding these ruptures in empathy or the alliance. Such help can be crucial in the repairing of a healing alliance and recognizing that all types of cultural oppression are not interchangeable (Comas-Díaz, 2012). Other breaks in the therapeutic alliance, including premature termination, need to be explored honestly and the feedback from a trusted colleague, consultant, or supervisor is an essential element in developing diversity competence. With such help, it might be possible to repair the therapeutic relationship. However, without help with the subtle and more overt breaks in the relationship, there can be a delay in the development of a psychologist's ability to display *radical empathy* (Koss-Chioino, 2006).

Feedback will help the psychologist avoid common missteps identified by Comas-Díaz (2012) such as:

- *not* using the client's vocabulary in the therapeutic dialogue;
- *not* displaying flexibility in shifting roles such as advisor, advocate, change agent, elder, expert of the heart, healer, guide, extended member of the family;
- *not* recognizing when *cultural fatigue* triggers missed empathic opportunities.

Openness to Deliberate Self-Monitoring

The influence of multicultural psychology is evident in research, practice, and training guidelines (APA, 2003; Sue & Sue, 2013; Sue, 2001; Vasquez, 2007). Some authors have underscored the neglect of ethnic minority and other diverse groups by evidence-based researchers and clinicians (Sue et al., 2006). With this in mind, what are we to assume we know about change and the need for self-reflection in the process of change? Particularly in regard to assessment, we must consider the important questions asked by Fontes (2008):

- Do we understand how our questions and our style of questioning reflect who we are as people?

- Do we express not only skillful professionalism but also care and respect?
- Do we know how our knowledge or lack of knowledge of a given diverse background affects the assessment process?

How do we know that our clinical interviewing skills or any battery of tests actually will lead to a fair, respectful, and accurate assessment? How do we put in place the deliberate self-monitoring needed to truly understand our personal strengths and weaknesses? Remembering that our work happens in the context of a trusting relationship, within a social context, should prompt us to schedule time for a deliberate self-monitoring of our work. Do we schedule this time carefully? How do we create the best atmosphere for self-monitoring? What tools can help us with this process?

We encourage the reader to schedule consistent self-monitoring time at the end of every work day. This deliberate self-monitoring time can happen by personal journaling, reviewing the day's high points and low points, or review of a checklist of patterns that you are observing and monitoring for yourself prior to consultation. Is the same client, or type of client, impacting you in a positive or negative manner? Do you see yourself struggling or excelling with some clients and not others? Clearly, it is easy to let self-monitoring slip with "too much already" or simply feeling like there is "nothing major coming to my attention." So, we are warned by Pope and Vasquez (2011), "We can balance our loyalty to our judgments if we search relentlessly for facts that do not fit, listen openly to those who disagree, and constantly ask ourselves what the other possibilities are" (p. 18). If we do less than this, we put our clients and our own professional growth in jeopardy.

Wondering out loud can be a wonderful form of self-monitoring and the framework of "curiosity or wondering" can actually take some of the sting from the bite of reality. Look for the patterns related to your working relationships. Are some of the "tough spots" found in your family of origin or in your personal relationships? Are some of the stresses in your personal life or life history coloring how you see certain clients or clinical situations? When was the last time you did a values clarification exercise for yourself or had a "heart to heart" discussion related to your worries, fears, or concerns? Do you see a pattern of neglecting yourself or neglecting those most like you or different from you? What are the risks of leaving all of these patterns unexplored? When are you most vulnerable to neglecting yourself or others? Getting out of the professional "comfort zone" is a sign that you are learning and our goal is life-long learning and refinement. Personal journaling and reflection can also provide some clarity. This is a great profession to grow old in as long as the emphasis is on "growing." We all need to remain students at heart.

Lewis, Virden, Hutchings, and Bhargava (2011) have outlined a method to teach students how to integrate reflective practice into the development of competencies in professional psychology. What is most exciting about their work is the systematic attempt to assess the concept of "reflection-in-action" as described by Schon's (1987) paradigm and the work of Erlandson and Beach (2008). Although a range of ability to self-reflect is an important competency, it has been suggested that deficits in this area can compromise healthy human maturity and development (Dimaggio, Vanheule, Lysaker, Carcione, & Nicolo, 2009).

Because self-reflection seems to lie along a developmental arc, a developmental framework might be the best way to conceptualize the aspects of self-reflection that are most critical in the assessment of ourselves and others. The following self-reflection exercises might appear to be simple questions. However, these questions are foundational pieces of preparing students for the *artistry* of self-reflection necessary for competent practice (Lewis et al., 2011; Schon, 1987). Methods for promoting self-reflection can be as structured because the actual competency-based methods provided in a training program or such methods can be cultivated and woven into a life-long learning approach. Below is a series of exercises designed to promote the self-reflection process.

Exercises for Self-Reflection

Comas-Díaz (2012) provided a method of self-reflection that is particularly important when working in a cross-cultural context. The *cultural genogram* she suggests places the therapist (and, we would add, assessor) as well as the client within their collective contexts. Among other variables, cultural genograms provide culture-specific information such as:

- activities of daily life;
- birth, marriage, death, and developmental milestones;
- meaning of cultural similarities and difference;
- communication style;
- cultural-racial ethnic-identity development;
- soul wounds;
- experience with oppression and privilege;
- internalization of oppression and privilege;
- orientation to time;
- spirituality and faith.

Comas-Díaz (2012) sees this exercise as both an assessment and treatment instrument where areas of overlap between the therapist and the client are within conscious awareness and are potent areas for self-reflection and self-correction. Comas-Díaz (2012) also recommends a *power differential analysis* (p. 132) that not only enhances a clinician's "cultural credibility" but clearly promotes the importance and necessity of self-reflection. A *power differential analysis* is conducted by examining closely the areas of overlap for the clinician and the client related to sources of oppression and sources of privilege. Some examples of sources of oppression and privilege identified by Comas-Díaz (2012) include the following:

Sources of oppression:

- race and ethnicity;
- socioeconomic status;

- skin color (phenotype);
- gender—sexual orientation;
- religion/spirituality;
- physical health issues;
- employment status;
- age;
- marital status;
- microaggressions.

Sources of privilege:

- all of the above; and
- intelligence;
- talents;
- language.

The *power differential analysis* (Comas-Díaz, 2012) will likely have dimensions that can be added to these lists of sources of oppression and sources of privilege. Nonetheless, it is the critical examination of both points on a continuum for you and your clients that will likely be illuminating and helpful in developing and enhancing multicultural clinical presence and competency.

Another model uses broad questions to get at the delicate balance between clinicians' self-assessment and assessment of diverse clients. Using an Awareness, Skill, Knowledge, Encounters, and Desire Method for ongoing cultural self-assessment, Campinha-Bacote (2002) asks the following questions:

1. Awareness: Am I aware of my biases?
2. Skill: Do I know how to conduct an effective multicultural assessment?
3. Knowledge: Do I know about the culture-specific information, ethnopsychopharmacology, and bicultural ecology?
4. Encounters: How many face-to-face encounters and interactions have I had with multicultural individuals?
5. Desire: Do I want to become culturally competent?

APA's (2003) multicultural guidelines recommend that we recognize when it is appropriate to adapt interventions to the cultural context of the client. Numerous recommendations for using empowerment as an important approach in multicultural care echo this ethical mandate (Cattaneo & Chapman, 2010; Comas-Díaz, 2012; Sue & Sue, 2013). Comas-Díaz (2012, p. 178) summarizes multicultural empowerment in the following points:

- Clients increase their access to resources.
- Clients develop options to exercise choice.
- Clients are affirmed in their cultural strengths.
- Clients strengthen their support systems.
- Clients are helped by promoting their cultural identity development.

- Clients are aided in fostering self-healing.
- Clients develop their own critical consciousness.
- Clients learn to overcome their own internalized oppression.
- Clients are motivated to improve individual and collective self-esteem.
- Clients are encouraged to engage in transformative actions.

Freire and Macedo (2000) note that oppression robs the oppressed of the opportunity to develop *critical consciousness*, or the ability to understand the larger framework of sociopolitical realities in which they live. Therefore, they describe the necessity of engaging in a dialogue and critical reflection of the client's issues against the backdrop of sociopolitical realities. The interaction of our "issues" as the clinician and those of our clients is incredibly complex. They are so complex that beginning clinicians might feel overwhelmed when they are merely trying to learn basic helping skills. However, it is important to begin to understand this complexity; therefore, the following areas of self-reflection are important to consider, ideally in the context of dialogue with a trusted colleague or supervisor. The parallel with Erik Erikson's stages of development (1963) and extensions of Erikson's work by Evans (1979) are intentional, with a similar understanding that the struggles of each stage are not linear. In fact, the tasks of each stage reappear so that, once again, we can attempt to move toward resolution and continued growth and development in relation to clients, ourselves, our loved ones, and colleagues.

Exercises for self-reflective practice

The premise for these self-reflective practices is to work on personal identity development that includes a degree of self-knowledge and ability to establish rapport and relationships that, according to Norcross, Koocher, and Garofalo (2006) have been shown to account for most of the positive change in therapy. We believe that looking introspectively at our own self-reflective development across time and context might be highly illuminating. Therefore, we present this integrative model below.

A developmental model of self-reflective tasks

1. *Trust vs. mistrust.* Look at your patterns of creating trust with yourself and with others. How have you grown to trust your instincts, abilities, and skills? Have you had experience trusting those who are very different from you? Has this enriched your life? Have you had some scars along the way? Are you able to get to a place of genuine self-acceptance and genuine, unconditional acceptance of the other?

2. *Humility vs. pride/self-humiliation.* Look at your patterns of professionally "carrying yourself." Do you see a pattern of strengths as well as limitations in your relationships with others? Do you allow yourself to admit mistakes? Do you demonstrate respect for privacy and freedom in your relationships? Do you

allow yourself to be vulnerable and close to others emotionally, intellectually, physically? Are you compelled to *play a role* where you have the power and control rather than humbly being yourself with others? Are you truly genuine and intimate with anybody? Who do you go to when you need help?

3. *Self-betrayal (vices) vs. being true to oneself (virtues).* Look at your patterns of personal failings. Have you been honest with yourself? Have you been honest with others? Are you too hard on yourself, generally? Generally, are you too easy on yourself (e.g., typically finding ways to avoid feedback and self-reflection)?

4. *Responsibility vs. reckless irresponsibility.* Look at your patterns of doing what you say you will do with fidelity or loyalty. Are you reliable when performing tasks for the benefit of others? Do you help with concerns within and for your community? Do you take initiative to contribute to a greater good? Are you generally avoidant and/or overscheduled? Do you rarely have "time to breathe?" Do you create chaos in groups and/or discord with others? Do your clients often discontinue without notice? Are you doing harm?

5. *Commitment vs. dissipation.* Look at your patterns of commitment. Do you get "tired" or "bored" with some people and not others? Are you feeling scattered, uncentered, and generally unfocused in your work and relationships? Are you struggling to be fully present with other people? Are you taking time to replenish and rejuvenate yourself physically, emotionally, and spiritually?

6. *Integration vs. alienation/isolation.* Look at your patterns of interpersonal engagement. Where, when, and with whom do you become avoidant? Do you choose to not share or avoid feedback or counsel? Are you a loner? What is the state of your personal relationships? Are you weaving a tapestry of complexity and diversity in your relationships at work and at play?

7. *Tolerance vs. celebration.* Look at your patterns of energy use, judgment, moods, and expressions of connection. Do you "put up" with some people? Do you "bite your tongue" with some people? Do you find yourself using a tone that is patronizing or infantilizing with some people? Whose strengths do you celebrate? Who gets your warmth and affection? Do you delight in all of creation?

8. *Devotion (movement toward liberation) vs. hopelessness (cynicism).* Look at your patterns of making meaning out of "the good, the bad, and the ugly." Are you opening doors (literally and figuratively)? Do you recognize the importance and value of potential and growth in yourself and others? Are you "stuck" or feeling "silenced and angry?" Are you experiencing sadness and finding yourself saying things that are harsh, sarcastic, and cynical? Are you lonely and tired and struggling with "why?"

Ideally, these questions are part of critical conversations that you have with your colleagues, friends, and loved ones, or part of your daily journaling efforts.

Feedback from multiple sources can be exceptionally helpful, particularly when there is a convergence of observations. When several people observe that you "look tired" it might be an invitation to talk, rest, have fun, or get out of the building into nature. Good feedback has two major components. One component is validation and confirmation that the struggle is worthy and noble. A second component is confrontation. Ideally, the confrontation is gentle and the intention is clear and caring. Usually, the feedback is expressed as a worry about you displaying behaviors that might be destructive to yourself or others. This difficult dialogue requires tremendous honesty and fundamental trust. Discussions about the consequences of our actions and needs to be more faithful to our better selves are critically important to maintaining integrity in our work. We cannot set forth on destructive paths without being challenged if we have good colleagues who often are excellent friends and professional consultants.

Practice Using the Developmental Model of Self-Reflective Tasks

Vignette #1

A colleague approaches you to look at the standardized test results of an elderly, rural, Mexican American woman. She does not appear to have a thought disorder, however, the test results indicate a "spike" on this particular scale score. What questions do you need answered before you help with the interpretation of this standardized test scale score that is part of a larger battery of tests?

Based on your reaction to this request, what developmental stage of self-reflection is your colleague working from? What level of self-reflective tasks characterizes your response? How can you help each other? How much time and thought has really gone into this consultation? Who else needs to be brought into the conversation?

Vignette #2

A black female practicum student who has experienced microaggressions in her workplace begins a course of therapy at her practicum site with another woman of color. The therapeutic rapport was building rapidly until the clinician presumed that the client's sexual orientation was heterosexual. The client was offended and indirectly asserted that she has "never had a boyfriend but my girlfriend is supportive of me being here." How might you react to this moment in the therapeutic encounter?

Based on your reaction to this request, what developmental stage of self-reflection is your colleague working from? What level of self-reflective tasks characterizes your response? How can you help each other? How much time and thought has really gone into this consultation? Who else needs to be brought into the conversation?

Vignette #3

A young American Indian woman is in a doctoral program in clinical psychology. While learning to give a standardized test for children, she finds out that none of the American Indian sample used for norms was from the Southwestern part of the country she lives and works in. In fact, the sample used for generating norms was from the northeastern part of the USA and the norming sample were all children raised in an urban area. She is asked to assess a 10-year-old child on the rural reservation of her own tribe using this same standardized test. When she writes a draft of an assessment report for her supervisor, she hesitates in revealing to her older, Irish American supervisor her true thoughts about the testing protocol. What should she do? Who can she consult on such matters? If she brings her dilemma to you, how do you feel?

Based on your reaction to this request, what developmental stage of self-reflection is your colleague working from? What level of self-reflective tasks characterizes your response? How can you help each other? How much time and thought has really gone into this consultation? Who else needs to be brought into the conversation?

Vignette #4

Your supervisee is a Latina graduate student who grew up in a poor family; she is working with a well-off, middle-aged White man for an assessment related to a custody case. She notes that several validity scales on his self-report personality measure were elevated and seeks input on how to discuss this with him and his legal team.

Based on your reaction to this request, what developmental stage of self-reflection is your supervisee working from? What level of self-reflective tasks characterizes your response? How can you help each other? How much time and thought has really gone into this consultation? Who else needs to be brought into the conversation?

Moving Forward

There are many Western practitioners who are seeking training in Eastern or indigenous therapies, such as mindfulness techniques. The ability to more accurately understand concepts cross-culturally is positive, however, the ability to self-reflect and self-correct with the aid of trusted colleagues and friends cannot be over-emphasized. Right-brain and left-brain processes emphasize different skill sets. The left-brain approach will always be more cognitive and logical and the right-brain will emphasize the harmonious, intuitive, and holistic approaches to healing. Clinical judgment is critical in learning the "art" of psychological assessment, particularly with underserved or vulnerable populations. The need to be particularly clear about what you are doing and *why* you are doing it is a critical self-assessment competency. Clarity around self-assessment, particularly when doing cross-cultural work, has been called for by many scholars (Gielen, Draguns, & Fish, 2008; Fontes, 2008; Wachtel, 2011).

The self-reflection stage model, questions, exercises, and vignettes introduced here are designed to prompt the type of self-assessment and discussion needed to be diversity-competent and ethical in the process of conducting psychological assessment. The clinical interview, testing, test interpretation, and report writing involve many choice points. How each of us makes sense of data within a context of a professional relationship and within a cultural/diversity context is indeed complex. This complexity cannot be underestimated, and diversity variables are fluid and change. Even changes in ancient cultures are happening at a faster pace than ever before. Mastering such complexity cannot be sought in isolation. If true self-reflection and self-correction are to occur, then ideally this happens with a trusted colleague(s) who are honest, gentle, and invested in the life-long learning process that characterize diversity competency in assessment.

Self-Reflection and Cultural Competent Practice

Given the commitment and dedication and discipline necessary for self-reflection, how can we assess if this results in an increase in cultural competency and diversity competency more generally? That is, how do we know if our self-reflection actually yields more competent care? What are some of the knowledge, skills, and attitudes that should develop and improve as a result of the self-reflective activities described above?

Like too few universities, the faculty in the first author's academic department does all of their instruction of graduate coursework with diversity in the forefront to foster the development of culturally competent psychologists. We believe the faculty has a responsibility to provide students with a dynamic model of diversity discourse. The model is unique in that it provides the expectation and structure for faculty, staff, and students to embody diversity in day-to-day interactions through experiential sharing and "walking it like we talk it." As the model begins to take shape, we begin to answer the following question: What exactly do faculty members need to do in order to provide the community with culturally competent psychologists? Although individual faculty members teach the concept with complete academic freedom, we find commonality based upon our shared values. Some of the general values and developmental goals that have been established include the following:

- Faculty choose to define diversity broadly, thus including issues of all persons who have been historically disenfranchised.
- Faculty model and create a sensitivity to diversity concerns.
- Faculty help students develop an awareness of diversity issues for themselves and in the conceptualization of client, participant, and student concerns.
- Faculty inspire social justice and advocacy efforts on behalf of their diverse clients and students.
- Faculty highlight and help students integrate the clinically relevant aspects of diversity.

- Faculty model a diversity dialogue rather than diversity debates.
- Faculty insist on ongoing assessment and development in the area of diversity, recognizing that all faculty and students will progress in their development at differing rates and in differing ways.

Moreover, we have concluded that:

- This method promotes cultural competency.
- Formal and informal dialogues lay the foundation for ongoing curiosity, advocacy, action, and ongoing development.
- Diversity awareness and sensitivity increase overall professional competence.
- Faculty engage with students regularly for critical conversations and both faculty and students assess their level of diversity competency throughout using the following model (Baca, Pinnell, & Lewis, 2003):

A developmental model of diversity competency in graduate education:

Level 1—*Characterized* as:

- unaware;
- little to no exposure to diversity of any sort;
- little work and/or life experience;
- diversity dialogue has never happened;
- naive;
- cautious,

DEVELOPMENTAL TASKS:

- Increase awareness in some areas with experiential exercises and education.
- Go outside of "comfort zone."
- Begin recognizing the need to have diversity dialogue with others.
- Begin to understand privilege and power dynamics.

Level 2—*Characterized* as:

- some awareness of some types of diversity;
- some exposure to diversity;
- some work and/or life experience;
- some diversity dialogue often in stereotypic terms;
- nonjudgmental.

DEVELOPMENTAL TASKS:

- Increase awareness of most types of diversity areas with experiential exercises and education.
- Seek diversity opportunities actively.

- Have good diversity experience in work and/or life.
- Engage in diversity dialogue without preconceptions and with full acknowledgment of privilege and power dynamics.
- Be open to learning.

Level 3—*Characterized* as:

- sensitive to all types of diversity;
- surrounded by diversity;
- seeks diversity self-reflection and open to feedback;
- makes a life-long commitment to diversity growth and development.

Even if your graduate program does not provide this type of framework for you (or if you are not a student anymore), you can still periodically evaluate your clinical practice, research, and teaching activities using this developmental model and measures such as the one we present in the Appendix. As we noted above, self-reflection is the first step to finding your position along this developmental continuum. It is important that you are as honest with yourself as you can be (and recruit others who can help you with this). In fact, we suggest that you err on the conservative side in assessing your developmental level. That is, given that a lack of cultural competence often comes with "blind spots," we might be inclined to assume we are more competent than might be the case. Therefore, assume that there is always more work to do, more reflection to be had, and more areas where you need to grow. Remember, competence is not something that can ever be fully achieved; it is merely a commitment to growth and learning.

Assessing Organizational Competency in Diversity

As psychologists, we often work as part of a larger organization, be it a hospital, school, clinic, or treatment team. In such settings, treatment is often delivered by a multidisciplinary group where not all group members share an ethical code, theoretical understanding, or even a shared understanding of goals and objectives. In those situations, it is incumbent on the psychologist to speak to, and evaluate, the competency of the organization in matters related to diversity. As is the case with individual psychologists, organizations lie along a continuum of competency and efforts must be made for ongoing dialogue, reflection, and evaluation.

Sue & Sue (2013) provide a stage model for evaluating organizations on their diversity competence. Proceeding from Stage One (Destructiveness) to Stage Six (Proficiency), this model allows psychologists to reflect on the organizations or groups in which they work:

Stage One: Cultural Destructiveness

- The group has a history of oppression.
- The group relies on forced assimilation (e.g., must speak English or "pass" to survive).
- Unethical behavior is done under the guise of research or "helping."

Stage Two: Cultural Incapacity

- The organization is not intentionally destructive but remains biased.
- There are discriminatory hiring process and treatment processes.
- Subtle messages that diversity is not valued or welcome.
- Beliefs and treatment based on stereotypes.

Stage Three: Cultural Blindness

- Provision of services with the express philosophy that "everyone is treated the same."
- Belief that methods used for treatment of the dominant culture are universally acceptable and applicable.
- Power remains with a few White men.

Stage Four: Cultural Precompetence

- Ethnic minorities are hired if they don't "rock the boat."
- Ethnic minorities must work harder to be seen as "equal" and must continually educate the dominant group "gently."
- Microaggressions occur to minority professionals, trainees, and clients.
- Microinvalidations are subtle but occur regularly.

Stage Five: Cultural Competence

- Self-assessment regarding diversity is ongoing and documented.
- Careful attention is paid to the dynamics of difference (e.g., language, acculturation status, historical oppression) in regular meetings regarding professionals, trainees, and clients.

Stage Six: Cultural Proficiency

- The organizational system focuses on adding research to the knowledge base on the assessment and treatment of diverse populations.
- There is advocacy for social justice and no tolerance for discrimination.
- Every person has training and competency in most areas of diversity and can document the continuing education efforts in this area.

According to the APA Ethics Code, psychologists have the responsibility to promote diversity and assure that the organizations they serve behave in a manner consistent with ethical principles. Although organizational change is difficult, particularly when we might lack status or power, it is vital that we seek to promote diversity competency by bringing these issues to the consciousness of our systems. When in a group, we might ask questions, such as:

What stage of diversity competency are we in? What efforts are being made toward achieving diversity competency? What is the plan/vision for diversity competency in the future? What are the obstacles for improvement?

Although such discussions can be challenging, they are also important and fruitful for giving voice to the highest of virtues.

Conclusions and Implications for Research and Practice

Now we are back to the role of self-reflection and self-evaluation and the importance of asking for feedback about our diversity blind spots. In fact, this chapter presents a full circle of work that is designed to ensure that the needs of institutions and practitioners are not met at the cost of the diverse clients, students, colleagues, and participants we serve. There are many changes that are taking place in the settings that need the skillsets of psychologists. We can only help create positive change if we are willing to do the hard work of ensuring that our work is done with recognition that good intentions are not enough.

The push for evidence-based practice carries with it a danger of imposing a "one size fits all" model for assessment and intervention in both educational and clinical health care settings. Diversity competency must remain in the forefront of our work if we are to abide by our ethical obligation to adhere to APA's ethics code and guidelines for multicultural competency, along with the Culturally and Linguistically Appropriate Services (CLAS) standards specified in the 1964 Civil Rights Act. This chapter has created an argument for the self-reflection and self-assessment work needed to work with our highest degree of professional integrity. Gaps both in our research knowledge and clinical scholarship can be filled in a number of ways. Innovations in teaching diversity knowledge, skills, and attitudes should be published to enhance diversity training. Research is needed using different research methods such as longitudinal designs, survey research, qualitative research, case studies, and cross-sectional research with underserved populations to help guide our assessment and intervention efforts.

The integrated health care movement will bring setting-specific challenges that are anticipated to bring stress related to doing assessment and intervention quickly. Going too fast and being too focused on pathology rather than building upon strengths will be most detrimental to those who have traditionally been underserved populations. Culturally and linguistically diverse clients will no longer be the "minority" client but rather a large percentage of the populations we serve. This chapter is designed to help us slow down enough to *not* cause harm to some of the most vulnerable populations. If we can build in appropriate self-reflection skills, appropriate self-evaluation skills and the critical conversations that need to accompany this work, then we can have some assurance of not being well intentioned but dangerously off base with regard to our work with diverse populations. Failure to do the self-reflection, self-correction, self-assessment, and critical conversation work will also continue the transgenerational "soul wound" that has characterized segments of the history of psychology (Duran & Duran, 1995). The power to assess and treat those who traditionally have been disenfranchised remains one of our most vital responsibilities. We should at least think about this regularly. The implications are staggering as we contemplate the increased diversity in our country based on increased demographic diversity in the next century. Our most noble goal as a profession will be to meet this diversity challenge.

We hope that this chapter has helped you consider and contemplate your competence and skills on working with people who might be different from you in self-definitional ways. Whether you are working with underserved populations or you are a member of an underrepresented group working with majority culture populations, questions of diversity sensitivity are salient for all of us. Given that these are often uncomfortable topics that raise issues of access, power, and privilege, it takes courage to begin this process of self-reflection. We applaud the reader for taking the steps toward greater understanding, sensitivity, and awareness.

References

American Psychological Association. (1990). *Guidelines for providers of psychological services to ethnic, linguistic, and culturally diverse populations.* Washington, DC: Author.

American Psychological Association. (2003). Guidelines on multicultural education, training, research, practice, and organizational change for psychologists. *American Psychologist, 58*, 377–402. doi: 10.1037/0003-066X.58.5.377

Baca, L., Pinnell, C., & Lewis, D. (October, 2003). *Creating a model of cultural competency in graduate education: A roundtable discussion.* Roundtable presented at the 2003 Argosy University Academic Conference, Washington, DC.

Campinha-Bacote, J. (2002). Cultural competence in psychiatric nursing: Have you ASKED the right questions? *Journal of the American Psychiatric Nurses Association, 8*, 183–187. doi:_10.1067/mpn.2002.130216

Cattaneo, L., & Chapman, A. (2010). The process of empowerment: A model for use in research and practice. *American Psychologist, 65*, 246–260. doi: http://dx.doi.org/10.1037/a0018854

Comas-Díaz, L. (2012). *Multicultural care: A clinician's guide to cultural competence.* Washington, DC: American Psychological Association.

Dimaggio, G., Vanheule, S., Lysaker, P., Carcione, A., & Nicolo, G. (2009). Impaired self-reflection in psychiatric disorders among adults: A proposal for the existence of a network of semi-independent functions. *Consciousness and Cognition: An International Journal, 18*, 653–664. doi: 10.1016/j.concg.2009.06.003

Dovidio, J. F., Gaertner, S. E., Kawakami, K., & Hodson, G. (2002). Why can't we just get along? Interpersonal biases and interracial distrust. *Cultural Diversity and Ethnic Minority Psychology, 8*, 88–102. http://dx.doi.org/10.1037/1099-9809.8.2.88

Duran, E., & Duran, B. (1995). *Native American postcolonial psychology.* Albany: State University of New York Press.

Erikson, E. (1963). *Childhood and society.* New York: Norton Press.

Erlandson, P., & Beach, D. (2008). The ambivalence of reflection: Rereading Schol. *Reflective Practice, 9*, 409–421. doi: 10.1080/14623940802475843

Evans, D. (1979). *Struggle and fulfillment.* London, UK: Williams Collins.

Falender, C. A., & Shafranske, E. P. (2008). Best practices of supervision. In C. A. Falender & E. P. Shafranske (Eds.), *Casebook for clinical supervision: A competency-based approach.* American Psychological Association, Washington, DC. doi: http://dx.doi.org/10.1037/11792-001

Fontes, L. A. (2008). *Interviewing clients across cultures: A practitioner's guide.* New York: Guilford Press.

Freire, P., & Macedo, D. (2000). Scientism and the ideological construction of violence, poverty, and racism. In S. Urso Spina (Ed.), *Smoke and mirrors: The hidden context of violence in schools and society* (pp. 163–175). Lanham, MD: Rowman & Littlefield. Retrieved from https://search.proquest.com/docview/60022050?accountid=14522

Gielen, U., Draguns, J., & Fish, J. (2008). *Principles of multicultural counseling and therapy.* New York: Taylor & Francis.

Kaufmann, W. (2003). *Freud, Adler, and Jung: Discovering the mind* (Vol. 3). London, UK: Transaction Publishers.

Koss-Chioino, J. (2006). Spiritual transformation, relation, and radical empathy: Core components of the ritual healing process. *Transcultural Psychiatry, 43,* 652–670. doi: 10.1177/1363461506070789

Lewis, D., Virden, T., Hutchings, P., & Bhargava, R. (2011). Competence assessment integrating reflective practice in a professional psychology program. *Journal of the Scholarship of Teaching and Learning, 11,* 86–106.

Liang, B., Tummala-Narra, P., & West, J. (2011). Revisiting community work from a psychodynamic perspective. *Professional Psychology: Research and Practice, 42,* 398–404. doi: 10.1037/a0024687

Liu, W. M., Soleck, G., Hopps, J., Dunston, K., & Pickett, T. (2004). A new framework to understand social class in counseling: The social class worldview model and modern classism theory. *Journal of Multicultural Counseling and Development, 32,* 95–122. doi: 10.1002/j.2161-1912.2004.tb00364.x

Norcross, J. C., Koocher, G. P., & Garofalo, A. (2006). Discredited psychological treatments and tests: A Delphi poll. *Professional Psychology: Research and Practice, 37,* 515–522. doi: 10.1037/0735-7028.37.5.515

Pope, K., & Vasquez, M. (2011). *Ethics in psychotherapy and counseling: A practical guide* (4th ed.). New York: John Wiley & Sons.

Reich, J., Zautra, A., & Hall, J. (Eds.) (2010). *Handbook of adult resilience.* New York: Guilford Press.

Rings, J., Genuchi, M., Hall, M., Angelo, M., & Cornish, J. (2009). Is there consensus among predoctoral internship training directors regarding clinical supervision competencies? A descriptive analysis. *Training and Education in Professional Psychology, 3*(3), 140–147. doi: 10.1037/a0015054

Rubin, J. (2008). Deepening listening: The marriage of Buddha and Freud. In J. Gielen, J. Draguns, & J. Fish (Eds.), *Principles of multicultural counseling and therapy.* New York: Taylor & Francis.

Schon, D. (1987). *Educating the reflective practitioner: Toward a new design for teaching and learning in professions.* San Francisco, CA: Jossey-Bass.

Sheikh, A., Milne, D., & MacGregor, B. (2007). A model of personal professional development in the systemic training of clinical psychologists. *Clinical Psychology and Psychotherapy, 14,* 278–287. doi: 10.1002/cpp.540

Sue, D. W. (2001). Multidimensional facets of cultural competence. *The Counseling Psychologist, 29,* 790–821. doi: 10.1177/0011000001296002

Sue, D., & Sue, D. W. (2013). *Counseling the culturally diverse: Theory and practice* (6th ed.). Hoboken, NJ: John Wiley & Sons Inc.

Sue, S., Zane, N., Levant, R. F., Silverstein, L. B., Brown, L. S., Olkin, R., & Taliaferro, G. (2006). How well do both evidence-based practices and treatment as usual satisfactorily address the various dimensions of diversity? In J. C. Norcross, L. E. Beutler, & R. F. Levant (Eds.), *Evidence-based practices in mental health: Debate and dialogue on the fundamental questions*. American Psychological Association, Washington, DC. http://dx.doi.org/10.1037/11265-008

Tummala-Narra, P. (2013). Psychoanalytic applications in a diverse society. *Psychoanalytic Psychology, 30*(3), 471–487. doi: 10.1037/a0031375

Vasquez, M. (2007). Cultural difference and the therapeutic alliance: An evidence-based analysis. *American Psychologist, 62*, 875–885. doi: 10.1037/0003-066X.62.8.878

Wachtel, P. L. (2010). Psychotherapy integration and integrative psychotherapy: Process or product? *Journal of Psychotherapy Integration, 20*, 406–416. doi: http://dx.doi.org/10.1037/a0022032

Wachtel, P. (2011). *Therapeutic communication: Knowing what to say when*. New York: The Guilford Press.

Yabusaki, A. S. (2010). Reflections on the importance of place. *Training and Education in Professional Psychology, 4*, 3–6. doi: http://dx.doi.org/10.1037/a0016976

Appendix

Diversity Competency Measure
Louise Baca, Ph.D. Argosy University/Phoenix
(Based on Sue & Sue, 2013)

Use the following scale to assess your growth and development in the areas assessed below:

1 = Strongly disagree
2 = Disagree
3 = Uncertain
4 = Agree
5 = Strongly agree

1. I am aware of sociopolitical forces impacting the diverse communities in this metropolitan area.
2. I am aware of the barriers diverse communities face in obtaining mental health care.
3. I recognize the roles of expertness, trustworthiness, and LACK of similarity between therapist and client upon the diverse client's receptivity to change/influence.
4. I understand the importance of worldview and cultural identity in the helping process.
5. I understand culture-bound syndromes and communication style differences among diverse groups.
6. I am aware of my own biases and negative attitudes.
7. I believe the helping process should be consistent with the **client's** values, life experiences, and culturally conditioned ways of responding.
8. I believe in using active methods beyond the traditional role of psychotherapist in order to help diverse clients.
9. I know my personal limitations and make appropriate referrals when necessary.

10. I use relevant and sensitive intervention strategies and skills in working with diverse clients.
11. I seek consultation, supervision, and continuing education in diversity areas.
12. I can generate a wide variety of verbal and nonverbal responses to diverse clients.
13. I can intervene at a systems level and advocate on behalf of diverse clients.
14. I can recognize the limits of my style and anticipate the impact on diverse clients.
15. I can facilitate work with indigenous healers and consult with them when necessary.
16. I work at an experiential level to widen my comfort zone in all areas of diversity.

________________1st Score ________________2nd Score*

**The higher the score the higher the diversity competency*

PART II

Client Contexts

CHAPTER 2

Asking Difficult Questions: Client Definitions

David M. Cimbora and Radhika Krishnamurthy

Instructors in doctoral-level personality assessment courses know that we are regularly tasked with emphasizing the critically important aspects of psychological assessment to our students. As students near the end of their three-semester assessment course sequence, the first author has often asked them the following question: "If you could only choose one assessment measure or technique across the large number that you have learned, which one would it be?" Very quickly, a student undoubtedly offers a correction, stating that no psychologist would base findings on only one measure or piece of data. After acknowledging such ethically minded thinking, the hypothetical is continued. Students throw out various ideas, including the most robust measures they have learned (e.g., MMPI-2, Rorschach, WAIS-IV). Typically, a small minority will often state (meekly) that they would want to simply conduct a thorough interview. This answer correctly identifies the binding "glue" that holds almost all assessments together. It is the interview that will be these students' most valuable resource for the vast majority of assessments they conduct. The importance of interview data has certainly been underscored in the current literature (e.g., Fontes, 2008; Karg, Wiens, & Blazei, 2013; Sharp, Williams, Rhyner, & Ilardi, 2013), and it is a central focus of this chapter.

The second author urges her graduate students to seek out diverse international students from the university population as volunteers for intelligence- and personality-testing course assignments. She finds that they are understandably apprehensive. They wonder if they would misconstrue interview data due to difficulty with their volunteers' accents or insufficient knowledge of their cultural backgrounds. They sweat over their analysis of test profiles ("Can I use the standard descriptions?") and especially their conclusions and recommendations ("Is it pathological if it is explainable by culture/gender/sexual orientation? Should I have sought more information in the interview?"). When they bravely charge ahead with the assessment task, they usually discover it to be an eye-opening experience.

What follows in this and the next chapter is a careful examination of cultural nuance in the interview process of clinical assessment, which is important for achieving accuracy in the eventual conceptualization of the person. The importance of cultural competence in professional psychology has been well established, as it is recognized as a focus of various competency rubrics (e.g., Fouad et al., 2009; Kenkel & Peterson, 2009), and most recently within the current Standards of Accreditation for Health Service Psychology (APA, 2015). In the assessment training context, we emphasize to students the importance of culturally competent interviewing among other aspects of the assessment. The main emphasis of the first of these two chapters is in understanding the cultural nuance of "client definitions," namely the manner in which clients define and identify themselves, and the meaning that they derive from such definitions and identifications. The second chapter emphasizes the cultural nuance of "client context." Client context refers to the settings and environments (both physical and psychological) that clients are immersed in, and the impact these contexts have upon client definitions. As an introduction, however, we will focus on the trainee's and professional's preparation for interviewing clients—how diversity-related awareness and willingness to explore clients' self-perspectives are necessary prerequisites for asking questions, facilitating responses, and hearing the other well.

Clinician Preparation for Conducting Interviews

A careful examination of graduate training curricula in professional psychology reveals a significant amount of focus on therapist preparation for relational dynamics within the *therapy* domain. Pre-practicum, beginning therapy techniques, and introduction to therapy are just a few of the courses in which graduate training prepares the neophyte clinician. As students mature in their abilities, they often can choose from a variety of modality- or orientation-specific course offerings. These courses, often offered throughout the students' graduate training, focus on broadening and refining students' skill sets and strengthening the impact of their interventions. However, *assessment* training is typically handled differently, often with only two required courses devoted to it (e.g., Ready & Veague, 2014). The indirect and perhaps unintentional message sent to students is that assessment competency, unlike therapy, can be obtained more quickly, or at the very least, is not amenable to classroom instruction—neither of which is true. Furthermore, the bulk of these few assessment courses often focus on the mechanics of test administration, scoring, interpretation, and report writing. Relatively little attention, if any, is devoted to the dynamics involved in the *assessment relationship*, let alone the cultural nuances that surface in an assessment. It is not a leap to conclude that educators assume that the training for the therapy relationship is easily transferable to the assessment context. However, one should not be so quick to make such an assumption; there are significant differences in the roles of therapist versus evaluator, the objectives and goals of each endeavor, and the methods to achieve such goals. We will explore the assessment relationship with an eye toward appropriate preparation for engagement. We then will shift focus to the interview itself, with a more specific inquiry into the issue of client definitions.

Self-Exploration and Self-Evaluation

As has been discussed in an earlier chapter, it is critical that evaluators pursue the complementary paths of self-exploration and self-evaluation prior to engagement with a client in the assessment context. For our purposes, we define self-exploration as a process of discovery of one's sense of self as an individual, rooted in one's cultural identity. Tied to this process is discovering our own implicit perceptions, reactions, biases, beliefs, values, assumptions, areas of ignorance (blind spots), emotional awareness, and a whole host of other factors (Comas-Díaz, 2012; Dadlani, Overtree, & Perry-Jenkins, 2012; Sigel, 1996). Furthermore, we understand our cultural identities to be multiple in nature; we do not identify solely as one characteristic (e.g., female), but as multiple (e.g., African-American, lesbian, female, from a rural area, etc.). Since the evaluator's self has a significant influence on the testing process and outcome, it is critical that the evaluator comes prepared with a thorough knowledge of the self.

We define self-evaluation as a critical examination of the potential benefits and hindrances our own multiple cultural identities might have on our clinical work. Through self-evaluation, we can examine the impact of the self in the assessment process and more accurately ascertain who the client actually is. While these ideas are typical fare in therapy training, we wonder how often this process is encouraged of trainees in the assessment context. When cultural competence is raised within the assessment context, it often centers on such themes as generalizability of tests to marginalized populations, language ability of clients, and the appropriateness of diagnostic categories for cultural minority groups (Branch, 2005; Dana, 2000, 2005; Suzuki, Onoue, & Hill, 2013). Although these are important, cultural competence also includes the ability to self-evaluate, particularly in the context of clinical interviewing. We term this process as understanding the "psychometrics of the self."

Psychometrics of the Self

In order to utilize a test, we must first ensure that the test has strong psychometrics. Within the context of the self, we must go through a similar process, determining both "self-validity and our self-reliability." Concerning self-validity, we need to ask how accurate we are in our self-evaluations. Inaccurate self-evaluation will undoubtedly lead to inaccuracy in our evaluations of others, as we would then be prone to misattribution errors, blind spots, and unrecognized biases. Receiving supervision, therapy, and consultation can all be helpful to us in becoming more accurate self-evaluators. In terms of self-reliability, do we offer our clients a fairly stable presentation over time, session-to-session, and client to client? Such stability offers a constant by which fluctuations in client presentations and differences between clients can be accurately assessed. In short, in order to effectively evaluate the meaning of clients' self-definitions, we must first understand our own and present in a stable and consistent manner.

Preparation to Ask

A common experience we have noted in training neophyte examiners is their reticence to engage in professional curiosity about clients' private lives. Trainees sometimes ask, "Who am *I* to ask?" When we inquire about the source of this question, students often respond with themes of professional or personal insecurity mixed with respect of others' privacy. It is important to educate trainees that maintaining professional curiosity is, in fact, their "job." Without the data gathered from direct verbal inquiry, the evaluation process is certainly hamstrung.

With a bit of encouragement, many trainees quickly assimilate to their role of professional curiosity. However, some trainees and some professionals still struggle with asking what we term "difficult questions." Their concern shifts from wondering "Who am *I* to ask?" to "Who am I to ask about *that?*" Often, the fear is of being too intrusive, that clients will find certain topics too personal and will be offended. To be fair, examiners' struggles might come from a benign sense of respecting the privacy of others. However, as said above, it is our job to pursue relevant lines of inquiry with our clients. We have noted that examiners typically have the most concern about asking questions regarding sexuality, criminality, finances, substance use, spirituality, and political views, to name a few. As an example, Lothian and Read (2002) found that two-thirds of clients had experienced a lifetime incidence of sexual, physical, or emotional abuse, but only 20% had been asked about abuse during their mental health assessment.

Although client discomfort might justify a clinician's avoidance of some questions in some cases, we posit that many clients are actually more comfortable in answering difficult questions than examiners are in asking them. Thus, projection of our own discomforts around various topics might be in play, particularly if such questions reveal limits to our understanding of diversity factors. It is important that we understand our own levels of comfort around such matters. With that understanding in mind, we also work toward effective relational techniques to effectively manage client reactions when these topics are brought up. We see this as part of understanding the psychometrics of the self.

Novice and experienced assessors alike might also be uncertain about, or negligent in, the "*what* to ask" aspect of the interview, especially when topics may have what appears to be little or indirect connection to psychopathology and diagnosis. This can occur because our personal assumptions might lead us to bypass certain areas of inquiry. For example, we might presume that a married woman is secure in her heterosexual identity, or that a middle-class White man has faced no discrimination, or that a highly religious person has no rebellious impulses. Upon looking at the personality test profiles in these instances, we might consequently fail to understand the underlying dynamics of the married woman's anxiety reactions, the middle-class White man's angry acting out, and the religious person's antisocial tendencies. Although interview time is finite, we must recognize that our notions of the client might not match his or her self-identity. Therefore, our assessment process should include soliciting the client's self-description within the broad framework of cultural and personal factors relevant to the client's sense of self.

Goals of the Interview

The goals of the interview typically focus on developing initial rapport, obtaining historical data, developing a clear diagnostic picture of the client, selecting treatment targets, and providing appropriate referrals (Maruish, 2008; Truax & Wright, 2007). We do not deny the importance of these goals. If this is all we do, however, we are only examining the client from our own Western-based medically oriented perspective, and we might miss out on the nuances afforded by the client's culture. A culturally sensitive approach must include an examination of clients' self-definition and how they understand their own identities. We now turn to these issues. First, we will explore client definitions as a function of culture and then of sub-cultural variations.

Client Definitions as a Function of Culture

Professional curiosity in the interview will help us understand how clients define themselves and the salient aspects of their identity. We have termed this "client definitions." This concept has a lexical content-based component, in that we are interested in the word choices and word meanings ascribed to the word choices that clients make. Thus, when a client uses a word such as "weird" to describe herself, it behooves us to query what she means by "weird." Similarly, when a client reports that his relationship with his mother was "good," we inquire further to ascertain his meaning of "good." However, content-based word queries do not necessarily help us understand the deeper cultural identifications of our clients. We believe that the ways in which clients define themselves can and should be seen as a function of culture. Simply put, identity is culturally driven (Hopkins & Reicher, 2011; McGoldrick & Ashton, 2012; Wing Sue & Sue, 2008).

Identity as a culturally driven variable

Many definitions of culture are provided in the literature, but for our purposes, we will define culture as an ideological dimension of the human condition that guides and motivates behavior. It is the values, worldviews, and traditions that help to define an individual or a group. Dimensions that are typically referred to when assessing culture include the following:

1. race/ethnicity/nationality
2. religion/spirituality
3. gender
4. sexual identity
5. socioeconomic status
6. ability
7. age

Later chapters will focus on each of these in depth, but for now we will focus on a brief overview. Some parts of cultural identity are typically visible (e.g., age, gender, race) while others might not be readily observed (e.g., spirituality, sexual identity, some forms of ability). In order to fully comprehend a client's self-definition, the evaluator needs to ascertain both the visible and less visible or invisible aspects of cultural identity.

Furthermore, evaluators need to remain curious even in the face of cultural variables that seem obvious. We are reminded of a colleague whose phenotype was "middle-Eastern." He talked openly about others assuming his ethnic heritage was Arabian. However, his true cultural identifications were more in keeping with Northern European heritage. He happened to be born in England and adopted early in his life by a family who strongly identified with a Scandinavian heritage, a culture with which he felt particularly aligned throughout his life. Interestingly enough, he was often sought out by his past educational and employment affiliations for public relations campaigns (e.g., photo shoots, interviews) as an example of ethnic minority representation. Few bothered to stop and ask him about his less visible or invisible cultural identifications, as most made conclusions based on the visible. Were they to do so, they would have discovered a wealth of knowledge, history, and appreciation for a culture they were not expecting.

Multiple Cultural Identities

Rarely is a client's cultural identity completely defined by a single factor; rather, we know that cultural identity is multiply determined (Falicov, 2014; Josselson & Harway, 2012; Yampolsky, Amiot, & de la Sablonniere, 2013). Multiple cultural identities is a term that describes our tendency to embrace multiple layers of self-definition, often spanning many and possibly all of the seven categories described above. Thus, a 38-year-old client might define herself initially as a mother, reflecting her primary self-definition. She might proceed to report that she and her husband immigrated from Bangladesh and are of the Muslim faith. Further inquiry might reveal she views herself as "old" (in contrast to the Western viewpoint of her chronological age) because her children are grown. Her middle-class status, implied by her husband's occupation, might be of little salience to her. Her cultural background is more relevant to her daily life activities, evident in the traditions she fosters in the home and her close friendships exclusively with women from Asian countries, regardless of their religion. This example demonstrates how diversity variables differ in their importance to the client's self-definition, which can be understood through thoughtful inquiry. As discussed by Grieger (2008), a conceptual framework for cultural assessment ("cultural" is used broadly to cover a host of diversity factors) would include the client's cultural self-definitions and preferred designations as well as the cultural factors most salient for the client.

The evaluator needs to be especially sensitive to possible conflict within a client's multiple cultural identities. Although aspects of cultural identity can harmoniously co-exist, this is not always the case. A common example of this can be seen in the intersection of spirituality/religion and sexual identity, particularly around gay, lesbian, bisexual, or transgender issues (e.g., Balkin, Watts, & Ali, 2014; Bieschke, Blasko, & Woodhouse, 2014). Another example involves tension between one's religious or spiritual beliefs and gender identity. Certain belief systems contain dogmas related to the public and private roles of men vis-à-vis women. Although a client might hold to his or her religious belief system's basic tenets, gender-based dogmas may cause tension with his or her cultural values around gender (e.g., Balkin, Watts, & Ali, 2014; Chong, 2006). Conflict can also occur within the same category of cultural identification. For example, a client might identify as having multiple ethnicities, and these could be in tension. Similarly, a client might experience being of full ability in one context (e.g., sports) but disability in another (e.g., the classroom). Other clients might report difficulty in embracing and integrating multiple religious faith systems in which they were raised. It is clear that our multiple cultural identities are complex and require sensitive and deliberate inquiry by the examiner. It is not enough that we obtain labels that seem to fit our clients, but instead we must pursue the true complexity and potential conflicts that exist within their multiple identifications.

Framework to Understanding Client Definitions of Cultural Identity

We all view the world through our ethnocentric lens, meaning a personal set of assumptions, beliefs, and ideologies that shape how we perceive, interpret, and react to our environment. Koss-Chioino and Vargas (1992) warn of the consequence of failing to recognize one's own ethnocentric lens in what they term the "Red Queen Syndrome." Taken from the literary fictional work of "Through the Looking-Glass" by Lewis Carroll, Koss-Chioino and Vargas describe the ethnocentric lens of the Red Queen. In her words to Alice, the Red Queen states, "I don't know what you mean by *your* way ... All the ways about here belong to me" (Carroll, 1981, p. 125; italics added). We as examiners can fall prey to the Red Queen Syndrome if we do not recognize our own ethnocentric lens through which we perceive, understand, and interpret the "ways" of our clients. Without such recognition, we run the risk of interpreting client self-definitions in ways that make sense to us but not necessarily with the meanings that were intended by the client. Not only must we recognize our own ethnocentric lens, but we must also be able to adopt the lenses of our clients, and in so doing, set aside our own culturally laden perceptions and interpretations.

A second part of our framework involves openness to the different ways clients' labels can be defined. Simply put, our definition of terms might not match those of our clients. For example, African-American and Black might not be interchangeable for a client, as both may have specific meanings with one being less applicable to a client than the other. Similarly, Hispanic, Mexican-American, Latino, and Chicano all have unique historical, socio-political, and cultural contexts. Christian, Evangelical, Southern Baptist, and "Born-again" all share similar foundations but are unique in their cultural nuances. Finally, gay, homosexual, queer-identified, and same-sex attracted are, similarly, not necessarily interchangeable terms. Pronoun use becomes critical when considering gender diversity, as some identify with traditional gender-based pronouns (e.g., he or she), while others might choose to define themselves outside of dichotomous labels (for example, prefer that their name be used). Furthermore, preferred gender pronouns might not always match physical appearance, as with some in the transgender community.

Examples like these show us the need for respectful inquiry and curiosity when clients use terminology, in order to fully grasp the uniqueness of our clients' self-definitions. The authors have found that trainees often struggle with asking clarification questions, such as "What does it mean to you to be African-American?" or "Can you help me understand what you mean by 'queer'?" Some of the struggle might be due to the examiner's own discomfort as discussed earlier, or to the examiner's fear of being seen as ignorant or insensitive, either by the client or by those evaluating the trainee. What we have found helpful is to encourage a stance of thoughtful humility paired with a comfort or an appreciation of "not-knowing." We have found that this stance typically lends itself to more robust explanations from clients and a growth in clients' belief that the examiner truly wants to understand without preconceptions.

Client Definitions as a Function of Sub-Culture

The seven categories of cultural identification listed earlier provide a thorough framework for understanding possibilities of client definitions. However, we realize that each of these categories holds a plethora of sub-groupings. It is rare indeed for clients to report having an identity that pertains to one of the seven categories without also having a more intricate definition that places them within a smaller yet still connected grouping. A client might express masculine phenotype and report to being identified as male in gender. Yet, within this client's self-definition could lie a host of stereotypically feminine qualities, traits, and interests that may become revealed in a personality test profile. As another example, a client might identify as lesbian, but the astute examiner would inquire about the degree to which the client is "out" to her community, both public and private. Similarly, a client might report as spiritual, but upon further inquiry, relate a Catholic identification. Even further inquiry could reveal a more specific identification, such as Roman Catholic or Eastern Orthodox. Understanding client sub-culture has unique implications for our interpretations about the client in general, not to mention specific behaviors, attitudes, and possibly even presenting symptomatology.

It is often true that sub-cultural groups may use idioms or have specific word meanings relevant to them. Adolescents, prison culture, religious groups, professional groups, and just about any collection of associated people can have a shared set of terms and meanings. It is critical that examiners inform themselves about these lexical nuances, either through preparation beforehand, inquiry to the client, or consultation with other resources. It is important to note that idioms and meanings can change over time in a sort of "lexical evolution;" examiners thus need to remain current.

In the last decade in particular, a relatively new set of sub-cultural groups has developed involving the Internet. Social media (e.g., currently Facebook, Pinterest, Twitter, Snapchat, and Instagram) allow for relational connections to be made across public and private Internet channels. These connections have resulted in the formation of sub-groups based upon common interests, values, positions, occupations, hobbies, and personalities, to name a few. We now turn to examine the ways in which the Internet and social media impact clients' self-expression and in turn, their self-definition.

Impact of Social Media on Self-Expression and Self-Definition

With the explosion of social media's popularity, it is important to realize that clients have multiple platforms for self-expression that were not available to them ten to fifteen years ago, for the most part. One characteristic of this Internet-based self-expression is the tendency to relay information that typically has been considered private into the public domain. Likes, dislikes, activities, personal facts, and a whole host of other pieces of information are shared in the public domain, potentially seen by millions of others. Even if a person avoids social media altogether, it is possible to still have a "digital footprint" if one has used the Internet at all, and this footprint might contain personal information such as website preferences, shopping tastes, and financial information. Maintaining completely private self-definitions is becoming more difficult as we continue to interface with the various Internet-based platforms. On the other hand, many embrace Internet-based public disclosure of information that in previous eras might have been considered "private." It is possible for some that the line between public and private identity is likely opaque. Areas of future study could include the impact this shift has on client disclosures in both assessment and therapy. Furthermore, it would be important to assess whether this trend results in clients experiencing less stigma about personal disclosures, particularly in the assessment and therapy contexts.

Online presence in social media might enhance or prove to be adaptive for one's identity. As one shares personal information in these formats, interpersonal connections can be made. These connections can help to solidify a sense of belonging and identification with a larger group. Shared interests, commonalities, and frequent or even instant access to similar others can strengthen one's identity. At the same time, online presence in social media poses some challenges and difficulties.

Fabrication of Self-Identity

Self-expression on the Internet tends to be characterized by anonymity and small levels of accountability. Usernames are not typically the actual name of the user. Statements about the self are neither typically verifiable nor subject to intense scrutiny. Most Internet-based means of self-expression are not regulated for validity—that is, one can write just about anything pertaining to the self and face little chance of verification from the typical Internet user. Thus, this context of self-expression is ripe for fabrication or falsification of the self (DeAndrea & Walther, 2011). Brunskill (2013) describes this as a "social avatar" or a false or exaggerated self. The construction of this falsehood is accomplished through a minimization or elimination of undesirable self-traits and a self-selection of favorable material.

Whether it is misrepresenting age, gender, interests, hobbies, beliefs, ideals, or any number of other characteristics, one's falsehoods stand little chance of being detected. Although such fabrications might involve elaborate lies, many users of the Internet engage in more subtle misrepresentations of self-definition. Using "Photoshopped" pictures of one's self to enhance one's appearance or over-stating one's educational or occupational accomplishments are examples of more subtle fabrications. Finally, some individuals adopt fabricated selves for the purpose of fantasy or escapism. This might take the form of character creation and adoption in video game playing. Some players invest more heavily into the qualities, attributes, wealth, possessions, and interpersonal connections of their virtual avatars than in their real-world identities. A little over a decade ago, few had ever heard of the idea of maintaining a virtual identity. Now, one can question whether virtual identities are a greater part of players' self-definition than their identity in real life.

On average, our clients are increasingly exposed to and engaged in a sub-culture that encourages personal and public self-expression, but that also allows for fabrication and misrepresentation of data with little consequence in many cases. One has to wonder to what extent the creation of false selves in the Internet context contributes to a difficulty in ascertaining accurate data in the testing context. As clients continue to define themselves behind anonymous computer keyboards and Internet firewalls, will this affect our ability to get accurate self-definitions from them when we meet for assessments? To what extent is the client aware of accurate self-definitions? To what extent are they able or willing to produce that data during the assessment? At what point does the fabricated self actually become the true self for the individual? These questions and others are ones the field needs to address.

The Assessment of Self-Definition

We now turn our discussion to the methods employed by professional psychologists to assess self-definition. First, we will look at the interview structure and style itself, and then we will focus on other methodologies such as test- and measure-based approaches.

Method of Interviews

Zalaquett, Chatters, and Ivey (2013) articulate a method for conducting interviews in therapy that can be generalized to assessment clients as well. First, the authors note that it is important that evaluators work "with" clients, and not "on" them. An evaluator's assessment of a client's self-definitions is a collaborative venture. The use of attending skills and listening skills is paramount. Attending skills can be organized into a framework called the basic listening sequence (BLS). The BLS includes (a) open and closed questions, (b) encouragement, (c) paraphrase, (d) reflection of feeling, and (e) summarization. We feel that such a method invites the client into the assessment process and into a collaborative frame. Each of these will be discussed separately.

By using both open and closed questions in the interview, we allow for two processes to unfold: (1) the client can explore self-definitions in an unfettered way (open questions), and (2) the evaluator still can maintain focus on specific targets of investigation (closed questions). Striking a balance between these is key, because an imbalance could lead to a lack of, or an over-abundance of, evaluator control in the interview—neither of which will likely yield informative outcomes. We might need to adopt a stance of encouragement through this questioning process, because such a stance may disarm client defenses and concerns.

Certainly a critical skill in the work of the interview is to paraphrase. With typical speech rates of 100–200 words per minute (slightly lower in young children; e.g., Martins, Vieira, Loureiro & Santos, 2007), we must paraphrase in order to capture the client's descriptions. Although direct quotes lend themselves to clear depictions of client definitions, an accurate paraphrase is inevitably useful for parsimony. Paraphrasing, however, needs to be confirmed by the client for accuracy, and thus the importance of the collaborative relationship. This is particularly important because the client actually paraphrases him- or herself prior to and while speaking out loud. Korba (1990) reported that an estimate of inner speech ("the private construction of elliptical thought") is around 4,000 words per minute. Thus, approximately 3,800 to 3,900 words per minute are either rejected or paraphrased by the client while the client speaks. Thus, it is possible that the evaluator's paraphrase does not capture the true intent and meaning of the client.

It is true that clients define themselves through cognitive-based descriptions, but much of the nuance of self-identity comes through the lens of emotion (e.g., Goldman & Greenberg, 2013; Kristjansson, 2010; Seaton & Beaumont, 2011). Statements like, "I'm a happy person," "I tend to be fairly content with life," or "I am typically jealous" are all examples of such emotionally based self-definition. However, such disclosures are mediated by culture, and they also require self-insight on the part of the client. Therefore, there is variability in the extent to which clients will produce emotionally based disclosures. It is common for the affect involved in a client's self-definition to be communicated non-verbally in the interview or through a process of nuanced or subtle word choice. In these cases, the interviewer would be well served to reflect his or her interpretations of the client's affective experience to assess for accuracy. When we are affectively attuned to our clients, it will likely lead to greater comfort in the interview and greater self-revelation.

A final skill involves summarization. Certainly the intake or assessment report is one such summarization. But the interviewer is required to make frequent and often cumulative summarizations during the course of the interview, adapting the summary to fit the new data the client produces. Our initial considerations of the client's self-definitions will likely be significantly altered by the time the interview and subsequent testing are completed.

All of these tasks need to be undertaken within a frame of open curiosity and humility. Outside of this frame, we are prone to misunderstandings, misattributions, and projections of the self onto the client. Resources exist that can aid evaluators in understanding their clients even before the initial session, thereby decreasing the likelihood of the errors above. Examples of such resources include literature on interviewing persons from specific populations such as Latina/o clients (e.g., Gallardo, 2013), Asian-American clients (e.g., Chang & O'Hara, 2013), and lesbian, gay, bisexual and transgender clients (e.g., Heck, Flentje, & Cochran, 2013).

Test and Measure Usage

Determining client self-definition often comes through interviewing, but tests and measures can be used conjunctively. It is critical that we put our tests and measures through careful psychometric scrutiny, just as we encourage careful scrutiny of the self. One area of scrutiny should be the degree to which the measure is embedded in a cultural context in its wording and content, or has culturally loaded delineations of the measured characteristics, which would determine its applicability for diverse populations. More important are the examiner's judgment about the appropriateness of the measure for a given individual and the contextual interpretation of a particular item or test score when the measure is reasonably suitable for use.

Each item within a measure lies somewhere along a continuum of cultural sensitivity. In the most basic sense, items are created by people with a particular cultural lens. This is a critical point, given that measure items should be seen as extensions of our own preconceived ideas and notions about human behavior. Thus, from the Western cultural lens, personality test descriptors such as independent and self-confident are often viewed as adaptive characteristics whereas conciliatory and self-deprecating characteristics are considered problematic. Much has been written about the topic of cultural bias in assessment measures (e.g., Dana, 2000; Suzuki, Onoue, & Hill, 2013). Although we maintain that "bias" arises more in application than from the measure itself, we must continue to take an item-by-item analysis of the extent to which measures obfuscate the true meaning of client definitions.

Our main focus here is on the demographics questionnaire, which often accompanies the initial interview. Demographics questionnaires are some of the most common methods in which client self-definitions are inaccurately reported. "Forced choice" methods of pre-determined ethnic categories are an example, as undoubtedly some individuals will identify with a term that is not represented on the form. Such clients are then forced to answer or mark a category that is inaccurate or opaque (e.g., "other"). Similar confusion can arise when asking other demographic questions, such as spirituality or religion. When considering gender, early conceptualizations considered it to be a dichotomous variable. This is often reflected in our demographics measures. However, some clients reject such bifurcation and would consider such items to be limiting. Ascertaining a client's primary language is critical to allowing the client the means by which to most fluently report their self-definitions on a demographics questionnaire, not to mention the interview. It is often difficult to assess for primary language, however. Whatever language the question is asked in could influence the client's response. In short, it behooves us to carefully examine our test measures, and in particular, our demographics questionnaires, at an item-by-item level to discern the cultural psychometric properties they have.

Concluding Thoughts and Recommendations

The cultural diversity literature has often been divided in discussing the way to improve our method of understanding our clients in context. Historically, one stream of thought has emphasized broadening our knowledge and experience of different cultures, variously referred to as culture-specific expertise (e.g., Sue, 1998) or demographic competency (e.g., Bieschke & Mintz, 2012). Another underscored maintaining an egalitarian, open, and sensitive attitude toward understanding and appreciating cultural differences (e.g., dynamic worldview inclusivity, Bieschke & Mintz, 2012; scientific-mindedness, Sue, 1998). The reality is that we cannot effectively acquire a deep understanding of the multitude of cultures and subcultures, nationalities, religions and religious denominations of the world, nor of the broad range of other diversities we might encounter in clinical practice. On the other hand, an attitude of openness and inquiry alone might not suffice, because the eventual knowledge we gain from our clients still requires our own understanding of broader cultural context. Thus, it is clear that we must do both, and this integration is reflected in professional guidelines (e.g., APA, 2003). However, even accomplishing these dual goals is not enough to ensure accuracy in understanding our clients.

In seeking to understand the meanings by which clients define themselves, we must first turn to examine how we define ourselves. Each of us may differently prioritize ethnicity, gender, age, socioeconomic status, religion, sexual preference, ability, and other variables in our core self-definition. We might also inspect how we describe ourselves in terms on personality test questionnaires (e.g., sensitive, angry, shy, warm, affectionate, demanding, tense), and what we mean when we endorse these words. Furthermore, we might reflect on how our self-definitions may differ from how others might categorize us. It is in assessing the psychometrics of the self that we will understand the filters, preconceived ideas and frameworks, biases, prejudices, and other lenses by which we make interpretations about the clients before us. The task that follows is one of changing those areas that inhibit or even prohibit us from making accurate appraisals of our clients. This is no easy task and is often a life-long journey. We must go through a similar process of evaluation and scrutiny with the measures and methods we employ.

Further steps include the creation of a "safe space" for clients to share their definitions with us. We often forget that our clients are evaluating us during the assessment, typically for signs of understanding, empathy, support, and acceptance. Awareness of the impact of our presence in the room can yield more comfort for the client, which likely leads to greater elaboration. We also need to keep in mind that our needs as evaluators sometimes do not match with the needs of our clients. Simply put, our need is to gather information and we therefore "need" clients to provide it. However, clients' needs might not necessarily align with producing information for us, and we must be careful to not enforce agendas that are grossly mismatched with clients' current need states or we run the risk of non-compliance.

It is critical for us to develop an appreciation for the multiple cultural identities of our clients. Simply put, people are not easily defined or categorized. The complexity of our "selves" must be maintained in awareness throughout the evaluation.

Finally, we emphasize the need for consultation. An important step in decreasing the likelihood of ethical violations in mental health practice is the act of professional consultation (Gutheil & Brodsky, 2008). In a similar way, we believe that assessment consultation likely decreases evaluator error. There is much to be learned from our clients about self-definitions that can be maximized when we also recognize that there is much to be learned from the professionals around us.

References

American Psychological Association. (2003). Guidelines on multicultural education, training, research, practice, and organizational change for psychologists. *American Psychologist, 58*, 377–402. doi: 1037/0003-066X.58.5.377

American Psychological Association. (2015). *Standards of Accreditation for Health Service Psychology*. Retrieved from www.apa.org/ed/accreditation/about/policies/standards-of-accreditation.pdf

Balkin, R. S., Watts, R. E., & Ali, S. R. (2014). A conversation about the intersection of faith, sexual orientation, and gender: Jewish, Christian, and Muslim perspectives. *Journal of Counseling and Development, 92*, 187–193. doi: 10.1002/j.1556-6676.2014.00147.x

Bieschke, K. J., & Mintz, L. B. (2012). Counseling psychology model training values statement addressing diversity: History, current use, and future directions. *Training and Education in Professional Psychology, 6*, 196–203. doi: 10.1037/a0030810

Bieschke, K. J., Blasko, K. A., & Woodhouse, S. S. (2014). A comprehensive approach to competently addressing sexual minority issues in clinical supervision. In C. A. Falender, E. P. Shafranske, & C. J. Falicov (Eds.), *Multiculturalism and diversity in clinical supervision: A competency-based approach* (pp. 209–230). Washington, DC: American Psychological Association. doi: 10.1037/14379-009

Branch, C. W. (2005). Racial-cultural issues in clinical assessment. In R. T. Carter (Ed.), *Handbook of racial-cultural psychology and counseling* (Vol. 2, pp. 316–339). Hoboken, NJ: Wiley & Sons.

Brunskill, D. (2013). Social media, social avatars, and the psyche: Is Facebook good for us? *Australasian Psychiatry, 21*, 527–532. doi: 10.1177/1039856213509289.

Carroll, L. (1981). *Alice's adventures in Wonderland & Through the looking-glass*. New York: Bantam Books.

Chang, C. Y., & O'Hara, C. (2013). The initial interview with Asian American clients. *Journal of Contemporary Psychotherapy, 43*, 33–42. doi: 0.1007/s10879-012-9221-9

Chong, K. H. (2006). Negotiating patriarchy: South Korean evangelical women and the politics of gender. *Gender and Society, 20*, 697–724. doi: 10.1177/0891243206291111

Comas-Díaz, L. (2012). Cultural self-assessment: Knowing others, knowing yourself. In *Multicultural care: A clinician's guide to cultural competence* (pp. 13–32). Washington, DC: American Psychological Association.

Dadlani, M. B., Overtree, C., & Perry-Jenkins, M. (2012). Culture at the center: A reformulation of diagnostic assessment. *Professional Psychology: Research and Practice, 43*, 175–182. doi: 10:1037/a0028152

Dana, R. H. (2000). Culture and methodology in personality assessment. In I. Cuellar & F. A. Paniagua (Eds.), *Handbook of multicultural mental health* (pp. 97–120). San Diego, CA: Academic Press. doi: 10.1016/B978-012199370-2/50007-9

Dana, R. H. (2005). *Multicultural assessment: Principles, applications, and examples.* Mahwah, NJ: Lawrence Erlbaum.

DeAndrea, D. C., & Walther, J. B. (2011). Attributions for inconsistencies between online and offline self-presentations. *Communication Research, 38,* 805–825. doi: 10.1177/0093650210385340

Falicov, C. J. (2014). Immigrant clients, supervisees, and supervisors. In C. A. Falender, E. P. Shafranske, & C. J. Falicov (Eds.), *Multiculturalism and diversity in clinical supervision: A competency-based approach* (pp. 111–144). Washington, DC: American Psychological Association. doi: 10.1037/14370-005

Fontes, L. A. (2008). *Interviewing clients across cultures: A practitioner's guide.* New York: Guildford Press.

Fouad, N. A., Grus, C. L., Hatcher, R. L., Kaslow, N. J., Hutchings, P. S., Madison, M., Collins, F. L., Jr., & Crossman, R. E. (2009). Competency benchmarks: A developmental model for understanding and measuring competence in professional psychology. *Training and Education in Professional Psychology, 3(4, Supplement),* S5-S26. doi: 10.1037/a0015832

Gallardo, M. E. (2013). Context and culture: The initial clinical interview with the Latina/o client. *Journal of Contemporary Psychotherapy, 43,* 43–53. doi: 10.1007/s10879-012-9222-8

Goldman, R. N., & Greenberg, L. (2013). Working with identity and self-soothing in Emotion-Focused Therapy for couples. *Family Process, 52,* 62–82. doi: 10.1111/famp.12021

Grieger, I. (2008). A cultural assessment framework and interview protocol. In L. A. Suzuki & J. G. Ponterotto (Eds.), *Handbook of multicultural assessment: Clinical, psychological, and educational applications* (pp. 132–161). San Francisco, CA: Jossey-Bass.

Gutheil, T. G., & Brodsky, A. (2008). *Preventing boundary violations in clinical practice.* New York: Guilford Press.

Heck, N. C., Flentje, A., & Cochran, B. N. (2013). Intake interviewing with lesbian, gay, bisexual, and transgender clients: Starting from a place of affirmation. *Journal of Contemporary Psychotherapy, 43,* 23–32. doi: 10.1007/s10879-012-9220-x

Hopkins, N., & Reicher, S. (2011). Identity, culture and contestation: Social identity as cross-cultural theory. *Psychological Studies, 56,* 36–43. doi: 10.1007/s12646-011-0068-z.

Karg, R. S., Wiens, A. N., & Blazei, R. W. (2013). Improving diagnostic and clinical interviewing. In G. P. Koocher, J. C. Norcross, & B. A. Greene (Eds.), *Psychologists' desk reference* (3rd ed., pp. 22–26). New York: Oxford University Press.

Kenkel, M. B., & Peterson, R. L. (Eds). (2009). *Competency-based education for professional psychology.* Washington, DC: American Psychological Association.

Korba, R. J. (1990). The rate of inner speech. *Perceptual and Motor Skills, 71,* 1043–1052. doi: 10.2466/PMS.71.7.1043-1052

Koss-Chioino, J. D., & Vargas, L. A. (1992). Through the cultural looking glass: A model for understanding culturally responsive psychotherapies. In L. A. Vargas & J. D. Koss-Chioino (Eds.), *Working with culture: Psychotherapeutic interventions with ethnic minority children and adolescents* (pp.1–22). San Francisco, CA: Jossey-Bass.

Kristjansson, K. (2010). *The self and its emotions.* New York: Cambridge University Press.

Josselson, R., & Harway, M. (2012). *Navigating multiple identities: Race, gender, culture, nationality, and roles.* New York: Oxford University Press. doi: 10.1093/acprof:oso/9780199732074.001.0001

Lothian, J., & Read, J. (2002). Asking about abuse during mental health assessments: Clients' views and experiences. *New Zealand Journal of Psychology, 31*, 98–103.

Martins, I., Vieira, R., Loureiro, C., & Santos, M. (2007). Speech rate and fluency in children and adolescents. *Child Neuropsychology, 13*, 319–332. doi: 10.1080/09297040600837370

Maruish, M. E. (2008). The clinical interview. In R. P. Archer & S. R. Smith (Eds.), *Personality assessment* (pp. 37–80). New York: Routledge/Taylor & Francis Group.

McGoldrick, M. & Ashton, D. (2012). Culture: A challenge to concepts of normality. *Normal family processes: Growing diversity and complexity* (4th ed.). New York, Guilford Press.

Ready, R. E., & Veague, H. B. (2014). Training in psychological assessment: Current practices of clinical psychology programs. *Professional Psychology: Research and Practice, 4*, 278–282. http://dx.doi.org/10.1037/a0037439

Seaton, C. L., & Beaumont, S. L. (2011). The link between identity style and intimacy: Does emotional intelligence provide the key? *Identity: An International Journal of Theory and Research, 11*, 311–332. doi: 10.1080/15283488.2011.613586

Sharp, K. L., Williams, A. J., Rhyner, K. T., & Ilardi, S. S. (2013). The clinical interview. In K. F. Geisinger et al. (Eds.), *APA handbook of testing and assessment in psychology* (Vol. 2, pp. 103–117). Washington, DC: American Psychological Association. doi: 10.1037/14048-007

Sigel, I. E. (1996). Applied developmental psychology graduate training should be grounded in a social-cultural framework. In C. B. Fisher, J. P. Murray, & I. E. Sigel (Eds.), *Applied developmental science: Graduate training for diverse disciplines and educational settings* (pp.189–219). Westport, CT: Ablex Publishing.

Sue, S. (1998). In search of cultural competence in psychotherapy and counseling. *American Psychologist, 53*, 440–448. http://dx.doi.org/10.1037/0003-066X.53.4.440

Suzuki, L. A., Onoue, M. A., & Hill, J. S. (2013). Clinical assessment: A multicultural perspective. In K. F. Geisinger, B. A. Bracken, J. F. Carlson, C. Hansen, & N. R. Kuncel (Eds.), *APA handbook of testing and assessment in psychology* (Vol. 2, pp. 193–212). Washington, DC: American Psychological Association. doi: 10.1037/14048-012.

Truax, P., & Wright, S. (2007). Selecting treatment targets and referral. In M. Hersen & J. C. Thomas (Eds.), *Handbook of clinical interviewing with adults* (pp. 79–94). Thousand Oaks, CA: Sage.

Wing Sue, D., & Sue, D. (2008). *Counseling the culturally diverse: Theory and practice* (5th ed.). Hoboken, NJ: John Wiley & Sons.

Yampolsky, M. A., Amiot, C. E., & de la Sablonniere, R. (2013). Multicultural identity integration and well-being: A qualitative exploration of variations in narrative coherence and multicultural identification. *Frontiers in Psychology, 4*, 1–15. doi: 10.3389/fpsyg.2013.00126

Zalaquett, C. P., Chatters, S. J., & Ivey, A. E. (2013). Psychotherapy integration: Using a diversity-sensitive developmental model in the initial interview. *Journal of Contemporary Psychotherapy, 43*, 53–62. doi: 10.1007/s10879-012-9224-6.

CHAPTER 3

The Importance of Client Context

David M. Cimbora and Radhika Krishnamurthy

As clinical psychologists, we immerse ourselves in the realm of psychological disorder. We are trained to perform diagnostic assessments focused on presenting problems and symptoms. Thus, our primary focus is to determine type and severity of dysfunction, identify maladaptive thoughts, feelings, and actions, and recommend suitable treatments. We are guided in identifying psychopathology by our personality assessment measures as well as criteria listed in diagnostic manuals. However, we are rarely urged, or guided, to contemplate the various contexts of the person who is troubled; at best, we might weigh the role of stressful life events as etiological or contributing factors. But do we know enough about the environment and world inhabited and experienced by the client, or, put another way, do we sufficiently consider the contexts in which the evaluation is embedded?

We begin this chapter with the premise that context matters. For the purposes of our discussion, our starting definition of "context" is environments and settings which clients choose or find themselves in. We also extend context to the entirety of the client's past contexts and experiences within them, as these likely have a significant bearing on current functioning.

Bronfenbrenner's (1979) social ecological perspective suggests the importance of environment on the development of our personal psychology. His model encourages psychologists to be simultaneously aware of clients, their environments, and interactions between clients and environments on many levels. A client's contexts can significantly influence his or her cognition, behavior, and emotional expression/experience. One might not ordinarily be angry, but after one has sat in traffic for hours only to find another vehicle cut in front, one might find a much greater propensity for rage. A star player on a football team may ordinarily be cooperative and harmonious. But after a six game losing streak, that same player might engage in blaming and scapegoating. An irresponsible student might develop greater study skills and think more clearly about the material if placed within a motivated study group.

It should come as no surprise, then, that context not only shapes our affect, thought, and action, but also our self-definitions. This is not a new revelation, as much of mental health endorses a biopsychosocial model of human development (e.g., Engel, 1980), where a significant element of the influence is from the environment. We posit that the influence of context on self-definition is gradual and more likely to result if the contexts are chronic in nature. Using the example of the football player above, his self-definition would not likely shift from a harmonious "team-player" to a blaming, scapegoating, divisive player unless the team was consistently mired in losing streaks.

In stating that our contexts influence our self-definition, we are also saying that they help to determine values, beliefs, worldviews, and the lenses one uses to interact with others. In this chapter, we will examine how context influences self-definitions of our clients and extends the overall cultural makeup of our clients. More specifically, context can influence self-definitions regarding gender, sexual orientation, religion, disability and ability, ethnicity (including nationality and regionalism), age, and social-economic status. We will briefly touch upon culture in general, whereas later chapters will examine each variable in detail. Finally, we will focus on methods for keeping client context at the fore of the psychological evaluation.

We begin with an examination of context itself. For our discussion, we partition context into three sub-categories: immediate, life, and psychological. Evaluators are encouraged to consider all three when assessing clients.

Immediate Context

Discussions of client context often dismiss or ignore the proximal role that the immediate context plays in the identifications and presentations of the client. By immediate context, we are referring specifically to the testing situation. As discussed by Bornstein (2011), the assessment setting extends from the actual physical setting to the client's perceptions and beliefs concerning the setting. Collectively, these factors influence the client's approach to, and participation in, the assessment.

We need to be carefully attuned to the impact that the testing environment can have on client presentation. Although it is unlikely that a time-limited experience such as a psychological evaluation can actually influence a client's core self-definition, we hold that the immediate context of the testing situation can influence the process by which a client shares information about him- or herself (e.g., the manner of sharing, the amount, the accuracy, etc.). This impact can be quite significant. If the immediate context affects client disclosure, then it has a consequential effect on conclusions the evaluator draws about the client's self-definitions, among other goals of the evaluation. Less than full and open disclosure on the part of the client can easily lead to faulty conclusions being made by the examiner.

To understand the impact of the testing context, the evaluator first needs to consider the qualities of the testing setting itself (Devlin & Nasar, 2012; Ryan, 1979). First, and perhaps most concretely, what type of building is the evaluation held in? Office buildings/private practices, school settings, community health agencies, hospitals, prisons, etc., all have unique qualities that may elicit different reactions from our clients. The first author's original private practice office was part of a group practice located in a converted residential house. The surrounding neighborhood was quiet and serene. The residential house maintained a sense of charm and warmth, as therapy offices were placed in the converted family room, living room, and even what used to be the garage and master bedroom. However, it lacked a sense of sophistication as, despite the renovation, it still looked very much like a home residence. David's second private practice office was in an office building connected to a medical facility. The surrounding neighborhood was comprised of mostly businesses. The reception area, billing office, therapy rooms, and assessment offices were updated with the latest furnishings and technologies. What it comparatively lacked in charm it made up for in professional presentation.

These two settings sent very different messages to clients as they entered. Although no studies were conducted determining statistically significant differences in client presentation, David's experience was that clients presented quite differently in the two settings. Clients presented very casually in the converted residential home as reflected in their verbal presentations and choice of dress. On the other hand, clients coming to the professional building presented more formally, both in physical appearance and verbal presentation.

The setting can also exert a potent influence on clients' perception of the evaluator's power. When working in a state psychiatric hospital, the second author found that patients responded to her as an authority figure, either with deference or rebellion. This was because, as a treatment team member, she was involved in decisions about length of stay, granting of privileges, etc., in addition to treatment decisions. The setting can also affect patients' responses to standardized assessments, particularly in cases of involuntary hospitalization, because of their awareness that assessment findings figure into treatment team decisions. Psychologists who conduct evaluations in correctional settings likely experience such issues of power dynamics even more strongly. These issues are discussed further in Chapter 13 "Assessment Contexts".

We must pay careful attention to the actual evaluation/testing room itself for possible impacts on client disclosure. The noise factor is one such variable to consider. For example, David's office can sometimes be interrupted with sirens from ambulances entering the medical complex. Such noise can cause significant distraction on the part of the client during evaluation, often interrupting thought flow and speech production. This can also result in client frustration or anxiety. Other aspects, such as lighting, type of furniture (comfortable or uncomfortable), décor, and even paint color could all impact the extent to which and manner by which a client reveals information. This extent and manner of revelation is ultimately interpreted by the assessor. Although office context might not directly relate to a client's cultural identifications, we have to acknowledge the impact of the immediate context on the client's experience of the evaluator and the client's subsequent reactions. Client reactions, in turn, get interpreted by the evaluator and may be incorporated into the evaluator's depictions of the client.

We must also be concerned with the larger environment outside the office. Clients can make assumptions and judgments about the evaluator based on the neighborhood and the building in which the evaluator works. For example, the assessor whose office is in a tall office building in a high socioeconomic status neighborhood might be viewed as successful and good at what he or she does, that he or she charges exorbitant amounts of money to be able to cover expenses, that he or she is affluent, or a variety of other assumptions. Assumptions such as these can impact the relationship between client and assessor, which then can impact the nature and quantity of disclosures by the client. Some trends in mental health suggest a way to bypass this interaction effect is to conduct mental health activities outside of the traditional office and meet within the client's typical environment (e.g., Brooks, 2010).

By shifting services to the client's typical contexts, it is expected that client familiarity and comfort would increase. For example, Leverentz (2010) noted that female ex-prisoners who desired rehabilitation often desired to remain in their old neighborhoods (as opposed to moving) in part due to the fact that the women found comfort in the familiar. Questions to be asked about one's office or work setting are: Is the neighborhood the facility is in familiar to the client, and can he or she find it easily? Are there people nearby (in the office or in the neighborhood) who resemble the client in some way, or does the client experience him- or herself as an outlier of sorts? Is the client's primary language one in use within the clinic or office? If the answers to these kinds of questions are "no," an evaluator would do well to consider ways in which to increase client comfort and familiarity. For example, the development of "in-home" services and neighborhood-based mobile clinics has come as a result of inquiries such as the ones above (Sheidow & Woodford, 2003).

Life Context

By life context, we are referring to the actual contexts in which a client lives, works, and otherwise spends significant time. We can understand life context within idiographic dimensions and nomothetic dimensions.

Idiographic Dimension

In considering idiographic dimensions of life context, we are concerned with factors that are particular to the individual. A significant idiographic context is a client's housing situation. An address tells us very little about the home context in which a client lives. Rather, we need to ask specific questions that reflect the experience of living within that address. How many people live in the home, and who are they? Does the home have room for privacy, or alternatively is there so much room that isolation is fairly common? What is the level of cleanliness? What are the kinds of entertainment that are available? Does the client have a permanent residence, or does he or she move frequently between places? Is the client experiencing homelessness? Does the physically disabled client's home support wheelchair-based mobility? Questions such as these are important to ask in order to obtain information about the nature of domestic life. Because clients typically spend significant amounts of time within their residence, it is likely that this variable has significant influence on cultural identity and self-definition. This idea is not new to psychology or sociology. Over eight decades ago, Plant (1930) described various negative psychological outcomes for children living in crowded situations. Loreto and Tonoli (1973) wrote of the importance of cleanliness in relation to mental health outcomes. Time-tested variables such as these continue to be important to evaluate.

Another aspect to a client's idiographic dimension of context involves his or her overall socioeconomic status, or SES. SES is a broad term that typically incorporates education, income, and occupation (Hollingshead & Redlich, 1958). It tends to symbolize the social standing of an individual, and often reflects the level of monetary and social resources the client has access to and can utilize. We know that, broadly speaking, SES has an inverse relationship with many mental health outcomes, but SES may also help shape a client's worldviews, beliefs, and values.

We need to directly ask clients about their monetary resource level, and not just for determining fees on a sliding scale. Asking about income, economic history, and access to money allows us information that can aid us in understanding our clients' worldviews and approaches to life. It can give us a clue to their sense of agency and locus of control. Ultimately, financial resources give us a window into foundational material on which cultural identities and self-definitions can be built.

But just as important to inquire about are social resources and social status. What is the client's social support network? Is the person relatively isolated from nurturing relationships, or is he or she immersed within a helpful environment? Are the person's social resources primarily electronically based (e.g., Facebook, texting, Twitter, Snapchat), or does contact come directly through face-to-face interaction? Furthermore, does the client have access to, and utilize, community resources such as church or religious/spiritual groups, libraries, activity centers, money lending sources, health centers, public or private transportation, public service (e.g., police/fire departments), and neighborhood watch programs, to name a few. All of these are considered within the context of SES and can directly contribute to a client's cultural identity and self-definition. For example, those without access (and without hope of access) might experience less agency and control (Greene & Murdock, 2013), less upward social mobility, and greater levels of distress (Drentea & Reynolds, 2012). Those with access and who choose to utilize resources might see themselves with internal loci of control and as having more power to influence systems.

Nomothetic Dimension

In addition to the idiographic variables above, it is important that we focus on variables of context to which larger groups of people, along with the client, belong. These nomothetic variables can be understood relative to the larger areas (local, regional, and national) in which the client resides. Each of these will be explored below.

Neighborhood Context

One can consider the neighborhood as a significant influence on a client's cultural identity (Nair, White, Roosa, & Zeiders, 2013). It is not uncommon to find clients having a strong affiliation with their home neighborhood, as might be the case with New Yorkers who hail from a borough, such as the Bronx or Manhattan. In some cases, neighborhoods will have a cultural identity all of their own, with words such as "tough" or "yuppie" that are used by those within or without to define the culture. It might be the case that those within those neighborhoods internalize such definitions as part of their own cultural identity.

Our inquiry into clients' neighborhoods should focus on factors likely to impact client identifications. Evaluators can have clients characterize their neighborhoods, asking specifically about neighborhood culture in general, but also specifics such as levels of crime and whether clients feel safe, availability and viability of transportation (cars, public transit, etc.), access to civic resources (police and fire departments, parks, libraries, businesses, government buildings, etc.), and relational styles of those in the neighborhood (e.g., private and secluded vs. socializing and available). These can all affect clients' living experiences and, ultimately, clients' views of themselves and the world around them. We suggest asking about specifics like these, but at the same time simply inquiring about clients' overall experiences of living where they do. At a level larger than the neighborhood, similar questions can be asked about the city in which the client lives. It is important to keep in mind, though, that cities are a microcosm of many neighborhoods, and it might not be sufficient to simply know that one is from the Los Angeles area, for example. Knowing that one lives in Chinatown, Compton, or Beverly Hills would paint a more specific picture of the client's life context than simply knowing the client hailed from the Los Angeles area.

Regional Context

Moving to the regional level, we can often gain better understanding of a client's self-definition by examining the larger geographic area in which he or she resides. For some, this is defined as a state, province, or territory. In the United States, we find various stereotypes about states or regions of the country. These stereotypes may have political dimensions (e.g., "red" state versus "blue" state), social-economic dimensions (Southern California or Silicon Valley being wealthy areas), or lifestyle (East Coast being active or "always on the go," while West Coast is more "laid-back"). It is important for the evaluator to understand the stereotypes of regions while also recognizing the client is an individual and not necessarily representative of others in the area. More importantly, the evaluator needs to carefully assess the extent to which the client might have internalized or even represent such stereotypes, or the extent to which he or she has remained distant from or opposed to them.

Beyond the issue of stereotypes, regions have actual characteristics that should be of focus during the interview, to the extent they influence client self-definition. Examiners should have some awareness of regional characteristics as they progress through the interview. This could be challenging if the examiner has had little experience with those regions him- or herself, or with others from those areas.

Humble curiosity with the client and consultation with other resources can be especially helpful.

One such dimension is the distinction between rural and urban lifestyles. Population density, access to resources, entertainment pursuits, and pace of life can all be important to explore. The way relationships are maintained and the extent to which an individual identifies with a larger community are both impacted by this rural/urban distinction. Part of how we see the world (our ethnocentric lens) is impacted by *what we see* (or what we are shown) of the world. Those in Southern California are not surprised to see expensive convertible automobiles, eight-lane highways, a plethora of fitness clubs and yoga studios, and lead news stories about Hollywood celebrities. Contrast this with a rural farming community where locals expect to see John Deere farm equipment stores, dirt roads, farm chores that double as a personal workout, and lead news stories about dew points, ground/soil temperature, and likelihood of frost.

Another characteristic is US national versus international life context. With the myriad cultural differences between countries, the competent examiner is careful to fully understand the impact of regional context. Furthermore, if an international client now resides in the United States, it is not sufficient to simply understand the client's country of origin. The examiner also needs to explore factors involved with the move itself (e.g., was the move voluntary or did the client feel he or she had no choice? Did the client come with or without resources? Do they have adequate resources now that they have relocated?). Understanding the client's acculturation process is just as important.

Acculturation involves the process of adjusting to new cultures, typically after a physical move or relocation, such as emigrating from one's native country or moving from one geographic area to another (e.g., moving from the Deep South in the US to Southern California). Current research depicts acculturation as a highly involved and complicated process (Birman & Simon, 2014; Broesch & Hadley, 2012; Schwartz, Unger, Zamboanga, & Szapocznik, 2010). Acculturation can be stressful, take considerable psychological resources, and ultimately can have a significant impact on one's cultural identity (e.g., de Abreu & Hale, 2011; Rosenbusch & Cseh, 2012). Of particular consideration are differing levels of acculturation across family members. The literature shows that parents and children may acculturate at different paces and in different ways following emigration, and that this can cause conflict (Bahrassa, Juan, & Lee, 2013; Telzer, 2011; Unger, Ritt-Olsen, Wagner, Soto, & Baezconde-Garbanati, 2009). Telzer's work in particular offers evaluators an appropriate frame for understanding this conflict, based on her review of the literature. It is widely known that children tend to acculturate faster than their parents in the host culture. However, Telzer articulates that this is just one possible finding of parent–child differences of acculturation. Another is that children are less acculturated than their parents in the host culture. Similarly, parents might be more or less acculturated in the native culture than their children. Considering such differences in host and native cultures can aid the evaluator in gaining a rich perspective on cultural identities of the family members.

Also important to consider is the client's goodness-of-fit with his or her regional setting. For example, a gay man might feel alienated from others in the religiously conservative small town where he has lived all his life. An unmarried, 35-year-old woman might feel right at home in a cosmopolitan city where many of her peers fit the same demographic. The issue of person–environment fit, discussed largely in the field of organizational psychology, deserves much more attention in clinical personality assessment than it has received to date. The limited literature on this topic includes empirical findings showing that person–society fit mediates the relationship between core self-evaluation and life satisfaction (Jiang & Jiang, 2015). Moreover, person–environment fit is found to be associated both with personality consistency over time and personality change in the direction of higher self-esteem, lower agreeableness, and lower neuroticism (Roberts & Robins, 2004).

As we have discussed, it is imperative that we investigate a client's physical context. These questions can sometimes seem "easy" to clients, as such questions are typically factual and not seen as invasive or overly sensitive. Yet, they can reveal a lot about client identity, particularly as the examiner asks about the experience of living within the settings that the client has. However, the physical environment is not the only area of inquiry regarding context. We will now turn to a more nuanced area of exploration, namely the client's psychological environment.

Psychological Context

With proper informed consent, clients are aware that they will be asked questions that might feel personal in nature. One such subset of these questions involves exploring a client's psychological context. By this, we mean a qualitative inquiry into the social, emotional, and cognitive elements of a client's environment. Although there are many psychological contexts, we will examine four in particular: family of origin, current family structure, work environment, and general environments of choice. These four topics are chosen due to our belief that these have a significant impact on the client's overall worldview, beliefs, attitudes, and other factors that impact cultural identity, and thus their self-definitions.

Family of Origin and Current Family

Perhaps the most significant area for exploration in terms of psychological context involves the client's family system, both family of origin and current family structure. For most clients, family systems have had a significant impact on their cultural identity development (e.g., Ensher & Clark, 2011). By *family of origin*, we are referring to the first family the client was a part of. Family of origin is not necessarily determined by just genetic relations, but might involve extended family members (e.g., aunts, cousins, grandparents, ancestors, etc.) and non-biological "family" members (e.g., friends, neighbors, priests, God-parents, etc.). Sometimes the most significant influences on identity come from relatives or significant others outside the nuclear family. Due to the retrospective (and therefore sometimes inaccurate) nature of client reporting in this area, it is sometimes helpful to have collateral interviews with other family members.

When assessing the family system as a client context, an important starting point is the attachment relationship between early caregivers and the client, which can be construed within a cultural framework (Hong, Fang, Yang, & Phua, 2013; Keller, 2013). Attachment has a significant impact on subsequent relational functioning, including approach, avoidance, expectations of need fulfillment, experience of relational safety and danger, and many others. The examiner should be sensitive to the fact that the parenting structure may take a variety of forms (e.g., two biological parents, single-parent, extended family member parent, no biological parent, gay or lesbian-identified parents, step-parents, etc.). Furthermore, attachment should continue to be assessed as one examines the client's relationships in adulthood. Much evidence supports the relationship between original attachment styles and attachment styles in adulthood (e.g., Fraley, Roisman, Booth-LaForce, Owen, & Holland, 2013).

Another variable of interest involves the sibling subsystem. Issues related to birth order and the client's position in that order, age-separation between siblings, and quality of sibling relationships all can have a significant impact in determining how a client's cultural identity develops (Brody, 1998).

Various qualitative variables should also be assessed. One such variable is the communication styles used by the family, both for internal communication and for external (family members to those outside the family). Other variables include access to information, power, boundaries, and hierarchies. Especially salient in the development of one's self-identity are a family's conflict resolution strategies (e.g., Katz, Kramer, & Gottman, 1992). The research has shown that conflict resolution is highly correlated with cultural identity (e.g., Kim-Jo, Benet-Martínez, & Ozer, 2010; McCarthy, Scheraga, & Gibson, 2010). Finally, issues related to trauma should be addressed as always, but remembering to also focus on the impact of trauma on the client's self-identity is important (Frie, 2011). Of course, the evaluator needs to keep in mind the sensitive nature of trauma and proceed carefully, as such exploration might not be possible for the client at the time of initial assessment.

Many of the same issues should be explored within the client's current family structure (assuming the client defines this experience as having his or her "own" family). Such clients have experienced new roles (e.g., parent, partner, grandparent, divorcee, widow, etc.). The examiner should assess changes in cultural identity and self-definition that may accompany those new roles. For example, seeing oneself as a provider for the first time (versus a consumer), becoming a widow or divorcee, or developing a will or living trust can shift the way someone defines themselves.

Employment Context

Understanding the impact of the client's place of employment is significant in that people in the United States spend an average of around 1,800 hours per year in employment (The American Workplace, 2006). However, it is not just the amount of time spent at work that makes this variable a critical one to explore with clients.

Some cultures stress the importance of placing extremely high value on work identity and work productivity. Therefore, it is not sufficient to ascertain simply what the client "does for a living," but to also inquire about the meaning it brings to the client, the extent to which he or she identifies as a worker, and the measure of personal satisfaction or dissatisfaction the work brings. As discussed in the previous chapter, we experience multiple cultural identities. For some clients, work and other parts of identity seamlessly intertwine. For other clients, their occupational identity comes into conflict with other roles or facets of cultural identity (e.g., Brown, 2014). Examples include the single parent whose time outside the home limits his experience of being an efficacious parent, the employee who experiences conflict between her personal values and the values of her employer, and tension between romantic partners about not having enough time for each other due to work obligations. Examiners should also keep in mind the tension that might occur across generations of a family regarding occupational identity (e.g., parents prescribing certain work roles for their adult children while the adult child would prefer something different, or one generation placing a higher value on work identity than another generation).

Contexts of Choice

The last psychological context we will explore involves the contexts that the client (1) voluntarily chooses to belong to and (2) derives some sense of gain or pleasure from. One could consider contexts of choice to be hobbies, interests, or areas of personal investment. While most examiners thoroughly explore family and work contexts, simply asking the client how he or she likes to spend his or her time can reveal much about cultural identity and self-definition. First, some clients' primary identification is within their hobby or interest area, as opposed to the familial or employment contexts. For such clients, the self-description might be primarily that of an athlete, artist, musician, nature-lover, vegetarian, council member, church elder, etc. For some clients, identity is drawn from relationships (e.g., being a good friend or a kind person). Thus, their context of choice may simply be in relationship with others. The evaluator's exploration of these chosen relationships that occur outside of the family unit is critical to understanding such clients.

Acculturation Issues within Contexts of Choice

We discussed acculturation previously within the frame of life context, as people move from one culturally identified locale to another. However, changes in physical environment are not the only causes of the process of acculturation. Acculturation can occur as one transitions from one psychological context to another. This can be seen as one shifts from one social sphere to another. For example, clients might report their experience of acculturating to life as a new member of a religious group, to a new level of authority at work (e.g., moving into senior leadership), to membership in a club or sports team at school, or to celebrity status for someone who has become famous. Acculturation can also occur as one transitions into a new phase of life. Examples of this include becoming a parent for the first time, identifying as a "senior citizen," leaving home to begin living independently, or transitioning into assisted-living. Each of these examples may include a change in the way the client perceives and relates to others, as well as the way others perceive and relate to the client.

Acculturation is not a dichotomous variable, but a continuous and fluid one. Evaluators should carefully assess for levels of acculturation while recognizing that acculturation in one life context might not be the same as the level in another. For example, a client may have fully acculturated to life as a parent but might still struggle with adapting to living in the United States for the first time.

Recommendations

We have suggested that in order to understand client definitions, the examiner needs to ascertain information about the client context. This begins with the immediate context, and then also considers life context and psychological context. In order to prepare for such inquiry, the examiner should engage in a process similar to the one articulated in the previous chapter. The process should involve self-assessment, information gathering, and consultation.

Self-Assessment

Prior to inquiring about context, the evaluator is encouraged to self-evaluate. Part of understanding the "psychometrics of the self" involves gaining insight into the impact of context in the evaluator's life. This should include a self-assessment of immediate, life, and psychological contexts. Doing so will inform the evaluator about his or her own preconceived notions of familiar contexts, which can likely be generalized to contexts he or she is less familiar with but which might be of extreme salience to his or her clients. This is crucial in order to inhibit the evaluator from projecting self-meaning onto the client, and to minimize the assumption that the evaluator "knows" what the client means. Such assumptions often lead to errors of omission in the inquiry process when evaluators do not ask clarification questions and instead "fill in the blanks" with their own personal experience. Finally, the self-assessment process leads to greater awareness of blind spots and areas of ignorance. This leads to the second step: information gathering.

Information Gathering

Evaluators are encouraged to become students of context impact. It is likely that clients will report contexts that are unfamiliar to the evaluator. Evaluators should not be loath to ask clients to offer clarity and expound upon the details of such contexts and their relative impacts. Although evaluators should be careful to not overstate their ignorance, a well-timed curious question on the part of the evaluator can be especially empowering to clients who already find themselves in an evaluation, and thus on the lower end of the power continuum. However, evaluators should not rely solely on clients to educate them about general processes of context impact. Part of demonstrating competency in working with clients is doing our due diligence in educating ourselves prior to seeing them. For example, if we know we are going to be working with Middle-Eastern immigrants, it would behoove us to familiarize ourselves first with the process of immigration and acculturation, and then more specifically to understand the nuances of the specific Middle-Eastern cultures of our clients and how they might experience acculturation. This may likely involve gathering print or media resources in addition to reading scholarly articles and books. However, another source of information is from the collective wisdom of our colleagues around us. This leads us to our third step: consultation.

Consultation

Consultation and supervision are critical as we attempt to gain insight into context impact. A young male trainee might not understand the implications of his 50-year-old female testing client's transition through menopause (which can be understood as a new psychological context or even possibly an issue of acculturation). In this case, the astute supervisor can offer supervision (or refer for appropriate consultation) on this cultural adjustment and its implications for self-definition and identity. Similarly, before assessing transgender clients, an evaluator might need to seek out supervision, or at the very least, consultation on the shifts in identity this population likely experiences, if in fact transgender issues were ones he had minimal familiarity with. It is true that all clients bring with them their unique physical and psychological contexts. The burden falls to us as evaluators to prepare ourselves for their story. Through self-assessment, information gathering, and consultation, we can best prepare ourselves for understanding client context and its impact on client self-definition.

References

The American workplace: How much time do Americans spend at work? (2006). Retrieved from http://jobs.stateuniversity.com/pages/17/American-Workplace-HOW-MUCH-TIME-DO-AMERICANS-SPEND-AT-WORK.html

Bahrassa, N. F., Juan, M. D., & Lee, R. M. (2013). Hmong American sons and daughters: Exploring mechanisms of parent–child acculturation conflicts. *Asian American Journal of Psychology, 4*, 100–108. doi: 10.1037/a0028451

Birman, D., & Simon, C. D. (2014). Acculturation research: Challenges, complexities, and possibilities. In F. L. Leong, L. Comas-Díaz, G. C. Nagayama Hall, V. C. McLoyd, J. E. Trimble, & F. L. Leong (Eds.), *APA handbook of multicultural psychology, Vol. 1: Theory and research* (pp. 207–230). Washington, DC: American Psychological Association. doi: 10.1037/14189-011

Bornstein, R. F. (2011). Toward a process-focused model of test score validity: Improving psychological assessment in science and practice. *Psychological Assessment, 23*, 532–544. doi: 10.1037/a0022402

Brody, G. H. (1998). Sibling relationship quality: Its causes and consequences. *Annual Review of Psychology, 49*, 1–24. doi: 10.1146/annurev.psych.49.1.1

Broesch, J., & Hadley, C. (2012). Putting culture back into acculturation: Identifying and overcoming gaps in the definition and measurement of acculturation. *The Social Science Journal, 49*, 375–385. doi: 10.1016/j.soscij.2012.02.004

Bronfenbrenner, U. (1979). Contexts of child rearing: Problems and prospects. *American Psychologist, 34*, 844–850. doi: 10.1037/0003-066X.32.10.844

Brooks, G. R. (2010). Therapeutic interventions outside the therapist's office. In G. Brooks (Ed.), *Beyond the crisis of masculinity: A transtheoretical model for male-friendly therapy* (pp. 47–67). Washington, DC: American Psychological Association. doi: 10.1037/12073-003

Brown, T. J. (2014). Work family conflict among parents of atypically developing children: Exploring the impact of worker, work, and child factors. *Journal of Child and Family Studies, 23*, 854–862. doi: 10.1007/s10826-013-9739-9

de Abreu, G., & Hale, H. (2011). Trajectories of cultural identity development of young immigrant people: The impact of family practices. *Psychological Studies, 56*, 53–61. doi: 10.1007/s12646-011-0061-6

Devlin, A. S., & Nasar, J. L. (2012). Impressions of psychotherapists' offices: Do therapists and clients agree? *Professional Psychology: Research and Practice, 43*, 118–122. doi: 10.1037/a0027292

Drentea, P., & Reynolds, J. R. (2012). Neither a borrower nor a lender be: The relative importance of debt and SES for mental health among older adults. *Journal of Aging and Health, 24*, 673–695. doi: 10.1177/0898264311431304

Engel, G. L. (1980). The clinical application of the biopsychosocial model. *The American Journal of Psychiatry, 137*, 535–544.

Ensher, G. L., & Clark, D. A. (2011). Diversity in context: What difference does a difference make in a family? In G. L. Ensher & D. A. Clark (Eds.), *Relationship-centered practices in early childhood: Working with families, infants, and young children at risk* (pp. 73–98). Baltimore, MD: Paul H. Brookes Publishing.

Fraley, R. C., Roisman, G. I., Booth-LaForce, C., Owen, M. T., & Holland, A. S. (2013). Interpersonal and genetic origins of adult attachment styles: A longitudinal study from infancy to early adulthood. *Journal of Personality and Social Psychology, 104*, 817–838. doi: 10.1037/a0031435

Frie, R. (2011). Irreducible cultural contexts: German-Jewish experience, identity, and trauma in a bilingual analysis. *International Journal of Psychoanalytic Self Psychology, 6*, 136–158. doi: 10.1080/15551024.2011.552175

Greene, C. A., & Murdock, K. K. (2013). Multidimensional control beliefs, socioeconomic status, and health. *American Journal of Health Behavior, 37*, 227–237.

Hollingshead, A. B., & Redlich, F. C. (1958). *Social class and mental illness: Community study.* Hoboken, NJ: John Wiley & Sons, Inc. doi: 10.1037/10645-000

Hong, Y., Fang, Y., Yang, Y., & Phua, D. Y. (2013). Cultural attachment: A new theory and method to understand cross-cultural competence. *Journal of Cross-Cultural Psychology, 44*, 1024–1044.

Jiang, Z., & Jiang, X. (2015). Core self-evaluation and life satisfaction: The person-environment fit perspective. *Personality and Individual Differences, 75*, 68–73. doi: http://dx.doi.org/10.1016/j.paid.2014.11.013

Katz, L. F., Kramer, L., & Gottman, J. M. (1992). Conflict and emotions in marital, sibling, and peer relationships. In C. U. Shantz, W. W. Hartup (Eds.), *Conflict in child and adolescent development* (pp. 122–149). New York: Cambridge University Press.

Keller, H. (2013). Attachment and culture. *Journal of Cross-Cultural Psychology, 44*, 175–194. doi: 10.1177/0022022112472253

Kim-Jo, T., Benet-Martínez, V., & Ozer, D. J. (2010). Culture and interpersonal conflict resolution styles: Role of acculturation. *Journal of Cross-Cultural Psychology, 41*, 264–269. doi: 10.1177/0022022109354643

Leverentz, A. (2010). People, places, and things: How female ex-prisoners negotiate their neighborhood context. *Journal of Contemporary Ethnography, 39*, 646–681. doi: 10.1177/0891241610377787.

Loreto, D. D., & Tonoli, C. C. (1973). Behavior theory and its clinical applications. *Neuropsichiatria, 29*, 1–26.

McCarthy, J. F., Scheraga, C. A., & Gibson, D. E. (2010). Culture, cognition and conflict: How neuroscience can help to explain cultural differences in negotiation and conflict management. In A. A. Stanton, M. Day, & I. M. Welpe (Eds.), *Neuroeconomics and the firm* (pp. 263–288). Northampton, MA: Edward Elgar Publishing.

Nair, R. L., White, R. B., Roosa, M. W., & Zeiders, K. H. (2013). Cultural stressors and mental health symptoms among Mexican Americans: A prospective study examining the impact of the family and neighborhood context. *Journal of Youth and Adolescence, 42*, 1611–1623. doi: 10.1007/s10964-012-9834-z.

Plant, J. S. (1930). Some psychiatric aspects of crowded living conditions. *The American Journal of Psychiatry, 9*, 849–860.

Roberts, B. W., & Robins, R. W. (2004). Person-environment fit and its implications for personality development: A longitudinal study. *Journal of Personality, 72*, 89–110. doi: http://dx.doi.org/10.1111/j.0022-3506.2004.00257.x

Rosenbusch, K., & Cseh, M. (2012). The cross-cultural adjustment process of expatriate families in a multinational organization: A family system theory perspective. *Human Resource Development International, 15*, 61–77. doi: 10.1080/13678868.2011.646895

Ryan, W. P. (1979). Therapist's office is a treatment variable. *Psychological Reports, 45*, 671–675. doi: 10.2466/pr0.1979.45.2.67

Schwartz, S. J., Unger, J. B., Zamboanga, B. L., & Szapocznik, J. (2010). Rethinking the concept of acculturation: Implications for theory and research. *American Psychologist, 65*, 237–251. doi: 10.1037/a0019330

Sheidow, A. J., & Woodford, M. S. (2003). Multisystemic therapy: An empirically supported, home-based family therapy approach. *The Family Journal, 11*, 257–263. doi: 10.1177/1066480703011003004

Telzer, E. H. (2011). Expanding the acculturation gap-distress model: An integrative review of research. *Human Development, 53*, 313–340. doi: 10.1159/000322476

Unger, J. B., Ritt-Olson, A., Wagner, K. D., Soto, D. W., & Baezconde-Garbanati, L. (2009). Parent-child acculturation patterns and substance use among Hispanic adolescents: A longitudinal analysis. *The Journal of Primary Prevention, 30*, 293–313. doi: 10.1007/s10935-009-0178-8

CHAPTER 4

Ethnicity and Personality Assessment

Joyce Chu, Lamisha Syeda Muquit, Vedant Agrawal, and Radhika Krishnamurthy

With a globalizing and diversifying population, the need for cultural competency in personality assessment is growing. Historically, personality disorders and assessments have largely been created with European American or Caucasian perspectives and samples, and recent growth in attention to cultural and diversity issues has been somewhat limited to language translations (Dana, 2000; Hall, Bansal, & López, 1999). Many existing assessment instruments and procedures do not go beyond language differences to consider how culture influences ethnic differences in beliefs and behaviors (Dana, 2000). Research is needed to examine and address cultural oversights in psychological assessments that could interfere with a reliable and valid interpretation of personality test results with diverse populations.

This chapter will address ethnic considerations related to the use of personality assessments. The chapter centers around three main sections: an examination of empirical data regarding assessments and ethnic variations, an exploration of the complexities of ethnic variations in clinical presentations and personality disorders, and discussion of clinical considerations for the use of personality assessments with people from different ethnic backgrounds.

Empirical Findings on Ethnicity and Personality Assessments

This section discusses the current state of knowledge regarding the effects of ethnicity on the validity of personality test scores. An examination of several personality assessment instruments including the Rorschach Inkblot Test, Thematic Apperception Test (TAT), Personality Assessment Inventory (PAI), Minnesota Multiphasic Personality Inventory-Second Edition (MMPI-2), and Indigenous Personality Assessment Inventories provides a window into what is currently and empirically known in the field.

Rorschach Inkblot Test

The Rorschach Inkblot Test was developed by Hermann Rorschach to evaluate implicit psychological processes through labeling ambiguous inkblots (Rorschach, 1942). Exner (1969) later developed the Rorschach Comprehensive System (CS) using 730 patients and 600 non-patients from different geographical regions and socioeconomic statuses within the United States. The Rorschach test is used clinically to assess coping and stress management, disordered thinking, affective engagement, self-esteem, and interpersonal capacities, although some validity concerns had been noted with some CS scores (McGrath & Carroll, 2012; Mihura, Meyer, Dumitrascu, & Bombel, 2013; Wood, Nezworski, & Stejskal, 1996). The latest development in the test's evolution is the Rorschach Performance Assessment System (R-PAS; Meyer, Viglione, Mihura, Erard, & Erdberg, 2011), for which international normative data are provided.

Studies exploring ethnicity in association to earlier versions of the Rorschach Inkblot Test utilizing the CS yielded evidence that suggested differences in response styles for the Rorschach test by culture. In a meta-analysis examining Rorschach score patterns, ethnic differences were observed among Korean native, Japanese native, Japanese American, Apache Indian, and Arab native individuals compared to European Americans (Day, Boyer, & De Vos, 1989; De Vos, 1989; De Vos & Miner, 1989; Garb, Wood, Nezworski, Grove, & Stejskal, 2001; Glass, Bieber, & Tkachuk, 1996; Moon & Cundick, 1983).

The Rorschach Performance Assessment System (R-PAS) was developed to address limitations of the CS, strengthen the test's empirical foundations further, and advance its research base (Meyer, Erdberg, & Shaffer, 2007). The R-PAS uses an internationally based normative sample for reference scores, which includes Argentina, Belgium, Brazil, Denmark, Finland, France, Greece, Israel, Italy, Portugal, Romania, Spain, and the United States (Meyer et al., 2007). Although the R-PAS has limited research on ethnic differences to date, two recent studies have provided evidence of the appropriateness of Rorschach use with diverse ethnic groups. Meyer, Giromini, Viglione, Reese, and Mihura (2015) reported that ethnicity had no reliable impact on the 60 Rorschach scores they examined in three clinical and nonclinical samples—the R-PAS international adult sample derived from 13 countries (N = 640), a clinical sample of inpatient and outpatient adults (N = 249), and an outpatient child and adolescent sample (N = 241). They concluded that R-PAS scores are minimally affected by cultural background or ethnic origin. In examining R-PAS measures of psychotic symptoms in a Taiwanese sample, Su and colleagues (2015) found that they validly reflected psychotic symptoms and severity of psychopathology in a sample of 75 psychiatric patients and 15 nonpatient adults. Furthermore, because the Rorschach and criterion measures were administered in the regional language, they concluded that their findings demonstrated the linguistic and cultural adaptability of the R-PAS and its appropriateness for using in an Asian country.

Despite the aforementioned evidence of valid use of the Rorschach with different ethnic groups, research on ethnicity and Rorschach scores has been relatively limited. The extant research, based largely on the CS, suggests that some differences across cultural groups might be expected based on their cultural characteristics and styles. For example, Meyer et al. (2015) noted that clinically relevant cultural references may appear in response verbalizations, which is an issue that deserves further study. We note that ethnic group differences of this kind, as well as small-magnitude Caucasian/non-Caucasian score differences found for a limited set of CS variables, do not necessarily indicate ethnic bias. Nonetheless, they warrant thoughtful attention by the test interpreter to achieve culturally responsive determinations in individual assessments.

Thematic Apperception Test (TAT)

Similar to the Rorschach, the TAT is used to reveal underlying, implicit psychological processes. The TAT contains a series of semi-ambiguous black and white pictures that display various situations and settings; the examinee is asked to tell a story about each picture (Murray, 1943). The test creator, Henry Murray, indicated that the purpose of this measure is to illuminate aspects of an individual's personality of which he or she might be unaware (Murray, 1943). This measure has widespread use nationally and internationally.

When administering the TAT, it is important to consider differences in cross-cultural motives and themes. De Vos (1995) found that after World War II, TAT stories by Japanese immigrants in the U.S. (Issei) were more motivated toward their cultural heritage in Japan than those of U.S.-born Japanese individuals (Nissei). De Vos, Wagatsuma, and Caudill (1973) examined a comparison between Japanese immigrants, Japanese Americans, and White Americans on the first "boy with the violin" TAT card. Japanese immigrants were found to have themes of competence and achievement in their stories while Japanese Americans expressed themes of parental pressure and control of being forced to play the violin.

Differences in themes are also observed between the youth of Latin America and the U.S. Suárez-Orozco and Todorova (2006) conducted multiple studies exploring narratives elicited from the TAT. In the first study, deprivation themes (e.g., not having an adult figure or financial support) were common in rural areas in Latin America (Suárez-Orozco, 1989; Suárez-Orozco & Todorova, 2006). Further, themes of nurturance and achievement were frequent in Central and South America. In contrast, U.S. themes were primarily related to autonomy and positive control, which highlighted values on success rather than effort and hard work. Suárez-Orozco and Suárez-Orozco (1995) also examined Mexican and U.S. cultural differences on TAT themes. Their study explored TAT stories from Mexicans, Mexican immigrants to the U.S., Mexican Americans, and Caucasian Americans. Mexican and Mexican immigrant participants' response data revolved around achievement and self-motivation, whereas Mexican Americans reported more negative themes such as failure. The authors discussed these thematic differences as consistent with changes due to acculturation, which affects one's perception of real-life experiences.

Recent TAT research has suggested differential validity of newer indices such as Cramer's (1991) Defense Mechanism Manual (DMM) for some ethnic groups in the United States. Hibbard et al.'s (2000) comparison of DMM scores of Asian American and White students indicated modest differential validity, with overprediction of desirable qualities for Asian Americans and underprediction of desirable qualities for Whites. These differences were not accounted for by acculturation and vocabulary. Again, findings of this nature do not necessarily indicate inapplicability of the test for a given ethnic group, but are useful in guiding test interpretation.

Overall, with limited sets of directions and ambiguity of the stimuli, linguistic equivalence is not typically a prominent concern with performance-based measures such as the Rorschach and TAT, and these tests and techniques may be more easily applied across different cultural backgrounds. However, limitations of some of these measures revolve around reliability and validity issues for scoring and interpretation, and difficulties in learning test scoring. While supporters of major performance-based measures advocate that there are adequate levels of reliability and validity for some questions with some populations, critics maintain that reliability and validity are difficult to establish due to the complex scoring guidelines.

Personality Assessment Inventory (PAI)

The Personality Assessment Inventory (PAI) is a 344-item four-point Likert scale questionnaire designed to provide clinical information regarding adult personality and psychopathology (Morey, 1999). Some research has found that the higher order structures of the PAI (e.g., an internalizing versus externalizing structure) are maintained across ethnic groups such as Latino/as versus White individuals (Hopwood & Moser, 2011). Yet, other research has shown statistically significant differences on multiple PAI indicators between Latino/a participants and White participants, or patterns of non-normative PAI responses among Latino/a individuals that might be attributable to cultural factors such as acculturation (see Correa & Rogers (2010) for a review). Indeed, a study by Estrada and Smith (2017) showed that Latino participants were found to endorse a greater level of distress than European Americans on the PAI, and another study found higher scores on the Negative Impression Management scale and the Paranoia, Anxiety, and Anxiety-Related Disorders PAI clinical scales, and lower scores on the Warmth scale, among a nonclinical sample of Asian American compared to Caucasian individuals (Chang & Smith, 2015). Furthermore, Chinese Americans with low acculturation have been found to have significantly higher scores on the interpersonal relatedness dimension than European Americans and Chinese Americans with high acculturation (Lin & Church, 2016). Despite this body of ethnicity-related research on the PAI, like many other assessment tools, the majority of ethnicity-related research on the PAI has focused on language translations that demonstrate linguistic equivalence (Morey, 1999).

Minnesota Multiphasic Personality Inventory-2 (MMPI-2)

The MMPI became one of the first self-report measures of its time to provide data on personality and psychopathology (Hathaway & McKinley, 1940). Goals of the MMPI were to allow clinicians and medical staff to examine a wide range of maladaptive behavior and psychiatric patterns of patients through a True/False questionnaire (Hathaway & McKinley, 1940; Dana, 2000).

While the MMPI provided useful information in psychiatric settings, it was originally normed on Caucasian populations (Hathaway & McKinley, 1940; Dana, 2000). Without incorporation of ethnic minorities in the original standardization sample, culture and ethnicity were ignored in the creation of the testing tool (Hall et al., 1999). When the measure was later redeveloped into the MMPI-2 (Butcher, Graham, Ben-Porath, Tellegen, Dahlstrom, & Kaemmer, 1989), items that contained racial bias were removed and ethnic minorities were included in the norming sample (Dana, 2000). The MMPI-2 is now one of the most researched personality assessment tools in the area of ethnic group differences.

Much of the cross-cultural research examining ethnic variations on the MMPI-2 has largely explored linguistic equivalence. These translations of the MMPI-2 have allowed for international use for individuals from different ethnicities or nationalities (Butcher, Cheung, & Lim, 2003). Research has shown translational congruence in test-retest reliability and similar test scores between MMPI and MMPI-2 translations in China, Japan, and Thailand compared to U.S. samples (Cheung, Song, & Zhang, 1996; Pongpanich, 1996; Shiota, Krauss, & Clark, 1996).

Limited equivalence or translational problems have been demonstrated, however, in other language versions of the MMPI-2 (e.g., Korean, Filipino (Tagalog), Vietnamese, and Hmong versions) (Butcher et al., 2003). For example, despite several retranslation attempts, the translation of the MMPI-2 in Korea has demonstrated sustained difficulties in literal translation (Butcher et al., 2003; Han, 1996). As one key example of these difficulties, many Korean college students skipped the "My sex life is satisfactory" item because of the rare occurrence of premarital sex in Korean communities (Butcher et al., 2003; Han, 1996). To reduce stigma of premarital sex, the item was retranslated into "If you are married, my sex life is satisfactory" and "If you are single, although I am not married, I am OK with my sex life the way it is." The Korean sample also displayed significantly elevated scores compared to the U.S. sample (Cheung et al., 1996). The Tagalog and Hmong versions of the MMPI have also demonstrated translational problems in their adaptations (Butcher et al., 2003). The Hmong version, for example, carried difficulties in translation because of limited literacy among the Hmong communities, partly because the written Hmong language has only existed for 40 years (Butcher et al., 2003). Due to the limited translation into the written form of Hmong, an audio version of the MMPI was created (Deinard, Butcher, Thao, Moua Vang, & Hang, 1996).

While the MMPI-2 has been adapted in many different languages and cultures, in an examination of the U.S. version, many studies have found contradictory evidence regarding ethnic differences on the measure (Hall et al., 1999). These ethnic differences make it difficult to discern abnormal from normal behaviors and personality traits in minority individuals (Timbrook & Graham, 1994). For example, Timbrook and Graham (1994) found that as compared to Caucasians, African American men scored higher on scale 8 (Schizophrenia), and African

American women scored higher on scales 4 (Psychopathic Deviate), 5 (Masculinity-Femininity), and 9 (Hypomania). On the other hand, a meta-analysis conducted by Hall and colleagues (1999) examined ethnic differences between African Americans, Latino Americans, and Caucasians, and found inconclusive results. The largest difference was found with scale 5, where male Latino Americans scored lower, suggesting the cultural phenomenon of machismo or masculinity. These cultural differences indicate a need for cultural guidelines of personality assessment to inform diagnosis and treatment.

It should be noted that, based on a comprehensive review of MMPI/MMPI-2 findings for ethnic groups, Greene (2011) cautioned against overstating the case of ethnic group differences in scores when (a) they reflect group averages, (b) often they do not reach the level of clinical significance, and (c) they are moderated by other demographic features. In our opinion, the bigger issue concerns the examiner's understanding of the client's cultural background and identification, so as to interpret findings in context.

Indigenous Personality Assessment Inventories

Some scholars have created indigenous (developed from the ground up) self-report inventories of personality assessment that recognize the existence of personality constructs unique to (rather than universal across) different cultural groups. The Chinese Personality Inventory (CPAI; Cheung, Song, & Zhang, 1996), for example, was created by initially identifying 150 personality characteristics through examination of Chinese literature, survey of Chinese individuals, and others. After the process of psychometric validation, the CPAI included personality constructs unique to Chinese individuals that are not found in predominantly Western-based personality assessments (Cheung et al., 1996). Interpersonal relatedness was highlighted as a personality construct particularly absent from Western measures (Cheung, Cheung, Leung, Ward, & Leong, 2003). The CPAI-2, for example, follows a four-factor model that considers Social Potency, Dependability, Accommodation, and Interpersonal Relatedness (Cheung et al., 2008). Subsequently, when the CPAI-2 was tested for applicability in other non-Western cultures, further cultural variability in factor structure was uncovered (Laher, 2015). For example, the Dutch and Romanian versions of the CPAI-2 were found to have five- and six-factor models, respectively, rather than the standard four-factor model.

Cultural and Interpersonal Presentation Factors in Personality

Much of the existing research on the influence of ethnicity in personality assessment tools has focused on language, population norms, and language translations—often exploring language differences in personality assessments as a proxy for the cultural factors related to ethnicity. Yet, other literature identifies *cultural* constructs that hold importance and influence on one's personality structure and expression of personality, and thus the validity of assessment responses. One such cultural construct is that of independent versus interdependent selfways.

Independent selfways that are more common in Western cultures, and interdependent selfways that are more common in Eastern cultures, refer to cultural rules for interpersonal presentations and self-construals that dictate personality-related values, cognitions, and behaviors for members of an ethnic group (Markus, Mullally, & Kitayama, 1997). For example, Western cultures strongly favor uniqueness, independence, and personal gains whereas Eastern cultures are more likely to favor different traits related to coordination, selflessness, and unity (Triandis, 1995). Ethnic groups that endorse individualistic beliefs have motivation toward self-enhancement, which is less common in collectivistic cultures (Sedikides, Gaertner, & Toguchi, 2003). For example, in the U.S., individuals typically focus on perceived strengths and successes while denying or ignoring negative attributions of themselves (Sedikides et al., 2003). On the other hand, Japanese culture holds opposite beliefs where they value "hitonami," or self-discipline and being average (Markus, Kitayama, & Heiman, 1996). Within the U.S., differences in level of individualism and collectivism among subgroups are noted, with some unexpected results. For example, Coon and Kemmelmeier (2001) reported higher collectivism among African Americans and Asian Americans but not Latino Americans compared to European Americans, and higher individualism among African Americans compared to European Americans and Asian Americans.

Given the differences in independent versus interdependent selfways and cultural beliefs, it is important to see how these differences translate to assessment measures. Collectivistic and individualistic differences, for example, are evident in self-report measures assessing for personality traits, such as the NEO Personality Inventory. In a study by Allik and McCrae (2004), the researchers found that European and American cultures endorsed higher extraversion and openness, and lower agreeableness compared to Asian and African cultures. An investigation of how acculturative struggles in navigating differing cultural values or practices may affect responses to personality assessments might be particularly important for understanding how ethnicity affects personality among immigrant or bicultural individuals. Van De Vijver and Phalet (2004) indicated that most psychological assessments fail to incorporate an acculturation measure to examine an individual's identification level of their native and host cultures. The researchers argued that adding an acculturation measure can strengthen the validity of psychological assessments.

The influence of cultural values in responses to personality assessments might be particularly evident in self-report response styles (Hamamura, Heine, & Paulhus, 2008). In a comparison between East Asians, North Americans with East Asian heritage, and European Americans, Hamamura and colleagues (2008) found stylistic differences in how participants responded to self-report measures involving Likert-style response options; East Asians responded to self-reports in a more ambivalent or moderate style, selecting the middle choices. Additionally, North Americans with East Asian heritage were also found to respond moderately and ambivalently, but also expressed extreme response choices similarly to European Americans (Hamamura et al., 2008). Individualistic cultures view conflict as a natural aspect of socializing with others and have traditionally resolved conflict by being assertive or confrontational (Triandis, 1995). Collectivistic cultures, on the other hand, view conflicts as a sign of disorganization and aim to avoid disagreements in order to reduce society discord (Triandis, 1995). The tendency to choose moderate and ambivalent answer choices in East Asian culture could be related to avoiding conflict and incorporating social desirability.

Ethnic differences in response styles might also be indicative of thought pattern variations. One particular thought approach is dialectical thinking, or the form of thought that holds contradictory beliefs (Hoffman, 1994). Individuals from collectivistic cultures, such as East Asians, have more dialectical thinking patterns in comparison to Caucasians (Hamamura et al., 2008; Peng & Nisbett, 1999). For example, East Asians were found to answer survey with responses that contain *both* positive and negative evaluations such as outgoing and shy, whereas Caucasians chose one evaluation of either shy or outgoing (Hamamura et al., 2008; Choi & Choi, 2002). The response styles that suggest dialectical thinking might reflect navigation of acculturative or bicultural conflicts between differing selfways such as that of collectivistic versus individualistic ideals.

Clearly, cultural constructs among ethnic groups, such as individualism versus collectivism, or acculturation, are important to consider in choosing, administering, and interpreting personality assessment tools and responses. Given that many personality assessments measure the psychopathological aspects of personality, it is also important to understand how cultural constructs among ethnic minorities affect the experience and presentation of psychopathology.

Ethnic Factors in the Clinical Presentation of Personality

Ethnic variations in clinical presentation of psychopathology aspects of personality, as well as differences in construct validity of psychopathology, can affect the valid interpretation of personality assessments. Ethnic differences in the clinical presentation of personality disorders are addressed below. In addition, four particular areas of consideration relevant to the consideration of ethnicity in assessment of psychopathology are discussed.

Ethnicity and Personality Disorders

The literature suggests differences in the diagnosis of personality disorders based on ethnicity. A meta-analysis conducted by McGilloway, Hall, Lee, and Bhui (2010) revealed higher prevalence of personality disorders among White groups compared to Black groups. In contrast, Raza, Demarce, Lash, and Parker (2014) found differences between symptom presentation and higher prevalence rates of Paranoid Personality Disorder among Black individuals compared to White individuals. This racial difference might be attributed to unique experiences among Black individuals such as racism, oppression, perceived discrimination, and spirituality. Differences in the rates of personality disorders diagnoses might also arise from the fact that what constitutes normal or abnormal personality is defined from a Western perspective (Ascoli et al., 2011).

Further evidence of differences in symptoms of personality disorders related to ethnic differences is seen in the clinical presentation of borderline personality disorder. Selby and Joiner's (2009) exploration of ethnic variations initially found a four-factor structure for borderline personality disorder generalizable among Caucasian, Hispanic, and African American participants that included affective dysregulation, cognitive disturbance, disturbed relatedness, and behavioral regulation. However, findings indicated differences between these primary symptom clusters between the different ethnic groups. Caucasian participants viewed "feelings of emptiness" as an affective dysregulation factor, but Hispanic and African Americans saw this as a cognitive disturbance factor. Additionally, Caucasians had higher symptom correlations in the affective and behavioral dysregulation domains of borderline personality disorder.

Widiger and Samuel (2005) asserted two important points about ethnicity and personality disorders: (1) Research on the impact of ethnicity/culture on the diagnosis or assessment of personality disorders is quite limited, and (2) much of the research has been limited to reports of ethnic group differences, and efforts to explain or account for these differences (e.g., as a function of racial discrimination or prejudice) are lacking. Given these constraints, we note that that the personality assessor's cultural competency acquires even greater significance.

Ethnicity and Psychopathology Aspects of Personality

Outside of personality disorders, research has also shown that ethnicity influences the assessment, interpretation, and experience of psychopathology as well—in four main ways. First, ethnic differences in symptom reporting style (e.g., under- or over-reporting) may yield differences in clinical presentation of psychopathology and personality on assessment instruments. As previously discussed, individuals from independent cultures tend to view themselves in terms of positive traits or self-enhancement perspectives, whereas collectivistic cultures value humility and self-criticism (Sedikides et al., 2003). Norasakkunkit and Kalick (2002) conducted a study exploring differences in personality traits between Asian Americans and European Americans via self-report measures for depression, social avoidance and distress, fear of negative evaluation, independent and interdependent self-construal, and a uniqueness or self-enhancement scale. Asian Americans endorsed higher levels of interdependent self-construal and social avoidance and distress than the European Americans, whereas the European Americans scored higher on independent self-construal and self-enhancement. These self-enhancement response styles yielded under-reporting of psychological distress. Further, with higher baseline scores in distress and social avoidance in collectivistic cultures such as Asian Americans, interdependent self-construals of modesty and self-criticism could be mistaken for over-reporting psychiatric symptoms and maladaptive behaviors or personality traits. These ethnic differences in response styles on self-report instruments reflect a potential confound between measurement and construct validity. It is difficult to determine whether ethnic differences in test scores are attributable to cultural variations in response styles, as opposed to actual differences in experience of a particular measured construct.

Second, cultural idioms (language or expressions) of distress can affect how individuals report and experience their mental health experiences and symptoms. The somatization of psychological distress in non-Western cultures as compared to psychologization in Western cultures (Ryder et al., 2008), for example, might be important when considering the validity of emotion-related items on personality assessments. Lee and colleagues (2009) concluded that approximately half of Asian patients diagnosed with Major Depressive Disorder (MDD) experienced painful physical symptoms as opposed to emotional symptoms of sadness. Another study found greater reports of somatic symptoms of depression in Latinos and African Americans compared to Caucasians (Myers et al., 2002). These results are also supported in an international study conducted by Simon, VonKorff, Piccinelli, Fullerton, and Ormel (1999). The researchers screened a total of 25,916 patients within 14 different countries and found that the range of patients diagnosed with depression that reported somatic symptoms was 45–95%. The majority of patients who reported somatic symptoms of depression were from non-Western countries.

Third, the construct validity of psychopathology assessed by personality instruments might deserve examination when symptoms are better explained by culturally normative factors rather than psychopathological processes. For example, research suggests that African Americans' increased reports of paranoia may be related to unique experiences of racism rather than true psychosis (USDHHS, 2001; Whaley, 2001). Without accounting for this influence of ethnicity factors on the validity of a diagnosis or set of psychotic symptoms, clinical bias via overdiagnosis of schizophrenia among African Americans may occur. Research with Latino/a individuals has also indicated the presence of symptoms of schizophrenia that may be culturally normative and better explained by ethnicity-related factors. Specifically, Betancourt and López (1993) found that symptoms of schizophrenia, such as auditory hallucinations, were found to be culturally normative among Latino/a participants due to their religious beliefs.

Research on ethnicity and histrionic personality disorder has yielded other examples of construct validity concerns in the clinical presentation of psychopathology. Among Latino populations, the cultural phenomenon of *machismo* might be misinterpreted as symptoms of histrionic personality disorder such as emotionality, attention-seeking, seductiveness, and impressionability (Paniagua, 2000). Machismo refers to strong masculine pride and exaggerated masculinity with responsibilities to provide and protect one's family (Torres, Solberg, & Carlstrom, 2002). Consistent with a cultural emphasis on machismo, it can be common for Latino men to be sexually seductive, display exaggeration in emotional expressions of aggression, and aim to be the focus of attention (Castillo, 1997; Paniagua, 2000). To determine if such behaviors are indicative of a personality disorder or a culturally normative expression of machismo, clinicians should examine whether these sets of behavior cause some form of functional impairment in an individual's life (APA, 2013).

As a final example of a construct validity concern, the behaviors of immigrants, refugees, and other ethnic minorities have been labeled as overly suspicious or odd, contributing to misdiagnosis of paranoid, schizoid, and schizotypal personality disorders (Paniagua, 2000). Castillo (1997) argues and illustrates this misdiagnosis in the case of members from Swat Pukhtun, tribal people who live in the mountains of Northern Pakistan. Men in this society all own guns, and are guarded, mistrusting and suspicious of others, and defensive of their community. In this community, if men do not own guns or display defensive mannerisms, it is viewed as abnormal. These cultural normative behaviors in the Swat Pukhtun community may be mistaken for maladaptive personality disorders according to the DSM-5. Further, many immigrants are often perceived as detached, socially awkward, and cold in the U.S., however these personality styles are not considered pathological in their respective cultures (Paniagua, 2000). For example, various ethnic groups have spiritual beliefs such as voodoo ceremonies, evil eye, and magical thinking (Paniagua, 2000). Uninformed clinicians might view these beliefs as consistent with schizotypal or schizoid personality disorders (Paniagua, 2000). Given these concerns, it will be important for clinicians to be aware of their own perceptions and biases when diagnosing individuals with personality disorders.

Fourth, ethnic variations in the expression or experience of psychopathology symptoms may be substantial enough to form entire culture-bound syndromes. For example, whereas social phobia in the U.S. is marked by fear of being judged or embarrassed by others, social anxiety among Japanese people can take the form of the culture-bound syndrome *taijin kyofusho*, and focus on how one's own actions offend, displease, or cause embarrassment for others (Kleinknecht, Dinnel, Kleinknecht, Hiruma, & Harada, 1997). There are four different subtypes within *taijin kyofusho* that reflect different fears or phobias of blushing, body appearance, eye-to-eye contact, and odor (Dinnel, Kleinknecht, & Tanaka-Matsumi, 2002). Japanese individuals experiencing *taijin kyofusho* might meet DSM-5 diagnosis for anxiety disorders such as social phobia and agoraphobia; however, this set of behaviors is unique to the Japanese culture.

Another culture-bound syndrome has been noted with individuals from Malaysia, Laos, Papua New Guinea, Polynesia, Philippines, and Puerto Rico who experience a dissociative-like episode involving outbursts of anger, violence, and aggression toward others (Saint Martin, 1999). This behavior has been called *amok* or *running amok*, defined as making "a furious and desperate charge" (Saint Martin, 1999, p. 66). In Malay mythology, amok is seen as an evil spirit entering an individual's body (Saint Martin, 1999). In other cultures, amok may be seen as a personality disorder or psychosis, even though it is a culturally conscribed experience (Saint Martin, 1999). Researchers have attempted to relate amok to suicide to disprove that it is culture-bound, but suicide was rarely present in primitive tribes compared to industrialized nations (Saint Martin, 1999). While suicide and amok have common elements such as risk factors and psychosocial stressors, these two behaviors are different (Saint Martin, 1999).

Clinical Considerations with Personality Assessments

Empirical findings regarding ethnic differences in personality assessment, the influence of cultural constructs on personality, and ethnic variations in psychopathology and personality suggest several areas of consideration when clinicians are choosing, administering, and interpreting personality assessment tools. First, examiners should conduct a literature search to familiarize themselves with the cross-cultural literature on a particular assessment instrument, in order to assess the reliability and validity of personality assessments across ethnicities. A literature review can assist the provider in identifying testing norms, language translations, and psychometric validation for the population of interest. Several existing tests and measures are reliable and valid even when administered across languages and cultures. One example is the Impact of Event Scale-Revised Japanese language version (IES-R-J), found to be a valid measure of posttraumatic stress disorder symptoms after a traumatic event for a Japanese sample (Asukai et al., 2002). However, this might not be the case for some other measures. A study by Schwarzer, Bäßler, Kwiatek, Schröder, and Zhang (1997) found that the reliability and validity estimates for the Assessment of Optimistic Self-Beliefs varied based on language, as well as the country of origin of the participant. The test was found to have the greatest internal consistency in Chinese, and to have greater validity when administered to the German sample compared to the Costa Rican sample. Among broadband measures such as the MMPI-2, although reliability and validity of scores for different ethnic/cultural groups have been demonstrated, the test user must consider that a modified interpretation of results might be indicated, for example, among Chinese participants (Cheung & Song, 1989).

Second, the intake process can be useful to note clients' cultural factors such as language preferences, degree of acculturation, familiarity with American culture, and cultural practices that might affect the testing environment. It is imperative for examiners to understand a client's language proficiency and preference, reading level, and cultural identity in order to determine which personality assessments and diagnoses are appropriate. Similarly, clinicians should carefully assess their own language match and competency to administer personality assessments to persons from different linguistic backgrounds. It is important for the examiner to not only be conversant in the language that the client is tested in, but also understand the challenges posed by linguistic barriers when complex symptoms and experiences are described.

Third, it is important for clinicians to examine potential ethnic differences in response style along with response biases that might appear depending on the format of an assessment tool. Asian or Asian American participants who may exhibit a central tendency bias to choose moderate or average response choices on Likert-style self-reports (Hamamura et al., 2008), for example, might benefit from multimodal assessment with conjunctive interviews, or the choice of True-False self-reports alternatives for assessments when available.

Fourth, ethnic minorities may under- or over-report personality or psychopathology constructs, or experience and express such constructs with culturally informed idioms of distress (e.g., somatization). Examiners should educate themselves about such cultural reporting and idiom of distress tendencies and their concomitant potential to yield under- or over-detection of personality constructs on assessment instruments.

Fifth, clinicians should pay careful attention to potential cultural constructs that could influence the content of assessment responses by some clients. Independent versus interdependent selfways, individualism versus collectivism, or acculturation level, for example, might be evident in lower extraversion and openness but higher agreeableness in Asian and African compared to European and American cultures (Allik & McCrae, 2004). In some cases, different response patterns have been found on personality assessments, with the underlying cultural mechanism for such ethnic differences as yet unknown. Some research suggests that assessment responses by ethnic minorities that appear more pathological in nature might be more normative in their cultural context, or vice versa; clinicians should titrate their interpretation of assessment results accordingly.

Finally, relationship factors between the examiner and examinee that constitute the testing environment can influence responses on personality assessment measures. Among Asian cultures, for example, perceptions of examiner as higher status might deter participants from asking clarifying questions, potentially affecting the efficacy of the test results due to lack of understanding of items (Bissell, May, & Noyce, 2004). Further, some ethnic minority groups such as African Americans have more mistrust of ethnically dissimilar Caucasian therapists compared to ethnically similar African American therapists (Whaley, 2001), which can yield discomfort in the testing environment. In these instances of perceived power differences or mistrust between examiner and examinee, it might be important for the therapist to consider the relationship between one's own cultural identity and minority status with that of the examinee, and attempt to establish a comforting and trusting relationship with the client accordingly. A more trusting relationship could facilitate participants' ability to clarify doubts, ask questions, and respond to the assessments as accurately as possible.

Given what we know about personality assessments and how they are affected by ethnic and cultural differences, clinicians are advised to maintain awareness about the influence of ethnic and cultural factors when choosing, administering, and interpreting personality assessments. Many existing personality assessments were designed based on a predominantly Caucasian sample with limitations in generalizability to a wider multicultural population (Dana, 2000). The administration and interpretation of personality assessments with ethnic minorities should take into account pre-existing cross-cultural literature, testing norms, test-taking abilities, and linguistic differences that could affect the accuracy of testing responses and scores. Further research will also be needed to advance the clinical practice of culturally competent personality assessments.

Conclusions

As the field of personality and psychopathology assessment continues to grow and become more culturally sensitive, it is important to consider the role of ethnicity in personality and psychopathological outcomes. Cultural considerations for assessment measures have predominantly focused on language related to ethnicity by translating tests to different languages, but cultural considerations for ethnicity should also include the influence of cultural beliefs, values, and practices. The MMPI-2, PAI, and NEO inventories, for example, have been adapted and translated into several different languages. While the language translation process involves several steps to determine if the translation is equivalent in item meanings as originally constructed, it does not systematically address variations in meanings of personality or psychopathology between ethnic groups. Given that most personality assessments were originally developed using Caucasian or European American samples, ethnic variations of symptom presentations and behaviors that are common in ethnic minority groups are not commonly accounted for. When using examining measures that do not require language adaptations, such as performance-based measures, the impact of acculturation and cultural beliefs on responses still needs to be considered.

With regard to research comparing ethnic differences between Caucasians and ethnic minorities, the evidence suggests that variations in clinical presentation and interpersonal styles (i.e., individualism versus collectivism) influence personality expression, and thus the validity of test scores. With regard to personality or psychiatric disorder in particular, it is important to consider the client's culturally influenced reporting styles, cultural idioms of distress, culture-bound syndromes, and the cultural validity of symptoms (including whether symptoms are better explained by culturally normative factors rather than psychopathological processes).

Finally, it is most important to consider what steps clinicians can take in regard to ethnic differences when assessing clinical symptoms and personality and psychiatric disorders to inform treatment. Competency in assessing personality and psychopathology includes an understanding of cultural differences and appropriate adaptation of assessments for clients with different ethnic backgrounds. These factors can involve specific variables related to test administration and test performance. Practitioners can make necessary adaptations such as having audiotapes of recorded assessment questions if clients cannot read or understand a language. Further, practitioners should take into account a client's cultural identity and understanding of U.S. culture, and interpret the results in ways that are culturally congruent with clients' specific needs.

As noted by Krishnamurthy and Meyer (2016), the assessment literature has to progress further in addressing diversity considerations extending beyond issues of scale development and validation with diverse clients, with emphasis on understanding the role of cultural influences on assessment results. Future personality assessment research should continue to examine differences between and within cultural groups, but with increased focus on explicating specific factors involved in these variations. Appropriate ethnic minority representation in sampling norms is needed in the creation and updating of personality assessments. Additionally, research should explore cultural personality constructs and theories and how these might affect the interpretation of current personality assessment results, taking cultural competence beyond language translation to that of cultural adaptation.

References

Allik, J., & McCrae, R. R. (2004). Toward a geography of personality traits patterns of profiles across 36 cultures. *Journal of Cross-Cultural Psychology, 35*(1), 13–28. doi: 10.1177/0022022103260382

American Psychiatric Association. (2013). *Diagnostic and statistical manual of mental disorders* (5th edition). Arlington, VA: American Psychiatric Publishing.

Ascoli, M., Lee, T., Warfa, N., Mairura, J., Persaud, A., & Bhui, K. (2011). Race, culture, ethnicity and personality disorder. *World Cultural Psychiatry Research Review, 6*(1), 52–60.

Asukai, N., Kato, H., Kawamura, N., Kim, Y., Yamamoto, K., Kishimoto, J., et al. (2002). Reliability and validity of the Japanese-language version of the Impact of Event Scale-Revised (IES-R-J): Four studies of different traumatic events. *The Journal of Nervous and Mental Disease, 190*(3), 175–182. doi: 10.1097/00005053-200203000-00006

Betancourt, H., & López, S. R. (1993). The study of culture, ethnicity, and race in American psychology. *American Psychologist, 48*(6), 629–637. doi: 10.1037//0003-066x.48.6.629

Bissell, P., May, C. R., & Noyce, P. R. (2004). From compliance to concordance: Barriers to accomplishing a re-framed model of health care interactions. *Social Science and Medicine, 58*(4), 851–862. doi: 10.1016/s0277-9536(03)00259-4

Butcher, J. N., Cheung, F. M., & Lim, J. (2003). Use of the MMPI-2 with Asian populations. *Psychological Assessment, 15*(3), 248. doi: 10.1037/1040-3590.15.3.248

Butcher, J. N., Graham, J. R., Ben-Porath, Y. S., Tellegen, A., Dahlstrom, W. G., & Kaemmer, B. (1989). *MMPI-2: Manual for administration and scoring*. Minneapolis: University of Minnesota Press.

Castillo, R. J. (1997). *Culture & mental illness: A client-centered approach*. Pacific Grove, CA: Thomson Brooks/Cole Publishing Co.

Chang, J., & Smith, S. R. (2015). An exploration of how Asian Americans respond on the Personality Assessment Inventory. *Asian American Journal of Psychology, 6*(1), 25–30. http://doi.org/10.1037/a0036173

Cheung, F. M., & Song, W. (1989). A review on the clinical applications of the Chinese MMPI. *Psychological Assessment, 1*(3), 230–237. doi: 10.1037//1040-3590.1.3.230

Cheung, F. M., Cheung, S. F., Leung, K., Ward, C., & Leong, F. (2003). The English version of the Chinese Personality Assessment Inventory. *Journal of Cross-Cultural Psychology, 34*(4), 433–452. doi: 10.1037/t27322-000

Cheung, F. M., Cheung, S. F., Zhang, J., Leung, K., Leong, F., & Kuang, H. Y. (2008). Relevance of openness as a personality dimension in Chinese culture: Aspects of its cultural relevance. *Journal of Cross-Cultural Psychology, 39*(1), 81–108. http://doi.org/10.1177/0022022107311968

Cheung, F. M., Song, W. Z., & Zhang, J. X. (1996). The Chinese MMPI–2: Research and applications in Hong Kong and the People's Republic of China. In J. N. Butcher (Ed.), *International adaptations of the MMPI–2: A handbook of research and applications* (pp. 137–161). Minneapolis: University of Minnesota Press.

Choi, I., & Choi, Y. (2002). Culture and self-concept flexibility. *Personality and Social Psychology Bulletin, 28*(11), 1508–1517. doi: 10.1177/014616702237578

Coon, H. M., & Kemmelmeier, M. (2001). Cultural orientations in the United States: (Re) examining differences among ethnic groups. *Journal of Cross-Cultural Psychology, 32*, 348–364. doi: 10.1177/0022022101032003006.

Correa, A. A., & Rogers, R. (2010). Cross-cultural applications of the PAI. In M. A. Blais, M. R. Baity, & C. J. Hopwood (Eds.), *Clinical applications of the Personality Assessment Inventory* (pp. 135–148). New York: Routledge.

Cramer, P. (1991). *The development of defense mechanisms: Theory, research, and assessment.* New York: Springer-Verlag.

Dana, R. H. (Ed.). (2000). *Handbook of cross-cultural and multicultural personality assessment.* Routledge. doi: 10.4324/9781410602374

Day, R., Boyer, L. B., & De Vos, G. A. (1989). Progressive constriction in Apache youth. In G. A. De Vos & L. B. Boyer (Eds.), *Symbolic analysis cross-culturally: The Rorschach test* (pp. 293–334). Berkeley, CA: University of California Press. doi: 10.2307/2072149

De Vos, G. A. (1989). Personality continuities and cultural change in Japanese Americans. In G. A. De Vos & L. B. Boyer (Eds.), *Symbolic analysis cross-culturally: The Rorschach test* (pp. 93–136). Berkeley, CA: University of California Press. doi: 10.2307/2072149

De Vos, G. A. (1995). Psychological anthropology: A professional odyssey. *The Psychoanalytic Study of Society, V. 19: Essays in Honor of George A. De Vos, 19,* 23.

De Vos, G. A., & Miner, H. (1989). Oasis and Casbah: Acculturative stress. In G. A. De Vos & L. B. Boyer (Eds.), *Symbolic analysis cross-culturally: The Rorschach test* (pp. 201–245). Berkeley, CA: University of California Press. doi: 10.2307/2072149

De Vos, G. A., Wagatsuma, H., & Caudill, W. (1973). *Socialization for achievement: Essays on the cultural psychology of the Japanese* (No. 7). University of California Press. doi: 10.1177/136346157401100217

Deinard, A. S., Butcher, J. N., Thao, U. D., Moua Vang, S. H., & Hang, K. (1996). Development of a Hmong translation of the MMPI-2. *International Adaptations of the MMPI-2,* 194–205.

Dinnel, D. L., Kleinknecht, R. A., & Tanaka-Matsumi, J. (2002). A cross-cultural comparison of social phobia symptoms. *Journal of Psychopathology and Behavioral Assessment, 24*(2), 75–84.

Estrada, A. R., & Smith, S. R. (2017). An exploration of Latina/o respondent scores on the Personality Assessment Inventory. *Current Psychology, 36*(1), 1–10.

Exner, J. E. (1969). *The Rorschach systems.* New York: Grune & Stratton.

Garb, H. N., Wood, J. M., Nezworski, M. T., Grove, W. M., & Stejskal, W. J. (2001). Toward a resolution of the Rorschach controversy. *Psychological Assessment, 13*(4), 433–448. doi: 10.1037/1040-3590.13.4.433

Glass, M. H., Bieber, S. L., & Tkachuk, M. J. (1996). Personality styles and dynamics of Alaska native and normative incarcerated men. *Journal of Personality Assessment, 66,* 583–603. doi: 10.1207/s15327752jpa6603_8

Greene, R. L. (2011). *The MMPI-2/MMPI-2-RF: An interpretive manual* (3rd ed.). Boston: Allyn & Bacon.

Hall, G. C. N., Bansal, A., & López, I. R. (1999). Ethnicity and psychopathology: A meta-analytic review of 31 years of comparative MMPI/MMPI-2 research. *Psychological Assessment.* doi: 10.1037//1040-3590.11.2.186

Hamamura, T., Heine, S. J., & Paulhus, D. L. (2008). Cultural differences in response styles: The role of dialectical thinking. *Personality and Individual Differences, 44*(4), 932–942. doi: 10.1016/j.paid.2007.10.034

Hambleton, R. K., Merenda, P. F., & Spielberger, C. (2005). Issues, designs, and technical guidelines for adapting tests into multiple languages and cultures. *Adapting Educational and Psychological Tests for Cross-Cultural Assessment, 1,* 3–38. doi: 10.4324/9781410611758

Han, K. (1996). The Korean MMPI-2. In J. N. Butcher (Ed.), *International adaptations of the MMPI–2: Research and clinical applications* (pp. 88–136). Minneapolis: University of Minnesota Press.

Hathaway, S. R., & McKinley, J. C. (1940). A multiphasic personality schedule (Minnesota): I. Construction of the schedule. *The Journal of Psychology, 10*(2), 249–254. doi: 10.1080/00223980.1940.9917000

Hibbard, S., Tang, P. C. Y., Latko, R., Park, J. H., Munn, S., Bolz, S., & Somerville, A. (2000). Differential validity of the Defense Mechanism Manual for the TAT between Asian Americans and Whites. *Journal of Personality Assessment, 75*, 351–372. doi: 10.1207/S15327752JPA7503_01.

Hoffman, I. Z. (1994). Dialectical thinking and therapeutic action in the psychoanalytic process. *Psychoanalytic Quarterly, 63*, 187–218. doi: 10.1002/j.2167-4086.2002.tb00021.x

Hopwood, C. J., & Moser, J. S. (2011). Personality Assessment Inventory internalizing and externalizing structure in college students: Invariance across sex and ethnicity. *Personality and Individual Differences, 50*(1), 116–119. http://doi.org/10.1016/j.paid.2010.08.013

Kleinknecht, R. A., Dinnel, D. L., Kleinknecht, E. E., Hiruma, N., & Harada, N. (1997). Cultural factors in social anxiety: A comparison of social phobia symptoms and Taijin Kyofusho. *Journal of Anxiety Disorders, 11*(2), 157–177. doi: 10.1016/S0887-6185(97)00004-2

Krishnamurthy, R., & Meyer, G. J. (2016). Psychopathology assessment. In J. C. Norcross, G. R. VandenBos, & D. K. Freedheim (Editors-in-Chief), R. Krishnamurthy (Associate Editor), *APA handbook of clinical psychology, Vol. 3: Applications and methods* (pp. 103–137). Washington, DC: American Psychological Association. doi: 10.1037/14861-000

Laher, S. (2015). Exploring the utility of the CPAI-2 in a South African sample: Implications for the FFM. *Personality and Individual Differences, 81*, 67–75. doi: 10.1016/j.paid.2014.12.010

Lee, P., Zhang, M., Hong, J. P., Chua, H.-C., Chen, K.-P., Tang, S. W., et al. (2009). Frequency of painful physical symptoms with major depressive disorder in Asia. *The Journal of Clinical Psychiatry, 70*(1), 83–91. doi: 10.4088/JCP.08m04114

Lin, E. J.-L., & Church, A. T. (2016). Are indigenous Chinese personality dimensions culture-specific? *Journal of Cross-Cultural Psychology, 35*(5), 586–605. http://doi.org/10.1177/0022022104268390

Markus, H. R., Kitayama, S., & Heiman, R. J. (1996). Culture and "basic" psychological principles. In E. T. Higgins & A. W. Kruglanski (Eds.), *Social psychology: Handbook of basic principles* (pp. 857–913). New York: Guilford Press.

Markus, H. R., Mullally, P., & Kitayama, S. (1997). Selfways: Diversity in modes of cultural participation. In U. Neisser & D. A. Jopling (Eds.), *The conceptual self in context: Culture, experience, self-understanding* (pp. 13–61). Cambridge, UK: Cambridge University Press.

McGilloway, A., Hall, R. E., Lee, T., & Bhui, K. S. (2010). A systematic review of personality disorder, race and ethnicity: Prevalence, aetiology and treatment. *BMC Psychiatry, 10*(1), 33.

McGrath, R. E., & Carroll, E. J. (2012). The current status of "projective tests." In H. Cooper et al. (Eds.), *APA handbook of research methods in psychology, Vol. 1: Foundations, planning, measures, and psychometrics* (pp. 329–348). Washington, DC: American Psychological Association.

Meyer, G. J., Erdberg, P., & Shaffer, T. W. (2007). Toward international normative reference data for the Comprehensive System. *Journal of Personality Assessment, 89*(S1), S201–S216. doi: 10.1080/00223890701629342

Meyer, G. J., Giromini, L., Viglione, D. J., Reese, J. B., & Mihura, J. L. (2015). The association of gender, ethnicity, age, and education with Rorschach scores. *Assessment, 22*(1), 46–64. doi: 10.1177/1073191114544358

Meyer, G. J., Viglione, D. J., Mihura, J. L., Erard, R. E., & Erdberg, P. (2011). *Rorschach Performance Assessment System: Administration, coding, interpretation, and technical manual.* Toledo, OH: Author.

Mihura, J. L., Meyer, G. J., Dumitrascu, N., & Bombel, G. (2013). The validity of individual Rorschach variables: Systematic reviews and meta-analyses of the Comprehensive System. *Psychological Bulletin, 139*(3), 548–605. doi: 10.1037/a0029406

Moon, T. I., & Cundick, B. P. (1983). Shifts and constancies in Rorschach responses as a function of culture and language. *Journal of Personality Assessment, 47*(4), 345–349. doi: 10.1207/s15327752jpa4704_2

Morey, L. C. (1999). *Personality Assessment Inventory (PAI).* New York: John Wiley & Sons, Inc.

Murray, H. A. (1943). *Manual for the Thematic Apperception Test.* Cambridge, MA: Harvard University Press.

Myers, H. F., Lesser, I., Rodriguez, N., Mira, C. B., Hwang, W.-C., Camp, C., et al. (2002). Ethnic differences in clinical presentation of depression in adult women. *Cultural Diversity & Ethnic Minority Psychology, 8*(2), 138–156. doi: 10.1037//1099-9809.8.2.138

Norasakkunkit, V., & Kalick, S. M. (2002). Culture, ethnicity, and emotional distress measures: The role of self-construal and self-enhancement. *Journal of Cross-Cultural Psychology, 33*(1), 56–70. doi: 10.1177/0022022102033001004

Paniagua, F. A. (2000). Culture-bound syndromes, cultural variations, and psychopathology. *Handbook of multicultural mental health: Assessment and treatment of diverse populations,* 139–169. doi: 10.1016/B978-012199370-2/50009-2

Peng, K., & Nisbett, R. E. (1999). Culture, dialectics, and reasoning about contradiction. *American Psychologist, 54*(9), 741. doi: 10.1037/0003-066X.54.9.741

Pongpanich, L. O. (1996). Use of the MMPI-2 in Thailand. In J. N. Butcher (Ed.), *International adaptations of the MMPI-2: Research and clinical applications:* (pp. 162–174). Minneapolis: University of Minnesota Press.

Raza, G. T., DeMarce, J. M., Lash, S. J., & Parker, J. D. (2014). Paranoid personality disorder in the United States: The role of race, illicit drug use, and income. *Journal of Ethnicity in Substance Abuse, 13*(3), 247–257.

Rorschach, H. (1942). *Psychodiagnostics: A diagnostic test based on perception.* Oxford, UK: Hans Huber. (Original work published 1921)

Ryder, A. G., Yang, J., Zhu, X., Yao, S., Yi, J., Heine, S. J., & Bagby, R. M. (2008). The cultural shaping of depressive symptoms: Somatization and psychologization in China and North America. *Journal of Abnormal Psychology, 117,* 300–313. doi: 10.1037/0021-843X.117.2.300

Saint Martin, M. L. (1999). Running amok: A modern perspective on a culture-bound syndrome. *Primary Care Companion to the Journal of Clinical Psychiatry, 1*(3), 66. doi: 10.4088/PCC.v01n0302

Schwarzer, R., Bäßler, J., Kwiatek, P., Schröder, K., & Zhang, J. X. (1997). The assessment of optimistic self-beliefs: Comparison of the German, Spanish, and Chinese versions of the general self-efficacy scale. *Applied Psychology, 46*(1), 69–88. doi: 10.1111/j.1464-0597.1997.tb01096.x

Sedikides, C., Gaertner, L., & Toguchi, Y. (2003). Pancultural self-enhancement. *Journal of Personality and Social Psychology, 84*(1), 60. doi: 10.1037/0022-3514.84.1.60

Selby, E. A., & Joiner, T. E. (2009). Ethnic variations in the structure of borderline personality disorder symptomatology. *Journal of Psychiatric Research, 43*(2), 115–123. doi: 10.1016/j.jpsychires.2008.03.005

Shiota, N. K., Krauss, S. S., & Clark, L. A. (1996). Adaptation and validation of the Japanese MMPI-2. *International adaptations of the MMPI-2: Research and clinical applications,* 67–87. doi: 10.1002/(SICI)1097-4679(199605)52:3<311::AID-JCLP8>3.0.CO;2-U

Simon, G. E., VonKorff, M., Piccinelli, M., Fullerton, C., & Ormel, J. (1999). An international study of the relation between somatic symptoms and depression. *New England Journal of Medicine, 341*(18), 1329–1335. doi: 10.1056/NEJM199910283411801

Su, W., Green, E. E., Su, J.-A., Viglione, D. J., Tam, W.-C. C., & Chang, Y.-C. (2015). Cultural and linguistic adaptability of the Rorschach Performance Assessment System as a measure of psychotic characteristics and severity of mental disturbance in Taiwan. *Psychological Assessment, 27*(4), 1273–1285. doi: 10.1037/pas0000144

Suárez-Orozco, C., & Todorova, I. L. (2006). Projecting the voices of Mexican-origin children. *Research in Human Development, 3*(4), 211–228. doi: 10.1207/s15427617rhd0304_3

Suárez-Orozco, C., & Suárez-Orozco, M. M. (1995). *Transformations: Immigration, family life, and achievement motivation among Latino adolescents*. Palo Alto, CA: Stanford University Press.

Suárez-Orozco, M. M. (1989). *Central American refugees and US high schools: A psychosocial study of motivation and achievement*. Palo Alto, CA: Stanford University Press.

Timbrook, R. E., & Graham, J. R. (1994). Ethnic differences on the MMPI-2? *Psychological Assessment, 6*(3), 212–217. doi: 10.1037/1040-3590.6.3.212

Torres, J. B., Solberg, V. S. H., & Carlstrom, A. H. (2002). The myth of sameness among Latino men and their machismo. *American Journal of Orthopsychiatry, 72*(2), 163. doi:10.1037/0002-9432.72.2.163

Triandis, H. C. (1995). *Individualism & collectivism*. Boulder, CO: Westview Press.

United States Census Bureau (2013). Retrieved September 07, 2016, from www.census.gov/topics/population/race/about.html

U.S. Department of Health and Human Services (USDHHS). (2001). *Mental health: Culture race, and ethnicity-A supplement to mental health. A report of the Surgeon General.* Rockville, MD: U.S. Department of Health and Human Services, Substance Abuse and Mental Health Services Administration, Center for Mental Health Services.

Van De Vijver, F. J. R., & Phalet, K. (2004). Assessment in multicultural groups: The role of acculturation. *Applied Psychology, 53*(2), 215–236. doi: 10.1111/j.1464-0597.2004.00169.x

Whaley, A. L. (2001). Cultural mistrust of white mental health clinicians among African Americans with severe mental illness. *American Journal of Orthopsychiatry, 71*(2), 252–256. doi: 10.1037/0002-9432.71.2.252

Widiger, T. A., & Samuel, D. B. (2005). Evidence-based assessment of personality disorders. *Psychological Assessment, 17*(3), 278–287. doi: 10.1037/1040-3590.17.3.278

Wood, B. J. M., Nezworski, M. T., & Stejskal, W. J. (1996). The comprehensive system for the Rorschach: A critical examination. *Psychological Science, 7*(1), 3–10. doi: 10.1111/j.1467-9280.1996.tb00658.x

CHAPTER 5

Gender and Personality Assessment

Kathleen A. Malloy and Radhika Krishnamurthy

When learning about psychological assessment we are often taught that assessment is objective. If we use reliable and valid measures and use the right norms to interpret test findings, we can understand a person from the data gathered from the standardized measures. Of course, assuring that the measures we use are statistically sound and that we use the most representative norms possible is important; they enable us to compare results to appropriate groups of people to determine if the individual we are assessing is similar to or different from others like her or him on the constructs being measured. However, it does not always allow us to grasp the etiology or meaning of those characteristics and symptoms for a given individual. In other words, it does not allow us to thoroughly assess a unique human being who functions within individual, familial, community, and cultural contexts that give meaning to his or her traits, behaviors, cognitions, emotions, and symptoms. This underscores the distinction between psychological testing (i.e., use of the test instruments for measurement) and psychological assessment (i.e., integration of multiple sources of information for developing a comprehensive conceptualization; Krishnamurthy & Meyer, 2016). Trying to understand that individual outside of the context within which he or she lives is limiting. Thoroughly understanding an individual requires exploring the meaning imposed by the context within which she or he exists and how that meaning is reflected in the data we collect. That context has many components, including, for example, individual history, family history, biological factors, and cultural variables. In this chapter the impact of one of those components, gender, is addressed.

Conceptual Considerations

In everyday discussions about gender, a common mistake that is made is to equate gender with sex. Thus, any discussion of gender should start with definitions describing what is meant by commonly used terms. Sex refers to the biological aspects of being male or female. Gender, on the other hand, is a socially constructed variable. Social construction theory proposes that meaning does not simply exist in nature, but rather that it is actively constructed by observers and participants and consistently reinforced within one's environment. Thus, gender is not "truth," but is a concept actively defined within a culture. The construction can then permeate a culture to the extent that it feels like truth or nature, even when it is not. Stereotypes develop when a belief becomes so ingrained that it leads to assumptions about others' traits and behaviors. Gender, then, refers to beliefs, characteristics, and roles determined to be appropriate for men and women, often based on gender-role stereotypes (Levant, 2011).

One indication of the socially constructed nature of gender is in the changes that occur over time in our understanding of what gender means. For example, at an earlier point in American history it was believed that women were high in nurturing, rendering them suitable for child rearing, but so low in logic that they were not capable of voting or holding office. While the stereotype that women are more nurturing and less logical than men persists today, the belief in the extent of those differences has changed significantly. Twenge (1997) found that women were more likely to describe their own personality as agentic than were women 20 years prior, but women's self-reported sense of communion had not changed over that period of time.

In addition to changing over time, gender is not a variable that is stagnant across other identity variables. Rather, the meaning given to gender interacts with multiple other socially constructed variables, including, but not limited to, race, ethnicity, economic status, ability status, sexual orientation, religious/spiritual beliefs, and age. Individuals are affected not only by cultural gendered expectations, but also by cultural understandings of other identity variables. African American women and men, for example, are impacted by gendered expectations while also dealing with the impact of racial expectations and racism (APA, 2007; DuBois, Burk-Braxton, Swenson, Tevendale, & Hardesty, 2002).

Gendered stereotypes are maintained in society in a variety of ways. One way is to exaggerate differences and minimize similarities between men and women, leading to the polarization of male and female gendered expectations (Deaux, 1984; Hare-Mustin and Marecek, 1988). Beliefs in exaggerated differences between the genders persist despite compelling findings to the contrary. For example, findings from a review of 46 meta-analyses on gender differences on a wide range of performance and personality variables indicated that 48% of effect sizes supporting gender differences were small and 30% were trivial, and that within-gender variability is typically greater than between-gender variability (Hyde, 2005). Such a polarization oversimplifies gender and obscures the complexity of human beings. Another way of maintaining stereotypes is to selectively remember information that is consistent with gendered stereotypes, making it difficult to disprove those stereotypes or to challenge a gender-based power structure. As a result, gendered stereotypes persist even in the face of evidence from large scale studies that have found that gender differences are not as dramatic or universal as asserted (Deaux, 1984).

As a socially constructed variable, gender is given meaning by the expectations of the broad culture regarding men and women. Those expectations define how an individual is to look, behave, feel, and think in order to be accepted as a "good" man or woman. They also impact how individuals expect others to behave and influence how they act when others do not adhere to gendered expectations. Traditional gender roles are reinforced through differential treatment of girls and boys (Levant, 1996; Pleck, Sonenstein, & Ku, 1994). They influence how parents, teachers, and peers socialize children and thus how children think, feel, and behave in situations related to gender. When individuals behave according to gendered expectations they are reinforced by others in their environments; when they do not, they often receive sanctions (Andersen & Hysock, 2010; Pleck, 1995). For example, boys who are perceived as too feminine are often called names such as "sissy" or "fag." As a result, individuals internalize gendered expectations, which are then enacted without self-awareness or conscious intention and become a part of how an individual values herself or himself (APA Task Force, 2010; Kite, Deaux, & Haines, 2008).

Gendered expectations become stereotypes that are both descriptive and prescriptive. They are descriptive in that they define for both the culture and for individuals within that culture what men and women are like, and prescriptive in that they define how men and women should be (Kite et al., 2008). Thus, individuals develop perceptions of who they are as men and women within their cultures and learn to strive to meet gendered expectations throughout their lives. In addition, they learn to expect that others will also strive to live up to gendered stereotypes and factor others' success in meeting those expectations into the esteem with which they regard them.

While all individuals who live within a culture are exposed to the ways in which gender is defined within that culture, individuals internalize gendered beliefs to varying degrees, ranging from rigid conformity to active rejection. The extent to which an individual internalizes gendered beliefs is impacted by many variables, some of which include family values, peer and community expectations, religious beliefs, and individual variables. In addition, the ability of some to achieve what the culture considers ideal gender roles are impacted by one's social class, race, ethnicity, sexual orientation, life stages, and historical eras (APA, 2007; Levant, 2011). Thus, gender *expression* may diverge from gender identity, and individual differences in gender *conformity* reflect the degree to which the gender stereotypical role is accepted (Brabender & Mihura, 2016)

Gender stereotypes are not value-neutral. Rather, values are assigned to stereotypical beliefs, with male gendered behaviors being judged as normative and female as nonstandard. Thus, characteristics such as autonomy and achievement are more culturally valued than characteristics such as interdependence and passivity (Deaux, 1984). Gender stereotypes are also used to justify differential treatment and expectations of women and men and to support culturally sanctioned power differences between the genders that allot greater social power to men (Hare-Mustin and Marecek, 1988).

Gender stereotypes and resulting expectations often lead to men and women having very different experiences, resulting in living in contexts that differ significantly based on gender. For example, women can be judged more negatively when they exhibit behaviors high in agency. Women high in agency are often seen as more competent, but are not liked (Matlin, 2012). On the other hand, women who exhibit more care-taking behaviors are seen as pleasant and warmer. The same behaviors on the part of men are judged differently, with men exhibiting more agency being seen as strong and capable while men exhibiting more care-taking behavior are seen as weak or unmanly. Lack of attention to those differences can limit mental health professionals' ability to recognize how psychological difficulties are affected by one's gender.

While individuals most often receive reinforcement for living up to cultural gendered expectations, not all consequences are positive (APA, 2007; Levant, 2011; Pleck, 1995). Over-conformity to gendered expectations prevents people from embracing a full range of belief systems and behaviors that would foster their personal growth and development. In addition, over-conforming with gendered expectations can lead to a narrowing of one's understanding of his/her own humanity and place restrictions on relationships with others. Thus, mental health problems can arise when women and men receive negative consequences for over-conforming to gendered expectations as well as when they do not adhere to those expectations.

Gender-Related Stereotypes and Expectations and their Impact on Mental Health

One way in which the meaning associated with gender affects psychological practice in general and assessment specifically is through its impact on diagnosis. Overall, differences in rates of diagnoses between women and men are in keeping with gendered stereotypes, with women being more likely to be diagnosed with disorders that are mediated by internalizing tendencies while men are diagnosed more often with disorders that involve externalizing tendencies (Eaton et al., 2012). Women are twice as likely to be diagnosed with depression as men, and girls are seven times more likely than boys to be depressed (Lewinsohn, Rhode, Seeley, & Baldwin, 2001). According to the U.S. Department of Health and Human Services, Office on Women's Health, women are also two to three times more likely to experience many types of anxiety disorders (cited in the report of APA's Task Force on Therapy with women and girls, 2010). Other diagnoses that women are more likely to receive than men include eating disorders, histrionic and borderline personality disorders, dissociative disorder, somatization disorder, premenstrual dysphoric syndrome, and agoraphobia. Men, on the other hand, are more likely to be diagnosed with both substance abuse disorders and antisocial disorders (Eaton et al., 2012). These differences have been found across racial and ethnic groups in the United States (Russo & Green, 1993). They can be attributed at least partly to gender biases within diagnostic criteria themselves when those criteria are not gender-neutral (Hartung & Widiger, 1998).

Differences in diagnoses suggest that women and men present for mental health services with different symptomatology. While biological differences might have some impact on differences in male and female experience, much of that difference can be accounted for by differing socially constructed gendered roles and social expectations experienced by women and men. As a result of those expectations, men and women are socialized differently from birth (Deaux & LaFrance, 1998).

That socialization impacts all areas of male and female experience, including how psychological distress is experienced and expressed.

Over the past several decades extensive research has examined the nature of gendered expectations and has found consistent stereotypes regarding women and men. In general, women are viewed as more expressive, communal, focused on others, gentle, understanding, devoted, and more emotional except when the emotion being expressed is anger or pride (Deaux & LaFrance, 1998). Girls are often socialized into patterns of nurturance, passivity, helplessness, and preoccupation with appearance (APA Task Force, 2010). Compared to boys, young adolescent girls have been found to report less favorable gender identity beliefs and lower self-esteem (Brown, 2003; Spence, Sheffield, & Donovan, 2002; Tolman & Brown, 2001). Multiple stressors rooted in gender stereotypes and sexualization experienced by girls and women that can negatively impact mental health include unrealistic media images of girls and women, discrimination and oppression, violence against women, devaluation, limited economic resources, role overload, and work inequities (APA, 2007; APA Task Force, 2010).

Historically, since women, especially White middle-class women, were deemed as more nurturing and less equipped to deal with the work world, they were expected to marry, have children, stay home and care for their families. That expectation has changed dramatically over the past several decades. However, male gendered expectations have not changed as dramatically, leading to many women experiencing stressors related to what has frequently been referred to as the "second shift," which burdens employed married women who are saddled with the brunt of child care and housework (Hochschild, 1989). Women continue to assume disproportionate responsibility for child care, elder care, household management, and partner/spouse relationships (Kulik, 2002; Sanderson & Sanders-Thompson, 2002; Steil, 2001). According to the 2013 United States Census report, women also comprise 82.5% of custodial single parents (Grall, 2016). Furthermore, full-time employed women earn only 80% of what men receive in income, as reported from 2016 United States Census figures (Semega, Fontenot, & Kollar, 2017). Chronic stress that is associated with role burden, housework inequalities, child care inequities, income inequities, parenting strains, and lack of affirmation in close relationships contribute to gender differences in depression (Nolen-Hoeksema, Larsen, & Grayson, 1999). It should be noted that while the expectation that women should stay home and nurture their families has been a part of the socially constructed definition of the female gender, ethnic minority women, single mothers, and low-income women often do not have the means or opportunities to eschew gainful employment. As a result they experience not only the stress related to filling multiple roles, but also the understanding that they cannot live up to what society deems as the most valued role for women. In addition, women who choose not to have children, not to maintain custody of their children, or not to take responsibility for the care of others are rejecting the expectation that they will be nurturers and are frequently misunderstood or judged negatively by others.

Both gender- and race-related stress have been linked to higher levels of emotional and behavioral problems among girls and women (DuBois et al., 2002).

Women who reported experiencing frequent sexism also reported higher levels of depression, anxiety, and somatization than either women who reported experiencing little sexism or men (Klonoff, Landrine, & Campbell, 2000). In fact, sexist discrimination was found to be a strong predictor of women's mental health symptoms, even when solely examining sexist stressors that virtually all women experience to some extent or another and excluding more extreme stressors frequently experienced by women, such as battering and rape (Landrine & Klonoff, 1997). One explanation posited for this finding is that stress in general has been found to contribute to psychiatric symptoms and that sexist stressors add significantly to the level of stress experienced by women. The experience of sexist stressors among women is extensive, suggesting that their impact on women's mental health is pervasive. Klonoff et al. (2000), for example, note that none of the 1,279 women in their various studies reported absolutely no sexist discrimination throughout their lives. Swim, Hyers, Cohen, and Ferguson (2001) surveyed undergraduate women and found that they reported experiencing an average of one or two nontrivial sexist remarks and behaviors every week, including traditional gender-stereotyped remarks, demeaning comments and behaviors, and sexual comments and behaviors. Harassment of women in public places is a common phenomenon that adds to the experience of gender stress by women. For example, Gardner (1995) interviewed 293 women across race, age, class, and sexual orientation and found that 100% could cite several examples of being harassed by unknown men in public and all but nine of the women classified those experiences as "troublesome." Nielsen (2004) found that 100% of 54 women she surveyed had been the target of offensive or sexually suggestive remarks at least occasionally, with 19% experiencing it every day. Roberson's (2005) survey of 168 girls and young women between the ages of 10 and 19, and interviews with an additional 34 participants, found that 86% had been catcalled on the street, 36% said men harassed them daily, and 60% said they felt unsafe walking in their neighborhoods. Sexual harassment also happens in the work environment. Ilies, Hauserman, Schwachau, and Stile (2003) performed a meta-analysis of studies exploring the occurrence of sexual harassment in the workplace. Based on more than 86,000 respondents from 55 studies, they found that, on average, 58% of women report having experienced potentially harassing behaviors and 24% report having experienced sexual harassment at work.

Women and girls are sexualized within U.S. culture. Sexualization is defined by the American Psychological Association's Task Force on the Sexualization of Girls and Women (2010) as encompassing the following four components: a person's value comes only from his or her sexual appeal or behavior, to the exclusion of other characteristics; a person is held to a standard that equates physical attractiveness (narrowly defined) with being sexy; a person is sexually objectified—that is, made into a thing for others' sexual use, rather than seen as a person with the capacity for independent acting and decision making; and/or sexuality is inappropriately imposed upon a person.

> Self-objectification in a culture in which a woman is a "good object" when she meets the salient cultural standard of "sexy" leads girls to evaluate and control their own bodies more in terms of their sexual desirability to others than in terms of their own desires, health, wellness, achievements, or competence.
> (APA Task Force, 2010, p. 20)

Sexualization can lead to girls expecting that, in order to be valued, they should have the perfect body and experiencing shame and disgust when they do not. As a result, the societal expectations regarding female bodies contribute to the higher rate of depression, anxiety, and eating disorders among girls and women.

Girls and women also experience interpersonal victimization and violence at higher rates than men. According to the Centers for Disease Control and Prevention (CDC), in the United States 19.3% of women have been raped during their lifetimes, 15.2% have been a victim of stalking, 8.8% experienced rape by an intimate partner, 22.3% have experienced severe physical violence perpetrated by an intimate partner (including acts such as being hit with something hard, being kicked or beaten, or being burned on purpose), and 9.2% were stalked by an intimate partner (Breiding et al., 2014). Experiences of abuse and violence can contribute to the occurrence of many of the disorders more frequently experienced by women, including eating disorders, depression, anxiety, and suicidal behavior (APA, 2007). Women are more than twice as likely as men to develop chronic posttraumatic stress disorder symptoms, likely as a result of the chronic nature of interpersonal violence (e.g., Hughes & Jones, 2000; Woods, 2005).

Stereotypes and traditional gendered expectations also exist for men. Similar to feminine gender roles, masculinity is a socially constructed variable that is developed and maintained within societies or cultural groups. What is expected by an individual to be judged as sufficiently masculine varies along multiple dimensions, including social class, race, ethnicity, sexual orientation, life stages, and historical eras, leading scholars in the field to talk about masculine ideologies, rather than stemming from one specific notion of what is meant by masculinity (Brod, 1987; Levant, 2011). However, there is also broad agreement in the field that while there are differences among masculine ideologies, those differences tend to be in degree of endorsing or placing emphasis upon pervasive norms rather than due to totally different sets of norms (Smiler, 2004). The basic expectations underlying various masculine ideologies are referred to as traditional masculinity. Traditional masculinity has been conceptualized as a multidimensional construct with four components: men should not be feminine; men should strive to be respected for successful achievement; men should never show weakness; and men should seek adventure and risk, even accepting violence if necessary (David & Brannon, 1976). As a result of these expectations, men are socialized to be strong, assertive, and independent (Zamarripa, Wampold, & Gregory, 2003). They are to be instrumental or agentic. Males are described as active, competitive, independent, self-confident, and assertive/controlling. Emphasis is placed on dominance, aggression, extreme self-reliance, and restrictive emotionality (Levant, 2011). According to Levant (2011), men are taught that if they adhere to these traditional roles they will be able to successfully perform the social expectations that men have historically been expected to fill across almost all cultures: procreation, provision, and protection. Traditional gender roles support a power-based gender structure that privileges men over women, especially White, heterosexual, upper-class, able-bodied, Christian men. Traditional gender roles also marginalize men who are unable to successfully fulfill the expected male roles, including those from ethnic minority groups, lower class men, men with disabilities, and gay men (Connell & Messerschmidt, 2005). Psychological strain results when men internalize traditional male norms and expectations and subsequently fail to live up to those internalized expectations (Pleck, 1995; Levant, 2011).

Pleck (1995) proposed that psychological strain also occurs when men are actually able to achieve traditional masculine expectations because many of the characteristics viewed as desirable in men actually have negative consequences for men and others. In further exploring ways that an adherence to traditional masculine expectations can be harmful to men, Levant and Richmond (2008) concluded from their extensive review of the literature that it is

> associated with a range of problematic individual and relational variables, including reluctance to discuss condom use with partners, fear of intimacy, lower relationship satisfaction, more negative beliefs about the father's role, lower paternal participation in child care, negative attitudes toward racial diversity and women's equality, attitudes conducive to sexual harassment, self-reports of sexual aggression, lower forgiveness of racial discrimination, alexithymia, and reluctance to seek psychological help.
>
> (p. 771)

O'Neil (2008) addressed four domains of what he refers to as Gender Role Conflict (GRC): success, power, and competition; restrictive emotionality; restrictive affectionate behavior between men; and conflict between work and family relations. He reviewed 232 empirical studies on GRC that were conducted over 25 years and concluded that it is significantly related to men's psychological and interpersonal problems. Affectively, GRC correlates with men's reports of anxiety, depression, homonegativity, negative identity, anger, and low self-esteem. Cognitively, GRC correlates with traditional attitudes toward women, stereotyping, antigay attitudes, homophobia, and low sex role egalitarianism. Behaviorally, it correlates with hostile behavior, spousal criticism, sexually aggressive behaviors, and health risk behavior. Given the impact of male socialization and conforming to traditional male gender roles, it is not surprising to find that men have long been disproportionately represented among many problem populations—parents estranged from their children; the homeless; substance abusers; perpetrators of violence; prisoners; sex addicts and sex offenders; victims of homicide, suicide, war, and fatal automobile accidents; and fatal victims of lifestyle and stress-related illnesses (Brooks & Silverstein, 1995).

Gender Effects in Personality Assessment Scores

As discussed by Krishnamurthy (2016), gendered experiences influence women's and men's responses to self-report personality measures through how frequently they endorse specific test items as applying to them, which in turn is influenced partially by gender-related response styles. Such differences are evident on widely used personality measures such as the Minnesota Multiphasic Personality Inventory, second edition (MMPI-2; Butcher, Dahlstrom, Graham, Tellegen, & Kaemmer, 1989) and Millon Clinical Multiaxial Inventory-III (MCMI-III, Millon, Davis, & Millon, 1997). It has an impact on scale scores, with women often scoring higher on scales measuring somatic, depressive, and histrionic symptoms and men often scoring higher on antisocial features. For example, Greene's (2011) overview of gender differences on the MMPI-2 indicates consistently higher endorsement of items on Hypochondriasis, Depression, Hysteria, and Psychasthenia scales by women than men in clinical settings, although only by two to three items. This pattern is also evident in clinical scale codetypes, with women producing internalizing-type codetypes (e.g., 2-3/3-2, 1-2/2-1 and 1-3/3-1) more often than men and men having higher rates of patterns involving behavioral disorganization and acting out (e.g., 6-8/8-6 and 7-8/8-7) than women. In the same vein, several MMPI-2 internalizing-type content and supplementary scales' scores are often slightly higher for women than men in clinical settings (e.g., Anxiety, Fears, Depression, Health Concerns, Low Self-Esteem, Post-Traumatic Stress Disorder-Keane), whereas externalizing type scale scores (e.g., Cynicism, Antisocial Practices, Type A, Hostility, MacAndrew Alcoholism-Revised, Addiction Potential) are often slightly higher for men than women. Such differences, although generally very small in effect size, reflect a pattern of greater subjective distress and negative affect reports by women and behavioral disturbances by men. With regards to the MCMI-III, Rossi, van der Ark, and Sloore's (2007) analysis of the Dutch-language version in a combined sample of patients and inmates revealed significantly different mean scale scores by gender for all but four scales, although the factor structure was consistent across gender. In a parental capacity evaluation sample, Blood (2008) found women to score higher than men on several MCMI-III pathology-related scales. Consistent with these findings, Howes and Krishnamurthy's (2014) analysis of MCMI-III, MMPI-2, and MMPI-2-RF scores in a sample of 168 child custody litigants showed significant higher scores for women particularly on MCMI-III and MMPI-2 scales of psychological disturbance; they cautioned that such profile patterns could result in adverse effects for women in custody outcomes if taken at face value.

In contrast to the gender-specific norms used for the MMPI-2 and earlier versions of the MCMI, non-gendered norms have come into use in recent years for tests such as the Personality Assessment Inventory (PAI; Morey, 1991), MCMI-III and the latest fourth edition of this test, and the Minnesota Multiphasic Personality Inventory-2-Restructured Form (MMPI-2-RF; Ben-Porath & Tellegen, 2008/2011). These norms (or the raw-to-T-score conversion formulae) seem to paradoxically[1] reduce gender differences in test scores (see Glassmire, Jhawar, Burchett, and

Tarescavage (2017) and Phillips, Sellbom, Ben-Porath, and Patrick (2014), for MMPI-2-RF forensic sample studies). Recent PAI studies (e.g., Hopwood & Moser, 2011) have demonstrated an invariant structure of scores across gender. However, non-gendered norms do not completely eliminate gender effects, as seen in the previously discussed MCMI-III studies. The important take-away point for the assessor from these research findings is that the pattern of higher scores for women across major personality tests does not necessarily equate with greater psychopathology in women as it is influenced by their greater *expression* of emotional distress (Krishnamurthy, 2016). In a practical sense, how the test results are used by the assessor becomes a more important issue than how the test norms are developed (Baker & Mason, 2010). At a descriptive level, the assessor might anticipate that women and men will differ in some personality dimensions, such as PAI-assessed Dominance and Warmth, as a function of gender socialization.

Gender effects are less prominent in contemporary performance-based personality measures such as the Rorschach Performance Assessment System (R-PAS; Meyer, Viglione, Mihura, Erard, & Erdberg, 2011), although they have been observed to a limited degree in some earlier Rorschach studies. This absence of gender effects is most evident in a recent study by Meyer, Giromini, Viglione, Reese, and Mihura (2015) that evaluated the associations of gender (alongside other demographic variables) with 60 Rorschach scores in multiple adult and child/adolescent samples and found no impact of gender on scores. The researchers suggested two possibilities for these findings as they are in contrast with those from self-report personality measures: (a) men and women differ in their self-conceptions, which is manifested in their self-report descriptions, but do not differ in their behavioral performance on the Rorschach task, and (b) the constructs assessed by self-report measures might be picking up on gendered differences better than Rorschach scores examined in their study. In explaining why gender does not appear to come into play on the Rorschach, Tuber, Boesch, Gagnon, and Harrison (2016) discussed that the implicit, unconscious associations evoked in the Rorschach task likely bypass a binary gender categorization; they suggested that, on an unconscious level, human representations cut across sexual boundaries. On the other hand, as discussed by Silverstein (2016), gender effects are more evident in performance-based tasks involving story-telling, such as the Thematic Apperception Test (TAT; Murray, 1943), and in figure-drawing tasks. Although the empirical literature on this topic is sparse, Silverstein's overview of prior findings noted higher levels of intimacy needs and motivations, affiliation needs, and nurturant interpersonal interactions among women on the TAT and gender identification by both sexes on human figure drawings. He proposed that "narrative verbalizations obtained from projective test instruments may be particularly well suited for explicating gender role functions and sexuality" (p. 186).

Practical Considerations

First, assessors must work to be aware of their own gendered beliefs and biases. As discussed above, gender is a socially constructed variable that is maintained in many ways that are often not visible to members of a given culture. Assessors are members of a culture and as such are inundated with gendered thinking, expectations, and stereotypes. Often, one's bias and expectations based on gender are not in conscious awareness. As a result, assessors must strive to understand the gendered messages present in their own cultures and to explore how they have internalized those messages. If they do not address their own biases, those biases will affect the assessment process and outcomes in significant ways without their awareness. If they are not aware of how a culture attributes value to gender and gendered behavior, assessors may transfer those cultural values into the work that they are doing, resulting in devaluing and over-pathologizing individuals who do not conform to gendered expectations. Conversely, assessors might not attend to gender-congruent behaviors or beliefs that cause distress. Ways in which assessors can uncover gendered biases include exploring the literature related to gender, participating in educational and/or therapeutic events that address gender, and consulting with colleagues who will help them to become aware of their own biases and how they impact their clinical work (APA, 2007).

In addition to understanding their own gender-related biases, assessors must explore with clients the clients' cultures, how those cultures address gender, and how cultural expectations have been internalized by their clients. In other words, assessors must make gender a salient variable by routinely asking about clients' gendered beliefs and experiences (Brown, 1990). This is usually accomplished by conducting a thorough interview that incorporates inquiries about gendered experiences and adherence to gendered stereotypes, norms, and expectations and explores consequences that clients experienced when either adhering to or rejecting gendered norms. Brown (1986, 1990) offers more detailed information on how to conduct gender-sensitive interviews when conducting psychological assessment. On clinical measures, research findings indicate women are more likely to score higher than men on mood disorder indices such as depression and anxiety, and men are more likely to score higher than women on behavioral acting out indices such as antisocial behavior and substance abuse. These differences, although relatively small, seem to reflect the influence of gender and gender-role conformity in a host of factors involved in the recognition, experience, and reporting of difficulty.

Often a primary goal of formal assessment is to determine accurate diagnoses. As a result, it is important to maintain vigilance regarding the impact of gendered expectations on diagnosis. Various symptoms have been conceptualized as exaggerations or stereotyping of traditional gender roles and behaviors and can lead to over-diagnosing. For example, female clients who overreact emotionally, attempt to sexually attract men, preserve romantic relationships at all costs, and placate others by internalizing, denying or inefficiently expressing anger might be behaving in ways that have been reinforced for women in their social contexts (APA, 2007). The same might be true of male clients who express very limited understanding of their own emotions, attribute their worth as human beings to their ability to accomplish, feel a need to control others to feel powerful, or rely on anger as their sole expression of emotion (Levant, 2011). As a result, an assessor should consider the possibility that symptoms that suggest the presence of a diagnosable disorder could in actuality be a client's attempt to meet gendered expectations. In addition, over-diagnosis can also occur when a client's problem behaviors are inconsistent with societal expectations. For example, women who react to discrimination with anger or men who cry when expressing sadness may be diagnosed more easily than women who respond in a more internalizing manner and men who respond in a more externalizing manner.

In addition to over-diagnosis, gendered expectations might lead to under-diagnosis. The specific needs and problems of girls may be overlooked and under-diagnosed because they are more likely than boys to internalize problems or to express problems with less overt symptoms (Brooks & Silverstein, 1995; Brown, 1990; Hartung & Widiger, 1998; Kite, Deaux, & Haines, 2008). Externalizing behaviors that are exhibited by boys might be written off as "boys will be boys" rather than as their attempt to express distress. Again, thoroughly exploring how individuals understand what it means to be male or female will help the assessor to determine the meaning of a client's behavior and the presence or absence of psychological disorders.

When conducting assessments, assessors are asked to make recommendations based on their findings that include productive ways to intervene with clients. In generating recommendations, assessors should communicate how cultural gendered expectations, stereotypes, and gendered self-expectations impact clients and contribute to the understanding of their assessment findings, including explaining symptomatology and providing diagnoses. Assessors should also be aware of and communicate about the need to educate clients regarding the impact of gender on their psychological functioning and to help them to understand how gendered expectations are established and internalized. In addition, it is important to help clients understand the nature and strength of gendered expectations and the consequences they might face from others in their families and/or communities if they choose to change the ways that they adhere to those expectations.

Note

1 Contrary to popular understanding, gender-specific norms rather than non-gendered norms serve to reduce gender influence in scores in terms of controlling for response-style effects.

References

American Psychological Association. (2007). Guidelines for psychological practice with girls and women. *American Psychologist, 62*(9), 949–979. doi: 10.1037/0003-066X.62.9.949

American Psychological Association Task Force on the Sexualization of Girls. (2010). *Report of the APA task force on the sexualization of girls.* Retrieved from www.apa.org/pi/women/programs/girls/report-full.pdf

Andersen, M. L., & Hysock, D. (2010). *The social construction of gender.* In B. Hutchison (Ed.), *Annual editions: Gender* (pp. 2–5). Boston, MA: McGraw-Hill.

Baker, N. L., & Mason, J. L. (2010). Gender issues in psychological testing of personality and abilities. In J. C. Chrisler and D. R. McCreary (Eds.), *Handbook of gender research in psychology* (pp. 63–88). New York: Springer.

Ben-Porath, Y. S., & Tellegen, A. (2008/2011). *Minnesota Multiphasic Personality Inventory-2-Restructured Form: Manual for administration, scoring, and interpretation.* Minneapolis: University of Minnesota Press.

Blood, L. (2008). The use of the MCMI-III in completing parenting capacity assessments. *Journal of Forensic Psychology Practice, 8,* 24–38. http://dx.doi.org/10.1080/15228930801947286

Brabender, V. M., & Mihura, J. L. (2016). The construction of gender and sex, and their implications for psychological assessment. In V. M. Brabender & J. L. Mihura (Eds.), *Handbook of gender and sexuality in psychological assessment* (pp. 3–43). New York: Routledge.

Breiding, M. J., Smith, S. G., Basile, K. C., Walters, M. L., Chen, J., & Merrick, M. T. (September 5, 2014). Prevalence and characteristics of sexual violence, stalking, and intimate partner violence victimization—National Intimate Partner and Sexual Violence Survey, United States, 2011. *Surveillance Summaries, 63*(SS08), 1–18.

Brod, H. (1987). *The making of the masculinities: The new men's studies.* Boston, MA: Unwin Hyman.

Brooks, G. R., & Silverstein, L. S. (1995). Understanding the dark side of masculinity: An interactive systems model. In R. F. Levant & W. S. Pollack (Eds.), *A new psychology of men* (pp. 280–333). New York: Basic Books.

Brown, L. M. (2003). *Girlfighting: Betrayal and rejection among girls.* New York: New York University Press.

Brown, L. S. (1986). Gender-role analysis: A neglected component of psychological assessment. *Psychotherapy, 23*(2), 243–248. doi: 10.1037/h0085604

Brown, L. S. (1990). Taking account of gender in the clinical assessment interview. *Professional Psychology: Research and Practice, 21*(1), 12–17. doi: 10.1037/0735-7028.21.1.12

Butcher, J. N., Dahlstrom, W. G., Graham, J. R., Tellegen, A., & Kaemmer, B. (1989). *Minnesota Multiphasic Personality Inventory-2 (MMPI-2): Manual for administration and scoring.* Minneapolis: University of Minnesota Press.

Connell, R. W., & Messerschmidt, J. W. (2005). Hegemonic masculinity: Rethinking the concept. *Gender & Society, 19,* 829–859. doi: 10.1177/0891243205278639

David, D., & Brannon, R. (1976). *The forty-nine percent majority: The male sex role.* Reading, MA: Addison-Wesley.

Deaux, K. (1984). From individual differences to social categories: Analysis of a decade's research on gender. *American Psychologist, 39,* 105–116. doi: 10.1037/0003-066X.39.2.105

Deaux, K., & LaFrance, M. (1998). *Gender.* In D. T. Gilbert, S. T. Fiske, & G. Lindzey (Eds.), *Handbook of social psychology* (4th ed., Vol. 1, pp. 788–827). Boston, MA: McGraw-Hill.

DuBois, D. L., Burk-Braxton, C., Swenson, L. P., Tevendale, H. D., & Hardesty, J. L. (2002). Race and gender influences on adjustment in early adolescence: Investigation of an integrated model. *Child Development, 73,* 1573–1592. doi: 10.1111/1467-8624.00491

Eaton, N. R., Keyes, K. M., Krueger, R. F., Balsis, S., Skodol, A. E., Markon, K. E., Grant, B. F., & Hasin, D. S. (2012). An invariant dimensional liability model of gender differences in mental disorder prevalence: Evidence from a national sample. *Journal of Abnormal Psychology, 121*(1), 282–288. doi: 10.1037/a0024780

Gardner, C. B. (1995). *Passing by: Gender and public harassment.* Berkeley, CA: University of California Press.

Glassmire, D. M., Jhawar, A., Burchett, D., & Tarescavage, A. (2017). Evaluating item endorsement rates for the MMPI-2-RF F-r and Fp-r scales across ethnic, gender, and diagnostic groups with a forensic inpatient sample. *Psychological Assessment, 29*, 500–508. http://dx.doi.org/10.1037/pas0000366

Grall, T. (2016, January). *Custodial mothers and fathers and their child support: 2013.* Retrieved from http://wikiurls.com/?https://www.census.gov/content/dam/Census/library/publications/2016/demo/P60-255.pdf

Greene, R. L. (2011). *The MMPI-2/MMPI-2-RF: An interpretive manual* (3rd ed.). Boston: Allyn & Bacon.

Hare-Mustin, R. T. & Marecek, J. (1988). The meaning of difference: Gender theory, postmodernism, and psychology. *American Psychologist, 43*, 455–464. doi: 10.1037/0003-066X.43.6.455

Hartung, C. M., & Widiger, T. A. (1998). Gender differences in the diagnosis of mental disorders: Conclusions and controversies of the DSM-IV. *Psychological Bulletin, 123*(3), 260–278. doi: 0033-2909/98/$3.00

Hochschild, A. (1989). *The second shift.* New York: Avon Books.

Hopwood, C. J., & Moser, J. S. (2011). Personality Assessment Inventory internalizing and externalizing structure in college students: Invariance across sex and ethnicity. *Personality and Individual Differences, 50*, 116–119. http://dx.doi.org/10.1016/j.paid.2010.08.013

Howes, R., & Krishnamurthy, R. (2014, March). *Gender differences in the MCMI-III, MMPI-2 and MMPI-2-RF profiles of child custody litigants.* Paper presented at the annual convention of the Society for Personality Assessment, Arlington, VA.

Hughes, M. J., & Jones, L. (2000). Women, domestic violence, and posttraumatic stress disorder (PTSD). *Family Therapy, 27*, 125–139.

Hyde, J. S. (2005). The gender similarities hypothesis. *American Psychologist, 60*, 581–592. doi: 10.1037/0003-066X.60.6.581

Ilies, R., Hauserman, N., Schwachau, S., & Stile, J. (2003). Reported incidence rates of work-related sexual harassment in the United States: Using meta-analysis to explain reported rate disparities. *Personnel Psychology, 56*(3), 607–631. doi: 10.1111/j.1744-6570.2003.tb00752.x

Kite, M. E., Deaux, K., & Haines, E. L. (2008). Gender stereotypes. In F. L. Denmark & M. A. Paludi (Eds.), *Psychology of women: A handbook of issues and theories* (pp. 205–236). London: Praeger.

Klonoff, E. A., Landrine, H., & Campbell, R. (2000). Sexist discrimination may account for well-known gender differences in psychiatric symptoms. *Psychology of Women Quarterly, 24*, 93–99. doi: 10.1111/j.1471-6402.2000.tb01025.x

Krishnamurthy, R. (2016). Gender considerations in self-report personality assessment interpretation. In V. M. Brabender & J. L. Mihura (Eds.), *Handbook of gender and sexuality in psychological assessment* (pp. 128–148). New York: Routledge.

Krishnamurthy, R., & Meyer, G. J. (2016). Psychopathology assessment. In J. C. Norcross, G. R. VandenBos, & D. K. Freedheim (Editors-in-Chief), R. Krishnamurthy (Associate Editor), *APA handbook of clinical psychology, Vol. 3: Applications and methods* (pp. 103–137). Washington, DC: American Psychological Association.

Kulik, L. (2002). The impact of social background on gender-role ideology. *Journal of Family Issues, 23*, 53–73. doi: 10.1177/0192513X02023001003

Landrine, H., & Klonoff, E. A. (1997). *Discrimination against women: Prevalence, consequences, remedies.* Thousand Oaks, CA: Sage.

Levant, R. F. (1996). The new psychology of men. *Professional Psychology: Research and Practice, 27*, 259–265. doi: 10.1037/0735-7028.27.3.259

Levant, R. F. (2011). Research in the psychology of men and masculinity using the gender role strain paradigm as a framework. *American Psychologist, 66*(8), 765–776. doi: 10.1037/a0025034

Levant, R. F., & Richmond, K. (2008). A review of research on masculinity ideologies using the Male Role Norms Inventory. *Journal of Men's Studies, 15*, 130–146. doi: 10.3149/jms.1502.130

Lewinsohn, P. M., Rohde, P., Seeley, J. R., & Baldwin, C. L. (2001). Gender differences in suicide attempts from adolescence to young adulthood. *Journal of the American Academy of Child & Adolescent Psychiatry, 40*(4), 427–434. doi: 10.1097/00004583-200104000-00011

Matlin, M. W. (2012). *The psychology of women* (7th ed. Belmont, CA: Wadsworth.

Meyer, G. J., Giromini, L., Viglione, D. J., Reese, J. B., & Mihura, J. L. (2015). The association of gender, ethnicity, age, and education with Rorschach scores. *Assessment, 22*, 46–64. doi: 10.1177/1073191114544358

Meyer, G. J., Viglione, D. J., Mihura, J. L., Erard, R. E., & Erdberg, P. (2011). *Rorschach Performance Assessment System: Administration, coding, interpretation and technical manual.* Toledo, OH: Rorschach Performance Assessment System.

Millon, T., Davis, R., & Millon, C. (1997). *Millon Clinical Multiaxial Inventory-III manual* (2nd ed.). Minneapolis: National Computer Systems

Morey, L. C. (1991). *Personality Assessment Inventory (PAI) professional manual.* Odessa, FL: Psychological Assessment Resources.

Murray, H. A. (1943). *Thematic Apperception Test: Manual.* Cambridge, MA: Harvard University Press.

Nielsen, L. B. (2004). *License to harass: Law, hierarchy, and offensive public speech.* Princeton, NJ: Princeton University Press.

Nolen-Hoeksema, S., Larsen, J., & Grayson, C. (1999). Explaining the gender differences in depressive symptoms. *Journal of Personality and Social Psychology, 77*, 1061–1072. doi: 10.1037/0022-3514.77.5.1061

O'Neil, J. M. (2008). Summarizing 25 years of research on men's gender role conflict using the gender role conflict scale: New research paradigms and clinical implications. *The Counseling Psychologist, 36*(3), 358–445. doi: 10.1177/0011000008317057

Phillips, T. R., Sellbom, M., Ben-Porath, Y. S., & Patrick, C. J. (2014). Further development and construct validation of MMPI-2-RF indices of global psychopathy, fearless-dominance, and impulsive-antisociality in a sample of incarcerated women. *Law and Human Behavior, 38*, 34–46. doi: 10.1037/lhb0000040

Pleck, J. H. (1995). The gender role strain paradigm: An update. In R. F. Levant & W. S. Pollack (Eds.), *The new psychology of men* (pp. 11–32). New York: Basic Books.

Pleck, J. H., Sonenstein, F. L., & Ku, L. C. (1994). Attitudes toward male roles: A discriminant validity analysis. *Sex Roles, 30*, 481–501. doi: 10.1007/BF01420798

Roberson, A. N. (2005). Anti-street harassment. *Off Our Backs*, June, p. 48.

Rossi, G., van der Ark, L. A., & Sloore, H. (2007). Factor analysis of the Dutch-language version of the MCMI-III. *Journal of Personality Assessment, 88*, 144–157. http://dx.doi.org/10.1080/00223890701267977

Russo, N. F., & Green, B. L. (1993). Women and mental health. In F. L. Denmark & M. A. Paludi (Eds.), *Psychology of women: A handbook of issues and theories* (pp. 379–436). Westport, CT: Greenwood Press.

Sanderson, S., & Sanders-Thompson, V. L. (2002). Factors associated with perceived paternal involvement in childrearing. *Sex Roles, 46*, 99–111. doi: 10.1023/A:1016569526920

Semega, J. L., Fontenot, K. R., & Kollar, M. A. (2017, January). *Income and poverty in the United States: 2016*. Retrieved from www.census.gov/content/dam/Census/library/publications/2017/demo/P60-259.pdf

Silverstein, M. L. (2016). Human figure drawings and Thematic Apperception Test narratives: Clinical uses for understanding gender roles and sexuality. In V. M. Brabender & J. L. Mihura (Eds.), *Handbook of gender and sexuality in psychological assessment* (pp. 166–189). New York: Routledge.

Smiler, A. P. (2004). Thirty years after the discovery of gender: Psychological concepts and measures of masculinity. *Sex Roles, 50*, 15–26. doi: 10.1023/B:SERS.0000011069.02279.4c

Spence, S. H., Sheffield, J., & Donovan, C. (2002). Problem-solving orientation and attributional style: Moderators of the impact of negative life events on the development of depressive symptoms in adolescence. *Journal of Clinical Child and Adolescent Psychology, 31*, 219–220. doi: 10.1207/S15374424JCCP3102_07

Steil, J. (2001). Marriage: Still "his" and "hers"? In J. Worell (Ed.), *Encyclopedia of women and gender* (pp. 677–686). San Diego, CA: Academic Press.

Swim, J. K., Hyers, L. L., Cohen, L. L., & Ferguson, M. J. (2001). Everyday sexism: Evidence for its incidence, nature, and psychological impact from three daily diary studies. *Journal of Social Issues, 57*, 31–53. doi: 10.1111/0022-4537.00200

Tolman, D. L., & Brown, L. M. (2001). Adolescent girls' voices: Resonating resistance in body and soul. In R. K. Unger (Ed.), *Handbook of the psychology of women and gender* (pp. 133–155). New York: Wiley.

Tuber, S., Boesch, K., Gagnon, G., & Harrison, D. (2016). Sex and gender distinctions and the Rorschach inkblot method. In V. M. Brabender & J. L. Mihura (Eds.), *Handbook of gender and sexuality in psychological assessment* (pp. 149–165). New York: Routledge.

Twenge, J. M. (1997). Changes in masculine and feminine traits over time: A meta-analysis. *Sex Roles, 36*, 305–325. doi: 10.1007/BF02766650

Woods, S. J. (2005). Intimate partner violence and post-traumatic stress disorder symptoms in women: What we know and need to know. *Journal of Interpersonal Violence, 20*, 394–402. doi: 10.1177/0886260504267882

Zamarripa, M. X., Wampold, B. E., & Gregory, E. (2003). Male gender role conflict, depression, and anxiety: Clarification and generalizability to women. *Journal of Counseling Psychology, 50*(3), 333–338. doi: 10.1037/0022-0167.50.3.333

CHAPTER 6

Queering Personality Assessment: Intersections between Personality Assessment, Sexual Orientations, and Gender Identity

Theodore R. Burnes and Steven R. Smith

Investigations of client satisfaction services have shown that current theoretical models of psychological practice (e.g., theories of psychotherapy, theories of personality) have caused many lesbian, gay, or bisexual (LGB) individuals to refrain from seeking mental health assessment services (Cochran, Sullivan, & Mays, 2003; Israel, Gorcheva, Burnes, & Walther, 2008). Transgender individuals are also extremely vulnerable to issues of psychological distress and mental health concerns (Budge, Adelson, & Howard, 2013). Concurrent with these findings, there is a growing need for practitioners to deliver assessment services (and to train future professional mental health clinicians to also deliver such services) that include an "assessment approach model that includes attention to … cultural components of health" (HSPEC, 2013, p. 411). Further, the literature has consistently documented that issues of sexual orientation and gender identity are not interpreted or contextualized correctly in the context of psychological assessment (Grant, Mottet et al., 2011; Kessler, Berglund, Demler, Jin, & Walters, 2005). These findings demonstrate the need for those providing health care services to pay particular attention to issues of sexual orientation and gender identity in psychological assessment. In response to this need, we will explore, in this chapter, issues of sexual orientation and gender identity in personality assessment and provide implications for clinicians.

Conceptual Considerations

When conceptualizing the intersections between personality assessment, sexual orientation, and gender identity, it is important for us to understand common language related to the identity and psychological well-being of LGBT people. *Sexual orientation* refers to one's social, emotional, and/or physical attraction to someone of the same sex, other sex, or multiple sexes (Diamond & Butterworth, 2008; Fassinger & Arsenau, 2007). This attraction has multiple components that overlap, but should be understood as distinct facets. *Sexual identity* is the label that individuals use to describe their identity, often (but not always) influenced by culture, environment, and community. Although there has been consistent documentation that these identities and attractions are often fixed within individuals, there is a growing documentation that highlights a series of identities that are relatively stable but may also be fluid and can change over time. Specifically, these identities demonstrate stability in terms of labeling and attraction, while there might be some fluidity in terms of who one is attracted to and how those attractions manifest over time (e.g., physical attraction, emotional attraction, behavioral engagement, etc.).

Scholars (e.g., Diamond & Butterworth, 2008; Dickey, Burnes, & Singh, 2012) have noted the importance in differentiating sexual orientation and gender identity. Although the four letters in the "LGBT" acronym are often grouped together due to their collective transcending of gender norms and experiences of verbal, physical, vocational, and societal harassment, those individuals who identify as transgender might not have any similarities, community, or identity related to those individuals who identify as lesbian, gay, or bisexual. As language in LGBT communities consistently changes and evolves, to define all necessary language for competent psychological assessment practices with LGBT communities would be outside the scope of this chapter; however, we suggest the comprehensive glossary put forth by the Gay and Lesbian Alliance Against Defamation (GLAAD's) Movement Advancement Project (2012). Specifically, one's attraction to another is different from that individual's *gender*, or "set of social, psychological, and emotional traits, often influenced by societal expectations that classify an individual as feminine, masculine, androgynous, or other" (American Counseling Association, 2010, p. 158).

Thus, *transgender* is broadly understood as an umbrella term used to describe those who transcend social gender norms, including genderqueer people, gender-nonconforming people, transsexuals, crossdressers, and so on. People must self-identify as transgender in order for the term to be appropriately used to describe them (American Counseling Association, 2010). These various understandings of sexual orientation and gender identity help clinicians who use personality assessments begin to understand the numerous and complex ways that gender and sexual orientation can impact the assessment process. These contemporary understandings of sexual orientation and gender identity have produced a routine critique of psychological and psychiatric discourses for using outdated and conflated definitions of sex, gender, and sexual orientation.

There is also consistent documentation that coping with oppression, stigma, and marginalization has presented itself in negative mental health experiences for LGBT people (Bullock & Wood, 2016). Specifically, the *minority stress model* (Meyer, 2003) conceptualizes the impact of stigmatization on their experiences of stress. In this model, "negative psychological symptoms increase as a result of experiences of discrimination, the anticipation of rejection, hiding or concealing the sexual minority identity, and the internalization of the negative societal views" (Riggle, Whitman, Olson, Rostosky, & Strong, 2008, p. 211). Such a model is critical when understanding certain symptoms of psychopathology for LGBT people in context.

Clinical Issues and/or Presentation

Historical trends in assessing sexual orientation and gender identity have traditionally stemmed from a pathological, heterosexist model (Grant, Flynn, Odlaug,

& Schreiber, 2011; APA, 2011). Although homosexuality was removed from the *Diagnostic and Statistical Manual of Mental Disorders* (DSM) in 1973, the tradition of pathologizing LGB individuals as impaired or deviant based on their sexual orientation continues within much current clinical practice (Israel et al., 2008; Mathy & Kerr, 2003). It has been consistently documented that LGBT people use psychological services at a greater rate than the general population, but that their continued use of services dramatically declines (resulting in premature termination; Greene & Britton, 2014). Although individuals who are L, G, B, and/or T seek therapy for many different reasons, there is continual documentation that therapists may tend to incorrectly interpret LGBT individuals' reasons for treatment based on their identities (e.g., a therapist does not ask about LGBT identity when it is an issue for treatment; a therapist tends to overly focus on LGBT identity with an LGBT client when it is not the focus of treatment; Morrow, 2012). These problems can result in clients immediately realizing their therapists' lack of education and training and prematurely terminating the psychological services in which they were engaged (Pachankis & Goldfried, 2004). As such, the need for clinicians to contextualize their clients' reasons for seeking treatment is critical for positive health care service delivery outcomes.

Compounded with issues related to being LGBT, scholars (e.g., Burnes & Chen, 2012; Cole, 2009) have noted the complexity of intersecting identities for individuals with differing degrees of marginalization and privilege. For LGBT clients who possess intersecting marginalized identities, they might often find themselves having to draw alliances with one identity over the other (e.g. identifying as a Black male, rather than as a Black gay male), which falls short in understanding the complexity of such issues, especially when working in applied settings with diverse populations (Collins, 2009; Crenshaw, 1991). Thus, the numerous complexities of working with LGBT clients' identities necessitate clinicians to assess how a client's unique combinations of marginalized and privileged identities impact their respective worldviews, environments, and relationships.

In addition, LGBT clients have a unique set of stressors based on their marginalized statuses that are often compounded by other marginalized identities such as race, class, and gender. Pachankis and Goldfried (2004) highlight some of these unique stressors, including fear of violence and discrimination in the forms of physical harassment, verbal harassment, or actual physical violence. Richmond, Burnes, and Carroll (2012) note that transgender individuals are almost four times as likely to suffer physical harassment as the general population. Further, Toomey, Ryan, Diaz, Card, and Russell (2010) note that there are specific stressors that impact the coming-out process for youth who are LGBT, including homelessness, family rejection, and increased incidence of major depression disorder and suicidal ideation.

These various clinical presentations present unique cultural variables for consideration during the delivery of psychological assessments. Concurrent with such considerations are problematic assumptions that are exemplified in current editions of widely used assessments. For example, the former version of the Minnesota Multiphasic Personality Inventory (MMPI; Hathaway & McKinley, 1942) assumed that sexual orientation, gender identity, and/or transgression of cultural and societal gender norms were deviant or pathological through the use of scale 5 (MF; Masculinity/Femininity), which assumed that gender non-conformity and transgression of masculinity and femininity were problematic (Bullock & Wood, 2016; Moradi & Parent, 2013). Although this inventory has been now been restructured (MMPI-2-RF; Tellegen & Ben-Porath, 2011), the restructured and newer scales of this measure do not explicitly make the connection between specific symptoms and cultural factors unique to LGBT communities. For example, scales such as the Ideas of Persecution (RC6), Self Doubt (SFD), and Disaffiliativeness (DSF) make suggestions about the etiology of symptoms they assess, but fail to consider how one's disclosure of LGBT identity or experience of minority stress and marginalization might impact the respondent's answers to test questions and the resulting profile.

The history of perceiving personality features related to sexual orientation for LGB individuals as crimes and mental disorders has been consistently documented as deeply embedded in Western cultural frameworks (Moradi & Parent, 2013). For example, scholars have documented how psychological symptoms related to coping with the coming-out process and societal homophobia and biphobia have been framed as diagnostic concerns and labeled as innate, individual-focused symptoms such as depression disorders, anxiety disorders, or personality disorders. Others (Balsam & Szymanski, 2005) have noted how LGB individuals who do not share their identities with others, and therefore do not connect readily in relationships, had problems with relating to others, often diagnosing them with characterological disorders. Such pathology-based understandings of assessment have influenced the training and practice of psychologists in seeing LGB individuals as deviant or mentally ill. More recently, scholars (e.g., Clausell & Roisman, 2009) have utilized a "framework of disclosure" for LGBT people as a context for understanding their personality. Notably, some personality assessment research has documented that individuals' disclosure to others as LGBT ("outing" themselves) is associated with more agreeable personalities, higher quality relationships, and displays of more positive affect (Clausell & Roisman, 2009).

Transgender clients have had even less luck with pathology-based models of psychological assessment. Transgender clients have reported inaccurate or biased interpretations about their personality related to their gender (Richmond, Burnes, & Carroll, 2012; Singh & McKleroy, 2011). For example, transgender individuals who are beginning to socially transition their gender (and might or might not later engage in medical interventions to have their physical sex match their core, authentic gender) might begin to experience fear of leaving their house due to possible harassment if they do not "pass" as their core, authentic gender. Although these symptoms may have agoraphobic similarities, the need for clinicians to understand these symptoms as a primary strategy to cope with harassment is paramount. Further, many psychologists do not have proper training to consider specific cultural factors when interpreting assessment results, thus traumatizing transgender clients (Burnes, Dexter, Richmond, Singh, & Cherrington, 2016).

Such pathology-based diagnoses have influenced the training and practice of psychologists in seeing LGB individuals as deviant or mentally ill (APA, 2011; Burnes, Peters-Long, & Schept, 2012). In the current managed care model of health care, the mental health service provider must diagnose a client with a mental disorder in order to be reimbursed for most services (Health Service Psychology Education Collaborative, 2013; APA, 2011). Such diagnostic practices often force the clinician to work from a pathology-based model with an LGB client who might instead be experiencing environmental and/or ecological stressors from being part of an oppressed group (Harper, 2005).

Empirical Findings

Although there is an increase in theoretical literature about how sexual orientation and gender identity can impact the personality assessment process, empirical research related to these understandings continues to be nascent. There is documented evidence that clinical symptoms related to both depression and anxiety are higher in LGBT people than the population as a whole (Kertzner, 2012; Nuttbrock et al., 2010). Further, scholars have shown that LGBT individuals have been dissatisfied with services in which their therapist operated from a pathology-based framework with regard to their sexual orientations and issues related to their LGB identity (Liddle, 1997, 1999; Maddux, 2002). To date, there is little extant literature on personality assessment profiles for individuals who identify as LGBT. The limited literature available is often theoretical in nature or presents single case studies (e.g., Prince & Potoczniak, 2012). Nonetheless, Krishnamurthy (2016) noted that the limited findings to date from self-report personality assessment research do not point to homosexuality, bisexuality, and transgender and gender-nonconforming identities being associated with any greater psychopathology than a heterosexual orientation.

Practical Considerations

The knowledge of culturally informed personality assessment can aid clinicians in considering the context of their clients' unique social and cultural frameworks. Specifically, diagnoses often used to pathologize LGB individuals should incorporate such social context into their criteria. For clinicians working with LGB clients, such a process must involve knowledge of personality characteristics that may occur in the coming-out process (e.g., paranoia, isolation, avoidance), or in learning about themselves within the context of same-sex sexual relationships (i.e., as sexual beings). A comprehensive clinical interview (Morrison, 2014) is vital to this approach, including questions related to: (a) the time of the client's life when the client first knew that the client was L, G, and/or B (e.g., "coming out to oneself"); (b) the process (if applicable) of the client' sharing their LGB identity with others (the assessor should ask about this disclosure in multiple arenas, including: work, school, home life, family, etc.); (c) how the process of coming out has impacted the client's mental health and well-being. Assessors should also inquire as to how an LGB client's identity might cause stress as it interacts with other cultural, familial, and societal identities. For example, has an African-American client who has come out to her ethnic community as a lesbian lost her community due to homophobia and thus lacks a vital support system to buffer against racism?

For clinicians working with transgender and gender-nonconforming clients, such a process would involve knowledge of how issues of gender have been found to impact personality and interpersonal functioning that may occur in the client's development, socialization, and overall expression (e.g., assertiveness, ability to form relationships, self-esteem, avoidance). Also, the individual conducting a personality assessment with transgender clients should be sure to assess how clients' transgender identities might cause stress that interacts with other cultural, familial, and societal identities. The need to understand both a client's lived and perceived experiences of gender and gender discrimination should also be carefully considered, as there might be some pathology which is perceived and could be a contextual factor for other psychological sequellae.

When conducting personality assessments with LGBT clients, the need to shift understandings of pathology to a resilience- and coping-focused framework becomes paramount (Riggle et al., 2008). Clinicians should apply theories of ecology (e.g., "family of choice"; LGBT culture and community: Fassinger & Arsenau, 2007) and the use of ecological frameworks to aid in the conceptualization of LGBT clients. Recent guidelines for psychological practice with LGB clients note that psychologists should recognize that the families of LGB people might include people who are not legally or biologically related (APA, 2012). In a case example, an 18-year-old African-American female presents inability to sleep and poor concentration as she decides to come out as lesbian to her family. As part of her clinical interview, the assessor notes that she exhibits nervousness as she explains her situation. However, as the assessor asks the client about her cultural support networks, the client is able to identify (and subsequently remember) the various sources of social support and close friends that she has upon whom she calls often.

When assessing LGBT clients using personality measures, we underscore the importance of the clinical interview and a plan for psychological assessment adapted to working with clients from marginalized communities (Sue & Sue, 2017). Assessment instruments focusing on personal strengths and human potential (affirmative clinical interviewing, valuing client strengths, assessments that are affirmative to the experiences of LGB people) can be extremely helpful. The concept of "Positive Clinical Interviewing," or the use of a form of the Structured Clinical Interview for the DSM-IV (SCID; First & Gibbon, 2004) from a positive psychology framework, becomes a unique and helpful application of culturally competent theory to personality assessment.

When using a culturally specific psychology approach with LGBT clients, assessors should adapt their clinical interview protocols to have specific semi-structured questions that focus on culture and community. Specifically, asking clients questions related to who is in their community (*"Who do you consider family? Can you tell me why this person/these people are family to you?"*), related to how and to what extent family have helped the client (*"Can you tell me about a specific instance when a family member has helped you through a difficult time?"*), and related to clients' unique relationship to culture (*"I know that we all have different ways that we engage with culture and the world around us. What are ways that you engage with your environment? How about your culture?"*). Further, asking clients questions in a clinical interview from a strength-based approach is equally important. Specifically, what is going well, strengths, and what they value in themselves helps people to comprehensively understand how their culture, environment, and context impact their personality and overall functioning. Finally, knowing how to use affirmative language when speaking of sexual orientation and gender identity has been documented as a critical process (Morrison, 2014).

In addition, one of the most glaring and complicated issues is that of gender-based norms for both adult and child assessment measures. On measures such as the MMPI-2 (Butcher et al., 1989) and most norm-based behavior rating scales for children and adolescents, separate norms have been typically provided for males and females. More recently, nongendered norms are available for this and most other personality measures. Nonetheless, most normative samples do not have much representation of LGBT individuals. Obviously, this norm-based scoring can over- or under-pathologize both adults and children who might not fit the stated, gendered profile if clinicians are not sensitive to the effects of gender role identification. It is important in such cases that clinicians interpret results as not "invalid," but as reflecting true differences from what is often seen as "typical." In concert with a thorough interview and history-taking, a test profile that reflects maladjustment might be a reflection that an LGBT client presents differently from others of their sex (although it is also important to be able to assess psychopathology in LGBT clients accurately). Rather than serving as a sign of pathology, this might open up a discussion about feeling different, misunderstood, or targeted. In some sense, assessment results are a reflection of a client's reality, so when their experience is different from what their culture deems as "normative," assessment results can yield a rich view of that experience. When an assessment measure might not be adequately normed on LGBT clients, it is incumbent upon the clinician to interpret the findings as sensitively as possible and to make sense of the results with the input of the client.

Prior to performing a self-report or behavior rating measure that might present heteronormative language (e.g., "mother and father" in the case of same-sex parenting), clinicians should discuss this with their clients. For example, a clinician might say:

> This measure has a lot of outdated and heterosexist language that may not apply to you and I'm sorry about that. But this measure can give us a place to start in our work. Rest assured, I'll discuss all results with you so that you can provide feedback on my initial interpretations. If you come across an item or two that really doesn't apply or makes you uncomfortable, please feel free to skip it and/or bring it up with me and we can talk about it.

This approach will help the client feel more empowered and communicate a certain degree of sensitivity on the part of the clinician. In keeping with the tenets of therapeutic and collaborative models of assessment (e.g., Finn, 2007; Finn, Fischer, & Handler, 2012), involving the client as an active collaborator can increase alliance and lead to meaningful dialogue, shared understanding, and change.

In addition to culturally competent data collections and the selection (or modification) of assessment instruments, clinicians should also be careful in their interpretation and writing of the assessment report when conducting psychological assessment with LGBT clients. The interpretation of test data for any client must be done from a framework of ethical decision-making that includes cultural knowledge, attitudes, and skills (Michaels, 2006). Clinical interpretation should be carefully checked and audited for cultural biases and assumptions, including those that are heterosexist, transphobic, and may include biases about gender roles, norms, and behaviors (Krishnamurthy, 2016). Such auditing should particularly occur with computer-aided scoring of personality assessments, given the basis for interpretive statements might not be clear (Lichtenberger, 2006).

It is important, both in written and verbal feedback, to examine the broader context in which the client lives. That is, although a clinician might make an effort to interpret test scores in a strength-based and culturally competent manner, he or she should also explore how a given profile of scores might leave clients "out of step" with the culture in which they live. Assessors should communicate acceptance of their clients while also recognizing that their schools, neighborhoods, or workplaces might not be as forgiving. This person-in-context analysis might allow clients to feel understood and normalized but also allows for a pragmatic discussion of how LGBT status might make them targets for implicit or explicit aggression or exclusion.

Finally, assessors must recognize that interpreting results and providing feedback to LGBT clients must be accompanied by feedback that is sensitive and helps the client to know that the feedback is being presented in a framework that is culturally sensitive. Allen, Montgomery, Tubman, Frazier, and Escovar (2003) note that clinicians' provision of verbal feedback concurrent with written interpretations of assessment data helps to strengthen the rapport between clinician and client and allows for questions to be answered thoroughly. For LGBT respondents, it might allow them additional information into how their answers to specific questions might have been interpreted from a framework that celebrates their sexual and gender identities instead of a psychological framework that has historically pathologized them.

In the context of feedback, it is important for the clinician to be aware of the client's sexual identity development. That is, some clients might be more uncomfortable with their sexual orientation and identity than is the clinician. Indeed, in some places and in some subcultures where non-heterosexual orientations are seen as sinful or pathological, clients might have a strong wish to reject their LGBT identity. We have heard cases of clients requesting conversion therapy, despite the fact that such "therapies" are unethical and even unlawful (McGeorge, Carlson, & Toomey, 2015). In such cases, clinicians have an even greater call to sensitivity, gentle education, and informed referral to ethical and LGBT-friendly psychological care.

Summary Points

Although many individuals are marginalized by their cultural identity in the diagnostic and assessment process, the discipline of culturally focused personality assessment has called for a needed change. The culturally intentional model for assessment and diagnosis with LGBT individuals is an important step in changing the history of pathologizing non-heterosexual sexual orientations and non-cisgender gender identities. Further, celebrating the strengths and communities of LGBT people can encourage health and well-being. Although this is the first step, we recognize the importance of trailblazing other steps in the process. We urge researchers, teachers, and practitioners to adopt a culture-specific framework in their assessment of clients and work with strengths early on in the assessment process. We hope that such a framework can be adopted into teaching and supervision practices to include strength-based assessment in the training of future counseling psychology professionals. Although the trail has endless possibilities, such a first step is necessary in creating competent services for LGB communities.

References

Allen, J. G., Montgomery, M., Tubman, J., Frazier, L., & Escovar, L. (2003). The effects of assessment feedback on rapport-building and self-enhancement process. *Journal of Mental Health Counseling, 25*, 165–182.

American Counseling Association. (2010). Counseling competencies with transgender clients. *Journal of LGBT Issues in Counseling, 4*(3), 135–159. doi: 10.1080/15538605.2010.524839

American Psychological Association (2011). *Guidelines for psychological practice in healthcare delivery systems.* Retrieved from www.apa.org/practice/guidelines/delivery-systems.aspx

American Psychological Association (2012). Guidelines for psychological practice with lesbian, gay, and bisexual clients. *American Psychologist, 67*(1), 10–42. doi: 10.1037/a0024659.

Balsam, K. F., & Szymanski, D. M. (2005). Relationship quality and domestic violence in women's same-sex relationships: The role of minority stress. *Psychology of Women Quarterly, 29*(3), 258–269.Budge, S. L., Adelson, J. L., & Howard, K. H. (2013). Anxiety and depression in transgender individuals: The roles of transition status, loss, social support, and coping. *Journal of Consulting and Clinical Psychology, 81*, 545–557.

Bullock, W., & Wood, N. (2016). Psychological assessment with trans people. In V. M. Brabender & J. L. Mihura (Eds.), *Handbook of gender and sexuality in psychological assessment* (pp. 489–510). New York: Routledge.

Burnes, T. R., & Chen, M. (2012). Multiple identities of transgender individuals: Incorporating a framework of intersectionality to gender crossing. In R. Josselson & M. Harway (Eds.), *Navigating multiple identities: Race, gender, culture, nationality and roles* (pp. 113–127). Oxford: Oxford University Press.

Burnes, T. R., Dexter, M. M., Richmond, K., Singh, A. A., & Cherrington, A. (2016). The experiences of transgender survivors of trauma who undergo social and medical transition. *Traumatology, 22*(1), 75.

Burnes, T. R., Peters-Long, S. L., & Schept, B. (2012). A resilience-based lens of sex work: Implications for professional psychologists. *Professional Psychology: Research and Practice, 43*(2), 137–144.

Butcher, J. N., Dahlstrom, W. G., Graham, J. R., Ben-Porath, Y. S., Tellegen, A., & Kaemmer, B. (1989). *Minnesota Multiphasic Personality Inventory-2 (MMPI-2): Manual for administration and scoring*. Minneapolis: University of Minnesota Press.

Clausell, E., & Roisman, G. I. (2009). Outness, big five personality traits, and same-sex relationship quality. *Journal of Social and Personal Relationships, 26*(2–3), 211–226.

Cochran, S., Sullivan, J., & Mays, V. (2003, February). Prevalence of mental disorders, psychological distress, and mental services use among lesbian, gay, and bisexual adults in the United States. *Journal of Consulting and Clinical Psychology, 71*(1), 53–61.

Cole, E. R. (2009). Intersectionality and research in psychology. *American Psychologist, 64*(3), 170–180.

Collins, P. H. (2009). Foreword: Emerging intersections—Building knowledge and transforming institutions. In B. T. Dill and R. E. Zambrana (Eds.), *Emerging intersections: Race, class and gender in theory, policy and practice* (pp. vii–xiv). New Brunswick, NJ: Rutgers University Press.

Crenshaw, K. (1991). Mapping the margins: Intersectionality, identity politics, and violence against women of color. *Stanford Law Review, 43*(6), 1241–1299.

Diamond, L. M., & Butterworth, M. (2008). *Questioning gender and sexual identity: Dynamic links over time. Sex Roles, 59*, 365–376.

Dickey, L. M., Burnes, T. R., & Singh, A. A. (2012). Sexual identity development of female-to-male transgender individuals: A grounded theory inquiry. *Journal of LGBT Issues in Counseling, 6*, 118–138.

Fassinger, R. E., & Arsenau, J. R. (2007). "I'd rather get wet than be under that umbrella": Differentiating the experiences and identities of lesbian, gay, bisexual, and transgender people. In K. J. Bieschke, R. M. Perez, & K. A. Debord (Eds.), *Handbook of counseling and psychotherapy with lesbian, gay, bisexual and transgender clients* (2nd ed.; pp. 19–50). Washington, DC: American Psychological Association.

Finn, S. E. (2007). *In our clients' shoes*. New York: Psychology Press.

Finn, S. E., Fischer, C. T., & Handler, L. (2012). *Collaborative/therapeutic assessment: A casebook and guide*. Hoboken, NJ: Wiley.

First, M. B., & Gibbon, M. (2004). The structured clinical interview for *DSM-IV* Axis I Disorders (SCID-I) and the Structured Clinical Interview for *DSM-IV* Axis-II Disorders (SCID-II). In M. J. Hilsenroth & D. L. Segal (Eds.), *Comprehensive handbook of psychological assessment, Vol. 2: Personality assessment* (pp. 134–143). Hoboken, NJ: Wiley.

GLAAD-Movement Advancement Project. (2012). An ally's guide to terminology: Talking about LGBT people and equality. Retrieved from: www.glaad.org/publications/talking about/terminology

Grant, J. E., Flynn, M., Odlaug, B. L., & Schreiber, L. R. N. (2011). Personality disorders in gay, lesbian, bisexual, and transgender chemically dependent patients. *The American Journal of Addictions, 20*(5), 405–411.

Grant, J. M., Mottet, L. A., Tanis, J., Harrison, J., Herman, J. L., & Keisling, M. (2011). *Injustice at every turn: A report of the National Transgender Discrimination Survey*. Washington, DC: National Center for Transgender Equality and National Gay and Lesbian Task Force.

Greene, D. C., & Britton, P. J. (2014). Self-regulation mediates LGBTQQ oppressive situations and psychological distress: Implications for psychotherapy. *Journal of Gay & Lesbian Mental Health, 18*(2), 121–141.

Harper, G. W. (2005). A journey towards liberation: Confronting heterosexism and the oppression of lesbian, gay, bisexual, and transgendered people. In G. Nelson & G. Prilleltensky (Eds.), *Community psychology: In pursuit of liberation and well-being* (pp. 382–404). New York: Palgrave Macmillan.

Hathaway, S. R., & McKinley, J. C. (1942). *The Minnesota Multiphasic Personality Inventory manual.* Minneapolis: University of Minnesota Press.

Health Service Psychology Education Collaborative. (2013). Professional psychology in health care services: A blueprint for education and training. *American Psychologist, 68*(6), 411–426. doi: 10.1037/a0033265.

Israel, T., Gorcheva, R., Burnes, T. R., & Walther, W. A. (2008). Helpful and unhelpful therapy experiences of LGBT clients. *Psychotherapy Research, 18*(3), 294–305.

Kertzner, R. M. (2012). Major depressive disorder: The unhappy ad man: Major depression in gay men. In P. Levounis, J. Descher, & M. E. Barber (Eds.), *The LGBT casebook* (pp. 121–130). Arlington, VA: American Psychiatric Publishing, Inc.

Kessler, R. C., Berglund, P., Demler, O., Jin, R., & Walters, E. E. (2005). Lifetime prevalence and age of-onset distributions of DSM-IV disorders in the national comorbidity survey replication. *Archives of General Psychiatry, 62*, 593–602.

Krishnamurthy, R. (2016). Gender considerations in self-report personality assessment interpretation. In V. M. Brabender & J. L. Mihura (Eds.), *Handbook of gender and sexuality in psychological assessment* (pp. 128–148). New York: Routledge.

Lichtenberger, E. O. (2006). Computer utilization and clinical judgment in psychological assessment reports. *Journal of Clinical Psychology, 62*(1), 19–32.

Liddle, B. J. (1999). Gay and lesbian clients' ratings of psychiatrists, psychologists, social workers, and counselors. *Journal of Gay & Lesbian Psychotherapy, 3*, 81–93.

Liddle, B. J. (1997). Gay and lesbian clients' selection of therapists and utilization of therapy. *Psychotherapy: Theory, Research, Practice, Training, 34*, 11–18; *43*, 394–401.

Maddux, J. E. (2002). Stopping the "madness": Positive psychology and the deconstruction of the illness ideology and the DSM. In C. R. Snyder & S. J. López (Eds.), *Handbook of positive psychology* (pp. 13–25). London: Oxford University Press.

Mathy, R. M., & Kerr, S. K. (2003). *Lesbian and bisexual women's mental health.* Binghamton, NY: Harrington Park Press.

McGeorge, C. R., Carlson, T. S., & Toomey, R. B. (2015). An exploration of family therapists' beliefs about the ethics of conversion therapy: The influence of negative beliefs and clinical competence with lesbian, gay, and bisexual clients. *Journal of Marital and Family Therapy, 41*, 42–56. doi: 10.1111/jmft.12040

Meyer, I. H. (2003). Prejudice, social stress, and mental health in lesbian, gay, and bisexual populations: Conceptual issues and research evidence. *Psychological Bulletin, 129*, 674–697.

Michaels, M. H. (2006). Ethical considerations in writing psychological assessment reports. *Journal of Clinical Psychology, 62*(1), 47–58. doi: 10.1002/jclp.20199.

Moradi, B., & Parent, M. C. (2013). Assessment of gender-related traits, attitudes, roles, norms, identity, and experiences. In K. F. Geisinger (Ed.), *APA handbook of testing and assessment in psychology: Vol. 2. Testing and assessment in clinical and counseling psychology* (pp. 467–488). Washington, DC: American Psychological Association.

Morrison, J. (2014). *The first interview* (4th ed.). New York: Guilford.

Morrow, S. L. (2012). Sexual orientations and identities. In E. Altmaier & J. Hansen (Eds.), *The Oxford handbook of counseling psychology* (pp. 409–433). New York: Oxford University Press.

Nuttbrock, L., Hwahng, S., Bockting, W., Rosenblum, A., Mason, M., Macri, M., & Becker, J. (2010). Psychiatric impact of gender-related abuse across the life course of male-to-female transgender persons. *Journal of Sex Research, 47*, 12–23.

Pachankis, J., & Goldfried, M. (2004). Clinical issues in working with lesbian, gay, and bisexual clients. *Psychotherapy: Theory, Research, Practice, Training, 41*(3), 227–246.

Prince, J. P., & Potoczniak, M. J. (2012). Using psychological assessment tools with lesbian, gay, bisexual, and transgender clients. In S. H. Dworkin and M. Pope (Eds.), *Casebook for counseling lesbian, gay, bisexual, and transgendered persons and their families*. Alexandria, VA: American Counseling Association.

Richmond, K., Burnes, T. R., & Carroll, K. (2012). Lost in translation: Interpreting systems of trauma for transgender clients. *Journal of Traumatology, 18*(1), 45–57.

Riggle, E. D. B., Whitman, J. S., Olson, A., Rostosky, S. S., & Strong, S. (2008). The positive aspects of being a lesbian or a gay man. *Professional Psychology: Research and Practice, 39*(2), 210–217.

Singh, A. A., & McKleroy, V. S. (2011). "Just getting out of bed is a revolutionary act": The resilience of transgender people of color who have survived traumatic life events. *Traumatology, 17*(2), 34–44.

Sue, D. W., & Sue, D. (2017). *Counseling the culturally diverse: Theory and practice* (7th ed.). New York: Wiley.

Tellegen, A., & Ben-Porath, Y. S. (2011). *MMPI-2-RF, Minnesota Multiphasic Personality Inventory-2-Restructured Form: Technical manual*. Minneapolis: University of Minnesota Press.

Toomey, R. B., Ryan, C., Diaz, R. M., Card, N. A., & Russell, S. T. (2010). Gender-nonconforming Lesbian, Gay, Bisexual, and Transgender youth: School victimization and young adult psychosocial adjustment. *Developmental Psychology, 46*(6), 1580–1589. doi: 10.1037/a0020705

CHAPTER 7

Religion and Personality Assessment

Tania Abouezzeddine, Peter C. Hill, Clark D. Campbell, and Steven R. Smith

Psychological assessment practice requires more than competence in rapport building, interviewing, test administration, scoring, and interpretation. Krishnamurthy and Yalof (2010) articulate that the entire process needs to be anchored in ethical principles and practices (APA, 2002) and multicultural sensitivity (APA, 2003). Because religion is an identified area of diversity (APA, 2013), religious aspects of clients should be considered in the assessment process. Rather than assessing a client's religion *per se*, this perspective suggests the need to understand the ways that a client experiences and expresses religiousness and spirituality and how it might influence his or her psychological functioning and approach to the psychological assessment process.

The relevance of considering a client's religious and spiritual identity during the assessment process is heightened when one considers the importance of religion and spirituality to the vast majority of Americans. Numerous national surveys have consistently shown that the vast majority of Americans believe in God (e.g., 90% according to the Gallup Daily Tracking project, cited in Newport, 2012) and believe that God is a personal God (e.g., 70% according to Kosmin & Keysar, 2009). The General Social Survey (GSS) conducted by the National Opinion Research Center (NORC), the most frequently cited source that studies religion and spirituality in America, found in 2010 that 31% of Americans attend church weekly (or more) and 71% attend church services at least once per year.

In reviewing the results of multiple surveys, Shafranske and Cummings (2013) concluded that although religion is very important or fairly important to the vast majority of Americans (80% to 88% in the surveys they reviewed), psychologists are considerably less likely to endorse the importance of religion (46% to 70% among those surveyed). Spirituality, however, is far more likely to be endorsed by psychologists, with the majority rating it as very important (48% to 61%) or fairly important (21% to 30%), such that the importance of spirituality to psychologists is comparable to the importance of religion (and spirituality) found in the general US populace. These findings raise some fundamental questions: What conceptions are generated when the terms religion and spirituality are used, given the differential reactions (at least for some people) that they generate? To what degree does the meaning of the two terms overlap? Is one term viewed more or less favorably than the other? Ultimately, what are the implications of religious or spiritual identification for personality assessment?

Conceptual Considerations

Although in many ways the USA continues to be a religious nation, it is clear that the religious landscape is changing. At the forefront of this change, accelerated in the past 40 years or so, is the bifurcation of religiousness and spirituality among a minority but gradually increasing percentage of Americans. Today, surveys estimate that between 20% and 35% of Americans consider themselves "spiritual, but not religious" (Ellison & McFarland, 2013). While such a decoupling indicates for some an alternative to traditional religion (primarily Christianity), it also reflects an emphasis on the interior life that is central to much religious belief; thus, the term does not necessarily suggest a non-religious alternative and, in fact, the majority of Americans still identify themselves as both spiritual and religious, with both concepts understood primarily within the context of Judeo-Christianity (Marler & Hadaway, 2002). Alternatives to the Judeo-Christian tradition have grown among the US populace, although the numbers remain relatively small (less than 5%; Ellison & McFarland, 2013). Included in this group are varieties of Eastern philosophies and religious traditions including Hinduism, Buddhism, and Jainism, Islamic and Zoroastrian faiths, Native American spirituality, and New Age thought and practices.

Even so, many people embrace some notion of spirituality that they see as distinct from religion. A common notion that has emerged is that the term "spiritual" refers to a subjectively personal and private feeling of connectedness to that which is perceived as sacred, and that declaring something sacred does not require institutional or doctrinal authority. In contrast to the experiential basis of spirituality, religion is viewed as a belief-based doctrinal system that has been sanctioned by institutional authority. However, both scientific and religious scholars (e.g., Hill et al., 2000; Smith, 1991; Zinnbauer & Pargament, 2005) caution against a strong decoupling of the two constructs and their polarizing connotations; instead, they contend that there is considerable overlap. Nevertheless, the "spiritual, but not religious" category deserves careful investigation in that it can include people from all corners of the religious/spiritual landscape, ranging from, for example, the evangelical Christian who stresses the interior life as opposed to church affiliation as the central feature of faith experience, to the self-identified atheist, agnostic, or apostate who conceives of spirituality as a domain far removed from traditional religious categories, such as an ecology (Streib & Klein, 2013).

Perhaps the most widely used conceptualization of spirituality and religion, offered by Pargament and colleagues (Hill et al., 2000; Pargament, 1997; Zinnbauer & Pargament, 2005), is that both concepts can be defined in terms of a search process. For example, Hill et al. (2000) suggest that both religion and spirituality involve

> feelings, thoughts, experiences, and behaviors that arise from a search for the sacred. The term 'search' refers to attempts to identify, articulate, maintain, or

> transform. The term 'sacred' refers to a divine being, divine object, Ultimate Reality, or Ultimate Truth as perceived by the individual.
>
> (p. 66)

What differentiates the two, according to Hill and colleagues, is that religion may also tend to be more prescriptive, usually through some organizational structure, not only in terms of how the sacred is to be understood but also in establishing and validating the means and methods of the search process itself. In the minds of many scholars, the intended goal of religion is to foster spirituality. For others, however, religious prescriptions may be seen as an obstacle to spiritual growth (Miller & Thoresen, 2003).

Religion as Culture and Meaning Systems

Religion and spirituality often become important sources of cultural identity. In fact, Cohen (2009) maintains that religion should be thought of as a cultural variable. Thus, the ability to freely practice one's religious faith without fear of repercussion or ostracism from the larger culture, to impart religious education to one's children, to mingle with other people of the same tradition, and to have access to places of worship are all important contributors to one's cultural identity (Tarakeshwar, 2013). To understand how religion and spirituality form and function within specific populations, it is crucial to understand their cultural manifestations in light of the major religious traditions within which they are embedded. Thus, for example, although a client who was born and raised in the United States might self-identify as "spiritual but not religious" even to the point of disavowing any affiliation with organized religion, that person's understanding and experience of spirituality might be heavily influenced by the Judeo-Christian culture in which that person is embedded.

It is, therefore, important to have at least a rudimentary knowledge and understanding of major world religions such as Buddhism, Christianity, Hinduism, Islam, and Judaism, and how those traditions have impacted the cultures where they are the predominant. Due diligence to the complexity and richness of major world religions and their cultures is impossible within the limits of this chapter. Those who wish to learn more about the psychology of each of these religious traditions are referred to Chapters 35 to 39 of Pargament (2013, Vol. I).

Both religion and spirituality can become important meaning systems that can influence the perceptions, emotions, and general well-being of clients. Hood, Hill, and Williamson (2005) describe a meaning system as a set of beliefs about the world and the self, which may impact how people see, interpret, and function within the world in which they live. They suggest that religion and spirituality are often successful meaning systems in that they can be seen as: comprehensive (a higher-order meaning system that contains other sources of meaning such as creativity, relationships, work, ideals, and values), a philosophical orientation (that provides the individual with a core schema or cognitive map to help them interpret and understand their experiences), a means of transcendence and association with what is beyond us, and a direct provider, with explicit claims, of meaning and purpose in life.

Given this perspective that religion is a meaning system, it is safe to say that although assessment of religious beliefs, practices, and functioning might appear simple, it is actually a very complex aspect of life and therefore requires a sophisticated assessment approach. A psychologist may simply ask, "What is your religion?" or "Do you belong to a particular church or denomination?" in order to get a sense of a client's religious beliefs. However, such an approach is far too simplistic and would likely lead to several misconceptions about the client. Rather, a more complex understanding of the role of religion in a client's life will lead to a more robust understanding of the client, preventing misinterpretation and the overpathologizing of what might be culturally and religiously appropriate. Issues to consider as part of this more complex and culturally sensitive understanding will now be presented.

Religion, Spirituality, and Personality

It is also imperative that the link between religion and personality be examined. Historically the literature has outlined two conflicting theories regarding the relationship between personality, religion, and spirituality. One theory, based on Freud's classic ideas on religion (Freud, 1950), suggested that religious belief was related to psychopathology, specifically neuroticism. A second, based on Jung's classic theories on religion and individuation, suggested that religious belief may promote psychological health and therefore might be negatively related to neuroticism (Jung, 1938). Over the decades there have been some attempts to test these theories and clarify the link between personality traits, religion, and spirituality.

Research examining the relationship between personality and these two constructs has been quite sparse, with a few seminal studies highlighting both positive and negative correlates. Personality traits of neuroticism, extraversion, openness, agreeableness, conscientiousness, and aggression were mainly examined. Religion and spirituality were subdivided into categories such as religious maturity, orientation, affiliation, and involvement (Saroglou, 2002; Taylor & MacDonald, 1999), as well as spiritual connectedness, forgiveness, experiences of sense and meaning, and hope (Unterrainer, Lewis, & Fink, 2014).

In a meta-analytic study by Saroglou (2002) certain healthy personality traits were found to be significantly linked to religion in 13 studies published between 1986 and 2001. Although the effect sizes were small, religiosity was identified as positively correlated with traits such as agreeableness, conscientiousness, and extraversion (Saroglou, 2002). Specifically religious affiliation and involvement were seen to more likely be associated with extraversion, while intrinsic religiosity was more likely linked to traits of agreeableness and conscientiousness (Saroglou, 2002; Taylor & MacDonald, 1999). In addition, open and mature religiosity was related to openness and emotional stability (Saroglou, 2002). In a more recent study utilizing the Multidimensional Inventory for Religious/Spiritual Well-Being (MI-RSWB), spiritual traits of hope and forgiveness were found to be positively correlated with extraversion and a sense of coherence (finding life understandable and manageable), while being negatively correlated with neuroticism (Unterrainer et al., 2014). The spiritual trait of forgiveness was also reported to be negatively associated with aggression. In a few studies Christianity's specific impact on emotional health was examined, with results indicating no link between this religious ideology and emotional instability (Francis & Jackson, 2003) but a positive link with happiness (Francis, Jones, & Wilcox, 2000).

On the other hand, some studies suggest that extrinsic religiosity and religious fundamentalism were, respectively, correlated with neurotic traits and individuals being less open (Saroglou, 2002). Taylor and MacDonald (1999) also examined correlates for individuals from various religious backgrounds and found that those with 'no religious' affiliation were more neurotic and shared common traits of being disagreeable and unconscientious with individuals who were less religiously involved in their communities.

The research in this area is still in its infancy, however there are findings that highlight the relationship between personality and religious or spiritual identity. This is an important aspect to keep in mind during assessment and diagnosis as it may shed light on patient subjective well-being and outcome.

Religious Aspects to Consider When Assessing Clients

Richards and Bergin (1997, 2005) described nine categories of religious information to consider when conducting psychological assessments:

1. Metaphysical worldview: beliefs about one's place in the universe and relationship to the divine (if any).
2. Religious affiliation: membership or identification with a particular faith tradition.
3. Religious orthodoxy: adherence (or attempts to adhere) to expectations and practices associated with a particular faith tradition.
4. Religious problem-solving: the use of religious coping strategies to deal with various problems in life.
5. Spiritual identity: the degree to which one sees oneself as a spiritual being.
6. God image: one's perception of God (personal/impersonal; active/inactive; judgmental/compassionate).
7. Value-lifestyle congruence: consistency between religious beliefs and behaviors.
8. Doctrinal knowledge: one's understanding of doctrines or theology related to a faith tradition.
9. Religious and spiritual health and maturity: awareness of one's spiritual progress or development (self-reflection about one's spiritual growth).

Although some clients may not be aware of, or able to articulate, the content of their beliefs and experiences of many of these categories, it will be helpful to consider these categories in making a comprehensive psychological evaluation of a client. It is also likely that some of these categories will be more significant than others, and therefore each category does not need to be fully assessed; rather, we should be cognizant of these various categories in an attempt to be sensitive to the religious aspects of the client's functioning. Moreover, although it is comprehensive to have this broader conception of religion in mind when evaluating clients, often there are time constraints that call for a more abbreviated way of evaluating the role of religion in a client's life. Pulchalski and Rommer (2001) describe such a brief assessment with the acronym *FICA*. An adaptation is provided here:

F = Faith ("Describe your faith tradition")
I = Importance ("How important is your faith to you and your family?")
C = Church ("What church or faith community do you belong to?")
A = Address ("How would you like these issues to be addressed in your evaluation?")

In addition to the gathering of religious information from the client, we should assess the level of devoutness or the fundamental nature of the patient's religious belief system. For example, although religious fundamentalism carries with it far reaching psychological implications that are often negative in nature, it also implies a powerful meaning system that highlights the structures of authority and truth that are most important to the client (Hood et al., 2005). For the fundamentalist, the religious text and its perceived absolute truths are seen as objective facts that provide a framework through which life and the world are attributed meaning.

Aspects of Religious Worldview that Might Impact Assessment

Object Relations theorists have described the significance of self and object (other) representations in psychological functioning. Self and other images are created early in psychological development as the infant and young child relates to his/her parents. Through these interactions, the child internalizes certain images, feelings, and beliefs about self in the world. These images and beliefs are culturally loaded and are significant for various aspects of diversity, such as gender, sexual identity, and religion. Thus, the views of self and others that have a strong religious component are often significant for clients who come for psychological assessment. Moreover, psychological explanations of health and pathology are likely conveyed early in life and co-exist with the views of self and other. These three views (self, other, and openness to psychological explanations) are highly connected to religious worldviews and should be considered in the assessment process.

View of Self

How does the client see himself/herself as a religious or spiritual being?

- What are the client's religious/spiritual views of self? Examples include such perspectives as: sinful, damaged beyond repair, completely holy (sanctified), growing in faith commitment, and questioning or doubting.

- What role does religious practice have in relation to the view of self? Religious practices may be a way of purifying the self or aligning with an all-good object. Alternatively, religious practice may be a way of avoiding "the world" and its temptations. Religious practices may also be a way for the client to demonstrate a commitment to religious beliefs so that there is consistency in belief and behavior.
- To what degree are religious practices motivated by intrinsic vs. extrinsic factors? Is the motivation to behave in certain ways a reflection of what the client believes and is therefore internally motivated? Or, is it a reflection of what religion does for the individual, a perceived obligation as per religious doctrine, or to manage the impressions one leaves on other people—all of which reflect external motivations for religious behavior.

View of Other

How does the religious client see others, particularly one in an authoritative and potentially judgmental role?

- Is the other all-powerful, and therefore god-like? If so, is the other all good (benevolent) or all bad (ruthless), or a mixture of both qualities?
- To what degree is there transference from the client's experience of authority to the authority vested in the psychological evaluator? How might this also be a reflection of the client's view of God or the divine?
- How does the client's view of the other impact the role behavior of the client? If the evaluator is seen as god-like and good, does it elicit a shame response in the client and a subservient role?

View of Psychological Explanations of Behavior

- Are naturalistic factors (e.g., psychological, biological) viewed as competing or complementary explanations with spiritual factors as explanations of behavior? How does the client view psychopathology? Is it the result of sin? If so, are all psychological problems the result of personal sins, or the sins of others, or the sins of political and systemic structures? To what extent are biological and psychological explanations accepted as factors?
- How does the client view psychological health? How does one become healthy—by one's own effort, by prayer, by religious devotion? What role does community support or supernatural intervention play in one becoming healthy? To what degree are psychological and spiritual health related to each other? Can one be psychologically healthy but spiritually unhealthy (or vice-versa)?

Each of these views is likely to be relevant at all stages of the assessment process. At the initial engagement with the psychological evaluator, these views might be evident in an individual's willingness to make an assessment appointment. If the client sees himself/herself as sinful and the evaluator as a secular authority, he/she might be reluctant to engage in the assessment process. Instead, this client might seek input from a pastor or priest.

During the clinical interview, a devoutly religious client may or may not be open to revealing aspects of his/her behavior or functioning for fear of judgment by the psychological evaluator and the ensuing feelings of guilt and shame. Conversely, the highly defended and devoutly religious client might try to convince the evaluator of the benefits of his/her religious beliefs and practices as a form of proselytization.

During the feedback of findings aspect of the assessment process, the religious client might want to incorporate the findings into religious language so that it becomes meaningful. This may require sensitivity and patience on the part of the assessor so that the client can benefit from the findings in a way that is personally useful.

As psychologists, it is our responsibility to ensure a holistic treatment of patients and that their beliefs are accounted for and respected. The assessment, interpretation, and diagnosis should all take into account the multidimensional aspects of the patient's personhood (holistic) and religious reality (context).

Empirical Findings

Review papers on the topics of culture and personality assessment consistently state that both domestic and international research have focused primarily on ethnicity and race as aspects of cultural diversity, with very little accounting of religion as its own specific cultural variable (e.g., Allik, Massoudi, Realo, & Rossier, 2012; Butcher 2004; Butcher, Derksen, Sloore & Sirigatti, 2003). The most common personality assessment tools utilized today are self-report measures such as the MMPI-2 and PAI and performance-based measures such as the Rorschach and Thematic Apperception Test. These measures, although used extensively across diverse cultures with several available linguistic translations and cultural adaptations (e.g. Butcher, 2004), do not sufficiently account for different cultural influences such as religious belief systems. Furthermore, the fact that these measures have been predominantly normed on Caucasian (non-Hispanic) populations, and that the questions or stimuli were developed from a Caucasian and Western perspective, has led to inaccurate interpretation of findings in domestic minority populations, such as African Americans (Reed, Walker, Williams, McLeod, & Jones, 1996; Whatley, Allen, & Dana, 2003), Hispanic Americans (Montgomery & Orozco, 1985; Velasquez et al., 2000), Asian Americans (Sue, Keefe, Enomoto, Durvasula, & Chao, 1996), and American Indians (Dana, 2000; Hill, Pace, & Robbins, 2010; Hoffmann, Dana, & Bolton, 1985; Pace et al., 2006), as well as international populations.

Some earlier research discussed the influence of the Christian belief system on personality assessment profiles. One early study (Groesch & Davis, 1977) looked specifically at MMPI profiles of Catholic versus Protestant drug-dependent and schizophrenic male patients. The study concluded that the profiles of their subjects reflected significant differences that were specifically related to their religious beliefs. Findings demonstrated differences on the Lie (L) scale and on scales 1 (Hypochondriasis), 2 (Depression), 5 (Masculinity-Femininity), 7 (Psychasthenia), and 8 (Schizophrenia). Religion was concluded to be an important variable that could potentially influence psychiatric diagnosis and treatment. This generated discussion as to whether separate norms should specifically be gathered to address religious populations, ideas put forward by Bier (1971).

Researchers have also looked at subcultural difference on the response of Christians on the MMPI's L scale. Early research documented a higher score on the L scale for bible-college students compared to non-religious students (e.g., Dahlstrom & Welsh, 1960; Delay, Pichot, Sadoun, & Perse, 1955). More recently, Bridges and Baum reported similar elevations among clinical Christian populations assessed in the early part of the 21st century (2013). These L scale results brought to question the validity of using the MMPI on individuals within certain religious communities (e.g., Hood, 1975). An elevation on the L scale, within the Christian subculture, was initially seen as an indication of naivety in response style, with a tendency of the Christian to try to 'fake good' (Dahlstrom & Welsh, 1960; Power & O'Donovan, 1969; Rigby, 1987). Others have attributed the high L score to poor insight and immaturity (Crookes & Buckley, 1976; Eysenck, Nias, & Eysenck, 1971; Francis, Pearson, & Kay, 1983; Francis, Pearson, & Stubbs, 1985; Rump & Court, 1971), as well as social conformity and compliance (Finlayson, 1972; Massey, 1980).

Other researchers have countered that the elevated MMPI L scale may be triggered by individuals responding to questions based on the norms within their belief system that emphasize honesty and sincerity (McCrae & Costa, 1985; O'Hagan & Edmunds, 1982), therefore reflecting a core meaning system rather than impression management efforts. For example, Duris, Bjorck, and Gorsuch (2007) conducted a multiple group factor analytic study of the items of the MMPI-2's L scale. Their findings demonstrated that seminary students, who self-identified as active and committed to their Christian faith, consistently responded differently on this scale compared to the MMPI-2's normative sample. In addition, six out of the 15 items on this scale were found to tap into religious motivation responses that are characteristic of individuals with a Christian belief system. The authors concluded that these individuals may interpret items on the MMPI-2's L scale differently than others and therefore analyzing their scores on this scale in the usual way (which influences the rest of the MMPI-2 profile) should be viewed as questionable.

Similar religious insensitivity in interpreting responses to MMPI-2 items was seen in a study conducted with American Indians, where concern was raised over the overpathologizing of experiences and perceptions that were linked to spiritual or religious practices (Dana, 2000; Pace et al., 2006). Hill and colleagues' (2010) item analyses of five MMPI-2 scales—Infrequency (F), 1, 6 (Paranoia), 8, and 9 (Hypomania)—obtained from a sample of American Indians from the Eastern Woodland Oklahoma tribe, revealed that a theme of spiritual 'core beliefs' impacted how American Indians responded to these items. For example, it would be spiritually appropriate for American Indians to affirmatively respond to an item asking if they believed that they receive communication via dreams (similar to an item on Scale 9 on the MMPI-2). Such an endorsement might be seen as pathological on the MMPI-2 even though it is appropriate given the individual's spiritual or religious context (based on a spiritual belief that individuals may be communicated with by ancestors via dreams). The authors of this study summarize that, instead of serving their intended purpose of diagnosing psychopathology, some items on the MMPI-2 bring up aspects of a minority group's core belief system that are positive or accepted within the culture (Hill et al., 2010).

MacDonald and Holland (2003) examined correlations between scores from the MMPI-2 clinical scales and the Expressions of Spirituality Inventory (ESI), a multidimensional measure of spirituality that identifies five central features that are believed to be at the core of spirituality. They found that individuals reporting active religious involvement had significantly lower T scores on scales 2, 4 (Psychopathic Deviate), 6, 7, and 8, whereas the non-religious participants were noted to have more clinically significant profiles indicating possible psychopathology. In addition, scores on all MMPI-2 clinical scales, with the exception of scales 5 and 9, were significantly associated with overall spirituality, with many displaying an inverse relationship with dimensions of Existential Well-Being and Religiousness. The one exception was the spiritual concept of Paranormal Beliefs which has a positive relationship with the MMPI-2 Paranoia scale.

A more recent study looked further into scores from the newer MMPI-2's restructured clinical (RC) scales and their relatedness to the ESI. They found that all spiritual dimensions on the ESI (both collectively and individually) had significant correlations (both positive and negative) with the MMPI-2 RC scales and that each RC scale was significantly correlated to at least one spiritual dimension represented on the ESI. A facet of spirituality (Existential Well Being) was negatively correlated with almost all the restructured clinical scales, with the only exception being the Hypomanic Activation RC9 scale. Other negative correlates were found to be consistent with the literature, where individuals with higher levels of spirituality reported higher levels of physical and psychological health and demonstrated less psychopathology and antisocial behaviors (Mendez & MacDonald, 2012). As with MacDonald and Holland's study, a few positive correlates between spirituality and the RC scale scores were also found. Specifically, individuals who scored high on the Experiential/Phenomenological dimensions on the ESI highly endorsed the restructured clinical scales of: Somatic Complaints (RC1), Aberrant Experiences (RC8), and Hypomanic Activation (RC9). In addition, and consistent with the earlier study examining traditional clinical scales, positive correlations were found between the ESI's Paranormal Beliefs dimension and performance on two restructured clinical scales: Ideas of Persecution and Aberrant Experiences (RC6 & RC8) (Mendez & MacDonald, 2012).

These examples might give us considerable pause in taking assessment data at face value without considering and taking into account the multidimensional nature of the populations we serve. At this time, given the limitations of the tools we have at hand, it is imperative that we continue to advance the research in this area and continue to utilize it in interpreting and understanding the populations we serve. In addition, we need to ensure the use of techniques that are culturally inclusive and sensitive, while focusing on nurturing a process-oriented way of thinking about the different dimensions of culture that might impact the assessment process. To that end, the rest of this chapter will be dedicated to outlining possible techniques to keep in mind while we navigate the various stages of the multicultural personality assessment process.

Practical Considerations: Taking into Account Religious Diversity—Stages of Assessment

In recent years therapists and assessors alike have begun to dialogue more frequently on how best to equip individuals in conducting ethical and valid multicultural assessment. López (2002) outlined three main conceptual issues that he believed should be covered when teaching graduate students to help them 'Shift their cultural lens': (1) establishing a solid foundation in traditional assessment theory and practice; (2) equipping future clinicians to discern what is important in their client's social and cultural world, learning to specify and test cultural differences without succumbing to group labels of ethnic/cultural groups; and (3) aiding students in learning to assess and formulate both cultural-specific and psychopathological hypotheses. To that end, we hope to be able to highlight some areas that would be advisable to think through when assessing individuals of diverse religious backgrounds.

In the Beginning, Know Thyself

In order to be able to discern the cultural and spiritual nuances in the life of the client, assessors must begin by examining their own culture and meaning systems. This imperative is supported by research conducted by Shafranske and Maloney (1990) who found that the variable that was most influential in providing treatment to spiritual or religious clients was the therapist's own spiritual belief system. The researchers pointed out that self-awareness regarding one's own spiritual values has been shown to decrease the likelihood of difficulties such as value clashes with the client and acting-out of the clinician's value conflicts, therefore allowing for the establishment and maintenance of good rapport, which is essential for a thorough and valid assessment.

Know Something about the 'Other'

Research in the United States indicates that a large percentage of clients believe therapists should be aware of their religious and spiritual concerns (Brown & Van Orden, 2007). However, spiritual and religious issues might never arise during the assessment process because of clients' preconceived misconceptions of religion being an unwelcome topic in psychology or because of distrust of the mental health professionals (e.g., Lindgren & Coursey, 1995). We cannot be expected to know all things regarding the possible religious or spiritual belief systems in the world. However, we should be open to learning and establishing some basic understanding of major religions represented in the communities within which we work, and particularly of the specific religious context and beliefs of the patients we assess. This would allow for a more culturally sensitive and relevant provision of assessment services. The training of professionals should not be limited to exposure from course content, guest lecturers or religiously diverse client populations alone (Worthington et al., 2009). Worthington and colleagues emphasize the need for supervision and mentorship that comes from a population of professionals that are exposed to and familiar with a diversity of religions and able to model appropriate techniques to their students.

Another important factor to keep in mind is the preference of the client regarding the spiritual belief system of the clinician. Research suggests that clinical populations that endorse spiritual belief systems may have preferences for therapists based on the spiritual beliefs of the therapists (e.g., Cinnirella & Loewenthal, 1999). For example, in a study by Worthington and colleagues (2009) of British citizens from diverse religious backgrounds, participants were seen to be divided among those who wished to be assessed by professionals within their religious group versus those who preferred professionals from a different religious group. Those with preferences for professionals from within their religious system felt that they would be better understood and that their cultural milieu would be accounted for in explaining their clinical presentation. The other subgroup, concerned that utilizing a professional from within their religious group would increase the risk of a breach of confidentiality, preferred a therapist who was outside their religious system. Worthington and colleagues (2009) found that highly religious patients preferred therapists who share their spiritual and religious values. Such religious and spiritual preferences should be assessed early on in the process to ensure an optimal testing environment.

Initiating Contact

Prior to beginning a diagnostic interview, it is important to verify a few variables that would impact the interview, assessment tools chosen, and hypotheses of diagnoses to be verified. Consistently and sensitively asking about social identities, language, and religious beliefs in the first interaction with patients will help lay a solid clinical foundation that acknowledges that issues of diversity will be addressed in the assessment process (Dadlani, Overtree, & Perry-Jenkins, 2012).

Religious Belief and Devoutness

In this chapter, we have emphasized the importance of asking patients about the belief systems that they subscribe to as well as their level of devotedness or faithfulness to those belief systems. Both religious and spiritual beliefs, as well as the level of devoutness, should be discerned early on in the process to keep any sociocultural errors or misdiagnosis on the part of the assessor at a minimum. Brown and Van Orden (2007, p. 65) recommend asking simple questions at the beginning of the interview (around the same time as other demographics are being gathered). Examples would be questions like: "Tell me about your religious beliefs" or "Tell me how spirituality relates to your life." It is important to be open, nonjudgmental, and professionally transparent while asking questions on this issue.

Understanding the role of religion in the client's life might also require knowledge about rituals and restrictions that could interfere with the assessment process. It is advisable that the clinician ask questions about such rituals or restrictions at intake. For example, a devout Muslim, either male or female, might believe that it is wrong to be in a room alone with an assessor of the opposite gender. Devout Muslims should also be allowed frequent breaks and a private space to offer prayer at the appropriate times according to their specific sect (Mahmood & Ahmed, 2012). Orthodox Jewish patients might have time restrictions specific to keeping the Sabbath, or major religious holidays, that would need to be accounted for when scheduling the assessment. Clinicians evaluating devout patients who come in for an assessment while observing fasting traditions would need to be aware of the hours the patient will be fasting for and ensure that the assessment process does not overlap with the allotted time for the 'breaking of the fast.' Members of some devout religious groups might be offended if they are touched by individuals of the opposite sex or different faiths, due to doctrines of cleanliness or being separate from the world. Such religious rituals need to be accounted for in order to ensure an uninterrupted assessment process and increase the likelihood of full patient participation and engagement.

Expectations for Assessment

Clarifying the reason for the assessment is important no matter the religious background of the patients seen. Knowing what the assessment will involve (how long the whole process will take, the different components of assessment, who will be included in the process) and what they will be receiving as a result of the assessment, is crucial to maintain the trust and cooperation of religious patients and their families. Individuals from certain cultural backgrounds might assume that the individual assessing them will also be the treatment provider (which might or might not be true), or that the assessment process itself will provide therapeutic relief and healing. These expectations should be discussed during intake or prior to the interview and false expectations should be addressed and corrected.

The Interview

Presenting Problems

The question of the presenting problem is one that sets the tone for the whole assessment process (including hypotheses considered and tools administered). Although there are many cross-cultural similarities in underlying personality profiles, culture and religious diversity might impact how patients exhibit symptoms related to certain psychopathologies (Butcher, Mosch, Tsai, & Nezami, 2006). In addition, based on some religious principles certain 'symptoms' that may be viewed as pathological in mainstream psychology may be viewed as normative within their cultural and religious contexts. For example, patients from certain religious backgrounds who display a high level of dependence or submission towards their spouses or fathers may meet the criteria indicated for a dependent personality disorder. However, these 'symptoms' may be highly normative, accepted, and in many ways expected within their religious worlds (e.g., Dwairy, 2006). Another example may be the patient endorsing miraculous encounters (e.g., visions) or hearing from God, that might be viewed as being normative within this person's religious setting but easily pathologized out of that context.

Other symptoms might not be viewed as religiously acceptable, such as feelings of hopelessness and sadness that are correlated with depression, since they may be seen as indicators of a weak faith. These symptoms may be manifested through physical symptoms that might be more culturally accepted (seen in both Asian and Middle Eastern cultures; e.g., Al-Krenawi & Graham, 2000; Lin & Cheung, 1999). Therefore, when gathering information regarding the presenting difficulties of patients, it is important that assessors use alternative clinical language and socio-culturally acceptable symptoms in order to assess clinical criteria. The assessor should strive to keep in mind the patient's religious and cultural belief system and that 'typical' symptoms might be manifesting in alternative ways.

Testing Environment

The question regarding who should be involved in the interview process is dependent on whether there are reasons a patient would or would not be comfortable being alone with the assessor. Devout Muslim and Orthodox Jewish patients might not be comfortable being alone in a room with a person of the other gender, and may prefer either having a family member in the room with them or having a window looking into the room in order to maintain propriety (Mahmood & Ahmed, 2012). Assessors should also be mindful of displaying religious artifacts in their testing room that could cause affront or distrust.

History Taking

There are times when family members are needed during the interview process in order to verify or fill in gaps in a patient's clinical history. Individuals of certain faiths or cultures might be open to bringing in family members (intertwined family systems), or opposed to it (sharing the information in public might bring dishonor and shame onto the family). The concept of shaming the family will also interfere with the accuracy and thoroughness of the history-taking interview. Topics such as sexual activity and substance abuse are especially shame-inducing to individuals who are devout. Great caution and wisdom need to be exercised during this process, and the groundwork for open dialogue between the assessor and patient should be established.

Assessment

Choosing Assessment Tools

At this time there are no personality tests that have been formulated or normed on specific religious populations. Assessors typically interpret their findings as carefully as possible and should examine test scales and scores carefully to determine which ones might be especially affected by religion and spirituality. This technique would decrease the chance of interpretive error and would allow for more culturally appropriate assessment.

Interpreting Data

The data collected from these measures need to be looked at qualitatively and within the cultural context of patients' belief systems. As discussed earlier, elevations of the L scale on the MMPI-2 are a typical finding among spiritual and religious individuals (Duris et al., 2007). In addition, individuals who have strong belief systems regarding the spiritual world (e.g., American Indians, devout Muslims, devout Christians, Buddhists) may elevate psychosis scales on the MMPI-2 and erroneously be given diagnoses that are consistent with psychotic disorders (e.g., Mahmood & Ahmed, 2012; Hill et al., 2010). Pathology on performance-based measures such as the Rorschach will be assessed based on a Western cultural perspective and, therefore, responses that are influenced by the patient's belief system may be misinterpreted and lead to misdiagnosis (e.g., Mahmood & Ahmed, 2012). Finally, any behavioral observations and accommodations made during the assessment session due to the patient's belief system should be accounted for when interpreting findings, writing reports, and formulating a diagnosis.

Report and Feedback

Patients' belief systems should be used as a framework within which the data and findings of the assessment are framed. When writing the report, clinicians should be sure to tailor recommendations to the religious context of the patient. For example, if recommendations of a personality assessment involve individual therapy, then the patient's preferences regarding the gender and belief system of the therapist should be directly addressed. In addition, within certain religious populations, using the family system (if it is a healthy one) as a source of support might be a preferred treatment method.

Beyond mere diagnostic assessments, if a patient is evaluated as part of an assessment to inform therapy or as a therapeutic intervention (e.g., Finn, Fischer, & Handler, 2012), the feedback session can be an invaluable opportunity to discuss the meaning of the assessment results. Both patients and their families can give active voice to the clinician's initial impressions, formulation, and viewpoint. By serving as a collaborator in the process, clients can ensure that their religious or spiritual worldview is at least seen and hopefully respected by the psychologist.

Finally, clients and their families can suggest ways in which their religious beliefs and/or communities could serve as healthy support and facilitators of change.

Summary Points

Religion and spirituality are identified as areas of diversity and meaning systems of clients that should be considered in the assessment process. The ways in which patients experience and express religiousness and spirituality may influence their psychological functioning and approach to the psychological assessment process, therefore making it crucial for them to be accounted for.

Both domestic and international research on assessment has primarily focused on ethnicity and race as aspects of cultural diversity, with little consideration of religion and spirituality as distinctive cultural variables. This is seen despite research demonstrating differences in assessment findings among individuals from diverse religious and spiritual backgrounds. This research gives us considerable pause in following assessment methods that do not take into account the various aspects of diversity of the populations we serve. We need to ensure the use of assessment methods that are sensitive to dimensions of culture including religious faith and spiritual beliefs that could impact the assessment process and results.

In this spirit, the authors of this chapter have outlined a few techniques and tips that would allow for a culturally inclusive and sensitive process. We suggest that assessors begin by examining their own culture and meaning systems while being open to learning and establishing some basic understanding of major religions represented in the communities in which they serve. In addition, prior to beginning a diagnostic assessment, assessors are encouraged to verify variables that would impact the interview process, assessment tools utilized, interpretations, and diagnostic hypotheses. Clinicians are also encouraged to consistently and sensitively ask about social identities, language, and religious beliefs in their very first interaction with patients. Religious beliefs, devoutness, expectations for assessment, and presenting problems should all be taken into account when putting together the diagnostic profile. Finally, religious and spiritual diversity should also be accounted for in the practical set up of testing environments, clinical history taking, assessment tool choices, interpretation of data, and the provision of applicable feedback and reports.

References

Al-Krenawi, A., & Graham, J. R. (2000). Culturally sensitive social work practice with Arab clients in mental health settings. *Health & Social Work, 25*, 9–22.

Allik, J., Massoudi, K., Realo, A., & Rossier, J. (2012). Personality and culture: Cross-cultural psychology at the next crossroads. *Swiss Journal of Psychology, 71*, 5–12. doi: 10.1024/1421-0185/a000069

American Psychological Association. (2002). *Ethical principles of psychologists and code of conduct. American Psychologist, 57*, 1060–1073. doi: 10.1037/0003-066X.57.12.1060

American Psychological Association. (2003). Guidelines on multicultural education, training, research, practice, and organizational change for psychologists. *American Psychologist, 58*, 377–402. doi: 10.1037/0003-066X.58.5.377

American Psychological Association Commission on Accreditation. (2013). *Guidelines and principles for accreditation of programs in professional psychology*. Washington, DC: Author.

Bier, W. C. (1971). A modified form of the Minnesota Multiphasic Personality Inventory for religious personnel. *Theological Education, 7*(2), 121–134.

Bridges, S. A., & Baum, L. J. (2013). An examination of MMPI-2-RF L-r scale in an outpatient Protestant sample. *Journal of Psychology and Christianity, 32*, 115–123. doi: 10.1037/t15121-000

Brown, J. S., & Van Orden, K. A. (2007). The assessment, diagnosis, and treatment of psychiatric disorders in religiously diverse clients. In J. D. Buckner, Y. Castro, J. M. Holm-Denoma, & T. R. Joiner (Eds.), *Mental health care for people of diverse backgrounds* (pp. 63–79). Milton Keynes, United Kingdom: Radcliffe Publishing.

Butcher, J. N. (2004). Personality assessment without borders: Adaptation of the MMPI-2 across cultures. *Journal of Personality Assessment, 83*, 90–104. doi: 10.1037/t15120-000

Butcher, J., Derksen, J., Sloore, H., & Sirigatti, S. (2003). Objective personality assessment of people in diverse cultures: European adaptations of the MMPI-2. *Behaviour Research and Therapy, 41*, 819–840. doi: 10.1037/t15120-000

Butcher, J. N., Mosch, S., Tsai, J., & Nezami, E. (2006). Cross-cultural applications of the MMPI-2. In J. N. Butcher (Ed.), *MMPI-2: A practitioner's guide* (pp. 505–537). Washington, DC: American Psychological Association.

Cinnirella, M., & Loewenthal, K. (1999). Religious and ethnic group influences on beliefs about mental illness: A qualitative interview study. *British Journal of Medical Psychology, 72*, 505–524. doi: 10.1348/000711299160202

Cohen, A. B. (2009). Many forms of culture. *American Psychologist, 64*, 194–204. doi: 10.1037/a0015308

Crookes, T. G., & Buckley, S. J. (1976). Lie score and insight. *The Irish Journal of Psychology, 3*, 134–136.

Dadlani, M., Overtree, C., & Perry-Jenkins, M. (2012). Culture at the center: A reformulation of diagnostic assessment. *Professional Psychology: Research and Practice, 43*, 175–182. doi: 10.1037/a0028152

Dahlstrom, W. G., & Welsh, G. S. (1960). *An MMPI handbook: A guide to use in clinical practice and research*. Minneapolis: University of Minnesota Press.

Dana, R. H. (2000). The cultural self as a locus for assessment and intervention with American Indians/Alaska Natives. *Journal of Multi-cultural Counseling and Assessment*, 28, 66–82. doi: 10.1002/j.2161-1912.2000.tb00608.x

Delay, J. J., Pichot, P. P., Sadoun, R. R., & Perse, J. J. (1955). Étude d'un groupe d'adeptes d'une secte religieuse. II. Étude psychométrique. (Study of a group of members of a religious sect. II. Psychometric study.) *Encephale, 44*, 254–265.

Duris, M., Bjorck, J. P., & Gorsuch, R. L. (2007). Christian subcultural differences in item perceptions of the MMPI-2 Lie Scale. *Journal of Psychology and Christianity, 26*, 356–366.

Dwairy, M. (2006). *Counseling and psychotherapy with Arabs and Muslims: A culturally sensitive approach*. New York: Teachers College Press.

Ellison, C. G., & McFarland, M. J. (2013). The social context of religion and spirituality in the United States. In K. Pargament (Ed.), *APA handbook of psychology, religion, and spirituality: Vol. 1. Context, theory, and research* (pp. 21–50). Washington, DC: American Psychological Association.

Eysenck, S. B., Nias, D. K., & Eysenck, H. J. (1971). The interpretation of children's Lie scale scores. *British Journal of Educational Psychology, 41*, 23–31. doi: 10.1111/j.2044-8279.1971.tb00654.x

Finlayson, D. S. (1972). Towards the interpretation of children's Lie Scale scores. *British Journal of Educational Psychology, 42*, 290–293. doi: 10.1111/j.2044-8279.1972.tb00721.x

Finn, S. E., Fischer, C. T., & Handler, L. (2012). *Collaborative/therapeutic assessment: A casebook and guide*. Hoboken, NJ: John Wiley & Sons Inc.

Francis, L. J., & Jackson, C. J. (2003). Eysenck's dimensional model of personality and religion: Are religious people more neurotic? *Mental Health, Religion & Culture, 6*, 87–100. doi: 10.1080/1367467031000086279

Francis, L. J., Jones, S. H., & Wilcox, C. (2000). Religiosity and happiness: During adolescence, young adulthood and later life. *Journal of Psychology and Christianity, 19*, 245–257.

Francis, L. J., Pearson, P. R., & Kay, W. K. (1983). Are religious children bigger liars? *Psychological Reports, 52*, 551–554. doi: 10.2466/pr0.1983.52.2.551

Francis, L. J., Pearson, P. R., & Stubbs, M. T. (1985). Personality and religion among low ability children in residential special schools. *British Journal of Mental Subnormality, 31*(60), 41–45.

Freud, S. (1950). *The future of an illusion*. New Haven, CT: Yale University Press.

Groesch, S. J., & Davis, W. E. (1977). Psychiatric patients' religion and MMPI responses. *Journal of Clinical Psychology, 33*, 168–171. doi: 10.1002/1097-4679(197701)33:1+<168::AID-JCLP2270330137>3.0.CO;2-9

Hill, J. S., Pace, T. M., & Robbins, R. R. (2010). Decolonizing personality assessment and honoring indigenous voices: A critical examination of the MMPI-2. *Cultural Diversity and Ethnic Minority Psychology, 16*, 16–25. doi: 10.1037/t15120-000

Hill, P. C., Pargament, K. I., Hood, R. W., McCullough, M. E., Swyers, J. P., Larson, D. B., & Zinnbauer, B. J. (2000). Conceptualizing religion and spirituality: Points of commonality, points of departure. *Journal for the Theory of Social Behaviour, 30*, 51–77. doi: 10.1111/1468-5914.00119

Hoffmann, T., Dana, R. H., & Bolton, B. (1985). Measured acculturation and MMPI-168 performance of Native American adults. *Journal of Cross-Cultural Psychology, 16*, 243–256. doi: 10.1177/0022002185016002007

Hood, R. W. (1975). The construction and preliminary validation of a measure of reported mystical experience. *Journal for the Scientific Study of Religion, 14*, 29–41. doi: 10.2307/1384454

Hood, R. W., Hill, P. C., & Williamson, W. P. (2005). *The psychology of religious fundamentalism*. New York: Guilford Press.

Jung, C. G. (1938). *Psychology and religion*. New Haven, CT: Yale University Press.

Kosmin, B. A., & Keysar, A. (2009, March). *American Religious Identification Survey [ARIS 2008]*. Retrieved from www.americanreligionsurvey-aris.org/reports/ARIS_Report_2008.pdf

Krishnamurthy, R., & Yalof, J. A. (2010). The assessment competency. In M. B. Kenkel & R. L. Peterson (Eds.), *Competency-based education for professional psychology* (pp. 87–104). Washington, DC: American Psychological Association.

Lin, K., & Cheung, F. (1999). Mental health issues for Asian Americans. *Psychiatric Services, 50*, 774–780.

Lindgren, K. N., & Coursey, R. D. (1995). Spirituality and serious mental illness: A two-part study. *Psychosocial Rehabilitation Journal, 18*, 93–111. doi: 10.1037/h0095498

López, S. R. (2002). Teaching culturally informed psychological assessment: Conceptual issues and demonstrations. *Journal of Personality Assessment, 79*, 226–234. doi: 10.1207/S15327752JPA7902_06

MacDonald, D. A., & Holland, D. (2003). Spirituality and the MMPI-2. *Journal of Clinical Psychology, 59*, 399–410. doi: 10.1002/jclp.10047

Mahmood, O. M., & Ahmed, S. R. (2012). Psychological testing and assessment. In S. Ahmed & M. M. Amer (Eds.), *Counseling Muslims: Handbook of mental health issues and interventions* (pp. 71–85). New York: Routledge/Taylor & Francis Group.

Marler, P. L., & Hadaway, C. K. (2002). "Being religious" or "being spiritual" in America: A zero-sum proposition? *Journal for the Scientific Study of Religion, 41*, 289–300. doi: 10.1111/1468-5906.00117

Massey, A. (1980). The Eysenck Personality Inventory Lie Scale: Lack of insight or . . .? *The Irish Journal of Psychology, 4*, 172–174.

McCrae, R. R., & Costa, P. T. (1985). Comparison of EPI and psychoticism scales with measures of the five-factor model of personality. *Personality and Individual Differences, 6*, 587–597. doi: 10.1016/0191-8869(85)90008-X

Mendez, D. M., & MacDonald, D. A. (2012). Spirituality and the MMPI-2 Restructured Clinical Scales. *International Journal of Transpersonal Studies, 31*, 1–10.

Miller, W. R., & Thoresen, C. E. (2003). Spirituality, religion, and health: An emerging research field. *American Psychologist, 58*(1), 24–35. doi: 10.1037/0003-066X.58.1.24

Montgomery, G. T., & Orozco, S. (1985). Mexican Americans' performance on the MMPI as a function of level of acculturation. *Journal of Clinical Psychology, 41*, 203–212. doi: 10.1002/1097-4679(198503)41:2<203::AID-JCLP2270410212>3.0.CO;2-7

Newport, F. (2012). *God is alive and well*. New York: Gallup Press.

O'Hagan, F. J., & Edmunds, G. (1982). Teachers' observations on pupils' untruthfulness in relation to the "Lie" scale. *Personality and Individual Differences, 3*, 335–338. doi: 10.1016/0191-8869(82)90057-5

Pace, T. M., Robbins, R. R., Choney, S. K., Hill, J. S., Lacey, K., & Blair, G. (2006). A cultural-contextual perspective on the validity of the MMPI-2 with American Indians. *Cultural Diversity and Ethnic Minority Psychology, 12*, 320–333. doi: 10.1037/1099-9809.12.2.320

Pargament, K. I. (1997). *The psychology of religion and coping*. New York: Guilford Press.

Pargament, K. I. (Ed.) (2013). *APA handbook of psychology, religion, and spirituality: Vol. 1. Context, theory, and research*. Washington, DC: American Psychological Association.

Power, R. P., & O'Donovan, D. D. (1969). Detection of simulation on the MPI by subjects given the rationale of the lie scale. *British Journal of Psychology, 60*, 535–541.

Pulchalski, C., & Rommer, A. L. (2001). Taking spiritual history allows clinicians to understand patients more fully. *Journal of Palliative Medicine, 3*, 129–137.

Reed, M. K., Walker, B., Williams, G., McLeod, S., & Jones, S. (1996). MMPI-2 patterns in African-American females. *Journal of Clinical Psychology, 52*, 437–441. doi: 10.1002/(SICI)1097-4679(199607)52:4<437::AID-JCLP8>3.0.CO;2-M

Richards, P. S., & Bergin, A. E. (1997). *A spiritual strategy for counseling and psychotherapy*. Washington, DC: American Psychological Association.

Richards, P. S., & Bergin, A. E. (2005). *A spiritual strategy for counseling and psychotherapy* (2nd ed.). Washington, DC: American Psychological Association. doi: 10.1037/11214-000

Rigby, K. K. (1987). "Faking good" with self-reported pro-authority attitudes and behaviours among schoolchildren. *Personality and Individual Differences, 8*, 445–447. doi: 10.1016/0191-8869(87)90049-3

Rump, E. E., & Court, J. (1971). The Eysenck Personality Inventory and social desirability response set with student and clinical groups. *British Journal of Social & Clinical Psychology, 10*, 42–54. doi: 10.1111/j.2044-8260.1971.tb00711.x

Saroglou, V. (2002). Religion and the five factors of personality: A meta-analytic review. *Personality and Individual Differences, 32*(1), 15–25. doi: 10.1016/S0191-8869(00)00233-6

Shafranske, E. P., & Cummings, J. P. (2013). Religious and spiritual beliefs, affiliations, and practices of psychologists. In K. Pargament (Ed.), *APA handbook of psychology, religion, and spirituality: Vol. 2. An applied psychology of religion and spirituality* (pp. 23–41). Washington, DC: American Psychological Association.

Shafranske, E. P., & Maloney, H. (1990). Clinical psychologists' religious and spiritual orientations and their practice of psychotherapy. *Psychotherapy, 27*, 72–78.

Smith, W. C. (1991). *The meaning and end of religion*. Minneapolis, MN: Fortress Press.

Streib, H., & Klein, C. (2013). Atheists, agnostics, and apostates. In K. Pargament (Ed.), *APA handbook of psychology, religion, and spirituality: Vol. 1. Context, theory, and research* (pp. 713–728). Washington, DC: American Psychological Association.

Sue, S., Keefe, K., Enomoto, K., Durvasula, R. S., & Chao, R. (1996). Asian American and White college students' performance on the MMPI-2. In J. B. Butcher (Ed.), *International adaptations of the MMPI-2* (pp. 206–218). Minneapolis: University of Minnesota Press.

Tarakeshwar, N. (2013). What does it mean to be a Hindu? A review of common Hindu beliefs and practices and their implications for health. In K. Pargament (Ed.), *APA handbook of psychology, religion, and spirituality: Vol. 1. Context, theory, and research* (pp. 653–664). Washington, DC: American Psychological Association.

Taylor, A., & MacDonald, D. A. (1999). Religion and the five-factor model of personality: An exploratory investigation using a Canadian university sample. *Personality and Individual Differences, 27*(6), 1243–1259. doi: 10.1016/S0191-8869(99)00068-9

Unterrainer, H. F., Lewis, A. J., & Fink, A. (2014). Religious/spiritual well-being, personality, and mental health: A review of results and conceptual issues. *Journal of Religion and Health, 53*(2), 382–392. doi: 10.1007/s10943-012-9642-5

Velasquez, R. J., Chavira, D. A., Karle, H. R., Callahan, W. J., Garcia, J. A., & Castellanos, J. (2000). Assessing bilingual and monolingual Latino students with translations of the MMPI-2: Initial data. *Cultural Diversity and Ethnic Minority Psychology, 6*, 65–72. doi: 10.1037/1099-9809.6.1.65

Whatley, P., Allen, J., & Dana, R. H. (2003). Racial identity and the MMPI in African American male college students. *Cultural Diversity and Ethnic Minority Psychology, 9*, 345–353. doi: 10.1037/1099-9809.6.1.65

Worthington, E. L. Jr., Sandage, S. J., Davis, D. E., Hook, J. N., Miller, A. J., Hall, M., & Hall, T. W. (2009). Training therapists to address spiritual concerns in clinical practice and research. In J. D. Aten & M. M. Leach (Eds.), *Spirituality and the therapeutic process: A comprehensive resource from intake to termination* (pp. 267–292). Washington, DC: American Psychological Association.

Zinnbauer, B. J., & Pargament, K. I. (2005). Religiousness and spirituality. In R. F. Paloutzian & C. L. Park (Eds.), *The handbook of the psychology of religion and spirituality* (pp. 21–42). New York: Guilford Press.

CHAPTER **8**

Cognitive or Physical Disabilities and Personality Assessment

Merith Cosden, Sarah Comunale, Lindsey Liles, and Steven R. Smith

We are aware that one single chapter that groups together both physical and cognitive impairments will likely be inadequate for all of these populations. However, we are also clear that the differently-abled are often neglected in discussions of diversity and marginalization. Therefore, the purpose of this chapter is to address some of the unique challenges of clients with disabilities and how these disabilities might impact the assessment process. For our purposes, we will address the unique challenges of those with cognitive disabilities, including attention-deficit/hyperactivity disorder (ADHD), specific learning disabilities (SLD), and traumatic brain injury (TBI), and those with physical disabilities, including visual and hearing impairments and mobility impairments.

Definition of Populations: Cognitive Disabilities

There are a number of conditions that can result in significant, but "invisible," cognitive impairments. Chief among those are ADHD, SLD, and TBI. Although these disorders can impact different facets of cognitive functioning, they also result in some shared concerns because they each create a risk for psychosocial problems and clinical disorders. Unless the personality assessor understands the nature of these disorders, there is a significant likelihood that he or she will misunderstand or misinterpret the client's needs during a personality assessment. Understanding the impact of these cognitive disorders on psychosocial functioning is critical in order to provide accurate test interpretations and useful recommendations.

Attention-Deficit/Hyperactivity Disorder (ADHD)

ADHD is a neurological disorder characterized by deficits in executive functioning associated with inattention, impulsivity, or hyperactivity. Cognitive processes affected in ADHD include self-regulation, behavioral inhibition, planning, working memory, and processing speed (Ramsay & Rostain, 2007, 2008). ADHD is one of the most frequently diagnosed disorders of childhood. Although it is most often identified during the elementary school years, it often persists into adulthood. People with ADHD also have an increased risk of psychosocial problems, such as difficulties with social skills and poor peer relationships. They also have an increased risk for psychological problems, such as depression, anxiety, and substance abuse (Cosden, 2001; Morrison & Cosden, 1997; Nigg et al., 2002; Sharps, Price-Sharps, Day, Villegas, & Nunes, 2005).

Assessment of ADHD focuses on the presence of symptoms delineated in the Diagnostic and Statistical Manual, 5th Edition (DSM-5; American Psychiatric Association, 2013), while also taking into account the severity of the symptoms with regard to functional impairment (Sowerby & Tripp, 2009). Background information is used to help rule out other explanations for symptoms associated with ADHD. The assessment process commonly involves interviews from multiple informants and use of rating scales, questionnaires, and behavioral observations of symptoms. Intelligence tests and other cognitive measures may also be administered when there are questions related to cognitive ability or academic difficulties. Neuropsychological tests are typically not included in routine assessment of ADHD but might be helpful when needed for measuring aspects of executive functioning, attention, and impulsivity.

Specific Learning Disabilities (SLD)

SLD is a group of neurologically based disorders that can affect cognitive processes differently across individuals, resulting in varied cognitive strengths and weaknesses. All SLDs are defined by a significant deficit in performance in one or more key academic areas (e.g., reading, mathematics, or written expression) relative to others, resulting in an uneven pattern of academic strengths as a function of these cognitive problems. There are many types of SLD, including what is commonly known as "dyslexia." As with ADHD, these disorders typically emerge in childhood but continue into adulthood. In children, these difficulties significantly impact academic performance, and in adults the academic skill difficulties may impact occupational performance or daily activities, as noted by the DSM-5 (American Psychiatric Association, 2013). Further, SLD can occur in individuals with a range of intellectual abilities including individuals that are intellectually gifted (National Joint Committee on Learning Disabilities, 2011). People with SLD also have an increased risk of psychosocial problems, such as difficulty interpreting social cues. They often also experience difficulties in their relationships with others, including a greater dependence on family into adulthood. People with SLD also have an increased risk of psychological problems, including depression and anxiety (Acklin, 1990; Cosden, 2001; Morrison & Cosden, 1997; Sharps, Price-Sharps, Day, Villegas, & Nunes, 2005).

Assessment and diagnosis of SLD has traditionally been based on the discrepancy model, with a significant difference between higher cognitive scores and lower achievement scores required, although alternative methods of identification have also been considered. Assessment of SLD commonly involves a clinical interview that addresses symptoms, a review of academic records and teacher reports, use of rating scales, and cognitive and achievement testing. Other explanations for academic failure, such as inadequate educational instruction, testing anxiety, or hearing or vision impairments, need to be ruled out.

Traumatic Brain Injury

TBI is an acquired brain injury[1] that persists after sudden trauma to the brain that has caused a disruption in brain functioning. The trauma could be as minor as a blow or jolt of the head during a fall, or as severe as a penetrating injury such as a gunshot wound. TBIs are classified as mild, moderate, or severe. A wide array of symptoms can follow TBIs. As described by Nolin, Villemure, and Heroux (2006), the lasting symptoms of mild TBI generally fall within three categories: (1) affective, including irritability, anger, depression, anxiety, and altered social functioning; (2) cognitive, including concentration, attention, and memory problems, slower processing speed, and altered problem-solving skills; and (3) physical, which often include headaches, sleep problems, fatigue, dizziness, nausea, blurred vision, and sensitivity to light and noise. Symptoms of moderate to severe TBI can include all of the above symptoms and might also include personality changes, convulsions or seizures, difficulty awakening from sleep, disruptions in speech, and loss of coordination. People with TBIs also frequently experience changes in psychosocial functioning, such as loss of relationships and social isolation and mood issues. All of these changes can have significant impacts on functioning that is secondary to the original injury.

Diagnosis of TBI generally entails an assessment of the initial brain injury, including assessment of the loss of consciousness, memory loss, and a Glasgow Coma Scale (GCS) score. The GCS assesses cognitive and motor functioning, such as the ability to follow directions, speak, and move eyes and limbs. Imaging tests, such as a computerized tomography scan are also commonly used to show brain bleeding, bruises, or other damage. Neuropsychological assessments can also help evaluate the impact of the brain injury on the individual's sensorimotor, cognitive, emotional, and general adaptive functioning (Vanderploeg, 2013).

Accommodations

The Individuals with Disabilities Education Improvement Act of 2004 (IDEA, 2004) includes SLD and TBI as disability categories and allows students with these disabilities to qualify for special services. The Americans with Disabilities Act (ADA) of 1990 also protects individuals with SLD, as the disability affects activities of daily living (National Joint Committee on Learning Disabilities, 2011), and individuals with TBI who have substantial limitations in a major life activity, as TBI is a physiological condition affecting neurologic function. Students with ADHD may qualify for school accommodations under Section 504 of the Rehabilitation Act of 1973 if the disorder substantially limits a life activity, such as learning or behavior in school.

Summary

Despite the diversity of cognitive skills and deficits within these populations, people with ADHD, SLD, and TBI share common concerns related to the impact of their disabilities on psychosocial functioning and, in some instances, clinical problems. It must be noted, too, that although each disorder can independently affect cognitive functioning, these disabilities can co-occur. TBI can co-occur with either or both of the other disorders, although the prevalence of this is not known. ADHD and SLD commonly co-occur. In a review of studies on populations affected by one or both disorders, Jakobson and Kikas (2007) reported that the prevalence of this comorbidity ranged from 10–80% across published studies. As might be expected, individuals with comorbid ADHD and SLD have more problems processing social information and with other aspects of psychosocial functioning than do individuals with either disorder alone (e.g., Crawford, Kaplan, & Dewey, 2006; McNamara, Willoughby, & Chalmers, 2005). Understanding "normative" characteristics of these populations can provide assessors with the context needed to accurately understand and interpret their personality assessments.

Interpersonal Presentation

All three cognitive disorders, ADHD, SLD, and TBI, can have an impact on social interactions in ways that create interpersonal problems. These interpersonal problems have been associated, in large part, with deficits in processing social information, although other factors, such as the stigma of being identified with special needs, may also contribute to problems in social relationships.

For people with ADHD and SLD, problems in psychosocial functioning often begin in childhood. Relative to youth without these disorders, youth with ADHD or SLD have a harder time making friends, eliciting positive responses from others, and relating positively to adults; they also demonstrate social skill deficits and are often socially isolated (Bryan, Burstein, & Ergul, 2004). The specific nature of the processing problems varies. For example, youth with SLD have problems encoding information in social situations, interpreting social cues, and generating interpretations of social scenarios. In general, those with social problems are less sensitive to social cues and less accurate than peers in interpreting social intentions (Bauminger & Kimhi-Kind, 2008; Bryan et al., 2004). Children with ADHD also display poor peer relationships and social isolation. Symptoms associated with ADHD such as poor impulse control, difficulties sustaining interest and attention, and emotional instability have been associated with these interpersonal difficulties (Barkley, Murphy, & Fischer, 2008; Brown, 2005; Weiss, Murray, & Weiss, 2002). Clearly, these cognitive problems can impair social relationships, resulting in inappropriate social interactions and limiting successful social relationships, and continue to do so into adulthood.

Psychosocial problems for this population can also result from other factors. After in-depth interviews with adults with these disorders, McNulty (2003) reported that psychosocial problems can also be associated with the stigma associated with being diagnosed, academic failures, and social misunderstandings. A wide range of responses were obtained, however, with some adults functioning well socially and others reporting ongoing concerns related to these disorders.

Finally, there are differences in the developmental needs of adolescents with and without ADHD and SLD for social support. Successful young adults with SLD are more likely to rely on family for support than are their same-age peers without these disabilities; young adults with ADHD or SLD tend to rely on social support more than do their non-disabled peers; successful adults with SLD report family, friends, teachers, and co-workers who served as mentors to help with ongoing challenges, and provide feedback and support across their lifespan (Goldberg, Higgins, Raskind, & Herman, 2003). It is important for assessors to conceptualize this longer period of dependence as normative for these populations, and not misinterpret it as being overly dependent.

TBI can also impact psychosocial functioning. Unlike ADHD and SLD, TBI can occur at any point in one's life; thus, rather than a life-long pattern of psychosocial problems, adults with TBI are more likely to demonstrate changes in psychosocial functioning before and after their injury. These differences may be difficult for friends and family to accept. Kersel, Marsh, Havill, and Sleigh (2001) found that one year after their injury 70% of adults with severe TBI reported job loss and over 30% relationship break-ups. While there are differences in recovery of function and subsequent behavioral problems, TBI has a long-term impact on social functioning for many individuals. In particular, high levels of loneliness, social withdrawal, and added family burden have been noted; for example, in a study following patients over a 10–20-year period after their TBI, 31% reported no friends at all while 8% stated experiencing complete social isolation (Hoofien, Gilboa, Vakil, & Donovick, 2001). Further, TBI is associated with certain types of psychopathology, including post-traumatic stress disorder (PTSD), with psychosocial problems related to this psychopathology in addition to the TBI itself (Bryant, Marosszeky, Crooks, Baguley, & Gurka, 2001; Pietrzak, Johnson, Goldstein, Malley, & Southwick, 2009).

Clinical Presentation

A majority of adults with ADHD, SLD, or TBI, like a majority of adults without those disabilities, do not have other clinical disorders. However, the presence of SLD, ADHD, or TBI can be considered risk factors for psychological problems including depression, serious anxiety, and substance abuse (Cosden, 2001; Morrison & Cosden, 1997; Sharps, Price-Sharps, Day, Villegas, & Nunes, 2005). Individuals with ADHD and SLD are overrepresented among those with depression and anxiety both as children (Nelson & Harwood, 2011) and as adults (Klassan, Tze, & Hannok, 2013), while adults with TBI are also overrepresented among those with clinical disorders even 10 years or more after the injury has occurred (Draper, Ponsford, & Schönberger, 2007; Hoofien et al., 2001), particularly for those who are not able to return to their pre-injury functioning (Ownsworth et al., 2011).

The disproportionate number of youth with ADHD or LD with internalizing problems has been attributed, in large part, to the high level of failure these students experience in the schools. Before students are identified as having a disorder it is not uncommon for them to spend several years in academic environments in which they experience frequent failure; in fact, it is a function of these failures that students are often referred for assessment to determine whether or not they qualify for special services. Even after students have had a disorder identified, schools often remain a challenging environment, as placements that are fully accommodating are rare (McNulty, 2003). When accompanied by social problems, failures across academic and social domains can impair self-esteem, resulting in higher levels of anxiety and depression.

Although ADHD and SLD are typically identified on the basis of school performance, problems with depression and anxiety often continue after youth leave school and into adulthood. Continued depression and anxiety in adults with ADHD and SLD reflect the impact of these disorders as life-long problems. Whether adult experiences of anxiety and depression are lower, the same, or higher than that of youth with ADHD or SLD depends on their ongoing environmental demands, supports, and stressors. Transition planning is particularly important for this population, as once school supports end, other supports to help compensate for their disorders might not be forthcoming without personal initiative and effort (Klassen et al., 2013).

Further, while anxiety and depression may develop as a function of social and academic failures, the presence of anxiety and depression might further debilitate the individual, causing them to avoid activities that would not have been directly affected by their disability. For example, persons with SLD that affects their ability to read might avoid collaborative work tasks that involve oral interactions even though these would not be affected by their disability. Relative to students without SLD, those with SLD have lower self-efficacy and report more negative mood and less hope even when controlling for academic achievement (Lackaye, Margalit, Ziv, & Ziman, 2006). Thus, in assessing individuals with ADHD or SLD, it is important to understand how their disabilities have contributed to their anxiety or depression, but it is also important to identify those aspects of behavior that are affected by depression and anxiety but which are not directly affected by these disabilities. Effective methods of intervention for problems that fall into either category would be expected to vary.

TBI has also been associated with psychiatric problems, particularly depression (Bryant et al., 2001; Hoofien et al., 2001; Kersel et al., 2001; Sigurdardottir, Andelic, Roe, & Schanke, 2013), anxiety (Hoofien et al., 2001), and PTSD (Bryant et al., 2001; Hoofien et al., 2001; Pietrzak et al., 2009). The presence of this psychopathology increases the likelihood of psychosocial problems among this population (Bryant et al., 2001; Hoofian et al., 2001; Pietrzak et al., 2009). In part, psychosocial problems associated with TBI may increase the likelihood of psychopathology. For example, the burden created by TBI on family and changes in one's temperament and behavior caused by TBI may increase social isolation and result in depression. In other instances, the traumatic event that caused the TBI might have independently resulted in other pathology. The most common instances of this would be military-related trauma, which can cause TBI as well as PTSD.

Finally, it is important to note that youth and adults with ADHD, SLD, and TBI may experience serious anxiety or depression for the same reasons as do other youth and adults. That is, they might have clinical disorders that are unrelated to having ADHD, SLD, or TBI. It is important to determine the manner and extent to which these disabilities affect other clinical problems in order to understand the clients' needs and make appropriate recommendations.

Definition of Populations: Physical Disabilities

There are many varieties of physical disability, ranging from quadriplegia to color blindness. We cannot cover all of these with adequate detail, but offer a few general points and highlights for the reader to keep in mind. For the purpose of this section, we define physical disabilities as sensory or movement impairments that substantially limit individuals in one or more major life activity.

Sensory Impairments: Visual and Hearing

There are many conditions that can result in enduring sensory impairments. These range from color blindness to congenital impairments that fully limit sensation. As is true for cognitive impairments, these can be either developmental (i.e., present from birth) or acquired (i.e., the result of disease or injury) and range from minor loss of acuity and/or range to complete impairment. Sensory impairments are more common in older adults and often co-occur with other medical complications or secondary to injury. Both the severity and origin of a client's impairment will have substantial impact on the assessment process.

Visual Impairments

The World Health Organization (2014) organizes visual impairments by severity in categories zero to five based on visual acuity (sharpness of vision) or visual field, or as a category nine for unqualified visual impairment. In 2010, the estimated number of individuals in the world with visual impairment was 285 million, 39 million blind and 246 million with low vision. The vast majority of visually impaired (65%) and blind (82%) individuals are over 50 years of age (Pascolini & Mariotti, 2010). Childhood blindness is an issue, however most blindness and visual impairment is related to ageing (Resnikoff et al., 2004). In the United States, approximately 22% of individuals over the age of 65 are visually impaired (Hung, Ross, Boockvar, & Siu, 2011). The primary causes of visual impairment are refractive errors (43%) and cataracts (33%). For blindness, cataracts are the cause nearly half the time (51%). The cause of blindness is undetermined approximately 20% of the time (Pascolini & Mariotti, 2010). With the increase in life expectancy over time, age-related macular degeneration is becoming a more significant cause of blindness, particularly in developed countries (Resnikoff et al., 2004).

Auditory Impairments

Auditory impairments range in severity from mild to profound as a result of genetic or environmental causes (Nance, 2003). Hearing impairments can be classified as conductive or perceptive based on the defective anatomical structures involved. Conductive hearing loss results from abnormalities in the middle or external ear and is typically mild to moderate in severity (Petit, 2006). Perceptive deafness is caused by a problem with the auditory pathway and ranges from mild to profound in severity. Profound hearing loss is characterized by an auditory deficit of >90#dB and an inability to detect sounds, even at volumes that would become painful for an individual with unimpaired hearing (Petit, 2006).

Hearing loss can occur pre- or post-lingually, meaning before or after the acquisition of speech (Fellinger et al., 2005). Approximately one in 2,700 children is born profoundly deaf. That ratio increases to one in 1,000 for deafness occurring for children within the first year of life (Hindley, 2005b). Prelingual deafness is associated with delays in language development for the 90% of deaf children born to hearing families (Du Feu & Fergusson, 2003). Mild, progressive hearing loss is common with ageing (Du Feu & Fergusson, 2003). Of adults 65 years and older, nearly 25% experience hearing loss. That percentage increases to 33% for adults 70 years and older (Campbell, Crews, Moriarty, Zack, & Blackman, 1999; Hung et al., 2011). Sudden and profound post-lingual deafness is not as common, but can occur due to an accident, injury, or illness.

Summary

The impact of auditory and visual impairments on development is determined by the interaction of four major factors: response of the developmental environment (parents, family, and teachers), age of onset, severity of the impairment, and the presence of associated impairments (e.g., CNS abnormalities; Hindley, 2005a). Independently, auditory and visual sensory impairments can significantly impact development and psychosocial functioning. Dual sensory impairment (DSI) has a cumulative effect. Approximately one in 100,000 children experiences both hearing and auditory impairments (Hindley, 2005a). Individuals who experience either auditory or visual impairments rely on their other senses to gather information about their environment. Research findings indicate that a large percentage of individuals with sensory impairments have co-occurring disabilities, health issues, or mental health problems (Flanagan, Jackson, & Hill, 2003; Hindley, 2000; Knoors & Vervloed, 2003).

Interpersonal Presentation

Both auditory and visual impairments impact an individual's interpersonal presentation. The acquisition of social skills and recognition of social cues play a large role in interpersonal development. Sensory impairments influence the way individuals collect information about the environment and interact with others. Hearing and vision loss are both associated with social isolation, anxiety, paranoia, and decreased self-esteem (Wallhagen, Strawbridge, Shema, Kurata, & Kaplan, 2001). The degree of the impact depends on the type and severity of the impairment, age of onset, presence of comorbid impairments, and the response of the individual's environment (Wright, 2008).

Interpersonally, blind children differ significantly depending on the presence or absence of comorbid impairments. About 50% of the children who are born blind have other disabilities that can limit their potential (Du Feu & Fergusson, 2003). Developmental delays in visually impaired children are sometimes related to experiential deprivation, but are more often related to co-occurring conditions and their associated brain abnormalities (Hindley, 2005a). Pinquart and Pfeiffer (2014) found that adolescents with visual impairment report higher levels of emotional problems, conduct problems, and difficulties with peers than do sighted adolescents.

Regarding the development of self-esteem and self-concept in children and adolescents, research provides conflicting findings. Some studies link the presence of visual impairment to negative impacts on self-concept in adolescents (Lifshitz, Hen, & Weisse, 2007). Other studies suggest the opposite, that there are no differences between the self-concepts or self-esteem of sighted and visually impaired adolescents (Garaigordobil & Bernarás, 2009; Griffin-Shirley & Nes, 2005). The discrepancies in the research findings could be due to other factors, such as severity of the impairment, age of onset, availability of social support, and presence of comorbid impairments. The assessor should keep in mind that a number of factors will play in to each individual's interpersonal presentation.

Sighted adults typically report higher self-esteem than those with blindness or low vision (Papadopoulos, Montgomery, & Chronopoulou, 2013). Additionally, the age at onset of visual impairment has been identified as a negative predictor of self-esteem, meaning that individuals who acquire visual impairments later in life have lower self-esteem than individuals born with visual impairments (Papadopoulos et al., 2013). It is likely easier to adjust to visual impairments from birth or in early childhood than in adolescence or adulthood. Acquired visual impairment can result in a bereavement response as well as an internal conflict between the need for assistance and the desire to maintain independence (Du Feu & Fergusson, 2003). In elderly populations, acquired visual impairment has been linked to loneliness, social isolation, lower morale, and diminished emotional security (Verstraten, Brinkmann, Stevens, & Schouten, 2005; Branch, Horowitz, & Carr, 1989).

Early communication skills are important to a child's social and emotional development. For this reason, a deaf child born to deaf parents will have a different interpersonal presentation than a deaf child born to hearing parents. Approximately 90% of deaf children are born into hearing families (Du Feu & Fergusson, 2003; Wright, 2008). These children typically experience delays in the development of their metacognitive skills, or ability to understand that others think and feel differently than they do. On average, hearing children develop this skill, or Theory of Mind, by age 4 or 5. Deaf children of hearing parents are typically three years behind, developing it around 7 or 8 years of age. Interestingly, deaf children born to deaf parents do not experience a delay (Lundy, 2002). The discrepancies in development are likely related to the communication difficulties faced in early years between parent and child. Because of this, the majority of deaf children have a more difficult time understanding the motivations and intentions of others.

Deaf children are more likely to exhibit decreased ability to understand, recognize, and regulate emotions than hearing children (Gray, Hosie, Russell, & Ormel, 2001). This can lead to interpersonal difficulties in later childhood, adolescence, and adulthood. Fellinger et al. (2005) found no differences in interpersonal relationships between deaf and hearing adult populations, indicating that the Deaf community is able to create satisfying relationships based on a common communication system. There is a cultural distinction between members of the Deaf community (who prefer American Sign Language, are typically prelingually deaf, and have a stronger deaf identity), and the hearing impaired (who typically prefer oral methods of communication) (Turner, Windfuhr, & Kapur, 2007). Although deaf children and adolescents can be as socially skilled as their hearing counterparts, they may experience anxiety if they suffer high levels of communication failure in settings with hearing peers. Deaf children in deaf education settings do not typically experience these difficulties but might have anxiety later in life when they transition into adulthood and increase their interactions with the hearing world (Hindley, 2000). Partially deaf children are typically placed in mainstream education settings and can experience bullying and feelings of isolation. Fellinger et al. (2005) found that deaf individuals possessed high interpersonal sensitivity, which was related to feelings of insecurity and inferiority.

Individuals born with dual sensory impairments (DSI) experience significant interpersonal difficulties due to limited opportunities to gather information from their environments. Development of DSI with old age is much more common than prelingual DSI. For elderly populations, DSI is more difficult to cope with than single sensory impairment because as both senses deteriorate the individual is robbed of compensatory strategies (Saunders & Echt, 2007). These individuals show decreased participation in social activities and an increase in cognitive and functional decline compared to those without sensory impairment (Congdon, Friedman, & Lietman, 2003).

Clinical Presentation

The presence of a visual or auditory impairment increases an individual's likelihood of experiencing psychological distress or maladjustment. Pinquart and Pfeiffer (2011) found in their meta-analysis that visually impaired individuals, especially older samples, have elevated levels of psychological distress compared to sighted individuals. The most common psychological symptom associated with significant vision loss is depression (Evans, Fletcher, & Wormald 2007; Hayman et al., 2007; Horowitz, Reinhardt, Boerner, & Travis, 2003). The prevalence of depression in visually impaired elderly individuals is 25–45% compared to less than 20% for sighted individuals (Evans et al., 2007). When the visual impairment is moderate or greater, adults are nearly 2 and 2.5 times more likely than non-impaired individuals to feel depressed and report fair or poor mental health (Wallhagen et al., 2001). Additionally, for older visually impaired individuals, lower levels of social support are related to higher levels of depression (Guerette & Smedema, 2011)

Although symptoms of depression are common in older individuals with vision loss, children and adolescents may respond differently. Garaigordobil and Bernarás (2009) found that visually impaired adolescents scored higher on symptoms of obsession-compulsion, hostility, paranoid ideation, and depression than their sighted peers. When paired with low self-esteem and low self-concept, these adolescents were more likely to have multiple psychopathological symptoms, a tendency toward neuroticism, and low extraversion compared to unimpaired individuals. The high level of symptomatology for adolescents may be partially explained by a compound effect of the stressors of this developmental stage (physical and social changes) paired with the stressors of being visually impaired (difficulty participating in activities, family control, and more dependence on others; Garaigordobil & Bernarás, 2009). Children who are born blind have a 50% chance of having an additional disability. In some cases, the condition that led to their blindness may also be associated with mental health problems. These cases account for a small percentage of the blind population, but an assessor should be aware of the possibility of co-occurring conditions.

Much like those who are blind and visually impaired, deaf and hearing-impaired individuals experience higher levels of psychological distress and are at greater risk for psychological disorder than unimpaired individuals (Fellinger et al., 2005). Deaf adults are more likely to experience depression than hearing adults (Lewis, Stephens, & McKenna, 1994). Deaf children are 1.5 to 2 times more likely to experience mental health problems related to organic issues, emotional, behavioral, psychological disorders, and delays in access to services (Hindley, 2000). When deafness is caused by a condition that also causes pervasive brain damage, a child is more vulnerable to mental health disorders such as Autism Spectrum Disorder and ADHD (Hindley, 2005b). During adolescence, deaf children are likely to be exposed to more risk factors for adjustment disorders (academic difficulties, low self-esteem, rejecting relationships, failure of age-appropriate development, and abuse) than hearing children (Du Feu & Fergusson, 2003). Deaf children raised within the Deaf community may experience fewer of these risk factors for adjustment disorders than hearing-impaired or deaf children in placed mainstream education settings.

Movement Impairments

Movement impairments are indicated by deficits in voluntary motor control, including difficulties with mobility, posture, reflexes, and the general functioning of body parts or limbs. A wide range of conditions, from illness to injury, can result in movement impairments. Although there are numerous ways to classify movement impairments, division into neuromotor and musculoskeletal conditions is common. Neuromotor impairments result from damage to the brain or spinal cord, limit muscle control or movement, and can be caused by cerebral palsy (CP), muscular dystrophy (MD), Parkinson's Disease, multiple sclerosis (MS), stroke, spinal cord injury, and other illnesses. Musculoskeletal conditions resulting in movement impairment include arthritis, limb deficiencies, and skeletal disorders (Smith, 2005). According to data from the National Health Interview Survey, nearly one-fifth of the adult population in the United States reports some type of movement difficulty (Altman & Bernstein, 2008).

Neuromotor Impairments

Neuromotor impairments result from damage to the brain or spinal cord. These conditions can be diagnosed at birth or during early childhood (e.g., spina bifida and CP), develop between adolescence and adulthood (e.g., MD, MS, and dystonia), onset later in life (e.g., tremor and Parkinson's Disease), or be acquired at some point due to illness or injury (e.g., Guillain-Barré, lupus, stroke, and spinal cord injury).

Neural tube defects (NTD) are the second most common birth defect among European American infants at approximately one in 1,000 births. The most common form of NTD, spina bifida (myelomeningocele), is characterized by an incomplete closure of the neural tube within the spinal column (Detrait et al., 2005). Cerebral palsy (CP) is another neurologic condition that might be present at birth. Less often, it can result from a brain injury within the first two years of life (Krigger, 2006). CP is defined as a group of permanent disorders that impact development of movement and posture, causing activity limitations (Rosembaun, Paneth, Levinton, Goldstein, & Max, 2007). It occurs in approximately two to three children per 1,000, and can result in spasticity, contractures, feeding difficulties, communication difficulties, decreased bone density, chronic pain, and gastrointestinal problems (Castle, Imms, & Howie, 2007; Krigger, 2006; Liptak, 2008). Nearly two-thirds of individuals with CP experience comorbid intellectual impairment (Krigger, 2006). Although it is not a progressive condition, individuals with CP often require intensive, life-long support from caregivers or a treatment team.

Multiple sclerosis (MS) is a disabling disease of the central nervous system that affects approximately 1 in 1,000 people (Mitchell, Benito-León, González, & Rivera-Navarro, 2005). It is typically diagnosed between 20 and 40 years of age and occurs about twice as often in women compared to men (Mohr & Cox, 2001). Symptoms of MS include sensory disturbances, visual difficulties, limb weakness, loss of coordination, loss of bladder and/or bowel control, fatigue, pain, emotional changes (including depression), and cognitive dysfunction (Mitchell et al., 2005; Mohr & Dick, 1998). The course of the disease can be benign, relapsing, progressive, or malignant, and symptom severity and outcome vary accordingly (Mohr & Cox, 2001).

Dystonia is a movement disorder associated with an excess of muscle activation that causes sustained or sporadic muscle spasms that lead to abnormal, and often repetitive, postures or movements. Dystonia can be classified according to clinical factors (age of onset, bodily distribution, temporal pattern, coexistence of other movement disorders, and other neurological manifestations) and etiology.

Parkinson's Disease (PD) is a degenerative neurological disorder caused by the progressive loss of specific neurons in the brain which leads to tremor, rigidity, bradykinesia (slowed movement), and motor dysfunction (Reichmann, Schneider, & Löhle, 2009; Tolosa, Wenning, & Poewe, 2006). PD increases in prevalence with age and is estimated to affect 1–2% of adults over 65 (Alves, Forsaa, Pedersen, Gjerstad, & Larsen, 2008). Nearly 90% of individuals with PD also experience non-motor problems including depression, psychotic symptoms, dementia, cognitive impairments, sleep disorders, and olfactory dysfunction (Alves et al., 2008; Reichmann et al., 2009).

The last group of conditions we will cover cause neuromotor impairments due to illness or injury. Systemic lupus erythematosus (SLE or lupus) is a severe rheumatic disease. Although the exact cause of SLE is unknown, it has been linked to certain infections and other environmental factors. SLE is most common in women, but tends to be more severe in men, pediatric, and late-onset cases (Pons-Estel, Alarcón, Scofield, Reinlib, & Cooper, 2010). Physical symptoms of SLE include fatigue, weakness, arthralgia, arthritis, and rash (Kone-Paut, Piram, Guillaume, & Tran, 2007). There is currently no cure for SLE, however with improvements to medical care and treatment, nearly 80% of individuals are expected to live at least 15 to 20 years after diagnosis (Pons-Estel et al., 2010). Guillain-Barré Syndrome (GBS) is an autoimmune disease that is typically preceded by a bacterial or viral illness. It affects males and females of all ages and causes rapidly progressing limb weakness over the course of a few days, up to four weeks. The muscle paralysis typically plateaus briefly and then gradually diminishes over a period of weeks to months. The muscle weakness associated with GBS leads to total paralysis and a 10% mortality rate due to respiratory failure. Most patients eventually recover, however 20% are left with lasting impairments (Kuwabara, 2004).

Musculoskeletal Conditions

Musculoskeletal conditions are associated with symptoms of pain and impaired functioning. Three common musculoskeletal conditions are osteoarthritis, rheumatoid arthritis, and osteoporosis. These conditions range in severity and duration, but typically become more prevalent with age (Woolf & Pfleger, 2003).

Accommodations

The biopsychosocial model of disability describes level of functioning as the result of the interaction between health conditions and contextual factors (World Health Organization, 2010). For many individuals with movement impairments, their surroundings can become a major barrier to engagement in daily activities. Accommodations to an individual's environment can significantly improve functioning and decrease the impact of their impairment. To accommodate students and adults with movement impairments, it is important that physical and learning environments be accessible and that individuals have access to specialized teaching, therapies, equipment, and technology (Smith, 2005). The IDEA ensures inclusive education for students with physical disabilities. Children with movement impairments are IDEA eligible if their impairment negatively impacts their performance in educational settings (IDEA, 2004). Section 504 of the Rehabilitation Act and the ADA apply within and outside of school settings. In 2008 the ADA was amended, broadening the interpretation of the definition of disability to apply to more individuals (ADA Amendments Act, 2008). After these amendments, some students not eligible for IDEA became eligible for Section 504 protections (Zirkel, 2009). Section 504 requires schools to eliminate barriers that prevent full participation in programs outside of school settings. The ADA prohibits discrimination on the basis of disability in employment, government, public accommodations, commercial facilities, transportation, and telecommunications. These laws protect individuals with movement impairments and ensure they are provided with appropriate accommodations.

Summary

There are many conditions that can lead to movement impairments. We have addressed a few of those above. Movement impairments vary in impact based on age of onset, severity, progression, duration, and presence of co-occurring conditions. In general, the prevalence of movement disorders increases with age, from approximately one in five individuals 50–59 years old to nearly half of 80–89-year-olds (Wenning et al., 2005). For nearly all of the conditions addressed, pain and decreased mobility are common symptoms. Independently, neuromotor impairments and musculoskeletal conditions can have an adverse impact on an individual's activities of daily living and overall quality of life. It is important to note that many of these conditions often co-occur with cognitive impairments and/or other medical problems. Chronic pain, illness, and loss of physical functioning can have a significant impact on an individual's psychosocial functioning and mental health. Certain behavioral and emotional responses are common in individuals with movement impairments. As clinicians, we should be aware of the ways in which this population differs from, and is similar to, the non-impaired population.

Interpersonal Presentation

Movement impairments can interfere with an individual's psychosocial functioning in a variety of ways. Individuals who are severely impaired from birth or early childhood might have limited interactions with similarly aged peers. Those coping with a sudden injury or illness can become socially withdrawn during an adjustment period. In large part, age of onset, severity, and disease progression will determine the impact a movement impairment has on an individual's psychosocial functioning.

The musculoskeletal conditions that lead to movement impairments generally have a less severe impact on interpersonal presentation than the neuromotor impairments. In older individuals, musculoskeletal conditions can negatively impact social function and decrease health-related quality of life. Pain plays a large role in how movement impairments impact psychosocial functioning. Individuals with osteoporosis, back pain, rheumatoid arthritis, or osteoarthritis might avoid leisure pursuits or withdraw from the workforce due to fragility and fear of injury or difficulty coping with painful symptoms. Without work or leisure pursuits, older individuals might have fewer opportunities to engage socially and they, therefore, become more withdrawn interpersonally (Woolfe & Pfleger, 2003).

Neuromotor impairments can have significant impacts on relationships and social functioning. Social isolation is a common occurrence for individuals with many of the neuromotor impairments we have discussed. Decreased social functioning or increased social withdrawal can occur in individuals with spina bifida, CP, MD, MS, dystonia, tremor, and PD (Boström & Ahlström, 2004; Grootenhuis, De Boone, & Van der Kooi, 2007; Hakim et al., 2000; Holmbeck, & Devine, 2010; Liptak, 2008; Lorenz, Schwieger, Moises, & Deuschl, 2006; Spliethoff-Kamminga, Zwinderman, Springer, & Roos, 2003; Zurowski, McDonald, Fox, & Marsh, 2013). For many of these individuals, the decrease in social function is related to low self-esteem, fear of social comparison, and prevalence of pain and difficulties related to mobility. Movement disorders in children have been linked to difficulties with attention, concentration, learning, and psychosocial adjustment (Boström & Ahlström, 2004; Dewey, Kaplan, Crawford, & Wilson, 2002; Holmbeck, & Devine, 2010; Mohr & Cox, 2001).

The presence or availability of social support is linked to improved outcomes and quality of life for many individuals with movement impairments. For spina bifida, MS, spinal cord injury, lupus, and GBS, social support is described as desired or helpful (Bénony et al., 2002; Hakim et al., 2000; Holmbeck & Devine, 2010; Manns & Chad, 2001; Seawell & Danoff-Burg, 2004; Weiss, Rastan, Müllges, Wagner, & Toyka, 2002).

Interpersonal relationships are important to an individual's overall quality of life. A study of individuals with spinal cord injury showed that among them, married individuals reported a higher quality of life than did their single counterparts (Holicky & Charlifue, 1999). Overall, physical disability is associated with difficulty establishing romantic relationships. Taleporos and McCabe (2001) found that physically disabled individuals may avoid romantic relationships due to fear of rejection and perception of negative attitudes associated with disability. Individuals who perceive their disability to be severe are less likely to be in relationships than are those who view their disability as less severe or are non-disabled (Taleporos & McCabe, 2003). Decreased self-esteem appears to play a large role in the ability and willingness of these individuals to engage socially. Additionally, the symptoms of pain that are present in most of these conditions are likely a barrier to social involvement. Despite these difficulties, it should be mentioned that individuals with MS, MD, and SCI were found to demonstrate resiliency and the ability to adapt and effectively cope with setbacks related to their illnesses (Boström & Ahlström, 2004; Finger, 1998; Manns & Chad, 2001).

Clinical Presentation

Movement impairments can lead to, or occur in conjunction with, mental health difficulties. Increased dependence on others and mobility limitations can restrict activity, result in isolation, depression, and anxiety, and contribute to poorer quality of life (Netuveli, Wiggins, Hildon, Montgomery, & Blane, 2006). The severity and prevalence of psychological symptoms varies depending on the disorder, age of onset, disease progression, and level of pain present on a daily basis. Chronic pain, a symptom of many movement impairments, is frequently associated with an increase in psychological distress and prevalence of depression. Pain severity is related to the extent of an individual's depressive symptoms (Lloyd, Waghorn, & McHugh, 2008). Studies examining individuals with musculoskeletal conditions report the prevalence of depressive symptoms between 40–60% with incidences of Major Depression occurring in 17–26% of individuals. Approximately 24% of those individuals met the criteria for anxiety disorder (Härter et al., 2002; Ozcetin et al., 2007).

The neuromotor conditions discussed are linked to a range of psychological symptoms. Multiple factors interact to influence the presentation of clinical symptoms for each individual. A review of the literature suggests that depression and anxiety are the main psychological difficulties encountered with neuromotor impairments. Youth with spina bifida are more likely to display behavioral problems, have higher levels of internalizing symptoms (depression and anxiety), and lower self-concept than are non-impaired children (Holmbeck et al., 2003; Shields, Taylor, & Dodd, 2008). Because of the variable nature of these diseases, it is impossible to determine the degree and severity of mental health issues associated with each impairment without doing a comprehensive assessment.

Research on Personality Assessment

Research on cognitive disability and personality assessment has a long history, dating back to Piotrowski's (1937) studies on the Rorschach in cases of brain dysfunction. Generally speaking, published work has fallen into three categories: (1) how personality assessment data can be used to diagnose disability-related conditions, (2) how personality assessment data can be used to describe the personalities of individuals with disabilities, and (3) how personality assessment can be used to address prognosis and rehabilitation. For example, Gass, Rogers, and Kinne (2017) found that patients with recent TBI showed marked changes on the MMPI-2, including a lack of insight and an overly positive view of the self. Similarly, PAI profiles showed distinct patterns of distress for US service members who had received a combat-related head trauma, leading to different courses of rehabilitation (Kennedy, Cooper, Reid, Tate, & Lange, 2015). However, in recent years, more and more research explores patients' ability to fake neurocognitive dysfunction on various personality measures in order to obtain services or for other secondary gain (Hopwood, Orlando, & Clark, 2010; Rogers, Gillard, Wooley, & Kelsey, 2013; Tarescavage, Wygant, Gervais, & Ben-Porath, 2013). For example, Aguerrevere and colleagues (2017) found that the MMPI-2-RF validity scales were able to distinguish between malingered and non-malingered profiles in a sample of chronic pain patients. To date, little has been written about adapting, modifying, or re-norming measures and procedures for those with physical or cognitive disabilities. The complexities of disabilities make such research challenging, which is why studies tend to focus on specific populations.

Practical Considerations

It is recommended that assessors utilize a risk and resilience framework instead of a "deficit" model to conceptualize clients with cognitive or physical disorders. That is, the presence of disability does not mean that individuals *will* have psychosocial problems or clinical disorders, but rather that their presence puts individuals *at risk* for certain types of difficulties, increasing their susceptibility to personal and social problems (Morrison & Cosden, 1997). Adults with ADHD, SLD, or TBI are most likely to seek assessments because they are not functioning as well as they would like in one or more psychosocial domains, for example, having problems socially, with family, or at work. It is important for assessors to keep in mind that while these cognitive disorders can contribute in significant ways to psychosocial problems, adults with these cognitive disorders can, and do, function well across professions and in higher education. Thus, rather than focus on client limitations, it is more appropriate to acknowledge clients' strengths and weaknesses; instead of advising clients what they can and cannot do, assessors can clarify to clients the effort it will take to engage in activities that they might find challenging as a function of their disability, allowing clients to make informed choices that might require more effort, compensatory strategies, or outside accommodations.

Although some disabilities are diagnosed in childhood, their impact is lifelong, as is the impact of TBI once it occurs at any age. For assessors attempting to integrate knowledge about these disabilities into a treatment plan, it is important to recognize that adults with ADHD, SLD, or TBI typically do not outgrow their problems any more than those with blindness or CP do. There is also great diversity in the functioning of youths and adults with these disabilities, however, so that an assessor cannot assume the nature or extent of continuing problems without individual analysis.

Not only does the assessor need to understand what it means to have a disability, the assessor might also need to help clients understand what it means to have one of those disorders. There are a number of reasons that individuals might not understand the nature of their disorders. In some instances, formal assessments may never have been conducted, and a disability suspected but not confirmed. This could be the case for individuals whose non-affected skills and general resilience have helped them to successfully compensate for their disabilities; in these instances, the impact of their disabilities might not be recognized until environmental requirements become too difficult to maintain with their typical compensatory strategies. For example, college students with undiagnosed ADHD or LD might find themselves challenged more than their peers and wonder, "What is wrong with me?" As part of the assessment process, it is important for the assessor to ask about the client's experiences in school, history of head trauma, and family history of ADHD or SLD, as well as to look for behavioral signs associated with these cognitive disorders. When appropriate, the assessor might need to refer for additional testing to identify the client's cognitive strengths and limitations, integrating this information into the personality assessment.

In other circumstances, it is possible that the client has been assessed and diagnosed with ADHD, SLD, or TBI but has not received sufficient information to help him or her understand the nature of the disorder. This is often the case for individuals identified while younger, in school, or in families where discussions of the disability were not encouraged. For example, in a study of children and adolescents with LD in two schools in southern California, a majority of the participants did not have an accurate understanding of their disability, and many of them stated that it had never been discussed with them (Cosden, Elliott, Noble, & Kelemen, 1999). In instances in which the individual does not have sufficient knowledge about their disorder, the assessor will need to explain to the client what the disability means and how it could impact his or her behavior across academic, vocational, and social domains.

Accurate self-understanding of one's disorder is important not only because it provides a context for understanding other aspects of one's personality; self-understanding of a disorder also contributes to self-esteem (Ingesson, 2007) and positive adult functioning (Goldberg et al., 2003; Toglia & Kirk, 2000). People with disabilities are often misunderstood by others, in part due to the unevenness of their skills, as well as either the invisibility or visibility of their disorders. It is not uncommon for children and adults with some disabilities to perform more poorly than expected in areas affected by their disorders; when the nature of the disorder is unknown to others, these individuals may be seen as "lazy" or "stupid," labels many report that they have been given over time. This is often exacerbated by frustration given the client's sense that he or she worked hard to achieve something, whether social, educational or vocational, even if it resulted in failure. Adults who have an accurate understanding of their disability are able to view it as circumscribed rather than as a global cognitive weakness, which contributes to positive self-perceptions and self-esteem (Cosden, Brown, & Elliott, 2002; Heyman, 1990; Goldberg et al., 2003; Wilczenski, 1993). With a clear understanding of their strengths and weaknesses, clients can advocate for themselves, selecting activities that utilize their strengths and obtaining resources as needed to help in areas in which they need accommodations. By providing, facilitating, and supporting this understanding through assessment and feedback, assessors contribute to the long-term positive functioning of their clients.

Clients might not disclose the presence of ADHD, SLD, or TBI to the assessor even when it is known to them. There are several possible reasons for this, from clients wanting to avoid the stigma of being labeled, to not seeing it as relevant to the question for which they are seeking assessment (Cosden, Patz, & Smith, 2009). However, as reflected throughout this chapter, the presence of LD or ADHD can impact all facets of personal functioning and provides important contextual information for understanding clients' problems and making appropriate recommendations. Thus, it is the responsibility of the assessor to help reduce the stigma associated with these disorders in order to make the discussion of the clients' needs as open as possible.

There are several special considerations for clients with TBI and physical disabilities. Although there are individual differences in recovery from TBI, some changes might be permanent and require ongoing intervention and compensation. This is also true for other disabilities that might worsen over time and even reduce lifespan. In addition, there may be interactive relationships between the psychosocial problems and clinical psychopathology exhibited by these clients. For example, problems with psychosocial functioning can increase depression, while longer periods of depression might cause psychosocial functioning to become worse. Thus, it is important to assess all aspects of functioning before and after interventions to determine whether change in one area (e.g., depression) has influenced improvements in others (e.g., psychosocial functioning).

If the client has a disability, there is a need to understand how that disability is reflected in the personality assessment. Given the complexity and heterogeneity of the disabilities discussed in this chapter, it is impossible to address all possible adaptations needed for an accurate personality assessment process. However, we offer a few reminders for the clinician:

1. Disabilities are often co-occurring with one another and with other health-related considerations.
2. Disabilities can limit a client's access to social exchanges either through communication or mobility.
3. Disabilities are stigmatizing and the client likely suffers the effects of prejudice, marginalization, or exclusion, which can manifest as depression, anxiety, or forms of psychological distress.
4. Clients with disabilities are often members of subcultures (e.g., the Deaf community) that have their own norms, values, and expectations.

Conclusions and Future Directions

The disabilities discussed in this chapter can have significant effects on psychosocial functioning, at times leading to serious anxiety or depression. It is important for assessors to be aware of the presence of these disabilities in order to accurately interpret their findings, particularly those related to self-perceptions and social relationships, and apply them toward determining prognosis for adjustment and developing effective treatment plans. Assessors need to ask clients about the possibility of one or more of these disabilities, even when the client does not offer this information, as the client might find it stigmatizing to be labeled, or not see the presence of the disability as related to the referral question. The assessor might also need to explain the relationship of that disorder to other aspects of life to the client, as it is not uncommon for clients to have insufficient understanding of the impact of their disability on psychosocial functioning. Depending on the nature of the findings, skill training to help the client develop appropriate social skills might be a part of recommendations. Future research needs to examine how individuals with disabilities receive and understand assessment feedback. That is, do these disabilities, with their impact on cognitive processing, interfere with the client's understanding of assessment interpretations and recommendations? Cosden et al. (2009) point out that clients with these cognitive disabilities might need special help to understand therapeutic interventions. Similar concerns are raised here, with more knowledge about this process needed to know how to effectively provide clients with disabilities assessment feedback.

Note

1 TBIs are increasingly referred to as "acquired brain injuries" to differentiate them from other trauma-related disorders (such as PTSD). However, we will use TBI in this chapter because it is still the most commonly used term.

References

Acklin, M. (1990). Personality dimensions in two types of learning-disabled children: A Rorschach study. *Journal of Personality Assessment, 54*, 67–77. doi: 10.1207/s15327752jpa5401&2_8

ADA Amendments Act of 2008, Pub. L. No. 110-325, 122 Stat. 3553. (2008).

Aguerrevere, L. E., Calamia, M. R., Greve, K. W., Bianchini, K. J., Curtis, K. L., & Ramirez, V. (2017). Clusters of financially incentivized chronic pain patients using the Minnesota Multiphasic Personality Inventory-2 Restructured Form (MMPI-2-RF). *Psychological Assessment*, June. doi: http://dx.doi.org/10.1037/pas0000509

Altman, B., & Bernstein, A. (2008). *Disability and health in the United States, 2001–2005*. National Center for Health Statistics.

Alves, G., Forsaa, E., Pedersen, K., Gjerstad, M., & Larsen, J. (2008). Epidemiology of Parkinson's disease. *Journal of Neurology, 255*(5), 18–32. doi: 10.1007/s00415-008-5004-3

American Psychiatric Association. (2013). *Diagnostic and statistical manual of mental disorders* (5th ed.). Arlington, VA: American Psychiatric Publishing.

Barkley, R., Murphy, K., & Fischer, M. (2008). *ADHD in adults: What the science says*. Guilford: New York.

Bauminger, N., & Kimhi-Kind, I. (2008). Social information processing, security of attachment, and emotion regulation in children with learning disabilities. *Journal of Learning Disabilities, 41*, 315–332. doi: 10.1177/0022219408316095

Bénony, H., Daloz, L., Bungener, C., Chahraoui, K., Frenay, C., & Auvin, J. (2002). Emotional factors and subjective quality of life in subjects with spinal cord injuries. *American Journal of Physical Medicine & Rehabilitation, 81*(6), 437–445.

Boström, K., & Ahlström, G. (2004). Living with a chronic deteriorating disease: The trajectory with muscular dystrophy over ten years. *Disability & Rehabilitation, 26*(23), 1388–1398. doi.org/10.1080/0963-8280400000898

Branch, L., Horowitz, A., & Carr, C. (1989). The implications for everyday life of incident self-reported visual decline among people over age 65 living in the community. *Gerontologist, 29*(3), 359–365. doi.org/10.1093/geront/29.3.359

Brown, T. (2005). *Attention Deficit Disorder: The unfocused mind in children and adults*. New Haven, CT: Yale University Press.

Bryan, T., Burstein, K., & Ergul, C. (2004). The social-emotional side of learning disabilities: A science-based presentation of the state of the art. *Learning Disability Quarterly, 27*, 45–51. doi: 10.2307/1593631

Bryant, R., Marosszeky, J., Crooks, J., Baguley, I., & Gurka, J. (2001). Posttraumatic stress disorder and psychosocial functioning after severe traumatic brain injury. *The Journal of Nervous and Mental Disease, 189*, 109–113. doi: 10.1097/00005053-200102000-00006

Campbell, V. A., Crews, J. E., Moriarty, D. G., Zack, M. M., & Blackman, D. K. (1999). Surveillance for sensory impairment, activity limitation, and health-related quality of life among older adults—United States, 1993–1997. *MMWR CDC Surveillance Summary, 48*(8), 131–156.

Castle, K., Imms, C., & Howie, L. (2007). Being in pain: A phenomenological study of young people with cerebral palsy. *Developmental Medicine & Child Neurology, 49*(6), 445–449. doi: 10.1111/j.1469-8749.2007.00445.x

Congdon, N., Friedman, D., & Lietman, T. (2003). Important causes of visual impairment in the world today. *Jama, 290*(15), 2057–2060. doi: 10.1001/jama.290.15.2057

Cosden, M. (2001). Risk and resilience for substance abuse among adolescents and adults with learning disabilities. *Journal of Learning Disabilities, 34*, 352–358. doi.org/10.1177/002221940103400410

Cosden, M., Brown, C., & Elliott, K. (2002). Developing self-understanding and self-esteem in children with learning disabilities. In B. Wong & M. Donahue (Eds.), *The social dimension of learning disabilities* (pp. 33–53). Mahwah, NJ: Erlbaum.

Cosden, M., Elliott, K., Noble, S., & Kelemen, E. (1999). Self-understanding and self-esteem in children with learning disabilities. *Learning Disability Quarterly, 22*, 279–291. doi.org/10.2307/1511262

Cosden, M., Patz, S., & Smith, S. (2009). Do problems with information processing affect the process of psychotherapy for adults with learning disabilities or attention deficit/hyperactivity disorder? *Learning Disabilities Research & Practice, 24*, 165–173. doi: 10.1111/j.1540-5826.2009.00290.x

Crawford, S., Kaplan, B., & Dewey, D. (2006). Effects of coexisting disorders on cognition and behavior in children with ADHD. *Journal of Attention Disorders, 10*, 192–199. doi.org/10.1177/1087054706289924

Detrait, E., George, T., Etchevers, H., Gilbert, J., Vekemans, M., & Speer, M. (2005). Human neural tube defects: Developmental biology, epidemiology, and genetics. *Neurotoxicology and Teratology, 27*(3), 515–524. doi.org/10.1016/j.ntt.2004.12.007

Dewey, D., Kaplan, B., Crawford, S., & Wilson, B. (2002). Developmental coordination disorder: Associated problems in attention, learning, and psychosocial adjustment. *Human Movement Science, 21*(5), 905–918. doi.org/10.1016/S0167-9457(02)00163-X

Draper, K., Ponsford, J., & Schönberger, M. (2007). Psychosocial and emotional outcomes 10 years following traumatic brain injury. *Journal of Head Trauma Rehabilitation, 22*, 278–287. doi: 10.1097/01.HTR.0000290972.63753.a7

Du Feu, M., & Fergusson, K. (2003). Sensory impairment and mental health. *Advances in Psychiatric Treatment, 9*(2), 95–103. doi: 10.1192/apt.01.03

Evans, J., Fletcher, A., & Wormald, R. (2007). Depression and anxiety in visually impaired older people. *Ophthalmology, 114*, 283–288. doi.org/10.1016/j.ophtha.2006.10.006

Fellinger, J., Holzinger, D., Dobner, U., Gerich, J., Lehner, R., Lenz, G., & Goldberg, D. (2005). Mental distress and quality of life in a deaf population. *Social Psychiatry and Psychiatric Epidemiology, 40*(9), 737–742. doi: 10.1007/s00127-005-0936-8

Finger, S. (1998). A happy state of mind: A history of mild elation, denial of disability, optimism, and laughing in multiple sclerosis. *Archives of Neurology, 55*(2), 241–250. doi.org/10.1001/archneur.55.2.241

Flanagan, N., Jackson, A., & Hill, A. (2003). Visual impairment in childhood: Insights from a community-based survey. *Child: Care, Health and Development, 29*, 493–499. doi: 10.1046/j.1365-2214.2003.00369.x

Garaigordobil, M., & Bernarás, E. (2009). Self-concept, self-esteem, personality traits and psychopathological symptoms in adolescents with and without visual impairment. *The Spanish Journal of Psychology, 12*, 149–160. doi.org/10.1017/S1138741600001566

Gass, C. S., Rogers, D., & Kinne, E. (2017). Psychological characteristics in acute mild traumatic brain injury: An MMPI-2 study. *Applied Neuropsychology: Adult, 24*(2), 108–115. doi: http://dx.doi.org/10.1080/23279095.2015.1107563

Goldberg, R., Higgins, E., Raskind, M., & Herman, K. (2003). Predictors of success in individuals with learning disabilities: A qualitative analysis of a 20-year longitudinal study. *Learning Disabilities Research & Practice, 18*, 222–236. doi: 10.1111/1540-5826.00077

Gray, C., Hosie, J., Russell, P., & Ormel, E. (2001). Emotional development in deaf children: Facial expressions, display rules, and theory of mind. In M. Clark, M. Marschark, & M. Karchmer (Eds.), *Context, cognition, and deafness* (pp. 135–160). Washington, DC: Gallaudet University Press.

Griffin-Shirley, N., & Nes, S. L. (2005). Self-esteem and empathy in sighted and visually impaired preadolescents. *Journal of Visual Impairment and Blindness, 99*(5), 276–285.

Grootenhuis, M., De Boone, J., & Van der Kooi, A. (2007). Living with muscular dystrophy: Health related quality of life consequences for children and adults. *Health and Quality of Life Outcomes, 5*, 31. doi: 10.1186/1477-7525-5-31

Guerette, A., & Smedema, S. (2011). The relationship of perceived social support with well-being in adults with visual impairments. *Journal of Visual Impairment & Blindness, 105*(7), 425–439.

Hakim, A., Bakheit, A., Bryant, T., Roberts, M., McIntosh-Michaelis, S., Spackman, A., ... McLellan, D. (2000). The social impact of multiple sclerosis: A study of 305 patients and their relatives. *Disability & Rehabilitation, 22*(6), 288–293. doi.org/10.1080/096382800296755

Härter, M., Reuter, K., Weisser, B., Schretzmann, B., Aschenbrenner, A., & Bengel, J. (2002). A descriptive study of psychiatric disorders and psychosocial burden in rehabilitation patients with musculoskeletal diseases. *Archives of Physical Medicine and Rehabilitation, 83*(4), 461–468. doi.org/10.1053/apmr.2002.30924

Hayman, K., Kerse, N., La Grow, S. J., Wouldes, T., Robertson, C., & Campbell, J. (2007). Depression in older people: Visual impairment and subjective ratings of health. *Optometry and Vision Science, 84*(11), 1024–1030. doi: 10.1097/OPX.0b013e318157a6b1

Heyman, W. B. (1990). The self-perception of a learning disability and its relationship to academic self-concept and self-esteem. *Journal of Learning Disabilities, 23*, 472–475. doi.org/10.1177/002221949002300804

Hindley, P. (2000). Child and adolescent psychiatry. In P. Hindley & N. Kitson (Eds.), *Mental health and deafness* (pp. 42–74). London: Whurr.

Hindley, P. (2005a). Development of deaf and blind children. *Psychiatry, 4*(7), 45–48. doi.org/10.1383/psyt.2005.4.7.45

Hindley, P. (2005b). Mental health problems in deaf children. *Current Paediatrics, 15*(2), 114–119. doi.org/10.1383/psyt.2005.4.7.45

Holicky, R., & Charlifue, S. (1999). Aging with spinal cord injury: The impact of spousal support. *Disability and Rehabilitation, 21*, 250–257. doi.org/10.1080/096382899297675

Holmbeck, G., & Devine, K. (2010). Psychosocial and family functioning in spina bifida. *Developmental Disabilities Research Reviews, 16*(1), 40–46. doi.apa.org

Holmbeck, G., Westhoven, V., Phillips, W., Bowers, R., Gruse, C., Nikolopoulos, T., ... Davison, K. (2003). A multimethod, multi-informant, and multidimensional perspective on psychosocial adjustment in preadolescents with spina bifida. *Journal of Consulting and Clinical Psychology, 71*(4), 782. doi.org/10.1037/0022-006X.71.4.782

Hoofien, D., Gilboa, A., Vakil, E., & Donovick, P. (2001). Traumatic brain injury (TBI) 10–20 years later: A comprehensive outcome study of psychiatric symptomatology, cognitive abilities and psychosocial functioning. *Brain Injury, 15*, 189–209. doi: 10.1080/026990501300005659

Hopwood, C., Orlando, M., & Clark, T. (2010). The detection of malingered pain-related disability with the Personality Assessment Inventory. *Rehabilitation Psychology, 55*, 307–310. doi.org/10.1037/a0020516

Horowitz, A., Reinhardt, J., Boerner, K., & Travis, L. (2003). The influence of health, social support quality and rehabilitation on depression among disabled elders. *Aging & Mental Health, 7*(5), 342–350. doi.org/10.1080/1360786031000150739

Hung, W., Ross, J., Boockvar, K., & Siu, A. (2011). Recent trends in chronic disease, impairment and disability among older adults in the United States. *BMC Geriatrics, 11*(1), 47. doi: 10.1186/1471-2318-11-47

Individuals with Disabilities Education Act (IDEA), 20 U.S.C. § 1400 (2004).

Ingesson, S. (2007). Growing up with dyslexia: Interviews with teenagers and young adults. *School Psychology International, 28*, 574–591. doi.org/10.1177/0143034307085659

Jakobson, A., & Kikas, E. (2007). Cognitive functioning in children with and without attention-deficit hyperactivity disorder with and without comorbid learning disabilities. *Journal of Learning Disabilities, 40*, 194–202. doi.org/10.1177/00222194070400030101

Kennedy, J. E., Cooper, D. B., Reid, M. W., Tate, D. F., & Lange, R. T. (2015). Profile analyses of the Personality Assessment Inventory following military-related traumatic brain injury. *Archives of Clinical Neuropsychology, 30*(3), 236–247. doi: http://dx.doi.org/10.1093/arclin/acv014

Kersel, D., Marsh, N., Havill, J., & Sleigh, J. (2001). Psychosocial functioning during the year following severe traumatic brain injury. *Brain Injury, 15*, 683–696. doi.org/10.1080/02699050121088

Klassen, R., Tze, V., & Hannok, W. (2013). Internalizing problems of adults with learning disabilities: A meta-analysis. *Journal of Learning Disabilities, 46*, 317–327. https://doi.org/10.1177/0022219411422260

Knoors, H., & Vervloed, M. (2003). Educational programming for deaf children with multiple disabilities: Accommodating special needs. In M. Marschark & P. E. Spencer (Eds.), *Oxford handbook of deaf studies, language, and education* (pp. 82–94). New York: Oxford University Press.

Kone-Paut, I., Piram, M., Guillaume, S., & Tran, T. A. (2007). Review: Lupus in adolescence. *Lupus, 16*(8), 606–612. doi: 10.1177/0961203307079562

Krigger, K. W. (2006). Cerebral palsy: An overview. *American Family Physician, 73*(1), 91–100.

Kuwabara, S. (2004). Guillain-Barré syndrome. *Drugs, 64*(6), 597–610. doi: 10.2165/00003495-200464060-00003

Lackaye, T., Margalit, M., Ziv, O., & Ziman, T. (2006). Comparisons of self-efficacy, mood, effort and hope between students with learning disabilities and their non-LD-matched peers. *Learning Disabilities Research and Practice, 21*, 111–121. doi: 10.1111/j.1540-5826.2006.00211.x

Lewis, J., Stephens, S., & McKenna, L. (1994). Tinnitus and suicide. *Clinical Otolaryngology & Allied Sciences, 19*(1), 50–54. doi: 10.1111/j.1365-2273.1994.tb01147.x

Lifshitz, H., Hen, I., & Weisse, I. (2007). Self-concept, self-esteem, personality traits and psychopathological symptoms in adolescents with and without vision impairment. *Journal of Visual Impairment and Blindness, 101*, 96–107.

Liptak, G. (2008). Health and wellbeing of adults with cerebral palsy. *Current Opinion in Neurology, 21*(2), 136–142. doi: 10.1097/WCO.0b013e3282f6a499

Lloyd, C., Waghorn, G., & McHugh, C. (2008). Musculoskeletal disorders and comorbid depression: Implications for practice. *Australian Occupational Therapy Journal, 55*, 23–29. doi: 10.1111/j.1440-1630.2006.00624.x

Lorenz, D., Schwieger, D., Moises, H., & Deuschl, G. (2006). Quality of life and personality in essential tremor patients. *Movement Disorders, 21*(8), 1114–1118. doi: 10.1002/mds.20884

Lundy, J. (2002). Age and language skills of deaf children in relation to theory of mind development. *Journal of Deaf Studies and Deaf Education, 7*(1), 41–56. doi.org/10.1093/deafed/7.1.41

Manns, P., & Chad, K. (2001). Components of quality of life for persons with a quadriplegic and paraplegic spinal cord injury. *Qualitative Health Research, 11*(6), 795–811. doi: 10.1177/104973201129119541

McNamara, J., Willoughby, T., & Chalmers, H. (2005). Psychosocial status of adolescents with learning disabilities with and without comorbid attention deficit hyperactivity disorder. *Learning Disabilities Research & Practice, 20*, 234–244. doi: 10.1111/j.1540-5826.2005.00139.x

McNulty, M. (2003). Dyslexia and the life course. *Journal of Learning Disabilities, 36*, 363–381. doi.org/10.1177/00222194030360040701

Mitchell, A., Benito-León, J., González, J., & Rivera-Navarro, J. (2005). Quality of life and its assessment in multiple sclerosis: Integrating physical and psychological components of wellbeing. *The Lancet Neurology, 4*(9), 556–566. doi: 10.1016/S1474-4422(05)70166-6

Mohr, D., & Cox, D. (2001). Multiple sclerosis: Empirical literature for the clinical health psychologist. *Journal of Clinical Psychology, 57*(4), 479–499. doi: 10.1002/jclp.1042

Mohr, D. C., & Dick, L. P. (1998). Multiple sclerosis. In P. M. Camic & S. Knight (Eds.), *Clinical handbook of health psychology: A practical guide to effective interventions* (pp. 313–348). Seattle: Hogrefe & Huber.

Morrison, G., & Cosden, M. (1997). Risk, resilience and adjustment of individuals with learning disabilities. *Learning Disability Quarterly, 20*, 43–60. doi.org/10.2307/1511092

Nance, W. E. (2003). The genetics of deafness. *Mental Retardation and Developmental Disabilities Research Reviews, 9*(2), 109–119. doi: 10.1002/mrdd.10067

National Joint Committee on Learning Disabilities (2011). Learning disabilities: Implications for policy regarding research and practice. *Learning Disability Quarterly, 34*, 237–241. doi.org/10.1177/0731948711421756

Nelson, J., & Harwood, H. (2011). Learning disabilities and anxiety: A meta-analysis. *Journal of Learning Disabilities, 44*, 3–17. doi: 10.1177/0022219409359939

Netuveli, G., Wiggins, R. D., Hildon, Z., Montgomery, S. M., & Blane, D. (2006). Quality of life at older ages: Evidence from the English longitudinal study of aging (wave 1). *Journal of Epidemiology and Community Health, 60*(4), 357–363. doi: 10.1136/jech.2005.040071

Nigg, J., John, O., Blaskey, L., Huang-Pollock, C., Willicut, E., Hinshaw, S., & Pennington, B. (2002). Big Five dimensions and ADHD symptoms: Links between personality traits and clinical symptoms. *Journal of Personality and Social Psychology, 83*, 451–469. doi: 10.1037/0022-3514.83.2.451

Nolin, P., Villemure, R., & Heroux, L. (2006). Determining long-term symptoms following mild traumatic brain injury: Method of interview affects self-report. *Brain Injury, 20*, 1147–1154. doi.org/10.1080/02699050601049247

Ownsworth, T., Fleming, J., Haines, T., Cornwell, P., Kendall, M., Nalder, E., & Gordon, C. (2011). Development of depressive symptoms during early community reintegration after traumatic brain injury. *Journal of the International Neuropsychological Society, 17,* 112–119. doi.org/10.1017/S1355617710001311

Ozcetin, A., Ataoglu, S., Kocer, E., Yazycy, S., Yildiz, O., Ataoglu, A., & Ycmeli, C. (2007). Effects of depression and anxiety on quality of life of patients with rheumatoid arthritis, knee osteoarthritis and fibromyalgia syndrome. *West Indian Medical Journal, 56*(2), 122–129. doi.org/10.1590/S0043-31442007000200004

Papadopoulos, K., Montgomery, A. J., & Chronopoulou, E. (2013). The impact of visual impairments in self-esteem and locus of control. *Research in Developmental Disabilities, 34,* 4565–4570. doi.org/10.1016/j.ridd.2013.09.036

Pascolini, D., & Mariotti, S. P. (2010). Global estimates of visual impairment: 2010. *British Journal of Ophthalmology, 96,* 614–618. doi: 10.1136/bjophthalmol-2011-300539

Petit, C. (2006). From deafness genes to hearing mechanisms: Harmony and counterpoint. *Trends in Molecular Medicine, 12*(2), 57–64. doi.org/10.1016/j.molmed.2005.12.006

Pietrzak, R., Johnson, D., Goldstein, M., Malley, J., & Southwick, M. (2009). Posttraumatic stress disorder mediates the relationship between mild traumatic brain injury and health and psychosocial functioning in veterans of Operation Enduring Freedom and Iraqi Freedom. *The Journal of Nervous and Mental Disease, 197,* 748–753. doi: 10.1097/NMD.0b013e3181b97a75

Pinquart, M., & Pfeiffer, J. P. (2011). Psychological well-being in visually impaired and unimpaired individuals: A meta-analysis. *British Journal of Visual Impairment, 29* (1), 27–45. doi: 10.1177/0264619610389572

Pinquart, M., & Pfeiffer, J. P. (2014). Change in psychological problems of adolescents with and without visual impairment. *European Child and Adolescent Psychiatry, 23,* 571–578. doi: 10.1007/s00787-013-0482-y

Piotrowski, Z. (1937). The Rorschach Inkblot Method in organic disturbances of the central nervous system. *Journal of Nervous and Mental Disease, 86,* 525–537.

Pons-Estel, G., Alarcón, G., Scofield, L., Reinlib, L., & Cooper, G. (2010). Understanding the epidemiology and progression of systemic lupus erythematosus. *Seminars in Arthritis and Rheumatism, 39*(4), 257–268. doi.org/10.1016/j.semarthrit.2008.10.007

Ramsay, J. R., & Rostain, A. L. (2007). Psychosocial treatment for attention-deficit/hyperactivity disorder in adults: Current evidence and future directions. *Professional Psychology: Research and Practice, 38,* 338–346. doi.org/10.1037/0735-7028.38.4.338

Ramsay, J. R., & Rostain, A. L. (2008). Adult ADHD research: Current status and future direction. *Journal of Attention Disorders, 11,* 624–627. doi.org/10.1177/1087054708314590

Reichmann, H., Schneider, C., & Löhle, M. (2009). Non-motor features of Parkinson's disease: Depression and dementia. *Parkinsonism & Related Disorders, 15,* S87–S92. doi.org/10.1016/S1353-8020(09)70789-8

Resnikoff, S., Pascolini, D., Etya'ale, D., Kocur, I., Pararajasegaram, R., Pokharel, G. P., & Mariotti, S. P. (2004). Global data on visual impairment in the year 2002. *Bulletin of the World Health Organization, 82*(11), 844–851. doi: /S0042-96862004001100009

Rogers, R., Gillard, N., Wooley, C., & Kelsey, K. (2013). Cross-validation of the PAI Negative Distortion Scale for feigned mental disorders: A research report. *Assessment, 20,* 36–42. doi: 10.1177/1073191112451493

Rosembaun, P., Paneth, N., Levinton, A., Goldstein, M., & Max, M. (2007). A report: The definition and classification of cerebral palsy. *Developmental Medicine & Child Neurology, 109,* 8–14.

Saunders, G. H., & Echt, K. V. (2007). An overview of dual sensory impairment in older adults: Perspectives for rehabilitation. *Trends in Amplification, 11*(4), 243–258. doi.org/10.1177/1084713807308365

Seawell, A. H., & Danoff-Burg, S. (2004). Psychosocial research on systemic lupus erythematosus: A literature review. *Lupus, 13*(12), 891–899. https://doi.org/10.1191/0961203304lu1083rr

Sharps, M. J., Price-Sharps, J. L., Day, S. S., Villegas, A. B., & Nunes, M. A. (2005). Cognitive predisposition to substance abuse in adult attention deficit hyperactivity disorder. *Addictive Behaviors, 30*, 355–359. doi.org/10.1016/j.addbeh.2004.05.003

Shields, N., Taylor, N. F., & Dodd, K. J. (2008). Self-concept in children with spina bifida compared with typically developing children. *Developmental Medicine and Child Neurology, 50*(10), 733–743. doi.org/10.1016/j.apmr.2007.11.056

Sigurdardottir, S., Andelic, N., Roe, C., & Schanke, A.-K. (2013). Depressive symptoms and psychological distress during the first five years after traumatic brain injury: Relationship with psychosocial stressors, fatigue and pain. *Journal of Rehabilitative Medicine, 45*, 808–814. doi.org/10.2340/16501977-1156

Smith, D. (2005). *Introduction to special education: Teaching in an age of opportunity* (5th edition). Boston, MA: Allyn & Bacon.

Sowerby, P., & Tripp, G. (2009). *Evidence-based assessment of Attention-deficit Hyperactivity Disorder*. (pp. 209–239). New York: Springer Science.

Spliethoff-Kamminga, N. G., Zwinderman, A. H., Springer, M. P., & Roos, R. A. (2003). Psychosocial problems in Parkinson's disease: Evaluation of a disease-specific questionnaire. *Movement Disorders, 18*(5), 503–509. doi: 10.1007/s00415-003-0165-6

Taleporos, G., & McCabe, M. P. (2001). Physical disability and sexual esteem. *Sexuality and Disability, 19*(2), 131–148. doi: 10.1023/A:1010677823338

Taleporos, G., & McCabe, M. (2003). Relationships, sexuality and adjustment among people with physical disability. *Sexual and Relationship Therapy, 18*(1), 25–43. doi.org/10.1080/1468199031000061245

Tarescavage, A., Wygant, D., Gervais, R., & Ben-Porath, Y. (2013). Association between the MMPI-2 Restructured Form (MMPI-2-RF) and malingered neurocognitive dysfunction among non-head injury disability claimants. *The Clinical Neuropsychologist*, 27, 313–335. doi.org/10.1080/13854046.2012.744099

Toglia, J., & Kirk, U. (2000). Understanding awareness deficits following brain injury. *NeuroRehabilitation, 15*, 57–70.

Tolosa, E., Wenning, G., & Poewe, W. (2006). The diagnosis of Parkinson's disease. *The Lancet Neurology, 5*(1), 75–86. doi.org/10.1016/S1474-4422(05)70285-4

Turner, O., Windfuhr, K., & Kapur, N. (2007). Suicide in deaf populations: A literature review. *Annals General Psychiatry, 6*(26), 1–9. doi: 10.1186/1744-859X-6-26

Vanderploeg, R. D. (2013). *Neuropsychological assessment*. Arlington, VA: American Psychiatric Publishing, Inc.

Verstraten, P., Brinkmann, W., Stevens, N., & Schouten, J. (2005). Loneliness, adaptation to vision impairment, social support and depression among visually impaired elderly. *International Congress Series*, 1282, 317–321. doi.org/10.1016/j.ics.2005.04.017

Wallhagen, M., Strawbridge, W., Shema, S., Kurata, J., & Kaplan, G. (2001). Comparative impact of hearing and vision impairment on subsequent functioning. *Journal of the American Geriatrics Society, 49*(8), 1086–1092. doi: 10.1046/j.1532-5415.2001.49213.x

Weiss, M., Murry, C., & Weiss, G. (2002). Adults with Attention-Deficit/Hyperactivity Disorder: Current concepts. *Journal of Psychiatric Practice, 8*, 99–111. doi.org/10.1097/00131746-200203000-00006

Weiss, H., Rastan, V., Müllges, W., Wagner, R. F., & Toyka, K. V. (2002). Psychotic symptoms and emotional distress in patients with Guillain-Barré syndrome. *European Neurology, 47*(2), 74–78. doi:10.1159/000047956

Wenning, G. K., Kiechl, S., Seppi, K., Müller, J., Högl, B., Saletu, M., . . . Poewe, W. (2005). Prevalence of movement disorders in men and women aged 50–89 years (Bruneck Study cohort): A population-based study. *The Lancet Neurology*, *4*(12), 815–820. doi.org/10.1016/S1474-4422(05)70226-X

Wilczenski, F. (1993). Coming to terms with an identity of "learning disabled" in college. *Journal of College Student Psychotherapy, 7*, 49–61. doi.org/10.1300/J035v07n01_06-

Woolf, A., & Pfleger, B. (2003). Burden of major musculoskeletal conditions. *Bulletin of the World Health Organization, 81*(9), 646–656. doi.org/10.1590/S0042-96862003000900007

World Health Organization. (2010). Towards a common language for functioning, disability and health: ICF. Geneva 2002.

World Health Organization. (2014). *International statistical classification of diseases and related health problems 10th revision (ICD-10).* Retrieved from http://www.who.int/classifications/icd/en/

Wright, B. (2008). Development in deaf and blind children. *Psychiatry, 7*(7), 286–289. doi.org/10.1016/j.mppsy.2008.05.007

Zirkel, P. (2009). Section 504: Student eligibility update. *The Clearing House: A Journal of Educational Strategies, Issues and Ideas, 82*(5), 209–211. doi.org/10.3200/TCHS.82.5.209-211

Zurowski, M., McDonald, W., Fox, S., & Marsh, L. (2013). Psychiatric comorbidities in dystonia: Emerging concepts. *Movement Disorders, 28*(7), 914–920. doi: 10.1002/mds.25501

CHAPTER 9

Nationality and Personality Assessment

Gargi Roysircar and Radhika Krishnamurthy

Psychologists engaged in psychological assessment work in clinical and counseling settings are, more than ever before, encountering clients from a multitude of national, cultural, and linguistic backgrounds. Published data show that the number of naturalized citizens in the United States (U.S.) totaled 730,259 in 2015, with the largest number, 261,374, from Asia (U.S. Department of Homeland Security, Office of Immigration Statistics, December, 2016). Additionally, the number of nonimmigrant international students in the U.S. totaled 1,043,839 in 2015/16, representing a 7% increase over the prior year; leading countries of origin were China, India, South Korea, and Saudi Arabia (Institute of International Education, 2017). Our professional work also brings us into contact with international persons on temporary work visas, asylum seekers, as well as undocumented immigrants (the latter group estimated at 11 million in 2015; Krogstad, Passel, & Cohn, 2017, April). Thus, the demands for mental health services, including assessment of personality and psychopathology, are on an upswing. However, some nationally diverse individuals, such as immigrants and their families, are reluctant to participate in assessment or seek therapy due to the stigma associated with mental health disorders, language problems, unfamiliarity with the idea of testing and assessment as well as with the U.S. mental health care system, perception of low cultural competence in psychologists, and their cultural distrust of mental health services and practitioners (APA, 2017).

Although the current psychological literature reflects significant advances in cross-cultural considerations, it is often at the level of broad cultures (e.g., Asian, Hispanic, etc.). The result has been both an increased understanding of cultural characteristics as they influence individual functioning, and overgeneralizations that obscure important distinctions within these groups. In this chapter we emphasize that nationality is one such variable of distinction. National context, with its attendant sociopolitical influences (e.g., democratic vs. communist nation, secular vs. religious state, indigenous vs. postcolonial influence, class differences, religious or ethnic cleansing, terrorist attacks), shapes the life experiences of its members in various ways, including attitudes and expectations, sense of personal agency, feelings of safety and security, and internalized oppression or self-stigma. Thus, for example, persons from the various countries comprising the Asian continent have distinct national histories and current societal contexts that need to be taken into consideration during psychological assessment.

Communities and individuals who are adapting to new sociocultural contexts need culture-informed psychological services. The role of mental health practitioners is to develop and maintain a high quality of assessment and service delivery with diverse nationality populations (Roysircar, 2013). Culturally "blind" applications of U.S. normed instruments with non-U.S. nationality populations, where there is little concern for their applicability to a different culture and no verification of the instruments' psychometric properties (i.e., reliability and validity) in new contexts, is simply bad practice.

Still, the idea that some tests are more suited for international assessment because of particular features, such as their format, mode of administration, and item contents covering global or broad presentations of personality, psychopathology, and human strengths, continues to underlie much of international assessment protocols and their interpretation (cf. Roysircar, Colvin, Afolayan, Thompson, & Robertson, 2017). Correspondingly, culture-specific measures have been assembled (cf. Kuo, Roysircar, & Newby-Clark, 2006; Kwan & Sodowsky, 1997; Sodowsky, Lai, & Plake, 1991; Sodowsky & Plake, 1991; see the Appendix for sample tests) or based on minor or major adaptations of existing measures such as the Minnesota Multiphasic Personality Inventory-2 for adults and the House-Tree-Person Test for children and adolescents. The adapted instruments contain various implicit references to, and meanings of, the European American culture of the test developers and their subsequent revising authors, and extensive revisions have been required for their use in other languages and cultures (Sodowsky, Kuo-Jackson, & Loya, 1996). Guidelines for assessing culturally diverse individuals with adapted U.S. measures have been recommended (Roysircar, 2005; Roysircar-Sodowsky & Kuo, 2001). Since 2000, the U.S. Department of Health and Human Services, through its Office of Minority Health (2013), has published and subsequently revised a list of 15 standards designed to improve care and assessment of marginalized groups. Entitled the Culturally and Linguistically Appropriate Services (CLAS) standards, they provide a blueprint for appropriate services, for example, stating that psychologists do not work in isolation from the community. From an organizational perspective there is a responsibility to ensure sufficient outreach to allow community feedback and monitoring of services, as well as to ensure that providers are well-versed in multiculturally informed practice, and that community members themselves have had educational opportunities designed to inform them of both the signs and symptoms of psychological difficulties and how to access services (Office of Minority Health, 2013).

This chapter addresses the social-emotional assessment of diverse nationality populations by discussing specific mental health presentations of Asian immigrant groups in the U.S. The intersectionality of individual acculturative adaptation and stress with ecological contexts of one's family, local nationality community, heritage culture, mainstream European American culture, and the host society's racist attitudes are critically analyzed. Finally, instruments that have been successfully utilized with various nationality groups are briefly presented in the Appendix to this chapter. The chapter is largely focused on immigrants naturalized through typical pathways (sponsorship through work or family in the United States). Space constraints prevent us from delving into the complexities of assessing asylum seekers/refugees and undocumented immigrants who seek psychological services, and for whom matters of access, persecution, and personal/family security hold great significance (see APA (2017) for this information). Nonetheless, we note that these individuals may be referred for assessment, even if they do not seek it voluntarily. Therefore, many of the issues discussed in this chapter are relevant to assessing them. However, we also recognize that issues related to national origin and cultural background cannot be easily separated from the contexts and experiences that brought these individuals to the U.S. or other Western countries for refuge. We emphasize to the reader that refugees and undocumented immigrants are likely to have had significantly traumatic experiences in their country of origin (e.g., war, genocide, famine in cases of asylum seekers/refugees) and in the U.S. (e.g., hate crimes, discrimination, exploitation in cases of undocumented immigrants), which requires considerable sensitivity and experience in trauma assessment on the part of the assessor.

Conceptual Considerations

Berry's Model of Acculturation for Immigrants

Berry's model of acculturation (i.e., Berry, Kim, & Boski, 1988) shows that both immigrants and the host society are confronted with two major issues: (1) maintenance of cultural group characteristics/identity and (2) contact/relationship between the two groups (Berry, 2001). Furthermore, there is mutual influence between both parties, which results in changes in both nationality groups (Berry, 2001).

Four major ways immigrants relate to the host culture have been identified: (a) *assimilation*—identifying only with the host culture and rejecting the native identity; (b) *marginalization*—rejecting relationship with the host society and the native identity; (c) *separation*—identifying only with the native identity and rejecting relationship with the host society; and (d) *integration*—becoming bicultural by maintaining traditions of own culture while selectively taking on customs of the host culture (Berry et al., 1988). However, when the host society restricts the type of relations immigrants can have with the host society, all four adaptation modes might not be viable. For instance, integration is only possible when the host society is open to multiculturalism and internationalism, which are periodically affected by nationalistic attitudes and immigration policies. Berry (1997), Farver, Xu, Bhadha, Narang, and Lieber (2007), and LaFromboise, Coleman, and Gerton, J. (1993) argue that the acculturation style of integration is psychologically the most adaptive.

In this bidimensional model, individuals select different components of both the host and native cultures in a way where increasing identification with one culture does not entail decreasing identification with the other. For example, a second-generation Asian Indian young adult living in the U.S. may enjoy participating in festivals of his or her heritage culture but might also choose to socialize with peers of diverse ethnic backgrounds (Kaling, 2011, 2016). As another example, many adolescents describe themselves with a bicultural identity (e.g., Chinese American, Vietnamese American, Korean American, Indian Caribbean American, Biracial Transgender Japanese) which may offer a sense of connection and belonging within multiple societal contexts. The experience of the bicultural identity further involves the salience of one particular aspect of identity over others, due to the influence of the specific context within which an individual interacts (APA, 2017). Furthermore, members of one family can adopt different acculturation adaptations. In addition, particular immigrant nationality groups display distinct patterns of acculturation adaptations. Immigrant families from India have collectivistic traditions that play a role in their acculturation adaptation as compared with those who are individualistic in their choices.

Empirical studies have demonstrated that *level* of acculturation also has an effect, evident in personality test scores. For example, Tsai and Pike (2000) reported that in a sample of Asian American college students (*N* = 90, primarily Chinese, Vietnamese, and Korean nationalities), low-acculturated students scored significantly higher on nine scales of the Minnesota Multiphasic Personality Assessment, second edition (MMPI-2; Butcher, Dahlstrom, Graham, Tellegen, & Kaemmer, 1989) compared to a matched sample of White students. Furthermore, they scored significantly higher than high-acculturated Asian students on five MMPI-2 scales. Thus, degree of acculturation appears to have an impact on profile elevations. In contrast are findings indicating that rather than traditional indices of acculturation, personality traits of extraversion and neuroticism exert a strong influence on psychological adjustment indicators, and that cultural *resistance* has a small impact on negative adjustment among Hispanic students (Ahadi & Puente-Diaz, 2011). Taken together, such findings suggest the need to consider the interaction of acculturation with various other factors, including individual personality makeup; another noted factor is that of experiences of discrimination (e.g., Fang, Friedlander, & Pieterse, 2016). Finally, a bidimensional model of acculturation (where heritage and mainstream cultural identities are considered independently) is empirically found to be a more comprehensive and valid representation of acculturation than a unidimensional model consisting of a single continuum (Ryder, Alden, & Paulhus, 2000).

Acculturation has been found to be a significant variable in determining attitudes toward therapy, help-seeking behaviors, and utilization of help resources by Asian international groups (Frey & Roysircar, 2006). Psychologists might find it facilitative to understand help-seeking attitudes of Asians that are determined by high versus low acculturation. Upon entering the United States, many immigrants face prejudice and discrimination based on both their immigrant status and nationality. United States citizens have expressed a fear that immigrants take jobs away from them, and there are pervasive negative stereotypes about immigrants being lazy and criminal in their conduct. Prejudicial attitudes like these create an unwelcoming environment for immigrants, and add to their acculturation adaptation difficulties and psychological distress (APA, 2017).

Acculturative Stress

Researchers have discovered that the process of learning to adapt to a new culture can create immense stress for individuals, families, and groups, also known as *acculturative stress* (Berry et al., 1988; Roysircar-Sodowsky & Maestas, 2000). Factors such as prejudice, discrimination, minority status, and pressure to learn English have been identified as contributing to stress in immigrant groups (Sodowsky, Lai, & Plake, 1991). Acculturation might be more stressful for some ethnic groups compared to others, and also differs at the individual level. Specifically, the greater the difference between the native and host cultures, the higher the level of expected stress (Berry, 1997; Sodowsky & Lai, 1997). In the same respect, a greater number of experienced difficulties is expected with psychological functioning (Farver, Bhadha, & Narang, 2002). Furthermore, children of immigrants, particularly those who came to the new country early in their lives or those who were born in the new country, often experience acculturative stress of a different nature (Sodowsky & Lai, 1997). These children often acquire the new language and culture faster than their parents, and may assist parents with writing, translating, or mediating cultures. Adult responsibilities for children may create significant changes in family structure and relationships, leading to potential family conflicts (Choi & Dancy, 2009). Hierarchically, a child might take on a more powerful role compared to her or his parents because of greater knowledge of the host culture. The parents become dependent on the child due to his or her English fluency and cultural knowledge. The difference in cultural knowledge and interactions with the host society and perhaps, as a result, in values, can create parent–child conflict.

Conceptual, Psychometric and Practical Considerations in Test Selection and Application

Effective psychological assessment of immigrants from other countries requires attention to issues of appropriateness of the test measure, including suitability of its items, constructs, norms, and language version. In the reverse direction, efforts to develop international adaptations and translations of Western personality measures have revealed the importance of conceptual and psychometric equivalence of test items for members of the nationality/cultural group for whom the test is to be applied (e.g., Butcher, 1996). Psychometric equivalence, a particular concern of bias in test scoring, refers to the level at which test scores can be compared across cultural groups and, hence, to the calibration of scales. If there is no bias, a given score is equivalent across cultural groups (Sodowsky & Impara, 1996). In other words, a score of 18 on the Beck Depression Scale would have the same psychological meaning across cultural groups, such as American and Chinese, who have been assessed.

We emphasize five issues for assessors to consider in selecting test measures and determining the suitability and scope of their yield in assessing immigrant populations. First, assessors need to be aware of the construct limitations of instruments they use, as the construct being measured might not be identical for different nationalities (Roysircar, 2005; Sodowsky et al., 1996). For instance, the Five-Factor Model in personality assessment, although found to have cross-national stability (e.g., Hendriks et al., 2003; McCrae et al., 1998) excludes aspects of functioning deemed salient in some Asian nationalities, such as Indian, Chinese, and South Korean. Interpersonal values and behaviors such as harmony, interdependent self-construal, loss of face, and cultural stigma are frequently observed in social practices and reactions in Asian collectivistic societies (Roysircar, 2013; Roysircar & Pignatiello, 2011). Thus, the Five-Factor model might not be sufficiently comprehensive in assessing persons from other (particularly Asian) countries of origin. Second, incomparable samples lead to sample bias. For instance, nationality populations can differ in educational background and income. Many U.S. instruments have been normed on European American middle-class people with at least an 8th grade English reading ability (Roysircar-Sodowsky & Kuo, 2001). Differences between this normative group and impoverished Spanish-speaking Latino immigrants with little to no education can confound real population differences on an assessed construct such as anxiety. Third, instrument bias involves stimulus familiarity. In many non-Western nationalities, displays of pictures or photographs or the drawing of human pictures is not common (Roysircar et al., 2017). European Americans who are familiar with such stimuli may obtain higher scores in the positive direction, for example, on global indices of adjustment on Figure Drawing tests, than those who have not had such exposure. Fourth, there is test administration bias. When test administrators and test takers have different first languages and cultural backgrounds, communication problems will occur when giving verbal tests or verbal instructions (Roysircar et al., 2017). Fifth, the assessment psychologist who uses a translated version of the test should use the appropriate translation. For example, there are different Spanish translations of the MMPI-2 for Mexico and Central America, for Spain and South America, and for the U.S. (University of Minnesota Press, Test Division, 2017), which are not interchangeable.

We also draw attention to the fact that responses to test items may arise from markedly different contexts. For example, people of different nationalities with similar experiences of trauma (disaster trauma, war, governmental neglect, persecution) may endorse trauma-related test items similarly but from different viewpoints. For instance, when the first author assesses the safety and security of girls in an international disaster setting such as Port-au-Prince, Haiti, a village in Southern India, a Nigerian city, or in the city of New Orleans, she asks the question, "Are you afraid when you walk alone on a road at night? What makes you afraid?" She gets different answers depending on the safety of the girls' neighborhoods even though the girls' scores are similar on a translated child trauma scale. Thus, while the score is the same, the meaning behind answered items is different. In summary, instrument properties (e.g., norms) can produce bias, but so can test-takers' characteristics and their contexts, and the way an instrument is administered.

Assessment of different nationality populations may entail more time and use of more tests than occurs in conventional testing procedures (Roysircar, Usher, & Geisinger, 2018). Test instructions might be longer, more examples might be included, and additional instruments might be required. Consultation with psychologists knowledgeable about the given nationality or culture might be necessary. The benefits of expanded assessment for clients have to do with the increase in the level of service delivery and the higher validity of interpretations based on test scores (Roysircar et al., 2017). Race relations in the locality of a clinic may improve. Claims can be validly made by the clinic that their psychologists are competent with the cultural heterogeneity of different nationalities. On the other hand, if existing assessment procedures are poor, the costs could include underutilization of services by specific nationality populations, additional training for test administrators, larger work load for supervisors, and a lack of evidence-based practice leading to decisions that need to be defended in court. There could be negative effect on a local community's race relations.

One Immigrant Nationality Group: The Case of Asian Indians

Asian immigrants are often categorized as one large ethnic and cultural group. There are values and beliefs that are common to most Asian cultures; these include "collectivism, conformity to norms, deference to authority, emotional self-control, family recognition through achievement, filial piety, humility, hierarchical relationships, and avoidance of shame" (Iwamoto & Liu, 2010, p. 82). However, Asian immigrants are comprised of individuals "from over 20 different nations, many distinct ethnicities, and (who) belong to at least two races" (Nandan, 2005, p. 176).

Within this vast group, Asian Indians are considered the third largest Asian nationality population residing in the United States. Within the Asian Indian nationality group, there is further heterogeneity in language usage, socioeconomic status (SES), education levels, dietary preferences and restrictions, religions, and celebration of festivals. Asian Indian immigrants from a working-class background and without a college education have been generally found to have fewer skills, less fluency in English, and lower SES than those who come to the United States as professionals. More importantly, nonprofessional immigrants appear to have more difficulty in adapting to the American culture (Nandan, 2005). Relatedly, among newly immigrated Asian Indian adults, 17.7% of those who were unemployed and underemployed were found to have depression, but suitably employed Asian Indians were 90.9% less likely to have symptoms of depression (Leung, Cheung, & Tsui, 2011).

Dasgupta (1998) noted that the professional Asian Indian population in the U.S. has been "able to carve a niche for itself as a technical and financial force" (p. 954). However successful they might be within American culture, many *first-generation* Asian Indians still prefer to socialize with members of their own nationality group and maintain regular contact with their homeland and relatives living there (Dasgupta, 1998). Asian Indian immigrants have invested much effort into keeping their culture alive in a foreign land. Nandan (2005) notes these immigrants appear to have only adapted to American culture in the physical dimension (e.g., clothing, transportation, housing, employment, professional behaviors) and not in implicit values.

Asian Indian immigrants vary in their levels of adaptation due to a range of possible factors. These factors include their reasons for migrating to the United States, the time and age of migration, the area where they settled in the U.S. (urban versus small town, Northeast versus the West Coast, the Midwest, or the Southern states), and physical distance to members of the same nationality group (Nandan, 2005). The children of Asian Indian immigrants who were either born in the United States or arrived at a young age, the *second generation*, may have more difficulty balancing both cultures compared with the *first generation*, who adapt physically to the U.S. culture and retain an implicit Indian culture, not being confused between the two. A cultural conflict can arise in second-generation children due to the strong differences between both cultures. The greater psychological difficulties of assimilated second-generation children of immigrants relative to their parents' effective functioning and outcomes has been called the "immigrant paradox." This phenomenon is explained in sections that follow.

Indian immigrant parents may experience various concerns for their children, such as the "fear of losing children to the U.S. culture, loss of parental authority over children, and loss of face within the Indian community due to children's violation of Indian cultural norms" (Varghese & Jenkins, 2009, p. 238). Furthermore, studies of second-generation adolescent and adult immigrants have found evidence of family conflicts resulting from clashes over parental control, poor communication, high expectations, and particularly marriage and dating. However, Thomas and Choi (2006) note that social support activities reduce the level of acculturative stress, with parental support being the most important predictive factor in determining the level of acculturative stress (see Kaling (2011) about types of parental support). Cultural and organizational activities are other important sources of social support for Indian youth that can moderate their level of acculturative stress (Thomas & Choi, 2006). Thus, the influence of the family environment and community are vital to the adjustment of second-generation Asian Indian youth.

Diaspora of Asian Indian Immigrant Youth

It is often assumed that the children of immigrants experience fewer daily obstacles because they are socialized and educated in the host culture. As a result, they are expected to be less vulnerable to psychological difficulties than their parents (Abouguendia & Noels, 2001). This might be true for individuals whose families are fairly well-acculturated into the dominant society and are of higher social class (cf. Kaling, 2011, 2016). However, second-generation youth can face particular challenges. A conflict in values between the child and family and the social environment, or both, can become problematic. Two primary sources of stress that the youth can experience include (1) the pressure from peers to assimilate to the host culture by rejecting their native culture and values and (2) the pressure from parents and other adults in their nationality community to follow their heritage culture's norms and traditions (Thomas & Choi, 2006).

Second-generation youth tend to experience the greatest struggles with reconciling the differences they perceive between the dominant culture and their family's cultural values compared with first- and third-generation youth (Willgerodt &

Thompson, 2006). Specifically, among Asian Indians there is an emphasis on the responsibilities and obligations family members have toward one another. Children from these families tend to feel a sense of duty to excel academically, obtain respectable and highly paid jobs, and take care of their parents financially and physically when the parents can no longer take care of themselves (Farver et al., 2007; Fuligni, 1998). However, the feeling of filial obligation does not necessarily translate to the behaviors these youth may hope to achieve.

Acculturative Family Distancing

As stated earlier, children of Asian Indian immigrants tend to acculturate faster than their parents (Roysircar, Carey, & Koroma, 2010). An "acculturation gap" is the discrepancy in the acculturation adaptation of immigrant parents and that of their children. Because they are immersed in the school environment, young children are prone to being influenced by the values of their school system. Furthermore, children are influenced by their school peers. Peer influence only increases with age as children move through adolescence. Acculturative family distancing (AFD; Hwang, 2006) is defined as "the problematic distancing that occurs between immigrant parents and children that is a consequence of ... cultural changes that become more salient over time" (p. 398). AFD consists of (a) a breakdown in communication and (b) incongruent cultural values that increase the risk for individual child psychopathology and family dysfunction.

Hwang (2006) notes that Asian American youth's communication problems can be either verbal or nonverbal. Verbally, the loss of a common language (i.e., native language vs. English) leads to a greater chance for misunderstandings and decreased family cohesion. Nonverbal communication styles include proxemics (the use and perception of interpersonal space), kinesics (bodily movements and facial expressions), paralanguage (vocal cues such as pauses, silences, and inflections), and high- and low-context communication (the degree to which explicit language is used vs. implied). Cultures differ in their emphasis on high-context communication (implied through nonverbal means, as in some Asian cultures) and low-context communications (more direct and explicit, as in the U.S. culture).

Parents and children can make interpretive errors regarding the meaning of different communication styles. For example, a mother might view her child's expression of feelings as disrespectful, while a child might view his or her mother's refusal to negotiate as unfair and uncaring. This may find expression in personality test profiles, such as a high score on the Family Problems scale of the Minnesota Multiphasic Personality Inventory-Adolescent (MMPI-A; Butcher et al., 1992), or as behavioral problems in a parent-reported personality measure such as the Personality Inventory for Children, second edition (PIC-2; Lachar & Gruber, 2001). Cumulative experiences of miscommunication result in a rupture in family cohesion as well as individual and family dysfunction (Hwang, 2006). As parents and children acculturate differently, incongruent value systems can arise. The degree to which value discrepancies exist depends on various factors, such as country of origin, age of immigration, nationality density of one's community, and persistence with which the family and community maintain, abandon, or change values (Hwang, 2006).

Developmental Clinical Presentations

The challenges that second-generation youth face may first become evident during the adolescent developmental period. In American culture, adolescence is a period where one attempts to establish one's own identity and seek autonomy. Adolescents desire to be accepted by their peers, and they are highly influenced by peers' attitudes, behaviors, and styles of dress. The values promoted in the U.S. culture, such as individualism and self-expression, are in stark contrast to Asian values of harmony and unity. However, Asian youth are expected to conform to American values in order to function in school and their future life endeavors.

Emotional and behavioral difficulties resulting from acculturative stress can intensify during young adulthood if they are not addressed in adolescence. Furthermore, new issues such as "dating, marriage, individualism, obedience to parents' wishes, and responsibility toward extended families" arise as important concerns within Asian communities as adulthood is approached (Dasgupta, 1998, p. 954). Atzaba-Poria, Pike, and Barrett (2004) suggest that there is increasing evidence that Asian Indian children of immigrants are at a high risk for internalized problems, such as depression and anxiety. The authors assert that these issues are "a natural expression of identity confusion, contradicting demands, and perhaps the prejudice that ethnic minority children experience" (p. 536). Internalized problems should be understood within the immigrant person's cultural context.

Asian immigrant youth's over-parenting in terms of their management of parents' controlling advice and over-involved assistance, their inadequate anticipatory personal problem-solving, and poor overall differentiation from the family are, clinically speaking, age-inappropriate (Sodowsky, 1991). Skowron (2004) found that ethnic minorities with higher levels of self-differentiation from their families were better skilled in social problem-solving and adjustment as well as in having a positive sense of cultural identity. Similarly, racial minority youth who adopted a differentiated stance managed better emotional reactivity to racist and discriminatory behaviors (Gushue et al., 2013). Thus, psychologists can help immigrant youth reduce their habituated reactive responses to racism by adopting differentiation from negative as well as positive stereotypes. Murdoch and Gore (2004) found that differentiation was related to coping with stress, with reflecting coping being related to greater differentiation of self, while suppressive and reactive coping was related to lower differentiation. Psychologists can help their Asian immigrant young adult clients to reflect on the tension and complementarity between family integrity and self-differentiation, whose dynamics can either result in logical reasoning or impact negative emotionality.

Other Negative Adjustments

While differences in parent and child acculturation adaptation is common (Hwang, 2006; Roysircar et al., 2010), it is not known empirically whether this difference leads to negative mental health in children. On the other hand, high educational and occupational achievements do not equate with positive adjustment (Sodowsky & Lai, 1997). Asian Indian youth in the United States are "confronted with situations that concern their race and skin color, language skills, ethnicity, and identity that may be confirming or disconfirming of the values of their culture of origin" (Farver et al., 2007, p. 186). Second-generation Asian Indian youth, who are born and socialized in this country, can find the acculturation process to be difficult because of the contrast between American (e.g., individualistic orientation) and Indian (e.g., collectivist orientation) cultural values. The contrast might not be as significant in future generations (i.e., third and fourth generations in the U.S.).

Tuan (1999) noted that Asian Americans who are not foreign-born can actively struggle with being defined by others as neither *real* Americans nor *real* Asians. They might be described within their immigrant nationality communities as "not Asian enough" because of their American behaviors and choices, and might be considered by non-Asians as closer to their heritage roots than their American roots (Tuan, 1999). Such labels can have an adverse effect on an individual Asian American's mental health.

The internalized symptoms of second-generation Asian Indian youth (i.e., withdrawal, somatic symptoms, anxiety, depression of Asian Indian Muslims and Muslims of other nationalities in the United States; cf. Herzig, Roysircar, Kosyluk, & Corrigan, 2013) have been found to be present in Asian Indian children in Britain as young as ages 7 through 9. For example, using the Child Behavior Checklist (CBCL; Achenbach & Rescorla, 2001) to identify internalized, externalized, and total problem behavior in children while also examining parental Indian language use and parental acculturation style, Atzaba-Poria et al. (2004) found these Indian children exhibited significantly higher levels of parent-reported internalizing behaviors when compared to their English peers.

While children might have greater cognitive resources when they reach adolescence, they can become particularly vulnerable to the opinions of their peer group at this point. New developmental experiences, such as pubertal changes and exposure to dating, substances (e.g., alcohol, cigarettes), or both can create conflicts within the teen as to how to behave. An interest in forming an individual identity can lead to conflict with parents if there is not an open and supportive relationship. Social support, namely parental but also organizational or cultural, becomes particularly important at this time. Emerging adults have significantly important decisions to make, such as career and marriage aspirations, which can be facilitated or impeded by parents (Roysircar et al., 2010; Herzig et al., 2013). The level of conflict between parent and child regarding these matters plays a crucial role in the mental health adjustment of second-generation Asian American youth.

Model Minority Myth's Negative Impact

The United States has long given Asian Americans the label of "model minority" because of the perception of this large group as non-threatening, quiet, well-behaved, hard-working, and successful. Asian Indians, in particular, are reported to have the greatest percentage of individuals who speak English "very well" (76.9%), the highest educational attainment (63.9% of Asian Indians have at least a bachelor's degree), and the highest percentage of employment in management, professional, and related occupations (59.9% according to the 2004 U.S Census Bureau) (Kumar & Nevid, 2010). While these are the current statistics, the label of "model minority" holds all Asian Americans to a high standard of character and behavior. The needs of individuals who might need support and assistance may be overlooked because of their membership in this "model minority" group (Saran, 2007). An Asian Indian adolescent girl who has internalized the model minority stereotype, or the notion that all Asian Indians are good in math and science and become doctors and computer programmers, may experience loss of self-esteem and feelings of isolation as she struggles with her academic work in math and science (Roysircar et al., 2010).

According to Qin (2008), there is a paradox in that Asian American students often report poor psychological and social adjustment despite their generally high levels of educational achievement. These students are often perceived as well adjusted because of their educational competence. This perception is reinforced by observations of a quiet demeanor, few acting out behaviors, and underutilization of mainstream psychological services. Studies with college students beginning in the 1970s have consistently shown that Asian American students reported higher levels of distress and emotional and social adjustment difficulties than White students (Qin, 2008). Some recent studies are showing similar results when levels of distress of Asian American students are compared with those of non-White students. Increased attention is being given to the psychological well-being of Asian American youth as stories increase of high-achieving, apparently well-adjusted students in these communities committing suicide (Roysircar et al., 2010; Qin, 2008).

Issues such as language barriers, the parent–child acculturation gap, and parent–child conflicts have become prevalent over time in many immigrant families. Qin (2008) noted in her longitudinal study with well-achieving Chinese immigrant adolescents that distressed youth reported discipline to be one of the most common factors leading to conflict at home. Specifically, parents were perceived by their children to be stricter and more controlling than American parents. Conflicts frequently arose around issues such as dating, appearance (mainly for girls), and spending money, particularly as children reached adolescence. Qin (2008) concluded from her study that parenting is a unique challenge in Asian immigrant families, influenced by the stressors parents are undergoing in adjusting to life in a new and different culture. Furthermore, parenting style after migration can contribute to different parent–child dynamics at home, resulting in different levels of psychological adjustment in children. Specifically, distressed adolescents had parents who were more strict and rigid in their parenting style (namely, following traditional Chinese parenting tenets). Such a style often led to high levels of parent–child conflict, poor communication, and distancing in parent–child relations. Non-distressed adolescents had parents with a more flexible and adaptive parenting modality, attending to the developmental needs of children, and the new cultural context. This approach allowed parents and children to maintain strong emotional connections after migration (Qin, 2008).

U.S. Socio-Environmental Factors of Psychological Distress

Racial and ethnic discrimination is a common stressor for immigrant youth in their adaptation to the majority culture. Racism does not exclude the second-generation immigrant youth. Increased evidence has been found linking racism with negative outcomes in Asian American college students and adults, such as lower social competence and self-esteem, and greater substance abuse, depressive symptoms, and risk for chronic illness (e.g., heart disease, respiratory illness) (Juang & Cookston, 2009).

The limited studies including Asian American adolescents have reported that these youth experienced higher levels of peer discrimination, in comparison with African American and Latino students (Juang & Cookston, 2009). These findings are concerning due to: (1) discrimination being linked to poorer adolescent adjustment, evidenced in lower self-esteem and greater depressive symptoms; (2) adolescents having fewer or less sophisticated skills in dealing with stressors than adults; and (3) reflective narratives of Asian American college students showing a lack of discussion about discrimination with parents when they were growing up (Juang & Cookston, 2009). However, despite discrimination occurring in both culturally diverse and homogeneous contexts, a culturally supportive environment may provide youth with the resources and support to develop a strong cultural identity. This belief is supported by evidence indicating that positive feelings toward one's cultural group buffers the negative effects of discrimination (Juang & Cookston, 2009).

Juang and Cookston (2009) also state the finding that second-generation Chinese American adolescents reported less perceived discrimination than first-generation adolescents (see also Roysircar et al.'s 2010 study on Asian Indian college students). However, two years later, the perceptions of the same second-generation adolescents rose to match those of the first generation. It is noted that immigrant adolescents born in the United States are often still considered to be foreigners (e.g., it is assumed that they do not speak English). Juang and Cookston (2009) describe the phenomenon of being the *perpetual foreigner* as a common source of discrimination for Asian American youth.

Symptom Presentations

While Asian Americans have been found to have rates of depression and anxiety comparable to those found among European Americans (Herzig et al., 2013), it is important to recognize that different cultural groups attribute different meanings to symptoms identified in U.S. assessment instruments. Some cultures may perceive these "symptoms" to be functional and a sign of positive social adjustment (Gee, 2004). For example, many Asian cultures socialize children to be attentive to the emotional states of others as well as to harmonious interactions. Gee (2004) notes the possibility that such socialization practices of Asian Americans increase their vulnerability to certain types of anxiety disorders, such as social anxiety.

In addition to the different perceptions among cultural groups of symptom expression, it is also important to be knowledgeable about the manifestations of psychological distress across different cultures. For example, Gee (2004) notes that the earliest symptoms of anxiety in Asian American adolescents may be somatic complaints and sleep and appetite disturbances. Mental health providers should also be aware of the existence of culture-bound syndromes, as identified in the *Diagnostic and Statistical Manual of Mental Disorders* (DSM-5; American Psychiatric Association, 2013).

Internalization

Many Asian Indian children's academic achievements may relate to their feeling responsibility to their parents for the sacrifices they made to provide them educational and economic opportunities in the United States (Fuligni, 1998). This outward success might disguise internal psychological conflict over balancing two different cultures as well as the prejudice and discrimination they may experience (Atzaba-Poria et al., 2004; Roysircar et al., 2010). Furthermore, Iwamoto and Liu (2010) noted the shared Asian values of collectivism, conformity to norms, deference to authority, emotional self-control, family recognition through achievement, filial piety, humility, and avoidance of shame. These values lend themselves to internalization (e.g., internal processing of difficulties) rather than externalization (acting out behaviors) of distress. Internalizing problems have been operationalized as three groups of behaviors indicating (a) depression and anxiety, (b) withdrawal, and (c) somatic complaints (Atzaba-Poria et al., 2004).

Depression

The prevalence rate of depression among Asian Americans is reported to at least meet that of White Americans (Lee, Lei, & Sue, 2001). Several studies have actually found that Asian Americans report higher levels of depressive symptoms than Whites (Aldwin & Greenberger, 1987, as cited by Lee et al., 2001; Okazaki, 1997). We reiterate here that applying standard assessment tools can lead to erroneous conclusions when the individual client belongs to a nationality group or groups that experience symptoms in ways different from the European American population in the U.S. For example, some populations, including Latino immigrant elders in particular but also older adults in general, are more likely to express somatic symptoms that really are indicative of depression (Liefland, Roberts, Ford, & Stevens, 2014). Depression measures that underrepresent somatic symptom expressions may, therefore, underestimate their depression.

Trait Anxiety

Similar to depression, cross-cultural studies have found Asian Americans to report higher degrees of anxiety than Caucasian Americans (Xie & Leong, 2008).

However, these studies tended to overlook ethnic heterogeneity or specific forms of anxiety. Xie and Leong (2008) further noted that trait anxiety for the Chinese is "the tendency to perceive stressful situations as dangerous or threatening, especially situations that involve being evaluated by other people or threats to one's self-esteem" (p. 54).

Somatization

As stated previously, somatic symptoms should be given particular attention as research has suggested that Asian Americans have a tendency to manifest their mental health symptoms through physical complaints (Uba, 1994). Conrad and Pacquiao (2005) note that somatization is very common in Asian cultures because of their disapproval of strong expressions of emotion, particularly negative emotions. Displays of negative emotion are believed to disrupt social and familial harmony and expose personal weakness. As such, Asians are believed to consciously or unconsciously "deny the experience and expression of emotions" (Lee et al., 2001, p. 165; see also, Kuo et al., 2006). It is also more socially acceptable to express emotional distress through the body than the mind (Lippincott & Mierzwa, 1995). Such somatic expressions of emotional difficulty have also been reported in studies of nonimmigrant Asian Indian college students in the U.S. For example, using the Minnesota Multiphasic Personality Inventory-2-Restructured Form (MMPI-2-RF; Ben-Porath & Tellegen, 2008), Taneja and Krishnamurthy (2017) reported a mean score of 65.92 (SD = 11.89) on Restructured Clinical (RC) Scale 1 (Somatic Complaints) in a sample of 48 Asian Indian students in the southeastern U.S., relative to the normative test score mean of 50 (SD = 10). They also found T scores > 60 on three of the five Somatic/Cognitive scales. RC1 scores for this sample correlated significantly with Family Problems, Anxiety, Depression, Suicidal Ideation, and Interpersonal Problems scale scores on the College Adjustment Scales (CAS; Anton & Reed, 1991).

Self-Critical Perfectionism

Self-critical perfectionism can be differentiated from adaptive perfectionism, which consists of high standards achievement motivation. Maladaptive perfectionists rigidly adhere to their standards and engage in "overly critical self-evaluations over a perceived failure to meet these standards" (Wang, Puri, Slaney, Methikalam, & Chadha, 2012, p. 34). Maladaptive perfectionists are reported to have higher levels of depression, anxiety, and interpersonal problems (Wang et al., 2012). Asian American college students have scored significantly higher than Caucasian American college students on measures of perfectionism (Castro & Rice, 2003; Chang, 1998). Furthermore, Asian Americans report extreme concerns about meeting the expectations of their parents (Castro & Rice, 2003).

A recent study by Chang and Smith (2015) examined the responses of Asian and Asian American college students (N = 41; primarily Chinese, Filipino, Vietnamese, Japanese, and Korean origins) to the Personality Assessment Inventory (Morey, 1991). The researchers hypothesized that this sample's scores, relative to those of a

European American comparison group, would reflect Asian cultural values of modesty, abasement, "saving face," and maintaining privacy, as well as features of anxiety, somatization, and affect restriction. Their results indicated higher scores on Anxiety, Anxiety-related Disorders, and Paranoia (i.e., internalizing features), alongside greater Negative Impression Management (i.e., abasement) and lower Interpersonal Warmth (i.e., greater privacy) compared to the European American comparison group. Findings such as these, and those of Taneja and Krishnamurthy (2017), provide direction for assessors using widely used personality measures in assessing Asian clients.

Identity Concerns

Several researchers have studied identity formation in American racial and ethnic minority groups (e.g., Aboud & Amato, 2001). However, the implications of racial and ethnic identity and their assessment for nationality groups, and especially those with complex intersectional identities (e.g., a gender questioning second-generation Asian Indian girl of low income status), are unclear. One of the leaders in developmental studies of ethnic identity, Phinney (1989; Phinney, Ong & Madden, 2000), influenced by Erickson's developmental theory, proposed an ethnic identity status model with four stages that reflect an individual's progress toward identity: identity diffusion (marked by a relative lack of thought about ethnic identity), identity foreclosure (marked by an uncritical acceptance of existing views about their ethnic identity), identity moratorium (marked by active exploration of one's ethnic identity), and identity achievement. The latter was viewed by Phinney (1989) as the highest level of ethnic identity. The psychologist is encouraged to recognize, however, that empirical tests of the Phinney model are relatively rare for nationality groups other than those defined by race or ethnicity (see the Appendix for nationality-specific identity measures). It is important to consider how developmental stages and cultural and political contexts inform identity and a re-definition of self within specific nationality groups. Self-definition and identity labels often contribute to individuals' relationships with others and psychological well-being (Kiang, 2008).

Guidelines for Assessment Practice

Building on our broad discussion of acculturation/acculturative stress and test selection considerations in the early part of this chapter, and extrapolating from our specific overview of Asian Indians, we offer the following guidelines for assessors:

1. Recognize that nationality has some specific impacts within the broader cultural (e.g. Asian, Hispanic) landscape, as countries differ in sociopolitical environments and national histories. For example, different life experiences can be expected for persons from democratic countries than those from communist countries or socialist republics, or for those from war zones versus those from stable political

environments. Different countries within a single continent might have different practices and laws related to various diversity variables such as issues of women and children, elders, and gay and lesbian individuals. Attention to these matters will help guard against overgeneralizations.

2. In both interview and testing components of assessment, give attention to the client's status with regard to their degree of integration into the new environment and retention of national identity, and level of stress experienced in the new living environment (including value conflicts and negative reactions from the majority group). In addition, consider whether the client is a first-, second-, or third-generation immigrant and examine the effects of immigration on the family as a whole, particularly when assessing children and adolescents. Such considerations give important contexts for interpreting test findings of psychological maladjustment accurately.

3. Use appropriate test instruments, language versions, and norms as indicated by the research literature. Supplement standard broad-band measures of personality and psychopathology with other measures as needed, such as to evaluate for cultural adjustment and coping methods, perceptions of prejudice and conflict, or alternative symptom presentations.

4. Consult additional resources (e.g., Evans & Hass, 2018; Vaisman-Tzachor, 2014) and/or undergo further training to develop competence for assessing asylum seekers and refugees.

Summary

In this chapter we have discussed assessment matters from the standpoint of nationality of origin as opposed to a broader cultural viewpoint that is more typical in the psychological literature. After reviewing acculturation issues common to both nationality and cultural background and discussing issues in test selection and use, we proceeded with an emphasis on Asian Americans, specifically focused on Asian Indians when possible. Our task was complicated by the fact that, despite a noteworthy growth in immigrants from Asian countries to the U.S. in the late 20th and 21st centuries, there has been relatively little personality assessment research on these populations. Asian Indians are particularly underrepresented in personality assessment research. From a practical perspective, assessors have relatively few empirical studies to guide them even as they seek to conduct diverse-sensitive assessments. We have attempted to bring in information from alternative literatures on developmental and psychological adjustment topics.

Our overarching emphasis is that consideration of nationality, with its attendant norms, values, social/cultural/political contexts, and personal experiences, enables competent assessment. At the level of the individual, it facilitates accuracy, sensitivity, and context-driven interpretations. At a broader level, the benefits for society of competent assessment of diverse nationalities are three-fold. First, such assessment better reflects the daily reality of an immigrant and multicultural society and the increasing internationalization of such a society. Second, a society benefits when all its members realize their potential and well-being, and competent assessment of diverse nationalities can help to reach this goal. Finally, the main benefit of culturally comprehensive assessment services for psychology as a profession is the higher level of quality of service delivery.

References

Aboud, F. E., & Amato, M. (2001). Developmental and socialization influences on intergroup biases. In R. Brown & S. L. Gaertner (Eds.). *Blackwell handbook of social psychology: Intergroup processes, Vol. 3* (pp. 65–88). Malden, MA: Blackwell.

Abouguendia, M., & Noels, K. A. (2001). General and acculturation-related daily hassles and psychological adjustment in first- and second-generation South Asian immigrants to Canada. *International Journal of Psychology, 36*(3), 163–173. doi: 10.1080/741930008

Achenbach, T. M., & Rescorla, L. A. (2001). *Manual for the ASEBA school-age forms & profiles*. Burlington, VT: University of Vermont, Research Center for Children, Youth, & Families.

Ahadi, S. A., & Puente-Diaz, R. (2011). Acculturation, personality, and psychological adjustment. *Psychological Reports, 109*, 842–862. doi: 10.2466/02.07.17.20.PRO.109.6. 842-862

American Psychiatric Association. (2013). *Diagnostic and statistical manual of mental disorders* (5th ed.). Arlington, VA: American Psychiatric Publishing.

American Psychological Association. (2017). Multicultural guidelines: An ecological approach to context, identity, and intersectionality. www.apa.org/about/policy/multicultural-guidelines.aspx.

Anton, W. D., & Reed, J. R. (1991). *College Adjustment Scales: Professional manual*. Odessa, FL: Psychological Assessment Resources.

Atzaba-Poria, N., Pike, A., & Barrett, M. (2004). Internalising and externalising problems in middle childhood: A study of Indian (ethnic minority) and English (ethnic majority) children living in Britain. *International Journal of Behavioral Development, 38*(5), 449–460. doi: 10.1080/01650250444000171

Ben-Porath, Y. S., & Tellegen, A. (2008). *Minnesota Multiphasic Personality Inventory-2-Restructured Form: Manual for administration, scoring, and interpretation*. Minneapolis: University of Minnesota Press.

Benet-Matinez, V., & Haritatos, J. (2005). Bicultural identity integration (BII): Components and psychosocial antecedents. *Journal of Personality Assessment, 73* (4), 1015–1050. doi: 10.1111/j.1467-6494.2005.00337.x

Berry, J. W. (1997). Immigration, acculturation, and adaptation. *Applied Psychology: An International Review, 46*, 5–34. doi: 10.1111/j.1464-0597.1997.tb01087.x

Berry, J. W. (2001). A psychology of immigration. *Journal of Social Issues, 57*(3), 615–631. doi: 10.1111/0022-4537.00231

Berry, J. W., Kim, U., & Boski, M. (1988). Acculturation and mental health: A review. In P. Dasen, J. W. Berry, & N. Sartorius (Eds.), *Cross-cultural psychology and health* (pp. 207–236). Newbury Park, CA: Sage.

Butcher, J. N. (1996). Translation and adaption of the MMPI-2 for international use. In J. N. Butcher (Ed.), *International adaptations of the MMPI-2*. Minneapolis: University of Minnesota Press.

Butcher, J. N., Dahlstrom, W. G., Graham, J. R., Tellegen, A., & Kaemmer, B. (1989). *Minnesota Multiphasic Personality Inventory-2 (MMPI-2): Manual for administration and scoring.* Minneapolis: University of Minnesota Press.

Butcher, J. N., Williams, C. L., Graham, J. R., Archer, R. P., Tellegen, A., Ben-Porath, Y. S., & Kaemmer, B. (1992). *MMPI-A (Minnesota Multiphasic Personality Inventory-Adolescent): Manual for administration, scoring, and interpretation.* Minneapolis: University of Minnesota Press.

Castro, J. R., & Rice, K. G. (2003). Perfectionism and ethnicity: Implications for depressive symptoms and self-reported academic achievement. *Cultural Diversity and Ethnic Minority Psychology, 9*(1), 64–78. doi: 10.1037/1099-9809.9.1.64

Chang, E. C. (1998). Cultural differences, perfectionism, and suicidal risk in a college population: Does social problem solving still matter? *Cognitive Therapy and Research, 22*(3), 237–254. doi: 10.1023/A:1018792709351

Chang, J., & Smith, S. R. (2015). An exploration of how Asian Americans respond to the Personality Assessment Inventory. *Asian American Journal of Psychology, 6*, 25–30. doi: 10.1037/a0036173

Choi, H., & Dancy, B. L. (2009). Korean American adolescents' and their parents' perceptions of acculturative stress. *Journal of Child and Adolescent Psychiatric Nursing, 22*(4), 203–210. doi: 10.1111/j.1744-6171.2009.00200.x

Conrad, M. M., & Pacquiao, D. F. (2005). Manifestation, attribution, and coping with depression among Asian Indians from the perspectives of health care practitioners. *Journal of Transcultural Nursing, 16*(1), 32–40. doi: 10.1177/1043659604271239

Dasgupta, S. D. (1998). Gender roles and cultural continuity in the Asian Indian immigrant community in the U.S. *Sex Roles, 38*(11/12), 953–974. doi: 10.1023/A:1018822525427

David, E. J. R., & Okazaki, S. (2006). The Colonial Mentality Scale (CMS) for Filipino Americans: Scale construction and psychological implications. Journal of Counseling Psychology, 53(2), 241–252. http://dx.doi.org/10.1037/0022-0167.53.2.241

del Prado, A. M., & Church, A. T. (2010). Development and validation of the Enculturation Scale for Filipino Americans. Journal of Counseling Psychology, 57(4), 469–483. http://dx.doi.org/10.1037/a0020940

Evans, B., & Hass, G. A. (2018). *Guide to forensic evaluations for immigration court: Ethical and evidence-based practice.* New York: Routledge.

Fang, K., Friedlander, M., & Pieterse, A. L. (2016). Contributions of acculturation, enculturation, discrimination, and personality traits to social anxiety among Chinese immigrants: A context-specific assessment. *Cultural Diversity and Ethnic Minority Psychology, 22*, 58–68. doi: 10.1037/cdp0000030

Farver, J. M., Bhadha, B. R., & Narang, S. K. (2002). Acculturation and psychological functioning in Asian Indian adolescents. *Social Development, 11*(1), 11–29. doi: 10.1111/1467-9507.00184

Farver, J. M., Xu, Y., Bhadha, B. R., Narang, S., & Lieber, E. (2007). Ethnic identity, acculturation, parenting beliefs, and adolescent adjustment. *Merrill-Palmer Quarterly, 53*(2), 184–215. doi: 10.1353.mpq.2007.0010

Frey, M., & Roysircar, G. (2006). South and East Asian international students' perceived prejudice, acculturation, and frequency of help resource utilization. *Journal of Multicultural Counseling and Development, 34*, 208–222. doi: 10.1002/j.2161-1912.2006.tb00040.x

Fuligni, A. J. (1998). The adjustment of children from immigrant families. *Current Directions in Psychological Science, 7*(4), 99–103. Retrieved from http://www.jstor.org/stable/20182516

Gee, C. B. (2004). Assessment of anxiety and depression in Asian American youth. *Journal of Clinical Child and Adolescent Psychology, 32*(2), 269–271. doi: 10.1207/s15374424 jccp3302_7

Green, D. E., Walkey, F. H., McCormick, I. A., & Taylor, A. J. W. (1988). Development and evaluation of the Hopkins Symptom Checklist with New Zealand and United States respondents. *Australian Journal of Psychology, 40*, 61–70. doi: 10.1080/00049538808259070

Gushue, G. V., Mejia-Smith, B. X., Fisher, A. C., Gonzalez-Mathews, M., Lee, Y.-J., Mancusi, L., . . . Johnson, V. (2013). Differentiation of self and racial identity. *Counselling Psychology Quarterly, 26*, 343–361. doi: 10.1080/09515070.2013.816839

Hendriks, A. A. J., Perugini, M., Angleitner, A., Ostenbdorf, F., Johnson, J. A., de Fruyt, F., . . . Ruisel, I. (2003). The Five-Factor Personality Inventory: Cross-cultural generalizability across 13 countries. *European Journal of Personality, 17*, 347–373. doi: 10.1002/per.491

Herzig, B. A., Roysircar, G., Kosyluk, K. A., & Corrigan, P. W. (2013). American Muslim college students: The impact of religiousness and stigma on active coping. *Journal of Muslim Mental Health, 7*(1), 33–42. doi: 10.3998/jmmh.10381607.0007.103

Huynh, U., & Roysircar, G. (2006). Community health promotion curriculum: A case study of Vietnamese and Cambodian refugees. In R. Toporek, L. H. Gerstein, N. A. Fouad, G. Roysircar, & T. Israel (Eds.), *Handbook for social justice in counseling psychology* (pp. 338–357). Thousand Oaks, CA: SAGE.

Hwang, W. (2006). Acculturative family distancing: Theory, research, and clinical practice. *Psychotherapy: Theory, Research, Practice, Training, 43*(4), 397–409. doi: 10.1037/0033-3204.43.4397

Hwang, W., & Wood, J. J. (2009). Acculturative family distancing: Links with self-reported symptomatology among Asian Americans and Latinos. *Child Psychiatry and Human Development, 40*, 123–138. doi: 10.1007/s10578-008-0115-8

Institute of International Education. (2017). *Open doors 2016 "fast facts": International students in the U.S.* Retrieved from www.iie.org/Research-and-Insights/Open-Doors/Data

Iwamoto, D. K., & Liu, W. M. (2010). The impact of racial identity, ethnic identity, Asian values and race-related stress on Asian Americans' well-being. *Journal of Counseling Psychology, 57*, 79–91. doi: 10.1037/a0017393

Janssen, R. (2011). Using a differential item functioning approach to investigate measurement invariance. In E. Davidov, P. Schmidt, & J. Billiet (Eds.), *Cross-cultural analysis: Methods and applications* (pp. 415–432). New York: Routledge.

Juang, L. P., & Cookston, J. T. (2009). A longitudinal study of family obligation and depressive symptoms among Chinese American adolescents. *Journal of Family Psychology, 23*(3), 369–404. doi: 10.1037/a0015814

Kaling, M. (2011). *Is everyone hanging out without me? (and other concerns).* New York: Crown Publishing.

Kaling, M. (2016). *Why not me?* New York: Three Rivers Press.

Kiang, L. (2008). Ethnic self-labeling in young American adults from Chinese backgrounds. *Journal of Youth and Adolescence, 37*, 97–111. doi: 10.1007/s10964-007-9219-x

Kim, G., DeCoster, J., Huang, C. H., & Chiriboga, D. A. (2011). Race/ethnicity and the factor structure of the Center for Epidemiologic Studies Depression Scale: A meta-analysis. Cultural Diversity and Ethnic Minority Psychology, 7, 381–396. doi: 10.1037/a0025434.

Kim, M. T. (2002). Measuring depression in Korean Americans: Development of the Kim Depression Scale for Korean Americans. *Journal of Transcultural Nursing, 13*(2), 109–117. doi: 10.1177/104365960201300203

Kim, S. Y., Chen, Q., Li, J., Huang, X., & Moon, U. J. (2009). Parent-child acculturation, parenting, and adolescent depressive symptoms in Chinese immigrant families. *Journal of Family Psychology, 23*(3), 426–437. doi: 10.1037/a0016019

Krogstad, J. M., Passel, J. S., & Cohn, D. (April 27, 2017). 5 facts about illegal immigration in the U.S. *Fact tank: News in the Numbers, Pew Research Center*. Retrieved from www.pewresearch.org/fact-tank/2017/04/27/5-facts-about-illegal-immigration-in-the-u-s/

Kumar, A., & Nevid, J. S. (2010). Acculturation, enculturation, and perceptions of mental disorders in Asian Indian immigrants. *Cultural Diversity and Ethnic Minority Psychology, 16*(2), 274–283. doi: 10.1037/a0017563

Kuo, B. C. H., Roysircar, G., & Newby-Clark, I. R. (2006). Development of the Cross-cultural Coping Scale: Collective, avoidance, and engagement coping. *Measurement and Evaluation in Counseling and Development, 39*,161–181. Retrieved from http://scholar.uwindsor.ca/psychologypub/21

Kwan, K. L., & Sodowsky, G. R. (1997). Internal and external ethnic identity and their correlates: A study of Chinese American immigrants. *Journal of Multicultural Counseling and Development, 25*, 52–68. doi: 10.1002/j.2161-1912.1997.tb00315.x

Lachar, D., & Gruber, C. P. (2001). *Personality Inventory for Children, second edition (PIC-2) manual*. Los Angeles, CA: Western Psychological Services.

LaFromboise, T., Coleman, H. L. K., & Gerton, J. (1993). Psychological impact of biculturalism: Evidence and theory. *Psychological Bulletin, 114*, 395–412. doi: 10.1037/0033-2909.114.3.395

Lee, J., Lei, A., & Sue, S. (2001). The current state of mental health research on Asian Americans. In N. Choi (Ed.), *Psychosocial aspects of the Asian-American experience* (pp. 159–178). New York: The Haworth Press.

Lee, R. M., Choe, J., Kim, G., & Ngo, V. (2000). Construction of the Asian American Family Conflicts Scale. *Journal of Counseling Psychology, 47*(2), 211–222. http://dx.doi.org/10.1037/0022-0167.47.2.211

Leung, P., Cheung, M., & Tsui, V. (2011). Asian Indians and depressive symptoms: Reframing mental health help-seeking behavior. *International Social Work, 55*(1), 53–70. doi: 10.1177/0020872811407940

Liefland, L., Roberts, D. L., Ford, R., & Stevens, B. J. (2014). Depressive symptoms among help-seeking Latinas in a disadvantaged, urban, Northeastern community mental health center. *Community Mental Health Journal, 50*, 331–335. doi: 10.1007/s10597-013-9655-x

Lippincott, J.A., & Mierzwa, J. A. (1995). Propensity for seeking counseling services: A comparison of Asian and American undergraduates. *Journal of American College Health, 43*, 201–204.

McCrae, R. R., Costa, P. T. Jr., Del Pilar, G. H., Rolland, J.-P., & Parker, W. D. (1998). Cross-cultural assessment of the five-factor model: The Revised NEO Personality Inventory. *Journal of Cross-Cultural Psychology, 29*, 171–188. doi: 10.1177/0022022198291009

Mollica, R. F., Caspi-Yavin, Y. (1991). Measuring torture and torture-related symptoms. *Psychological Assessment: A Journal of Consulting and Clinical Psychology, 3*(4): 581–587. http://dx.doi.org/10.1037/1040-3590.3.4.581

Mollica, R. F., Reczycki, M., & Lavelle, J. (2000). Health Promotion Confidence Form. *Statewide network of local care to survivors of torture funded by the federal Office of Refugee Resettlement*. Cambridge, MA: Massachusetts General Hospital.

Morey, L. C. (1991). *Personality Assessment Inventory*. Lutz, FL: Psychological Assessment Resources.

Murdoch, N. L., & Gore, P. A. (2004). Stress, coping, and differentiation: A test of Bowen's theory. *Contemporary Family Therapy, 26*(3), 319–335. https://doi.org/10.1023/B:COFT.0000037918.53929.18

Nandan, M. (2005). Adaptation to American culture: Voices of Asian Indian immigrants. *Journal of Gerontological Social Work, 44*(3/4), 175–202. doi: 10.1300/J083v44n03_11

Office of Minority Health. (2013). *National standards for culturally and linguistically appropriate services (CLAS) in health and health care*. U.S. Department of Health and Human Services Office of Minority Health. Retrieved from www.thinkculturalhealth.hhs.gov/pdfs/EnhancedNationalCLASStandards.pdf

Okazaki, S. (1997). Sources of ethnic differences between Asian American and White American college students on measures of depression and social anxiety. *Journal of Abnormal Psychology, 106*(1), 52–60. doi: 10.1037/0021-843X.106.1.52

Phinney, J. S. (1989). Stages of ethnic identity in minority group adolescents. *Journal of Early Adolescence, 9*, 34–49. doi: 10.1177/0272431689091004

Phinney, J. S., Ong, A., & Madden, T. (2000). Cultural values and intergenerational value discrepancies in immigrant and non-immigrant families. *Child Development, 71*(2), 528–539. doi: 10.1111/1467-8624.00162

Qin, D. B. (2008). Doing well vs. feeling well: Understanding family dynamics and the psychological adjustment of Chinese immigrant adolescents. *Journal of Youth and Adolescence, 37*, 22–35. doi: 10.1007/s10964-007-9220-4

Radloff, L. S. (1977). The CES-D Scale: A self-report depression scale for research in the general population. *Applied Psychological Measurement, 1*(3), 385–401. doi: 10.1177/014662167700100306

Roysircar, G. (2005). Culturally sensitive assessment, diagnosis, and guidelines. In M. G. Constantine & D. W. Sue (Eds.), *Strategies for building multicultural competence in mental health and educational settings* (pp. 19–38). Hoboken, NJ: John Wiley & Sons.

Roysircar, G. (2013). Multicultural assessment: Individual and contextual dynamic sizing. In F. T. L. Leong & J. Trimble (Eds.), *APA handbook of multicultural psychology. Vol. 1. Theory & Research* (pp. 141–160). Washington, DC: APA.

Roysircar, G., Carey, J., & Koroma, S. (2010). Asian Indian college students' science and math preferences: Influences of cultural contexts. *Journal of Career Development, 36*(4), 324–347. doi: 10.1177/0894845309345671

Roysircar, G., Colvin, K. F., Afolayan, A. G., Thompson, A., & Robertson, T. W. (2017). Haitian children's resilience and vulnerability assessed with House-Tree-Person (HTP) drawings. *Traumatology, 23*(1), 68–81. htpp://dx.doi.org/10.1037//trm0000090

Roysircar, G., & Pignatiello, V. (2011). A multicultural-ecological tool: Conceptualization and practice with an Indian immigrant woman. *Journal of Multicultural Counseling and Development, 39*(3), 167–179. doi: 10.1002/j.2161-1912.2011.tb00149.x

Roysircar, G., Usher, B.-J., & Geisinger, K. (2018, submitted). Multidimensional scaling of projective and objective assessment with children in Haiti. *Psychological Assessment*.

Roysircar-Sodowsky, G., & Kuo, P. Y. (2001). Determining cultural validity of personality assessment: Some guidelines. D. Pope-Davis & H. Coleman (Eds.), *The intersection of race, class, & gender: Implications for multicultural counseling* (pp. 213–239). Thousand Oaks, CA: SAGE.

Roysircar-Sodowsky, G., & Maestas, M. (2000). Acculturation, ethnic identity, and acculturative stress: Evidence and measurement. In R. H. Dana (Ed.), *Handbook of cross-cultural and multicultural personality assessment* (pp. 131–172). Mahwah, NJ: Lawrence Erlbaum.

Ryder, A. G., Alden, L. E., & Paulhus, D. L. (2000). Is acculturation unidimensional or bidimensional? A head-to-head comparison in the prediction of personality, self-identity, and adjustment. *Journal of Personality and Social Psychology, 79*, 49–65. doi: 10.1037//0022-3514.79.1.49

Saran, R. (2007). Model minority imaging in New York: The situation with second generation Asian Indian learners in middle and secondary schools. *Anthropologist (Special Issue), 2*, 67–79. Retrieved from www.krepublishers.com/06-Special%20Volume-Journal/T-Anth-00-Special%20Volumes/Anth-SI-02-Indian%20Diaspora-Web/T-Anth-SI-02-06-067-079-Saran-R/T-Anth-SI-02-06-067-079-Saran-R-Tt.pdf

Singelis, T. M. (1994). The measurement of independent and interdependent self-construals. *Personality and Social Psychology Bulletin, 20*(5), 580–591. http://dx.doi.org/10.1177/0146167294205014

Skowron, E. A. (2004). Differentiation of self, personal adjustment, problem-solving, and ethnic group belonging among people of color. *Journal of Counseling and Development, 82*(4), 447–456. doi: 10.1002/j.1556-6678.2004.tb00333.x

Slaney, R. B., Rice, K. G., Mobley, M., Trippi, J., & Ashby, J. S. (2001). The Revised Almost Perfect Scale. *Measurement and Evaluation in Counseling and Development, 34*, 130–145. Retrieved from http://proquest.com

Sodowsky, G. R. (1991). Effects of culturally consistent counseling tasks on American and international student observers' perception of counselor credibility: A preliminary investigation. *Journal of Counseling and Development, 69*, 253–256. http://dx.doi.org/10.1002/j.1556-6676.1991.tb01498.x

Sodowsky, G. R., & Impara, J. C. (Eds.). (1996). *Multicultural assessment in counseling and clinical psychology*. Lincoln, NE: Buros Institute of Mental Measurements, University of Nebraska.

Sodowsky, G. R., Kuo-Jackson, Y. P., & Loya, G. J. (1996). Outcome of training in the philosophy of assessment: Multicultural counseling competencies. In D. Pope-Davis & H. Coleman (Eds.), *Multicultural counseling competencies: Assessment, education and training, and supervision*. Thousand Oaks, CA: SAGE.

Sodowsky, G. R., & Lai, E. W. M. (1997). Asian immigrant variables and structural models of cross-cultural distress. In A. Booth, A. C. Crouter, & N. Landale (Eds.), *Immigration and the family: Research and policy on U.S. immigrants* (pp. 211–237). Mahwah, NJ: Lawrence Erlbaum.

Sodowsky, G. R., Lai, E. W. M., & Plake, B. (1991). Moderating effects of sociocultural variables on acculturation attitudes of Hispanics and Asian Americans. *Journal of Counseling and Development, 70*, 194–204. doi: 10.1002/j.1556-6676.1991.tb01583.x

Sodowsky, G. R., & Plake, B. (1991). Psychometric properties of the American-International Relations Scale. *Educational and Psychological Measurement, 51*, 207–216. doi: 10.1177/001314491511020

Taneja, S., & Krishnamurthy, R. (2017, March). External test correlates of MMPI-2-RF scores for Asian Indian college students. In K. Bolinskey (chair), *MMPI assessment*. Paper presented at the annual convention of the Society for Personality Assessment, San Francisco, CA.

Thomas, M., & Choi, J. B. (2006). Acculturative stress and social support among Korean and Indian immigrant adolescents in the United States. *Journal of Sociology and Social Welfare, 33*(2), 123–143.

Tsai, D. C., & Pike, P. L. (2000). Effects of acculturation on the MMPI-2 scores of Asian American students. *Journal of Personality Assessment, 74*, 216–230. doi: 10.1207/S15327752JPA7402_4

Tuan, M. (1999). Neither real Americans nor real Asians? Multigenerational Asian ethnics navigating the terrain of authenticity. *Qualitative Sociology, 22*(2), 105–125. doi: 10.1023/A:1022020023990

Uba, L. (1994). *Asian Americans: Personality patterns, identity, and mental health.* New York: Guilford Press.

United States Department of Homeland Security. (December, 2016). Yearbook of immigration statistics: 2015. Washington, DC: U.S. Department of Homeland Security, Office of Immigration Statistics. Retrieved from www.dhs.gov/immigration-statistics/yearbook/2015

University of Minnesota Press, Test Division. (2017, August 25). Available translations. Retrieved from www.upress.umn.edu/test-division/translations-permissions/available-translations

Vaisman-Tzachor, R. (2014). Psychological assessment protocol for asylum applications in federal immigration courts. *Annals of Psychotherapy & Integrative Health,* 34–39.

Varghese, A., & Jenkins, S. R. (2009). Parental overprotection, cultural value conflict, and psychological adaptation among Asian Indian women in America. *Sex Roles, 61,* 235–251. doi: 10.1007/s11199-009-9620-x

Wang, K. T. (2010). The Family Almost Perfect Scale: Development, psychometric properties, and comparing Asian and European Americans. *Asian American Journal of Psychology, 1*(3), 186–199. http://dx.doi.org/10.1037/a0020732

Wang, K. T., Puri, R., Slaney, R. B., Methikalam, B., & Chadha, N. (2012). Cultural validity of perfectionism among Indian students: Examining personal and family aspects through a collectivistic perspective. *Measurement and Evaluation in Counseling and Development, 45,* 32–48. doi: 10.1177/0748175611423109

Willgerodt, M. A., & Thompson, E. A. (2006). Ethnic and generational influences on emotional distress and risk behaviors among Chinese and Filipino American adolescents. *Research in Nursing and Health, 29,* 311–324. doi: 10.1002/nur.20146

Xie, D., & Leong, F. T. L. (2008). A cross-cultural study of anxiety among Chinese and Caucasian American university students. *Journal of Multicultural Counseling and Development, 36*(1), 52–63. doi: 10.1002/j.2161-1912.2008.tb00069.x

Appendix: Suggested Measures for Assessing Cultural Indicators

Acculturation-Related Measures

Vancouver Index of Acculturation (VIA: Ryder, Alden, & Paulhus, 2000). The VIA is a 20-item measure of bidirectional acculturation that assesses orientation toward mainstream culture as well as heritage culture. Major dimensions include values, social relationships, and adherence to tradition. Items are rated according to degree of agreement on a Likert-type scale ranging between 1 and 9. The VIA evidenced congruent validity with the Suinn-Lew Asian Self-Identity Acculturation Scale, which is a unidimensional measure of acculturation.

Perceived Prejudice Subscale of American-International Relations Scale (AIRS: Sodowsky & Plake, 1991). The AIRS is a multidimensional instrument designed to measure international individuals' perception of their relationship with White Americans, as well as their acculturation to the dominant culture, including the English language. Primarily used with first- and second-generation Asian Indians as well as other immigrant and sojourner groups, the AIRS has evidenced strong concurrent and predictive validity with other related measures. Within the Perceived Prejudice subscale, items include experiences of stereotypes, discrimination, and isolation derived through factor and confirmatory factor analyses with the AIRS. Items are rated on a 6-point Likert-type scale.

The Enculturation Scale for Filipino Americans (ESFA: Del Prado & Church, 2010). The ESFA is a 73-item scale that assesses the degree to which individuals, specifically Filipino Americans, adhere to their heritage culture in three key areas: connection with homeland, interpersonal norms, and social conservatism. A shortened, 30-item form was also developed. Items are rated on a 6-point Likert-type scale. The EFSA evidenced construct validity with items obtained through factor analysis.

Colonial Mentality Scale (CMS: David &Okazaki, 2006). The CMS is a 36-item scale which assesses in Filipino Americans the presence of a form of internalized oppression stemming from a perception of cultural and national inferiority as a consequence of centuries of European colonization. This measure was developed through exploratory factor analysis. Items are rated on a 6-point Likert scale. Concurrent and discriminant validity have been evidenced. Negative correlations between CM and Collective Self-Esteem evidenced that as CM increases, positive perceptions of one's own culture decreases.

Acculturative Family Distancing Youth Report (AFD-YR: Hwang, 2006). The AFD-YR is a 46-item measure consisting of two subscales, Communication Difficulties (CD) and Incongruent Cultural Values (ICV). Items are rated on a 7-point Likert-type scale. The measure evidenced parent–child agreements and, thus, consistency between parent and child forms. Hwang and Wood (2009) used structural equation modeling to measure the effects of AFD on Asian and Latino American college students, finding a 14% prevalence of depression. The AFD was also found to be related to higher rates of psychological distress.

Asian American Family Conflict Scale (FCS: Lee, Choe, Kim, & Ngo, 2000). The FCS is comprised of two 10-item subscales, FCS-Likelihood and FCS-Seriousness, and was developed through confirmatory factor analysis. The Likelihood subscale measures the potential for familial conflict, and the Seriousness subscale measures the conflict's degree of severity. Both scales' items are rated on a 5-point Likert-type scale. Convergent and divergent validity was evidenced through correlations with the Social, Attitudinal, Familial, and Environmental Acculturation Stress Scale.

Cultural Adjustment Difficulties Checklist (CADC: Sodowsky & Lai, 1997). The CADC is a 48-item measure of acculturative stress among immigrants in the United States, including from India, China, Taiwan, and Hong Kong. This checklist specifically assesses intercultural conflict in three major areas: interpersonal problems, alienation from heritage culture, and self-efficacy and performance within the dominant cultural context. This measure includes two subscales: Acculturative Distress and Intercultural Competence Concerns, with the two subscales negatively correlating with each other. Items are rated on a 6-point Likert-type scale. Regarding discriminant and convergent validity, structural equation modeling evidenced Acculturative Distress correlated with general and cultural stress, and negatively with self-esteem and sense of belonging to an identity group.

Riverside Acculturation Stress Inventory (RASI: Benet-Matinez & Haritatos, 2005). The RASI is a 15-item questionnaire that reflects the interpersonal, intellectual, professional, and structural pressures associated with acculturative stress. It consists of five subscales: language skills, work challenges, intercultural relations, discrimination, and cultural/ethnic composition of relationships. Items are rated on a 5-point Likert scale. Reliability and validity have been evidenced with the Asian American population.

The Cross-Cultural Coping Scale (CCCS: Kuo, Roysircar, & Newby-Clark, 2006). The CCCS is a scenario-based instrument and includes three subscales: Collective, Avoidance, and Engagement Coping. Test-takers are presented with stress-triggering scenarios and assessed for coping strategies through a 20-item questionnaire. These items are rated on a 6-point Likert-type scale. This CCCS was developed through exploratory and confirmatory factor analyses. The criterion-related validity with other measures was predicted by the CCCS scores of Chinese Canadian adolescents, Chinese Canadian college students, as well as international students at a Midwestern university in the United States. The CCCS subscales' correlations with the Self-Construal Scale's (SCS: Singelis, 1994) independent and interdependent self-construal subscales indicated convergent, divergent, and discriminant validity.

Measures of Internalization

Center for Epidemiological Studies-Depression Scale (CES-D: Radloff, 1977). The CES-D is a 20-item measure of depressive symptoms that has been successfully used with Asian American college students. The CES-D has shown internal consistency and reliability across diverse populations, with consistent test-retest reliability. The CES-D differentiates between clinical and non-clinical populations with consistency, and shows concurrent validity with other measures of depression. The CES-D has also demonstrated predictive validity, evidenced by correlations between items and total scores for self-esteem and trait anxiety. Items are rated using a 4-point Likert-type scale.

Kim and colleagues (2009, 2011) found differential item functioning in 80% of items from the CES-D scale when comparing Mexican American and European American elderly participants, but that only 10% of items displayed differential responses when Blacks and European Americans were compared. While the significance of differential item responses is ambiguous, the differences raise the possibility that instrument scores might not reflect underlying problems across different groups (Janssen, 2011). Investigating prior use of the instrument with the target audience can be informative.

The Kim Depression Scale for Korean Americans (KDSKA: Kim, 2002) is a 25-item self-report measure that assesses depression in Korean Americans, consisting of four subscales: emotional, cognitive, behavioral, and somatic symptoms. Test-takers check responses that most accurately describe their experiences of the past week in the symptom areas. Convergent validity was evidenced by correlations between the four subscales and other measures, such as the CES-D. A confirmatory factor analysis indicated the KDSKA's construct validity.

Discrepancy Subscale of the Almost Perfect Scale-Revised (APS-R: Slaney, Rice, Mobley, Trippi, & Ashby, 2001). The APS-R is a measure of self-critical perfectionism, a characteristic shown to have higher rates in Asian immigrant youth and emerging adults. The Discrepancy subscale measures the extent to which individuals might view themselves as falling behind personal performance expectations. Items are rated on a 7-point Likert-type scale. This scale correlates significantly with the Self-Oriented and Socially Prescribed Perfectionism subscales on the Multidimensional Perfectionism Scale.

Family Almost Perfect Scale (FAPS: Wang, 2010). The FAPS is a 17-item measure of the perceived level of perfectionistic standards of one's family. These standards include familial attitudes, beliefs, and values. The items are rated on a 7-point Likert-type scale. Factorial validity was established through the use of multiple group confirmatory factorial analysis using the scores of two samples, European American and Asian American, to cross-validate measurement properties.

Somatic Distress Subscale (SDS) of the Hopkins Symptom Checklist-21 (HSCL-21; Green, Walkey, McCormick, & Taylor, 1988). Due to the prevalence of somatic symptoms in some Asian cultures, the SDS may serve as a useful measure. It is a 7-item self-report inventory that utilizes a 4-point Likert-type scale. It has evidenced convergent and divergent validity with various measures of psychological and physical health for clinical and normative samples.

Refugee Trauma Assessment

Harvard Program in Refugee Trauma (HPRT) Depression/Torture Screening Instrument (Mollica & Caspi-Yavin, 1991). The HPRT was intended to provide health care providers with a self-report screening tool to detect symptoms of depression and PTSD among Vietnamese and Cambodian refugees in the United States. Several of the depression and the PTSD-related items were taken from the Hopkins Symptom Checklist-25 (HSCL-25) (Parloff, Kelman, & Frank, 1954). The HPRT depression scale consists of 15 items, using the cut-off score of 1.75 and greater for positive symptomatology of depression, which is consistent with HSCL-25 data obtained from a random general population sample in California (Derogatis, Lipman, & Rickels, 1974). The second half of the HPRT asks Yes/No questions related to exposure to torture and symptoms of PTSD. Those who identify three out of five items are categorized in the PTSD-symptom group. Three translated versions of the HPRT (Vietnamese, Kru/Khmer, Laotian) were validated on an Indochinese DSM-diagnosed psychiatric sample. As such, the sensitivity and specificity of the HPRT for this sample (using either an anxiety score, depression score, or total score of greater than 1.75) were 0.93 and 0.76, respectively. Test-retest coefficients for the three language groups combined were 0.89 for PTSD/torture, 0.84 for anxiety, and 0.82 for depression.

CHAPTER **10**

Regionalism and Personality Assessment: A Matter of Place

Shannon McClain, Collette Chapman-Hilliard, and Steven R. Smith

> Tina is a 32-year-old self-identified biracial woman who has been experiencing recent changes in her mood and behavior, including depressive and anxiety symptoms. She was born in and resided in a small southern U.S. town until several months ago, when she moved to an urban community in the Pacific Northwest region for a job opportunity. She has been referred to you for personality assessment to help guide her diagnosis and treatment. You complete Tina's evaluation and prepare to write a report of your findings. As you prepare to write the report, what kinds of issues will you consider about the role of Tina's regional context to help you interpret and understand the results of the personality assessment?

To begin this discussion, we highlight that the accuracy of any type of psychological assessment and subsequent interpretation of the assessment findings is predicated upon the consideration of multiple contextual factors. Due to the relatively brief nature of the interaction between client and assessor in the assessment context, the possibility of misinterpretation can be amplified (Society for Personality Assessment, 2006). Therefore, it is important to consider a variety of client background factors that may influence the assessment findings.

In personality research, person-in-environment factors have been an area of particular interest that supports the interactionist approach to personality theory. From an interactionist perspective, individual differences in personality traits are expressed in environments where those traits are perceived as relevant (Snyder & Ickes, 1985). For example, Holland's (1985) work on career paths and vocational interests suggested that people with specific types of personality traits seek work environments that will encourage the expression of their individual personality characteristics. Hence, an important tenet of the interactionist perspective is that personality traits and environmental settings are interconnected.

In recent years, personality researchers have begun to more closely examine person-in-environment factors, specifically attending to the relationship between personality and "place." These researchers ask, "Are there differences in personality expression by region of the United States?" In short, the answer is *yes*. In our discussion of the role of place in personality assessment, we will review the body of research exploring the relation between place and personality, as well as corresponding psychological and behavioral correlates. Furthermore, we view *place* as a cultural variable in itself that is important to diversity-sensitive personality assessment.

Psychologists have identified multicultural competence as integral to the quality of services provided in clinical work (Sue, 2003; Vera & Speight, 2003). As such, the field has seen an increased emphasis in scholarship and training addressing multicultural considerations in clinical work, including psychological assessment (Lee, Rosen, & Burns, 2013; Suzuki & Ponterotto, 2008). Despite this significant shift in the field and the growing attention to the importance of integrating issues of social identity and diversity into clinical work, there has been a consistent lack of attention to social identity related to place. Although there is an established literature addressing cross-cultural differences in personality and culture (e.g., variation between nations and regions of the world; Allen & Walsh, 2000; Church, 2001; van de Vijver & van Hemert, 2008), psychology as a field has largely ignored the possibility and implications of within-nation regional variation and its impact on clinical work. The absence of region as a topic related to personality assessment within the literature suggests it has historically been perceived as less important or relevant to psychology.

In this chapter, we assert that regionalism is an important cultural variable and address its relevance to personality assessment. In our discussion of place and its relevance to personality assessment, this chapter examines: (1) definitions of region, (2) region as a cultural variable, (3) place and interpersonal presentation, and (4) practical considerations for psychologists considering region in personality assessment.

Conceptual Considerations

Defining Region

Individual differences in personality traits are often expressed in environments or places where those traits are perceived as germane, allowing for one to adapt to a particular context (Holland, 1985; Snyder & Ickes, 1985). *Place*, in this sense, is interconnected with the expression of personality and personality traits. *Region* as a representation of place is of particular significance, as all clients with whom clinical assessors interact live within a particular regional context. For example, as matter of standard practice or conversational pleasantry, when we meet clients for the first time, we often ask, "Where are you from?" Although this question may elicit several different kinds of responses, people often respond by naming their hometown. Within the US, the hometowns to which people refer might reflect large urban areas, small rural towns, or specific areas of the country such as the West Coast or Midwest. Further, specific referents to place tend to elicit common stereotypical images of the people who reside in these areas. From the kindness of Midwestern small town folks to the brashness of New England city dwellers, information about where a person is from creates for many people, consciously or unconsciously, a mental image of another person's experiences, behaviors, and even beliefs—all based on one's perception of a particular region.

The origin of the word "region" derives from the Latin verb *rego* meaning to rule or steer and the term later became associated with *regio*, a Latin noun referring to a district, boundary or line. Contemporarily, region can refer to geographical space, government jurisdiction, or social and cultural norms and characteristics. Social scientists from a range of disciplines—sociologists, political scientists, and anthropologists—have put forth definitions for the term region and have demonstrated that people who live in different regions differ from one another in important ways. Odum and Moore (1938) suggest that region reflects commonality among elements such as wealth, access to natural resources, subcultures, and economy based on a geographical space. Other definitions highlight specific areas or geographic spaces that possess cohesion among cultural features and are distinct from other areas (Hartshorne, 1959; Paasi, 1986). Hence, regions may be demarcated by a collection of states defined by geography, such as South, West, Northeast; regions may reflect population density such as an area being classified as urban or rural; and regions may also denote areas with similar values or cultural norms, such as the "Bible Belt." Across definitions, there appears emphasis on cohesiveness and common experience that is unique to a particular region. With such distinctiveness or difference highlighted in distinguishing one region from another, it stands to reason that such variation would be present among residents.

Regional variation has significant implications for psychological, behavioral, and affective expression often demonstrated through personality traits (Park & Peterson, 2010; Rentfrow, 2010). Hence, region is much more than topography, geography, and cohesiveness among residents. Region represents a kind of "mental landscape" (Morrissey, 1997) upon which people express their individual differences and/or learn to adapt to their environmental context. The relationship between persons and regions is one in which personality is analogous to regionality in that both demonstrate elements of uniqueness by a particular entity (Langenhove, 2013). Furthermore, more than a geographical boundary, a core characteristic of region is identity: "region operates as a generator and communicator of identity" (Langenhove, 2013, p. 484). As such, the cultural products that arise from regions (e.g., institutions, symbols, texts) influence how individuals think and express who they are. This theory of region illustrates the reciprocal relationship between place, personality, and other identity-related characteristics (e.g., values). The expression of individuals' personality characteristics is influenced to some degree by place and contributes variation in personal/regional expression. For the purpose of this chapter, region reflects both definitions influenced by population density (e.g., urban and rural environments) and geographical location or a collection of states (e.g., Southeast). The complexity of the person–region relationship and the subsequent expression of and/or adaptation of personality characteristics based on regional context demonstrates regionalism as an important issue in personality assessment and, more broadly, clinical cultural competence.

Interpersonal Presentation by U.S. Region

Although we can easily conjure to mind ideas about language, dress, cuisine, attitudes, and personality traits for different regions within the United States, for many the question is whether these are meaningful cultural differences or irrelevant stereotypes (Vandello, Hettinger, & Michniewicz, 2014). The United States is often portrayed as a homogeneous cultural context (Plaut, Markus, Treadway, & Fu, 2012) and researchers frequently conflate culture and nation or nationality (Triandis, 1995). One reason for confusion around whether US region constitutes a cultural variable (or a relevant cultural variable) is the existence of many varied definitions of culture, ranging from very narrow to very broad definitions from the perspectives of various fields, such as anthropology, sociology, and psychology. Although there is no one established definition of culture within any field, we refer to the psychological definition of Helms and Cook (1999), which defines culture as "the values, beliefs, language, rituals, traditions, and other behaviors that are passed from one generation to another within any social group" (p. 24).

Through this lens, we can begin to understand the relevance of region as a cultural variable in psychology. Kitayama, Conway, Pietromonaco, Park, and Plaut, (2010) note that although the U.S. is relatively homogeneous in its implicit ethos, or individuals' tacit cultural practices and associated mental habits, there is quite a bit of regional variation in its explicit ethos, or individuals' explicitly held values and the behaviors that are influenced by these values. Recent literature has increasingly demonstrated that there is robust within-nation regional variation in values, norms, attitudes, behavior, and personality traits.

Values

Individualism versus collectivism

The constructs of individualism and collectivism are the most studied in cultural and cross-cultural psychology. However, they have typically been studied in the context of comparing Eastern and Western cultures, often at the national level. Broadly, individuals in individualist cultures tend to be more autonomous and independent from their in-groups, show a tendency to prioritize their own individual goals over those of their in-groups, and base their attitudes and behavior on their own attitudes rather than in-group norms. On the other hand, those in collectivist cultures show interdependence within their in-groups, tend to prioritize the goals of their in-groups, and are particularly concerned with maintaining interpersonal relationships (e.g., are concerned with maintaining harmony, reducing conflict, and tend to shape their behavior based on in-group norms; Triandis, 2001).

The United States is often touted as a quintessential individualistic nation (Hofstede, 1980). Although a national culture of individualism, independence, egalitarianism, personal control, personal responsibility, and individual achievement is a pervasive cultural force in the U.S. (Bellah, Madsen, Sullivan, Swidler, & Tipton,

1985; Hofstede, 1980), research increasingly suggests that this might be an oversimplification, because individualism and collectivism vary on a regional and/or statewide level, as well as by racial-ethnic group within the U.S. (Coon & Kemmelmeier, 2001; Vandello & Cohen, 1999).

Vandello and Cohen (1999) created the U.S. Collectivism Index and sought to understand statewide differences across the U.S., as measured by variables including the percentage of people living alone, percentage of people with a religious affiliation, and divorce to marriage ratio. They found significant variation among states and regions, such that Hawaii, the "Deep South" (e.g., Louisiana, Mississippi, etc.), and Utah were particularly collectivistic, while the Mountain West and Great Plains (e.g., Montana, Oregon, Nebraska, etc.) were particularly individualistic. Furthermore, scholars have suggested that regionally, Appalachian residents (e.g., from eastern Kentucky, eastern Tennessee, western North Carolina, etc.) are more likely to endorse collectivistic values and behavior (Keefe, 1988; Wilson & Peterson, 2000). While Gore, Wilburn, Treadway, and Plaut (2011) reported that Appalachian students endorsed only marginally higher collectivism than non-Appalachian students, they found that the relation between collectivism and academic attitudes (e.g., academic efficacy, school connectedness) was stronger for Appalachian students compared to non-Appalachian students. This demonstrates the ways that regional culture, and the extent to which people internalize and express their regional culture, has implications for broader types of attitudes and outcomes.

Endorsement of collectivistic values within the U.S. is correlated with a slower pace of life, a focus on affiliation over achievement, and being more receptive to higher levels of government involvement (Conway, Ryder, Tweed, & Sokol, 2001; Conway, Sexton, & Tweed, 2006). Scholars examining Appalachian and Southern culture have also found that individuals in these locales tend to strongly identify with their families, communities, and region, have a particularly high desire to avoid conflict, have a strong sense of personal and religious values, and engage in higher rates of cosleeping (i.e., parents sleeping in close proximity with children, which may include bed-sharing) (Halperin, 1998; Keefe, 1998; Montgomery, 2000). On the other hand, individuals in the Mountain West, who are more likely to be highly individualistic, are particularly likely to espouse values in line with an ethos of independence, such as the importance of self-direction, self-expression, and self-reliance (Kitayama et al., 2010).

Honor and Retribution

Among the most thoroughly researched constructs in the literature on variations in within-nation values are honor and retribution. A body of research suggests that individuals in the South more highly value honor and retribution, and Southerners are more likely to respond to threats to their reputation or honor (or that of their family, in-group, or property) with violence (Cohen, 1996, 2001; Nisbett, 1993). Cohen, Nisbett, Bowdle, and Schwarz (1996) conducted three studies, including a lab experiment, field experiment, and a survey study, that support this notion. For instance, compared to their Northern counterparts, Southern men: (1) were more likely to endorse the importance of fighting someone who insulted their wife, (2) tended to respond to an insult with anger rather than amusement or confusion, and (3) experienced a spike in hormones related to stress and aggression (i.e., cortisol and testosterone) and became more confrontational or aggressive in the presence of a physically intimidating research confederate. This research points to a unique regional culture that impacts values, emotion, and behavior. However, it must be noted that an examination of cultural differences may become value-laden, such that Southerners might be portrayed or viewed as dominant culture out-group members who are too aggressive. Thus, it might be equally important to understand and assess factors that contribute to a Northern culture of passivity, including outcomes related to such interpersonal styles within this American subculture.

Tolerance and Openness

The U.S. is thought to be a culturally diverse nation and one that touts advocacy for all persons to experience freedoms regardless of race, religion, affectional orientation, creed, and/or gender (Alesina, Devleeschauwer, Easterly, Kurlat, & Wacziarg, 2003). However, scholars remain curious about whether this sentiment of increased tolerance and openness translates across regions.

Early studies conducted on attitudes toward difference demonstrated that residents of urban regions tended to be more open-minded and flexible than their non-urban or rural counterparts (Stouffer, 1955; Wirth, 1938). More recent studies examining the effects of urbanism on attitudes of tolerance are consistent with previous research, suggesting that urban dwellers tend to be more tolerant of diverse religions, political ideologies, and groups of people (Carter & Borch, 2005; Carter, Scott, Mulkey, & Borch, 2005; Twenge, 1997; Wilson, 1985, 1991). This research is also consistent with investigations that have examined regions by state. For example, Rentfrow and colleagues (2008) found that *Openness* (e.g., curiosity, flexibility, creativity, etc.) tended to be highest among the Northeast and West Coast regions of the U.S.; areas in which there are higher frequencies of urban areas.

Tightness versus Looseness

Recent research in social psychology suggests that within-nation regional differences in values, personality, and behavior might be explained by another value-laden construct: tightness versus looseness. Cultures that are *tight* are defined by having many enforced rules or regulations implicit in the culture, in addition to little tolerance (i.e., more punishment) for nonconformity to such rules. On the other hand, *loose* cultures have few strongly enforced rules or regulations and greater tolerance (i.e., less punishment) for nonconformity.

In the first study to apply this construct to U.S. regional culture, Harrington and Gelfand (2014) suggest this construct is distinct from individualism versus collectivism or tolerance and openness and has important implications for understanding regional culture. This study found a high degree of variability across U.S. states in tightness–looseness, distinct from the aforementioned constructs. States scoring very high in tightness tended to be located in the South, such as Mississippi, Alabama, and Arkansas while states scoring very low on tightness included West Coast states such as California, Oregon, and Washington. The authors found that tightness–looseness was related to ecological and historical factors (e.g., availability of resources, health vulnerabilities), psychological characteristics (e.g., personality traits), and psychosocial outcomes (e.g., substance abuse, perceived discrimination, incarceration rates).

Such regional differences in the valuing of implicit cultural rules and regulations may also influence other attitudinal regional differences. For instance, scholars have found attitudes toward corporal punishment vary widely in the U.S., with Southerners particularly likely to endorse corporal punishment and those from the Northeast particularly unlikely to endorse corporal punishment (Douglas, 2006; Flynn, 1994). Similarly, the construct of tightness/looseness might influence regional differences in gender role attitudes, as research suggests that those living outside the South and those living in more urban areas are more likely to hold more egalitarian or liberal gender role attitudes that are more accepting of changing roles in the family and larger society compared to those in the South and rural regions (Carter & Borch, 2005; Powers et al., 2003; Rice & Coates, 1995).

Personality and Place: Regional Differences in Traits

For psychologists seeking to understand the influence of regional culture in personality assessment, it becomes important to understand the diversity in interpersonal presentation of those within various regional cultures. Although psychologists have only recently been exploring to what extent personality traits vary by region, a convincing body of research has been built that supports regional variation of personality traits in the U.S.

Currently, four empirical studies provide support for the variation of personality traits by U.S. region. Three of these studies, which vary in methodology, compare regions or states on individual traits (Krug & Kulhavy, 1973; Plaut, Markus, & Lachman, 2002; Rentfrow et al., 2008). Rentfrow and colleagues (2008) utilized the Big Five Inventory (BFI; John & Srivastava, 1999) with a sample of 620,000 Internet respondents surveyed between 1999 and 2005, while Plaut and colleagues (2002) examined traits by utilizing a national dataset of telephone and paper survey respondents self-rating on personality attributes (items from MIDI Personality Scales) representing the Big Five personality factors.

Despite some variation among the methodology and results, Rentfrow and colleagues (2013) note that the results of these studies are notably consistent. The findings collectively suggest that Neuroticism is highest in the Northeast and Southeast and lowest in the Midwest and West; Openness is highest in New England, the Mid-Atlantic, and Pacific regions, and lower in the Great Plains, Midwest, and Southeastern states; and Agreeableness tends to be higher in the South, while lower in the Northeast. Findings regarding Extraversion and Conscientiousness were inconsistent across these studies.

The most recent study examining personality and U.S. region was the first to attempt to map distinct psychological regions within the U.S. by examining configurations of traits, or psychological profiles, and outcomes related to such configurations, rather than focusing solely on individual traits (Rentfrow et al., 2013). By examining systematic variation in personality traits, as well as political, economic, social, and health (PESH) factors, the authors demonstrate that regions are far more than arbitrarily delineated spaces, but can represent their own culture, with differing traits, values, and demographics. In their study, Rentfrow and colleagues examined traits at the statewide level, such that states with similar psychological profiles that are near each other were considered a part of the same psychological region, defined by their shared psychological trait profile. They found three distinct psychological regions, which they termed the (1) Friendly and Conventional region, (2) Relaxed and Creative region, and (3) Temperamental and Uninhibited region.

The *Friendly and Conventional* region mirrors the Midwest, as it is comprised of states in the geographic center of the U.S. This psychological profile is marked by socially conservative values and defined by moderately high levels of Extraversion, Agreeableness, and Conscientiousness, moderately low Neuroticism, and very low Openness, noting that the profile "portrays the sort of person who is sociable, considerate, dutiful, and traditional" (p. 1006). With regard to PESH factors, the study found this region to be marked by relatively low levels of education, wealth, economic innovation, and social tolerance, a predominantly White population, and a tendency to adhere to unhealthy lifestyles.

The *Relaxed and Creative* region generally includes states in the West Coast, Rocky Mountain, and Sunbelt regions. This profile is defined by low scores on Extraversion and Agreeableness, very low Neuroticism, and very high Openness scores, denoting a region "where open-mindedness, tolerance, individualism, and happiness are valued" (p. 1007). PESH factor correlates indicated that this region includes a high proportion of non-Whites as well as individuals with higher levels of wealth and education. Residents were generally described as liberal and healthy relative to other regions, both psychologically and physically. The region was noted for its low social capital but high tolerance for diversity in culture and lifestyle.

Finally, the *Temperamental and Uninhibited* region generally includes states in the Mid-Atlantic and Northeast regions. This profile is defined by low Extraversion scores, very low Agreeableness and Conscientiousness, very high Neuroticism, and moderately high Openness, and "depicts the type of person who is reserved, aloof, impulsive, irritable, and inquisitive" as well as "passionate, competitive, and liberal" (p. 1008). PESH factor correlates indicated that this region is fairly liberal and marked by relatively high proportions of wealthy individuals and college graduates, as well as women and older adults.

Clinical Issues and Presentation by Region

Psychologists have become increasingly interested in understanding the ways in which regional context impacts psychological and social outcomes (Vandello et al.,

2014). Having data on regional personality differences has allowed psychologists to understand regional variation in a variety of outcomes, including psychological well-being (Pesta, McDaniel, & Bertsch, 2010) and social capital (Rentfrow, 2010).

Place and Emotional Well-Being

At the U.S. state level, neuroticism in particular has been found to contribute strongly to regional variation in emotional health and well-being (McCann, 2011; Rentfrow, Mellander, & Florida, 2009), such that states such as West Virginia, Mississippi, and Kentucky that are high in measured neuroticism have lower rates of emotional health, while states such as Utah, with low levels of neuroticism, show high levels of emotional health. These studies also point to the influence of demographic variables in regional mental health, with socioeconomic status (SES) having a particularly strong influence. However, when controlling for such demographic variables, personality variables such as neuroticism still have a strong influence.

Also of significance, this literature suggests that subjective psychological well-being varies regionally, signifying a cultural construction of well-being. As discussed earlier, research suggests that states vary with regard to levels of individualism and collectivism. As the cross-cultural literature has shown, these factors impact the ways in which the self and subjective well-being are constructed (Markus & Kitayama, 1991). That is, research has found significant differences in the extent to which individuals from individualistic and collectivistic cultures report level of subjective well-being, as well as variance in factors that contribute to their well-being (Park, Peterson, & Ruch, 2009). Although Americans show some general consistency with regard to what contributes to well-being, evidence shows it is shaped by our more immediate regional worlds.

Plaut and colleagues (2002) reported the following distinctions in subjective well-being by U.S. region: (a) New England (e.g., Connecticut, Massachusetts, Maine) emphasized autonomy-focused well-being (i.e., ability to not be constrained) and showed the highest levels of social well-being and positive relations with others; (b) The Mountain region (e.g., Colorado, Utah, Wyoming) emphasized self-satisfaction and autonomy-focused well-being (i.e., independent thinking and being in charge of one's situation); (c) The West-South Central (e.g., Texas, Arkansas, Oklahoma, Louisiana) emphasized self-focused well-being (i.e., the opportunity for personal growth and opportunity), high levels of emotion-focused well-being (i.e., feeling cheerful and happy; absence of nervousness/restlessness), and high other-focused well-being; (d) The West-North Central region (e.g., Minnesota, Nebraska, Missouri) did not emphasize autonomy or personal growth, but rather self-focused well-being (i.e., self-satisfaction and self-acceptance) and emotion-focused well-being (i.e., feeling calm, peaceful, and satisfied); and (e) The East-South Central region (e.g., Kentucky, Tennessee, Mississippi) is particularly distinctive for its high emphasis on social responsibility, especially contribution to the welfare and well-being of others; this region's profile is distinguished by relatively low scores on all other aspects of well-being.

Differences in subjective well-being have also been found when the level of analysis is reduced to individual cities. For example, Plaut and colleagues (2012) examined culture in the context of city of residence as it relates to constructions of self and well-being in a comparison of Boston and San Francisco. The authors found that those living in Boston derive self-satisfaction based on education, finances, work, family, and community. This emotional pattern is described as a contingent self-worth, with more attention to fitting in with others and support of regulation by establishment. This stronger sense that what is expected by others is connected to one's own sense of well-being may be experienced as constraint, as well-being may rise with the relative absence of negative social contingencies and fall with the presence of these contingencies. On the other hand, those living in San Francisco showed a sense of self-evaluation and self-worth that is relatively noncontingent on family, finances, or community (but is related to work), with well-being understood in terms of the presence of events that produce good feelings.

Collectively, this body of research suggests that place matters in determining how we think of ourselves and what we value with regard to psychological health. As we consider the role of place in personality assessment, it becomes important to consider not only individual differences in personality traits but the ways in which factors that contribute to well-being can vary and the various ways in which the environment might influence these factors. For example, in their theory to explain how regional variation in personality traits might emerge and persist, Rentfrow and colleagues (2008) hypothesized that higher frequencies of individuals high in neuroticism may lower the average emotional health in the state. One explanation is that in states with higher frequencies of neurotic individuals, a more tense or unstable environment might be created in which those who are not particularly high on this trait may experience shifts in their thoughts, feelings, and behaviors, thus influencing their emotional health. The latter hypothesis is consistent with the person-in-environment or interactionist perspective of personality and environment. The potential for incongruence of environment, personality trait expression, and the likelihood for subsequent psychological distress, is an area of significance for personality assessors particularly given the high mobility of people in the U.S.

Relevant questions for psychologists to consider include: What do individuals in this region value and does this particular individual's values align or misalign with those of the region (e.g., do they value close social connections)? What social forces might be in play that contribute to or function to support psychological well-being? What social forces might inhibit psychological well-being? For example, Rentfrow and colleagues (2013) note that, broadly, the Relaxed and Creative region showed evidence of good health, while the Friendly and Conventional region showed evidence of poor psychological well-being and health. For individuals in these regions, understanding both their personal traits and the social forces influencing their well-being is important, reflecting a shift in the ways in which many psychologists conceptualize their clients' presenting problems. In the personality assessment context, one might ask, in what ways are clients influenced by others with traits that do or do not foster positive coping and health behaviors in the place where they live?

Place and Psychopathology

Mental illness does not impact all communities equally. Psychologists have found mental illness differentially affects individuals based on a number of cultural and social identity variables including race, ethnicity, SES and, although relatively understudied, place (i.e., region and community type; Hudson, 2012). Scholars have questioned whether such disparities related to place are due to the complex interaction of such aforementioned variables (i.e., geographic variation in race, education, SES, geographic isolation of community, etc.) or whether place matters above and beyond such demographic variables? The answer appears to be *both.*

Mental Health and Regional Personality Trait Distribution

The literature suggests statewide differences in serious mental illness, such that the highest rates are found in more isolated regions of the country (e.g., Appalachia and some sparsely populated Western states), and the lower Mississippi Valley regions (e.g., Louisiana and Mississippi), while the lowest rates are found in the coastal area between Virginia and Massachusetts and in Florida and California (Hudson, 2009; Moriarty et al., 2009). Rentfrow and colleagues (2013) suggest that differences in health outcomes might be, in part, due to personality differences. For example, in examining a state such as California in the "Relaxed and Creative" region, which is marked by low scores on Neuroticism and high Openness, this region would have an unusually high number of residents who tend to cope well and typically refrain from overreacting to difficult events. The environment fostered by these individuals might help to promote health in other individuals in the region. However, it must be noted that there are substantial regional differences in both SES and access to mental health care that also contribute to rates of mental illness.

Regional differences in mental health also include stark differences in rates of suicide completion. Research suggests that regional variation in suicide rates can, in part, be attributed to variation in personality traits. More specifically, a negative association is found between states' level of both neuroticism and agreeableness and states' rates of suicide completion, even when accounting for the influence of demographics such as race, urban versus rural population, SES, and higher depression rates (Lester & Voracek, 2013; McCann, 2010; Voracek, 2009). In trying to further understand this relationship between person and place, Shrira and Christenfeld (2010) examined suicide completions in the regions with the highest and lowest rates of suicide completions (i.e., states within the Mountain West and New England, respectively), comparing residents who died inside the region, residents who died outside the region, and visitors to the region. Their findings suggested that in the high suicide region, all three groups had elevated levels of death by suicide, suggesting that both being a resident of the region and short-term exposure to the region predicted suicide. On the other hand, short-term exposure to the low suicide region was not a protective factor (i.e., no decrease in suicide among visitors). However, for residents of the region, suicides completed in the region were significantly reduced, while their suicide rates drastically rose outside of their geographic home. The authors suggest that both individual and contextual factors specific to the region contribute to low or high rates of suicide. For instance, the high and low suicide completion regions represent the most densely and most sparsely populated regions, respectively. Further, these regions drastically differ in firearm availability and use.

Mental Health in Rural and Urban Communities

Generally, research suggests that geographic areas that are more isolated or more sparsely populated are at increased risk for disproportionately high levels of mental illness. This could be due to the influence of SES, lower levels of social integration (Stack, 2000) or inadequate access to treatment (Hoyt, Conger, Valde, & Weihs, 1997). Turchik, Karpenko, Hammers, and McNamara (2007) highlight a number of challenges unique to providing quality psychological assessment services to rural communities, including heightened stigmatization of seeking out psychological services, increased likelihood of seeing clients with limited or no access to health care or transportation, a shortage of mental health professionals in rural communities, and increased isolation of health care providers with less opportunity to consult with other professionals. Turchik and colleagues (2007) also note that providers in these regions might be more likely to work in practices with fewer resources and, thus, might find themselves confronted with ethical dilemmas such as using psychological assessments that are outdated. Although an explication of all the specific differences in urban and rural mental health is beyond the scope of this chapter, there are broad differences in the characteristics of the population and physical environment that have implications for personality assessment service delivery.

According to the U.S. Census Bureau (2010), persons living in areas with 50,000 or more inhabitants and in close proximity to areas with at least 2,500 inhabitants are considered urban areas. In contrast, rural areas consist of persons residing in places with fewer than 2,500 inhabitants, typically surrounded by uninhabited or unincorporated land. People residing in both urban and rural regions represent a range of heterogeneity in culture, occupation, and lifestyle. However, the type and degree of heterogeneity differs for urban and rural environments on various social and geographical indicators. Population characteristic indicators range from attitudes toward mental health/helping and coping beliefs to demographic variables such as age, race, and sex. For example, rural communities tend to have larger populations who are either older adults or youth/adolescents (Coward, DeWeaver, Schmidt, & Jackson, 1983). This is in contrast to urban regions whose inhabitants tend to be predominantly young adults entering the workforce (Park & Peterson, 2010). Additionally, in recent decades, there has been a sharp increase in the ethnic minority and immigrant populations in both rural and urban regions, resulting in the need for residents of these communities and health care professionals to directly and indirectly address culture and diversity (Shrestha, 2011).

The geographical pictures of urban and rural communities lend insight into the ways in which the characteristics of a region may inform service delivery. One of the most frequently cited barriers to the delivery of psychological health services in rural communities is geography, as people in these regions tend to be widely dispersed and isolated (Coward et al., 1983; Murray & Keller, 1991). In contrast, a major challenge to service delivery in urban settings comes from population density, with the number of people in need of services far outweighing the number of people available to provide psychological services. These situations create a plethora of dilemmas for psychologists, one of which is efficiently and effectively providing personality evaluations to meet the mental health demands of each of these regions while also addressing the diversity in these respective regions. As such, important questions are raised for those who engage in personality assessment: What is the impact of regional demography on the expression of personality traits? Do geographical factors influence the ways in which distress or psychopathology is perceived and thus reported? As the heterogeneity of both urban and rural regions increases, should there be a shift in the ways in which personality assessments are conducted and should this differ across urban and rural settings? Are the assumptions that underlie the responses to personality assessments consistent with the norms and experiences of people living in different regions of the U.S.?

Given some of the differences in the features of urban and rural environments, studies have compared perceptions of mental health and clinical symptomatology in these areas. For example, Swaim and Stanley (2011) found that adolescents living in rural communities were slightly more likely to drink alcohol and experience drunkenness than their non-rural counterparts. In addition, individuals living in rural communities perceived drinking alcohol as more adaptive in managing challenging situations in comparison to individuals living in non-rural environments (Chimonides & Frank, 1998). Although the samples for these studies were small and certainly not representative of all rural populations, it appears that adolescents in rural communities may approach coping differently than their non-rural counterparts, which has implications for the ways in which personality assessors interpret elevations on certain clinical scales for this population. These authors also found that urban adolescents viewed depression as a more normative response to life circumstances than study participants from small cities or towns, who perceived depressive symptoms as unhealthier or more problematic than their urban counterparts.

For psychologists engaging in personality assessment, it is integral to acknowledge and understand the intersection of cultural factors related to where they practice or the place where their clients reside. This includes disparities in the necessity and accessibility of services, differing conceptions of well-being, and protective and risk factors for mental illness and suicide that may be unique to that region/place. Furthermore, given the highly mobile nature of many families, our clients might live in a region that is not their region of origin (or that of their parents), such that their personal values and personality traits are in opposition to the culture of the region. In such cases, the cultural characteristics of a particular region might be more or less in harmony with the values of a given client, potentially leading to increased isolation, frustration, and stress. As is true in all cases, we must conduct thorough interviews prior to test interpretation so that we can begin to understand the person-in-context variables for our clients.

Personality Assessment Instruments

Psychology highly emphasizes the importance of utilizing appropriately normed and standardized testing instruments in psychological assessment, allowing psychologists to make valid interpretations of individuals' test scores (APA, 2002; Cicchetti, 1994). In an attempt to minimize test bias, test developers are generally encouraged to stratify the test standardization samples on important demographic variables including geographic region in addition to race, ethnicity, SES, and level of education. The goal is for tests to represent the general population with which the measure will be used. Historically, many widely used personality assessment instruments did not include sufficient sampling by region in deriving their standardization samples. For example, the Minnesota Multiphasic Personality Inventory (MMPI) was originally normed on a sample derived from Minnesota (Hathaway & McKinley, 1940). Today, widely used personality assessment measures have shown significant improvement in geographic representativeness, which has become common practice for psychological test construction. For example, the restandardized MMPI-2 (Butcher, Dahlstrom, Graham, Tellegen, & Kaemmer, 1989) was standardized on 2,600 individuals from seven U.S. states, using national census parameters in data collection. Similarly, the MMPI-A (Williams et al., 1992) was standardized on a sample of 1,620 adolescents residing in eight U.S. states. Development of the Personality Assessment Inventory (PAI; Morey, 1991) involved representation of individuals from 12 states across the U.S. in its standardization sample.

There are virtually no studies on the ways in which individual personality assessment outcomes and responses may vary by region. In a single investigation we found, researchers compared participants' responses on the performance-based assessment, Draw-A-Person in the Rain (DAPR), based on regional patterns of precipitation. Participants who lived in regions with more frequently stormy weather responded to the DAPR stimuli with drawings characteristic of more distress (e.g., participants' drawings included images of more inclement weather) in comparison to their counterparts who resided in environments where it rained less often (Graves, Jones, & Kaplan, 2013).

Practical Considerations

Almost all practitioners providing personality assessments are trained in a model wherein science and practice inform one another. As a field, we have much work to do to better engage psychological science in the dialogue about regional differences in psychological and social outcomes. Although there is a small but growing body of literature on region and personality (see Rentfrow and colleagues), this literature is not specific to clinical applications. Moreover, little is written about the intersection of regional influences with other diversity variables such as gender (i.e., are there differences in gender role conformity, evident in personality test profiles, across regions?). As such, the bridge between science and practice, at present, is one that is in continued development.

To contribute to the building blocks of this bridge, we have provided some suggestions for considering region in personality assessment (see Table 10.1).

Although it is typical to gather some general background information with regard to place, psychological assessors are encouraged to develop a practice standard of gathering information in the clinical interview with regard to both place or origin, current place of residence, and the extent to which these are important parts of clients' identities. If psychologists are unfamiliar with the place or regional culture, they should seek to gain some understanding to provide perspective about the client's history and current experience.

As psychologists work toward improving their multicultural competency and sensitivity to diversity, it is integral to understand and acknowledge their own assumptions and values, as well as biases they might have toward another cultural

Table 10.1 Suggestions for Considering Regional Influences in Personality Assessment

- Develop a practice standard of determining your clients' place of origin and where they currently reside.
- If your clients are from a region with which you are unfamiliar, consider learning more from your client about the significance of that regional environment for them.
- Identify and acknowledge your biases about certain regions and perceived characteristics of individuals residing in those regions.
- Identify and acknowledge the ways in which your own culture, based on place or region, could influence your conceptualizations of and recommendations for clients.
- Seek to understand the ways in which a client's traits and/or values align or misalign with those of the place or region where the client resides.
- Take into account various sociocultural forces that contribute to or function to support or inhibit psychological well-being in the place where the client resides.
- Consider the ways in which place serves as a protective or risk factor.
- Garner an understanding of how physical environment may contribute to expressed personality dimensions.
- Carefully consider the difference between clinically significant information as expressed through personality versus regional variation in expression of specific traits.
- Understand the extent to which tests are normed and standardized on geographically representative samples, including region and community type.
- Learn about the region/place in which you practice by seeking to acknowledge and understand the intersection of cultural factors in the area in which many of your clients reside.

group (Arredondo, 1999). This also relates to the cultural context of region. A psychologist's own worldview may color his or her interactions with, and conceptualization of, clients, particularly those from different regions. Although Americans tend to have much in common with regard to values and constructions of self, it is important for psychologists to recognize the ways in which clients' values and behavior might vary as a function of place.

It might be incorrectly assumed that all of our domestic clients ascribe to individualistic values as a function of being a part of American culture. This may be particularly true of psychologists who live in regions that more highly value individualism (e.g., the Mountain West region). However, such an assumption might lead psychologists engaging in personality assessment to overpathologize or incorrectly interpret certain behavior, or to provide recommendations for clients that impose different values onto them or their families. For example, revisiting the case of "Tina" presented at the beginning of this chapter, a psychologist in Tina's new cultural environment, which is likely highly individualistic in comparison to her small town Southern background, might be quick to pathologize her family relationships as enmeshed or suggest methods for setting "appropriate" boundaries in relationships. However, the psychologist might not be taking into account that it could be normative in her regional culture of origin to strongly identify or align the self with family or community, to value avoiding conflict, and maintain harmony. Furthermore, it is important to consider that Tina may be particularly likely to identify with her connectedness to place and social groups. Thus, if she is now living alone, a far distance from home and family, and removed from important social institutions such as her church, these changes might present as stressors above and beyond the typical stress associated with adjustment to a new place. In this circumstance, the psychologist should work to understand and highlight Tina's cultural strengths, working within a value system that honors the client's worldview and helps her adjust to her new cultural environment.

An understanding of regional values adds an important context to a psychologist's work with clients that is relevant to personality assessment, particularly when there is a difference in regional culture within the clinical dyad. For instance, understanding that the way individuals respond to threats to their honor, or by extension the honor of their family, will vary by regional culture. It may give context to an individual's emotional response or behavior that might otherwise seem confusing or excessive to someone outside of a particular regional culture. As such, whether an individual is perceived as excessively aggressive or excessively passive or meek will likely relate to regional cultural values. An appreciation of what is at the core of such emotion and behavior allows psychologists engaging in personality assessment to achieve an accurate understanding of behavior and to make appropriate recommendations.

Similarly, understanding the broader regional context from an individual's home region, as well as where an individual currently resides, offers rich context that is relevant to personality assessment. For example, an understanding of place allows for a framework from which psychologists might understand social forces that act as stressors or that function to support well-being, thus aiding the conceptualization.

For clients with marginalized identities, understanding the cultural context of tolerance or openness where a client resides or was raised might be important. Further, an understanding of PESH factors within a given region might also help clinicians understand environmental contexts that might be relevant to their clients. In the case of Tina, while she is likely to have moved to a region considered to be more tolerant and open, it is noteworthy that she might have moved to a region with fewer racial-ethnic minorities. Thus, it will be helpful to gain a sense of Tina's racial and ethnic identity as a biracial woman in seeking to understand how this intersects with place in her recent transition.

Understanding the personality, attitudinal, and behavioral tendencies of the region in which a client lives might provide context to a client's traits and behavior. For example, Tina has moved from a U.S. region that is tight to a region that is loose (i.e., from a region that enforces implicit cultural rules with little toleration for nonconformity to a region with few strongly enforced implicit cultural rules or regulations and greater tolerance for nonconformity). What might it mean for her to have been surrounded previously by a high proportion of individuals who fit her own attitudinal and behavioral profile and now be living in an environment with a high proportion of individuals who do not? It will be important to understand how this potential shift in the expectations and worldview of those around her could have implications for Tina's mood, behavior, and relationships with others. We invite assessors to be curious as to how their conceptualization can be informed by such information. However, not all residents of a region will fit this general personality, attitudinal, or behavioral profile. It might be helpful for psychologists to consider what it means for a person to fit well with a regional profile or to have very different traits or characteristics from those commonly observed in regions where they live. For individuals who fit a regional trait profile, they might feel very "at home" interpersonally, emotionally, and behaviorally in their region, which could be a protective factor. However, there might also be ways in which characteristics of their region promote unhealthy behavior or contribute to distress. For individuals whose personality traits, values, and behavior are in stark contrast to that of the region in which they live, whether they are long-time residents or have recently moved to the area, an understanding of conflicting traits or values may help contextualize difficulty adjusting to a new environment, interpersonal difficulties, or a decreased sense of well-being.

Psychologists should consider the many different ways that individuals derive meaning and a sense of well-being in their lives. Will well-being be heavily influenced by adaptations to the place of residence? Again, individuals who do not fit the typical profile of their region might experience psychological distress based in part on incongruity in what is meaningful with regard to wellness compared to their peers. If Tina is an individual who derives meaning from and whose happiness is contingent on community, family, and connection, but moves to a region where this is not as highly valued, she could feel quite unsettled. Psychologists might be biased by their own subjective sense of well-being, which could be influenced by their own region or place of origin. It is important that psychologists seek to understand their client's worldview and do not seek to privilege their own worldview over the client's.

We encourage psychological assessors to consider how place serves as a protective or risk factor. When engaging in risk assessment, understanding the relation between place, as it influences lifestyle, could be helpful particularly for clients at high risk for suicide. As such, we recommend considering the ways in which the physical environment has implications for personality assessment service delivery. This might be particularly relevant when considering community type, such as rural and urban communities. Regional factors such as population density and firearm availability could contribute to individuals in certain states being at higher risk. An understanding of regional protective or risk factors also includes taking into consideration the accessibility of services and conceptions of mental health services for any given place. These factors should help shape the conceptualization and recommendations offered in the assessment. While Tina has moved to an urban area where mental health resources are more likely to be accessible to her, it will be important to gauge her perception of seeking out and receiving mental health services. If she has internalized views from a regional culture where mental health is less likely to be explicitly discussed and more likely to be stigmatized, this could impact her receptiveness to, and persistence in, therapy.

In considering place as a protective or risk factor, it will also be important to consider the intersection of place with other types of identity (e.g., SES or immigration status). In communities with limited availability of psychological services or fewer resources, as in rural communities, psychologists might face ethical dilemmas such as how to help clients who may be unable to pay for services or whether or not to use outdated or copyright-violated versions of tests when few funds or resources are available (Turchik et al., 2007). In considering regional population and available resources, it is also important to note that some regions will have large immigrant populations. As such, there might be a practical demand for bilingual assessors in some states/regions (e.g., large Asian immigrant populations in states such as California and large Latino immigrant populations in states such as Texas, Arizona, Florida, and California). Research suggests that limited English proficiency serves as a barrier to seeking out and receiving quality psychological services, particularly among Latino immigrants (Kim et al., 2011). Thus, considering the availability and importance of bilingual psychologists and interpreters remains vital in some regions.

With regard to the use of personality assessment measures, it is important that psychologists understand the extent to which tests are normed and standardized on geographically representative samples, including region and community type. For places with unique factors (culture, language, etc.), psychologists should seek to understand how results may be biased/skewed for individuals from this region. In addition, when using performance-based and/or measures that rely on verbal responses, psychologists should be aware of regional idioms that might impact scoring or interpretation. This is particularly applicable when assessing children who might not have been exposed to speech or language outside of their immediate context.

Finally, practitioners engaging in personality assessment are encouraged to acquaint themselves with the norms of the regions where they practice. For practitioners who have moved to a new area, taking time to learn about the local culture, values, language, and resources is necessary for providing quality care for the community.

The considerations and recommendations discussed are general guidelines that should be treated as areas of inquiry or hypotheses, rather than used to make assumptions or vague generalizations about clients from various regions. Individuals within a region will have unique histories and presentations that contribute to their personalities, interpersonal presentation, and presenting problems.

Summary Points

In this chapter, we had two primary goals: to introduce region or place as a cultural variable and to examine the relevance of place in the context of personality assessment. To further integrate region as a cultural variable into the dialogue within psychology, and specifically in personality assessment, it is important that psychologists and health care professionals consider the influence of region not just on a macro public health level, but also on a micro individual psychologist–client care level. Scholars have provided evidence for regional variance in values and personality traits that have relevance to personality assessment through their influence on emotional well-being, mental illness, and behavior. The individuals who enter our offices for personality assessments represent a multiplicity of identities and, although it has often been ignored, one such identity is a *regional identity*. As we confront our biases and become curious about the ways in which traits and behavior might vary based on place, we should understand the importance of moving beyond stereotypes to have a more nuanced understanding of the role of regional culture in individuals' lives.

References

Alesina, A., Devleeschauwer, A., Easterly, W., Kurlat, S., & Wacziarg, R. (2003). Fractionalization. *Journal of Economic growth, 8*(2), 155–194. http://dx.doi.org/10.1023/A:1024471506938

Allen, J., & Walsh, J. A. (2000). A construct-based approach to equivalence: Methodologies for cross-cultural/multicultural personality assessment research. In J. H. Dana (Ed.), *Handbook of cross-cultural and multicultural assessment* (pp. 63–85). Mahwah, NJ: Lawrence Erlbaum.

American Psychological Association. (2002). Ethical principles of psychologists and code of conduct. *American Psychologist, 57*, 1060–1073. doi: 10.1037/0003-066x.57.12.1060

Arredondo, P. (1999). Multicultural counseling competencies as tools to address oppression and racism. *Journal of Counseling & Development, 77*, 102–108. http://dx.doi.org/10.1002/j.1556-6676.1999.tb02427.x

Bellah, R. N., Madsen, R., Sullivan, W. M., Swidler, A., & Tipton, S. M. (1985). *Habits of the heart: Individualism and commitment in American life*. Berkeley, CA: University of California Press.

Butcher, J. N., Dahlstrom, W. G., Graham, J. R., Tellegen, A., & Kaemmer, B. (1989). *MMPI-2: Manual for administration and scoring*. Minneapolis: University of Minnesota Press.

Carter, J., & Borch, C. (2005). Assessing the effects of urbanism and regionalism on gender role attitudes, 1974–1998. *Sociological Inquiry, 75*, 548–563. http://dx.doi.org/10.1111/j.1475-682X.2005.00136.x

Carter, J., Scott, L., Mulkey, L., & Borch, C. (2005). When the rubber meets the road: The differential effects of urbanism and region on principle and implementation measure of racial tolerance. *Social Science Research, 34*, 408–425. http://dx.doi.org/10.1016/j.ssresearch.2004.04.004

Chimonides, K., & Frank, D. (1998). Rural and urban adolescents' perceptions of mental health. *Adolescence, 33*, 823–832.

Church, A. T. (2001). Personality measurement in cross-cultural perspective. *Journal of Personality, 69*(6), 979–1006. http://dx.doi.org/10.1111/1467-6494.696172

Cicchetti, D. V. (1994). Guidelines, criteria, and rules of thumb for evaluating normed and standardized assessment instruments in psychology. *Psychological Assessment, 6*(4), 284. http://dx.doi.org/10.1037/1040-3590.6.4.284

Cohen, A. B. (2009). Many forms of culture. *American Psychologist, 64*(3), 194–204. http://dx.doi.org/10.1037/a0015308

Cohen, D. (1996). Law, social policy, and violence: The impact of regional cultures. *Journal of Personality and Social Psychology, 70*, 961–978. http://dx.doi.org/10.1037/0022-3514.70.5.961

Cohen, D. (2001). Cultural variation: Considerations and implications. *Psychological Bulletin, 127*, 451–471. http://dx.doi.org/10.1037/0033-2909.127.4.451

Cohen, D., Nisbett, R. E., Bowdle, B. F., & Schwarz, N. (1996). Insult, aggression, and the Southern culture of honor: An "experimental ethnography." *Journal of Personality and Social Psychology, 70*, 945–960. http://dx.doi.org/10.1037/0022-3514.70.5.945

Conway, L. G. III, Ryder, A. G., Tweed, R. G., & Sokol, B. W. (2001). Intranational cultural variation: Exploring further implications within the United States. *Journal of Cross-Cultural Psychology, 32*, 681–697. http://dx.doi.org/10.1177/0022022101032006003

Conway, L. G. III, Sexton, S. M., Tweed, R. G. (2006). Collectivism and governmentally initiated restrictions: A cross-sectional and longitudinal analysis across nations and within a nation. *Journal of Cross-Cultural Psychology, 37*, 20–41. http://dx.doi.org/10.1177/0022022105282293

Coon, H. M., & Kemmelmeier, M. (2001). Cultural orientations in the United States (re) examining differences among ethnic groups. *Journal of Cross-Cultural Psychology, 32*(3), 348–364. http://dx.doi.org/10.1177/0022022101032003006

Coward, R. T., DeWeaver, K. L., Schmidt, F. E., & Jackson, R. W. (1983). Distinctive features of rural environments: A frame of reference for mental health practice. *International Journal of Mental Health, 12*, 3–24.

Douglas, E. M. (2006). Familial violence socialization in childhood and later life approval of corporal punishment: A cross-cultural perspective. *American Journal of Orthopsychiatry, 76*(1), 23. http://dx.doi.org/10.1037/0002-9432.76.1.23

Flynn, C. P. (1994). Regional differences in attitudes toward corporal punishment. *Journal of Marriage and the Family, 56*(2), 314–324. http://dx.doi.org/10.2307/353102

Gore, J. S., Wilburn, K. R., Treadway, J., & Plaut, V. (2011). Regional collectivism in Appalachia and academic attitudes. *Cross-Cultural Research, 45*(4), 376–398. http://dx.doi.org/10.1177/1069397111403396

Graves, A., Jones, L., & Kaplan, F. F. (2013). Draw-a-Person-in-the-Rain: Does geographic location matter? *Art Therapy, 30*(3), 107–113. http://dx.doi.org/10.1080/07421656.2013.819282

Halperin, R. H. (1998). *Practicing community: Class, culture, and power in an urban neighborhood.* Austin: University of Texas Press.

Harrington, J. R., & Gelfand, M. J. (2014). Tightness–looseness across the 50 United States. *Proceedings of the National Academy of Sciences, 111*(22), 7990–7995. http://dx.doi.org/10.1073/pnas.1317937111

Hartshorne, R. (1959). *Perspective on the nature of geography.* Chicago: Rand McNally.

Hathaway, S. R., & McKinley, J. C. (1940). A multiphasic personality schedule (Minnesota): I. Construction of the schedule. *Journal of Psychology, 10,* 249–254. http://dx.doi.org/10.1080/00223980.1940.9917000

Helms, J. E., & Cook, D. A. (1999). *Using race and culture in counseling and psychotherapy: Theory and process.* Needham, MA: Allyn & Bacon.

Hofstede, G. (1980). *Culture's consequences.* Beverly Hills, CA: Sage.

Holland, J. L. (1985). *Making vocational choices: A theory of vocational personalities and work environments* (2nd ed.). Englewood Cliffs, NJ: Prentice-Hall.

Hoyt, D. R., Conger, R. D., Valde, J. G., & Weihs, K. (1997). Psychological distress and help seeking in rural America. *American Journal of Community Psychology, 25,* 449–470. http://dx.doi.org/10.1023/A:1024655521619

Hudson, C. G. (2009). Validation of a model for estimating state and local prevalence of serious mental illness. *International Journal of Methods in Psychiatric Research, 18,* 251–264. http://dx.doi.org/10.1002/mpr.294

Hudson, C. G. (2012). Disparities in the geography of mental health: Implications for social work. *Social Work, 57*(2), 107–119. http://dx.doi.org/10.1093/sw/sws001

John, O. P., & Srivastava, S. (1999). The Big Five Trait taxonomy: History, measurement, and theoretical perspectives. In L. A. Pervin & O. P. John (Eds.), *Handbook of personality: Theory and research* (2nd ed., pp. 102–139). New York: Guilford.

Keefe, S. E. (1988). Appalachian family ties. In S. E. Keefe (Ed.), *Appalachian mental health* (pp. 24–35). Lexington, KY: The University Press of Kentucky.

Keefe, S. E. (1998). Appalachian Americans: The formation of "reluctant ethnics." In G. R. Campbell (Ed.), *Many Americas: Critical perspectives on race, racism, and ethnicity* (pp. 129–153). Dubuque, IA: Kendall/Hunt.

Kim, G., Loi, C. X. A., Chiriboga, D. A., Jang, Y., Parmelee, P., & Allen, R. S. (2011). Limited English proficiency as a barrier to mental health service use: A study of Latino and Asian immigrants with psychiatric disorders. *Journal of Psychiatric Research, 45*(1), 104–110. http://dx.doi.org/10.1016/j.jpsychires.2010.04.031

Kitayama, S., Conway, L. G. III, Pietromonaco, P. R., Park, H., & Plaut, V. C. (2010). Ethos of independence across regions in the United States: The production-adoption model of cultural change. *American Psychologist, 65*(6), 559. http://dx.doi.org/10.1037/a0020277

Krug, S. E., & Kulhavy, R. W. (1973). Personality differences across regions of the United States. *Journal of Social Psychology, 91,* 73–79. http://dx.doi.org/10.1080/00224545.1973.9922648

Langenhove, L. (2013). What is region? Towards a statehood theory of regions. *Contemporary Politics, 19,* 474–490. http://dx.doi.org/10.1080/13569775.2013.853392

Lee, D. L., Rosen, A. D., & Burns, V. (2013). Over a half-century encapsulated: A multicultural content analysis of the *Journal of Counseling Psychology,* 1954–2009. *Journal of Counseling Psychology, 60*(1), 154. http://dx.doi.org/10.1037/a0031002

Lester, D., & Voracek, M. (2013). Big five personality scores and rates of suicidality in the United States. *Psychological Reports, 112*(2), 637–639. http://dx.doi.org/10.2466/12.09.PR0.112.2.637-639

Markus, H. R., & Kitayama, S. (1991). Culture and the self: Implications for cognition, emotion, and motivation. *Psychological Review, 98*, 224–253. http://dx.doi.org/10.1037/0033295X.98.2.224

McCann, S. J. (2010). Suicide, big five personality factors, and depression at the American state level. *Archives of Suicide Research, 14*(4), 368–374. http://dx.doi.org/10.1080/13811118.2010.524070

McCann, S. J. H. (2011). Emotional health and the big five personality factors at the American state level. *Journal of Happiness Studies, 12*(4), 547–560. http://dx.doi.org/10.1007/s10902-010-9215-9

Montgomery, M. (2000). The idea of Appalachian isolation. *Appalachian Heritage, 28*(2), 20–31. http://dx.doi.org/10.1353/aph.2000.0071

Morey, L. C. (1991). *Personality assessment inventory (PAI) professional manual.* Odessa, FL: Psychological Assessment Resources.

Moriarty, D. G., Zack, M. M., Holt, James B., Chapman, D. P., & Safran, M. A. (2009). Geographic patterns or frequent mental distress. *American Journal of Preventive Medicine, 36*(6), 497–505. http://dx.doi.org/10.1016/j.amepre.2009.01.038

Morrissey, K. G. (1997). *Mental territories: Mapping the inland empire.* Ithaca, NY: Cornell University Press.

Murray, J., & Keller, P. (1991). Psychology and rural American: Current status and future directions, *American Psychologist, 46*, 220–231. http://dx.doi.org/10.1037/0003-066X.46.3.220

Nisbett, R. E. (1993). Violence and US regional culture. *American Psychologist, 48*(4), 441–449. http://dx.doi.org/10.1037/0003-066X.48.4.441

Odum, H., & Moore, H. (1938). *American regionalism.* New York: Holt.

Paasi, A. (1986). The institutionalization of regions: A theoretical framework for understanding the emergence of regions and the constitution of regional identity. *Fennia, 164*, 105–146.

Park, N., Peterson, C., & Ruch, W. (2009). Orientations to happiness and life satisfaction in twenty-seven nations. *The Journal of Positive Psychology, 4*(4), 273–279. http://dx.doi.org/10.1080/17439760902933690

Park, N., & Peterson, C. (2010). Does where we live matter? The urban psychology of character strengths. *American Psychologist, 65*(6), 535–547. http://dx.doi.org/10.1037/a0019621

Pesta, B. J., McDaniel, M. A., & Bertsch, S. (2010). Toward an index of well-being for the fifty U.S. states. *Intelligence, 38*, 160–168. http://dx.doi.org/10.1016/j.intell.2009.09.006

Plaut, V. C., Markus, H. R., & Lachman, M. E. (2002). Place matters: Consensual features and regional variation in American well-being and self. *Journal of Personality and Social Psychology, 83*(1), 160. http://dx.doi.org/10.1037/0022-3514.83.1.160

Plaut, V. C., Markus, H. R., Treadway, J. R., & Fu, A. S. (2012). The cultural construction of self and well-being: A tale of two cities. *Personality and Social Psychology Bulletin, 38*(12), 1644–1658. http://dx.doi.org/10.1177/0146167212458125

Powers, R. S., Suitor, J. J., Guerra, S., Shackelford, M., Mecom, D., & Gusman, K. (2003). Regional differences in gender-role attitudes: Variations by gender and race. *Gender Issues, 21*(2), 40–54. http://dx.doi.org/10.1007/s12147-003-0015-y

Rentfrow, P. J. (2010). Statewide differences in personality: Toward a psychological geography of the United States. *American Psychologist, 65*(6), 548–558. http://dx.doi.org/10.1037/a0018194

Rentfrow, P. J., Gosling, S. D., Jokela, M., Stillwell, D. J., Kosinski, M., & Potter, J. (2013). Divided we stand: Three psychological regions of the United States and their political, economic, social, and health correlates. *Journal of Personality and Social Psychology, 105*(6), 996–1012. http://dx.doi.org/10.1037/a0034434

Rentfrow, P. J., Gosling, S. D., & Potter, J. (2008). A theory of the emergence, persistence, and expression of geographic variation in psychological characteristics. *Perspectives on Psychological Science, 3*(5), 339–369. http://dx.doi.org/10.1111/j.1745-6924.2008.00084.x

Rentfrow, P. J., Mellander, C., & Florida, R. (2009). Happy states of America: A state-level analysis of psychological, economic, and social well-being. *Journal of Research in Personality, 43*(6), 1073–1082. http://dx.doi.org/10.1016/j.jrp.2009.08.005

Rice, T. W., & Coates, D. L. (1995). Gender role attitudes in the southern United States. *Gender & Society, 9*(6), 744–756. http://dx.doi.org/10.1177/089124395009006007

Shrestha, L. B. (2011). *Changing demographic profile of the United States*. DIANE Publishing.

Shrira, I., & Christenfeld, N. (2010). Disentangling the person and the place as explanations for regional differences in suicide. *Suicide and Life-Threatening Behavior, 40*(3), 287–297. http://dx.doi.org/10.1521/suli.2010.40.3.287

Snyder, M., & Ickes, W. (1985). Personality and social behavior. In G. Lindzey & E. Aronson (Eds.), *Handbook of social psychology* (3rd edition, Vol. 2, pp. 883–948). New York: Plenum Press.

Society for Personality Assessment. (2006). Standards for Education and Training in Psychological Assessment: Position of the Society for Personality Assessment. *Journal of Personality Assessment, 87*, 355–357. http://dx.doi.org/10.1207/s15327752jpa8703_17

Stack, S. (2000). Suicide: A 15-year review of the sociological literature. Part II: Modernization and social integration perspectives. *Suicide and Life-Threatening Behavior, 30*, 163–176.

Stouffer, S. (1955). *Communism, conformity, and civil liberties*. New York: Doubleday.

Sue, S. (2003). In defense of cultural competency in psychotherapy and treatment. *American Psychologist, 58*(11), 964. http://dx.doi.org/10.1037/0003-066X.58.11.964

Suzuki, L. A., & Ponterotto, J. G. (Eds.). (2008). *Handbook of multicultural assessment: Clinical, psychological, and educational applications*. San Francisco, CA: Jossey-Bass.

Swaim, R., & Stanley, L. (2011). Rurality, region, ethnic community make-up and alcohol use among rural youth. *The Journal of Rural Health, 27*, 91–102. http://dx.doi.org/10.1111/j.1748-0361.2010.00324.x

Triandis, H. C. (1995). *Individualism and collectivism*. Boulder, CO: Westview.

Triandis, H. C. (2001). Individualism-collectivism and personality. *Journal of Personality, 69*(6), 907–924. http://dx.doi.org/10.1111/1467-6494.696169

Turchik, J. A., Karpenko, V., Hammers, D., & McNamara, J. R. (2007). Practical and ethical assessment issues in rural, impoverished, and managed care settings. *Professional Psychology: Research and Practice, 38*(2), 158. http://dx.doi.org/10.1037/0735-7028.38.2.158

Twenge, J. (1997). Attitudes toward women, 1970–1995. *Psychology of Women Quarterly, 21*, 35–51. http://dx.doi.org/10.1111/j.1471-6402.1997.tb00099.x

U.S. Census Bureau. (2010). Census urban and rural classification and urban area criteria. Retrieved February 2014 from www.census.gov/geo/reference/ua/urban-rural-2010.html.

Vandello, J. A., & Cohen, D. (1999). Patterns of individualism and collectivism across the United States. *Journal of Personality and Social Psychology, 77*(2), 279–292. http://dx.doi.org/10.1037/0022-3514.77.2.279

van de Vijver, F. J., & van Hemert, D. A. (2008). Cross-cultural personality assessment. *The SAGE handbook of personality theory and assessment, 2*, 55–72. http://dx.doi.org/10.4135/9781849200479.n3

Vandello, J. A., Hettinger, V. E., & Michniewicz, K. (2014). Regional culture. In A. B. Cohen (Ed.), *Culture Reexamined: Broadening Our Understanding of Social and Evolutionary Influences* (pp. 77–91). Washington, DC: American Psychological Association. http://dx.doi.org/10.1037/14274-004

Vera, E. M., & Speight, S. L. (2003). Multicultural competence, social justice, and counseling psychology: Expanding our roles. *The Counseling Psychologist, 31*(3), 253–272. http://dx.doi.org/10.1177/0011000003031003001

Voracek, M. (2009). Big five personality factors and suicide rates in the United States: A state-level analysis. *Perceptual and Motor Skills, 109*(1), 208–212. http://dx.doi.org/10.2466/pms.109.1.208-212

Williams, C. L., Graham, J. R., Archer, R. P., Tellegen, A., Ben-Porath, Y. S., & Kaemmer, B. (1992). *MMPI-A: Minnesota Multiphasic Personality Inventory-Adolescent: Manual for administration, scoring, and interpretation*. Minneapolis: University of Minnesota Press.

Wilson, S. M., & Peterson, G. W. (2000). Growing up in Appalachia: Ecological influences on adolescent development. In R. Montemayor, G. R. Adams, T. P. Gullotta (Eds.), *Adolescent diversity in ethnic, economic, and cultural contexts* (pp. 75–109). Thousand Oaks, CA: Sage Publications. http://dx.doi.org/10.4135/9781452225647.n4

Wilson, T. (1991). Urbanism, migration, and tolerance: A reassessment. *American Sociological Review, 56*, 117–123. http://dx.doi.org/10.2307/2095677

Wilson, T. (1985). Urbanism and tolerance: A test of some hypotheses drawn from Wirth and Stouffer. *American Sociological Review, 50*, 117–123. http://dx.doi.org/10.2307/2095345

Wirth, L. (1938). Urbanism as a way of life. *The American Journal of Sociology, 44*, 1–24. http://dx.doi.org/10.1086/217913

CHAPTER 11

Age as Diversity in Psychological Assessment

Verónica Portillo Reyes, Radhika Krishnamurthy, and Antonio E. Puente

The individuals we assess in behavioral health settings undoubtedly vary in age across the lifespan spectrum. In fact, the traditional age range of clients receiving psychological assessment has progressively expanded over time, both downward to infancy and upward to older adulthood. Given that children are being tested at younger ages than ever before for early identification of developmental risks, and evaluation of older adults has increased in response to a growing aging population, questions arise such as: Are we sufficiently attuned to the developmental context of children and adolescents and the needs of older adults? Are we considering generational characteristics and their effects that might influence interactions with the individual, evaluation methods, and interpretation of test results? Are we using suitable test measures and norms?

A number of practical issues come into play when conducting assessments with individuals of different ages. Consider the following scenarios:

1. A seven-year-old boy is referred for assessment for refusal to go to school. During the assessment interview, he clings to his mother and is visibly anxious when asked to come into the testing room alone. Can the assessor depart from standard testing procedures to permit the mother's presence during testing? Will the presence of the observing parent have an impact on the validity of test results?
2. A 15-year-old girl being assessed for an eating disorder does not want her parents to be informed of assessment results. Given the adolescent's status as a minor, how might the assessor balance issues of the parents' right to information and the client's need for privacy?
3. A 72-year-old man experiencing acute depression and cognitive confusion is scheduled for a testing session in which personality and neuropsychological tests are to be administered. Test results are needed quickly to guide dispositional decisions. After two hours of testing, the client has completed only 150 items on the Minnesota Multiphasic Personality Inventory, 2nd edition (MMPI-2) and reports eye strain, fatigue, and problems keeping up with the demands of testing. What steps can the assessor take to accommodate the client while achieving timely completion of testing?

4. A 20-year-old man is referred for pre-employment screening as part of his application for a police officer position. Results of the personality assessment indicate narcissistic traits and autonomy-proneness, which might be viewed as undesirable in this context. What information related to generation/cohort effects should the assessor contemplate to make a fair assessment of the individual?

These scenarios speak to the need for knowledge and sensitivity to age considerations. Potential errors and oversights could have adverse effects such as overdiagnosis of psychopathology in children and adolescents or ageist biases in assessing older adults.

In this chapter, we discuss the role of age as a diversity variable and its implications for personality assessment methods and interpretations. We posit that regardless of what other conditions of diversity are present in an assessment situation, such as culture and gender, age is involved in all of them. Therefore, although diversity is a broad-ranging variable, the focus will eventually include age as a variable in question.

Conceptual Considerations

The typical organization of age across the lifespan is by groupings such as childhood, adolescence, and adulthood. However, as populations in the United States and worldwide evolve, we find shifts in the composition of these age groupings, both in their relative size and in their diversity makeup. Among adults, for example, the 2010 U.S. Census report indicates that the number of persons age 65 and over was greater in 2010 than in any previous census; between 2000 and 2010, this segment of the population grew at a faster rate than the total U.S. population (Werner, November 2011), and it is projected to reach 88.5 million in 2050 (Vincent & Velkoff, May 2010). It is also anticipated that by 2060, 64% of children under age 18 will belong to racial or ethnic minorities (Colby & Ortman, March 2015). Furthermore, modern generations such as the Millennial cohort, born between 1982 and the early 2000s, are becoming the prevalent generation represented in society today. Indeed, with greater projected additions to the Millennial population from immigration than any other cohort, this group is expected to peak in 2036 at 81.1 million (Fry, 2016). With increased globalization and mobility, populations in the U.S. and worldwide have become more culturally diverse; between 2014 and 2060, the foreign-born population in the U.S. is projected to increase by 36 million people (Colby & Ortman, March 2015). These forms of diversity, in turn, interface with and affect the characteristics of the individual being assessed. We understand diversity to include the recognition of individuals' uniqueness in terms of their age, disability, ethnicity, gender identity, language, race, sexual orientation, religion, and socioeconomic status (Daniel, Roysircar, Abeles, & Boyd, 2004). Chronological age, therefore, bears consideration in assessment work, in parallel with the characteristics of the individual's generation and in intersection with other diversity variables.

In this chapter, we use the organization of conventional age groupings—childhood, adolescence, adulthood and geriatric—to define developmental epochs. We do so for several reasons. (1) They are most often considered major developmental periods; (2) these periods are often marked by distinct behavioral, cognitive, neuropsychological, and personality characteristics; (3) psychopathology can be more easily grouped into these four developmental periods. However, even within these chosen periods, there are subsets. For example, childhood could be further subdivided into infancy, early, middle, and late childhood, and boundaries are also drawn between young adulthood, middle age, and older adulthood. As a further caveat, we note the following important points: (a) developmental age can differ from chronological age, as often discussed in the area of child assessment (e.g., Petermann & Macha, 2008); (b) older adults' current conceptions of their chronological age might differ from those in previous eras, as influenced by their individual viewpoints of what constitutes being old but also by shifting societal views of old age. Therefore, standard cut-offs for different age groups can be seen as arbitrary (Levy & Macdonald, 2016). In an alternative self-categorization model, Giles and Reid (2005) describe salient age categories as a series of overlapping continua; this is schematically presented as overlapping distributions with identified prototypic positions that might or might not lie in the center of the distribution.

While chronological age is a necessary consideration when assessing psychological characteristics of an individual, it is not sufficient. The individual must also be placed within the context of the period within which he or she was born and developed. This shared location in historical context creates a "peer personality" which differs from generation to generation (Strauss & Howe, 2008). Howe and Strauss (2007) explain that these unique characteristics arise from the shared experiences of the age cohort; for example, the Baby Boomer generation (born 1943–1960) grew up during the civil rights movement, the Vietnam War, the sexual revolution, and the Cold War. This generation's experiences in the workforce consisted of many women entering male-dominated workplaces, and both sexes started in value-centric careers. During the 1980s, as deregulation and free enterprise increased, this generation evolved into the yuppie individualists, followed by the 1990s where politics and culture were of great cultural focus. As parents, this generation valued very close parenting styles and has experienced a large decline in economic prosperity. One must be attentive to the culture of the individual's generation during the process of evaluation as an important factor of diversity.

According to Howe and Strauss (2000), there are five generations in current American society. The Silent Generation represents the oldest in society who were born 1942 or before, the Baby Boomer generation represents those born from 1943 to 1960, Generation X are individuals born from 1961 to 1981, Millennials are those born from 1982 to 2002, and Generation Z are those born from 2003 onwards. Each generation exhibits trends in characteristics such as values, beliefs, expectations, communication style, motivation, and personality traits which are the result of their development in a historical context (Howe & Strauss, 2000). Increases in diversity have led researchers to use the unique generational characteristics to better integrate individuals in workplaces and refine methods of education (e.g., Johnson &

Romanello, 2005; Lyons & Kuron, 2014); these differences in generation-related culture are also relevant for personality test interpretations.

The growing awareness of societal biases against older adults has, in recent decades, intensified the literature on ageism in relation to the elderly population. Ageism has been conceptually defined as:

> negative or positive stereotypes, prejudice and/or discrimination against (or to the advantage of) elderly people on the basis of a perception of them as being 'old' or 'elderly.' Ageism can be implicit or explicit and can be expressed on a micro-, meso- or macro-level.
>
> (Iversen, Larsen, & Solem, 2009, p. 15)

Negative stereotypes about the elderly often include exaggerated notions of impaired functioning, disability, or incompetence, with the associated assumption that they are a burden on personal and public resources. Such stereotypes are found even among health care professionals (Chrisler, Barney, & Palatino, 2016). Ageism finds expression in actions such as patronizing and disrespectful behavior toward older adults, discriminatory hiring practices and forced early retirements, and deficient health care services (Levy & Macdonald, 2016). Furthermore, because the majority of older adults are women, they are likely to experience cumulative stress effects of both ageism and gender disparities (Chrisler et al., 2016). Ageism is embedded in our culture such that the stereotypes can become internalized by older adults to the detriment of their health and functioning (Palmore, 2015); documented adverse effects of internalized ageism include decline in memory performance, increased cardiovascular response to stress over time, and problems with activities of daily living (Butler, 2009; Nelson, 2016). Conversely, maintaining a positive view of aging has been associated with a lower likelihood of developing psychiatric problems, better functional health, and increased longevity (Nelson, 2016). The psychological assessor should take note of any ageist stereotypes he or she might hold that could introduce bias into the evaluation process. Ageism is a factor that is typically not considered, but it can result in distorted test findings and inadequate mental health treatment (Robb, Chen, & Haley, 2002).

Age and Development

Age-related developmental effects are well documented with regard to cognitive development in children and potential declines among older adults. In the case of children, for example, executive function does not start to develop until about the age of seven (Best, Miller, & Jones, 2009) and complex problem solving emerges clearly by adolescence (Frischkorn, Greiff, & Wüstenberg, 2014). Information processing capacities, including processing speed and effectiveness, are found to increase from childhood into adolescence, and adolescents also demonstrate improved performance on decision-making tasks relative to younger children (Kuhn, 2006). In contrast to children and adolescents, older adults often experience a decline in some aspects of cognitive performance and possible changes in personality. Older adults are less able than the young to store new information and recall it later (Rosselli & Ardila, 2010). Increases in age in older adulthood are generally associated with slower motor speed, reduced perceptual information processing speed, and increased reaction times (Ardila, 2007). In investigating the effect of age on normative scores on the Wechsler Adult Intelligence Scale-III, Ryan, Sattler, and López (2000) found that processing speed and perceptual organization scores decreased among older adults. However, verbal subtest scores changed minimally with age. It should be noted that age effects on cognitive functioning can be influenced by education level and cultural context. For example, Ostrosky-Solís et al.'s (2007) study of 521 Spanish-speaking participants in Mexico aged 6–85 years found interactions between age and years of education for the 16–30 and 31–55 age ranges in general orientation and memory performance; between 56 and 85 years, the age effect was seen to be more potent than education.

Evidence of age effects is also found in the research literature on personality development and psychopathology. For example, recent articles note that adolescents experience normative increases in moral judgment and ego development, but also greater frequency of increased conflicts with parents, risk-taking and law-breaking behaviors, and depression than in earlier or later periods (McCrae et al., 2002). McCrae et al. (2002) presented evidence of increased Openness to Experience between age 12 and 18 for both girls and boys and increased Neuroticism among girls, which were generalizable to other Western cultures. Problems in emotion regulation can also intensify in adolescence. Among those with a degree of personality dysfunction, the threshold for exhibiting symptoms has been found to be lower in adolescence than in adulthood for Self and Interpersonal domains of the Severity Indices for Personality Problems-118 (Debast, Rossi, Feenstra, & Hutsebaut, 2017). Other studies have documented significantly lower constraint and lower positive emotionality in adolescents compared to young adults (Ryan, 2009). Among older adults, mean-level trends are found in the direction of increasing neuroticism and decreasing extraversion, agreeableness, openness, and conscientiousness relative to younger and middle-aged adults (Kandler, Kornadt, Hagemeyer, & Neyer, 2015).

In a related topic on personality development and age but with a somewhat different slant, an issue discussed in the personality literature concerns the degree of continuity versus change in personality patterns over the course of the lifespan. Some (e.g., McCrae & Costa, 1994) have provided the perspective that significant change is more likely to occur early in development and that stability, especially in personality traits, becomes established during adulthood. This viewpoint has strong empirical support, with accompanying evidence of cross-cultural and cross-language universality of personality trait structure (McCrae & Costa, 1997). Others (e.g., Debast et al., 2014) provide information about both continuities and discontinuities in adaptive and maladaptive personality traits throughout the lifespan, whereby manifested behaviors may vary even as the underlying structure remains constant. It is, therefore, fair to say that the impact of age as an important variable in assessment can vary significantly across the lifespan and within each developmental epoch. The original concept proposed by early personality theorists as to the stability of personality and cognition throughout the lifespan after early epochs might be oversimplistic in terms of not appreciating the robustness and complexity of age effects. Therefore, age should be considered as an important variable affecting the measurement of a construct (e.g., personality and psychopathology, intelligence, and neuropsychological status).

With regard to generational effects, Jean Twenge, a forerunner in this area of study, and other researchers have demonstrated that there are differences between generations in aspects of psychopathology and personality. Using meta-analyses to compare cross-temporal scores from high school and college students over the past 70 years, Twenge et al. (2010) demonstrated that findings from previous studies on depression (i.e., Lewinsohn, Rohde, Seeley & Fischer, 1993; Robins et al., 1984; Wickramaratne, Weissman, Leaf, & Holford, 1989) could be verified as the result of generational changes. Furthermore, they demonstrated that scores on MMPI clinical scales including Psychopathic Deviate, Paranoia, Schizophrenia, and Hypomania, are, on average, more than a standard deviation higher for current generations of college students than previous ones, when controlling for social desirability and defensive responding. A similar pattern was found for high school students for Paranoia, Hysteria, Hypochondriasis, and Depression scales. Anxiety has also been seen to have risen approximately a standard deviation from the 1950s to the 1990s (Twenge, 2000). Twenge and colleagues (2010) summarized that the increased emphasis on extrinsic goals and individualism in modern American culture appears to be co-occurring with increased psychopathology (as discussed also by Eckersley & Dear, 2002; Kasser, 2006; Myers, 2000; Seligman, 1990). Researchers have also demonstrated that narcissism has been increasing from generation to generation (Trzesniewski, Donnellan, & Robins, 2008; Twenge & Foster, 2010; Twenge, Miller, and Campbell, 2014). Some go as far as to say that there is an epidemic of narcissism; Twenge and Campbell (2009) reason that modern parenting strategies, media, and social networking foster individualism and might lead Millennials and Generation Z to demonstrate increased narcissistic traits as compared to previous generations.

Age and Personality Assessment

There is well-documented evidence of age effects on self-report personality measures such as the MMPI-2 (Butcher, Dahlstrom, Graham, Tellegen, & Kaemmer, 1989). Greene's (2011) review of age effects on the MMPI-2 identifies several important differences in *T* scores of adult age groups from the normative sample and a large clinical sample, clustered in ten-year intervals. Among notable findings, the 18–19-year-old cohort produced higher *T* scores than other age groups on several validity scales measuring self-unfavorable reporting of psychopathology, particularly in the clinical sample, and several clinical, content, and supplementary scales. Scale 1 (Hypochondriasis) scores and 1-2/2-1 and 1-3/3-1 code types increasing in frequency among older age groups whereas Scale 4 (Psychopathic Deviate) and all code types involving this scale decreased with age. Similarly, scores on the Health Problems content scale increased by an average of six *T*-score points from the 20–29 age range to the 50–59 age range, and the PSY-5 Psychoticism and Disconstraint scale scores showed consistent decrease between ages 20–29 and 80+ across samples. Greene summarized that (a) age effects are similar across clinical and normal samples for most MMPI-2 scales, (b) the youngest age group (age 18–19) routinely elevate scale scores more than 20–29 year olds and older age groups, (c) scores on several scales measuring behavioral activation decrease by 5–10 *T*-score points across ages 20–29 to 80+. These findings reflect the real impact of age on personality and symptomatic expressions of psychopathology.

Friedman, Bolinskey, Levak, and Nichols (2015) further summarized that psychopathology in adults as measured by the MMPI-2 declines with age, along with decreased acting out and alienation in both men and women. On the other hand, preoccupation with health/illness increases, along with slight increments in pessimism. Friedman et al. noted that age-related differences are not large enough to warrant use of age-corrected norms for adults, but age should, nonetheless, be considered as a moderator variable in the interpretation of the test profiles. They suggested, for example, that moderate elevations on depression and somatic scales are likely less pathological in a person over age 70 than in a young adult. This is because they may reflect realistic changes in health concerns and energy levels and attitudes that often accompany age progression (Graham, 2012).

Age-related findings are also found for other self-report personality measures. Davis and Greenblatt's (1990) investigation of age effects on the MCMI scores of psychiatric inpatients showed that older adult age groups (age 36+) obtained lower symptom scale scores than younger adult groups (age 35 and below). Investigations of psychopathy using measures such as the Hare Psychopathy Checklist (PCL) have also reported age effects in the direction of lower scores at older ages. Harpur and Hare's (1994) analysis of PCL scores in samples of male prison inmates and forensic psychiatric inpatients showed that although Factor 1 (affective/interpersonal) scores were stable across ages, Factor 2 (unstable and antisocial lifestyle) scores and the prevalence of antisocial personality disorder significantly decreased with age. They discussed that the latter findings could be attributed in part to reductions in personality characteristics of impulsivity and sensation seeking with age. Coid, Yang, Ullrich, Roberts, and Hare (2009) similarly reported lower PCL: Screening Version (PCL:SV) scores for adults ages 55–74 than younger age groups, particularly in Lifestyle and Antisocial factors. A recent research report further exemplified the role of chronological age in personality and psychopathy test score connections. In their investigation of Psychopathic Personality Inventory-Revised (PPI-R) correlates of the Personality Assessment Inventory (PAI) in a community sample, Irvin and Krishnamurthy (2014) found score associations to be stronger and more numerous for younger (ages 20–39) than older (age 50+) participants. The pattern and strength of associations were fairly consistent with the expectation that younger adults are more likely to act out behaviorally in antisocial or socially deviant ways than older adults, evidenced also in significantly higher scores for the younger age group on the PAI Antisocial Features scale and its Stimulus Seeking subscale and on the PPI-R Fearlessness scale.

In performance-based personality measures such as the Rorschach, the effects of age and developmental status are addressed by using age-appropriate norms when empirically determined to be necessary. In fact, developmental trends in normative responses to the Rorschach stimuli were noted at the time of the test's development and have been supported by decades of research with children and adolescents (Tibon-Czopp & Weiner, 2016). The Comprehensive System workbook (Exner, 2001) provides separate norms by age for ages 5 through 16, and a single set of norms are used for ages 17 and older. The newer Rorschach Performance Assessment System (Meyer, Viglione, Mihura, Erard, & Erdberg, 2011) currently has a set of transitional child and adolescent norms across ages 6 through 17 (Meyer, Viglione, & Giromini, 2016 February). Other performance-based measures, such as apperceptive techniques, have developmentally appropriate alternative forms for use with different age groups. For example, alternatives to the Thematic Apperception Test (TAT), which is best used with adults, include the Children's Apperception Test (CAT) for children and Senior Apperception Technique (SAT) for elderly individuals (Bellak & Abrams, 1997). Overall, the assessor would need to attend to issues of test version and test norms for administering, scoring, and interpreting personality tests accurately for different age groups.

Assessment Considerations

An obvious issue in assessing individuals across the age spectrum is to use age-appropriate instruments. In terms of self-report personality assessment, this means evaluating adolescents with measures designed for this age group (e.g., the Minnesota Multiphasic Personality Inventory-Adolescent/Restructured Form [MMPI-A/MMPI-A-RF], Personality Assessment Inventory-Adolescent [PAI-A], Adolescent Psychopathology Scale [APS], or Millon Adolescent Clinical Inventory [MACI]) instead of the counterparts designed for adults, regardless of the perceived maturity of the teenage client, as their item content and norms are appropriate to adolescent age and developmental levels. For older adults, a useful review of appropriate assessment instruments is provided by Edelstein et al. (2008), which covers assessment of anxiety, depression, suicidal ideation, sleep disorders, normal and maladaptive personality functioning. A recent overview of child/adolescent and adult measures for assessing personality and psychopathology is also provided by Krishnamurthy and Meyer (2016).

Tests must match the developmental period both from a theoretical as well as a practical standpoint. For example, a test intended for complex problem solving, such as the Category Test, must be modified substantially to address the cognitive patterns of younger individuals to align with their developmental capacities. Commonly used tests for adaptive function such as the Vineland Adaptive Behavior Scales and the Adaptive Behavior Assessment System were intended to measure deficits in children. However, they have sometimes been used to retrospectively determine adaptive deficits before the age of 18 for individuals older than 18. We emphasize that tests developed for one developmental epoch should not be used for another epoch unless research studies support the appropriateness of such "adaptation." Most likely such an application would not result in an "accommodation" that, according to the Standards for Educational and Psychological Testing (AERA, APA, & NCME, 2014), preserves the measured construct, but would instead result in a "modification" that changes the construct.

With regard to variables that are considered during the assessment process, the literature appears to indicate that the following three variables are critical in the measurement of human behavior, in order of importance: (1) age, (2) culture, and (3) education. Culture in this context not only refers to the society and behavioral norms but also generational characteristics. The task of the assessor is to meaningfully integrate these variables into the assessment findings instead of having them operate as confounds, such as misrepresenting depression in an older adult as normal affect for the elderly.

The use of psychometrically sound instruments in the evaluation process is essential to diminish the possibility of confounding age or generation status with the intended construct being measured (e.g., maladjustment) or other forms of diversity as well as with other constructs in question. In turn, if diversity influences could be isolated from development features, then a truer within-development comparison would exist. This would reduce construct irrelevance and increase understanding of the question being pursued (although, in actuality, various attributes and experiences of the individual tend to be intertwined or overlapping). With this awareness, the use of universal tests is likely to be much less suitable for all purposes and circumstances as well as across all developmental periods. That is, for different populations and contexts, clinicians will need to make additional adjustments to meet the characteristics of these individuals or contexts. Therefore, these considered characteristics such as age, generation, race, ethnicity, gender, education, and income, should be acknowledged throughout the evaluation process (i.e., in test administration, scoring, interpretation, and use) so that any limitations within the process can be minimized and test score validity may not be skewed by any type of bias (AERA et al., 2014). In fact, recent guidelines for evidence-based assessment of children and adolescents emphasize consideration of age, gender, ethnicity, and culture, with attention to how they might influence the scope of assessment and use of assessment findings in developing intervention plans (Mash & Hunsley, 2005). With older adults, additional consideration needs to be given to health status and its effects on functioning and well-being, particularly illnesses and diseases such as heart disease and stroke for which there is increased risk with age (Black, 2000).

Tests must also have appropriate norms. Specifically, it has been suggested that normative samples represent the different proposed epochs in equal numbers. Normative data collection should include more comprehensive groups to better reflect the populations with whom the test may be used (Hsieh & Tori, 2007). Norms should not be based on samples of convenience but should, at the minimum, address a cross-section of the variables previously addressed, namely, cultural and educational variables. That is, norms should be stratified by age with cultural/generational and educational factors embedded within age groups if not considered as separate variables. Norms must be age-specific when empirically determined to

Table 11.1 A Proposed Model for Norms

Variable	*Developmental Periods*			
	Childhood	*Adolescence*	*Adulthood*	*Geriatric*
Age				
Culture/Generation Status				
Education				

be necessary. As Table 11.1 illustrates, the best-case scenario would be that norms include 12 different cells: four developmental periods × three demographic variables. An alternative to this model would be to embed culture/generation status and education within the four developmental periods.

In terms of assessment methods, the norm is to obtain multi-informant data in assessing children, typically involving parent and teacher reports to supplement observations and individual testing (Achenbach, 2005). This approach has evolved from the recognition of limits to the reliability and accuracy of children's reports, depending on their age and developmental level. At the other end of the continuum, assessing older adults requires a different set of considerations; issues such as cessation of driving or limited ambulatory capacity can interfere with the older adult's ability to come to the testing site. Among hospitalized older adults and those in nursing care facilities, bedside testing might be necessary. This approach is usually discussed in relation to mental status examinations and cognitive/neuropsychological testing, and efforts have even been undertaken to develop specific bedside tests for use in rehabilitation settings (e.g., Leibovitch, Vasquez, Ebert, Beresford, & Black, 2012). However, it is rarely addressed in terms of personality assessment. The current trend toward use of technology in supplying tablet-based test administration modes could prove facilitative, providing that the individual from an older age cohort has sufficient comfort and experience with such an alternative mode. A specific example provided in the Standards (AERA et al., 2014) that might be relevant to older age is to provide user-selected font sizes in technology-based tests to reduce construct irrelevance. Also important to note is that because psychological symptoms cannot be easily separated from medical/health problems among older adults, the assessment should ideally include consultation and coordination with other health care professionals (Hinrichsen, 2016).

Policy and Standards

The American Psychological Association (APA) has published several important position papers that affect the role of age in assessment. The APA Council of Representatives approved two major documents: Guidelines on Multicultural Education, Training, Research, Practice and Organizational Change for Psychologists (American Psychological Association, 2003a); and the Guidelines for Psychological

Practice with Older Adults (American Psychological Association, 2003b). The Council of National Psychological Associations for the Advancement of Ethnic Minority Issues (CNPAAEMI) has published relevant documents such as the Guidelines for Research in Ethnic Minority Communities (Council of National Psychological Associations for the Advancement of Ethnic Minority Issues, 2000). The Standards for Educational and Psychological Testing (AERA et al., 2014) introduced in its most recent revision an entire chapter on fairness in testing, and age figures among the diversity variables that warrant fairness considerations. Each of these provides important pieces to addressing age and assessment. Of these four, the guidelines for practicing with older adults and the standards for testing are particularly important.

The position paper on older adults was primarily generated by individuals who were developmentally focused on this age bracket more so than a specific specialty (e.g., neuropsychology). As a consequence, its strongest point is in emphasizing the uniqueness of geriatric individuals, ranging from personality and cognitive abilities and limitations to specific behavioral and physical characteristics that require understanding their special situation. For example, neuropsychological evaluations previously lasted close to 15 hours in length. Such lengthy evaluations not only do not make sense for older adults due to, among other things, their stamina, but also such lengthy evaluations do not fit into the facilities and disease processes of older adults that require a different approach.

The third author of the chapter was on the Committee for the Revision of Standards of Educational and Psychological Tests. When the 1999 revision "call for input" was sent out, a major concern for the Management Team was "fairness." Not surprisingly, groups representing more traditional diversity (e.g., ethnic-minority) areas appropriately weighed-in on their concerns. A group that previously had not apparently been very vocal in terms of the idea of diversity consisted of those within APA representing older adults. Of interest was the idea of including age as a form of diversity. When age was added to the traditional list, it became obvious to the committee that it would be impossible to address all types of diversity specifically, and that the committee could simply address "fairness," a more contemporary and expanded view. In doing so, age easily was included and helped introduce the idea that ageism is an issue warranting attention. Again, the concept was to make sure that measurement error did not confound developmental changes with another construct. For example, arthritis of the hands would seriously affect Finger Tapping Test results, which could be interpreted as a motor dysfunction and not simply as arthritis. Likewise, contextual knowledge of the individual's generation status might help explain maladaptation seen in personality testing.

The remaining two APA documents, especially the multicultural guidelines, emphasize the critical role of cultural (and linguistic) variance but do not specifically speak to the concept of age as diversity. It is anticipated that ageism will be considered an increasingly central concern in diversity awareness. As indicated previously, age is not only a diversity variable but also interfaces, affects, and confounds the role of age on assessment. Hence, understanding of the four documents in unison reflects the previously proposed multi-modal approach of the psychological assessment of age and other forms of diversity.

Practical Implications

It is critical to remember that psychological tests are only tools that aid in the diagnostic and descriptive process. The task of the examiner is to understand the individual and his or her life context in a holistic manner, with consideration of multiple interacting diversity influences. Earlier in the chapter, we noted that there are situations involving age and life context that complicate the evaluator's goal of achieving fairness in testing and obtaining unbiased test scores. We underscore the following points:

1. Being diversity-sensitive in doing personality assessment with regards to age factors means maintaining awareness of one's age-related stereotypes and biases and inhibiting their influence on the assessment process and results. It means interacting in ways that facilitate rapport with individuals of different ages—being sensitive to young children's potential anxiety in being alone with the examiner in a testing room, avoiding an overly authoritarian as well as an overly laissez-faire approach with adolescents, and responding to elderly adults in a respectful and non-condescending manner. The examiner should keep in mind the dual goals of achieving clients' full involvement in the assessment and enabling them to preserve a sense of safety and dignity.
2. In assessing children, provide the supports needed for successful assessment, such as periodic breaks to accommodate for lapses in attention or onset of fatigue. In assessing older adults, check to see that they have vision- and hearing-support devices if needed. As discussed earlier, try to provide enhanced formats of test materials such as large print booklets, electronic devices with adjustable text size and brightness, or audio presentations of test questions.
3. Keep up with the literature not only about the role of age in psychological testing but also culture, generation status, and education.
4. Know what tests meet the minimum proposed requirements, which include (a) that the test must theoretically reflect the developmental period of the person being evaluated, and (b) that norms are age stratified or age sensitive and, if possible, that culture, generation status, and education are embedded or considered in the normative equation.
5. Consider the limitations of your knowledge, the test, and the norms, and include those limitations in the final report. Alternatively, refer out if feasible or consult with others more knowledgeable of the particular age-related circumstances.

Conclusions and Future Directions

In this chapter we have discussed age as a central diversity factor in psychological assessment, in interaction with cultural background and generation status. Education is added as a third and critical variable in diversity-sensitive personality assessment.

Among older adults in particular, disease processes appear to further interact with age but the primary influence of age remains salient. As previously indicated, the interaction of age and generation with other forms of diversity pose significant challenges for accurate personality and neuropsychological assessment. Special care should be taken when a non-majority group is being represented in the evaluation process. Here the literature is sparse and only beginning to emerge. With some groups burgeoning in the U.S. population, such as Hispanics and modern generations of young adults, these issues are going to become increasingly clinically relevant.

Given that diversity includes age and development across the entire lifespan, great sensitivity and care are needed in interpreting psychological assessment results. Much research, training, and clinical growth is in front of psychology and psychologists. As we proceed forward to accepting this challenge, it is refreshing and exciting to bring age and generation status into the fold of diversity.

References

Achenbach, T. M. (2005). Advancing assessment of children and adolescents: Commentary on evidence-based assessment of child and adolescent disorders. *Journal of Clinical Child and Adolescent Psychology, 34*(3), 541–547. doi: 10.1207/s15374424jccp3403_9

American Educational Research Association, American Psychological Association, & National Council on Measurement in Education (2014). *Standards for educational and psychological testing*. Washington, DC: American Educational Research Association.

American Psychological Association. (2003a). Guidelines on multicultural education, training, research, practice, and organizational change for psychologists. *American Psychologist, 58*(5), 377–402. Retrieved from http://www.apa.org/pi/multiculturalguidelines.pdf

American Psychological Association. (2003b). *Guidelines for psychological practice with older adults*. Washington, DC: Author. Retrieved from http://www.apa.org/pi

Ardila, A. (2007). Normal aging increases cognitive heterogeneity: Analysis of dispersion in WAIS-III scores across age. *Archives of Clinical Neuropsychology, 22*(8), 1003–1011. doi: 10.1016/j.acn.2007.08.004

Bellak, L., & Abrams, D. M. (1997). *The T.A.T., C.A.T., and S.A.T. in clinical use* (6th ed.). Boston: Allyn & Bacon.

Best, J. R., Miller, P. H., & Jones, L. L. (2009). Executive functions after age 5: Changes and correlates. *Developmental Review, 29*(3), 180–200. doi: 10.1016/j.dr.2009.05.002

Black, S. A. (2000). The mental health of culturally diverse elderly: Research and clinical issues. In I. Cuellar & F. A. Paniagua (Eds.), *Handbook of multicultural mental health: Assessment and treatment of diverse populations* (pp. 326–339). San Diego, CA: Academic Press.

Butcher, J. N., Dahlstrom, W. G., Graham, J. R., Tellegen, A., & Kaemmer, B. (1989). *Minnesota Multiphasic Personality Inventory-2 (MMPI-2): Manual for administration and scoring*. Minneapolis: University of Minnesota Press.

Butler, R. N. (2009). Combating ageism. *International Psychogeriatrics, 21*(2), 211. doi: 0.1017/S104161020800731X

Chrisler, J. C., Barney, A., & Palatino, B. (2016). Ageism can be hazardous to women's health: Ageism, sexism, and stereotypes of older women in the healthcare system. *Journal of Social Issues, 72*(1), 86–104. doi: 10.1111/josi.12157

Coid, J., Yang, M., Ullrich, S., Roberts, A., & Hare, R. D. (2009). Prevalence and correlates of psychopathic traits in the household population of Great Britain. *International Journal of Law and Psychiatry, 32*, 65–73. doi: 10.1016/j.ijlp.2009.01.002

Colby, S. L., & Ortman, J. M. (March, 2015). Projections of the size and composition of the U.S. population: 2014–2060. *U.S. Census Bureau*. Retrieved from www.census.gov/content/dam/Census/library/publications/2015/demo/p25-1143.pdf

Council of National Psychological Associations for the Advancement of Ethnic Minority Issues. (2000). *Guidelines for research in ethnic minority communities*. Washington, DC: American Psychological Association.

Daniel, J. H., Roysircar, G., Abeles, N., & Boyd, C. (2004). Individual and cultural-diversity competency: Focus on the therapist. *Journal of Clinical Psychology, 60*(7), 755–770. doi: 10.1002/jclp.20014

Davis, W. E., & Greenblatt, R. L. (1990). Age differences among psychiatric inpatients on the MCMI. *Journal of Clinical Psychology, 46*, 770–774. doi: 10.1002/1097-4679(199011)46:6<770::AID-JCLP2270460611>3.0.CO;2-I

Debast, I., Rossi, G., Feenstra, D., & Hutsebaut, J. (2017). Developmentally sensitive markers of personality functioning in adolescents: Age-specific and age-neutral expressions. *Personality Disorders: Theory, Research, and Treatment, 8*(2), 162–171. http://dx.doi.org/10.1037/per0000187

Debast, I., van Alphen, S. P., Rossi, G., Tummers, J. H., Bolwerk, N., Derksen, J. J., & Rosowsky, E. (2014). Personality traits and personality disorders in late middle and old age: Do they remain stable? A literature review. *Clinical Gerontologist, 37*(3), 253–271. doi: 10.1080/07317115.2014.885917

Eckersley, R., & Dear, K. (2002). Cultural correlates of youth suicide. *Social Science and Medicine, 55*, 1891–1904. doi: 10.1016/S0277-9536(01)00319-7

Edelstein, B. A., Woodhead, E. L., Segal, D. L., Heisel, M. J., Bower, E. H., Lowery, A. J., & Stoner, S. A. (2008). Older adult psychological assessment: Current instrument status and related considerations. *Clinical Gerontologist, 31*(3), 1–35. doi: 10.1080/07317110802072108

Exner, J. E. Jr. (2001). *A Rorschach workbook for the Comprehensive System* (5th ed.). Asheville, NC: Rorschach Workshops.

Friedman, A. F., Bolinskey, P. K., Levak, R. W., & Nichols, D. S. (2015). *Psychological assessment with the MMPI-2/MMPI-2-RF* (3rd ed.). New York: Routledge.

Frischkorn, G. T., Greiff, S., & Wüstenberg, S. (2014). The development of complex problem solving in adolescence: A latent growth curve analysis. *Journal of Educational Psychology, 106*(4), 1007. http://dx.doi.org/10.1037/a0037114

Fry, R. (2016). Millennials overtake Baby Boomers as America's largest generation. *Pew Research Center, 25*.

Giles, H., & Reid, S. A. (2005). Ageism across the lifespan: Towards a self-categorization model of ageing. *Journal of Social Issues, 61*(2), 389–404. doi: 10.1111/j.1540-4560.2005.00412.x

Graham, J. R. (2012). *MMPI-2: Assessing personality and psychopathology*. New York: Oxford University Press.

Greene, R. L. (2011). *The MMPI-2/MMPI-2-RF: An interpretive manual* (3rd ed.). Boston: Allyn & Bacon.

Harpur, T. J., & Hare, R. D. (1994). Assessment of psychopathy as a function of age. *Journal of Abnormal Psychology, 103*, 604–609. doi: 10.1037/0021-843X.103.4.604

Hinrichsen, G. A. (2016). Clinical geropsychology. In J. C. Norcross, G. R. VandenBos, & D. K. Freedheim (Editors-in-Chief), M. Domenech Rodriguez (Associate Editor), *APA handbook of clinical psychology, Vol. 1: Roots and branches* (pp. 159–177). Washington, DC: American Psychological Association.

Howe, N., & Strauss, W. (2000). *Millennials rising: The next great generation*. New York: Vintage Books.

Howe, N., & Strauss, W. (2007). The next 20 years. *Harvard Business Review, 85*, 41–52.

Hsieh, S. L. J., & Tori, C. D. (2007). Normative data on cross-cultural neuropsychological tests obtained from Mandarin-speaking adults across the life span. *Archives of Clinical Neuropsychology, 22*(3), 283–296. doi: 10.1016/j.acn.2007.01.004

Irvin, K., & Krishnamurthy, R. (2014, March). *Psychopathic Personality Inventory Revised (PPI-R) correlates of the PAI in a community sample*. In M. Baity (chair), *The Personality Assessment Inventory*. Paper presented at the annual convention of the Society for Personality Assessment, Arlington, VA.

Iversen, T. N., Larsen, L., & Solem, P. E. (2009). A conceptual analysis of ageism. *Nordic Psychology, 61*, 4–22. doi: 10.1027/1901-2276.61.3.4

Johnson, S. A., & Romanello, M. L. (2005). Generational diversity: Teaching and learning approaches. *Nurse Educator, 30*(5), 212–216. doi: 10.1097/00006223-200509000-00009

Kandler, C., Kornadt, A. E., Hagemeyer, B., & Neyer, F. J. (2015). Patterns and sources of personality development in old age. *Personality and Social Psychology, 109*(1), 175–191. http://dx.doi.org/10.1037/pspp0000028

Kasser, T. (2006). *The high price of materialism*. Cambridge, MA: MIT Press.

Krishnamurthy, R., & Meyer, G. J. (2016). Psychopathology assessment. In J. C. Norcross, G. R. VandenBos, & D. K. Freedheim (Editors-in-Chief), R. Krishnamurthy (Associate Editor), *APA handbook of clinical psychology, Vol. 3: Applications and methods* (pp. 103–137). Washington, DC: American Psychological Association.

Kuhn, D. (2006). Do cognitive changes accompany developments in the adolescent brain? *Perspectives on Psychological Science, 1*(1), 59–67. doi: 10.1111/j.1745-6924.2006.t01-2-.x

Leibovitch, F. S., Vasquez, B. P., Ebert, P. L., Beresford, K. L., & Black, S. E. (2012). A short bedside battery for visuoconstructive hemispatial neglect: Sunnybrook Neglect Assessment Procedure (SNAP). *Journal of Clinical and Experimental Neuropsychology, 34*(4), 359–368. http://dx.doi.org/10.1080/13803395.2011.645016

Levy, S. R., & Macdonald, J. L. (2016). Progress on understanding ageism. *Journal of Social Issues, 72*(1), 5–25. doi: 10.1111/josi.12153

Lewinsohn, P. M., Rohde, P., Seeley, J. R., & Fischer, S. A. (1993). Age-cohort changes in the lifetime occurrence of depression and other mental disorders. *Journal of Abnormal Psychology, 102*(1), 110. doi: 10.1037/0021-843X.102.1.110

Lyons, S., & Kuron, L. (2014). Generational differences in the workplace: A review of the evidence and directions for future research. *Journal of Organizational Behavior, 35*(S1). doi: 10.1002/job.1913

Mash, E. J., & Hunsley, H. (2005). Evidence-based assessment of child and adolescent disorders: Issues and challenges. *Journal of Clinical Child and Adolescent Psychology, 34*(3), 362–379. doi: 10.1207/s15374424jccp3403_1

McCrae, R. R., & Costa, P. T. Jr. (1994). The stability of personality: Observations and evaluations. *Current Directions in Psychological Science, 3*(6), 173–175. doi: 10.1111/1467-8721.ep10770693

McCrae, R. R., & Costa, P. T. Jr. (1997). Personality trait structure as a human universal. *American Psychologist, 5*(5), 509–516. http://dx.doi.org/10.1037/0003-066X.52.5.509

McCrae, R. R., Costa, P. T. Jr., Terraciano, A., Parker, W. D., Mills, C. J., De Fruyt, F., & Mervielde, I. (2002). Personality trait development from age 12 to age 18: Longitudinal, cross-sectional, and cross-cultural analyses. *Journal of Personality and Social Psychology, 83*(6), 1456–1468. doi: 10.1037//0022-3514.83.6.1456

Meyer, G. J., Viglione, D. J., & Giromini, L. (2016, February). Current R-PAS® transitional child and adolescent norms. Retrieved from www.r-pas.org/CurrentChildNorms.aspx

Meyer, G. J., Viglione, D. J., Mihura, J. L., Erard, R. E., & Erdberg, P. (2011). *Rorschach Performance Assessment System: Administration, coding, interpretation, and technical manual.* Toledo, OH: Rorschach Performance Assessment System, LLC.

Myers, D. G. (2000). The funds, friends, and faith of happy people. *American Psychologist, 55*(1), 56. doi: 10.1037//0003-066X.55,1.56

Nelson, T. D. (2016). Promoting healthy aging by confronting ageism. *American Psychologist, 71*(4), 276–282. http://dx.doi.org/10.1037/a0040221

Ostrosky-Solís, F., Esther Gómez-Pérez, M., Matute, E., Rosselli, M., Ardila, A., & Pineda, D. (2007). Neuropsi attention and memory: A neuropsychological test battery in Spanish with norms by age and educational level. *Applied Neuropsychology, 14*(3), 156–170. doi: 10.1080/09084280701508655

Palmore, E. (2015). Ageism comes of age. *Journal of Gerontology: Social Sciences, 70*(6), 873–875. doi: 10.1093/geronb/gbv079

Petermann, F., & Macha, T. (2008). Developmental assessment: A general framework. *Zeitschrift für Psychologie/Journal of Psychology, 216*(3), 127–134. doi: 10.1027/0044-3409.216.3.127

Robb, C., Chen, H., & Haley, W. E. (2002). Ageism in mental health and health care: A critical review. *Journal of Clinical Geropsychology, 8*(1), 1–12. doi: 10.1023/A:1013013322947

Robins, L. N., Helzer, J. E., Weissman, M. M., Orvaschel, H., Gruenberg, E., Burke, J. D., & Regier, D. A. (1984). Lifetime prevalence of specific psychiatric disorders in three sites. *Archives of General Psychiatry, 41*(10), 949–958. doi: 10.1001/archpsyc.1984.01790210031005

Rosselli, M., & Ardila, A. (2010). La detección temprana de las demencias desde la perspectiva neuropsicológica. *Acta Neruológica Colombiana, 26*(3), 59–68.

Ryan, J. J., Sattler, J. M., & López, S. J. (2000). Age effects on Wechsler Adult Intelligence Scales-III subtests. *Archives of Clinical Neuropsychology, 15*(4), 311–317. doi: 10.1016/S0887-6177(99)00019-0

Ryan, R. G. (2009). Age differences in personality: Adolescents and young adults. *Personality and Individual Differences, 47*, 331–335. doi: 10.1016/j.paid.2009.03.023

Seligman, M. E. (1990). Why is there so much depression today? The waxing of the individual and the waning of the commons. In R. E. Ingram (Ed.), *Contemporary psychological approaches to depression: Theory, research, and treatment* (pp. 1–9). New York: Plenum Press.

Strauss, W., & Howe, N. (2008). *Generations: The history of America's future, 1584 to 2069.* New York: William Morrow.

Tibon-Czopp, S., & Weiner, I. B. (2016). *Rorschach assessment of adolescents: Theory, research, and practice.* New York: Springer.

Trzesniewski, K. H., Donnellan, M. B., & Robins, R. W. (2008). Is "Generation Me" really more narcissistic than previous generations? *Journal of Personality, 76*(4), 903–918. doi: 10.1111/j.1467-6494.2008.00508.x

Twenge, J. M. (2000). The age of anxiety? The birth cohort change in anxiety and neuroticism, 1952–1993. *Journal of Personality and Social Psychology, 79*(6), 1007–1021. doi: 10.1037/0022-3514.79.6.1007

Twenge, J. M., & Campbell, W. K. (2009). *The narcissism epidemic: Living in the age of entitlement.* New York: Simon & Schuster.

Twenge, J. M., & Foster, J. D. (2010). Birth cohort increases in narcissistic personality traits among American college students, 1982–2009. *Social Psychological and Personality Science, 1*(1), 99–106. doi: 10.1177/1948550609355719

Twenge, J. M., Gentile, B., DeWall, C. N., Ma, D., Lacefield, K., & Schurtz, D. R. (2010). Birth cohort increases in psychopathology among young Americans, 1938–2007: A cross-temporal meta-analysis of the MMPI. *Clinical Psychology Review, 30*(2), 145–154. doi: 10.1016/j.cpr.2009.10.005

Twenge, J. M., Miller, J. D., & Campbell, W. K. (2014). The narcissism epidemic: Commentary on modernity and narcissistic personality disorder. *Personality Disorders: Theory, Research, and Treatment, 5*(2), 227–229. doi: 10.1037/per0000008

Vincent, G. K., & Velkoff, V. A. (May, 2010). The older population in the United States: 2010 to 2050, population estimates and projections. *U.S. Census Bureau*. Retrieved from www.census.gov/prod/2010pubs/p25-1138.pdf

Werner, C. A. (November, 2011). The older population: 2010. *U.S. Census Bureau*. Retrieved from www.census.gov/prod/cen2010/briefs/c2010br-09.pdf

Wickramaratne, P. J., Weissman, M. M., Leaf, P. J., & Holford, T. R. (1989). Age, period and cohort effects on the risk of major depression: Results from five United States communities. *Journal of Clinical Epidemiology, 42*(4), 333–343. doi: 10.1016/0895-4356(89)90038-3

CHAPTER 12

Socioeconomic Considerations in Personality Assessment

Claudia Porras Pyland, Sally D. Stabb, and Steven R. Smith

In this chapter, conceptual and definitional issues as they pertain to socioeconomic status (SES) and personality assessment are presented initially, followed by a discussion of the interpersonal presentation and clinical issues that may be unique to clients across the SES spectrum. Empirical findings that are relevant to SES and personality assessment are noted. Practical considerations in conducting personality assessment across the SES spectrum are provided, framed in terms of the American Psychological Association's revised Benchmark Competencies (APA, 2012). Throughout, the emphasis is on the MMPI-2 and the Rorschach as the most well-known and widely utilized self-report and performance-based personality measures, although some discussion of other tests, such as the NEO-PI-R, is included. The chapter concludes with a summary and recommendations for moving forward.

Conceptual Considerations

Although definitions of personality and the fuzzy boundary between personality and psychopathology are legitimate areas for theoretical debate, the primary conceptual consideration in this chapter is specific to SES. SES is notoriously difficult to define. The term is often used interchangeably with a host of others, including social class, income, wealth, poverty/the poor, and economic (dis)advantage (Pope & Arthur, 2009). For example, in their content analysis of the social class literature in Counseling Psychology, Liu and colleagues (2004) found 448 different words used to indicate some version of the concept; it has been operationalized in countless ways. We searched a number of on-line dictionaries to examine definitions of SES, and virtually all included income, education, and occupation. A representative example would be: "An individual's or group's position within a hierarchical social structure. SES depends on a combination of variables, including occupation, education, income, wealth, and place of residence" (Dictionary.com, n.d.). It becomes clear that SES contains many elements, but exactly which ones are definitive remains controversial.

Class is considered a more inclusive term than SES and incorporates dimensions of power into its definition. There are various forms of classism, as per Lott (2012, pp. 654–655):

> *Institutional classism* is the maintenance and reinforcement of low status by social institutions that present barriers to increase the difficulty of accessing resources. *Interpersonal classism* is identified by *prejudice* (negative attitudes), *stereotypes* (widely shared negative beliefs), and *discrimination* (distancing, excluding, or denigrating behavior).

From a sociological perspective, Grusky and Ku (2000) present a multidimensional view of the advantage/disadvantage spectrum, by noting eight different types of assets that distinguish people along this dimension, including wealth, power, social, cultural, honorific, civil, human, and physical assets.

Specific to personality assessment, almost 25 years ago Dana and Whatley (1991) reviewed the ways in which SES was operationalized in 21 studies of the MMPI. They concluded that there was "no clarity with regard to the measurement of social stratification and ... no reasonable group comparability" (pp. 401–402) between these measures. Although acknowledging that SES was an important moderator in interpreting MMPI profiles, they noted that the underlying issues in the measurement of SES suggest caution. Our own review indicates that this situation has not improved.

We are not in a position to settle the definitional debate here and have pulled data from sources that use multiple terms. However, readers will at least be aware of the issues from this brief overview. We included studies related to class and classism in addition to those on SES, as these writings have been primary in understanding the diversity-sensitive application of psychological interventions, including assessment.

Most of the research on SES in psychology is about the poor. There is a small body of work on the wealthy. The middle class appears to be ignored, in the sense that the vast majority of research done in the field historically uses middle-class participants, who are implicitly assumed to represent normality; their SES is thus not discussed.

Although practitioners are likely to continue to see many middle-class clients, statistics support the popular idea that the wealth gap in the U.S. is growing. Using U.S. Census data for example, Bishaw (2013) reports that in the last dozen years, the percentage of people in poverty increased from 3.7% to a current level of 15.9%, while the number of people in poverty increased by 15.5 million people to reach 48.8 million in 2012. Fry and Taylor (2013) of the Pew Research Center, cite data indicating that between 2009 and 2011, the mean net worth of the upper 7% of households grew by approximately 28%, while the mean net worth of the remaining 93% of households fell by 4%. This means there will be more people in poverty who need access to mental health treatment and assessment in the future, and these individuals are historically less likely to seek mental health treatment than those with more resources (Weintraub & Goodman, 2010). When individuals on either end of the SES spectrum present for assessment or treatment, understanding their unique concerns is important, yet most practitioners' training has not consistently addressed class issues (Goodman, Pugach & Smith, 2013; Smith, 2013; Stabb & Reimers, 2013). Thus, we turn now to considering the interpersonal and clinical presentations of these individuals.

Interpersonal and Clinical Presentations

Psychopathology and personality have been found to interact with SES in clear ways. Below is an account of this interaction, considering each side of the SES spectrum as well as general information about the relationships between SES and personality.

General Information

The complex relationship between SES and personality has been highlighted in various ways in the literature. For example, personality impacts how much satisfaction people derive from increases in income, with those high in Conscientiousness being most satisfied by such increases (Boyce & Wood, 2011). Using the NEO-PI, Boyce and Wood (2011) found gender effects, in that women who scored high on Introversion, Neuroticism, and Openness to Experience had lower satisfaction from income increases. Boyce and Wood used a large, middle-class sample for this study. Earlier, Hathaway and Monachesi (1963) found that high-SES individuals presented as having better self-management, fewer somatic concerns, and fewer fears than low-SES individuals. There is also an interrelationship between parental education, income, and personality. For example, Jonassaint, Siegler, Barefoot, Edwards, and Williams (2011) found that high-SES participants with highly educated mothers scored higher on Extraversion and Openness on the NEO-PI-R. In contrast, low-SES participants with poorly educated fathers scored higher on Neuroticism and lower on Conscientiousness.

Low SES

Although the directionality of the relationship between SES and psychopathology remains unclear, a review of the literature reveals consistent patterns of distinct experiences of psychopathology within this group, as well as unique expressions of said psychopathology. For example, people of low SES are more likely to meet diagnostic criteria for psychiatric disorders than people of high SES, even after adjusting for other diversity variables (Kohn, Dohrenwend, & Mirotznik, 1998). Two hypotheses, the social selection hypothesis and the social causation hypothesis, have been proposed for explaining SES differences in rates of psychopathology. The social selection hypothesis suggests that people with psychopathology drift down the social ladder as a result of an inability to meet social and role obligations (Dohrenwend et al., 1992). On the other hand, the social causation hypothesis poses that living in poor conditions results in increased psychopathology, either by causing or activating inherent psychopathology (Wadsworth & Achenbach, 2005). There is substantial empirical support for the social causation model. Stigmatized and with less power in multiple domains than those in higher social strata, the social exclusion routinely experienced by the poor can "contribute to self-defeating behavior, unhealthy styles of living, and emotional numbness" (Smith, 2013, p. 14).

Research consistently shows that chronic exposure to the prolonged stress brought on by the inability to meet basic needs and by living in chaotic, substandard environments impacts the physical and mental health of those living in poverty (Goodman et al., 2013; Lott 2012). This results in understandably elevated rates of trauma, relational instability, anxiety, depression, hostility and suspicion, internalized powerlessness, and feelings of low self-worth. These impacts are further exacerbated by racism in communities of color (Goodman et al., 2013). Growing up in a low-SES community appears to have long-term effects, regardless of whether an individual is able to climb the social ladder later in life. This may take form in the perception of less social support and in the individual's tendency to employ passive coping strategies over proactive strategies when dealing with stressors in adulthood (Beatty, Kamarck, Matthews, & Shiffman, 2011).

However, the relationship between stress and SES is complex and bidirectional. In their study of low-income families, Wadsworth, Raviv, DeCarlo, and Etter (2011) found complicated interactions between poverty-related stress, primary and secondary coping, and internalizing and externalizing distress. Coping style and the degree of sensitivity to stress play a role in the negative effects of poverty for low-income individuals. Sensitivity to stress or neuroticism has also been linked to depression in low-income individuals, and an active or primary coping style has been associated with reduced sensitivity to stress for high-SES groups (Jokela & Keltikangas-Järvinen, 2011). Unfortunately, employing active coping strategies may not reduce sensitivity to stress or depression for low-SES individuals as it does for high-SES persons (Jokela & Keltikangas-Järvinen, 2011; Stanton, Jonassaint, Williams, & James, 2010). Active coping is likely ineffective for low-SES individuals because they are faced with chronic stressors that require a great deal of energy and resources to manage and are often out of their control. Over time, this leads to negative emotionality and health risks (Bennett et al., 2004; Stanton et al., 2010). On the other hand, secondary control coping, such as reframing, acceptance and distraction, can be implemented at any time and with any stressor, which is most helpful for chronic stressors or those out of an individual's control (Wadsworth et al., 2011). Therefore, secondary control coping may have a stronger buffering effect against stress for low-income individuals.

An additional layer to the social causation hypothesis is that people of low SES who suffer from psychopathology face barriers to psychological treatment and/or might not recover as quickly as those from higher SES, thereby increasing the differential incidence of psychopathology in people of low SES (Chen & Paterson, 2006; Wadsworth & Achenbach, 2005). The poor underutilize mental health services (Goodman et al., 2013), and face barriers that are not only practical or financial. Psycho-social barriers can include fear of insensitive treatment and mistrust of authority figures. These psycho-social barriers become heightened in correctional settings, where personality assessment is frequently used for treatment planning, and which include a disproportionately high number of individuals from low-SES backgrounds. In such cases, clients are unable to provide true informed consent for assessments, have serious concerns about how assessment data might be used, and likely have court-appointed attorneys who might not dedicate the time and support to them that would be given by private legal representation (A. Williams, personal communication, February 3, 2014). Physical barriers can include the limited or nonexistent availability of therapists trained to handle the unique obstacles that commonly arise in low-SES communities as well as the limited availability of valid assessment tools and procedures appropriate for use with low-SES communities. This can often result in biased conceptualizations, inaccurate diagnoses, and impractical treatment plans (Goodman et al., 2013; Smith, Chambers, & Brantini, 2009).

High SES

Turning to the other end of the class spectrum, when looking at wealthy adults and adolescents, a number of relationships with mental health are notable. Using a multigenerational object relations framework, Kleefeld (2001) found that neglectful, superficial, and often absent affluent parents generated children who crave recognition, but lack support or positive role models. As adults, high rates of depression/suicide, narcissism, addictions, anti-social personality patterns, low self-esteem, and low tolerance for frustration were prevalent. These problems were compounded by perceived needs for secrecy, given their families' prominence, and focus on outward appearances. Similarly, Ullrich, Farrington, and Coid (2007) found that in adults, obsessive, narcissistic, and avoidant personality traits have been correlated with wealth and status.

Lott (2012) summarized data from the National Science Foundation indicating that high levels of wealth may be linked to a sense of entitlement, including some forms of unethical behavior. Piff, Stancato, Martinez, Kraus, and Keltner (2012) found that the wealthy prefer to depend on their material resources when life becomes chaotic, rather than reaching out for relational, community supports. Affluent teens appear driven by pressures to excel/achieve, which in combination with disconnection from parents, can lead to high rates of anxiety, depression, maladaptive perfectionism, and substance abuse (Levine, 2006; Luthar & Latendresse, 2002; Luthar & Sexton, 2004; Zelman, 2008).

Although we should not assume that all persons who are wealthy have materialistic values, inverse relationships have been found between materialism and subjective well-being. In his classic article "If We're So Rich, Why Aren't We Happy?", Csikszentmihalyi (1999) cites research that the most wealthy people are not more happy than others, and that in fact, upper-middle-class adolescents are unhappier than their peers in other socioeconomic levels. Furthermore, when income inequality grows, constant upward social comparisons lead to increased unhappiness.

More recently, researchers have found that competitiveness and aggression are tied to materialistic values (Saunders, Allen, & Pozzebon, 2008).

This review of the literature has provided for some understanding of personality and psychopathology with individuals of varying class levels, but the question, "What does this mean for the application of personality assessment with individuals across the SES spectrum?" remains. Although differences in personality types and in the experience of psychopathology for people across the SES spectrum have been empirically supported over a multitude of research studies, it is possible that some of the differences researchers have found are inaccurate, misconstrued or inflated by errors and biases in assessment tools and procedures. The next section addresses both foundational and functional competencies needed to begin to uncover some of these biases, as well as suggestions for what to do to minimize future errors.

Personality Assessment Competencies

The American Psychological Association's Revised Competency Benchmarks (APA, 2012) are used to frame this section. As a result, the section is broken down by a discussion of foundational and functional competencies in personality assessment. Foundational competencies are awareness- and knowledge-based. Here, we present key features of critical self-reflective skills, literature regarding the psychometrics of personality tests as they relate to SES, and the limitations regarding assessment methods with people at different ends of the class spectrum. Functional competencies reflect application. In discussing functional competencies, we present concrete and behavioral suggestions about what clinicians should do when administering, scoring, and interpreting personality assessments in light of SES considerations. The benchmarks are constructed to attend to differing levels of trainee and professional development; the considerations given here also apply to the independently functioning professional and have been tailored specifically to personality assessment.

Foundational Competency: Awareness

Hansen (2002) makes the critical point that overarching all competencies, examiners should have awareness of how their own cultural heritage, gender, class, ethnic or racial identity, sexual orientation, disability, language, and age cohort shape their personal values, assumptions, and biases related to other SES groups. They should have the ability to accurately self-assess their own multicultural competence, including knowing when circumstances (e.g., personal biases; class; stage of ethnic identity; sociopolitical influences; or lack of requisite knowledge, skills, or language fluency) are negatively influencing professional activities, and adapt accordingly. Examiners should be aware of biases about low-SES clients, such as a misconception that they are apathetic to the therapeutic process, and recognize the prevalence of institutional and social classism and its impact on the lives of those they assess (Pope & Arthur, 2009). The importance of this type of self-reflection is underscored by the APA Benchmark Competencies (2012), which place awareness of individual and cultural differences in self, others, and relationships as a foundational competency in and of itself, with application to all other domains and competencies. The need for awareness about class and classism is echoed by numerous experts in the field (Goodman et al., 2013; Lott & Bullock, 2007; Smith, 2010; Stabb & Reimers, 2013).

SES biases can arise at both ends of the spectrum. For example, one of the authors of this chapter (S. Stabb) served a wealthy clientele during internship. Coming from a middle-class background, she had to negotiate day-to-day reactivity to a student parking lot filled with luxury vehicles, reminding herself that these students could still have serious problems despite their affluence. One particularly striking encounter in doing vocational/personality assessment occurred with a student who presented with a career goal of becoming an international ambassador. Although it would have been easy for the author to assume this student was narcissistic and grandiose, and even though research supports the prevalence of narcissism in very high-SES populations, this did not turn out to be the case. The student already had connections and an entrée into the world of international relations and a quite realistic plan for proceeding. The author also had to wrestle with both internal intimidation and irritation when entitled and influential parents called the counseling and testing center demanding information on their (adult) child's assessments or therapy and had to be firmly reminded of confidentiality rules.

Foundational Competencies: Knowledge of Measurement, Psychometrics and Assessment Methods

The foundational competencies here include: (a) a general understanding of the literature regarding the unique considerations that need to be made when assessing people on various points of the class spectrum, (b) the theoretical and scientific underpinning of the personality assessments used, including test construction, administration and scoring protocols, and the reliability and validity issues of instruments, and (c) competencies related to selection of personality assessment measures, such as understanding the strengths and limitations of different tests, particularly in terms of social context and responsivity to diversity concerns. Further, recognizing that our comprehension of the relationship between SES and personality assessment continues to evolve, cultural sensitivity in psychological assessment is a life-long learning process. Examiners should maintain a growing understanding of how assessment tools and procedures might be biased toward SES groups. This understanding should extend to knowledge of how to accurately assess or measure variables of special relevance to different SES groups (Hansen, 2002).

The two most common tactics researchers have employed to evaluate the use of personality assessment instruments with the poor are: (1) administer the assessment to a spectrum of SES participants and compare those in the highest and lowest categories and/or determine relationships based on SES as a continuous variable, or (2) administer the assessment to a group of exclusively low-SES persons.

We found a handful of articles where the focus is on examining the reliability, validity, or utility of the personality measures per se. We chose articles that demonstrated clear attention to both SES and personality in their titles or abstracts. There are undoubtedly hundreds of articles that have used personality assessments with a sample that happened to include some variability in SES of participants; however, unless this relationship was a focus of analysis or discussion, it was not included in the present review (see the Appendix). In general, when researchers report their studies, gender and race are most often noted in demographic data, with SES a distant third. Furthermore, analyses using SES as a categorical variable are far less common than those using gender or race (Reimers & Stabb, 2007). Unfortunately, there are limited data on the wide range of personality assessments currently in use vis à vis SES.

Even after taking into account actual differences in the extent and severity of psychopathology in people of low SES (see previous section), there continues to be a disproportionate amount of inaccurate assessment data for this group. A thorough review of the literature on SES points to four factors that impact assessment results for low-SES clients: (1) biased assessment results that yield spurious and shortsighted interpretations of people from low SES, (2) different personality structures within the class spectrum that result in varying responses to test stimuli, (3) higher interpersonal anxiety or distrust in the psychological assessment, and (4) examiner bias against the low-SES clients during testing and in interpreting results (Hillerbrand, 1988; Jonassaint et al., 2011; Levy, 1970; Löckenhoff et al., 2008; Sladen, 1982). We will begin this discussion by reviewing the literature on SES-related findings and potential biases in personality assessment measures.

MMPI

Information on the first version of the Minnesota Multiphasic Personality Inventory (MMPI; Hathaway & McKinley, 1943) and social class is scattered. Hathaway and Monachesi (1963) found that an elevated score on scale 8 (Schizophrenia; Sc) was predictive of low SES later in life. Joshi and Singh (1966) found elevations on scales 1 (Hypochondriasis; Hs), 3 (Hysteria; Hy), 5 (Masculinity/Femininity; Mf), and 4 (Psychopathic Deviate; Pd) in their comparison of low-SES adolescent boys versus those boys in three higher SES groups. Using a mini MMPI, Adams and Horovitz (1980) studied relationships between psychopathology and father absence in low-SES adolescent boys, but concluded that poverty and maternal psychopathology were the primary predictors of these boys' aggression.

There is disagreement about whether the MMPI-2 (Butcher, Dahlstrom, Graham, Tellegen, & Kaemmer, 1989) is biased or if it identifies actual individual differences among groups on the class spectrum. For example, Timbrook and Graham (1994) argue that differences between groups are indicative of important individual characteristics. It is worth mentioning, however, that the two most disparate features of the MMPI-2's normative sample are in educational background and income, the two factors that are most often attributed to SES. There is an overrepresentation of individuals with a post-college education and hardly any representation of individuals without a high school education, with only 5% of participants having a high school education (Butcher et al., 1989).

Although several scales on the MMPI-2 have been found to result in disproportionate differences across the class spectrum, researchers have consistently found class differences for the validity scales F (Infrequency), K (Correction), L (Lie), and clinical scale Sc (Long & Graham, 1994). Saba (as cited in Caldwell, 1997) also found that people of low SES who did not have a psychiatric disorder produced elevations on Sc (T = 70). Other discrepancies in scores due to SES are found for clinical scales Hs, Mf, Ma (Mania), and Si (Social Introversion) and supplementary scales Es (Ego Strength), and Welsh's A (Anxiety) (Long & Graham, 1994). Long and Graham (1994) also found that participants of higher income levels scored higher on scale K, which is intended to measure defensiveness, than those of lower income levels (T-score difference of 5 points). Given the consistency in this elevation for high-SES individuals in the literature, it is likely that K is not representative of defensiveness for higher SES people but instead may be more attributable to positive coping. The Socioeconomic Status scale (Ss) may be useful in distinguishing between true emotional constraint and defensiveness associated with a high K score among upper SES individuals (Friedman, Bolinskey, Levak, & Nichols, 2015).

Rorschach

Early research findings point to interpretation bias when using the older Rorschach scoring systems with low-income individuals. In a study by Levy and Kahn (1970), Rorschach raters tended to score protocols as more psychotic and as having more personality disorders when they were told the patients were low-income than when they were told they were middle-class (Levy & Kahn, 1970). Further, Gibbs (1982) found that the Developmental Level (DL) score, using Friedman's Developmental Scoring System, was not useful in differentiating between personality functioning because it was biased for those with low intelligence scores. They did not assess for education level, therefore, the impact of education on DL is unknown. In 1994, George Frank identified a need to consider how the Rorschach may be biased with individuals of low-SES backgrounds and urged that more research be done in this area. However, in our review of the literature, we could not find any research within the last two decades that evaluates the psychometric properties of the Rorschach when used with different SES groups. Given that these older studies were conducted with out-of-date scoring systems, research using the newer Rorschach Performance Assessment System (R-PAS; Meyer, Viglione, Mihura, Erard, & Erdberg, 2011) is needed.

NEO-PI-R

Regarding styles of reporting, African American groups with limited education tended to produce invalid results on the NEO-Personality Inventory-Revised (NEO-PI-R; Costa & McCrae, 1992) due to an acquiescent response style; however, the relevant literature suggests this invalidity and acquiescence is due to limited education (a factor commonly used to characterize SES) rather than ethnicity (Löckenhoff et al., 2008; Sutin, Costa, Evans, & Zonderman, 2013). For example, Sutin et al. (2013) found that NEO-PI-R items associated with the Openness to Experience scale required a higher reading level (2.5 grade levels above the reading level required for other scales) than did the other four scales. Further, internal consistency of the Big Five personality factors also tend to be lower for groups with limited education (Löckenhoff et al., 2008). Self-report personality measures, which comprise the majority of commonly used measures of personality, require clients to have a good understanding of the content and meaning of items. Unfortunately, the issue of literacy has not been well researched. As is true for much of the literature on test bias, research with the NEO-PI-R has explored characteristics that correlate with SES (e.g., ethnicity and education) without fully exploring SES per se.

PAI and Other Tests

The Personality Assessment Inventory (PAI; Morey, 1991) was standardized using three samples: a normative sample, a college sample, and a clinical sample. The mean educational attainment was 13.7 years (Morey, 2007). Alterman et al. (1995) found questionable or marginal internal consistency for scales measuring drug problems (DRG), perceived lack of social support (NON), treatment rejection (RXR), and warmth (WRM) scales for low-income African American and Latino methadone maintenance patients. These patients scored significantly lower on RXR and WRM and higher on all other clinical, treatment, and interpersonal scales than the PAI's normative sample. The questionable validity for DRG might be explained by the constricted variance range found in drug treatment facilities. Concurrent validity was satisfactory. Although some differences were found between African Americans and Latinos, no gender differences were found. Overall, there are very few empirical studies that have investigated the PAI's applicability with people from extreme ends of the SES spectrum. Given the middle-class and largely White norm sample for the PAI, conclusions about its applicability to low- (or very high-) SES individuals are hard to make and should therefore be a focus of future research.

The Relationship Profile Test (RPT; Bornstein & Languirand, 2003) and the Personality Assessment Screener (PAS; Morey, 1997) have been found to be adequate tools to use with low-income, African American women and low-income urban primary care clients, respectively (Bornstein, Porcerelli, Huprich, & Markova, 2009; Porcerelli, Kurtz, Cogan, Markova, & Mickens, 2012). Porcerelli et al. (2012) found that the PAS was effective in identifying major forms of psychopathology in a low-income urban primary care setting, including patients with mood disorders, cluster B personality disorders, and alcohol use disorders. The authors recommended, however, that a cut-off score of 20 be used instead of the intended cut-off score of 19, in order to improve diagnostic accuracy. The 10 PAS element scores showed good convergent and discriminant correlations with the reference measures.

Functional Competencies: Application, Conceptualization and Diagnosis

The competencies in this area include the clinician's ability to independently select which measure(s) will best answer the diagnostic and/or referral question at hand, and to integrate the results of such testing to inform both conceptualization and treatment planning. Competencies here include attending to developmental context as well as diversity factors in understanding normal/abnormal behavior when moving forward with clinical decision-making (APA, 2012).

Skills

Hansen (2002) has delineated specific skills needed for diversity-sensitive assessment. For example, examiners should cultivate skills related to establishing rapport, diagnosis and conceptualization, and communication of assessment findings.

Preparing for the Assessment and Establishing Rapport

Rapport can be an issue at any point on the SES spectrum. With high-SES clients, for example, examiners should be aware that clients may be especially concerned about confidentiality and the possibility that any testing results might be used against them in reviews of their character and fitness in occupations such as law and medicine. Examiners should be prepared to discuss these concerns at some length.

For low-SES clients, examiners should make efforts to address barriers to seeking services, such as providing transport, offering flexible scheduling options, on-site child care, or making home visits (Goodman et al., 2013).When necessary, examiners should have the ability to modify assessment procedures. For example, examiners should consider administering the assessment orally for those with limited literacy (Sutin et al., 2013). Literacy concerns should be kept in mind when administering tests such as the NEO-PI-R that have been found to have shortcomings related to literacy.

Examiners should be able to convey appreciation for and understanding of clients' lived experiences in culturally sensitive ways while taking into account the intersectionality of SES and other cultural factors, such as ethnicity, gender, and disability. Examiners may do this via culture-bound interpretations of verbal and nonverbal cues, personal space, and eye contact. They should be able to accurately identify when their own biases are so dominant that continuing the assessment process would be unethical and a referral is necessary (Hansen, 2002; Pope & Arthur, 2009). When the examiner determines that biases could be impacting the assessment procedures, he or she should minimize these biases by obtaining needed information through literature or continuing education and seeking consultation and supervision.

An excellent example of the application of functional personality assessment competencies was given to us by a colleague who works in the court system doing assessments with a low-SES, primarily ethnic minority population. Some of her observations fit with literature already reviewed; many, however, have never been directly addressed by research. She (A. Williams, personal communication, February 3, 2014) describes taking the following points into routine consideration:

- Does the client need glasses to read the test, but has not been able to afford them?
- Client's reported education level might not reflect his/her actual ability, which is often lower than actual educational attainment.
- The MMPI-2 might be overwhelming for people because it is so long, however the Yes/No format might be easier for some people than assessments with wider ranges of choices for response.
- The PAI's wider range of possible responses can be a problem for clients experiencing exceptionally elevated environmental stress as a result of living in poverty. Such stressors can lead to processing difficulties or difficulties focusing, which might make choosing one of multiple responses difficult.
- Many scales on the MCMI-III can be raised in low-SES clients because living in chronic poverty can fundamentally change one's perception of the world. Many of the definitions of personality disorders are vague and fit many people. It is unclear whether a problematic characteristic is an enduring personality trait or the impact of a client's environment.
- Standardized assessment procedures might be problematic. Examiners should consider providing additional information and explanation for the testing situation, which is completely out of most people's experiences and is very foreign. Many will not do well in such a novel situation, so additional normalization and support should be provided.

Diagnosing and Conceptualization

Examiners should qualify conclusions appropriately (including empirical support, where available) in assessing different SES groups. Examiners should ascertain effects of language differences on psychological assessment and intervention (Sutin et al., 2013). Descriptions of behaviors should always be offered in support of conceptualization. Additional considerations when conceptualizing and diagnosing low-SES clients are noted below (from A. Williams, personal communication, February 3, 2014):

- It is important to gather context and collateral information and take it into account more heavily when conceptualizing. For example, gender, immigration status, and physical disability are closely tied to SES (see also Pope & Arthur,

2009). Considerations regarding the intersectionality of these cultural identities on emotional well-being and functioning should be made.

- Client's living conditions: Is the client homeless? If so, has s/he had anything to eat? If not, s/he might have difficulty concentrating during the test and thought processes might not be clear. Indicators that might look like schizophrenia symptoms, such as being disheveled or unkempt, might be a result of being homeless and not mental illness.
- Clients living in high crime areas might look paranoid but this is appropriate to their living situations.
- The wording of items on personality tests can elevate paranoia scales, because they may pull for the kinds of experiences that are normative in low-SES peoples' lives.
- Review the client's responses with the client and ask why they answered as they did on critical items instead of taking them at face value.
- Consider co-occurring impact of substance use/abuse.
- Trauma histories might be severe for many low-SES clients, but especially for women; for example, more recent sexual trauma might lead to elevation of paranoia and anxiety scales, but this is normative for such experiences. Clients might also find it hard to process information well if trauma is recent.
- Many low-SES clients go through multiple stressors at once, and this can look like depression, so pay attention to the timing of the testing to avoid over-diagnosing.

Communication of Assessment Findings

Examiners should be able to explain results in an SES-sensitive, contextual manner so as not to inadvertently perpetuate prejudice and discrimination. Further, examiners should avoid offering opinions about clients that are not based on data obtained from the assessment battery. Reports should attend accurately to diversity concerns (Hansen, 2002).

Summary and Future Directions

In summary, there are strikingly few empirical studies on the psychometric properties and interpretive accuracy of personality assessment for different SES groups. Much of the literature available points to shortcomings in assessment tools and procedures, but few offer suggestions for improvement. Future directions should clearly include additional, systematic and substantive research on the psychometric properties of established personality measures in socioeconomically diverse populations, particularly among those with low levels of literacy (Sutin et al., 2013), and with the Rorschach, which has not been empirically studied in relation to SES for over 20 years. We simply do not have enough data here to provide effective, empirically based recommendations to current practitioners using personality assessment measures about the vast majority of specifics regarding scale or profile interpretations in light of SES factors.

Equally important, training in class-competent assessment is a must. Even if the knowledge base regarding the psychometric properties of personality assessment instruments is or remains incomplete, it is incumbent upon all practitioners (and researchers) doing personality assessment to develop self-awareness about the impact of their own social class, to understand the social and psychological impacts of SES and classism, and to continue to develop their own understanding of effective interventions across the class spectrum (Goodman et al., 2013; Hansen, 2002). These competencies should be integrated with an intersectional approach, recognizing that social locations such as gender, race, and class do not function independently and therefore must be considered in an integrated fashion (Cole, 2009; Dana & Whatley, 1991). From start to finish, the assessment situation must include a constant checking in with ourselves about the possibilities of bias, stereotyping, and over- or under-pathologizing our clients based on their position on the SES continuum. It must also include interpersonal skills in creating a welcoming environment, establishing and maintaining rapport, and understanding the unique concerns of our clientele at all class levels. In conclusion, consistent contextualization is likely to be the hallmark of class-competent personality assessment.

References

Adams, P. L., & Horovitz, J. H. (1980). Psychopathology and fatherlessness in poor boys. *Child Psychiatry & Human Development, 10*, 135–143. doi: 10.1007/BF01433626

Alterman, A. I., Zaballero, A. R., Lin, M. M., ... McDermott, P. A. (1995). Personality Assessment Inventory (PAI) scores of lower-socioeconomic African American and Latino methadone maintenance patients. *Assessment, 2*, 91–100. doi: 10.1177/1073191 195002001009

American Psychological Association. (2012). *Revised competency benchmarks*. Retrieved on January 16, 2014 from www.apa.org/ed/graduate/revised-competency-benchmarks.doc

Beatty, D., Kamarck, T. W., Matthews, K. A., & Shiffman, S. (2011).Childhood socioeconomic status is associated with psychosocial resources in African Americans: The Pittsburgh Healthy Heart Project. *Health Psychology, 30*, 472–480. doi: 10.1037/a0024304

Bennett, G. G., Merritt, M. M., Sollers, J. J., Edwards, C. L., Whitfield, K. E., Brandon, D. T., & Tucker, R. D. (2004). Stress, coping, and health outcomes among African-Americans: A review of the John Henryism hypothesis. *Psychology and Health*, 19, 369–383. doi: 10.1080/0887044042000193505

Bishaw, A. (2013). Poverty 2000–2012. *U.S. Department of Commerce Economics and Statistics Administration*. Retrieved January 21, 2014 from www.census.gov/prod/2013pubs/acsbr12-01.pdf

Bornstein, R. F., & Languirand, M. A. (2003). *Healthy dependency*. New York: Newmarket Press.

Bornstein, R. F., Porcerelli, J. H., Huprich, S. K., & Markova, T. (2009). Construct validity of the Relationship Profile Test: Correlates of overdependence, detachment, and healthy dependency in low income urban women seeking medical services. *Journal of Personality Assessment, 91*, 537–345. doi: 10.1080/00223890903228406

Boyce, C. J., & Wood, A. M. (2011). Personality and the marginal utility of income: Personality interacts with increases in household income to determine life satisfaction. *Journal of Economic Behavior and Organization, 78*, 183–191. doi: 10.1016/j.jebo.2011.01.004

Butcher, J. N., Dahlstrom, W. G., Graham, J. R., Tellegen, A., & Kaemmer, B. (1989). *Minnesota Multiphasic Personality Inventory-2 (MMPI-2): Manual for administration and scoring.* Minneapolis: University of Minnesota Press.

Caldwell, A. B. (1997). Whither goest our redoubtable mentor, the MMPI/MMPI-2? *Journal of Personality Assessment, 68,* 47–68. doi: 10.1207/s15327752jpa6801_5

Chen, E., & Paterson, L. Q. (2006). Neighborhood, family, and subjective socioeconomic status: How do they relate to adolescent health? *Health Psychology, 25,* 704–714. doi: 10.1037/0278-6133.25.6.704

Cole, E. R. (2009). Intersectionality and research in psychology. *American Psychologist, 64,* 170–180. doi: 10.1037/a0014564

Costa, P. T. Jr., & McCrae, R. R. (1992). *Revised NEO Personality Inventory (NEO-PI-R) and NEO Five-Factor Inventory (NEO-FFI) professional manual.* Odessa, FL: Psychological Assessment Resources.

Csikszentmihalyi, M. (1999). If we are so rich, why aren't we happy? *American Psychologist, 54,* 821–827. doi: 10.1037/0003-066X.54.10.821

Dana, R. H., & Whatley, P. R. (1991). When does a difference make a difference? MMPI scores and African Americans. *Journal of Clinical Psychology, 47,* 400–406. doi: 10.1037/a0014564

Dictionary.com. (n.d.). *Socioeconomic status.* Retrieved January 21, 2014 from http://dictionary.reference.com/browse/socioeconomic+status

Dohrenwend, B. P., Levav, I., Shrout, P. E., Schwartz, S., Naveh, G., Link, B. G., et al. (1992). Socioeconomic status and psychiatric disorders: The causation-selection issue. *Science, 255,* 946–952. doi: 10.1126/science.1546291

Frank, G. (1994). Socioeconomic status and the Rorschach. *Psychological Reports, 74,* 95–98. doi: 10.2466/pr0.1994.74.1.95

Friedman, A. F., Bolinskey, P. K., Levak, R. W., & Nichols, D. S. (2015). *Psychological assessment with the MMPI-2/MMPI-2-RF.* New York: Routledge.

Fry, R., & Taylor, P. (2013). A rise in wealth for the wealthy; declines for the lower 93%: An uneven recovery 2009–2011. *Pew Research Center.* Retrieved January 21, 2014 from: www.pewsocialtrends.org/2013/04/23/a-rise-in-wealth-for-the-wealthydeclines-for-the-lower-93/

Gibbs, J. T. (1982). Personality patterns of delinquent females: Ethnic and sociocultural variations. *Journal of Clinical Psychology, 8,* 197–206.

Goodman, L. A., Pugach, M. S., & Smith, L. (2013). Poverty and mental health practice: Within and beyond the 50-minute hour. *Journal of Clinical Psychology, 69,* 182–190. doi: 10.1002/jclp.21957

Grusky, D. B., & Ku, M. C. (2000). Gloom, doom, and inequality. In D. B. Grusky, M. C. Ku, & S. Szelenyi (Eds.), *Social stratification: Class, race and gender in sociological perspective* (pp. 2–28). Boulder, CO: Westview Press.

Hansen, N. D. (2002). Teaching cultural sensitivity in psychological assessment: A modular approach used in a distance education program. *Journal of Personality Assessment, 79,* 200–206. doi: 10.1207/S15327752JPA7902_03

Hathaway, S. R., & McKinley, J. C. (1943). *Manual for the Minnesota Multiphasic Personality Inventory.* New York: Psychological Corporation.

Hathaway, S. R., & Monachesi, E. D. (1963). *Adolescent personality and behavior: MMPI patterns of normal, delinquent, dropout, and other outcomes.* Minneapolis, MN: University of Minnesota Press.

Hillerbrand, E. (1988). The relationship between socioeconomic status and counseling variables at a university counseling center. *Journal of College Student Development, 29,* 250–254.

Jokela, M., & Keltikangas-Järvinen, L. (2011). The association between low socioeconomic status and depressive symptoms depends on temperament and personality traits. *Personality and Individual Differences, 51*, 302–308. doi: 10.1016/j.paid.2010.05.004

Jonassaint, C. R., Siegler, I., Barefoot, J., Edwards, C., & Williams, R. B. (2011). Low life course socioeconomic status (SES) is associated with negative NEO PI-R personality patterns. *International Journal of Behavioral Medicine, 18*, 13–22. doi: 10.1007/s12529-009-9069-x

Joshi, M. C., & Singh, B. (1966). Influence of socioeconomic background on the scores of so MMPI scales. *Journal of Social Psychology, 70*, 241–247. doi: 10.1080/00224545.1966.9712421

Kleefeld, C. A. (2001). The psychopathology of affluence. *Dissertation Abstracts International: Section B: The Sciences and Engineering, Vol. 62*(3-B), p. 1583.

Kohn, R., Dohrenwend, B. P., & Mirotznik, J. (1998). Epidemiological findings on selected psychiatric disorders in the general population. In B. P. Dohrenwend (Ed.), *Adversity, stress, and psychopathology* (pp. 235–284). London: Oxford Press.

Levine, M. (2006). *The price of privilege: How parental pressure and material advantage are creating a generation of disconnected and unhappy kids.* New York: Harper Collins Publishers.

Levy, M. R. (1970). Issues in the personality assessment of lower-class patients. *Journal of Projective Techniques & Personality Assessment, 34*, 6–9. doi: 10.1080/0091651X.1970.10380196

Levy, M. R., & Kahn, M. W. (1970). Interpreter bias on the Rorschach test as a function of patients' socioeconomic status. *Journal of Projective Techniques and Personality Assessment, 34*, 106–112. doi: 10.1080/0091651X.1970.10380218

Liu, W. M., Ali, S., Soleck, G., Hopps, J., Dunston, K., & Pickett, T. Jr. (2004). Using social class in counseling psychology research. *Journal of Counseling Psychology, 51*, 3–18. doi: 10.1037/0022-0167.51.1.3

Löckenhoff, C. E., Terracciano, A., Bienvenu, O. J., Patriciu, N. S., Nestadt, G., McCrae, et al. (2008). Ethnicity, education, and the temporal stability of personality traits in the East Baltimore epidemiologic catchment area study. *Journal of Research in Personality, 42*, 577–598. doi: 10.1016/j.jrp.2007.09.004

Long, K. A., & Graham, J. R. (1994). Socioeconomic status and MMPI-2 interpretation. *Measurement and Evaluation in Counseling and Development, 27*, 158–177.

Lott, B. (2012). The social psychology of class and classism. *American Psychologist, 67*, 650–658. doi: 10.1037/a0029369

Lott, B., & Bullock, H. E. (2007). *Psychology and economic injustice: Personal, professional, and political intersections.* Washington, DC: American Psychological Association. doi:10.1037/11501-000

Luthar, S. S., & Latendresse, S. J. (2002). Adolescent risk: The cost of affluence. *New Directions for Youth Development, 95*, 101–121. doi: 10.1002/yd.18

Luthar, S. S., & Sexton, C. C. (2004). *Advances in child development and behavior.* R. V. Kail (Ed.). San Diego, CA: Elsevier Academic Press.

Meyer, G. J., Viglione, D. J., Mihura, J. L., Erard, R. E., & Erdberg, P. (2011). *Rorschach Performance Assessment System: Administration, coding, interpretation, and technical manual.* Toledo, OH: Rorschach Performance Assessment System.

Morey, L. C. (1991). *Personality Assessment Inventory: Professional manual.* Odessa, FL: Psychological Assessment Resources.

Morey, L. C. (1997). *The Personality Assessment Screener: Professional manual.* Odessa, FL: Psychological Assessment Resources.

Morey, L. C. (2007). *Personality Assessment Inventory (PAI): Professional manual* (2nd ed.). Lutz, FL: Psychological Assessment Resources, Inc.

Piff, P. K., Stancato, D. M., Martinez, A. G., Kraus, M. W., & Keltner, D. (2012). Class, chaos, and the construction of community. *Journal of Personality and Social Psychology, 103*, 949–962. doi: 10.1037/a0029673

Pope, J. F., & Arthur, N. (2009). Socioeconomic status and class: A challenge for the practice of psychology in Canada. *Canadian Psychology, 50*(2), 55–65. doi. 10.1037/a0014222

Porcerelli, J. H., Kurtz, J. E., Cogan, R., Markova, T., & Mickens, L. (2012). Personality assessment screener in a primary care sample of low-income urban women. *Journal of Personality Assessment, 94*, 262–266. doi: 10.1080/00223891.2011.650304

Reimers, F. A., & Stabb, S. D. (2007, August). *A content analysis of class variables in the Counseling Psychology literature.* Symposium presentation at the APA annual convention, San Francisco.

Saunders, S. A., Allen, M. W., & Pozzebon, K. (2008). An exploratory look at the relationship between materialistic values and goals and type A behaviour. *Journal of Pacific Rim Psychology, 2*, 47–52. doi: 10.1375/prp.2.2.47

Sladen, B. J. (1982). Effects of race and socioeconomic status on the perception of process variables in counseling. *Journal of Counseling Psychology, 29*, 560–566. doi: 10.1037/0022-0167.29.6.560

Smith, L. (2010). *Psychology, poverty, and the end of social exclusion: Putting our practice to work.* New York: Teachers College Press.

Smith, L. (2013). So close and yet so far away: Social class, social exclusion, and mental health practice. *American Journal of Orthopsychiatry, 83*, 11–16. doi: 10.1111/ajop.12008

Smith, L., Chambers, D., & Brantini, L. (2009). When oppression is the pathogen: The participatory development of socially just mental health practice. *American Journal of Orthopsychiatry, 79*, 159–168. doi: 10.1037/a0015353

Stabb, S. D., & Reimers, F. A. (2013). Competent poverty training. *Journal of Clinical Psychology: In Session, 69*, 172–181. doi: 10.1002/jclp.21956

Stanton, M. V., Jonassaint, C. R., Williams, R. B., & James, S. A. (2010). Socioeconomic status moderates the association between John Henryism and NEOPI-R personality domains. *Psychosomatic Medicine, 72*, 141–147. doi: 10.1097/PSY.0b013e3181cdc00e

Sutin, A. R., Costa, P. T., Evans, M. K., & Zonderman, A. B. (2013). Personality assessment in a diverse urban sample. *Psychological Assessment, 25*, 1007–1012. doi: 10.1037/a0032396

Timbrook, R. E., & Graham, J. R. (1994). Ethnic differences on the MMPI-2? *Psychological Assessment, 6*, 212–217. doi: 10.1037/1040-3590.6.3.212

Ullrich, S., Farrington, D. P., & Coid, J. W. (2007). Dimensions of DSM-IV personality disorders and life-success. Journal of Personality Disorders, *21*, 657–663. doi: 10.1521/pedi.2007.21.6.657

Wadsworth, M. E., & Achenbach, T. M. (2005). Explaining the link between low socioeconomic status and psychopathology. *Journal of Consulting and Clinical Psychology, 73*, 1146–1153. doi: 10.1037/0022-006X.73.6.1146

Wadsworth, M. E., Raviv, T. S., DeCarlo, C., & Etter, E. M. (2011). Testing the adaptation to poverty-related stress model: Predicting psychopathology symptoms in families facing economic hardship. *Journal of Clinical Child and Adolescent Psychology, 40*, 646–657. doi: 10.1080/15374416.2011.581622

Weintraub, S. R., & Goodman, L. A. (2010). Working with and for: Student advocates' experience of relationship-centered advocacy with low-income women. *American Journal of Orthopsychiatry, 80*, 46–60. doi: 10.1111/j.1939-0025.2010.01006.x

Zelman, D. B. (2008). Mental health help seeking among affluent adolescents. *Dissertation Abstracts International Section A: Humanities and Social Sciences, Vol. 69*(1-A), AAI3299310.

Appendix

Table 12.1 Summary of Studies Using Personality Assessment Instruments with Low-Income Samples

Authors and Date	*Personality Measure(s)*	*Focus of Study*	*Sample Characteristics*	*Results*
Adams & Horovitz (1980)	Mini MMPI Louisville Aggression Survey Schedule–1 (LASS1) (instruments translated to Spanish were needed)	Relationships between boys' psychopathology (aggression), father presence/absence and SES	454 households (mothers, fathers if present, male children); 55% Black, 45% "Cuban/White;" all Medicaid-eligible "slum dwellers"	No effect of father presence or absence, ethnicity or age. Authors ascribe primary effects to poverty and mother's psychopathology.
Alterman et al. (1995)	Personality Assessment Inventory (PAI) NIMH Diagnostic Interview Schedule Addictions Severity Index	Reliability, concurrent validity, and other psychometric properties of the PAI with low-SES addict population; compared scores to other instruments and to three reference samples (normal, clinical, substance-dependent)	229 inpatient heroin addicts undergoing methadone treatment; roughly half Black and half Latino/a; 39% women, 61% men; average monthly income $100; median income $0	7/11 clinical scales had adequate reliability. Questionable or marginal reliability found for DRG, RXR, NON, and WRM scales. Concurrent validity was satisfactory. Current sample PAI scores were similar to other clinical and substance-dependent groups and clearly elevated in comparison to normal group. Latinos had higher scores than Blacks on SOM, ANX, DEP, ALC, and SUI. No gender differences.

(continued)

Table 12.1 Summary of Studies Using Personality Assessment Instruments with Low-Income Samples *(continued)*

Authors and Date	*Personality Measure(s)*	*Focus of Study*	*Sample Characteristics*	*Results*
Bornstein, Porcerelli, Huprich, & Markova (2009)	Relationship Profile Test–Subscale scores: Destructive Overdependence (DO) Dysfunctional Detachment (DD) Healthy Dependency (HD)	Determining construct validity of the RPT in a low-income sample	143 predominantly Black, Medicaid-eligible women with annual incomes under \$20,000; family medicine clinic patients	Construct validity of the PRT supported with this population. High correlations of DO and DD unique to this population.
Gibbs (1982)	Diagnostic Interview for Borderlines Rorschach WAIS or WISC-R	Ethnic and sociocultural patterns in delinquent girls	48 White, Hispanic, and Black adjudicated delinquent girls ages 13–18; 3 SES levels: lower, working, and middle/upper	Only interpretable results related to SES were that middle/upper class girls were more neurotic than lower class girls.
Jokela & Keltikangas-Järvinen (2011)	Beck Depression Inventory Temperament and Character Inventory Big 5 Personality Inventory	Personality mediators of the relationship between low SES and depression	2,678 participants (1,510 women and 1,168 men); measured education, occupation, and income. Range of SES represented	Focused on the findings that in low-SES participants, depression was highest in those with high harm avoidance and neuroticism.

Authors and Date	*Personality Measure(s)*	*Focus of Study*	*Sample Characteristics*	*Results*
Jonassaint, Siegler, Barefoot, Edwards, & Williams (2011)	NEO-PI-R	Relationship of personality variables to SES over the life-course; compared high-SES to low-SES (determined by median split at 40th percentile of income in the geographic area; parental education)	233 participants, ages 18–50 years; 145 high SES and 88 low SES; 113 female, 120 male, 141 African American, and 92 White	Low father education and low life-course SES were disproportionately associated with high neuroticism and low conscientiousness. No gender or race effects.
Joshi & Singh (1966)	MMPI (Indian adaptation) Subscales: Hypochondriasis (HS) Hysteria (HY) Masculinity-Femininity (MF) Psychopathic Deviance (PD) Lie Scale (L)	Relationship of MMPI subscales to SES	2,018 urban boys 16–26 years old divided into four SES groupings	Boys in the lowest SES bracket had significantly higher elevations on HS, HY, and MF than the other three groups. Boys in the lowest SES bracket had significantly higher elevations on PD than boys in the uppermost SES bracket. No differences were found on the L-scale.

(continued)

Table 12.1 Summary of Studies Using Personality Assessment Instruments with Low-Income Samples *(continued)*

Authors and Date	*Personality Measure(s)*	*Focus of Study*	*Sample Characteristics*	*Results*
Porcerelli, Kurtz, Cogan, Markova, & Mickens (2012)	Personality Assessment Screener (PAS) Patient Health Questionnaire (PHQ) Personality Diagnostic Questionnaire-4 (PDQ4) Alcohol Use Disorders Identification Test (AUDIT)	Assess the convergent validity, and other psychometric properties of the 10 PAS element scores and compare with three other instruments. Assess the diagnostic efficacy of the recommended cut-off score and two additional cut-off scores.	110 women seeking treatment at an urban family medicine training clinic; 89% African American, earned less than $20,000/year and were unemployed	The PAS was found to be an adequate screening tool for use in a primary care setting. The recommended cut-off score of 20 was found to be the most conservative and warranted score for groups with similar demographics. No discussion of SES.
Stanton, Jonassaint, Williams, & James (2010)	NEO-PI-R Active Coping (John Henryism; JH) Scale	Explore relationships between NEO-PI personality domains, John Henryism, and SES with a focus on lower SES	233 community volunteers, mean age 33 yrs; 61% Black and 39% White; created two categorical SES groups based on current household income and education	SES moderated the association between JH and Neuroticism (N). Among low-SES individuals, mean N scores changed little as mean JH scores increased, whereas among high-SES individuals, mean N scores decreased as mean JH scores increased.

Authors and Date	*Personality Measure(s)*	*Focus of Study*	*Sample Characteristics*	*Results*
Sutin, Costa, Evans, & Zonderman (2013)	NEO-PI-R	Quality of data and replicability of the NEO-PI–R factor structure in a sample that varied in ethnicity, SES, and literacy.	546 men (35%) and women (65%); Urban African American (58%) and White (42%). 49% living above and 51% below 125% of the federal poverty line	Subscale: Openness to Experience required a higher reading level (2.5 grade levels above the reading level required for other factors) than did the other four factors. Factor structure in general well-replicated; internal consistency good.

PART III

Interpersonal Contexts

CHAPTER 13

Assessment Contexts

Matthew R. Baity, Alexander L. Hsieh, and Samantha M. Swanson

In this chapter, we consider several ways to highlight the importance of the context in which an assessment occurs. As we have defined it, a *context* is a sociocultural perspective that is relevant for a particular patient in a particular situation. That is, an assessment takes place at a particular time for both clinician and patient, and at the time of assessment, a patient's particular background and reason for assessment intersect with the time and place of the assessment. Taken together, these form the context in which the assessment occurs. This definition recognizes that patient (and clinician) identities are in flux, changing, and reactive. For example, a young adult female being evaluated over concerns about having borderline personality disorder might be facing shame around receiving a diagnosis, concern about the stigma of mental illness, and stigma considering young adult social culture. Additionally, she might be facing the loss of freedom should an inpatient stay be necessary, and the future repercussions of the stigma associated with being in inpatient care. What if we were to also fold in the fact that this patient identifies her own mother's institutionalization as a significant contributor to her father's substance abuse and his subsequent abandonment of the family? What if the culture of the family was not accepting of Western health care? The lack of sensitivity to cultural differences between clinician (giving the diagnosis) and patient (receiving the diagnosis) might also contribute to the patient's rejection of said diagnosis originating from a Western dominant ideology. Traditional psychological assessment instruments provide scores for comparison against normative samples, but clinicians invested in being responsive to their patients must also consider the larger contexts at play to bring a deeper meaning to the data (Stiles, Honos-Webb, & Surko, 1998).

A more straightforward approach to this chapter would be to list out the potential contexts that are present in various settings. However, this is unlikely to be successful for three reasons. First, identifying the contexts in ordinal fashion presumes that this list appears somewhere in the literature (either in part or in whole) already and that we would just need to summarize and cite the sources for readers to look up in their own time. Despite our best efforts (and hopes), such a list has not been created. Given the range of contexts that are present in any particular case, producing such a list would go well beyond the scope of this or any chapter hoping to keep the readers' interest. Second, even if a list was created, it would be difficult to hierarchically arrange the various contexts by order of importance because every patient is different. The loss of freedom might be relevant for two different patients of the same ethnicity, but perhaps more so if one of those patients has had multiple family members incarcerated. Or, as in our case below, loss of freedom might also impact continued enrollment at a university as the first person in the family to attend college. This complexity leads to our final reason for not creating a simple list: it would negate the importance of how these contexts intersect and impact one another in a given case. The intersectionality of characteristics and cultural perspectives creates a much more complex palette for clinicians to consider. Therefore, we have chosen a more experiential route to this chapter. First, we present a case and describe what a traditional approach might look like based on the training a typical psychologist is likely to receive in graduate school. Then we discuss the various contexts and their intersections that seem relevant for the case, and take a second look at how the clinician might better understand and interact with the patient.

Historical Links to Emotion

Before discussing specific contexts of assessment, we feel it is necessary to at least summarize some historical elements that all clinicians should consider and become more aware of in the various settings and situations of assessment. A common thread of the major theoretical orientations in understanding human behavior is that emotions, thoughts, and behavior are connected in some way. Interestingly, Darwin had a lot to say about emotions in humans that was not always directly linked to his ideas in *The Origin of Species* (1859). He posited that emotions were reflexive, innate, and, at one point in our ancestral past, directly useful for survival. However, not all expressions of emotions continue to have a distinct purpose in modern adult humans. For example, raised body hair after perceiving a fear stimulus in humans is a leftover response from animals where puffing out hair or fur is instinctual behavior to make them appear bigger and more intimidating when their survival is threatened. Darwin saw these examples of emotions as vestigial and therefore evidence for evolution (Darwin, 1872/1998). He believed that emotional expressions were signals to us and others, and in that sense serve the purpose of facilitating communications and building relationships. So, although we can argue that emotions are not primarily tied to survival in humans in the same way as in our animal ancestors, emotional expression still plays a vital role in helping us understand our environment.

A substantial amount of research from several different fields of psychology (social, experimental, personality, etc.) since Darwin has identified a basic set of emotions that seem to be innate in humans, with neurological correlates also found in other species. For several decades the universality hypothesis dictated that anger, sadness, joy, disgust, fear, and occasionally surprise led to distinct facial expressions that were identifiable across a wide range of cultures (Ekman & Friesen, 1971; Ekman, Sorenson, & Friesen, 1969; Elfenbein & Ambady, 2002, 2003;

Izard, 1994). Although the existence of these basic emotions is not under scrutiny, the universal expression of them has been the source of numerous debates. Individualistic societies value emotional expression and encourage individual goal attainment while collectivistic societies reinforce group harmony where the actions of the individual are less important. As might be expected, participants from individualistic societies are more accurate in judging photos of facial expressions (Matsumoto, 1989) than collectivistic members, presumably because outward displays of emotion are more reinforced in Western culture. Other research has demonstrated distinct differences in facial muscle activation with collectivistic individuals using subtler (and less obvious) eye movements to display emotion as opposed to their individualistic counterparts (Jack, Garrod, Caldara, & Schyns, 2012). Experimental manipulation of the environment (i.e., context) has also been shown to influence the verbal and physiological expression of emotion across stereotypically individualistic and collectivistic samples (Masuda et al., 2008; Scherer, Matsumoto, Wallbott, & Kudoh, 1988). Ekman (1989) provides an eloquent summary of the field of emotion expression and presented data to suggest that individuals from different cultures displayed and experienced emotions based on the "rules" taught by the culture with which they most identify. As one might expect, individuals tend to have greater difficulty identifying the emotions of someone who has a "rule set" that is different from their own. Interestingly enough, there are some data to suggest that certain emotions are more readily identified than others that, in part, depend on how the emotion is expressed (e.g., audio only, visual only, or audio and visual; Abelin, 2004). This pattern is also seen in some research on psychotherapy with patients of color where dropout rates tend to be higher when the perceived ethnicity of the therapist and patient are dissimilar (Owen, Imel, Adelson, & Rodolfa, 2012; Wintersteen, Mensinger, & Diamond, 2005). However, there are also data to suggest that patient–therapist match does not have a significant effect on dropout rates (Gottheil, Sterling, Weinstein, & Kurtz, 1995; Maramba & Nagayama Hall, 2002). This is not to say that we are bound to experience emotion based on the culture we grew up with, but it is very influential in how we perceive our environment. For example, American-born children of immigrant families can face the dilemma of managing different "rule sets" on a day-to-day basis. This can be particularly stressful for families if there is pressure to maintain the native culture at the expense of interfacing with the dominant culture. When we are open to and respectful of "rule sets" that are different from our own, it not only becomes easier to acquire knowledge about different perspectives but also reduces the chances of misinterpreting our patients' behaviors.

Social Constructivism

We would posit that those "rule sets" have their roots in social constructivist theory (SCT); that our learned knowledge about the world is constructed by those around us. We begin learning about our environment at an early age and, through both interpersonal exchanges (SCT) and observational learning (e.g., Bandura), children form schemas about how the world works, what relationships should be like, what to expect, what is dangerous, etc. This happens regardless of the environment, so children from Beverly Hills, to Baghdad, to Beijing will learn how to understand their environment based on what they experience. SCT also suggests that the elements of evaluation are idiographic experiences so that there are both inter- and intracultural differences. Two children raised in the same family environment and exposed to similar experiences can have very different ways of evaluating the world. This makes the argument that the emotions one feels in a given situation (as well as the connected behavior) is a function of a culture-based evaluation with no guarantees that individuals from similar cultures are coming to similar conclusions. Therefore, making assumptions about individuals based on their perceived group membership (i.e., social class, race, diagnoses, etc.), or assuming that patients adhere to the tenets of the clinician's dominant culture without clarifying how the individual evaluates their environment, can lead to a range of miscalculated assumptions. A recent example was experienced by the first author at a treatment team meeting where many team members were convinced that a suicidal patient with a series of recent admissions was "borderline" and just seeking attention, but curiously overlooked the fact that this patient was known to have very low intellectual functioning. Some brief testing also revealed this patient also had gross cognitive impairment, particularly in memory and executive functioning. In other words, her extreme behavior and poor affect regulation were likely a product of her poor cognitive foundation more than a stereotypical character pathology. She even reported that her most recent suicide attempt (trying to hang herself with a shoelace on a shower curtain rod that instantly gave way) was because she wanted to have someone to talk to that day. Despite attempts to explain this to the psychiatrist, the attitude toward this patient remained unchanged.

How this all applies to considering the context in psychological assessment is to be sensitive to the ideas that the where, when, and why an assessment is conducted likely influences not only the findings from the tests, but also how clinicians obtain this information. Primary emotions (anger, fear, disgust, joy, sadness) are, for the most part, universal but not universally expressed or experienced the same way. Secondary emotions (e.g., love, shame, contentment, etc.) are even more defined and prioritized by cultural "rule sets." Which emotions are experienced is based largely on an evaluation of the context; the parameters for which are also both culturally defined and idiosyncratic. Situations that are determined to be aligned with goals tend to elicit pleasurable emotions while incongruence with goals evokes more painful ones. The term "culture" here does not necessarily refer to ethnic heritage, but to the various groups one identifies with and how they prioritize the goals from those groups. A transgender Latino female being evaluated in a rural community might have greater concerns about how they are accepted by others, than if they are in a larger metropolitan area. If that same person also recently found out they were HIV positive, concerns about how they will be treated in the community or gender-related issues may increase, decrease, or be integrated into the identity spectrum. Add homelessness, unemployment, or severe mental illness and the relevant goals might change yet again. Given the likelihood of a patient spontaneously providing a listing of their identities and how they are prioritized is quite low, the burden of determining how patients' rule sets factor into the context of assessment rests firmly on the shoulders of clinicians.

Aside from a select number of settings where the length and time required for an assessment is not a major issue, many of us are not able to conduct a comprehensive cultural identity interview for a variety of reasons. A number of culturally specific instruments are available for review both within this text and in the broader literature for clinicians looking to add relevant measures to a testing battery that might address some of the issues we are raising. It is an important starting point and an increased recognition of how the complexities that cultural identities bring to a case has broadened our dialogue in the field. However, clinicians should be aware of several issues when choosing to use such measures, which are typically self-report. First, as with adding any new measure, clinicians should review the literature on the development of the measure they are considering in order to evaluate its psychometric properties. What is the theory behind the instrument? What is the sample size and make-up on which the primary analyses were done? What are the statistical procedures used and how realistic are the conclusions based on the analyses conducted (e.g., are definitive findings drawn from correlative analyses? Have there been studies of invariance with other samples?)? Our main concern with using these cultural measures, is that they are stagnant representations with (typically) limited assessment of social desirability or impression management. As discussed earlier, appraisal of one's environment is a fluid, ongoing process that is unlikely to be fully represented on a measure of cultural identity. The risk here is that clinicians might not see these results as a snapshot and could be vulnerable to confirmation biases without considering the context in which the person is being evaluated.

Case Background

A.S. was a 19-year-old African American male hospitalized at a locked inpatient psychiatric institute for new onset psychosis in the wake of excessive alcohol and cocaine use. Mr. S was found stumbling outside of a large fraternity party on the local college campus yelling loudly and walking into oncoming traffic. Witnesses to this event described Mr. S as incoherent and aggressive. Attempts from other party attendees to remove Mr. S from the road resulted in an altercation and Mr. S leaving the scene. Upon returning to the dorm room, Mr. S's roommate found him semi-conscious on the floor. Paramedics were called, and Mr. S was described as combative and resistant to intervention. After being cleared medically in the ER, Mr. S continued to appear confused and disorganized. He denied any recollection of the previous night's events and asked that he be allowed to go home. After reportedly describing vague plans for suicide with intent, Mr. S was transferred to the locked inpatient psychiatric unit for further evaluation. After three days in the psychiatric unit, Mr. S's mood continued to remain poor but his level of comprehension and responsiveness improved. He began to make requests that he be discharged from the unit because he was "not crazy, [and] just had a bad night." When asked directly about his suicidal thinking Mr. S said, "I'm not going to kill myself right now and even if I was, I wouldn't tell you!" Despite his recent aggressive behavior, he did not display any outbursts on the unit. He was "quietly compliant" with staff and treaters on the psychiatric unit, but tended to keep to himself and only communicated when directly spoken to.

What initial thoughts did you have when reading this case? Just a series of poor decisions by a college student? Signs of a serious addiction problem? Early onset psychosis? Angry Black man? How would your impression change if Mr. S was Asian or Latino? If ethnicity was not provided, would you have assumed he was White because he was a college student? Mr. S had a shift in his attitude where he was more communicative, but remained somewhat disengaged from the milieu. He was no longer intoxicated, which might account for some or all of the shift. However, if his goal was to leave, why was he not being more overt in demonstrating improvement? Was his defiance about reporting his suicidality a sign of psychosis, depression, antisocial personality, or mistrust of authority? Perhaps Mr. S was responding (consciously or not) to the broader issue of uneven incarceration rates for people of color, especially Black men. Maybe he just thought this was the best way to get out as quickly as possible. Obviously these questions cannot be answered from the small amount of information provided and no psychological test is going to give us direct information about why Mr. S chose this approach. What we can surmise is that he evaluated his situation in some way based on his prior experience and knowledge, there was emotion involved, and he chose a course of action based on that evaluation. We will not make claims about whether emotion or thought came first with the hopes of avoiding a cognitive vs. psychodynamic argument. What really matters is the thought-feeling appraisal of being involuntarily committed that is informing his behavior. Next, we consider some additional information about Mr. S that was gathered in a brief interview.

Sociocultural Information

Mr. S's parents described him as a quiet but social child who made friends easily, participated in recreational sports, and never had any worrisome incidents until recently. Due to his academic promise, Mr. S's parents took great care to support his interest by enrolling him in a wide range of summer camps and workshops with the intention of helping him choose a career early. In his teenage years, Mr. S became fascinated with the game of chess and would play relentlessly when he was at home. According to Mr. S, this interest originally led to tension within his peer group because none of his friends played. Although he reportedly was able to find peers to play with, they would not be what he would call "his crew" because he had difficulty relating to them in ways other than a combined interest in chess. This resulted in him essentially having two separate peer groups; one that he played chess with and one that he would spend the majority of his social time with. Because of his academic success and offer for a scholarship, he reportedly felt compelled to attend college but remained hesitant as he felt this choice would put him at further odds with his primary social group. Mr. S described that the freedom of being away from home, and the lack of an established peer group (beyond the other students using substances) led him quickly to the point where he started "skipping classes, doing coke, and playing video games all day long." He reported that his alcohol use increased at this time as well. Mr. S estimated that he was drinking up to a 12-pack of beer and snorting10 lines of cocaine in a 24-hour period. He reportedly recognized the direction that he was heading but felt that he could not stop himself.

Guilt from letting down his family and himself resulted in increased feelings of depression and suicidal thinking. He failed his first semester of college, resulting in the loss of his academic scholarship. However, he kept this information from his parents out of shame, and told them he wanted to move into an apartment off campus so he could get more money from them to support his habit. This maneuver reportedly left Mr. S with even greater feelings of guilt and shame that began to turn more violent. The night he was hospitalized, Mr. S had set out to do this very thing. He had reportedly run out of money and thought that he would go to a fraternity party on campus to find drugs. He denied any clear memories after that moment, but did recall that "I was going to go out with a bang." Although he did not deny the events of the rest of the evening, he continued to report that he did not recall what happened. When he described his first conversation with his parents after his arrest, he began to cry openly which was the first expression of emotion seen since his hospitalization. He continued to be ambiguous when asked about his current suicidal ideation, stating that he does still think about it, but that he did not know for sure whether he would ever act on these feelings. He denied having any current plans or intention, but stated "I never had a plan, I just decided to do it."

Traditional Approach

Mr. S's testing data did not suggest the presence of psychosis but did highlight limited psychological resources, a slight tendency to misperceive his environment, and social isolation. More specific diagnostic testing indicated the presence of a ruminative anxiety, dysphoria, and a complement to the social isolation in the form of both avoidant and schizoidal personality disorder traits. There was little information from the assessment and/or clinical observations that would help justify a continued involuntary hospitalization, but his limited psychological resources and tendency toward social isolation were seen as primary concerns. If this were to remain unchanged for Mr. S, his risk for returning to another acute state was thought to be high.

The treatment recommendations from the testing were primarily focused on establishing support systems to prevent a repeat decline in functioning including academic tutoring services, outpatient therapy, psychiatric evaluation, and substance abuse support groups. Mr. S agreed with the findings and was discharged from the hospital shortly thereafter.

At a broad level there was nothing wrong with the assessment; commonly accepted instruments were selected to answer the referral question in a timely manner; recommendations were made to the treatment team, and feedback was offered to the patient who reported agreement with the results. At a more culture-centric level, what choice did Mr. S really have? He was a Black man being held against his will by a team dominated by White treaters who had the ability to keep him or release him. There is no clear data pointing to how much racial or power differences influenced the results, but the absence of this evidence should not be considered evidence of its absence. He was also facing an uncertain academic future given that his primary means to get a college education was through the scholarship that he lost. What were Mr. S's plans to address this after being discharged? When he cried after speaking to his parents following his hospital admission, was this embarrassment over getting caught or did it run deeper than that?

Know Your Patient

The task of assessing your patient begins with acknowledgment and understanding of your patient's cultural identities as well as how those identities interact with the context in which the patient will be assessed. As other chapters in this volume and the extant literature on diversity highlight, clinicians should be mindful to not initially label patients based on perceived physical diversity attributes without more thorough questioning. Despite outward appearances (also prone to clinician biases), patients may or may not identify with their cultural background or might have a difficult time assimilating to the dominant culture (Burkard & Ponterotto, 2008), and further assessment must be conducted before progressing into the treatment stages of therapy. Although understanding our patients from a culturally competent perspective pays respect and attention to diversity, context would give great meaning to the expression of culture for our patients.

First, clinicians need to identify potential cultural considerations to be paid during the process of assessment. There are several different categories of diversity clinicians must keep in mind when assessing for patient's acculturation. Individuals will present uniquely and no two patients have the same exact cultural identity. As a clinically competent assessment clinician, one must be open and mindful of these various cultural identities. Clinicians should start by allowing the patient to define these cultural identities he or she connects with and allow the patient to inform the clinician on how these major themes define them (Sciarra & Simon, 2008). Drawing from our case study, socioeconomic status and education are critical cultural identities that Mr. S identified with. His decision to pursue a college education (the first of his generation) is a component of the patient's identity that he brings to the psychiatric evaluation, as is the extent to which Mr. S identifies with traditional African American values (e.g., family support, filial piety, generational hierarchy, and strong sense of pride). Thus, questions could be asked about Mr. S's family support, being first generation college attendee, and perhaps religious affiliations. Culturally, these are important assessments because they give insight into how much Mr. S identifies and aligns himself with his African American culture, how the rules of his various identities might influence his appraisal of his environment, and ultimately his decision to act on his appraisal. The culturally competent therapist perceives culture and acculturation on a spectrum when conducting assessments and understands that the patient's cultural identities interact with the patient's context. Pertaining to this case, we will look specifically at the power dynamic regarding the patient's context.

Power

Power, especially social power, should be a major consideration in psychiatric evaluations, given that it can be a significant component toward the outcome of the evaluation. Traditionally, social power is seen as a function of ethnicity, but more importantly, power is a dynamic perception dependent on the assessment context. When individuals have certain levels of perceived power (or are relatively ignorant to its influence), they are propelled to make more decisive choices and enact deeper desires. With less perceived power, individuals tend to more actively manage others' impressions of them, that might range from more closely editing the information they share to a paranoid level of hypervigilance. The relationship between a clinician and patient exhibits natural differences in power, but given a specific context, that imbalance of power may be diminished or amplified. In most contexts, it is the patient's perception of this power imbalance that will be most relevant.

Closely related to the balance of power in psychological assessment are the potential outcomes or recommendations from the testing. This evaluation of the patient's perceived power becomes especially paramount give certain psychiatric contexts, such as an inpatient psychiatric unit. Despite Mr. S's stated desire to leave, he was unable to just walk off the unit before an evaluation could be completed, thus temporarily taking power from Mr. S. Had this situation been a part of Mr. S's cognitive appraisal, it would make sense that he might meet the evaluation and the evaluator with resistance. Consequently, this resistance might have influenced his engagement in the assessment, which could increase the risk of painting an illusion of psychopathology (e.g., anger, paranoia, "faking good," etc.) and ultimately influencing the timeline of his hospital discharge.

Bidimensional Model of Acculturation

Acculturation should be best understood as a bidimensional model rather than a unidimensional one (Kim, Newhill, & López, 2013). The bidimensional model of acculturation accounts for an individual's identification with both the dominant and biological culture. This model can best be understood with intersecting axes of an individual's biological culture with one's surrounding dominant culture (see Figure 13.1). The intersecting axes pattern individuals into four acculturation identities (assimilation, separation, marginalization, and integration). People are considered to be in the *assimilation* gradient when they have fully embraced the dominant cultural practices while abandoning their inherent cultural principles. The *separation* dimension is typified by individuals who still adhere to their native cultural norms while shunning the dominant cultural practices. *Marginalization* patterns occur when individuals stray from both dominant culture and their inherent cultural practices. Finally, patients with *integration* acculturation patterns typically maintain their native cultural values while adopting mainstream practices as well. This pattern is typically categorized as biculturalism or multiculturalism (Kim et al., 2013). A thorough understanding of acculturation patterns can give the clinician insight into how the context of an assessment might be impacted by a patient's motivations, expectations, and concerns. For example, a patient who identifies with a native culture that conceptualizes mental health differently from Western practices might be expected to view a personality assessment with great trepidation. Assigning a diagnosis to this individual might bring about concerns of shame to his family. Recommendations for therapy or inpatient hospitalization for an individual with personal experiences of loss of freedom in their native country could result in a re-traumatization. Ideally, the clinician assesses for acculturation through semi-structured interviews with the patient by evaluating the patient's own identity with key cultural values and tendencies.

Awareness of our patient and understanding the various gradients of the bidimensional approach is key to acknowledgment of our various biases. Assessment clinicians can then begin to understand the various processes with which our diverse patients struggle. The bidimensional approach gives clinicians a better

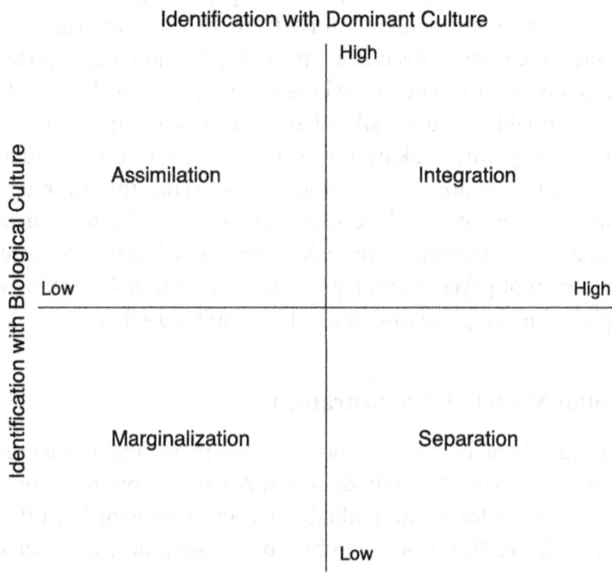

Figure 13.1 Bidimensional Model of Acculturation

understanding of the impact acculturation has on their patients and the various patients' identity developments. For example, an assimilated Chinese patient presenting with depressive symptoms would be more open to diagnosis and treatment than a separation Chinese patient since, culturally, such a diagnosis would be rejected by the individual and family because it represents weakness and could stigmatize the entire family.

When we work from a bidimensional framework, we open the possibility of culturally sensitive treatments. Methodology becomes multidimensional because we have a multidimensional perspective into the acculturation dynamic of our patients. Because early assessments are critical to the prognosis of treatment, understanding the bidimensional approach and proper assessment of our patients' acculturation levels becomes essential. We then acknowledge the diverse components of our patients, check our own biases, and treat from a culturally informed perspective, understanding that treatment needs to take into account the individual patient's acculturation pattern. By adopting the bidimensional model of acculturation, we not only make assessment a culturally sensitive process but also use assessment to guide the treatment process.

Intersection Approach to Diversity

The bidimensional approach to acculturation gives assessment psychologists a better understanding of patients' acculturation experiences, but clinicians also need to understand how various diversity patterns intersect. Basic diversity characteristics are gender, race, and class but should also be extended to sexual orientation, ability/disability, religion, language coherence, and age. The intersection theory introduces the ideal that minority groups experience various discriminations based on multiple traits, creating an exponential diversity barrier (Toren, 2009). The intersection theory paints a more complex identity model for patients. Toren (2009) states that the intersection model deems "identities are malleable and can be organized through a multiplicity of interpretive frameworks and in relation to social conditions that are inherently unstable" (p. 154).

The multitude of diversity categories within each individual intersect in a nearly infinite number of ways depending on the context, such that each patient has a unique identity even if they share one or more diversity characteristics with others. For example, male patients with a similar racial and ethnic background and at the same age in development will exhibit vastly different internal qualities if one comes from an urban atmosphere and the other a rural standard. These interactions of diversity categories will create contrasting narratives which the patient must be the expert in illustrating for the clinician.

Here we see how Mr. S's cultural identity interacts with his context of perceived power. Historically, African Americans have less social power than the dominant culture, and in instances where distribution of power is contextually unequal, African Americans have been disproportionately represented. For example, African Americans tend to have a high prison incarceration rate compared to other ethnicities and they tend to be paid significantly less compared to their White counterparts on similar jobs. The two context examples, the prison system and job workplace, demonstrate environments where power can be a key social component. As referenced earlier, an inpatient care facility demonstrates another environment of power differential, which is at play with the historical cultural perception of African Americans and power struggle, as well as Mr. S jeopardizing his identification as a first generation college student, and facing the stigma of having a mental illness. Now, perhaps his perceived resistance is not entirely based on his mistrust of the system, but also a reluctance to return to life outside the hospital where he will have to face the consequences of his decisions. This transition will require careful monitoring of his instinct to escape into substances to manage uncomfortable affect.

The answer for clinicians would be to consider both the power dynamic as well as the patient's cultural identity. By perceiving these elements from an interaction model, the clinician can provide a more thorough assessment. Part of the power differential can be avoided if the clinician empowers the patient toward a more collaborative approach in assessment. Fostering a positive clinician–patient relationship would contribute to offsetting the clinician–patient power differential, in the hope that the patient will be more responsive in the assessment.

The assessment process thus becomes relative because of the extensive complexity of the intersection model. To an assessment clinician, patients will not present the same because of the various intersections that might or might not play a role in the their identities. For example, Mr. S's cultural identity supports strong sense of family values and family cohesion, demonstrated by his interactions and feelings of shame and guilt over betrayals because of lies previously told. In addition, Mr. S experienced a loss of power because of mandatory hospitalization, bringing up the experience of social power loss. Furthermore, the cultural and family stigma associated with a mental health diagnosis (with a history of an uncle who struggled with drugs and alcohol), taken together with the previously stated cultural identities, paints a complicated perception of resistance.

Identifying the various diversity characteristics and their various points of intersection would be critical in understanding our patients in identity and cultural development. We must take into account how these individual characteristics impact our patients on a horizontal and vertical level as well as how these intersecting points create the complexity. We take into account the relativity that our patients experience and understand that experiences are impacted by the various intersecting points of diversity. These intersecting diversity points might create quintessential identity characteristics for some patients, but be completely irrelevant for others. We should proceed from the curious perspective and leave space for understanding from the patient's perspective by allowing our patients to guide us.

Understanding the complexity of diversity and the interactional effect with context can help give us an insight into our patients' experiences and, with it, a better understanding of our patients. A broader, more comprehensive, and detailed depiction of diversity offers complexity toward understanding diversity. Diversity no longer becomes a singular unit capable of being captured by one approach and one perspective. Contrarily, the bidimensional acculturation approach and intersection of diversity presents patients as a complex but comprehensive entity. Therefore, it becomes paramount for clinicians to include both these models when conceptualizing diversity in their patients. The interaction of an individual's cultural identity with the setting creates a more complex but complete picture given the context. From our case study and example, we can see the complexities associated with a bidimensional model. When we establish an understanding of our patient's cultural identity, we gain more insight and can have a greater grasp of how that intersects and interacts with the patient's context and setting. This allows for a more comprehensive assessment: one that accounts for minority culture, dominant culture, integration of both (or multiple) cultures, the interaction between cultures, the patient's context and setting, and the interaction between all the variables.

References

Abelin, Å. (2004). Cross-cultural multimodal interpretations of emotional expressions: An experimental study of Spanish and Swedish. In *Proceedings of Speech Prosody*. ISCA, March 23–26, Naran.

Burkard, A. W., & Ponterotto, J. G. (2008). Recent developments in the assessment of racial identity, ethnic identity, and the multicultural personality. In L. A. Suzuki, J. G. Ponterotto, & J. Mueller (Eds.), *Handbook of multicultural assessment: Clinical, psychological, and educational applications* (3rd ed.) (pp. 52–72). Thousand Oaks, CA: Sage.

Darwin, C. (1859). *On the origin of species by means of natural selection or the preservation of favored races in the struggle for life* (1st ed). London: John Murray. doi: 10.1037/14088-000

Darwin, C. (1872/1998). *The expression of emotions in man and animals* (3rd ed.). New York: Oxford University Press. doi: 10.1037/10001-000 (1872)

Ekman, P. (1989). The argument and evidence about universals in facial expression of emotion. In H. Wager and A. Manstead (Eds). *Handbook of social psychophysiology*. Chichester: Wiley.

Ekman, P., & Friesen, W. V. (1971). Constants across culture in the face and emotion. *Journal of Personality and Social Psychology, 17*, 124–129. doi: 10.1037/h0030377

Ekman, P., Sorenson, E. R., & Friesen, W. V. (1969). Pan-cultural elements in the facial displays of emotion. *Science, 164*, 86–88. doi: 10.1126/science.164.3875.86

Elfenbein, H. A., & Ambady, N. (2002). On the universality and cultural specificity of emotion recognition: A meta-analysis. *Psychological Bulletin, 128*, 203–235. doi: 10.1037/0033-2909.128.2.203

Elfenbein, H. A., & Ambady, N. (2003). Universals and cultural differences in recognizing emotions. *Current Directions in Psychological Science, 12*, 159–164. doi: 10.1111/1467-8721.01252

Gottheil, E., Sterling, R. C., Weinstein, S. P., & Kurtz, J. W. (1995). Therapist/patient matching and early treatment dropout. *Journal of Addictive Diseases, 13*(4), 169–176. doi: 10.1300/j069v13n04_05

Izard, C. E. (1994). Innate and universal facial expressions: Evidence from developmental and cross-cultural research. *Psychological Bulletin, 115*, 288–299. doi: 10.1037/0033-2909.115.2.288

Jack, R. E., Garrod, O. G. B., Caldara, R., & Schyns, P. G. (2012). Facial expressions of emotions are not culturally universal. *Proceedings of the National Academy of Sciences, 109*(19), 7241–7244. doi: 10.1073/pnas.1200155109

Kim, Y. M., Newhill, C., & López, F. (2013). Latino acculturation and perceived educational achievement: Evidence for a bidimensional model of acculturation among Mexican-American children. *Journal of Human Behavior in the Social Environment, 23*(1), 37–52. doi: 10.1080/10911359.2012.739531

Maramba, G. G., & Nagayama Hall, G. C. (2002). Meta-analyses of ethnic match as a predictor of dropout, utilization, and level of functioning. *Cultural Diversity and Ethnic Minority Psychology, 8*(3), 290–297. doi: 10.1037/1099-9809.8.3.290

Masuda, T., Ellsworth, P. C., Mesquite, B., Leu, J., Tanida, S., & van de Veerdonk, E. (2008). Placing the face in context: Cultural differences in the perception of facial emotion. *Journal of Personality and Social Psychology, 94*, 365–381. doi: 10.1037/0022-3514.94.3.365

Matsumoto, D. (1989). Cultural influences on the perception of emotion. *Journal of Cross-Cultural Psychology, 20*(1), 92–105. doi: 10.1177/0022022189201006

Owen, J., Imel, Z., Adelson, J., & Rodolfa, E. (2012). "No-show": Therapist racial/ethnic disparities in client unilateral termination. *Journal of Counseling Psychology, 59*(2), 314–320. doi: 10.1037/a0027091

Scherer, K. R., Matsumoto, D., Wallbott, H. G., & Kudoh, T. (1988). Emotional experience in cultural context: A comparison between Europe, Japan, and the United States. In Scherer K.R. (Ed.), *Facets of emotion: Recent research* (pp. 5–30). Hillsdale, NJ: Lawrence Erlbaum Associates, Inc.

Sciarra, D. T., & Simon, G. M. (2008). Assessment of diverse family systems. In L. A. Suzuki & J. G. Ponterotto (Eds.), *Handbook of multicultural assessment: Clinical, psychological, and educational applications* (3rd ed., pp. 247–272). San Francisco, CA: Jossey-Bass.

Stiles, W. B., Honos-Webb, L., & Surko, M. (1998). Responsiveness in psychotherapy. *Clinical Psychology: Science and Practice, 5*(4), 439–458. doi: 10.1111/j.1468-2850.1998.tb00166.x

Toren, N. (2009). Intersection of ethnicity, gender and class: Oriental faculty women in Israel. *Gender Issues, 26*, 152–166. doi: 10.1007/s12147-009-9073-0

Wintersteen, M. B., Mensinger, J. L., & Diamond, G. S. (2005). Do gender and racial differences between patient and therapist affect therapeutic alliance and treatment retention in adolescents? *Professional Psychology: Research and Practice, 36*(4), 400–408. doi: 10.1037/0735-7028.36.4.400

CHAPTER **14**

The Interpersonal Context of Assessment

Aaron Estrada

The purpose of this chapter is to explore and consider how personality assessment process and outcome are influenced by the unique characteristics of examinee and examiner, their interpersonal interaction, and the larger context in which that interaction occurs. Personality assessment is a combination of an examinee, an examiner, and assessment tools. Of these three primary components, the varied pairings that can be constructed (i.e. examinee–assessment; examiner–assessment; and examinee–examiner) are distinct, yet interdependent, relationships (Husain, 2009). Furthermore, all of these combinations exist within a context or setting that offers a unique flavor to the assessment. In this chapter, I will focus on the examinee–examiner pairing and some of the central aspects that influence the nature and quality of the interaction between the two. The assessment context should not solely focus on client characteristics and the referral question, but should also take into account the influential features clinicians bring to the encounter, such as physical characteristics and interpersonal style (Masling, 1992). Unpacking the interpersonal context of assessment is useful because how client and clinician experience each other impacts the assessment process and ultimate results (Groth-Marnat, 2009).

I consider *interpersonal context* to encompass how examinee and examiner perceive and understand themselves as individuals, how that understanding influences how they experience and behave in relation to one another, and how interaction influences each member's experience of the assessment. Both bring personal histories and experiences, unique social identities, and culturally defined realities into the encounter. As clinicians, we must endeavor to understand the interpersonal context of assessment because it can enhance our clinical techniques and effectiveness (Hopwood, 2010). In what follows, I will address the interpersonal context of personality assessment via interpersonal style, power, status characteristics, stereotype threat, and setting.

Interpersonal Style

Although it is largely accepted that, as clinicians, we occupy the powerful position of expert, considerations vary in regard to the status of examinees. Hierarchical positioning of the assessment dyad can range from a vertical to an increasingly horizontal arrangement with the examinee viewed as a passive target of services, or conversely as an active collaborator, respectively. Depending on orientation, clinicians might view the assessment as something that is done *to*, versus *with*, examinees. Clinicians' approaches to engaging examinees range from neutrally detached to relational, either of which influences examinees' interactions with examiners and the process. The impact of warm and cold interactions between examiner and examinee on the administration, scoring, and interpretation of personality testing have long been known (Masling, 1957).

On one level, interpersonal context might be thought of in terms of the tone between examiner and examinee throughout the assessment. Hopwood (2010) provides a useful application of the interpersonal circumplex in taking the construct of complementarity from interpersonal theory in psychotherapy and relating it to personality assessment. The circumplex model posits that interpersonal interaction occurs via reciprocal determinism in that the behavior of one member dictates the subsequent response behavior in the other in a predictable fashion. This model is structured on a Cartesian plane with vertical and horizontal axes defined as *Agency* and *Communion*, respectively, wherein *Agency* can be defined by dominance, power, and control and *Communion* by nurturance, friendliness, and affiliation (Gurtman & Lee, 2009).

Hopwood's (2010) application of the circumplex model to assessment proposes that examiners' approaches to communion, a continuum ranging from a warm to cold style of interaction, suggests a predictable mirroring of interactional style by examinees (i.e., warmth is met with warmth). In addressing the second axis, agency defines a continuum ranging from poles of dominance to submissiveness. Contrary to communion-based matching of interactional style, agency predicts an opposite effect such that dominance by one member begets submissiveness in the other. Ultimately, given our position of power as expert, we often initiate and set the tone of an assessment. As such, we must consider how our interpersonal style serves to call forth predictable responses from examinees, because our approach influences the way examinees engage and respond to us as well as the assessment process. While useful, a challenge of applying the interpersonal circumplex to assessment, particularly assessment of members of marginalized groups, is that the agency axis (dominant vs. submissive) can be complicated by a societal status system that allocates even more power to clinicians.

Power

Exploring the interpersonal context of assessment necessitates reflecting upon issues of power because the assessment is not set on neutral turf. French and Raven (1959) posit in their widely applied framework that social power is defined by the prospect of getting someone to do something they might not have done without influence. Taking a social perspective on power is an appropriate lens here given that assessment is an interpersonal event. French and Raven's (1959) system identifies both Holders and Targets of power wherein the former possesses a degree of power or influence while the latter is who the influence is aimed at. The authors further suggest that contrary to a rigidly fixed allocation of power, when people interact they actually alternate between the two roles depending upon the resources available to each member throughout interaction. French and Raven's (1959) original system described the five bases of Reward power (the ability to give or withhold reward based on the Target's compliance with the Holder's aims), Coercive power (the power to punish), Referent power (the liking and wanting to be like the Holder in some way), Legitimate power (the power of position or social role), and Expert power (the power of knowledge). Raven (1965) later differentiated Informational power from Expert power and described it as its own form (based on important data or logic). Although extensive application of this framework goes beyond the scope of this chapter, the purpose of including it even in this limited form is to unpack and delineate the concept of power. Rather than being a singular concept that is static and fixed in terms of who can access it, power appears more accurately understood as a multifaceted and relatively fluid construct. Clinician and client hold power in some regard for five out of the six bases previously outlined, with perhaps Legitimate power being reserved for the clinician alone.

Whereas the other five bases of power occur and alternate at the more immediate level of ongoing interchange between client and clinician, I differentiate Legitimate power because it is fixed at a societal level in defining the expectations, rights, and roles associated with the generic statuses of examinee and examiner. So, although in some regards the holder of power might vary throughout the assessment process, the interpersonal dynamic of power is set in an established system that is inherently hierarchical, wherein the role of examinee is arguably innately one of subordination. Legitimate power resides in the position of a psychologist within a social structure that accepts the practice of psychological assessment as a valid and broadly consistent enterprise conducted within established ethical and legal parameters. Examiners' role-based power extends the right to give directions and ask personal questions. In accord, examinees' role-based responsibility is to follow examiners' directions and provide the personal information that is requested of them. Ardila (2005) described the expectations underlying this process as operating from a background of authority. In this, relative to the client, the clinician is in a position of power to dictate the who, what, when, where, why, and how of an assessment. Ultimately, at the conclusion of the process, the expertise and legitimized position of authority conveys upon the clinician the right to diagnose and recommend, which influences subsequent processes and experiences for the examinee.

Despite best efforts to empower clients, or at the very least to maintain an approach grounded in neutrality, power inequity in psychological assessment, as in all psychological service provision, is inherent and influential (Prilleltensky, 2008). At a basic level, this inequity can be understood as deriving from one party's seeking out or having been referred to the specialized services offered by the other. Still, albeit skewed, power is not dichotomously distributed in absolute terms such that the clinician is in a position of omnipotence and impervious to the influence of the situation or the behavior of the client. For example, examinees have the task of negotiating how to interact with the examiner, so, via the power of choice, the examinee controls what and how much to convey about themselves. Phenomenologically speaking, examinees might be seen as the holders of Expert and Information power in that they know themselves better than anyone else and the decision regarding degree and accuracy of self-disclosure is in their hands. Yet even in this example of examinee control over personal information, clinician power trumps examinees' in that our interpretations and recommendations carry the final word.

Beyond the assessment-specific temporary roles of examiner and examinee, both members of the assessment dyad hold other more permanent identities. Structural factors related to social identities and group memberships determine the different levels of power people experience (Prilleltensky, 2008) beyond the roles defined and allocated within assessment. Hays (1996, 2008) developed the ADDRESSING acronym (Age and generation; Disability status—developmental; Disability status—acquired; Religion; Ethnicity; SES; Sexual orientation; Indigenous heritage; National origin; Gender) to acknowledge the multiple group memberships and identities of both patients and clinicians. Each of these identity dimensions is present within each of us, but can vary in regard to which are particularly salient to any given individual. Identity salience also varies as a function of setting or interpersonal context. Within the domain of assessment, clinicians should reflect on what is salient in their understanding of themselves, their clients, and how the identities of each member interact in terms of current societal circumstances and historical sociopolitical relationships. Because it is a relational process, the identities, assumptions, and characteristics of the examiner should be considered at least as influential as those of the examinee (Groth-Marnat, 2009). Perceived similarity or difference on any of these identity markers might have implications for examiner and examinee behavior and therefore the overall interpersonal context of the assessment experience.

There is a power imbalance that systematically and consistently plays out in favor of a particular group or identity in its relation to and interaction with others. Hays (2008) provides Table 14.1, which describes power relations and privilege status in the US.

Outlining all of the possible permutations and constellations between clinician and client is not necessary in understanding that the assessment dyad is composed of two distinct individuals, each member holding a variety of social identities that are imbued with varying degrees of status and power. How the various identities of patient and clinician intersect influences the power dynamics of the assessment dyad beyond their assessment-specific roles. The identities and associated power are culturally defined and founded in current and historical contexts of relations between the groups that each member belongs to. Borrowing a useful elaboration from psychotherapy, DeVaris (1994) describes the complex interaction of power associated with the generic roles and specific personal identities through the lens of gender:

> There is a socially prescribed power differential when a [clinician] and a patient are of different genders. The male in the dyad has more socially prescribed power than the female. This power differential may be balanced when the [clinician] and the patient are of the same gender. In mixed-gender pairs, when the patient is a female, the power balance is skewed toward the male [clinician] and when the patient is male, the power balance is skewed toward the male patient.
>
> (p. 590)

Of course, we might go to the previously provided table of power and privilege and interchange any of the listed identities with that of gender as it is used in the

Table 14.1 ADDRESSING Framework

Cultural Characteristic	*More Power and Privilege*	*Less Power and Privilege*
Age and generational influences	Adults (not elders)	Children, adolescents, elders
Developmental disabilities	Able-bodied Able-minded	People with developmental disabilities
Disabilities acquired later in life	Able-bodied Able-minded	People with disabilities acquired later in life
Religion and spiritual orientation	Christian sects	Religious minority cultures
Ethnic and racial identity	European American	Ethnic and racial minority cultures; may include acculturation considerations
Socioeconomic status	Upper & middle class; access to higher education	People of lower status because of class, occupation, income, or rural habitat; limited access to higher education
Sexual orientation	Heterosexual people	Gay, lesbian, bisexual, transgender people
Indigenous background	Non-native	Indigenous, Aboriginal, native people
National origin	U.S. born	Refugees, immigrants, international students
Gender	Male	Female, transgender, intersex people

Adapted from Hays (2008, p. 18).

example here. In reality, each of us simultaneously occupies and identifies with each identity category, which only adds further complexity to the power dynamic and distribution. From this we see that power allocation and negotiation operate on multiple levels simultaneously as our diverse identities intersect. So, just as the labels of examiner and examinee convey the ordering of an established power system, so too do the other personal and salient identities that each member brings into assessment. These personal statuses either expand or reduce the power differential between clinician and client depending upon societal privilege and power associated with particular identities.

Status Characteristics

In going beyond general roles, we should aim to understand examinee and examiner in terms of salient personal characteristics that could influence interactions between them. At a basic level, we might ask: Do these personal characteristics represent similarity or difference between examiner and examinee? Ardila (2005) proposed that the distance between examiner and examinee has the potential to impact the testing situation and outcome. Distance here does not refer to physical proximity, rather it reflects perceptions of similarity or difference of life experience and group membership.

Status characteristics theory (Berger, Cohen, & Zelditch, 1972) suggests that people classify one another according to age, ethnicity, sex, and other visibly identifiable factors in order to attempt to understand whom the person is that they are interacting with. Once ascribed, these statuses or identities influence degree of participation, influence, and prestige among people engaged in a variety of tasks, including performance on standardized assessment (Lovaglia, Lucas, Houser, Thye, & Markovsky, 1998). The theory posits that people tend to interact with stereotypes and preconceived notions they hold about the groups that they perceive others to be members of, rather than characterizing the unique qualities of that individual. It is an intrapsychic process of figuring out, if not temporarily creating whom a stranger is, so we can gauge and conduct our behavior and interactions with who we perceive them to be. Some status characteristics are imbued with privilege when associated esteem affords social advantages, such as power and access to resources (Lovaglia et al., 1998). According to the theory, how examinees and examiners perceive each other influences how they might behave during assessment, regardless of the accuracy of their perceptions.

The influence of status characteristics can be further detailed in our propensity to feel safer and trust others who we perceive as similar to ourselves. In the assessment context, an experience of safety and trust might yield an openness wherein clients put forth more accurate and undefended accounts of themselves. Perceived similarities and differences might be visible and quite salient, as in the case of age, ethnicity, or gender, and even minor, superficial similarities such as given or surnames can generate a sense of safety and positive attitudes toward strangers (Moss, Garivaldis, & Toukhsati, 2007). Conversely, people tend to become more guarded and anxious around others that they perceive as different from themselves. So, when a patient experiences discomfort due to their perception of being different from their clinician, they might be more closed off to assessment. Moss et al. (2007) described how sensitivity toward a threat might be enhanced in demanding situations, such as a personality assessment, and how it can exaggerate the identification of interpersonal differences. The experience of this threat and how examinees process with it has implications for their engagement, performance, and self-presentation in assessment and associated results.

Stereotype Threat

Stereotype threat operates in conditions where an individual is concerned about not measuring up to or potentially performing down to an undesirable expectation. The theory describes how people experience threat related to confirming a negative stereotype about themselves that is held in regard to broader groups of which they are members (Steele & Aronson, 1995). Experiencing this threat negatively impacts individuals in stereotype-relevant contexts such that their performance is not representative of their actual abilities. Stereotype threat was originally developed to examine the standardized test experience of African Americans (1995), but has since been used to describe a variety of identity statuses including but not limited to race and ethnicity, age, SES, gender, as well as influence of multiple vulnerable identities.

Aronson et al. (1999) suggest the following two conditions as necessary and sufficient for the experience of stereotype threat: (1) the person being evaluated identifies with and cares about the domain they are being assessed in and, (2) there is a potentially compromising situation-relevant stereotype. Generally speaking, the more a person identifies with the domain being assessed, the greater the experience and negative effect of the threat on their performance (Armenta, 2010). Although research has consistently supported the notion that identification with a stigmatized social identity heightens the likelihood of, and vulnerability to, experiencing stereotype threat, situational factors (not group membership) are largely responsible for the experience of threat. In short, anyone from any group can be vulnerable given the situation. While the majority of stereotype threat research has been focused on performance in cognitive and intelligence domains, the negative impact of stereotype threat has also been established with athletic performance (Stone, Lynch, Sjomeling, & Darley, 1999). This latter point suggests that stereotype effects are not reserved for intelligence or cognitive ability alone and that the threat holds sway in other domains. So, what then of circumstances where assessing abilities is replaced with an aim to evaluate personality?

In contrast to aptitude and abilities-based testing, personality assessment is not geared toward identifying what a person can do, rather it is oriented to elucidating who the person *is*. To this end, personality assessment is generally conducted to identify ways of being, thinking, feeling, and relating to others that are consistent across time and situations. Regarding Aronson et al.'s (1999) first necessary condition for stereotype threat, we might safely assume that people typically tend to care about how they understand and perceive themselves, as well as how they are perceived by others. As for the second condition, stereotypes about personality traits and social identities abound and could hardly be more situation-relevant than a personality assessment. Because personality assessment is conducted with an explicit question in mind and within a specific context, examinees might experience a threat regarding expectations or concerns about the clinician's perceptions of them and possible consequences related to assessment outcome.

Although there are clearly significant distinctions between the aims of personality- and ability-based testing, one important common ground between the two might be patients' awareness that assessment results will hold implications for their subsequent life experiences. In as much, examinees might not only be concerned about being perceived in a negative stereotypical light, but their concern also extends into the likelihood of being treated in accord with said negative perception. Herein lies a reflection of the power differential previously discussed. It is not merely examinees' fear of confirming negative stereotypes about themselves, but what that confirmation means for them beyond the assessment. The threat resides in our findings and opinions as based in our powerful position of expert. For clinicians, the assessment experience ends once feedback and recommendations are provided to the client or referral source, but the same is not true for examinees. While the process of assessment also ends for examinees after feedback, the influence of results continue to ripple across various domains of their lives indefinitely.

Consideration of patients' motives relative to assessment perhaps aids in expanding our understanding beyond the threat of merely confirming a stereotype about oneself into appreciating what might be at stake for examinees in their broader life context. Speculatively, if an examinee experiences a threat about confirming a negative stereotype, as well as a threat that such confirmation will negatively impact his life, he might strive to represent himself in opposition to that stereotype, or more generally in what he perceives to be a flattering or acceptable likeness. The latter point essentially relates to examinees engaging in socially desirable responding or faking good. Examples that come to mind are cases of child custody or visitation assessment and employment-related evaluations where examinees stand to benefit by gaining access to their children or getting a job, respectively, if they can positively influence an examiner's perception of them regardless of the accuracy of said perception. Such intentional self-presentation is centrally moderated by the examinee's choice and motivation. Personality assessment affords examinees the opportunity to attempt to enhance or undermine the perception they present of themselves. In endorsing how "like me" or "not like me" a self-report item is, examinees make item-to-item decisions to reveal or withhold accurate personal information. The same is true of implicit, narrative measures where examinees make the choice of whether or not to openly reveal what they see in an inkblot or to offer the narrative that "spontaneously" comes to mind. If the decision is to withhold accurate self-information in favor of an inauthentic version of self, socially desirable responding and impression management might be considered in light of motivations related to expected or imagined consequences associated with self-disclosure and representation.

Although stereotype threat as it is understood and researched to date has yet to enter into the realm of personality assessment, the consistent findings from the social psychological and aptitude testing literature provide food for thought. Throughout the testing process, examinees often assess their similarity or difference from examiners, monitor how they are representing themselves, and remain cognizant of the possible consequences of the assessment outcome as based on said self-representation. Although what I have written here is a departure from its origins, stereotype threat might hold some useful implications and considerations for the domain of personality assessment.

Assessment Setting

We must consider how the setting influences the process and results of assessment as the environment is defined by the setting's goals and mission. Brabender and Bricklin (2001) describe the complexity that setting adds to contextualizing assessment in stating:

> Each setting in which assessment referrals are made has its own set of recurrent problems related to why assessments are being done in the setting, who is being assessed, who gets to see the assessment, and the traditional values and beliefs of the setting as well as the potential consequences for the client of assessments in that setting.
>
> (p. 193)

By developing familiarity with the different types of settings and contextual factors unique among, yet common within each, clinicians can gain clarity in regard to the referral question and source, as well as develop a relevant approach to the assessment (Groth-Marnat, 2009). Ultimately, recognizing how contextual factors relate to and impact the process and interpretation of assessment is a measure of clinical competence (Meyer et al., 2001).

Regarding examinee–examiner interpersonal context, the assessment is likely to be colored by the preexisting relationship and prior experiences between the examinee and the system in which they are being assessed. The setting and the circumstances related to the assessment become entwined with the motivations of the examinee, as well as for administrators or other decision-makers in situations where the assessment is requested by someone other than the examinee. In the latter circumstance, we must consider how the motives of the examinee either align with or counter those of the requesting body.

Thus far, I have primarily addressed the interpersonal context of the assessment dyad alone. In actual practice, the number and type of people involved varies as a function of the setting and reason for referral. Due to the need to gather relevant information from a variety of sources, complexities related to initiating and carrying out a personality assessment, and coordinating treatment among professionals from other disciplines, psychologists routinely interact with collateral sources and individuals other than the examinee. Because interactions with key individuals related to the process are influential, I will briefly address collateral sources and actors along with the interpersonal context of the assessment dyad as I next discuss some general themes distinct to conducting assessment in medical settings, schools, forensic settings, and clinics.

Medical Settings

Personality and psychological assessment in medical settings often relates to measuring the presence, source, and influence of both physical and psychological health factors. More broadly, assessment in these settings is often requested to identify, differentiate, or rule out the degree to which psychological factors might be contributing to the somatic presenting issues for patients, or to determine if psychological factors are due to the physical complications patients are experiencing. For example, a psychologist might be called upon to differentiate factitious disorder, where examinees consciously produce or feign physical symptoms in order to play the patient role, from conversion disorder, where clients experience the somatic ailments they report despite having no physical cause, or to ascertain that health problems are organic in nature. Another example might be for a clinician to clarify whether depression is a cause of compromised physical health due to lifestyle and poor self-care or if depression is a consequence of health complications.

In these settings, the interaction between clinician and patient might be impacted by factors related to the patient's capacity for insight, diagnosis, level of resistance, degree impairment, and reason for hospitalization (Groth-Marnat, 2009). Medical settings are further influenced by patients' openness and motivation for assessment as well as the impact of people outside of the clinician-patient dyad including the patient's family, nurses, treating physicians, and social workers, to name central and common players.

A challenge inherent to assessment in medical settings lies in their being composed of a variety of specialized units. Each sub-setting requires consideration for their potential influence on our interactions with patients. Sweet, Tovian, Guidotti-Breting, and Suchy (2013) address and differentiate the influence of specific physiological diagnostic considerations and typical relationships to psychological presentations. For example, conducting a personality assessment with a patient presenting with dual-diagnosis of psychological challenges and chemical dependence is a different interactive process than that occurring on a gerontology unit or a wing dedicated to caring for oncology patients. Because of our own personal life histories, we should consider how different types of patients presenting with varied medical diagnoses and diverse backgrounds might differentially impact us and, in turn, influence our approach.

The interpersonal context of the assessment is influenced by patients' perceptions of whether personality assessment is relevant to their situation. For example, a patient presenting with seizures might wonder why they have been referred for a personality assessment. Patients' perceptions of personality assessment as potentially useful and relevant may influence their view of the clinician as a helpful resource, whereas patient views of an assessment as unrelated to the purpose of their hospitalization might result in seeing the examiner as unnecessary and intrusive. Patient uncertainty and confusion regarding the inclusion of seemingly irrelevant personality assessment might arouse their suspicions, which in turn could result in patient resistance (Groth-Marnat, 2009). Such challenges might be avoided or ameliorated if clinicians clarify the rationale for the assessment upfront.

Interpersonal context of assessment within hospitals often involves multidisciplinary treatment teams composed of physicians, psychiatrists, nurses, and social workers among other specialists. Ideally, these teams are composed of competent practitioners who come together with a commitment to cooperating with the other members so as to achieve the best possible treatment outcomes for patients. Conversely, at times, members' allegiance to their disciplines or interpersonal conflict can result in interactions that are competitive and challenging. The atmosphere of treatment teams can have a lingering effect on clinicians' moods and attitudes that carries beyond team meetings. Should we find we are facing such challenges, we must be aware of how these feelings might compromise our interactions with patients if we are not careful.

Finally, a treating physician, psychiatrist, or administrator generally requests psychological assessments in medical settings. That is, patients rarely (if ever) request their own evaluations. Along with issues of consent and access to records, these third-party requests can also raise questions about patient motivation to engage in the assessment. The issue of motivation for the completion of assessment is an important one in this setting because patient motivations might be different from the requesting party's motivations, reflecting the varied agendas of the two. We must consider how the motives of the examinee either align with or counter those of the requesting body. For example, a patient might be motivated to stay in the hospital whereas the hospital is motivated for discharge and each act to meet their goal. Such motives clearly impact the assessing clinician's interactions with each entity.

Schools

Psychological assessment in school settings is generally fixed in a psychoeducational context such that any assessment must be made relevant under the guise of learning and education, whereas addressing issues of personality and psychopathology appears to fall increasingly to clinical assessment settings outside of the school, such as community clinics and private practices (Flanagan, 2007). Assessment in schools is broadly approached with the aim of evaluating students' areas of strength, or conversely to explain why students might be struggling with educational tasks and, as a result, if current classroom placement is appropriate. A central reason to initiate school-based evaluation is to identify if a student does or does not have a disability as defined by the Individuals with Disabilities Education Act (IDEA). In approaching assessment in a school-based setting, we must take into account the age of the child, gender, race and ethnicity, and interaction and involvement with influential collateral sources.

An essential power dimension that is particularly important in the school setting is age. Of course, age is important when considering interpersonal dynamics because the examinee is a child being assessed by an adult. It is clear that children have no power in the assessment process because those who refuse to participate are typically evaluated by other means, such as behavioral observation or parent, teacher, and peer rating scales (Knauss, 2001; although these sources are often included regardless of the degree of examinee engagement). Although this example might highlight an absence of student examinee autonomy, outright refusal to participate in assessment may be considered a rather infrequent occurrence given that students are no doubt aware that they are struggling in some way. Further, given the crowded nature of classrooms and student-to-teacher ratios, students are likely to appreciate a one-on-one interaction and embrace individual time with the assessor (Fagan & Wise, 2007). Still, this might vary depending upon developmental stage and age with younger children being particularly receptive to focused attention, whereas adolescents might be less so, given their desire to increasingly fit in and identify with their peers instead of adults. Despite this developmental distinction, the hierarchical position of a student means the examinee is always in a one-down position in relation to important powerful adults who are consistently overseeing the educational and social spheres of the student's life.

Similar to issues of power and status related to age, so too must sex, gender, race, and ethnicity be considered when conducting assessment in schools. Regarding trends of the types of students identified for assessment, Fagan and Wise (2007) suggest that young, elementary school-age children are referred more often than older students and that boys are more typically referred than girls. In terms of power and bias, the dimensions of ethnicity and race must be addressed given the history of discrimination in the U.S. because some groups are referred for assessment more than others. In a state-specific example, in response to systematic assessment bias resulting in overrepresentation of both African American (*Larry P. v. Riles*) and Latino (*Diana v. State Board of Education*) students being placed in Special Education classrooms, California court litigation has established limitations on intelligence-based testing for the purposes of such placements for these ethnic groups. The overrepresentation of underrepresented groups in Special Education was not based on actual deficits in the children's abilities, but instead represented access to resources, language of origin, and different cultural realities and knowledge bases. Clearly, when conducting personality or other forms of assessment in school settings we should strive to be cognizant and sensitive to U.S. cultural history of pathologizing difference.

Beyond the obvious inclusion of the student examinee, the interpersonal context of assessment in schools also includes parents and/or guardians, teachers and administrators, and peers. Collaboration between home and school represents the challenge of working with independent, yet interrelated systems that encompass students' lives. Years ago, Knoff (1983) suggested an ecological approach (Bronfenbrenner, 1979) to account for the influence of these overlapping systems on the student, the interactions between various systems, and the assessment process itself. In addressing barriers to parent–school collaboration, Burke (2012) states that culturally and linguistically diverse parents might be less likely to engage in an Individualized Education Program (IEP) and Special Education planning for a variety of reasons. Among the factors undermining successful parent–school partnerships are challenges in communication, both in terms of interpersonal communication and inadequate translation of documentation, lack of availability of competent interpreters, parents might experience limited involvement in decision making, and ultimately because parents feel a lack of respect from school personnel. Parent and student cooperation throughout the assessment process can be fostered by school personnel committing to respectful, understandable communication starting with informed consent, continuing through a discussion and endorsement of options, involvement in decision making, and follow through to ultimate intervention goals (Burke, 2012; Knauss, 2001). Last, because teachers and school administrators are largely responsible for creating and maintaining the various school environments students experience day-to-day, they must be considered in regard to the influence and impact they are having on the student.

In closing with the actual assessment dyad's interaction during assessment, we must be sure that the student does not get lost and ignored, with adults speaking around and about her, yet not directly to the student herself. We need to keep the examinee central to the process and should be as clear as possible about the purpose, ultimate goals, and potential benefits the student might experience as a result of engaging in the assessment openly and honestly. In short, student examinees should have a clear understanding about why assessment is relevant to the challenges they might be facing at school, as well as in life in a broader sense. By being clear with the student that the focus is on them, with the desired outcome to be an improvement in their overall academic experience, it might be easier for them to buy into and fully engage in the assessment.

Legal and Forensic Settings

Assessment in forensic settings is a broad consideration given that forensic psychology encompasses all psycho-legal domains. Under the broad categories of criminal and civil legal proceedings, forensic personality assessment addresses issues such as child custody and access, insanity and competency to stand trial, parole hearings, and prisoner safety assessments, whereas regarding employment, fitness for duty evaluations might be the aim. Clearly, what falls under the umbrella term of forensic evaluation is substantial. What follows here is a brief account of some of the significant factors, such as the role of third parties, general tone of interaction, examinee motivations, and influential identity statuses relevant to the interpersonal context of assessment in forensic and legal settings.

Ethical and legal guidelines specific to forensic assessment vary from other settings and because of the legal context, unique concerns arise. For instance, often in forensic evaluations the examinee is not the client. Instead, an influential third party, such as a judge, employer, representative (e.g., attorney), or a family member might step in to use information provided from assessment and ultimately make determinations about the examinee. When such third-party requests are mandated, informed consent is generally not required from adult examinees, nor is there the therapeutic relationship that might exist in other settings (Kalmbach & Lyons, 2006). Such circumstances convey a lack of examinee autonomy and may result in a less relational interpersonal context between clinician and examinee than might be present in other assessment settings.

Kalmbach and Lyons (2006) suggest, "the forensic evaluation involves limited contact, an adversarial forum, an impartial stance, and a critical, evaluative style that includes reliance on collateral and corroborated information rather than mere assertions by the examinee" (p. 261). Examinees might view consulting examiners as agents of a system that is interfering with their freedom, family, and other areas of life. Similarly, examiners might be seen by the examinees as obstacles between them and some goal or desired outcome. Such a view of the assessor no doubt lends to the typically adversarial quality of the assessment and evaluation in forensic settings.

Of course, the absence of rapport is not the absolute norm, as in the case of child custody, civil cases, and the like. Assessments of this ilk are, conversely, specifically requested and intended with the interests of the clients in mind (e.g., self-referred plaintiffs in civil liability cases) and rapport in assessment is needed. Assessment in child custody cases necessitates that clinicians build a rapport with the youth being evaluated in order to accurately assess them and provide opinions to the court. As for related parental assessments, the possibility that examinees might produce self-enhancing presentations in an effort to win over or sway the clinician in their favor must be entertained. The interpersonal atmosphere is in part dictated by examinees' motivations, expectations or hopes about what desired or unfavorable consequences or circumstances may come subsequent and dependent upon the assessment results and recommendations.

Accuracy of examinee self-representation, both positive and negative, is a particularly important consideration in forensic evaluations because of the often high stakes of decisions and subsequent life circumstances for examinees associated with assessment outcomes. "Faking good" is a possibility when examinees might benefit from complimentary assessment reports, whereas "faking bad" is a concern when examinees stand to gain from conveying compromised well being. "Malingering is almost always a rule-out in any forensic evaluation" (Conroy & Kwartner, 2006, p. 29). Still, examinee and requesting party motivations alone cannot account for all that transpires to impact the interpersonal context of the assessment.

In turning to salient power and identity dimensions in forensic settings, gender and sex are particularly relevant because men tend to be arrested and convicted at a significantly higher rate than do women, and men are more highly represented in criminal and violent populations. Taken together with the steadily increasing numbers of female psychologists serving as clinicians in forensic settings, the influence of sex and gender on the interpersonal context of assessment and legal decision making is of increasing importance. For example, gender effects have been found influential in that clinicians tend to assess the same case information as more indicative of legal insanity if the offender is a woman than if they are a man (Yourstone, Lindholm, Grann, & Svenson, 2008).

Economic status is an important characteristic because people from low-SES backgrounds are more vulnerable to involvement with the legal system than are those of middle and high SES. Conversely, clinicians generally occupy higher economic classes than most incarcerated individuals, resulting in financially privileged examiners assessing examinees who may be struggling with poverty and a lack of basic resources. Coming from dissimilar economic classes can be equated with coming from different worlds or cultures (Kalmbach & Lyons, 2006) and can result in unproductive, untenable assessment and other service provision (e.g., psychotherapy; Mathias & Sindberg, 1985).

Last, ethnic and racial disparities regarding psychologists and the incarcerated appear to be inverse for African Americans and Latinos as compared to Caucasians. Morgan, Beer, Fitzgerald, and Mandracchia (2007) reported that Caucasians accounted for 79% of students within two years of graduation from forensic and correctional psychology graduate programs, whereas Latino and African Americans accounted for only 5.7% and 4.6%, respectively. Conversely, African Americans (38.2%) and Latinos (20.7%) account for a combined 59% of the total population of incarcerated individuals in the U.S. according to Census data as of 2010. These figures indicate significant overrepresentation of these ethnic and racial groups in the U.S. legal system as compared to their representation in the general population (13.6% African American; 16.3% Latino or Hispanic per the US Census 2010). In simple terms, these trends convey a consistent and systematic reproduction of who is an examinee and who is an evaluator.

Clinics

Community outpatient psychology clinics are intended to treat and serve a wide range of presentations and perform a variety of functions. Serving the general community means that clientele is often a diverse group and, therefore, we must reflect on a variety of multicultural factors that influence interpersonal processes. In many cases, a community psychology clinic might strive to reduce barriers to service by offering a reduced cost or sliding scale, which clearly implies that identities and experiences related to SES might be central to the clients' lives.

Quite often, but not exclusively, a clinic might be associated with a university. Clinic settings simultaneously serve as both a provider of psychological services for the general community as well as a training site for graduate students in various fields of applied psychology. When clinicians are graduate students, clients must be informed of the supervisory aspect wherein a licensed clinician will have access to, and closely review, test data and assessment reports. This brings a third party into the assessment relationship. With this third entity inclusion, the client might experience a reduction in privacy and perceived power that could have implications for the degree of disclosure of intimate information in the assessment. Power should also be considered on the part of the training clinician, where knowing your work is to be scrutinized by a supervisor might undercut confidence and competence in interacting with examinees. Clinicians, therefore, need to be aware of how multiple bodies involved in the process might impact the client's, as well as their own, experience of assessment. Clients' potential for reservation when overseen by multiple clinicians might be reduced by the fact that they are typically self-referred and motivated to engage openly. The clinic setting is, arguably, the most autonomous for both client and clinician and thus allows for the focus to solely be on the personality assessment, as opposed to other settings where assessment might only be a support or conducted to inform other interventions or services being provided.

In contrast to the settings previously discussed, when conducting assessments in a clinic setting, we have the greatest potential to operate autonomously and play the role not only of examiner, but also of primary decision maker (Groth-Marnat, 2009) in terms of applying assessment findings and producing recommendations. Similarly, the clinic tends to be the least coercive for the client as they are typically self-referred and invested in the process. Enhanced autonomy for both examiner and examinee might also serve to enrich collaboration where both parties look to develop a shared understanding of the issue, preferred scenario, and realistic goals. Therefore, the likelihood of endorsing, adhering to, and following through with assessment-informed recommendations is heightened. Even in the case where a third party is involved, the context of the clinic still provides opportunity for the clinician to approach personality assessment as a treatment intervention in and of itself. Assessment in clinics might also be conducted as a part of ongoing psychotherapy and can facilitate development of the therapeutic relationship and working alliance between clinician and client (Ackerman, Hilsenroth, Baity, & Blagys, 2000). In short, the relational component between examiner and examinee and important collateral sources of information (e.g., parents, guardians, intimate partners, etc.) is enhanced in the clinic as opposed to other settings where third parties largely have a more impactful and potentially disruptive, or at least distancing, presence.

In closing, settings add an important layer of information to the conceptualization and understanding of the interpersonal context of personality assessment and psychological assessment in general. Each setting has a specific set of common factors and consistent issues relating to organizational identity and mission, reasons for referral, goals of assessment, who the examinee is and whether or not he or she is also the client, and associated consequences for the examinee (Brabender & Bricklin, 2001). Clinicians should aim to familiarize themselves with setting specific factors and interpersonal considerations in efforts to enhance their ability to conduct competent and appropriate assessments relevant to the needs and aims of both examinees and setting representatives.

Recommendations and Considerations

1. Assessment is an interpersonal interaction and not solely based on the characteristics of the examinee or their engagement with assessment tools.
2. Examiners' interpersonal style can yield predictable responses from examinees in their interaction with both examiner and assessment.
3. Power is inherent to the assessment process, skewed in favor of examiners, and can impact examinees' performance and participation throughout the assessment.

4. Consider issues related to social identities and diversity-based similarity or difference between examiner and examinee.
5. Contextualize patients' behavior during assessment and the results within the framework of their diverse identities intersecting those of examiners.
6. Examinee concerns about self-presentation, confirming group stereotypes, and the implications of results might influence their approach to assessment.
7. Setting is essential in understanding motivations of examinees as well as of third parties that request assessment when examinees are not the identified client.
8. Examinee behavior during assessment is influenced by their unique identities, life history, socio-political-historical context, characteristics of examiners, the interpersonal context, and the setting.

Conclusion

Individuals might undertake personality assessment for a variety of reasons. How and why people ultimately arrive at an assessment has implications for how they might behave and engage in the process. Examinees can either self-refer or they might be mandated to undertake assessment by legal and governing bodies, such as the courts or school systems. From the perspective of examinees, the reasons why they initiate or have had the assessment process initiated for them, their choice or lack of choice in participating in the assessment process, their beliefs and attitudes about the assessment and the clinician, and potential subsequent consequences or stakes all influence the interpersonal atmosphere of the assessment process.

Personality assessment takes place between two people wherein each member has their own identity and history that come into contact with those of the other in the frame of the assessment. Considering the interpersonal context of assessment takes a step beyond conceptualization of the examiner as neutral and acknowledges that they are impacted by the examinees' diverse characteristics and interpersonal styles. Similarly, characteristics of examiners are influential in terms of what examinees choose to disclose and withhold, as well as how they approach and engage the personality assessment process at large. The interpersonal context requires consideration of issues related to client awareness and concern about how they are being perceived by the clinician, and possible consequences and outcomes associated with that perception. Power needs to be a central consideration within the interpersonal context as well, and although the clinician is in a position of privilege in terms of interpersonal power, the client is not completely powerless. Personality assessment is dependent upon the information provided by examinees (Groth-Marnat, 2009), which puts them in a powerful position regarding degree and accuracy of self-disclosure. Still, the interpretation of information provided and subsequent recommendations falls to examiners. Finally, consideration of the setting in which personality assessment is conducted is essential because of common themes and missions inherent to each site, interpersonal interaction and context beyond that of the examinee–examiner relationship, the definition of our roles and functions as examiners, and the goals of the assessment within the broader context of services provided therein.

References

Ackerman, S., Hilsenroth, M., Baity, M., & Blagys, M. (2000). Interaction of therapeutic process and alliance during psychological assessment. *Journal of Personality Assessment, 75*(1), 82–109. doi: 10.1207/S15327752JPA7501_7

Ardila, A. (2005). Cultural values underlying psychometric cognitive testing. *Neuropsychology Review, 15*(4), 180–195. doi: 10.1007/s11065-005-9180-y

Armenta, B. (2010). Stereotype boost and stereotype threat effects: The moderating role of ethnic identity. *Cultural Diversity & Ethnic Minority Psychology, 16*(1), 94–98. doi: 10.1037/a0017564

Aronson, J., Lustina, M. J., Good, C., Keough, K., Steele, C. M., & Brown, J. (1999). When white men can't do math: Necessary and sufficient factors in stereotype threat. *Journal of Experimental Social Psychology, 35*(1), 29–46. doi: 10.1006/jesp.1998.1371

Berger, J., Cohen, B. P., & Zelditch, M. (1972). Status characteristics and social interaction. *American Sociological Review, 37*(3), 241–255. doi: 10.2307/2093465

Brabender, V., & Bricklin, P. (2001). Ethical issues in psychological assessment in different settings. *Journal of Personality Assessment, 77*(2), 192–194. doi: 10.1207/S15327752JPA7702_02

Bronfenbrenner, U. (1979). *The ecology of human development: Experiments by nature and design*. Cambridge, MA: Harvard University Press.

Burke, M. M. (2012). Examining family involvement in regular and special education: Lessons to be learned for both sides. *International Review of Research in Developmental Disabilities, 43*, 187–218. doi: 10.1016/B978-0-12-398261-2.00005-2

Conroy, M. A., & Kwartner, P. P. (2006). Malingering. Applied Psychology in Criminal Justice, *2*(3), 29–51. Retrieved from www.apcj.org

Department of Justice. Bureau of Justice Statistics. (2010). *Prisoners in 2009*. Retrieved from www.bjs.gov/content/pub/pdf/p09.pdf

DeVaris, J. (1994). The dynamics of power in psychotherapy. *Psychotherapy, 31*(4), 588–593. doi: 10.1037/0033-3204.31.4.588

Fagan, T. K., & Wise, P. S. (2007). *School psychology: Past, present, and future* (3rd ed.). Bethesda, MD: National Association of School Psychologists.

Flanagan, R. (2007). Comments on the miniseries: Personality assessment in school psychology. *Psychology in the Schools, 44*(3), 311–318. doi: 10.1002/pits.20225

French, J. R. P., & Raven, B. H. (1959). The bases of social power. In D. Cartwright & A. Zander (Eds.), *Group dynamics* (pp. 150–167). New York: Harper & Row. doi: 10.1111/j.1540-4560.1993.tb01191.x

Groth-Marnat, G. (2009). *Handbook of psychological assessment* (5th ed.). New York: J. Wiley.

Gurtman, M., & Lee, D. (2009). Sex differences in interpersonal problems: A circumplex analysis. *Psychological Assessment, 21*(4), 515–527. doi: 10.1037/a0017085

Hays, P. A. (1996). Addressing the complexities of culture and gender in counseling. *Journal of Counseling & Development, 74*, 332–338. doi: 10.1002/j.1556-6676.1996.tb01876.x

Hays, P. A. (2008). *Addressing cultural complexities in practice, Second edition: Assessment, diagnosis, and therapy.* Washington, DC: American Psychological Association.

Hopwood, C. J. (2010). An interpersonal perspective on the personality assessment process. *Journal of Personality Assessment, 92*(6), 471–479. doi: 10.1080/00223891.2010.513284

Husain, O. (2009). Paul Lerner and the heart of assessment: A tale of three relations. *Journal of Personality Assessment, 91*(1), 30–34. doi: 10.1080/00223890802483441

Kalmbach, K. C., & Lyons, P. M. (2006). Ethical issues in conducting forensic evaluations. *Applied Psychology in Criminal Justice, 2*(3), 261–290. Retrieved from www.apcj.org

Knauss, L. (2001). Ethical issues in psychological assessment in school settings. *Journal of Personality Assessment, 77*(2), 231–241. doi: 10.1207/S15327752JPA7702_06

Knoff, H. M. (1983). Personality assessment in the schools: Issues and procedures for school psychologists. *School Psychology Review, 12*(4), 391–397. Retrieved from www.nasponline.org

Lovaglia, M. J., Lucas, J. W., Houser, J. A., Thye, S. R., & Markovsky, B. (1998). Status processes and mental ability test scores. *American Journal of Sociology, 104* (1), 195–228. doi: 10.1086/210006

Masling, J. (1957). The influence of warm and cold interaction on the interpretation of a projective protocol. *Journal of Projective Techniques, 21*, 377–383. doi: 10.1080/08853126.1957.10380804

Masling, J. (1992). The influence of situational and interpersonal variables in projective testing. *Journal of Personality Assessment, 59*(3), 616–640. doi: 10.1207/s15327752jpa5903_14

Mathias, R. E., & Sindberg, R. H. (1985). Psychotherapy in correctional settings. *International Journal of Offender Therapy and Comparative Criminology, 29*(1), 265–275. doi: 10.1177/0306624X8502900309

Meyer, G. J., Finn, S. E., Eyde, L. D., Kay, G. G., Moreland, K. L., Dies, R. R., Eisman, E. J., Kubiszyn, T. W., & Reed, G. M. (2001). Psychological testing and psychological assessment: A review of evidence and issues. *American Psychologist, 56*(2), 128–165. doi: 10.1037/0003-066X.56.2.128

Morgan, R. D., Beer, A. M., Fitzgerald, K. L., & Mandracchia, J. T. (2007). Graduate students' experiences, interests, and attitudes towards correctional/forensic psychology. *Criminal Justice and Behavior, 34*, 96–107. doi: 10.1177/0093854806289831

Moss, S. A., Garivaldis, F. J., & Toukhsati, S. R. (2007). The perceived similarity of other individuals: The contaminating effects of familiarity and neuroticism. *Personality and Individual Differences*, 43, 401–412. doi: 10.1016/j.paid.2006.12.008

Prilleltensky, I. (2008). The role of power in wellness, oppression, and liberation: The promise of psychopolitical validity. *Journal of Community Psychology, 36*(2), 116–136. doi: 10.1002/jcop.20225

Raven, B. H. (1965). Social influence and power. In I. D. Steiner & M. Fishbein (Eds.), *Current studies in social psychology* (pp. 371–381). New York: Holt, Rinehart, & Winston.

Steele, C. M., & Aronson, J. (1995). Stereotype threat and the intellectual test performance of African Americans. *Journal of Personality and Social Psychology, 69*, 797–811. doi: 10.1037/0022-3514.69.5.797

Stone, J., Lynch, C. I., Sjomeling, M., & Darley, J. M. (1999). Stereotype threat effects on black and white athletic performance. *Journal of Personality and Social Psychology, 77*, 1213–1227. doi: 10.1037/0022-3514.77.6.1213

Sweet, J. J., Tovian, S. M., Guidotti-Breting, L. M., Suchy, Y. (2013). Psychological assessment in medical settings. In J. R. Graham, J. A. Naglieri, & I. B. Weiner (Eds.), *Handbook of psychology, Volume 10: Assessment psychology* (2nd ed.) (pp. 315–346). Hoboken, NJ: John Wiley & Sons Inc.

Yourstone, J., Lindholm, T., Grann, M., & Svenson, O. (2008). Evidence of gender bias in legal insanity evaluations: A case vignette study of clinicians, judges and students. *Nordic Journal of Psychiatry, 62*(4), 273–278. doi: 10.1080/08039480801963135

CHAPTER 15

Collaborative/Therapeutic Assessment and Diversity: The Complexity of Being Human

Hale Martin

Diversity is the underpinning of any work in clinical psychology. The struggle to accurately understand our clients is magnified in psychological assessment, which requires us to arrive relatively quickly at important conclusions about the people we evaluate. We are usually working with people who are at a difficult time in their lives. Often when clients come for an assessment, their problems seem to them to be impossible to conquer, and hope is in short supply. Some are in great pain, some are angry, some are scared, some are confused about why their lives do not work as they think they should. Some do not think anything is wrong despite plenty of evidence to the contrary. Often clients are trapped in ineffective strategies to which they cling tenaciously. Sometimes they look to us for miraculous insights, while at the same time rejecting what we have to offer.

On top of this, there always seem to be time pressures arising from the referring therapist, the client, and from our own busy schedule. Managed care provides little compensation if any, clients struggle to pay, and we do what we can with as few instruments as possible to save time and expense. Report writing frequently hangs over us. We are often behind and pressing to get on to the next task. Furthermore, it can be deeply challenging for assessors to share closely in clients' lived experience in a helpful way. Exposure to the horrible experiences many of our clients have had is wearing and at times traumatizing for the assessor. We look to protect ourselves from the painful realities of our clients. And in this situation we stand, as fallible human beings, with our own personal histories and limitations.

Given the difficult work of psychological assessment, the pressure to use stereotypes to understand the client in front of us is great. We also are hardwired to stereotype. Categorizing is a way humans parse the world into useful distinctions. It organizes and simplifies our world. It makes manageable the enormous amount of information constantly coming at us. Thus, we discriminate, which at its root is a reflexive mental function of awareness and thought. As we develop, we apply our past experiential knowledge to think about and interact with a person, object, or situation. Each experience informs the next until we have reflexive understandings. We can work for new understanding, but it requires attention, energy, and new neuronal pathways. This effort to understand anew seems to diminish as we age and gather a bigger pool of experience to rely upon. It is easier and more efficient to apply our past experience to current circumstances (assimilate) than to consider new possibilities (accommodate). We can rarely if ever bring completely new eyes to our experience. The nuances of stereotyping are well documented (see Fiske & Tablante (2015) for a current review of stereotyping research).

And yet when we do rely on stereotypes, we do our clients a disservice. We risk making inaccurate attributions about our clients that distort our understanding of them and leave them feeling misunderstood as the unique individuals they are. Even though we know that using a prototype to diagnosis a disorder rather than carefully assessing the client's symptoms and experiences increases error in our work (Meyer et al., 1998), we seek ways to be efficient in order to ease our burden a bit by using convenient categories and strategies. Relying on stereotypes associated with race, class, age, gender, and sexuality, which are the most commonly studied "out-groups," according to Fiske and Tablante (2015), introduces a potentially large source of error in understanding the person in front of us. However, given the difficult work of psychological assessment, the enormous complexity many cases involve, and the unrelenting pressures, it is easier and feels safer to rely on sanctioned understandings (i.e., stereotypes) than to tailor findings to the individual client. It is easy to ignore complexity for the sake of efficiency.

A further complication regarding reliance on group stereotypes is the possibility of multiple cultures, categories, or groups. If we look deeper at less well-studied categories that are ripe for stereotyping (attractiveness, intelligence, physical fitness, birth order, and a host of other ways people and their life contexts differ), there are certain to be multiple categories into which a client fits. The interaction effects among all the categories to which a client belongs produce overwhelming complexity. Thus, there is great difficulty balancing stereotypic, nomothetic information with personal, idiographic information. Unfortunately, the well-intended emphasis on diversity in clinical training today can exaggerate reliance on stereotypes. Although multiculturalism is a very important social phenomenon and deserves great attention, its emphasis in clinical work too often leads students to see their clients through a distorting lens. The challenge is to walk the line between allowing group differences to inform us of possibilities, while not obscuring the actual lived experience of each individual client. If we ignore the information available about cultural differences, we are not well prepared to work with a client from a culture or group different from our own. But if we place too large an emphasis on stereotypes and social out-groups, we risk missing our client's life experience. For example, prejudice is an unfortunate common experience in out-groups, but what is important in clinical work is not the assessor's understanding of prejudice or what she/he read in a book, but rather the *client's* experience of prejudice. Clients from "out-groups" often have very different experiences of prejudice from others and, even when the experiences are similar, what they make of them can vary enormously. Thus, openness to the client's actual experience is important to have accurate empathy, which allows us to understand our client and which can be healing in itself. Thus, I strongly believe that training should emphasize psychological factors rather than categories that often tell us little about a specific person.

The only effective way to deal with all these complexities is to ask questions and listen carefully. We cannot be of service to our clients if we jump to conclusions and impose our own fantasies on them. There is no way around spending the time to deeply listen to our client's story, despite how contrary to our expectations it might be or how painful it is to hear. Clients' unique experiences and what they have made of them are the bottom line. Although nomothetic data are valuable, they are not enough. They are no substitute for the client's lived experience. If we want to understand and help the client, we cannot take the tempting shortcuts, no matter how sanctioned they might be. We have to accept our uncertainty and drop our pretensions in order to connect with and understand our fellow human. As Finn (2007) asserts, we have to get into "our client's shoes."

In this chapter, I would like to describe collaborative assessment (Fischer, 1985, 2000) and Therapeutic Assessment (TA; Finn, 2007), together referred to as C/TA, which represent an evolving approach to assessment that I think provides an excellent solution to this challenge of diversity. This approach involves both nomothetic and idiographic perspectives, it requires knowledge of group differences but also recognition that group differences are only one influence of many that make people who they are. At its core, C/TA is an effort to meet a unique person in his/her unique place and to work with that individual to find realistic, adaptive solutions to the problem areas in his/her life.

In this effort, C/TA offers an avenue to understanding a client—or more importantly, helping a person understand themselves. It is a process of reconciling our knowledge from books and our own personal experience, with the nooks and crannies of the client's experience. It requires patience and time, but the results go beyond what anyone might expect. C/TA also provides a richly rewarding experience for the assessor in the ringside seat to the awe-inspiring panorama of human diversity.

In the following pages I will discuss the philosophy underlying the collaborative approach to assessment pioneered by Constance Fischer. Then I will describe the advances of TA developed by Stephen Finn (2006) and briefly summarize the growing empirical evidence that supports these approaches. Then I will review work that illustrates and refines these approaches as they apply to diversity. Finally, I will present a case that demonstrates TA with a young man belonging to a number of recognized groups along with his own uniqueness. I hope to provide an appreciation of TA and the solutions it offers in balancing the nomothetic with the idiographic in assessment. One can then better judge the value of TA in assessing the complexity of being human.

Collaborative Psychological Assessment: Phenomenology, Collaboration, and Context

Constance Fischer's revolutionary thinking about assessment came together in her 1985 book *Individualizing Psychological Assessment*, in which she advocates a phenomenological approach to assessment grounded in collaboration with the client. She believed that important relationships emerge in the assessment process—between the assessor and the client as well as between the client and her/his life. The assessor–client relationship involves seeking optimal working relationships, which Fischer (1982) understood as sharing a common cause while respecting the other's abilities and limits; privacy, which she saw as an undefended mental state that has no fear of judgment or intrusion; and intimacy, which she defined as sharing the essence of one's life. Fischer (1982) believed that these three ways to be present together are important to effective assessment. Her focus on relationship is quite a departure from traditional assessment. It also was prophetic of subsequent understandings, such as that offered by intersubjectivity.

Fischer (1985) believed that psychological tests are simplified versions of the challenges clients face in their real lives and provoke similar feelings and behaviors. Thus, if the assessor can be present to the client's experience during testing, the assessor can observe typical ways the client reacts to the world. By noticing these reactions and bringing them to the client's attention (in a moment of shared privacy), the client can become aware of patterns of behavior—and realize they are not immutable. Behavior can change to more effectively address a repetitive problem in living. It takes collaborative relationship to bring problem "comportment" into focus in the shared privacy that allows effective change.

Fischer also believed that clients, like all people, are not a collection of static traits but rather are constantly in flux; so, understanding the context of problem behavior rather than talking about traits or abstract dynamics is essential if we hope to help clients find some viable alternative to problematic behavior. As Fischer eloquently claimed, "For an optional route to be personally viable, it must be a variation of present approaches; it must branch off from where the client is now, and it must accommodate familiar action" (Fischer, 1985/1994, p. 100). This is analogous to giving someone directions to a new location. If you do not start at a point known to the person, the directions are useless.

Thus, this approach brings us quite close to the client's lived experience and leaves little room for stereotyping. We are working with one person's life experience and not labels. With her revolutionary thinking, Fischer set a new course for psychological assessment. It is a course that offers an answer to the question about what to do with the overwhelming complexity we face as assessors. And it provides a solution to the balance between nomothetic and idiographic information. The goal of assessment, in Fischer's mind, was not finding absolute truths but rather identifying patterns related to a client's problems in living so that viable, more adaptive patterns for the individual can be developed and implemented.

Therapeutic Assessment

Stephen Finn (2006) furthered the paradigm shift that Fischer began by blending it with his own thinking and experience to develop Therapeutic Assessment (TA). He then empirically demonstrated the significant therapeutic effect this collaborative approach can have (Finn & Tonsager, 1992). TA is a semi-structured approach to assessment that incorporates many of Fischer's ideas. It is grounded in six principles: collaboration, curiosity, compassion, humility, openness, and respect (Finn, 2009). Collaboration begins with the first contact and is emphasized in the initial session in which clients are helped to articulate their burning questions about their problems in living. Formulating questions that are most important to them with the aid of a caring professional begins an important interpersonal process and gives clients hope that the results will be connected to their concerns and not merely abstractions that do not practically relate to their lives. Their questions then guide the entire assessment process, which becomes a quest for the best answers the assessor and client working jointly can puzzle together.

From here the structure of a TA is tailored to the client, but it typically involves, first, gathering nomothetic data that critically inform the answers to the questions. However, the nomothetic must be integrated with the idiographic concerns of the client, thus, limiting room for stereotyping to intrude. One way to do this is what Finn calls the "extended inquiry." After a test is completed, simply asking the client about puzzling responses or behaviors during a test can provide helpful insight for both the assessor and the client that otherwise might be lost. The fact that traditional assessors often do not ask about specific answers or test behaviors that seem odd or pregnant with undisclosed meaning can leave important stones unturned.

Another way to relate the findings to the client's unique life in a meaningful way that limits the intrusion of stereotyping is what Finn (2006) called the assessment intervention session or AIS. In an AIS a testing procedure is used to elicit some important experience for the client in the testing room that is related to a central question he/she posed. This session offers both the client and the assessor the opportunity to more deeply understand the client and their problem and to work together to develop new approaches to the problem.

The assessor works with the client's personal experience provoked by the assessment measure to help the client see something she/he is experiencing in vivo. They then work together to understand the experience in new ways and to develop and practice alternative approaches that are more adaptive. This session can make accessible to the client assessment findings that they might not grasp in a traditional feedback session. With the client's blind spot activated, a collaborative relationship with a compassionate and respectful assessor, and a context grounded in the client's real life, the assessor has created optimal conditions for significant change. Notice here that the focus is on the client's unique experience, not on textbook understandings or stereotypical generalizations.

These experiential stepping stones intimately related to the client's lived experience pave the way to the summary discussion session (referred to in traditional assessment as the feedback session). During this session, answers to the questions are discussed, not proclaimed. The assessor and the client together weave understanding meaningful to the client's life. The assessor uses the client's words, images, and metaphors and seeks to contextualize the answers in the client's life with the client's help. Throughout the assessment, the assessor is non-judging and supportive.

The written results are in the form of a personal letter to the client recapping the summary discussion session. It is written in first person and avoids jargon and abstract concepts that are not recognizable to the client. Again, the words, images, and metaphors of the client, especially those that were developed in the summary discussion are used. These capture more than mere words and are used to provide deeply meaningful anchors that facilitate the client repeatedly finding their way back to this new perspective. Also the client's contributions to understanding the assessment results, both in the summary discussion session and previous ones, are amply referenced in the feedback letter. These written summaries provide the client with clear information intimately connected to their lives to which the client can refer back over time.

The TA model can be applied to a wide range of assessments, including personality, cognitive, and neuropsychological assessment. It is especially well suited to cases in which diversity issues are prominent. An examination below of accumulating insights into how TA is best applied in assessments in which diversity is prominent will highlight its utility in these situations. Notice that the heart of the work is focusing on the unique individual in our presence with his/her multitude of life influences that otherwise would be impossible to sort out in any meaningful way. Attunement, responsiveness, and respect for the client as a unique person are central.

Empirical Evidence Supporting the Therapeutic Efficacy of TA

Does TA actually work? Is it helpful to harness the penetrating insights that assessment measures have been honed to provide and to apply those insights in a supportive holding environment to a client's personal questions about their struggles in life? Research has consistently found significant therapeutic effects resulting from TA. Finn and Tonsager (1992) demonstrated that a brief TA (two sessions) involving only the MMPI-2 had a significant positive effect in college students, including decreased symptomatology (effect size .85) and increases in self-esteem (effect size .46), while the control group who got equal clinical attention showed no significant changes. Newman and Greenway (1997) replicated Finn and Tonsager's study. Studies have shown TA is more effective than traditional assessment in increasing compliance with treatment recommendations (effect size = .42; Ackerman, Hilsenroth, Baity, & Blagys, 2000); in enhancing the therapeutic alliance with a therapist following the assessment (effect size = 1.02; Hilsenroth, Peters, & Ackerman, 2004); and in prompting self-harming adolescents admitted to emergency rooms to follow through with subsequent therapy ($p < .05$; Ougrin, Ng, & Low, 2008). A randomized clinical trial compared TA to a structured goal-focused pretreatment intervention. Results showed that TA demonstrated superior ability to raise outcome expectations and patient perceptions of progress toward treatment (Cohen's d 0.65 and 0.56, respectively) and yielded higher satisfaction ($d = 0.68$); however, symptomatology was the same in both groups after treatment (De Saeger et al., 2014).

The TA model has been adapted to children and families as well as adolescents and couples (Finn, 2007; Tharinger et al., 2009). It has been used in a range of settings, including forensic assessment (Chudzik, 2016; Evans, 2016) with good results. In work with latency aged children and their families, TA has proved effective in decreasing symptomatology in both children and mothers, while also decreasing family conflict and enhancing family communication (Tharinger et al., 2009). Smith, Handler, and Nash (2010) used a time-series analysis to find that boys diagnosed with Oppositional Defiant Disorder showed decreases in symptomatology and improved family relationships after a TA.

Such research demonstrating the power of TA has accumulated rapidly. A meta-analysis of studies of C/TA (which includes both collaborative assessment and TA), including some simply using enhanced feedback techniques and some as short as two sessions, showed C/TA had a robust overall Cohen's *d* effect size of .43 (Poston & Hansen, 2010). The authors of the analysis concluded that assessors should seek training in therapeutic models of assessment, that training programs should teach this approach, and that managed care policy makers should consider the therapeutic model of assessment in future policy and reimbursement decisions. In short, C/TA offers an evidenced-based, brief intervention that is highly effective in comparison to other therapeutic approaches seeking behavior change.

Therapeutic Assessment with Diverse Cultures and Groups

Rosenberg, Almeida, and Macdonald (2012) wrote a seminal article about the application of C/TA to clients from marginalized groups. The authors worked in an inner-city clinic whose clients were largely Black, Hispanic, or Asian, and who lived in an impoverished and too often violent community. Rosenberg and her colleagues contended that "bridging the wide gap between cultures and overcoming cultural mistrust starts in building the assessor–client relationship and taking both world views into account as a way to create meaning from the assessment results" (Rosenberg et al., 2012, p. 223). The components of TA they used involved collaborating with the family throughout the assessment, which included initially gathering questions that the family and even the child/adolescent would like addressed, discussing the findings and suggested answers to the questions with the caregivers, and providing in writing the answers they reached together in the form of a letter to the caregivers and a fable for the child. As is common in TA, they also sometimes wrote formal reports for involved third parties, such as schools and social workers.

Like Fischer (1982), these clinicians saw the key to their success residing in the relational experience that evolves during the assessment process. The obstacles the relationship must overcome were racial distrust and language issues, but more importantly what they referred to as "translation," which is communication of meaning beyond words, with the goal of crossing cultural barriers. This crossing often involves finding a meaningful metaphor that captures important issues, lends itself to a deeper level of meaning than words can provide, and bridges the differences between the assessor and the client. The resulting "co-created meanings" have a powerful effect on both the client and the assessor.

Rosenberg et al. contended that translation requires assessors to suspend their Eurocentric understanding of the world and to put themselves as much as possible in their client's shoes. By attuning to the client in her/his world, the assessor opens the possibility of meaningful connection, and with that, the hope for new understanding and possibilities emerges. Change happens, mistrust turns to connection, being trapped gives way to new options, and diverse cultures converge into shared humanness. Successful communication across a wide cultural gap happens and allows the client to make important adjustments that would not otherwise have happened.

Rosenberg et al. (2012) believed four factors are involved in the co-creation of meaning:

1. the assessor abandoning the expert stance and letting the client teach the assessor about her/his life;
2. changing the focus from "what does this mean" to "what experience am I in with this person?" (p. 231);
3. finding a metaphor that relates the findings to the client's life experience;
4. experiencing the power of co-created meaning in the present.

Co-creating meaning is an effective way to connect with, understand, and help the client. It is facilitated by the philosophy and techniques of collaborative assessment and TA. Without it assessors are limited to a few nomothetic probabilities that might have little connection to the client's true experience and offer no real options for change. When a co-created understanding is reached, powerful therapeutic effects result.

Finn (2016) offers additional insights into the use of TA with diverse populations in a case study with a transgender client. The salient lessons from his work start with the importance of multicultural training focused on the specific population with which one is working. Of course, this often requires substantial on-the-job effort, given there are many groups to which a client can belong. His work demonstrated beautifully the value of detailed nomothetic knowledge of the group of interest, but adapting that knowledge to fit the client's unique experience. Importantly, Finn also had thought through his own feelings about this type of assessment. This preparation played a central role in creating space for the client to articulate key questions and develop the shared privacy that facilitates change. By being attuned to the complicated social pressures and issues transgender clients often face, and open to and versed in a range of options, he was well prepared to listen carefully to the client's concerns. The results in this case were closely tailored to the client and provided helpful insights related to her questions.

For an illuminating series of case studies involving TA with diverse clients, the reader is directed to a 2016 special edition of the *Journal of Personality Assessment* (Volume 98; Issue 6). Cases presented by Fantini (2016), Chudzik (2016), and Evans (2016) offer clinically relevant explorations of how the TA approach embodies the flexibility needed to meet clients where they are and to navigate the cultural differences between clients and assessors. Fantini (2016) discusses the subtle dangers of stereotyping presented by microcultural differences. She describes how humility, self-reflection, attunement to the client's reactions, and confirming assumptions with the client (as the expert on themselves) can repair significant ruptures in the assessment alliance. Chudzik (2016) reports on the assessment of a violent criminal offender. By approaching this challenging case with the core values of TA, collaboration, curiosity, compassion, humility, openness, and respect, Chudzik was able to discover with the client the developmental root of his behavior, which created the possibility that the client's behavior could change. Evans (2016) describes a forensic assessment case of an Ethiopian woman who had been brutally tortured and was seeking asylum in the United States. The attuned, compassionate, and respectful relationship advocated by TA, promoted a more accurate assessment than traditional forensic approaches would have allowed and one that was healing for the client. Aschieri (2016) helps us understand aspects of traditional assessment that can inadvertently trigger shame in clients, which impairs the assessment process and can leave the client feeling disempowered, less hopeful, and even abused. All of these contributions provide excellent insights into the dynamics and value of TA with clients from diverse life experiences.

Many cases involve multiple aspects of diversity, the understanding of which can become quite complex. The following section provides a detailed example of one such case.

Therapeutic Assessment Involving Multiple Life Issues: A Case Study

The real world is rarely simple and linear. An assessment case that illustrates this point is one involving a 27-year-old man we have called Pouya that a doctoral student completed under my supervision (Martin & Jacklin, 2012). Pouya fit a number of major out-group categories. He was born with a rare genetic disorder that caused notable physical characteristics, such as short stature and unique facial features, and it led others, particularly his family, to lower expectations of him. He also was an immigrant. His family emigrated to the United States from a Middle Eastern country when he was a young boy with the hope of finding better medical care for him than was available in their homeland. Thus, he grew up with a foot in two very different cultures. He also had experienced significant academic problems that suggested low intellectual functioning.

Pouya initially presented for a learning disability assessment with hope he might qualify for additional time for the GED test he hoped to pass. He had dropped out of high school in the tenth grade. However, in the initial interview, he jumped at the opportunity to pose other questions for the assessment. His questions included:

1. Do I have a learning disability and if so, what can I do about it?
2. Am I depressed?
3. Why do I become frustrated around authority and stop listening to them?

4. Why haven't I been in a serious relationship, and why am I so scared and self-conscious about myself?
5. What can I do to have somebody beside me in my life in a healthy, 50/50 relationship?

(Martin & Jacklin, 2012, p. 159)

He was clearly motivated to understand himself and open to collaboration—he brought pages of background information about these questions after the initial interview. His questions and his demeanor did not fit with someone of limited intelligence.

Pouya had a long history of unsuccessful interventions to address his problems that had been forced upon him by his concerned parents. He had undergone various outpatient treatments, inpatient treatment, and drug rehabilitation programs with little success. He also reported great difficulty maintaining friendships. He had a very close relationship with his parents, to whom he spoke on the phone three to four times per day. We learned that close family connections are common in Middle Eastern culture, but Pouya admitted that the relationships with his parents were conflictual and that he manipulated them into giving him what he wanted. He also admitted defiant relationships with authority figures starting before high school.

After the initial interview, the assessor, Erin, noted that Pouya seemed much younger than his age but also demonstrated surprising strengths. As his questions suggested, he showed some self-awareness, but he seemed to lack insight into the motivations of others. He expected that others could see his needs and was frustrated when he felt they were purposely withholding what he needed. Erin liked his openness and vulnerability but noted in herself a pull to take care of him. She also felt put off by him at times as well. She noticed ambivalence in his expressed wish to stop manipulating others vs. his apparent pride about how good he was at it. When asked, he admitted he was reluctant to give up his well-developed skill at manipulating others to get his needs met.

Because a potential learning disability prompted his seeking assessment, we started with cognitive testing. The standardized testing showed a WAIS-IV (Wechsler Adult Intelligence Scale, Fourth edition; Wechsler, 2008) Full Scale IQ in the low average range but with variability. While his Verbal Comprehension Index and Perceptual Reasoning Index were both a standard score of 81, and his Processing Speed Index was 79, his Working Memory Index was 97 and his Similarities subtest was a scaled score of 9, which is within the normal range. His achievement scores were about what would be predicted by his IQ. We were a bit perplexed by his pattern of scores and their incongruity with the articulate and thoughtful person in the room, so Erin administered the Stanford Binet-5 (Roid, 2003). Once again he showed personal strengths in working memory but also in quantitative reasoning, both of which were in the average range. His lowest score was on the Visual Spatial Processing Index (standard score = 74). We came to see that Pouya's difficulties lay with non-verbally mediated tasks, which, along with ineffective schooling and perhaps some cultural effects, likely caused his full scale

IQ to be an underestimate of his true ability. True to the TA model, we had let our curiosity lead us to test further than we had planned in order to puzzle out an influence that affected Pouya's performance and, further, his feelings about himself. It was likely a factor in dropping out of school.

The personality testing showed inconsistency between a self-report measure (MMPI-2; Butcher et al., 2001) and a performance-based measure (Exner, 2002), with the MMPI-2 reflecting much more distress and dysfunction than the Rorschach. The Rorschach showed indications of developmental deficits, poor judgment, and less than ideal reality testing but good positive resources, including the capacity to reflect on himself and a focus on relationships. We understood these results in the context of his admitted manipulativeness, to suggest that Pouya found connection to others by crying for help. He likely had come to believe what his early environment had suggested to him: that he was not capable, when actually he had more positive resources than he knew. His academic struggles might have further reinforced the idea that he was not as capable as others. Testing also suggested that Pouya was not confident that others could be trusted to meet his strong dependency needs. His response to card VIII of the Rorschach—"an unreachable fish in the ice" which suggested starvation—captures his frustration. So, we came to see what Pouya and others called "manipulation" was actually his best effort to get his needs met in an environment where he believed that direct requests would not be responded to positively.

The Rorschach extended inquiry helped us understand this dilemma more clearly. His differences from peers as an immigrant and with his physical characteristics had left him vulnerable to teasing, bullying, and being left out early in life. The extended inquiry also gave us insight into his experience of love, vulnerability, and survival. The discussion poignantly connected Pouya with his painful life, and gave him a powerful experience of sharing his inner state with Erin, who handled it in a way that he felt understood and accepted.

Near the end of the assessment, Pouya lobbied Erin to meet with him and his parents when they visited. He wanted help explaining to them the emerging results, particularly his manipulative behavior. In TAs with adult clients, we do not typically have family sessions; but they are not unheard of and flexibility and responding to the uniqueness of every case is a hallmark of TA. A family session might well have been normative in his Middle Eastern culture, and we felt that for him and his situation it was worth the effort in any event. Erin understood the caretaking involved with this, but we agreed to proceed with it. So she facilitated a conversation between Pouya and his parents, hoping to shift the family story about Pouya to a more accurate account that would be more conducive to his growth. The meeting provided a number of insights for his parents and for Pouya. For example, when Pouya told his father that he was angry that his father had not objected to his lying about stealing money from his father's drawer as a child, his father was surprised, and said he was unaware Pouya had lied about it. This shocked Pouya and allowed him to see that he had drawn firm conclusions about his father's actions that were inaccurate. The session ended with Pouya and his parents setting ground rules for future interactions, and it introduced Pouya to new ways of being with his parents.

We planned an assessment intervention session using the Thematic Apperception Test to try to get Pouya's characteristic behavior patterns and relationship expectations active in the room. This would give the opportunity to explore them together before we discussed the results and to see where change might be possible. His stories illustrated beautifully how his entrenched ideas about relationships and himself impaired his ability to create and maintain satisfying friendships and romantic relationships. Erin and Pouya were able to enter together that shared privacy Fischer describes, which allowed Pouya to drop defenses and to see deeply into his motivations and behavior. As a result, he was able to "rewind" some of his stories and figure out how the characters could have more mature and effective interactions, negotiating meeting each other's needs. The ensuing discussion identified Pouya's "automatic pilot" and allowed Erin and him together to plan how he might notice when he goes on automatic pilot and ways he could turn it off. They related these insights to a recent break with a friend and thought through together how Pouya could handle it differently. Pouya planned to practice the new ways he was learning by addressing his misunderstanding with the friend outside the session.

With all this work, the summary/discussion session went smoothly, cementing the advances Pouya had realized and translating them further into his real world. Erin's letter at the end of the assessment included:

> Learning to appropriately assert yourself and ask directly for what you need from others will allow you to create a more flexible and effective approach to others. Learning to do this will help you manage conflict without reverting to manipulation. It may also allow you to feel more comfortable being close to others. Furthermore, feeling increasingly confident that you can hold your own in the event of any conflict, may allow you to better express negative emotions in relationships than you currently do.
>
> (p. 174)

This statement reflects the reality that Pouya was likely caught between cultures in untenable ways. In some Middle Eastern countries directness is not polite and interactions are more subtle than Erin was advocating. Such cultural conflicts likely had added to his confusion and to his interpersonal struggles in the United States. Having met his parents, we had seen first-hand that they were open to directness. Thus, Erin's words might have helped him clarify a confusing cultural difference and given him some important tools to succeed in his present life. The shared privacy between Pouya and Erin made these changes possible and smoothed the lessons.

The follow-up session revealed that Pouya had substantially benefitted from the assessment. New options for living had been understood and integrated into his life. He was working to have healthier relationships that avoided manipulation with his parents and with others. His self-confidence and self-esteem were growing as was his hope that healthy 50/50 relationships were within reach.

This case shows the inevitable confluence of many unique influences in a client's life. Not just from a rare genetic disorder, learning differences, or as an immigrant, but rather the unique meaning Pouya made of all these influences and more. Influences, coping strategies, and feelings went well beyond prototypical templates one might expect from these various out-groups. But knowledge of out-group influences played a role in sensitizing the assessor to possibilities. The flexibility of TA offers a sensitive and flexible phenomenological lens to understand the nuances of multiple cultural influences on development.

Summary

There is substantial evidence that TA can be a culturally responsive intervention and thus is well-suited to cases involving clients whose histories and identities are widely discrepant from the assessor's. Diverse clients working with middle-class White assessors can benefit from the values and techniques of TA because it addresses many of the challenges in cross-cultural assessment, such as stereotyping, misleading nomothetic data, and rigid thinking, that have led many psychologists who work with diverse clients to abandon and disavow assessment. TA works to avoid stereotyping. We stay close to the client's experiences and the meaning of those experiences to the client, thus reducing stereotype-based assumptions. In addition, our focus generally is not on diagnosis, although this is sometimes an important client question. Rather, we seek to intimately understand the client's world and the forces that have acted on the client. We do this by inquiring, listening, and believing the client.

TA also addresses the traditional power differential inherent in psychological assessment by engaging the person who has sought help as an essential part of the assessment process. By collaborating with clients and recognizing their expertise, the assessor reduces the power gap clients might otherwise feel in the assessment relationship. This has many benefits ranging from getting more accurate data to empowering clients, which can be therapeutic in itself. In TA we shift the notion that we know truth to a humble search with clients for what is true and possible for them in their world. By enlisting their expertise on themselves and focusing on their concerns, TA stays in touch with who they are and what they struggle with, regardless of the demographic categories to which they belong. We work with them, not on them, and thus reduce the power differential that exists in traditional assessment. In this regard TA is well-suited to groups that too often feel marginalized. This single effort changes the dynamics in the assessment process, empowering clients to work with us toward the common goal of alleviating their problems in living.

As is apparent, TA is extremely flexible in its application and in the understanding it provides. While we find nomothetic tests essential in providing important information and keeping us anchored in important ways, we do not apply them rigidly. Idiographic data are equally important in keeping the focus on the individual client. Tailoring the testing results to clients using their input, assessors are at much less risk for making erroneous attribution of test results to clients. Although TA assessors are still mindful of what norms they use with a client, they are careful to avoid misapplying test results. Thus, thoughtful application of the best nomothetic data we can acquire is balanced by extended inquiries, assessment interventions sessions, and the entire collaborative process with the client.

Respect is another tenet of TA that is important in working with those who have been disenfranchised or feel different from others. It is an antidote for the disregard and lack of importance they might have felt in their lives and may feel in traditional assessment, which can be painfully isolating. Along with respect, TA strives to attend to the shame that many clients of every ilk face, and to actively work to reduce it (Finn, 2007).

Several other components stand out as particularly applicable, if not essential to effective assessment with diverse populations. These include assessors educating themselves through good training and life experience. Education begins with exposure and openness in our lives to diverse ways of being, and it is deepened in formal training in the nomothetic tendencies of various groups. This prepares us to be available to our client in helpful ways. But if we stop here, we have failed because the most meaningful education is what we learn on the job, intently listening and learning from the client with whom we are working. It is essential to understand what the client did with all the experiences which she/he lived. Extended inquiries and assessment intervention sessions are excellent techniques to accomplish this.

With the attuned presence of an assessor who is open, flexible, and authentic, the client is most likely to feel understood and the work will have its important impact. In short, the willingness to step into the client's shoes, to strive to understand what the client experiences, and then to blend it with what an assessor has to offer from all her/his training, allows the client to more effectively approach his/her problems in living. The work requires the assessor to work outside the restricted, traditional approach. It demands unusual openness and flexibility in thinking to work with the client from the inside. Many assessors find this challenge exciting and, as you can perhaps now appreciate, the rewards for the client and the assessor are substantial. Clients are helped more than they could have anticipated, and assessors have powerful experiences that change their lives in at least some small ways.

Smith (2016, p. 563) rightly highlights

> the need to practice assessment with multicultural competence, and the potential benefits of using an assessment model (e.g., TA) that is itself culturally responsive. As the world continues to become more culturally diverse through changing demographics and the recognition and evolution of different subcultures, the need to practice assessment using these concepts will only become more central.

References

Ackerman, S. J., Hilsenroth, M. J., Baity, M. R., & Blagys, M. D. (2000). Interaction of therapeutic process and alliance during psychological assessment. *Journal of Personality Assessment, 75*, 82–109.

Aschieri, F. (2016). Shame as a cultural artifact: A call for self-awareness and reflexivity in personality assessment. *Journal of Personality Assessment, 98*(6), 567–575. doi: 10.1080/00223891.2016.1146289.

Butcher, J. N., Graham, J. R., Ben-Porath, Y. S., Tellegen, A., Dahlstrom, W. G., & Kaemmer, B. (2001). *MMPI-2: Manual for administration, scoring, and interpretation, revised edition.* Minneapolis: University of Minnesota Press.

Chudzik, L. (2016). Therapeutic Assessment of a violent criminal offender: Managing the cultural narrative of evil. *Journal of Personality Assessment, 98*(6), 585–589. doi: 10.1080/00223891.2016.1215321.

De Saeger, H., Kamphuis, J. H., Finn, S. E., Smith, J. D., Verheul, R., van Busschbach, J. J., et al. (2014). Therapeutic Assessment promotes treatment readiness but does not affect symptom change in patients with personality disorders: Findings from a randomized clinical trial. *Psychological Assessment, 26*(2), 474–483. doi: 10.1037/a35667

Evans, F. B. (2016). What torture survivors teach assessors about being more fully human. *Journal of Personality Assessment, 98*(6), 590–593. doi: 10.1080/00223891.2016.1180527.

Exner, J. E. (2002). *The Rorschach: Basic foundations and principles of interpretation.* New York: Wiley.

Fantini, F. (2016). Family traditions, cultural values, and the clinician's countertransference: Therapeutic Assessment of a young Sicilian woman. *Journal of Personality Assessment, 98*(6), 576–584. doi: 10.1080/00223891.2016.1178128.

Finn, S. E. (2006). Master Lecture at Society for Personality Assessment. March, 2006. San Diego, CA.

Finn, S. E. (2007). *In our clients' shoes: Theory and techniques of Therapeutic Assessment.* Mawah, NJ: Erlbaum.

Finn, S. E. (2009). Core values in Therapeutic Assessment. Retrieved from www.therapeuticassessment.com

Finn, S. E. (2016). Using Therapeutic Assessment in psychological assessments required for sex reassignment surgery. In V. Brabender & J. L. Mihura (Eds.), *Handbook of gender and sexuality in psychological assessment* (pp. 511–533). New York: Routledge.

Finn, S. E., & Tonsager, S. E. (1992). The therapeutic effects of providing MMPI-2 test feedback to college students awaiting psychotherapy. *Psychological Assessment, 4*, 278–287.

Fischer, C. T. (1982). Intimacy in psychological assessment. In M. Fisher & G. Stricker (Eds.), *Intimacy* (pp. 443–460). New York: Plenum.

Fischer, C. T. (1985/1994). *Individualizing psychological assessment.* Mahwah, NJ: Erlbaum.

Fischer, C. T. (2000). Collaborative, individualized assessment. *Journal of Personality Assessment, 74*, 2–14.

Fiske, S. T., & Tablante, C. B. (2015). Stereotyping: Process and content. In M. Mikulincer & P. R. Shaver (Eds.), *APA handbook of personality and social psychology, volume 1: Attitudes and social cognition* (pp. 457–507). Washington, DC: American Psychological Association.

Hilsenroth, M. J., Peters, E. J., & Ackerman, S. J. (2004). The development of therapeutic alliance during psychological assessment: Patient and therapist perspectives across treatment. *Journal of Personality Assessment, 83*, 332–344.

Martin, H., & Jacklin, E. (2012). Therapeutic Assessment involving multiple life issues: Coming to terms with problems of health, culture, and earning. In S. Finn, C. Fischer, & L. Handler (Eds.), *Collaborative/Therapeutic Assessment: A casebook and guide* (pp. 157–177). Hoboken, NJ: John Wiley & Sons, Inc.

Meyer, G. J., Finn, S. E., Eyde, L. D., Kay, G. G., Kubiszyn, T. W., Moreland, K. L., et al. (1998). Benefits and costs of psychological assessment in healthcare delivery. APA Report, June 1998.

Newman, M. L., & Greenway, P. (1997). Therapeutic effects of providing MMPI-2 test feedback to clients in a university counseling service: A collaborative approach. *Psychological Assessment, 9*, 122–131.

Ougrin, D., Ng, A. V., & Low, J. (2008). Therapeutic assessment based on cognitive-analytic therapy for young people presenting with self-harm: Pilot study. *Psychiatric Bulletin, 32*, 423–426.

Poston, J. M., & Hanson, W. M. (2010). Meta-analysis of psychological assessment as a therapeutic intervention. *Psychological Assessment, 22*, 203–212. doi: 10.1037/a0018679.

Roid, G. H (2003). *Stanford-Binet Intelligence Scales, Fifth Edition*. Itasca, IL: Riverside.

Rosenberg, A., Almeida, A., & Macdonald, H. (2012). Crossing the cultural divide: Issues in translation, mistrust, and co-creation of meaning in cross-cultural Therapeutic Assessment. *Journal of Personality Assessment, 94*(3), 223–231. doi: 10.1080/00223891.2011.648293.

Smith, J. D. (2016). Introduction to the special section on cultural considerations in collaborative and Therapeutic Assessment. *Journal of Personality Assessment, 98*(6), 563–566. doi: 10.1080/00223891.2016.1196455.

Smith, J. D., Handler, L., & Nash, M. R. (2010). Family Therapeutic Assessment for preadolescent boys with oppositional defiant disorder: A replicated single-case time-series design. *Psychological Assessment, 22*, 593–602. doi: 10.1037/a0019697.

Tharinger, D. J., Finn, S. E., Gentry, L., Hamilton, A., Fowler, J., Matson, M., et al. (2009). Therapeutic Assessment with children: A pilot study of treatment acceptability and outcome. *Journal of Personality Assessment, 91*, 238–244. doi: 10.1080/00223890902794275.

Wechsler, D. (2008). *Wechsler Adult Intelligence Scale, Fourth Edition*. San Antonio, TX: Psychological Corporation.

CHAPTER **16**

Culturally Responsive Personality Assessment: Blending Competence with Humility

Hadas Pade

Sara, a licensed psychologist, got a call from a potential assessment client. The man on the phone said his therapist suggested he seek an assessment to better understand some of his "relationship issues." During this initial conversation, he described himself as a White male in his 30s with a Master's degree who is conservative and religious. He went on to express his concern about "the terrible state of our society." When Sara asked for clarification, he explained that "certain groups were taking over," "we are killing unborn babies," and "White Christians need to arm themselves and make America right again." Sarah, a White female in her 30s who happens to be an unwavering Democrat who believes in pro-choice, pro-immigration, and equality, and had recently participated in a rally protecting the rights of Muslim Americans, was hesitant. Was this man displaying paranoia and his opinions part of a potential psychiatric diagnosis, or are those his sincere views on the world? If the latter was the case, would she be able to administer, score, interpret, integrate, write a report, and provide feedback without significant bias? Would she end up in a heated political discussion during testing sessions? Even if such verbalizations were indeed "symptoms," and regardless of her clinical expertise, is she the right fit for this client?

Introduction and Definitions

According to Suzuki and Ponterotto (2008, p. 26), "Clinicians face the ethical challenge of adequately balancing and integrating in their assessments clients' private and ecological experience." What about the clinicians' own private and ecological experience? There is much written about the vulnerability of diverse clients, and rightly so. But what about the assessor? Although it is true that we hold the power in the assessment interaction, there are important characteristics to consider on that end as well.

The term *Culturally Responsive Assessment* (CRA) is not as common in the field of clinical psychology or psychological assessment, but is frequently used in the field of education where increased consideration has been given to using assessment approaches that are culturally sensitive and responsive. In general, being culturally responsive in the context of education involves being student-focused and acknowledging students' differences in order to systematically reduce bias within the broader assessment framework of learning outcomes (Montenegro & Jankowski, 2017). Suzuki and Ponterotto (2008) included this term when discussing psychological assessment, and this chapter will consider it with respect to personality assessment, but in a broader sense. In general, this concept is similar to an individualized and person-focused approach in psychological assessment discussed later on in this chapter.

Handler and Hilsenroth (1998) discussed the unique interaction between client and examiner during assessment. They referenced Schafer's work from 1954 and his acknowledgment of the idiosyncratic personal history of each of the participants that is part of the testing session. There have been increasing efforts to acknowledge diversity and multiculturalism in psychological assessment (Dana, 2005; Suzuki & Ponterotto, 2008). However, the focus almost always is on the client and on particular diversity factors. In this chapter, I explore the diversity of the examiner, client, and particularly the interaction of such various diversity factors that might be relevant in the assessment context.

In order to have a meaningful discussion about competence and humility in the context of culturally responsive personality assessment, it would be helpful to first define such terms. According to the 2006 Final Report by the American Psychological Association (APA) Task Force on the Assessment of Competence in Professional Psychology: "competence refers to the professional's overall suitability for the profession, which is a reflection of the individual's knowledge, skills, "and attitudes and their integration" (p. 11). The APA report further indicated that "competence is both developmental and incremental in that what is expected of the professional differs depending on the individual's stage of professional development and subsequent functioning" (2006, p. 11). This can be directly applied to competence in personality assessment, referring to a lengthy list of knowledge and skills noted as necessary for psychologists to possess (Krishnamurthy et al., 2004).

In terms of *cultural competence*, the APA (2002) expects psychologists in the practice of psychological testing to have "an understanding of factors associated with age, gender, gender identity, race, ethnicity, cultural, national origin, religion, sexual orientation, disability, language, or socioeconomic status ... for effective implementation of their services" (APA Ethics Code, Standard 2.01b). A multicultural focus on openness to the other is closely related to the concept of reflection and humility (Hook, Davis, Owen, Worthington, & Utsey, 2013). According to the 2005 Presidential Task Force on Evidence-Based Practice (EBP) Final Report, "clinical expertise requires the ability to reflect on one's own experience, knowledge, hypotheses, inferences, emotional reactions, and behaviors and to use that reflection to modify one's practices accordingly" (p. 12). Such reflection is linked directly to a sense of humility and "an awareness of the limits of one's knowledge and skills as well as the recognition of the heuristics and biases (both cognitive and affective) that can affect clinical judgment" (p. 12). In this chapter, humility will refer to a recognition of one's own competence boundaries as an assessment psychologist. I encourage you to consider these terms and your own assessment practice as you read on.

"Having the competence necessary for becoming culturally sensitive in assessment procedure is not an easy task" (Suzuki & Ponterotto, 2008, p. 16). Add to that actually utilizing and applying that sensitivity in a culturally responsive way and the challenge is further increased. The term cultural competence and its application to clinical practice, including assessment, are discussed by several authors (APA, 2002; Dana, 2005; Groth-Marnat, 2009; Sue & Sue, 2003; Suzuki & Ponterotto, 2008). Fisher-Borne, Cain, and Martin (2015) argued that "[m]any cultural competency frameworks fail to encourage critical self-awareness . . . these frameworks often fail to explore ways in which cultural values and structural forces shape not only client experiences and opportunities but also providers' approaches and capacity for care" (p. 169). Tervalon and Murray-Garcia (1998) introduced the concept of *cultural humility*, which takes into account the fluidity of culture. Several authors in the field of social work have critiqued the concept of cultural competency as offering too narrow a view and focus on practitioners learning about "others" (Fisher-Borne et al., 2015; Hook, 2014; Hook et al., 2013; Tervalon & Murray-Garcia, 1998). Instead, the term cultural humility offers "an alternative approach that focuses on knowledge of oneself in relation to others" (Fisher-Borne et al., 2015, p. 170). Elements of cultural humility include self-reflection and self-critique, learning from clients, and partnership building, as part of a life-long process (Chang, Simon, & Dong, 2012). Cultural humility is comprised of intrapersonal and interpersonal components (Hook et al., 2013). On the intrapersonal level, humble individuals have an accurate view of themselves. The interpersonal level is characterized by respect for others and a lack of superiority (Davis et al., 2011). In order to develop cultural humility, providers need to become more aware of their own cultural worldviews (Hook, 2014).

Hook (2014) emphasized the importance of self-awareness of one's own background and experiences. Furlong and Wight (2011) further discussed the importance of one's level of critical awareness in terms of cultural humility. They argued that acknowledging one's own cultural sense of self includes a "complex and dynamic interrogation of 'where I am coming from'—a critical dialogue entailing an engagement with one's social, cultural, ideological, and professional dimensions" (p. 50). The authors recognized that such a periodic dialogue might be uncomfortable (Furlong & Wight, 2011). Fisher-Borne et al. (2015) agreed that "cultural humility challenges us to ask difficult questions instead of reducing our clients to a set of norms" (p. 177). This expanded notion of humility is relevant to this chapter and the emphasis on critical self-reflection. Handler and Hilsenroth (1998) acknowledged how often literature has discussed countertransference issues and possible "acting out" behaviors in psychologists in a therapy setting, but not in the context of test administration, scoring, and interpretation. It seems that such countertransference issues could be directly related to cultural and self-awareness and the concept of cultural humility. The cases included in this chapter are intended to illustrate such issues.

Context and Purpose

The foundation for this chapter is based on one of the interpretive principles in the R-PAS manual (Meyer, Viglione, Mihura, Erard, & Erdberg, 2011). Meyer et al. (2011) recommended a combined person-focused and test-focused approach as a basis for interpretation when conducting personality assessment. They argued that "this approach allows us to formulate individually tailored, helpful, salient, and meaningful interpretations" (p. 318). They encourage psychologists interpreting test data to "focus on *this* particular person with *these* particular characteristics in *this* particular context and with *these* particular assessment questions and their implications" (p. 318). A similar approach can apply to the psychologist conducting the assessment. Considering the examiner's *particular* characteristics with a *particular* client and a *particular* assessment, would allow for individually tailored, helpful, salient, and meaningful reflections on our role as evaluators. Such reflections can assist when choosing to accept a certain assessment case as well as consider potential impact of various diversity factors on the multiple steps in the assessment process. More often than not, both clients and psychologists are more complicated than one or two diversity factors. I suggest that it is the *combination* of such factors that is the most relevant in a personality assessment case.

Certain client, examiner, or more importantly, the combination of such cultural characteristics' impact on the collaborative assessment relationship may be more or less influential depending on the context. Diversity factors must always be considered, but understanding where they fall on a continuum in terms of specific assessment goals and framework is helpful. In some cases, diversity factors or combination of factors would be so significant that a psychologist needs to consider their level of competence and appropriateness in accepting a case, thus practice humility. An example of this comes later in the chapter in the case of Dr. Davis and Raul. This type of recognition is the product of thoughtful and honest reflection, the importance of which is one of the goals in this chapter. That said, there are likely many cases where certain characteristics might not come to light until later on in the assessment process. Therefore, reflection and ethical considerations throughout the assessment process are necessary. Several hypothetical cases with some basis in reality are presented in this chapter. Some cases are more detailed, encompassing several steps in the assessment process, while others include only brief scenarios.

Of course, we have some resources about multicultural assessment (APA, 2002; Dana, 2005; Suzuki & Ponterotto, 2008) and, at least in theory, we know what we are supposed to do and not do. But what happens in reality? How much do we follow what we know (or are supposed to know)? How do we apply or not apply some of what has been researched and recommended? The cases below attempt to address exactly those sorts of dilemmas. Many experienced psychologists might dismiss certain scenarios as obvious or having simple and easily identifiable interventions and solutions, which is likely true when we are completely removed from the case. However, most of us can probably describe situations where a psychologist was working outside their competence and with limited humility, and perhaps that psychologist was us.

Consider a scenario where the client has a physical disability, such as a visual impairment. Under what circumstances would it be appropriate for a psychologist with no such assessment experience to accept such a case? What if the impairment is minimal and simple accommodations are easily obtained with no impact on standardized administration of typical measures? Would the type and severity of the visual impairment be sufficient factors in making a decision? What additional information would a psychologist need to consider in such a case? The main idea in such a situation is not necessarily to encourage or discourage a psychologist to take the case but, rather, to reflect and consider the various factors and characteristics that might be relevant. In addition to the factors mentioned above, and along with personal skills and expertise, the psychologist would need to consider their own diversity characteristics and how those might impact each step of the assessment process. The scenario above is one situation where ethnicity, the most widely written about diversity factor, might have little to no relevance.

With respect to test use, significant problems can occur when psychologists erroneously dismiss certain measures due to clients' diversity factors or utilize measures in which they are not well versed. In such cases, their choices, although considerate of the client, might negatively impact administration, and thus findings, without them even knowing it. Trying to accommodate clients in ways that break standardized administration and scoring is also problematic. Similarly, such positive intentions on behalf of the psychologist might end up being problematic when interpreting and integrating data and writing reports. Suzuki and Ponterotto (2008) mentioned several types of judgment errors, including overemphasizing or minimizing the cultural influence on clients' psychological presentation and idiographic experience. Dana (1998) stated that "bias appears in psychological assessment reports as stereotypy, caricature, pathologization, or failure to diagnose" (p. 325). Allyn (2012) discussed the importance of attitude and tone when writing reports including particular choice of words, terminology, and level of formality used.

My purpose here is not to increase assessment psychologists' self-doubts to the point we cannot do our work, stretch outside our comfort zone, or challenge ourselves. Rather, as noted previously, the goal is to think about and consider various factors that are not often covered in graduate school or any aspect of our training as assessment psychologists. Obviously, our training cannot address and prepare us for every assessment situation possible. However, literature has suggested that many aspects of diversity-related factors are not addressed in a systematic manner (Weiner & Greene, 2008), and thus warrant increased attention.

I can easily reflect on my experience and identify situations where my own demographics, or personal perspective of my cultural characteristics, were relevant to my assessment work. For example, during my training, I conducted assessments in a juvenile detention center. I recall being quite upset at the fact that the adolescents I met with, most of whom were members of ethnic minority groups, saw me as another White person who is part of the "system." At least that is what I assumed. This especially bothered me because I never even considered myself as "White" until I came to North America. I often found myself wishing I had more of an accent, thinking of ways to let them know that I was not American, not part of the system, and I could relate to them without judgment. On one occasion, I was so focused on this that I actually tuned out during an adolescent's detailed response to one of my clinical interview questions. I felt embarrassed and did not tell anyone about it. I did not ask the adolescent to repeat himself, and who knows what vital information I might have missed. I, of course, realized how ridiculous that was and that the focus should be on them and their needs rather than mine, but it was hard to let go. Over a decade later, when I returned to doing similar evaluations as a licensed psychologist, the same feelings and thoughts returned and still accompany me regularly. I think and hope that I manage to put them aside and focus on the individual across from (and sometimes next to) me. I still wonder how they view me as a person and whether it impacts their willingness to disclose and work with me, and thus the relevance to the validity of my findings and reports. It would be ignorant to think it does not, at least in some manner. Although reflecting on this issue does not necessarily resolve it, I do believe it increases my awareness and hopefully reduces potential negative impact. Moreover, it allows me to enter challenging dialogues with my clients and opens the door for important discussions.

So, ask yourself as you read the following cases: What issues do you foresee as challenging for yourself (not just for the examiner discussed)? What did the psychologist in the various scenarios do well and what could they have done better? How would you have handled the situation differently? When in your training or practice have you been exposed to such issues and how have you learned to handle them? Finally, what particular diversity factors do you tend to empathize with or ignore, and how relevant is it in the context of the personality assessments you conduct?

Illustrative Assessment Cases

Case 1: Dr. Edwards and John

Dr. Derek Edwards, a White, homosexual male, in his early 30s, from a large urban metropolitan background who has been surrounded by a liberal mindset growing up, secured a position as a psychologist at a community mental health center in another fairly large metropolitan city. As we would expect given that he has been licensed for only three years, Dr. Edwards still experiences some self-doubt and uncertainty in his assessment skills and as a psychologist, generally. John, his first assessment client in this setting is a White heterosexual male in his early 40s. Upon initial contact it seems the two have quite a bit in common: gender, ethnicity, academic experience, and even socioeconomic standing. John was seeking an assessment to better understand the periodic episodes of depression he has been experiencing, which have impacted his work and relationships. Dr. Edwards is a particularly compassionate individual and he is eager to use his therapeutic skills to establish a collaborative relationship and get the most out of the testing data to address his client's needs. As the clinical interview unfolds, Dr. Edwards slowly discovers that John has strong opinions and convictions that include very negative views about homosexuals, which he expresses frequently, at times using offensive language toward the LGBTQ community.

Dr. Edwards is unsure how to proceed. Should he confront and challenge John's views or ignore them? As John continues with his prejudicial comments, Dr. Edwards recognizes that some of his forgotten feelings from early adolescence are resurfacing. He recalls the teasing and bullying he endured throughout middle school that he worked so hard to overcome. He felt caught off guard. Nothing in his training prepared him for what he was experiencing with this client. Dr. Edwards was blindsided and did not necessarily consider how this might impact the assessment process. Who can blame him? Dr. Edwards has always been respectful of others' beliefs and opinions and he was not about to change that now. But he was irritated. He tried to put aside the negative feelings he was experiencing and decided to just administer, score, and interpret the measures he had chosen, just as he was trained.

As testing continues, Dr. Edwards struggles to balance his growing apprehension toward John with professional conduct and compassion. While sharing his prejudiced views with Dr. Edwards, John also gets tearful when talking about past events in his life that have caused him significant emotional pain. Dr. Edwards is conflicted about getting help with this case versus "toughing it out" on his own. He feels that because he has been licensed for a while, he needs to deal with such issues himself. Yet he periodically reflects on his strong emotions in sessions and potential implications on his administration of the various measures in his battery. He recalls being quite short with John when clarifying various items on the MMPI-2RF.

The last session included the Rorschach. Dr. Edwards has always appreciated the rich data he gathered via this measure but he is also challenged by it, plagued with worries about over- and under-clarifying responses. Dr. Edwards is quite consumed with such worries and seems to let go of any concerns regarding his now fairly deep resentment toward John. It is as if he has become completely "blind" to it. During administration, Dr. Edwards is focused on the clarification phase and feels he has done a pretty good job. He decides to consult with a colleague with respect to his scoring. His colleague asks about some of the cognitive codes Dr. Edwards assigned to quite a few of the responses. Upon re-examination of the client's responses, Dr. Edwards cannot defend his scores. He is confused, slightly embarrassed, and becomes somewhat angry as well. He wonders if perhaps he is not as competent as he thought he was. Oddly enough, Dr. Edwards has not considered the possibility that he assigned certain scores in a somewhat "punitive" way to John who has been unknowingly attacking that which Dr. Edwards has been passionately advocating for the past two decades or so.

Much has been written and discussed about working with a "resistant" client in a therapeutic setting, but what about working with a prejudiced client, specifically in an assessment setting? How do we as trained psychologists handle that situation? How could it potentially impact the assessment process? Dana (1998) noted that "there are profound differences in world views, life histories, health/illness beliefs, expectations for services, values, first languages, self-concept, and encounters with oppression" (p. 326). Hook (2014) noted that "practicing cultural humility can be difficult, especially in situations in which the client's worldview and goals are markedly discrepant from the worldview and goals of the therapist" (p. 279). Such discrepancies and differences need to be considered when we aim for CRA. If you were in Dr. Edwards' place, would you have chosen to address John's views in some manner? What additional diversity factors might have played a role in this case impacting Dr. Edwards' decisions?

Case 2: Dr. Zharkov and Andy

Dr. Anya Zharkov, a well-established psychologist, was born in the United States, but her parents were from Eastern Europe. They immigrated shortly before she was born. The family struggled financially while Dr. Zharkov was growing up, often relying on welfare and food stamps, and she worked extremely hard to pay for her education and establish her career. As a single mother of two, now grown, boys she continued to appreciate the power of money. She was assigned yet another assessment for juvenile probation. Andy, was a 17-year-old White male who was in custody for violating his probation. His prior offenses included breaking and entering and vandalism, both related to ongoing severe substance use. Dr. Zharkov has always been compassionate toward these teenagers who, more often than not, had a sad and chaotic upbringing filled with trauma and lack of positive role modeling.

Upon reviewing Andy's case records, Dr. Zharkov was surprised to learn that he was from an affluent family, growing up in an intact home where both parents were highly educated professionals. His father was the main provider and his mother a stay-at-home mother. According to records, Andy had the "best of everything" growing up. In early adolescence, he began using drugs with a few friends and that spiraled out of control into a severe addiction of hardcore substances. Dr. Zharkov struggled to understand Andy's choices considering all the resources available to him. Of course, she knew that simply growing up in a wealthy family did not guarantee a successful and positive lifestyle. She was intrigued to learn more about Andy and perhaps challenge some of what she recognized was stereotypical thinking on her part.

The first session with Andy included an in-depth clinical interview. He was forthcoming with information, but displayed what Dr. Zharkov considered as a sense of entitlement. As the interview continued, Dr. Zharkov sensed a familiar feeling seeping in but in an unfamiliar context. She was often angry at the circumstances that brought the teens she assessed into custody, but this was different. She felt angry *at* this teenager. He had everything, was privileged, and he threw it all away. Dr. Zharkov could not help but think of her two sons when they were that age. How humble and appreciative they were, hardworking, and focused! The session shifted into testing, and when Andy made some remarks and jokes about various items on the PAI-A, she just about had it with him. She forgot many of the other teens had done the same thing. Before she knew it, Dr. Zharkov found herself lecturing this adolescent about his choices and his views on life, and Andy quickly tuned her out. The self-report she scored later turned out to have high scores on indicators of validity. A collateral phone call with Andy's mother left her further conflicted. She felt compassion for his mother and yet also blamed her for what happened to Andy. Was it also possible she had strong personal feelings about, and toward, this woman who was quite privileged in many ways and reminded Dr. Zharkov of her personal trials in life?

When the time came for interpretation, integration, and report writing, Dr. Zharkov's challenge was to separate herself from the case. She had evaluated many adolescents and had always been proud of her level of knowledge, compassion, and professionalism. But in this case, she was disappointed in herself and somewhat ashamed, which did not improve with how she felt about Andy and the report-writing process. She felt embarrassed to consult with a colleague so late in the process. In the end, she believed that she was able to produce a report that was not reflective of her emotional state and negative feelings about Andy. However, the report also did not entirely reflect Andy's unique situation and needs including considering any underlying mental health or sense of self issues leading to his drug use. At that point, Dr. Zharkov just wanted to complete this case and move on. A few weeks later, she continued to dwell on her work with Andy. She was still puzzled as to why or how that had happened. How could she, a seasoned, professional, compassionate psychologist allow her feelings to get in the way in this manner?

Using or keeping at bay personal narratives as well as emotions is something we somehow learn to do as part of training. But how realistic or problematic is it to keep such information outside of our decision-making process when such information includes particular and perhaps vital diversity factors to consider for assessment cases? Schafer recognized that "each of us brings a good deal of personal baggage to the testing session" (as cited in Handler & Hilsenroth, 1998, p. 123). Dana (1998) suggested that "[m]any assessors have learned an impersonal behavior-cognitive service delivery stance that diminishes human complexity in order to control the response process and provide more reliable sources of data" (p. 326). To be meaningful, responsible, and ethical, our work must keep human complexity in the assessment interaction process, which means that we must acknowledge our "baggage."

Case 3: Laura, Dr. Hill, and Rachel

Laura has always been an ambitious individual and her pursuit of a doctorate degree in clinical psychology was no surprise to anyone who knew her. What was a surprise, at least to Laura, was her experience as a pre-doctoral intern at a prestigious outpatient assessment clinic. Laura has a medical condition that somewhat limits her fine motor skills and has a slight impact on her expressive speech. In her application, Laura provided information about her condition and accommodations she utilized for assessments in her previous training placements. Although it was visible, the nature of her disability was not completely clear to an observer. Even though her supervisor, Dr. Hill, did not express concern directly about her ability to conduct personality assessments, Laura could not help but get the sense she had some.

During the initial two weeks of training activities, her supervisor often paired her with a fellow intern. This was not a problem, but none of the other interns were paired. In individual supervision, Laura felt that her supervisor reviewed basic components of assessment and various measures quite slowly as if she thought Laura might have some sort of a cognitive delay. It so happens that Laura is quite bright and was an honor student throughout her academic career. Her disability had no relevance whatsoever to her intelligence and comprehension capacity. Laura was insulted. But, this was her supervisor and this internship, which she worked so hard to get, was a critical part of her training and future plans. So she was respectful and compliant in the beginning. She decided that if things continued in this manner, she would address it with the supervisor directly.

Eventually, she was assigned an assessment case (later than her fellow interns). Her new client, Rachel, was a well-educated White woman in her early 40s seeking clarity regarding her depressive symptoms. It seemed to be a fairly straightforward case and cases assigned to Laura's fellow interns appeared to be more complex. Laura's supervisor asked that she video record all of her sessions as part of her training, which was also fine. Interestingly, Laura learned that her peers were instructed to video record one session of their choice.

At the first session, Laura introduced herself, explained that she was working under supervision and then described the assessment process. Rachel asked if she could contact the supervisor if she had any questions. Laura said yes, although she clarified that she was available to address any questions as well. Rachel politely thanked her and they proceeded with the clinical interview. Laura was a skilled clinician, but the past few weeks of training and supervision took a toll. She felt tense and her speech impediment was more pronounced than usual. Regardless, Laura thought that she established rapport and gathered helpful information about her client. Rachel also seemed pleased about the collaborative approach Laura described and she came up with a couple of insightful assessment questions.

At the second session, which entailed testing, Dr. Hill showed up to observe. Unbeknown to Laura, she had communicated with the client prior to the session. After Laura clearly explained the directions, Rachel completed the MCMI-III in silence. Following this, Laura used her laptop to record Rachel's TAT stories because handwriting in a timely manner was a particular challenge for her. She was not sure if Dr. Hill had actually rolled her eyes or it was just her imagination when she asked the client to slow down or repeat herself so she could type everything.

The Rorschach was planned for the third session. The day before, Dr. Hill suggested it might be better if she did the administration given that Laura had only done a handful of them previously. Laura was not sure how to respond. Her voice cracked as she tried to speak. Perhaps it was related to her disability or maybe her emotional state at that moment ... probably both. Laura then raised her voice, which was completely out of character. She told her supervisor that she chose this particular internship so she could enhance her assessment skills and that she did not feel that she was given a fair opportunity thus far. Dr. Hill looked surprised, but Laura continued. She expressed her frustration that the supervisor's bias and lack of confidence in her negatively impacted her relationship with the client, both directly and indirectly, calling into question the entire assessment process. Dr. Hill asked for an example and Laura provided a number of them without hesitation. Dr. Hill replied that maybe it would be best if they postponed the Rorschach and meet again tomorrow to discuss this matter further along with the program director. The next day, Laura was told that she was removed from the case due to her "emotional outburst" in supervision and statements about discriminatory treatment that needed to be addressed. One of her fellow interns was assigned to complete the case. The client would be told that "something came up" and that Laura would not be seeing the case through.

What is the role of the supervisor when it comes to CRA? What does CRA supervision look like? Supervision support can have a tremendous impact on the confidence of an assessment psychologist in training and thus the assessment itself. Supervisors are supposed to question supervisees' decisions and skills, but what happens when they question those for the wrong reasons?

Case 4: Dr. Rodriguez & Carl

Dr. Rosa Rodriguez was a newly licensed psychologist who was excited to begin her private practice. She completed her doctorate degree and training in the United States, but English was her second language. She was well aware of her accent and the important role that played in many of the assessments she completed during her training, especially when explaining directions and with certain measures or tasks (e.g., Vocabulary and Digit Span). She often found that slowing down when speaking helped with clarity. Dr. Rodriguez was trained in a collaborative therapeutic model of assessment and had always received high praise from her supervisors for her skills. Her first client as a private practitioner was an older African American man from a lower socioeconomic status working toward his GED. He was twice divorced and a father of three grown children. Dr. Rodriguez felt confident because she had worked with diverse clientele during her internship and post doc and had several courses about multicultural psychotherapy. Carl was seeking an assessment due to periodic anxiety attacks and increasingly angry responses toward others around him that recently jeopardized his position as a school custodian. In the first session, Dr. Rodriguez worked with Carl to reframe and clarify his assessment goals into meaningful questions, just as she had learned.

When selecting measures, she thoughtfully considered current research and consulted with colleagues. Dr. Rodriguez felt that testing went smoothly. She explained the purpose of the measures used, checked in with Carl throughout, and consulted with a previous supervisor as needed. During the interview and testing, Dr. Rodriguez often referenced her doctoral training experience. On some level, she seemed to know that she was trying to "prove" herself to both Carl and herself to reassure herself that she was ready for independent practice. By the end of testing, Dr. Rodriguez felt that she really understood Carl and that he appreciated her care. When interpreting testing data, Dr. Rodriguez was considerate of the norms available and those lacking. She integrated findings with Carl's particular background to individualize the written report. She could not wait to have the feedback session and believed most of what she had to say would not be too unexpected to Carl.

As the feedback session began, Dr. Rodriguez sensed that Carl seemed irritated, but figured that he was just a bit nervous. But she continued as she had planned the day before. When Carl still did not respond much, she decided to stop and check in with him. She did not expect his response; Carl was upset, even angry. He felt that she was overly focused on his ethnicity and socioeconomic status. He felt that Dr. Rodriguez thought she was "better than him" because he barely had a GED and she kept talking about her advanced degree and training. He also felt that she was "talking down to [him]" often speaking slowly "as if [he] was dumb." Dr. Rodriguez was shocked. She felt tears well in the corner of her eyes and did everything she could to keep it together. She could not figure out what went wrong and how the two of them could have experienced things so differently.

Have you ever had an assessment case where you felt really good and so confident about your work? Perhaps you were pleased with how collaborative and therapeutic you were throughout testing and that your writing might even be a published model for an individualized and meaningful report, and then discovered that your client did not have the same experience at all. How does one handle such a situation and learn from it for future cases? Can such a scenario and relationship with the client be "repaired?" How did you feel about the discrepancy between Dr. Rodriguez's view of the assessment relationship and Carl's?

Case 5: Dr. Jones and Justin

Dr. Raymond Jones has always been known as "one of the nicest guys around." His clinical practice primarily included therapy work, but he took on an assessment case fairly regularly. As an African American man in his late 40s, he felt he was particularly sensitive to cultural diversity issues and individual differences. He had amassed an impressive collection of literature about multicultural issues in psychology. The majority of his clients were either African American or Hispanic, mostly due to the location of his office but also his reputation as someone knowledgeable with minority groups. Therefore, Dr. Jones was quite pleased when he got a call from Justin, an Asian American client seeking an assessment. Although he was not directly experienced with this "population," Dr. Jones felt confident and well prepared. Prior to the first session with Justin, Dr. Jones reviewed several chapters and articles about working with Asian Americans in therapy. Throughout the assessment process, he referred back to the research he had readily available.

Dr. Jones learned that Justin was born in the United States, but his family was originally from Vietnam. He had attended prestigious schools over the years and was an average student. His main concern included limited meaningful interpersonal relationships with family members and in general. Justin wanted to understand some underlying contributing factors and possible interventions. Dr. Jones carefully selected a battery of tests and was cautious about limited norms available for Asian Americans. He frequently checked with the various resources he had about specific issues to consider with this ethnic group. He also felt that his personal awareness of discrimination against ethnic minorities in the United States would be of benefit in this case.

At the feedback session, Dr. Jones diligently presented assessment findings referencing evidenced-based interpretations in commonly used psychology texts. In fact, Dr. Jones went above and beyond incorporating well-established understanding of Asian American cultural values including a collectivistic orientation, the role of family hierarchy, an emphasis on education and excellence, and particular importance of parenting style (Sue & Sue, 2003), as related to Justin's problematic interpersonal relationship issues. When Dr. Jones asked Justin how the presented information fit with his experience, Justin did not hold back. In what sounded like a resentful tone, Justin reminded Dr. Jones that although he is of Asian American descent and his great grandparents immigrated from a small village in Vietnam, his family has been in the United States for four generations, residing in a large city, and no one in their family even speaks Vietnamese. Justin went on to emphasize that although he attended prestigious private schools, they were actually quite diverse and the only marginalization and oppression he felt were due to his average grades. He talked about how his parents could not have been more Westernized in their parenting approach and thus, he was quite puzzled about Dr. Jones's interpretations regarding the significant impact of coming from a homogeneous culture, and his "fluid self as becoming" viewpoints and relevance to his experience. Justin said he wished Dr. Jones had asked more about such things rather than assume.

Rogler, Malgady, Costantino, and Blumenthal (1987) suggested that "[w]ithout an individualized approach to culturally sensitive assessment and diagnosis, the unsuspecting clinician can easily be led down the proverbial well-intentioned pavement of the path to hell—cultural sensitivity is not stereotypy" (p. 121). Fisher-Borne et. al. (2015) advocated that "a focus solely on race and/or ethnicity often ignores disparities that exist in regards to other aspects of identity" (p. 170). Keeping that in mind, let us consider Dr. Jones, the well-meaning psychologist who is familiar with multiculturalism literature and makes great efforts to incorporate such information into his assessment practice. When does what seems to be an admirable, ethical, and helpful approach become not much more than a stereotype and narrow view of a client? Had Dr. Jones practiced cultural humility in this case? Would that have made a difference?

Case 6: Dr. Davis and Raul

Dr. Norm Davis was a seasoned psychologist, who has conducted, taught, and supervised personality assessments for over 25 years. He was well published and had earned advanced credentials in the field of assessment. Therefore, Dr. Davis did not shy away from complex assessment cases that he felt challenged his skills. A colleague of his called and asked if Dr. Davis could take on a unique and complicated case. The client, named Raul, was a 20-year-old male who was in a serious accident where he suffered a mild head injury as well as severe burns to several parts of his body. Raul was admitted to a local hospital a few months prior. It so happened that he was from a small and fairly poor town in South America where a particular dialect of Spanish was spoken, and his English was quite limited. His parents, who resided abroad were only reached a few days prior and could not afford to make the trip to the United States. Raul was on a trip with a friend, first time away from his home, when the accident occurred. His friend was assisting with translation because his English was slightly better. The physicians at the hospital were concerned about Raul's progress, even though medically he was improving and their interventions were effective. Although they suspected depression, which was highly likely and even expected considering the circumstances, they were also concerned about his thought process and felt they needed a greater understanding of underlying contributing factors to some of his odd reactions to those around him. His friend mentioned that Raul was always known as a bit "weird" back home, but harmless. The decision was made to conduct a personality assessment and perhaps shed some light on his needs, including possible recommendations for psychiatric medications.

Dr. Davis was well aware of the multiple variables and factors that complicated this case and that would likely impact the assessment every step of the way. He decided to at least meet Raul before making a determination. Almost as soon as he began the assessment, Dr. Davis stopped. He realized the complicating diversity factors described along with other variables for this case were simply overwhelming. Among the multiple other issues, he recognized that he would not be able to administer most measures in anywhere near a standardized manner due to the language and translation barriers, as well as physical issues related to Raul's injury. Dr. Davis realized that without some background information aside from his friend's recollection, any findings would be limited at best and could potentially be more harmful than helpful. Dr. Davis felt terrible. He offered to try to help find another psychologist, but given the time constraints of a short inpatient stay for an uninsured patient, there would not be opportunity for an evaluation to help the medical team. Much to the consternation of the physicians and Dr. Davis's colleague who referred him, discharge planning began without valuable information related to Raul's psychological functioning. It was unlikely that Dr. Davis would be consulted again by that particular hospital team any time soon.

Some psychologists might argue that regardless of such factors, we could still "do some good" with an assessment, particularly when using a collaborative or therapeutic approach, and there is not always a need to rely on specific measures. But what if diversity factors get in the way of establishing and following through with such an approach? If the process of forming meaningful questions together is jeopardized or compromised, is it ethical to proceed? Is it about our egos or in our client's best interest? Finn (2007) stated: "If a client's full cooperation and motivation cannot be gained during an assessment … perhaps we should think twice about whether it's appropriate to conduct the assessment at all" (p. 63).

Although Finn was writing about defensive clients' protocols, this type of thinking can be quite relevant to conducting CRAs and considering diversity factors in this respect. Is it possible that a *challenge* is not always the appropriate term and regardless of how competent and proficient and even advanced an assessment psychologist is, perhaps certain cases are simply beyond their scope? Most of us would probably say yes, of course it is possible. But what about such a psychologist not recognizing that when taking on such a case? Is that a possibility?

Reflections and Discussion

Suzuki and Ponterotto (2008) argued that: "Culture exerts a powerful but often overlooked or misunderstood influence on psychological assessment" (p. 25). Keeping that in mind, what do we as psychologists, or most of the psychologists portrayed in these cases, have in common? What are the factors that at times lead us to minimize and perhaps even blindly ignore diversity issues during an assessment case, whether clients' or our own? There are several possible reasons for this. It is very likely that our natural desire to help others is a key component. It is also possible that we like to challenge ourselves and appear competent to ourselves and others. Finally, perhaps we think that if we do not take the case someone even less qualified might, and that would be worse. It sounds a bit arrogant and perhaps it is, but there is some truth to that as well. Even so, it certainly is not a good enough reason to accept a case.

Finn (2007) reminds us of the fascinating fact that most psychologists "are not great at asking for help" and "that many of us will wait until we are completely stumped, confused or exasperated by a client until we ask for a consultation from a colleague" (p.100). Schafer (as cited in Handler & Hilsenroth, 1998) discussed several characteristics or descriptors of assessors, a couple of which seem most relevant here: "The examiner must seem like an *oracle* to test takers, with the ability to draw momentous and portentous inferences from signs or symbols;" and "In agreeing to help test takers with their problems and dilemmas, the examiner takes on a *saintly* aspect" (p. 121). Who does not want to be considered as an oracle or have saintly aspects?

Regardless of the reasons and our difficulty asking for help, consultation would likely have been helpful in each of the cases described. At the very least, consultation might have simply allowed the assessor necessary space to vent frustration or conflicts and hopefully reduce potential impact of those on the assessment. Consultation might have also helped identify issues and develop ways to address them. Finally, consultation could have led to removing oneself from the case if this was determined to be the ethical and most appropriate course of action and in the best interest of the client. The EBP Task Force (APA, 2005) supports this notion with the emphasis that "consultation for the psychologist is a means to monitor, and correct if necessary, cognitive and affective biases" (p. 13). In each case it was not just one or two or even three diversity factors to consider with respect to the assessor, client, or the match. Instead, it was a collection of factors and the interaction of such factors including one's personal experiences in general that produced a compounded effect.

As I was writing this chapter, I was teaching an assessment course where students conduct clinical psychological assessments with me as supervisor. Expectedly, there was some pressure to get cases assigned. One potential case entailed an individual with a significant trauma history who spoke limited English. This person has been waiting for an assessment for a while and was eager to participate. There was talk of having another student, not in the class and without assessment training, assist with the case as she spoke the client's native language. I will practice humility here and fully admit the main reason I said "no" with limited uncertainty was because I was immersed at the time with these cases. I suspect that I might have been pulled differently otherwise. I would have wanted to help and maintain the relationship with the particular referral source. I would have been empathic to the client and possibly talked myself into dangerously minimizing the risks and concerns for the client's best interest as well as the student's and finally myself as supervisor. By the way, although I felt good and proud of this decision, a few days later, I found myself thinking about it and wondering "what if?"

Implications for the Future

As noted previously, it is impossible to cover everything or even near that in training. But even one article or chapter discussing this, or an instructor or supervisor sharing a case, showing humility in the face of diversity, would make some positive impact. Regardless of whether they indeed acted in a humble and culturally responsive manner or not, the sheer exposure would likely be valuable. Handler and Hilsenroth (1998) proposed that "[c]onsiderable empirical evidence supports the importance of the examiner's personality on professional performance" (p. 123). Dana (1998) argued that we cannot ignore the fact that "[e]ach of us has a cultural self that provides a contextual reality for our life experiences" (p. 326). Dana (2005) further explained that the development of the cultural self-system is important in the assessment context. I will only add that it is important to consider the cultural self of both client and assessor to better understand the relationship dynamic within the assessment process. Traditional assessments have not focused on relationships, thus the idea of cultural responsiveness was not much of a concern. The assessing psychologist was often discouraged from showing humility and instead considered as an expert gathering information from a client to better inform others about him or her (Finn, 2007; Fischer, 2000). However, as we thankfully continue to shift toward a more collaborative, individualized, and therapeutic assessment model, these issues are recognized to be just as critical as the testing data we collect.

Suzuki and Ponterotto (2008) concluded that "[p]sychological assessment is a complex decision-making process, influenced by subtle sociopsychological variables often not accounted for in the process" (p. 24). That much was illustrated by the cases included in this chapter. So how do we blend competency, awareness, and humility in the process of personality assessment? The other chapters in this book provide much needed and valuable information and insight to at least begin the journey to answers. In this chapter, I offer a few recommendations:

- Explore and acknowledge the various diversity aspects all participants bring to assessment sessions.
- Try to determine how a meaningful and productive assessment relationship can be developed.
- Overcome shame or embarrassment and talk to someone (something we expect our clients to do).
- Use critical self-reflection including questions such as: "What might be triggering for you?" "How will you know that you are in too deep?" "Who would you call or consult with about this?"
- Finally, consider your level of cultural sensitivity, awareness, competence, and responsiveness and incorporate humility into assessment work. The APA EBP Task Force (2005) also includes the importance of continual self-reflection and acquiring skills in the process of competency and humility.

Hopefully the cases included in this chapter illustrated the importance of an individualized, collaborative, and culturally informed approach to assessment. Culturally responsive psychological assessment is comprised of clinical assessment competence as well as cultural humility. The latter requires that "individuals continually engage in self-reflection and self-critique" (Tervalon & Murray-Garcia, 1998, p. 118). It would take increased efforts and a shift in thinking throughout assessment training and practice to further incorporate and apply such concepts to the benefit of assessment clients. In addition to ongoing learning and critical self-reflection, Fisher-Borne et al. (2015) noted a sense of accountability as part of humility. They suggested several essential questions for critical self-reflection. Such questions included: "What are my cultural identities? How do my cultural identities shape my worldview? How does my own background help or hinder my connection to clients? What are my initial reactions to clients, specifically those who are culturally different from me? What do I learn about myself through listening to clients who are different from me?" (Fisher-Borne et al., 2015, p. 176). These questions can be adjusted specifically for assessment and incorporated into assessment coursework and field training as well as in ongoing practice. These questions are similar to those asked throughout the chapter and can help increase one's sense of humility and related accountability. Hook et al. (2013) explained the paradoxical impact of cultural humility and that providers "who are culturally humble not only strive to be effective but also cultivate a growing awareness that they are inevitably limited in their knowledge and understanding of a client's cultural background, which motivates them to interpersonally attune themselves to the client in a quest to understand the individual client's cultural background and experience" (p. 354). Perhaps we can all take a personal journey to better understand the various aspects of ourselves that led us to where we are today and, most importantly, the potential relevance and impact of such aspects to our assessment clients and our work.

References

Allyn, J. B. (2012). *Writing to clients and referring professionals about psychological assessment results: A handbook of style and grammar*. New York: Routledge.

American Psychological Association (APA). (2002). Ethical principles of psychologists and code of conduct. *American Psychologist, 57*, 1060–1073.

American Psychological Association. (2005). *Report of the 2005 Presidential Task Force on Evidence-Based Practice*. Washington, DC: American Psychological Association. Retrieved from: www.apa.org/practice/resources/evidence/evidence-based-report.pdf

American Psychological Association. (2006). *Final Report of the 2006 Task Force on the Assessment of Competence in Professional*. Washington, DC: American Psychological Association. Retrieved from: www.apa.org/ed/resources/competency-revised.pdf

Chang, E., Simon, M., & Dong, X. (2012). Integrating cultural humility into health care professional education and training. *Advances in Health Sciences Education, 17*(2), 269–278. doi: 10.1007/s10459-010-9264-1

Dana, R. H. (1998). Personality assessment and the cultural self: Emic and etic contexts as learning resources. In L. Handler & M. J. Hilsenroth (Eds.), *Teaching and learning personality assessment* (PP. 325–346). New York: Routledge.

Dana, R. H. (2005). *Multicultural assessment: Principles, applications, and examples*. Mahwah, NJ: Lawrence Erlbaum Associates.

Davis, D. E., Hook, J. N., Worthington, E. L. Jr., Van Tongeren, D. R., Gartner, A. L., Jennings, D. J. II., & Emmons, R. A. (2011). Relational humility: Conceptualizing and measuring humility as a personality judgment. *Journal of Personality Assessment, 93*, 225–234. doi: 10.1081/00223891.2011.558871

Finn, S. E. (2007). *In our clients' shoes: Theory and techniques of Therapeutic Assessment*. Mahwah, NJ: Erlbaum.

Fischer, C.T. (2000). Collaborative, individualized assessment. *Journal of Personality Assessment*, 74(1), 2–14.

Fisher-Borne, M., Cain, J. M., & Martin, S. L. (2015). From mastery to accountability: Cultural humility as an alternative to cultural competence. *Social Work Education, 34*(2), 165–181. doi: http://dx.doi.org/10.1080/02615479.2014.977244

Furlong, M., & Wight, J. (2011). Promoting "critical awareness" and critiquing "cultural competence": Towards disrupting received professional knowledges. *Australian Social Work, 64*(1), 38–54. doi: 10.1080/0312407X.2010.537352

Groth-Marnat, G. (2009). *Handbook of psychological assessment* (5th ed.). New York: Wiley.

Handler, L., & Hilsenroth, M. (1998). *Teaching and learning personality assessment*. New York: Routledge.

Hook, J. N. (2014). Engaging clients with cultural humility. *Journal of Psychology and Christianity, 33*(3), 277–280.

Hook, J. N., Davis, D. E., Owen, J., Worthington, E. J., & Utsey, S. O. (2013). Cultural humility: Measuring openness to culturally diverse clients. *Journal of Counseling Psychology, 60*(3), 353–366. doi: 10.1037/a0032595

Krishnamurthy, R., VandeCreek, L., Kaslow, N. J., Tazeau, Y. N., Miville, M. L., Kerns, R., et al. (2004). Achieving competency in psychological assessment: Directions for education and training. *Journal of Clinical Psychology, 60*(7), 725–739.

Meyer, G. J., Viglione, D. J., Mihura, J. L., Erard, R. E., & Erdberg, P. (2011). Rorschach performance assessment system: Administration, coding, interpretation, and technical manual. Toledo, OH: Rorschach Performance Assessment System, LLC.

Montenegro, E., & Jankowski, N. A. (2017, January). Equity and assessment: Moving towards culturally responsive assessment (Occasional Paper No. 29). Urbana, IL: University of Illinois and Indiana University, National Institute for Learning Outcomes Assessment (NILOA).

Rogler, L. H., Malgady, R. G., Costantino, G., & Blumenthal, R. (1987). What do culturally sensitive mental health services mean? The case of Hispanics. *American Psychologist, 42*(6), 565–570.

Sue, D. W., & Sue, D. (2003). *Counseling the culturally diverse: Theory and practice* (4th ed.). Hoboken, NJ: John Wiley & Sons.

Sue, S. (2006). Cultural competency: From philosophy to research and practice. *Journal of Community Psychology, 34*(2), 237–245.

Suzuki, L., & Ponterotto, J. G. (Eds.) (2008). *Handbook of multicultural assessment: Clinical, psychological, and educational applications*. San Francisco, CA: Wiley & Sons.

Tervalon, M., & Murray-Garcia, J. (1998). Cultural humility versus cultural competence: A critical distinction in defining physician training outcomes in multicultural education. *Journal of Health Care for the Poor and Underserved, 9*, 117–125.

Weiner, I., & Greene, R. (2008). *Handbook of personality assessment*. Hoboken, NJ: Wiley.

PART IV

Professional Contexts

CHAPTER 17

Writing for an N of 1: Cultural Competence in Personality Assessment Report Writing

Collette Chapman-Hilliard, Shannon McClain, Alissa Sherry, Susan Broyles, and Stacey Jackson

In a sense, personality assessment (PA) is akin to a mixed methods research study with an N of 1, and should incorporate a balance of both quantitative and qualitative approaches. However, such an approach is much easier conceptually discussed than employed in practice. In fact, a great challenge exists for assessors in determining *how* to convey findings or results in a PA report using both objective and subjective data. PAs yield, oftentimes, deeply personal information about one's cognitive, affective, and behavioral characteristics (Ownby, 2009). This process, consequently, from initial client meeting to the assessor completing a final written report, is highly complex and involves the consideration of multiple proximal and distal variables. A client's cultural context is one such variable that might appear either proximal or distal contingent upon the individual's lived experiences and interactions within the assessment context.

With increasing necessity for PAs to serve as the evidence base for intervention as well as mounting pressures from managed care systems for efficient and cost-effective services, it is not uncommon for an assessor to spend less time with clients, ask fewer questions, and write more concise, sometimes "cookie cutter" reports. As a result, assessors might feel they do not have the time to address proximal and distal cultural issues, and may therefore tell themselves these issues are irrelevant or secondary to the task at hand. Although this sentiment might be common, it could not be farther from the truth. Assessors have an ethical duty to conduct culturally competent assessments. While the American Psychological Association has reinforced the importance of multicultural competence and diversity-sensitive work via publications such as *Ethical Principles of Psychologists and Code of Conduct* (APA, 2002) and *Guidelines for Providers of Psychological Services to Ethnic, Linguistic, and Culturally Diverse Populations* (APA, 1993), there has been less focus on report writing and the specific structure of a written report that highlights the significance of culture. For the purpose of this chapter, *structure* is broadly defined as the arrangement and construction of assessment data (i.e., subjective and objective sources of clinical information) with attention to cultural contexts. Thus, as assessors seek to construct written reports that attend to the cultural dynamics present in the assessment context and optimally respond to a referral question(s), it is imperative for them to determine: (a) the purpose of a PA report, (b) for whom the PA report is written, (c) the role of the assessor in the PA report-writing process, and (d) the format of the PA report.

For What Reason?

PAs are required to answer questions regarding differential diagnosis, to inform and monitor psychological/psychiatric treatment, or to identify the need for services within an educational setting (Meyer et al., 2001; Weiner & Greene, 2011). Oftentimes the reason for a PA is defined by a referral question or questions. These questions represent one of the most discernable guides available for readers of PAs to determine the reason a report has been written. Referral questions are significant in determining the type of personality measures that will be administered and consequently these measures influence the type and quality of the information included in a written report. Generally speaking, a well-written assessment report clearly links referral questions with answers to those referral questions (Groth-Marnat, 2009). However, how to write a report that adequately addresses cultural dynamics germane to a given referral question is less clear, particularly when referral questions for PAs often fail to inquire about the role of culture to understand a client's clinical picture. Examples of common referral questions for PAs may include: *Is there a presence of cognitive impairment or a thought disorder? What is the quality and extent of depression, anxiety, or trauma for a client? What is the predicted responsiveness to treatment?* While referral questions, like the aforementioned, from which most assessors develop their assessment batteries and subsequently write their reports, are necessary to support clients' psychological health, such questions often lack a focus on cultural experiences or narratives. Consequently, in culturally competent PA report writing great importance must be placed on how the written document links the answers to referral questions with clients' cultural contexts. Given that the written results of most PA reports are used to communicate information about a client's mental health and prognosis, two areas—clinical diagnosis and treatment considerations—are of particular concern in considering cultural competence and *for what reason* a report is written.

Chief among the information communicated in a PA report is that of clinical diagnosis. The diagnostic process involves the collection of data from various sources including test scores, interview responses, and the assessor's impressions. Historically, many culturally diverse group members have been marginalized and overly pathologized in the diagnostic process (Escobar, 2012; Whaley, 1997) due to cultural bias in assessment administration (e.g., assessor bias) and in assessment measures (Monnot, Quirk, Hoerger, & Brewer, 2009). In particular, the victimization of culturally diverse groups through the use of measures standardized on homogeneous, White, middle-upper-class Americans is well-documented in the literature (Guthrie, 2004). Such measures can yield findings that suggest racially or culturally diverse individuals are deviant or dysfunctional when compared to majority culture groups. The Minnesota Multiphasic Personality Inventory, 2nd edition (MMPI-2), for example, is among the most widely and routinely used PAs to make important diagnostic decisions, and has been found to demonstrate differences in the clinical significance of symptoms by race and ethnicity. Among clinical populations, the MMPI-2 appears to differentially and less accurately predict psychiatric disorders among African American men as compared to White American men (Monnot et al., 2009). In another study, also using the MMPI-2, Tsai and Pike (2000) found that less acculturated Asian American students (e.g., resided in the U.S. less than five years) scored higher on clinical scales such as Scale 1 (Hypochondriasis; Hs), Scale 5 (Masculinity-Femininity; Mf) and Scale 8 (Schizophrenia; Sc) when compared to their White counterparts. As with objective PAs, scholars have also cited challenges with performance-based PAs (i.e., Rorschach) in terms of attention to cultural diversity and possible bias in assessment instruments (Allen & Dana, 2004; Wood & Lilienfeld, 1999).

Extending these research findings to the report-writing context, assessors should keep in mind alternative or additive cultural explanations of assessment results as they respond to referral questions and provide information about diagnoses. Consider as an illustration elevated Scale 8 (Sc) scores on the MMPI-2 and content on the Rorschach suggesting detachment in a client who recently immigrated to the U.S. At first glance, these data might suggest a personality profile demonstrative of confusion, anxiety, emotional instability, and poor interpersonal skills. However, considering these data alongside the client's cultural narrative an alternative explanation is possible; could it be that the assessment data reflect the feelings of a newly immigrated person? Certainly, it is likely that an individual who recently immigrated to a new place would experience feelings of confusion, uncertainty, isolation, and changing emotions, a pattern sometimes discussed as *culture shock* (Whaley, 1998). Hence, culturally competent PA report writing requires consideration of cultural narratives as well as the possibility of more serious pathology when interpreting and documenting findings from assessment measures to support diagnoses.

In addition to grounding PA findings within cultural contexts, assessors must give the same consideration to utilizing and integrating information from the *Diagnostic and Statistics Manual for Mental Disorders* (DSM) into PA reports. Despite a long history of controversy about diagnostic categories in psychology, particularly as discussed in the DSM, these categories work rather well when they are appropriately applied to the persons for whom they were designed—persons with Western values and predominantly privileged identity statuses. The further a person diverges from this type of identity, the less diagnostic labels can be applied without excessively pathologizing and fundamentally misrepresenting clients' experiences. Take for instance psychosis-related symptomatology; some symptoms that would indicate delusions according to conventional criteria might be considered normative for certain cultural groups. For bereaved people from certain Southeast Asian and Native American cultures, seeing or hearing the voices of deceased loved ones might be a normal experience and not indicative of psychopathology (Carpenter-Song, Schwallie, & Longhofer, 2008).

Beyond documenting clinical diagnoses in a written report, another significant reason PA reports are written is to provide treatment recommendations. It is largely the work of the assessor to develop treatment recommendations within an appropriate cultural context. In outlining guidelines for diagnostic assessment and treatment planning, Dadlani, Overtree, and Perry-Jenkins (2012) posit that all clients (and assessors) exist within a particular cultural context that must be carefully examined in the assessment process. Before rendering any recommendation, assessors are encouraged to explore carefully cultural explanations for a client's condition. Assessors might inquire about areas such as: symptom expression (e.g., somatic complaints, nervios or nerves, paranoia, etc.), specific cultural meanings associated with symptom expression, and local diagnostic or non-Western categorizations of symptomatology (Allen, 2002; American Psychiatric Association, 2013). These questions provide local or culturally specific norms and patterns of distress that can either qualify standardized test interpretations or provide a pathway for culture-centered treatment recommendations (Allen, 2002).

To illustrate the aforementioned points, consider the hypothetical case of a 35-year-old, second-generation, unemployed, and widowed woman living with her elderly parents, who was referred for an assessment for chronic difficulties in social relationships and mood symptoms. The personality testing revealed intrapsychic conflicts about separation, an internalizing coping style, and perfectionism—a personality profile upon initial review that might lead an assessor to propose a treatment recommendation suggesting intensive individual insight-oriented therapy. However, from the purview of culturally competent PA report writing, this recommendation is incomplete; there is room to explore further the role of cultural context to determine more comprehensive treatment recommendations. With the current example, the treatment recommendation fails to take into account, for instance, the client's reasons for living with her parents as an adult and her second-generation status (e.g., the client's parents were born outside of the U.S. and the client was born in the U.S.). There is potential for each of these pieces of information to help contextualize her test results and provide more meaningful treatment recommendations. Perhaps, within the client's family of origin and native religious traditions, it is customary for adult daughters to care for their parents or live with their parents if not living with a husband. Thus, a more comprehensive treatment recommendation might include insight-oriented therapy that addresses the client's experience of negotiating Western and non-Western values, family sessions to address potential separation concerns, and culture-specific consultations for the therapist to explore effective non-Western therapeutic techniques.

Additionally, the DSM-5 (American Psychiatric Association, 2013) provides another helpful tool for assessors to utilize in gathering cultural data to support the diagnostic process and treatment planning. The DSM-5's *Cultural Formulation Interview* (CFI) for clinicians and assessors aids in the process of gathering thorough information about clients' cultural contexts. The CFI allows assessors to gather information about cultural identity, cultural explanations of a client's condition, cultural factors related to a client's environment, and cultural influences relevant to the client–assessor relationship. The utility of the CFI can be seen in treatment recommendations that include attention to concepts such as racial and ethnic identity, gender identity, religiosity and spirituality, and cultural mistrust, to name a few. A clinical case documented by Newhill (1990) illustrates the utility of cultural information in discerning treatment recommendations. In this case example, a man of African descent presented with beliefs that his wife was unfaithful despite no evidence for it, and beliefs that others were conspiring against him in the workplace due to his race. Without assessing these areas further through a cultural lens, an assessor might falsely conclude that this client was experiencing delusions that included content related to his marriage and the workplace. However, by asking additional questions about the nature of the client's experiences, particularly as they related to race and racism as well as interpersonal relationships, the client was referred for legal assistance for the workplace issue and therapy for suspected delusional thinking regarding his wife. This example demonstrates the significance of utilizing information from a client's cultural narrative to discern symptoms of paranoia along a continuum (e.g., from mild symptoms expressed due to systemic injustice, to potentially clinically significant psychotic symptoms) and develop appropriate, culturally congruent treatment recommendations (Whaley, 1998).

Cultural information is also vital to making treatment decisions regarding client risk and safety, and documenting them in the written report. While research highlights cultural differences in suicide rates (Bhui, Dinos, & McKenzie, 2012), rarely are cultural considerations expressly discussed when determining plans for client safety (Chu et al., 2013). To address this gap, Chu and colleagues (2013) developed the *Cultural Assessment of Risk and Suicide* (CARS) which is based on the Cultural Theory and Model of Suicide (Chu, Goldblum, Floyd, & Bongar, 2010). This measure (and theory) importantly provides a clinical tool and, more broadly, a particular cultural lens through which assessors may begin to better understand suicidal symptomatology across cultural and/or marginalized groups. Consider, for instance, that a gay youth who reports experiencing bullying and suicidal thoughts related to significant minority stress might benefit from a suicide-prevention plan that integrates coping with minority identity related stressors as well as psychoeducation about various forms of discrimination and the influence of such discriminatory experiences on an individual's affective, behavioral, and cognitive responses. Such a recommendation demonstrates Chu and colleagues' (2010, 2013) perspective and calls assessors to write treatment recommendations that address the relationship between minority identity related stressors, suicidality, and other forms of client risk.

For Whom?

As a matter of professional practice and in line with standards in the field of psychological assessment, a well-written report should include: (a) identifying information, (b) reason for evaluation and referring provider, (c) assessment measures and procedures employed, (d) findings and results yielded from measures used, (e) interpretation of results, including the implications of such results to the specific referral question, and (f) treatment recommendations. These elements are basic components of any psychological assessment report and are said to provide enough information for clinicians to effectively communicate with, and determine treatment plans for, their clients. However, we challenge this notion to ask the question, for whom is the product of a PA procedure written?

Ownby (2009) suggests that the purpose of a psychological report is to communicate and disseminate the results of an assessment procedure in a manner that provides the reader with evidence (e.g., data) and encourages the reader to take action toward a specific recommendation. Other scholars contend that the process of assessment and, by extension, the written clinical report yielded centers on the client's needs and lived experiences (Finn & Tonsager, 1997, 2002; Fischer, 2000). Interestingly, these scholars similarly emphasize the client as an important reader. This is not to say that assessors should not consider that their clinical evaluations will be read by other practitioners; it is more to emphasize the importance of clients as the primary audience that assessors aim to reach through their clinical writing.

Engaging in any aspect of clinical assessment and treatment has been demonstrated as more effective for clients when the practitioner is culturally aware and the experience is culturally congruent for the client (Cardemil & Battle, 2003; Takeuchi, Sue, & Yeh, 1995; Tucker, Marsiske, Rice, Nielson, & Herman, 2011). Further, culture-centered collaboration in the client–assessor dynamic strengthens the therapeutic alliance and increases the likelihood of accurate and successful outcomes (Fischer, 2000; Frey, 2013). Although the client is not often physically present for the report-writing process, his or her cultural and lived experiences remain influential to determining the structure of the report. That is, report writing and the specific structure of the report are an extension of the assessment process. An assessor might choose to modify the language used in a report for a client from a non-Western, collectivist culture to include more language that engenders interdependence and interconnectedness as a means of improving the reader's connection with that which is written (e.g., cultural congruence). For example, a traditional Western report excerpt might read (in a hypothetical case):

> The client can be described as having an anxious temperament and dependency needs involving familial relationships that appear enmeshed, and as a result the client has a difficult time with independent decision making, which likely exacerbates feelings of nervousness.

The preceding statement not only includes jargon-laden language but also lacks consideration of cultural context. An alternative description to capture a more collectivist stance could read:

> The client's closeness to family appears significant to their view of the world. As a result, this client tends to seek social support from others, particularly family members when making decisions; however, when close others are unavailable to help, the client is less certain as to how to go about making decisions, leading to feelings of anxiety.

A minor change such as this to the structure of one's report supports the goal of connecting with the primary intended audience (i.e., clients) and is also likely to provide further credibility to the report.

With clients being important readers of PA reports, assessors should also keep in mind the significance of writing for client advocacy. In recent years, there has been an increased focus on writing for advocacy—that is, using written psychological reports as tools to educate clients (and professionals) when appropriate. Report writing for advocacy can include opportunities for psychoeducation in working to be an active change agent in the assessment process. At a basic level, writing for advocacy might include consciousness-raising or aiding clients in understanding the ways in which their individual difficulties are influenced by, or rooted in, larger historical, systemic, and social forces (Goodman et al., 2004; Helms & Cook, 1999). Thus, part of a report can be used as a psychoeducational tool to add critical context to the difficulties some clients might experience that are grounded in culture-bound social and political histories. For instance, a report might be written to include an explanation of specific symptomatology in both clinical and cultural terms, noting the ways that racism, homophobia, and ageism may intersect and impact a client's psychosocial functioning. By emphasizing the client as the primary audience, assessors are more likely to accurately capture cultural narratives, write in a manner that is accessible to the client, and advocate for their clients in their interpretation of findings and in the development of treatment recommendations.

What About the Assessor?

Assessors must be willing to openly acknowledge the power inherent not only in the role of the "expert" but also in the written word proffered in this role. This is a fundamental starting point of culturally competent assessment, as unacknowledged privilege can contribute to insensitive and potentially oppressive interpretations and conclusions that, in their written form, may follow a client and be used by other professionals throughout their medical and/or mental health history. An important part of examining power in the assessment context includes, at minimum, the internal acknowledgment of bias, stigmatization, and marginalization that impacts the lives of diverse client populations as well as a sense of one's role within marginalizing systems. This includes oppression at the individual, cultural, and institutional levels (Constantine, Hage, Kindaichi, & Bryant, 2007). In this acknowledgment, it is also integral to consider the ways in which assessors might inadvertently marginalize clients and/or readers of their assessment reports by utilizing carelessly placed remarks or poorly worded phrases (Krishnamurthy, 2012). When an assessor is working within his, her, or hir own Western, privileged cultural reference point to document the experiences of people from other cultural frames, personality and behavioral variables can be easily misconstrued. Consider when an assessor documents a father's parenting skills as poor or inadequate because he can only work the night shift, describes a family environment as chaotic because multiple generations live in a single home, or notes a client to be indifferent or passive in the assessment situation when, in fact, the client fears authority.

Another way that assessors can inadvertently marginalize clients in report writing is by failing to share power. Sharing power is an important facet of social justice and cultural competence, and includes resisting temptations to abuse the power inherent in the relationship between an assessor and client (Ivey, D'Andrea, Bradford Ivey, & Simek-Morgan, 2002). While many assessors and practitioners are socialized to identify as an expert (or clients may view them as an expert), sharing power means acknowledging clients as experts of their own lives. Assessors tend to spend a very brief period of time with clients and presenting oneself as expert on clients' lives and their functioning can be off-putting, particularly for clients who have been oppressed. Appropriately utilizing naming prefixes, particularly upon initial client meeting, is an example of sharing power and demonstrating respect, and this should carry over into the written report. Among ageing adult clients who have been historically marginalized, addressing the client by their first name could be construed as a sign of disrespect. Equally, some female clients might find it demeaning when male assessors refer to them by their first names while introducing themselves with a proper prefix (Fontes, 2008). In situations like these, and more generally, assessors are advised to ask the client how they would prefer to be addressed and utilize that same language throughout the report-writing process. Thus, the more assessors can seek to learn from clients, including using their words and their stories in report writing, the more assessors are sharing power.

In addition to acknowledging and sharing power, assessors are encouraged to practice outwardly stating their areas of expertise, clinical framework, and the limitations of their knowledge. The PA report-writing process is inherently subjective and requires the *involvement* of the writer. Even as we write this chapter, there is involvement, or purposeful choice informed by a set of subjective experiences in the use of specific words and phrases. For example, the use of the word "client" as opposed to "consumer" or "patient" provides information about our positionality with regard to our view of persons who seek help from clinical professionals. Hence, the involvement and positionality of the assessor is another important area to examine when discussing cultural competence in the PA report-writing process. While documenting the assessor's involvement in the assessment process as a matter of standard practice is uncommon in the structure of PA reports, this practice is suggested in writing culturally competent PA reports. Being called upon to make interpretations about clients based on clinical data (including behavioral observations) and clinical judgment, assessors engage in a subjective process and are required to structure and write reports based on their own positionality, training experiences, and biases. Sample positionality statements are shared below and might be included in the diagnostic impressions or recommendation and prognoses section of a PA report.

> *Statement 1—Focus on Assessor Training*
> The assessment interpretations and clinical impressions documented in this report reflect the perspective of an assessor trained from a psychodynamic

approach to psychological treatment with expertise in multicultural counseling. The findings yielded from the assessment measures are reported using the standardized notations as per the assessment measure guidelines. Given my clinical focus and training, my interpretations of these findings seek to integrate assessment data with cultural and early developmental narratives to help explain the assessment findings.

Statement 2—Focus on Assessor Worldview
As an assessor, I acknowledge the influence of both my marginalized and privileged identity statuses, including the power that I hold in writing this report. I include this statement to note that my treatment recommendations are based both on clinical expertise and discussions with the client about the feasibility of the recommendations outlined. My approach reflects attention to how power and social location in the client–assessor dynamic may impact treatment recommendations and client outcomes. My recommendations therefore do not specify a particular theoretical treatment orientation but focus on themes of inequity and injustice experienced by the client that should be addressed in treatment.

There may be multiple approaches to writing a positionality statement that vary in length and level of disclosure. In an assessment report, this might include information about the race, socioeconomic status, ethnic, religious, and cultural background of the assessor as well as the training and experience relevant to the current assessment at hand. Areas that might present particular limitations in a given evaluation should be highlighted, such as the need for interpreters or vastly different acculturation experiences (for example, a White upper-middle-class male psychologist evaluating a newly immigrated female trauma victim seeking asylum from an Asian country who does not speak English). Theory underpinning qualitative research provides a framework for documenting the assessor's involvement in the assessment context and is consistent with a mixed-methodological approach. Qualitative researchers are apt to attend to subjectivity such that they may carefully examine whose experiences or perceptions are being described by a set of findings (Landén, 2011; Morrow, 2005). Guidelines suggested by Elliott, Fischer, & Rennie (1999) for conducting and publishing qualitative research in psychology are applicable to this discussion of cultural competence in PA report writing. These guidelines include: "(a) owning one's perspective, (b) situating the sample, (c) grounding in examples, (d) providing credibility checks, (e) coherence, (f) accomplishing general versus specific research tasks, and (g) resonating with readers" (p. 220). Table 17.1 illustrates how these tasks translate to the PA report-writing process.

Which Format and What to Communicate?

Almost any scholar who has written guidelines for clinical report writing has discussed the limited effectiveness of jargon, the problems with a lack of practical examples to support objective assessment data, and the use of generic treatment

Table 17.1 Qualitative Tasks of the Assessor (adapted from the work of Elliott et al., 1999)

Qualitative Task	*Central Question in Personality Assessment*	*Application to Report Structure*
Owning one's perspective	Who is the assessor and what cultural biases are introduced with the assessor's presence?	Disclosure of personal characteristics, clinical theoretical orientation, and values, as well as known and perceived cultural similarities and differences. Disclosure about how cultural dynamics influence one's perspective
Situating the sample	Who is the client and what cultural dynamics are introduced into the assessment context with the client's presence?	Inclusion of complete demographic, cultural, social, and contextual information about the client
Grounding in examples	What data supports the assessor's interpretations?	Documentation of assessment evidence from measurement tools such as the PAI, MMPI, MCMI, Rorschach, etc., and culturally congruent behavioral observations
Credibility checks	Are the assessor's interpretations plausible?	Collaborate with client to determine plausibility of conclusions and recommendations
Coherence	How do the pieces of a client's narrative interact?	Allow the client to help determine the congruence of the relationships among assessment findings, one's cultural and social context, and lived experiences
General vs. specific tasks	What are the limitations to the assessor's findings?	Assessor documents possible limitations to assessment conclusions based on client report and/or empirical investigation regarding the reliability or validity of a measure for a particular group
Resonate with readers	Does the written narrative demonstrate an appreciation for the client's cultural context and lived experience while also addressing the assessment question(s)?	Write in first person, using active voice regularly citing examples and employing the use of verbs rather than concepts. Note specific cultural strengths and evidence of resilience. Avoid the use of technical or jargon-laden terminology

recommendations in reports. In fact, the structure of psychological reports shifted from being largely jargon filled and pathology focused in the 1950s and 60s (Fischer, 2000) to less jargon focused in later decades (Ownby, 2009); yet, the structure of PA reports has remained relatively inaccessible to clients and failed to integrate cultural dynamics. Contextualization, collaboration, and creativity are skills that can support assessors in remedying these shortcomings. Research on culturally sensitive and collaborative approaches to clinical assessment and therapy have increased in the last several decades (Finn & Tonsager, 1997, 2002; Fischer, 2000; Jordan, 1997). This work challenges conventionality in clinical assessment and the structure of written reports.

Imagine for a moment preparing to write a PA report and having your client sitting with you as you write the document. Together, you determine how to interpret the findings and determine treatment recommendations. While engaging this process, you realize that your textbook interpretation of your Haitian client's elevated clinical scores on some of the MMPI-2 subscales were less about clinical distress and more issues of acculturation and cultural mistrust. As suggested by Fischer (2000), you provide a contextualized example of your client's experience related to acculturating to the U.S. along with the data from the PA measures. You glean this information by collaborating with your client and engaging a process that qualitative researchers refer to as "thick description" (Geertz, 1983). Thick description involves detailing a person's individual construction of his, her, or hir lived experiences as well as detailing the cultural and social contexts in which those experiences occur. Using the previous example, a statement reflecting thick description might document that the client immigrated to the U.S. six months prior to the current evaluation during a time of civil unrest, leaving behind a wife and three children who the client describes as his world, and leaving social capital because his degree is not acknowledged in the U.S., all of which the client discusses in terms of shame and confusion. This statement lends further insight into the client's narrative and provides potential additive or alternative explanations for clinical findings. Hence, by writing from a lens that more readily engages the client's narrative, assessors can provide clients with a potential therapeutic experience as well as generate valid interpretations of assessment results.

Although such an approach might seem counter to that which many assessors learned in their graduate training, collaborative, individualized assessment (Fischer, 1979), and later, therapeutic assessment (Finn & Tonsager, 1997) are approaches that extend the bounds of traditional assessment, humanizing the client beyond the subject of a report and providing clients with voice and greater autonomy (Finn & Tonsager, 2002; Fischer, 2000). In collaborative, individualized assessment the assessor and client work together to co-construct productive understandings of one's cognitions, affective responses, and behaviors (Fischer, 1979, 2000). Fischer (2000) translates this approach into clinical report writing, suggesting that the structure of a report should not just be "experience near but life near" (p. 10) and as a result reports may be formulated in multiple ways. In some cultural groups, the expression of narrative story-telling is a traditional means of learning and providing information. Employing a collaborative, individualized assessment approach, an assessor might choose to write the PA report as a story or fable (e.g., Long ago, there lived a wise man, about 60 years old, who dedicated his life to his community . . .). Other report structures include reports written as a letter to the client or written with a section for the client's impressions (Fischer, 2000). Using these creative approaches allows for both a culturally sensitive and "thick" communication of an individual's lived experience beyond data from various PA measures.

In a similar vein, therapeutic assessment is a technique in which the assessment itself is considered an intervention (Finn & Tonsager, 1997). Therapeutic assessment aims to foster self-awareness in clients that subsequently supports them in making life changes. The primary role of the assessor is to provide clients with growth opportunities in the assessment context. This too extends to a report's structure. Assessors should consider carefully if the written product encourages opportunity for growth and further exploration for their clients. Specifically, an assessor might include a section in a PA report reflecting the process of how findings were interpreted. The section might include a description of the assessor's aim to reduce power, particularly in a majority group and non-majority group assessment pairing or by having the clients provide their initial impression of the findings in the context of their cultural and lived experiences. Further, this could include a statement from the assessor contextualizing the reliability and validity of a set of findings for certain groups. As an example, since practitioners are aware that chronic experience of "isms" increases distress among certain marginalized group members and these can appear as elevations on personality clinical scales, it is imperative to include in one's PA report the cautious consumption of such findings when there is report or suspicion of systemic bias or other prejudicial experiences.

As alluded to earlier (see section entitled *For Whom?*), assessors might also consider writing reports from a collective frame as a means of attending to cultural diversity. A collectivist focused report would take into consideration who the client is in relation to others. This requires taking a multi-systems perspective that acknowledges the ways that systems contribute to clients' problems (i.e., social problems and marginalization within systems) (Kiselica & Robinson, 2001). Additionally, assessors could benefit from considering a systems approach in their treatment recommendations. By expanding the level of analysis beyond an individual client, assessors might come to understand the various ways clients may experience healing, including the ways in which clients' own cultural practices or communities might be involved in the healing process. Constantine and colleagues (2007) suggest that it is important that mental health professionals not only actively seek to obtain knowledge of cultural or indigenous models of health and healing, but also seek to collaborate with such entities or individuals when appropriate. Examples of culturally relevant sources/services might include extended family, a cultural/indigenous support group, a religious support group, or a peer-facilitated group. Relatedly, report writing that highlights clients' strengths and the strengths of clients' communities reflects attention to the interaction between individuals and their surroundings. Information about a client's or community's orientation toward interconnectedness, resilience, or spirituality and/or religiosity can all be considered strengths relevant to a client's treatment plan, and should be discussed by assessors alongside assessment findings.

Language is another significant topic to consider in culturally competent PA report writing. Culture and language are inextricably intertwined and co-constructed through interactions with others (Reboul, 2012). From this perspective, culturally competent PA report writing represents a unique opportunity to understand clients through a shared meaning-making process between assessor and client that is culturally and/or cross-culturally constructed through language (e.g., the written report). The process of engaging the culturally situated notions of language and shared meaning making, however, is challenged by the field's heavy reliance on verbal and written communication. According to Sue and Sue (2008) clients are expected to be able to "verbalize their thoughts and feelings to a practitioner in order to receive the necessary help" (p. 136). This poses an even greater problem when the assessor and client do not speak the same language. The use of translators and interpreters has been incorporated in an effort to address this problem, but many translation approaches fail to consider the cultural component that underlies language (Betancourt & López, 1993). In writing a report, assessors should clearly document the interpreter's involvement in the assessment proceedings and potential biases in translating, issues related to semantic equivalence, and the manner in which the interpretation occurred (simultaneous vs. consecutive). For instance, a written report should detail if there are occurrences in which concepts or terms must be explained differently because there is no English (or vice versa with other languages) equivalent (Fontes, 2008). Further, if because of language barriers the assessor remains unclear about how to interpret or integrate assessment findings with a client's narrative, it is advised to make treatment recommendations to further assess the gaps in information remaining from the assessment proceedings.

Language is also expressed via word choice and notational phrases utilized by assessors in their written reports. Fontes (2008) suggests that notational phrases may reflect notational bias when assessors are limited in their ability to describe an experience or when assessors utilize shorthand to describe problems. Oftentimes, objective PA measures and structured or semi-structured interviews do not allow for clients to report areas of in-between statuses. For example, if clients are asked to indicate if their parents are married or unmarried—there is no clear opportunity for them to share that their parents live together on occasion. Failing to have this option represents a form of bias. Such bias can also be evident in word choice, which is of particular consequence for PA report writing. An assessor's choice of words to interpret findings or make treatment recommendations can provide evidence of one's cultural competence. Assessors must choose words that do not contribute further to a client's experiences of marginalization. Sometimes assessors will use terms such as "at-risk" or "inner-city" in their interpretations, observations, or recommendations. While such terms are used in everyday language, they carry a connotation that tends to be associated with marginalized groups in the U.S. context. Other terms that convey the same message but are less pejorative include words or phrases such as "resource poor" or "underserved community." More specific terms that describe the condition or experience the assessor is aiming to illustrate often add clarity to the writing and better capture clients' narratives. To this end, the format and content communicated in a PA report may include many variations to accommodate the needs of a range of clients and systems. The end goal, though, for assessors remains the same—to structure reports in which the words and format are meaningful, accurate, and culturally sensitive.

Conclusion

Writing for an N of 1 is an approach to PA report writing that privileges the experiences of clients' cultural contexts to elucidate and add richness to assessment findings. However, engaging the task of assessment report writing from a culturally competent frame is not without its challenges. As articulated by Delpit (1995), "one of the most difficult tasks we face as human beings is communicating meaning across our individual differences, a task confounded immeasurably when we attempt to communicate across social lines, racial lines, cultural lines, or lines of unequal power" (p. 66). Cultural competence in report writing requires assessors to communicate across the lines through their writing, and to do so, sometimes, with inadequate tools. Assessors must attend to cultural narratives and social justice concepts in the report-writing process and document the role of these narratives and concepts in their reports. As discussed, acknowledging cultural dynamics in a PA report in practice might look like a statement regarding the assessor's positionality, acknowledging the limitations of diagnostic categories or language, or utilizing a less traditional approach to conveying report findings. Each of these practical applications to cultural competence in PA report writing lends itself to reducing assessor bias, limiting cross-cultural and inter-cultural misunderstandings, and increasing client advocacy. PA reports exist in perpetuity, potentially having long-term implications for the clients assessors serve. Thus, it is imperative to remain up-to-date and curious about culture, make use of available resources on measurement and diagnosis, and most of all, view clients not only nomothetically, but also idiographically, as complex and unique individuals, impacted by larger systems.

Recommendations for Culturally Competent Personality Assessment Report Writing

As you engage the report-writing process or review your final document, ask yourself the following questions:

- Have you used DSM-5 resources such as culture-related diagnostic issues, gender-related diagnostic issues, and the Cultural Formulation Interview (CFI) to contextualize assessment findings?
- Have you considered additive or alternative cultural explanations of elevated or depressed findings on assessment measures as you interpret assessment findings?

- How did you share power with your client in the assessment context? Did you document the shared experience in your report?
- Who are you considering to be the audience for your written report?
- Have you written your report in language that is accessible to your client?
- Will the structure of your report support a therapeutic experience for your client?
- Does your report accurately capture the client's cultural experiences (e.g., the experiences discussed by the client or "thick description")?
- Have you documented cultural information and provided specific examples to help readers understand report findings?
- Do your treatment recommendations answer the referral questions with consideration for the client's cultural context?
- Have you considered your positionality in writing this report? Should you document aspects of your training (or limitations), cultural, and/or social contexts in a positionality statement?
- Did you consider non-traditional (or a combination of traditional and non-traditional) approaches to presenting report findings?
- Did you collaborate with your client to better understand assessment findings and determine the feasibility of treatment recommendations?
- Does your report advocate for your client, attending to specific cultural narratives?
- Did you include multiple systems in writing your treatment recommendations, catalyzing the client, family, and broader community as appropriate?
- What does the language of your report communicate to clients and other health care professionals about your cultural competence?
- Have you included specific rather than general, colloquial language? Did you avoid the use of jargon?

References

Allen, J. (2002). Assessment training for practice in American Indian and Alaska native settings. *Journal of Personality Assessment, 79*(2), 216–225. doi: 10.1207/s15327752 jpa7902_05

Allen, J., & Dana, R. H. (2004). Methodological issues in cross-cultural and multicultural Rorschach research. *Journal of Personality Assessment, 82*(2), 189–206. doi:10.1207/s15327752jpa8202_7

American Psychiatric Association. (2013). *Diagnostic and statistical manual of mental disorders* (5th edition). Arlington, VA: American Psychiatric Publishing.

American Psychological Association (APA). (1993). Guidelines for providers of psychological services to ethnic, linguistic and culturally diverse populations. *American Psychologist, 48*, 45–48. doi: 10.1037/0003-066X.48.1.45

American Psychological Association (APA). (2002). Ethical principles of psychologists and code of conduct. *American Psychologist, 47*, 1060–1073. doi: 10.1037/003-066X.57.12.1060

Betancourt, H., & López, S. R. (1993). The study of culture, ethnicity, and race in American psychology. *American Psychologist*, 48, 629–637. doi: 10.1037/0003-066X.48.6.629.

Bhui, K. S., Dinos, S., & McKenzie, K. (2012). Ethnicity and its influence on suicide rates and risk. *Ethnicity & Health, 17*(1–2), 141–148. doi: 10.1080/13557858.2011.645151

Cardemil, E. V., & Battle, C. L. (2003). Guess who's coming to therapy? Getting comfortable with conversations about race and ethnicity in psychotherapy. *Professional Psychology: Research and Practice, 34*(3), 278–286. doi: 10.1037/0735-7028.34.3.278

Carpenter-Song, E., Schwallie, M. N., & Longhofer, J. L. (2008). Using care with culture. In M. Sajatovic & S. Loue (Eds.), *Diversity issues in the diagnosis, treatment, and research of mood disorders* (pp. 17–31). New York: Oxford University Press.

Chu, J., Floyd, R., Diep, H., Pardo, S., Goldblum, P., & Bongar, B. (2013). A tool for the culturally competent assessment of suicide: The Cultural Assessment of Risk for Suicide (CARS) measure. *Psychological Assessment, 25*(2), 424–434. doi: 10.1037/a0031264

Chu, J. P., Goldblum, P., Floyd, R., & Bongar, B. (2010). A cultural theory and model of suicide. *Applied and Preventive Psychology, 14*, 25–40.

Constantine, M. G., Hage, S. M., Kindaichi, M. M., & Bryant, R. M. (2007). Social justice and multicultural issues: Implications for the practice and training of counselors and counseling psychologists. *Journal of Counseling & Development, 85*(1), 24–29. doi: 10.1002/j.1556-6678.2007.tb00440.x

Dadlani, M. B., Overtree, C., & Perry-Jenkins, M. (2012). Culture at the center: A reformulation of diagnostic assessment. *Professional Psychology: Research & Practice, 43*(3), 175–182. doi: 10.1037/a0028152

Delpit, L. D. (1995). *Other people's children: Cultural conflict in the classroom*. New York: The New Press.

Elliott, R., Fischer, C. T., & Rennie, D. L. (1999). Evolving guidelines for publication of qualitative research studies in psychology and related fields. *British Journal of Clinical Psychology, 38*, 215–229. doi: 10.1348/014466599162782

Escobar, J. I. (2012). Diagnostic bias: Racial and cultural issues. *Psychiatric Services, 63*(9), 847. doi: 10.1176/appi.ps.20120p847

Finn, S. E., & Tonsager, M. E. (1997). Information-gathering and therapeutic models of assessment: Complementary paradigms. *Psychological Assessment, 9*(4), 374–385. doi: 10.1037/1040-3590.9.4.374

Finn, S. E., & Tonsager, M. E. (2002). How therapeutic assessment became humanistic. *The Humanistic Psychologist, 30*(1–2), 10–22. doi: 10.1080/08873267.2002.9977019

Fischer, C. T. (1979). Individualized assessment and phenomenological psychology. *Journal of Personality Assessment, 43*(2), 115–122. doi: 10.1207/s15327752jpa4302_1

Fischer, C. (2000). Collaborative, individualized assessment. *Journal of Personality Assessment, 74*, 2–14. doi: 10.1207/S15327752JPA740102

Fontes, L. A. (2008). *Interviewing clients across cultures: A practitioner's guide*. New York: The Guilford Press.

Frey, L. L. (2013). Relational-cultural therapy: Theory, research, and application to counseling competencies. *Professional Psychology: Research and Practice, 44*(3), 177. doi: 10.1037/a0033121

Geertz, C. (1983). *Local knowledge: Further essays in interpretive anthropology*. New York: Basic Books.

Goodman, L. A., Liang, B., Helms, J. E., Latta, R. E., Sparks, E., & Weintraub, S. R. (2004). Training counseling psychologists as social justice agents: Feminist and multicultural principles in action. *The Counseling Psychologist, 32*(6), 793–836. doi: 10.1177/0011000004268802

Groth-Marnat, G. (2009). The five assessment issues you meet when you go to heaven. *Journal of Personality Assessment, 91*(4), 303–310. doi: 10.1080/00223890902935662

Guthrie, R. (2004). *Even the rat was white: A historical view of psychology*. Boston, MA: Pearson Education, Inc.

Helms, J. E., & Cook, D. A. (1999). *Using race and culture in counseling and psychotherapy: Theory and process*. Boston, MA: Allyn & Bacon.

Ivey, A. E., D'Andrea, M., Bradford Ivey, M., & Simek-Morgan, L. (2002). *Theories of counseling and psychotherapy: A multicultural perspective* (5th edition). Boston, MA: Allyn & Bacon.

Jordan, J. V. (1997). A relational perspective for understanding women's development. In J. V. Jordan (Ed.), *Women's growth in diversity: More writings from the Stone Center* (pp. 9–24). New York, NY: Guilford Press.

Kiselica, M. S., & Robinson, M. (2001). Bringing advocacy counseling to life: The history, issues, and human dramas of social justice work in counseling. *Journal of Counseling & Development, 79*(4), 387–397. doi: 10.1002/j.1556-6676.2001.tb01985.x

Krishnamurthy, R. (2012, Summer). The Dharma of good personality assessment: Address to the Society for Personality Assessment annual meeting. *SPA Exchange, 24*(2), 1, 9–11.

Landén, A. S. (2011). From ethnographic "self"-discovery to processes of identification. *Qualitative Research, 11*(5), 536–551. doi: 10.1177/1468794111413238

Meyer, G. J., Finn, S. E., Eyde, L., Kay, G. G., Moreland, K. L., Dies, R. R., et al. (2001). Psychological testing and psychological assessment: A review of evidence and issues. *American Psychologist, 56*(2), 128–165. doi: 10.1037/0003-066X.56.2

Monnot, M. J., Quirk, S. W., Hoerger, M., & Brewer, L. (2009). Racial bias in personality assessment: Using the MMPI-2 to predict psychiatric diagnoses of African American and Caucasian chemical dependency inpatients. *Psychological Assessment, 21*(2), 137–151. doi: 10.1037/a0015316

Morrow, S. L. (2005). Quality and trustworthiness in qualitative research in counseling psychology. *Journal of Counseling Psychology, 52*(2), 250–260. doi: 10.1037/0022-0167.52.2.250

Newhill, C. E. (1990). The role of culture in the development of paranoid symptomatology. *American Journal of Orthopsychiatry, 60*(2), 176–185. doi: 10.1037/h0079170

Ownby, R. L. (2009). Writing clinical reports. In J. N. Butcher (Ed.), *Oxford handbook of personality assessment* (pp. 684–692). New York: Oxford University Press.

Reboul, A. (2012). Language: Between cognition, communication and culture. *Pragmatics & Cognition, 20*(2), 295–316.

Sue, D. W., & Sue, D. (2008). *Counseling the culturally diverse: Theory and practice* (5th ed.). Hoboken, NJ: John Wiley & Sons, Inc.

Takeuchi, D. T., Sue, S., & Yeh, M. (1995). Return rates and outcomes from ethnicity-specific mental health programs in Los Angeles. *American Journal of Public Health, 85*(5), 638–643. doi: 10.2105/ajph.85.5.638

Tsai, D. C., & Pike, P. L. (2000). Effects of acculturation on the MMPI-2 scores of Asian American students. *Journal of Personality Assessment, 74*(2), 216–230. doi: 10.1207/s15327752jpa7402_4

Tucker, C. M., Marsiske, M., Rice, K. G., Nielson, J. J., & Herman, K. (2011). Patient-centered culturally sensitive health care: Model testing and refinement. *Health Psychology, 30*(3), 342–350. doi: 10.1037/a0022967

Weiner, I. B., & Greene, R. L. (2011). *Handbook of personality assessment*. Hoboken, NJ: John Wiley & Sons.

Whaley, A. L. (1997). Ethnicity/race, paranoia, and psychiatric diagnoses: Clinician bias versus sociocultural differences. *Journal of Psychopathology and Behavioral Assessment, 19*(1), 1–20. doi: 10.1007/bf02263226

Whaley, A. L. (1998). Cross-cultural perspective on paranoia: A focus on the Black American experience. *Psychiatric Quarterly, 69*(4), 325–343. doi: 10.1023/a:1022134231763

Wood, J. M., & Lilienfeld, S. O. (1999). The Rorschach Inkblot Test: A case of overstatement? *Assessment, 6*(4), 341–351. doi: 10.1177/107319119900600405

CHAPTER **18**

Ethics in Diversity-Sensitive Assessment

Virginia Brabender

Diversity awareness and ethical decision-making in assessment are inextricably tied. The connection between ethics and diversity is necessarily close because assessors' decision-making concerns people who are complex and different from one another in many ways. They are constituted of a multiplicity of facets, many of which are woven into their personal identities. Facets such as race, ethnicity, socioeconomic status, generation, or immigration status shape how the person sees him or herself, and how others regard that individual. Assessors for whom ethical decision-making is simply the application of a set of rules, or who attempt to make ethical decisions insensible of these identity facets, are likely to fail to serve optimally the well-being of the client; the person has not been regarded in his or her fullness in this situation.

In the first section of this chapter, we see how the intimate tie between ethics and diversity is rooted in the major ethical system employed by psychologists, including assessment psychologists: principle ethics (Beauchamp & Childress, 2001; see Brabender & Bricklin, 2001, for general application to personality assessment). With this background in mind, we proceed to an examination of two lines of research that illumine the processes by which assessors do or do not take into account identity information in making decisions that have ethical implications. In the heart of this chapter, we follow an assessor through the various stages of conducting an assessment and seeing how ethical issues might emerge that require his or her diversity sensitivity. Finally, we consider all of the material explored in this chapter in terms of its implications for how (a) assessors' heightened diversity awareness might increase their capacities for sound ethical decision-making; and (b) future lines of investigation might create greater potential for intimacy to be achieved between ethics and diversity in the assessor's everyday practice.

Conceptual Considerations and Definitions

Most, if not all, human service professions embrace the system of principle ethics, a set of core values whose observance leads to the highest levels of ethical conduct (Beauchamp & Childress, 2001). Among the human service professionals who subscribe to principle ethics are clinical psychologists. The "Ethical principles of psychologists and code of conduct" (American Psychological Association, 2010) describes five principles to which all psychologists should aspire to adhere. These principles are: Beneficence and Nonmaleficence, Fidelity and Responsibility, Integrity, Justice, and Respect for People's Rights and Dignity. As will be shown through a few examples, diversity considerations run through these principles.

Beneficence and Nonmaleficence, which instruct us to benefit clients as we avoid harming them, entails an awareness of obstacles to these aspirations: "Because psychologists' scientific and professional judgments and actions may affect the lives of others, they are alert to and guard against personal, financial, social, organizational, or political factors that might lead to misuse of their influence" (APA, 2010, p. 3). For personality assessors, the translation of the principle requires attending to how assessment findings might be used not simply by the client, but by others in the client's life. For example, when an employer seeks an assessment on an employee in an effort to frame her complaints about gender discrimination as a reflection of her psychopathology, the assessor aware of this dynamic must very seriously consider whether taking on this case is ethically defensible.

The principle of Justice requires that all people have the opportunity to benefit from psychological assessment services, not simply those who can afford it by dint of socioeconomic status or other differentiating factors. Justice also demands that the recipients of psychological assessment services not be subject to assessor biases that could limit the benefit a person could derive from psychological assessment, or even produce harm. We will see later in this chapter how biases can operate unconsciously but, even then, the assessor must be open to processes that will help him or her to identify and modify them. Respect for People's Rights and Dignity imposes on the assessor the need to safeguard the client's right to "privacy, confidentiality, and self-determination." This principle lists a variety of identity variables such as ethnicity, sexuality orientation, and race and stresses the importance of the psychologist's respectful attitude toward these facets of the client as the psychologist pursues clinical work.

In sum, then, when psychologists adhere to a core principle model of ethics, their focus on diversity must be (a) intensive in examining deeply the ways in which identity facets influence them; (b) extensive in look at the full range of factors that define identity; and (c) consistent in being an unfailingly present aspect of their view of the client.

Psychological assessors must continually consider whether their actions honor the core ethical principles of their profession. At times, circumstances will occur when it might be difficult to identify a course of action that will satisfy all principles. Adhering to one principle may violate another. This situation is what constitutes an *ethical dilemma or quandary*. One tool that psychologists use to resolve a dilemma is the hierarchy of principles. For example, generally, Respect for People's Rights and Dignity is seen as having ascendancy over every ethical principle but Nonmaleficence (as expressed in the notion, first do no harm). Suppose an assessor felt that input from a potential informant would benefit an assessment, but the client did not want to give permission to the assessor to contact that party. The hierarchy would dictate that honoring the client's request trumps the benefit that could be gleaned from garnering the additional information. From a diversity perspective, it is important to recognize that hierarchies of ethical principles can vary from culture to culture, and even within subcultures of a given culture. To a Western sensibility, the privileging of individualism makes a great deal of sense; intuitively, it seems correct. Yet, in more collectivist cultures, the importance of respecting autonomy is accorded less emphasis than other values such as fostering the common well-being. When the client's cultural background differs from that of the assessor, a hierarchy clash can occur, leading to great ambiguity about the most ethically sound resolution of a dilemma.

Even when hierarchies are used to resolve ethical dilemmas, those principles that are subordinated to others should not be ignored. The psychologist strives always to balance principles, finding that course of action that maximally honors all principles and violates each principle least. The formulation of these carefully sculpted courses of action typically requires that the assessor garner considerable information about the client's context and person. In other words, developing a plan of ethical action requires that the assessor thoroughly reckon with the client's diversity.

Empirical Considerations

The empirical literature on the role of diversity in ethical decision-making in assessment is scant. How assessors actually go about taking into account diversity factors, or the extent to which they do, is unknown. Are particular diversity factors more salient than others? Are particular assessment situations more conducive than others to the assessor's cognizance of diversity factors that should be taken into account in resolving ethical dilemmas?

Even though these questions remain unanswered, findings in two realms of inquiry provide a basis for our enhanced understanding of the intersection of ethics and diversity in psychological assessment. One area emphasizes ethics and the other, diversity.

Processing Errors

The first line of research concerns information-processing factors that could impinge upon ethical decision-making, especially as it applies to diversity. Researchers have uncovered particular errors to which human beings are subject in making judgments. The broader the assessor's scope of consideration, the more ethically grounded his or her decision is likely to be. However, assessors are subject to the phenomenon of *diagnostic overshadowing* (Jones, Howard, & Thornicroft, 2008) in which one identity facet can obscure an assessor's awareness of another facet of the client.

> For example, the director of an outpatient clinic tells a psychological assessor that she is seeking referrals for her psychotherapy group for individuals who are struggling with their sexual orientations. The assessor has just evaluated a

> client with a diagnosis of schizophrenia who has talked about having this very issue. However, the salience of the schizophrenia in the mind of the assessor overshadows other issues, in the same way that this diagnosis prevents health service professionals from addressing the wide array of physical and life style problems schizophrenic individuals tend to have. In fact, the assessor might assume that the sexual orientation questioning is part and parcel of the schizophrenia when this might not be the case at all. Of course, the schizophrenic client might not be a candidate for the group because of level of functioning issues. However, the assessor must ensure that the diagnosis of schizophrenia is not obscuring an issue that the client could benefit from addressing. Ethnic minority groups have also been shown to fall victim to overshadowing. Even when other factors such as client preferences are controlled, Latinos and African Americans are less likely to be referred for a variety of services (Ashton et al., 2003).

Overshadowing is an example of a diagnostic error with ethical implications. Investigators have documented other types of nonrational processing biases that may have their roots in affective factors (Rogerson, Gottlieb, Handelsman, Knapp, & Younggren, 2011). That is, factors such as fear might give rise to the assessor's focusing intensively on a certain piece of information while neglecting others. Once assessors become aware of a potential processing bias, an ethical posture demands their effort to compensate for it. In the example, given that schizophrenia is a diagnosis that often overshadows other problems, especially physical problems, the ethical assessor takes this bias into account and strives to attend assiduously to other potential problem areas. In doing so, the assessor honors the ethical principle of Justice, ensuring equal provision of services to all human beings.

Training Research

The more we know about how diversity-sensitive, ethical decision-making proceeds in psychological practice, the better we will be able to foster it. If, for example, particular gaps are identified in what diversity facets assessors register or circumstances in which they are less attentive to diversity issues altogether, then training programs can strategically address these problems. Even before such information accrues, training programs seeking to develop diversity-sensitive ethical assessors can make use of a rapidly burgeoning literature on the broader topic of fostering multicultural awareness in students. This literature is potentially relevant because if particular techniques and methods are effective in producing diversity-sensitive practitioners, then, it is likely this sensitivity would extend to assessment activities.

Can students be taught to be more sensitive to diversity issues? Smith, Constantine, Dunn, Dinehart, and Montoya (2006) suggest on the basis of their two meta-analyses that they can. A meta-analysis of 45 studies, each of which examined the effectiveness of multicultural education by comparing individuals who had versus had not participated in multicultural education, yielded an effect size of 0.49 (SE = 04, p < 001). Dependent variables were measures of multicultural competence, racial/ethnic identity, racial prejudice, client–counselor relationship, or some combination of these. A second meta-analysis comprised 37 studies, each of which included a pretest evaluation, multicultural intervention, and post-test evaluation. For this analysis, the effect size was .92 (SE = 0.10, p < 001). Notably, a limitation of this second meta-analysis was that the majority of studies were based on self-report data, and only ten used observation or client reports. Sammons and Speight (2008) conducted qualitative interviews of 124 trainees from a variety of graduate programs. They inquired if trainees had undergone change from participating in multicultural courses and examined the types of changes they experienced. These students saw themselves as having not only expanded their knowledge bases but also as having altered their attitudes and behaviors as a function of course participation. Gatmon and colleagues' (2001) student-interviewees reported that supervisors infrequently discussed with them factors such as culture, sexual orientation, and gender but when they did, the supervisory alliance was strengthened and they felt more satisfied with the supervision.

Comment

As noted in the introduction of this section, although each of these areas holds promise for advancing our understanding of diversity awareness and ethical decision-making, they do not shed light on the intersection of these dimensions. Future research is needed to ascertain how an awareness of diversity issues in general and diversity-related information-processing biases could strengthen the assessor's capacity to make decisions that serve the highest ethical ideals, including those ideas that specifically reference diversity.

Practical Considerations: Grappling with Ethical Nodal Points

Within every assessment, certain key junctures exist in which an assessor makes a set of decisions that determine that assessor's activity within the subsequent stage of the assessment. These junctures might be thought of as *assessment nodal points* in their capacity to organize the energies of both the assessor and client. Typically, some of the decisions made by the assessor upon reaching a nodal point have an ethical aspect. That is, the assessor might be faced with one or more ethical dilemmas. At issue is whether in resolving the dilemma, the assessor factors in information about diversity, that is, data about the identity facets of the person and his or her individual context.

In the sections that follow, a sample of nodal points that occur in most assessments is presented with an illustration of the kinds of ethical dilemmas that might confront the practitioner at these junctures. The ethical principles activated by these dilemmas, and how diversity information might be integrated into the contemplation and ultimate resolution of the dilemma, are explored.

Accepting the Referral

A crucial decision any assessor makes is whether or not to accept a referral. Rarely is it an action that should be taken without deliberation. Considering whether to accept a referral entails the application of the ethical principles of Nonmaleficence and Beneficence in that the assessor would want to ensure that his or her assessment work would help and not hurt the client. To accomplish these goals—doing good and avoiding harm—the assessor must be competent to do the assessment. An aspect of this competence is the capacity to work effectively with the client in the context of that client's identity, that is, all of the facets that define that client as a person. In some cases, the decision to accept or reject a referral may entail significant contemplation:

> An assessor at a community health clinic receives a referral for an assessment from a man from The Gambia who had been in the United States for three years. His English was at a basic level. Because the Gambians represent a substantial subpopulation of individuals who receive services at the clinic, a translator was present on-site. The translator was a mental health professional, but not an assessor. No assessors were present on-site who spoke Wolof (the client's language), and in fact, none could be located in the larger metropolitan area. Furthermore, no standard translation of the various tests the psychologist was going to use existed in Wolof. The assessor recognized that in the absence of a standard translation, plenty of room existed for misinterpretation that could limit the validity of the test results. The assessor struggled with whether information garnered under these conditions could be used to describe in accurate terms the internal workings of the client.

In taking a pause and carefully considering all aspects of the possible assessment situation, the assessor is acting ethically. Her evaluation of whether the conditions would enable a valid portrait to be drawn operates in the service of Beneficence and Nonmaleficence: were the client's personality or symptom pattern to be captured incompletely or worse, inaccurately, he would be very unlikely to receive benefit from the assessment and could even be harmed. Still, to reject the referral out of hand simply because the conditions were more complicated would be an infringement upon the principle of Justice in that the client by virtue of his identity would be denied a potentially valuable service. Rosenberg, Almeida, and Macdonald (2012) describe a case in which an assessor used translation difficulties with a client as a tool for enhancing empathy with the client. The language translation served as a metaphor for the translation of self that is inherent in the assessment process for both client and assessor. In this way, they served not only the principle of Justice but also that of Beneficence.

Resolving the translation issue, however, does not satisfy the need for diversity awareness. The client's worldview, use of idioms and metaphors, and other aspects of his culture must be fully appreciated to understand him accurately and fully. Although the assessor might not have this knowledge prior to the assessment request, she could make a commitment to acquiring it over the course of the assessment. Such a commitment, though, would require access to resources for cultivating such knowledge. For example, would others in the clinic be able to educate her about Gambian culture?

In circumstances in which an assessor is faced with an ethical decision that is not easily made, a useful step is consultation with colleagues, mentors, or supervisors (Russ, 2001). Perhaps others have faced this type of situation, even if it is not exactly the same as the current situation. Having done so, these assessors might have identified ways of balancing ethical principles that may not have occurred to the present assessor. For example, Hays (2005) suggests that to achieve maximum benefit from the use of a translator, the assessor and translator should have a pre-assessment meeting in which the assessor learns about various aspects of the relevant culture. The implementation of such a suggestion would serve the principle of Beneficence. Consultants may also play a role in identifying any decision-making biases that the current assessor cannot recognize. Another useful step is to consult any codes or regulatory guidelines that might address the circumstance of translator-facilitated assessment. For example, in the "Ethical Principles of Psychologists and Code of Conduct" (APA, 2010), Ethical Standard 9.03 addresses use of translators in assessment and stipulates that the informed consent make provision for the introduction of this element. Specifically it indicates:

> Psychologists using the services of an interpreter obtain informed consent from the client/patient to use that interpreter, ensure that confidentiality of test results and test security are maintained, and include in their recommendations, reports, and diagnostic or evaluative statement, including forensic testimony, discussion of any limitations on the data obtained.
>
> (p. 12)

By heeding this standard, the assessment practitioner would use an interpreter in a way that respects the client's autonomy or capacity to direct events in his or her life. The assessor would also need to acknowledge in the report and in communications with the client in feedback any concerns about limitations in assessment data validity that the use of the translator created (Knauss, 2001). Moreover, the assessor ought to be careful in striking the appropriate level of caution in relation to her interpretations.

The quandary of whether or not to do an assessment via a translator highlights that rarely is an ethical decision simply a binary choice. More commonly, it necessitates the development of a complex plan of action that gives both sides of the quandary their due. If, for example, the assessor decided that she could not perform the assessment, she or some professionals within the organization would still have to grapple with how to get this client's psychological needs met in a way that takes into account the diversity he presents. In this way, she would be avoiding whatever problems were associated with using a translator while still ensuring that the client had the benefit of the assessment. If she decided to proceed with the translator-mediated assessment, she would put into place some of the safeguards mentioned above so that the risks associated with the use of the translator were minimized.

Obtaining the Informed Consent

The informed consent lays the ethical foundation for an assessment. It is the means by which the client's autonomy is respected and the possibilities for harm are lessened. Conducting an effective informed consent in which both elements are satisfied—the client gets the information he or she needs to make a decision and the client makes a decision without coercion of any kind—relies upon diversity awareness, as the following example illustrates:

> Pilar, a 25-year-old woman, came to the first session of an assessment accompanied by her parents, first generation immigrants from Mexico. The assessor called Pilar into her office and her parents rose, presuming they would be attending this meeting. The assessor politely indicated that she would be happy to speak with them, but first wished to speak with Pilar. The assessor reminded Pilar that in this the first session, she would be asked to sign an informed consent. Pilar was given the written informed consent and the assessor discussed with her its key elements. In a space in which the client could write down the names of third parties who could be present at the assessment or read a copy of the report, Pilar listed her parents. When the assessor asked Pilar about her thoughts about including them, she responded off-handedly: "Oh, I thought I might just put them down, too. After all, they're paying for most of it." The assessor then engaged Pilar in a rather full discussion of how her anticipation of her parents' receiving the information about the assessment might influence her participation throughout. She agreed that her openness in the process might be influenced by the knowledge that they would be privy to what she and the assessor learned. But she also admitted that she knew it was an expectation of theirs to be feedback recipients. She talked about such a parental expectation within her culture not being unusual, particularly because she was single.
>
> The assessor perceived Pilar's consent to have her parents' unlimited involvement in the feedback as less than wholehearted. She discussed with Pilar the possibility of deferring the decision until later in the assessment. She and Pilar worked out a plan in which she would meet with the assessor for several feedback sessions and through this process, they would decide what might be shared with the parents, if anything. They did agree that the assessor would talk about the assessment process with the parents and explain the need to take a flexible stance with what would be ultimately shared with them.

Diversity awareness requires a moment-to-moment sensitivity on the part of the assessor to the client's unfolding reactions. This assessor was able to obtain a full-throated consent from the client by the awareness both of her tentativeness and its connection to cultural forces that might have shaped her assumptions about the testing process and the participation of her parents. We see that knowledge of groups is important but insufficient. Attunement to the individual client's stance in relation to the group is also essential for ethical decision-making. Pilar, in this case, had an ambivalent stance in relation to a cultural prescription, her challenging of which enhanced her motivation to participate fully.

Establishing a Test Battery

The instruments the assessor selects to answer the assessment questions must be ones that are tailored not to some notion of a generic client but the specific client being evaluated. In this regard, let us continue to follow our assessor from the last section who is designing an assessment experience for Pilar.

> In discussing with the assessor whether or not to have her parents at the feedback session, Pilar expressed sympathy for her parents' perspective and indicated that were she to have a child, she might feel similarly. At the same time, she stated that she wanted greater independence from them and longed to forge her own path. The assessor was struck by her sense that Pilar seemed torn between two worlds, and she wondered if this conflict accounted for at least some of her difficulties. In fact, being caught between two worlds seemed critically connected to Pilar's assessment question: Why can't I select a direction for myself in life? Why am I floundering? In thinking about how she might obtain information relevant to these questions, the assessor looked at some of the instruments she commonly used. She doubted whether they would capture the nature of Pilar's struggle, a struggle that the assessor felt should be articulated as finely as possible. She researched a variety of instruments and selected a measure of acculturation that yielded information on Pilar's degree of identification with each of her cultures, was normed on an appropriate population, and possessed good psychometric qualities.

Our assessor's situation does not constitute a bona fide ethical dilemma, but does have ethical dimensions nonetheless. She could have taken the easier route of employing her customary and familiar instruments. Indeed, according to a survey by Hansen et al. (2006), 86% of psychologists avoided taking into account multicultural information when it was relevant to a case. In delving into what was less charted terrain for this assessment psychologist, she was able to individualize the assessment more fully and thereby enhance the potential of the assessment to be useful—a line of action in the service of Beneficence. Both Justice and Respect for People's Rights and Dignity are served by the assessor's awareness that the potential conflict second-generation individuals often experience can be linked to particular psychological problems.

Our current assessor was fortunate in that she was able to find a suitable instrument—the empirical base on scales of acculturation for Hispanics and even subgroups of Hispanics (e.g., Mexican Americans) is robust (Wallace, Pomery, Latimer, Martinez, & Salovey, 2010). However, for other ethnic groups, such measures are lacking altogether or are in a very rudimentary stage of development. For example, the assessor seeking an acculturation measure to incorporate into the testing of the Gambian client would have been hard pressed to find something suitable. Indeed, psychological assessors have given sustained and deep attention to diversity factors only recently (Dana, 2000), and it is therefore likely that many questions clients and their assessors might pose are not entirely addressable. In such circumstances, the assessor—in the service of the principle of Integrity—carries an ethical burden to disclose, both in the informed consent and in any communications about the test findings, what gaps might exist in the data collected.

Interpreting the Data

The following vignette illustrates how the interpretive stage of the assessment process can invite the emergence of diversity-related assessor biases and how a good supervisory relationship can address them. This vignette is more extended than the prior ones because it addresses issues pertaining both to interpretation and supervision of assessment. It also illustrates how the broader training context can influence diversity-sensitive ethical decision-making.

> Dr. Sneed had been supervising Luke for four months. During that time, Luke had conducted a number of personality assessments of adult clients, both male and female. Dr. Sneed began to note a pattern over time. When the configuration of variables suggested self-sufficiency in a man, Luke described it as such. Women who appeared in similar fashion to their male counterparts were described as counterdependent. That is, Luke saw them as rejecting their strong dependency urges. Dr. Sneed was puzzled by these different clinical profiles and pulled the charts to examine the data more closely. Upon once again finding no appreciable difference among the men and women, she concluded that Luke might be operating under the sway of gender stereotypes. She wondered whether for him, women who show independence are suspect—the independence might not be all that it seems and likely possesses a defensive character. She decided she would sensitively broach her impression with Luke.

Adequate functioning as a professional psychologist requires not only a knowledge base and skill set but also, the professional attitudes that enable the most successful use of knowledge and skills (Kaslow, 2004). Luke's attitude toward female clients could quite possibly exert a negative influence on their overall well-being in that functioning that is likely to be in the service of adaptation—the ability to attempt to meet one's own needs—is seen and presented to the client in pathological terms. All assessors are likely to be the victims of their own cultural experiences if they leave unchallenged the assumptions they bring about various individuals. The time that these assumptions are most likely to be exposed is during the training years when, by definition, the clinician is in a period of receiving feedback. In years subsequent to one's training years, adverse outcomes might occur but the framework might not be present for the clinician to realize what these outcomes are saying about his or her practice. Assessment supervisors may be in a privileged role in being able to identify biases in that they are exposed to a student's work across a number of cases. They thereby can see the student's potentially differential response to the variability among human beings.

Understanding how any assessment practitioner goes about the task of making an ethical decision when diversity issues are engaged might be enhanced by considering Kurt Lewin's (1947) *force field* framework of thinking about the forces that lead an individual to progress toward a goal. In this case, the goal is the formation of a diversity-sensitive ethical decision, and the carrying out of that decision. What will influence the assessment practitioner in moving toward that goal is the balance of restraining forces and driving forces that operate within that assessor's context.

Restraining Forces on Explorations

Supervisors might be reluctant to work with a supervisee about the latter's biases for many reasons. They might doubt their own perceptions. They might feel that supervision is not a forum in which such problems can be addressed intensively and thoroughly. They might worry about the supervisee's possible defensiveness and the potential for such explorations to undermine the relationship. They might fear that the supervisee will give the supervisor a negative evaluation or take some other retaliatory action against the supervisor (Knauss, 2001). Given that faculty have very different ways of responding to competency incidents (e.g., Forrest et al., 2013), particularly those related to diversity (Shen-Miller, Forrest, & Burt, 2012), she might have feared that other faculty may have objected to her taking up with the student the bias in his assessments. At a more internal level, the supervisor might have feared that she had sensitivity, perhaps undue sensitivity, toward the supervisee's stance toward women because she was a woman. She might be concerned that she was introducing her own issues into the supervisor relationship. All of these apprehensions are understandable and, to some extent, go with the supervisory territory. Still, the consequence of the supervisor's failure to make these matters part of supervision is that the supervisee might allow his or her prejudices to influence negatively his or her clinical work throughout that clinician's career—a circumstance at odds with the ethical principles of Justice and Respect for People's Rights and Dignity (APA, 2002). Hence, the stakes are high.

Driving Forces on Explorations

Although supervisors have many reasons for avoiding a serious discussion with a student about a diversity issue, embracing the challenge of doing so is an ethical responsibility for all supervisors, including assessment supervisors. In fact, as Jacobs et al. (2011) note in their article on difficult conversations with trainees, the ability to participate in such conversations is a core competency of supervisors. These authors recognize that in addressing these problems with trainees, the supervisor is adhering to those general ethical principles that should inform all psychologists' behaviors. For example, Dr. Sneed, in helping Luke to identify and modify his gender-based assumptions, would be avoiding that harm that would result from seeing women and their assessment results through the lens of a sexual stereotype.

Rather than succumbing to these apprehensions, the trainer might seek ways to ameliorate them. One means is to develop with students a supervisory contract that anticipates for them the possibility that they will receive feedback concerning biases affecting assessment work. The supervisor may say something like, "When all of us begin learning assessment, we are the products of our backgrounds and carry worldviews that will affect the assessment work we do. One of my roles is to identify elements of that worldview that I see as operating in a given assessment or across different assessments that is important for your investigation." Such a statement can have a salubrious effect on the supervisor's willingness to confront sensitive topics and the supervisee's nondefensive reception of such areas of exploration.

Also part of that initial contract will be a specification of how, upon their identification, such areas are to be treated. A source of anxiety for both supervisors and supervisees is when supervision devolves to psychotherapy with all of the difficulties therein. Supervisors can establish for themselves and their supervisees that supervision will identify areas of concern, which psychotherapy can explore further. The identification of a problem is a powerful step; many supervisees will make the necessary adjustments simply by recognizing a certain unwholesome stance. For others, more work is needed and it is important that programs have in place affordable means for students to accomplish that work.

The Contribution of the Program

Supervisors perform their training functions in broader systems such as doctoral programs, and those systems play a large role in how diversity-related assessment problems are pursued. However, the training program in which the faculty member is embedded also has a big role in whether issues at the intersection of diversity and ethics can be productively addressed by faculty. In this way, programs themselves can vary in their ethical responsiveness. Supportive programs recognize that such issues will emerge in students' work and regard it as a faculty responsibility to address those problems (Forrest et al., 2013). In such programs, discussions occur among faculty regularly on how students can be abetted in fruitful self-examination in regard to their diversity-related attitudes and behaviors. These programs also make a commitment to students' developing what Bieschke and Mintz (2012) term "demographic competence" and require students to have an array of clients with a range of demographic characteristics. It is this circumstance that enables the students' attitudes to reveal themselves, attitudes that are then available for exploration.

The Assessment Practitioner

Even if Dr. Sneed provided Luke with abundant information about his biases, once Luke was functioning more independently, he would continue to need to be vigilant. New clinical experiences could invite the emergence of previously unexamined prejudices toward classes of individuals. Assessment practitioners require an internalized Dr. Sneed who continually reflects not only on individual cases but also on patterns, so as to detect preconceived views that influence the data on which the assessor focuses and the data he or she ignores.

Although this example pertained to supervision, in fact many of the essential points apply to assessor practitioners as well. The most essential point is that the assessment practitioner needs to recognize that he or she is likely to have biases. These biases can be the result of idiosyncratic experience or the internalization of societal stereotypes about particular groups. A level of assessor humility and awareness of the fallibility of clinical judgment will aid that practitioner in the process of taking stock—that is, looking at patterns of practice and seeing emotional or attitudinal features that could impair clinical judgment.

Another essential point is that even if an assessment practitioner is not in a supervisory relationship with a co-worker but sees that co-worker engage in diversity-insensitive practices (for example, along the lines of Luke in the prior vignette), then that assessment practitioner has an ethical obligation to help the co-worker recognize the need to respond in more helpful ways to his or her client's multiple identities. If an organization in which an assessor practitioner offers services exhibits diversity insensitivities that affect the assessment practitioner's ability to conduct ethical assessments, then that assessment practitioner is obligated to educate the organization on diversity sensitivity.

Providing Feedback

The assessment practitioner has an obligation to provide feedback to his or her assessment clients. The diversity that the client presents might require significant adaptations on how feedback is typically given. Even if the client has impediments in receiving feedback in the way the feedback is customarily provided, the obligation to offer feedback nonetheless exists.

> Mrs. Thack, a woman in her mid-eighties, had been exhibiting signs of depression and difficulty performing everyday tasks. Her son, observing these difficulties, arranges for a psychological assessment to obtain a picture of her problems, and Mrs. Thack readily agrees. She proceeds through the assessment process cooperatively. The assessor is aware that Mrs. Thack might find the feedback difficult to understand, both cognitively and emotionally. Mrs. Thack's son indicates that the assessor should give the feedback to him and he will tell her "whatever she needs to know. That way Mother won't get upset."

The feedback session is an element of the assessment that should be agreed upon at the commencement of the assessment. Still, circumstances arise where one party or another seeks a change in the agreed-upon arrangement. The assessor is then faced with the dilemma of whether to accede to the request for an alteration or whether to continue with the original plan, which in this case involved the assessor giving Mrs. Thack direct feedback.

In this circumstance, the assessment practitioner might be tempted to acquiesce to the son's plan. The assessor might wish to please the son or avoid conflict with him. Additionally, the assessor may wish to lessen or eliminate his anxiety over giving Mrs. Thack what might well be difficult information. Of course, the concern about subjecting Mrs. Thack to unnecessary discomfort comes from the assessor's recognition of the principle of Nonmaleficence—to do no harm. The assessor might also be under the sway of an internalized ageist attitude that leads him to treat elderly individuals in patronizing ways (Languirand, 2016). What is key is the assessment practitioner's capacity to be aware of these factors so that they are less likely to lead the assessor to behave in a way at odds with his ethical duty. Like the supervisor in the last vignette, some insight into these factors might be achieved by studying practice patterns. For example, the assessor might ask himself whether his feedback sessions with elderly individuals or perhaps, more specifically, elderly women, departs in some way from his feedback protocol with other individuals. Were he to discern some differences, he could then reflect upon their possible emotional and attitudinal roots. He might also seek out consultation with another assessment practitioner to explore the matter further.

Additional factors might be important for the assessor to recognize in that they could provide that assessor the means to honor not only Nonmaleficence but also Respect for People's Rights and Dignity, and Beneficence. A first consideration is that the presence of some difficulties on the part of the client in understanding feedback does not remove the assessor's obligation to provide it, an obligation which, when fulfilled, honors Respect for People's Rights and Dignity. Rather, it simply necessitates that the assessor be thoughtful in developing a feedback plan. Presumably, the assessor has already had some conversation with Mrs. Thack about her performance during the assessment process. The assessor's experience of what she was able to both receive and offer would provide the basis for customizing a form of feedback that would be effective. In designing a useful feedback plan, the assessor honors the principle of Beneficence. Another consideration is that Mrs. Thack herself is likely to have a healthy curiosity about the assessor's findings and this curiosity might well not be satisfied by her son's overview of the findings. The assessor, too, is in need of Mrs. Thack's input at the time of the feedback. How she responds to various observations about her could be useful to the assessor in refining his observations. Finally, the assessor might realize that he enjoys a position of relative neutrality. Family members are stakeholders, often seeking data that may fit their preconceived ideas and plans. For example, Mrs. Thack's son might have a desire to have her placed in assisted living and be seeking evidence to support this agenda. The assessment practitioner lacks the kind of personal investment that could contribute to a skewed presentation of findings.

Conclusions and Future Directions

Diversity attunement is key to the formation of sound judgments and the development of effective courses of ethical action. This truth is solidly ensconced in the ethical principles that inspire psychologists to practice according to the highest ideals of their profession. Despite the acknowledgment of the intimate tie between diversity awareness and ethical decision-making, research on how or even whether assessors factor in diversity information in ethical thinking, does not exist. The field would benefit from data on how assessors incorporate diversity information in their ethical decision-making. However, ethical, diversity-sensitive decision-making cannot wait for the accrual of researched data. In the meantime, assessors and their clients would be well served by their application of knowledge that has been amassed on clinical judgments and ethical decision-making, such as the errors to which assessors are prone in their weighting of different factors as they confront various ethical nodal points across the assessment process.

References

American Psychological Association. (2010). Ethical principles of psychologists and code of conduct. Accessed at www.apa.org/ethics/code/principles.pdf. doi:10.1037/0003-066X.47.12.1597

Ashton, C. M., Haidet, P., Paterniti, D. A., Collins, T. C., Gordon, H. S., O'Malley, K., et al. (2003). Racial and ethnic disparities in the use of health services. *Journal of general internal medicine, 18*(2), 146–152. doi: 10.1046/j.1525-1497.2003.20532.x

Beauchamp, T. L., & Childress, J. F. (2001). *Principles of biomedical ethics* (5th ed.). New York: Oxford.

Bieschke, K. J., & Mintz, L. B. (2012). Counseling psychology model training values statement addressing diversity: History, current use, and future directions. *Training and Education in Professional Psychology, 6*(4), 196–203. doi: 10.1037/a0030810

Brabender, V., & Bricklin, P. (2001). Ethical issues in psychological assessment in different settings. *Journal of Personality Assessment, 77*(2), 192–194. doi: 10.1207/S15327752JPA7702_02

Dana, R. (2000). *Handbook of cross-cultural and multicultural personality assessment.* Mahwah, NJ: Lawrence Erlbaum.

Forrest, L., Elman, N. S., Huprich, S. K., Veilleux, J. C., Jacobs, S. C., & Kaslow, N. J. (2013). Training directors' perceptions of faculty behaviors when dealing with trainee competence problems: A mixed method pilot study. *Training and Education in Professional Psychology, 7*(1), 23–32. doi: 10.1037/a0032068

Gatmon, D., Koshkarian, L., Martos-Perry, N., Molina, A., Patel, N., & Rodolfa, E. (2001). Exploring ethnic, gender, and sexual orientation variables in supervision: Do they really matter? *Journal of Multicultural Counseling and Development, 29*(2), 102–113. doi: 10.1002/j.2161-1912.2001.tb00508.x

Hansen, N. D., Randazzo, K. V., Schwartz, A., Marshall, M., Kalis, D., Frazier, R., et al. (2006). Do we practice what we preach? An exploratory survey of multicultural psychotherapy competencies. *Professional Psychology: Research and Practice, 37*(1), 66–74. doi: 10.1037/0735-7028.37.1.66

Hays, P. A. (2005). *Addressing cultural complexities in practice: A framework for clinicians and counselors* (2nd ed.). Washington, DC: American Psychological Association.

Jacobs, S. C., Huprich, S. K., Grus, C. L., Cage, E. A., Elman, N. S., Forrest, L., et al. (2011). Trainees with professional competency problems: Preparing trainers for difficult but necessary conversations. *Training and Education in Professional Psychology, 5*(3), 175–184. doi: 10.1037/a0024656

Jones, S., Howard, L., & Thornicroft, G. (2008). "Diagnostic overshadowing": Worse physical health care for people with mental illness. *Acta Psychiatrica Scandinavica, 118*(3), 169–171. doi: 10.1111/j.1600-0447.2008.01211.x

Kaslow, N. J. (2004). Competencies in professional psychology. *American Psychologist, 59*, 774–781. doi: 10.1037/0003-066X.59.8.774

Knauss, L. (2001). Ethical issues in psychological assessment in school settings. *Journal of Personality Assessment, 77*(2), 231–241. doi: 10.1207/S15327752JPA7702_06

Knauss, L. (2013, Summer). Ethics, remediation, and competency in assessment. *SPA Exchange, 25*(2), 4; 12–13.

Languirand, M. (2016). Who I was, who I am: Gender and generativity in the assessment of older adults. In V. M. Brabender & J. L. Mihura (Eds.), *Handbook of gender and sexuality in psychological assessment*. (pp. 578–602). New York: Routledge.

Lewin, K. (1947). Frontiers of group dynamics: Concept, method and reality in social science, social equilibria, and social change. *Human Relations, 1*, 5–41.

Rogerson, M. D., Gottlieb, M. C., Handelsman, M. M., Knapp, S., & Younggren, J. (2011). Nonrational processes in ethical decision-making. *American Psychologist, 66*(7), 614–623. doi: 10.1037/a0025215

Rosenberg, A., Almeida, A., & Macdonald, H. (2012). Crossing the cultural divide: Issues in translation, mistrust, and cocreation of meaning in cross-cultural therapeutic assessment. *Journal of Personality Assessment, 94*(3), 223–231. doi: 10.1080/00223891.2011.648293

Russ, S. W. (2001). Tackling ethical dilemmas in personality assessment. *Journal of Personality Assessment, 77*(2), 255–258. doi: 10.1207/S15327752JPA7702_08

Sammons, C. C., & Speight, S. L. (2008). A qualitative investigation of graduate-student changes associated with multicultural counseling courses. *The Counseling Psychologist, 36*(6), 814–838.

Shen-Miller, D. S., Forrest, L., & Burt, M. (2012). Contextual influences on faculty diversity conceptualizations when working with trainee competence problems. *The Counseling Psychologist, 40*, 1181–1219. doi: 10.1177/0011000011431832

Smith, T. B., Constantine, M. G., Dunn, T. W., Dinehart, J. M., & Montoya, J. A. (2006). Multicultural education in the mental health professions: A meta-analytic review. *Journal of Counseling Psychology, 53*(1), 132–145. doi: 10.1037/0022-0167.53.1.132

Wallace, P. M., Pomery, E. A., Latimer, A. E., Martinez, J. L., & Salovey, P. (2010). A review of acculturation measures and their utility in studies promoting Latino health. *Hispanic Journal of Behavioral Sciences, 32*(1), 37–54.

CHAPTER 19

Supervision and Training of Personality Assessment with Multicultural and Diverse Clients

Jed Yalof

Watkins, writing in 1991, asked the question: "Psychodiagnostic assessment supervision: What do we really know about it?" Watkins noted the discrepancy between therapy and assessment literatures in favor of therapy. Now, almost 25 years later, not much has changed. A psychologist searching for guidance in the area of psychotherapy supervision will be welcomed by an extensive literature that paints a broad stroke over the supervision canvas, including its models, techniques, and outcome measures. In contrast, this same psychologist would have to search far and wide to uncover an empirical base for the supervision of psychological assessment. Whereas the psychotherapy supervisor has scholarly texts (e.g., Falender & Shafranske, 2004; Ladany, Friedlander, & Nelson, 2005; Watkins, 1997) as supplements to the high volume of peer-reviewed citations that comprise an empirical base, the assessment supervisor must rely on a handful of articles sampling assessment supervision, including stages (Finkelstein & Tuckman, 1997), competencies (Krishnamurthy & Yalof, 2010), and techniques (e.g., Yalof & Abraham, 2009).

This discrepancy between psychotherapy and assessment supervision is played out even more so in the area of multiculturalism and diversity. Psychotherapy texts (e.g., Comas-Diaz, 2012; Sue & Sue, 1999) supplement a rich, journal-based scholarship that dwarfs the multicultural assessment supervision literature. The situation becomes more myopic when the search targets multicultural supervision of personality assessment as a narrow scope within the broader field of psychological assessment (e.g., Allen, 2007; Dana, 2005). Thus, while it might be an overstatement that psychologists supervising multicultural personality assessment have nowhere to turn, there is no doubting the disadvantage they face when it comes to identifying a coherent literature in this area.

This chapter organizes a literature for psychologists who supervise and train developing psychologists in multicultural personality assessment. The range of people to whom the term "culturally diverse" might apply was described broadly by López (1997, p. 570) as "those from the U.S. ethnic and racial groups other than the majority group of Euro-American backgrounds." First, practice guidelines, ethics and standards, competency with multicultural and diverse clients, education and training benchmarks, and models of supervision are discussed. Second, a review of the literature on personality assessment with multicultural and diverse clients is offered, including applications to different tests and measures and supervision techniques. Third, a clinical vignette is provided that integrates the literature review. Fourth, different dimensions are recommended for evaluating supervisee competency in the areas of diversity, multiculturalism, and personality assessment.

General Supervisory Considerations

Practice Guidelines

The assessment supervisor has flexibility when it comes to determining the focus of a supervisory session, but the supervision process itself is subject to practice guidelines that inform clinical work with all clients. The American Psychological Association (APA) has published competency guidelines and definitions that address multiculturalism and diversity (American Psychological Association, 2003), lesbian, gay, and bisexual clients (2012a), individuals with disabilities (2012b) with applications to psychological assessment, and, most recently guidelines for supervision in health service psychology (2015; see Domain B: Diversity). The APA (2003) stated that "Multiculturalism, in an absolute sense, recognized the broad scope of dimensions of race, ethnicity, language, sexual orientation, gender, age, disability, class status, education, religious/spiritual orientation, and other cultural dimensions" (p. 380).

The APA (2003) further encouraged psychologists, under Guideline 5, to apply "culturally appropriate skills" (p. 390) and included assessment under this guideline. Specifically, psychologists are encouraged to be sensitive to the limitations of assessment with respect to particular groups, as well as "test bias, test fairness, and cultural equivalence" (p. 391). Fair use in assessment was discussed recently in detail (American Educational Research Association, American Psychological Association, & National Council on Measurement in Education, 2014). Challenges associated with applying tests and measures cross-culturally have been discussed in some detail by Byrne et al. (2009) and Leong, Leung, and Cheung (2010).

Ethics and Standards

The APA's practice guidelines are implemented against a backdrop of professional ethics. With respect to clinical assessment, the APA's (2010) "Ethical Principles of Psychologists and Code of Conduct" addresses many general practice considerations that interface with personality testing, including human relations, competence, informed consent, privacy and confidentiality, record keeping, and therapy-intervention under different standards. In particular, Standard 9 focuses on assessment. Here, the psychologist must consider the following standards when practicing, teaching, or supervising assessment: (9.01) bases for assessment, (9.02) use of assessments, (9.03) informed consent in assessments, (9.04) release of test data, (9.05) test construction, (9.06) interpreting assessment results, (9.07) assessment by unqualified persons, (9.08) obsolete tests and outdated test results, (9.09) test scoring and interpretation services, (9.10) explaining assessment results, and (9.11) maintaining test security.

The APA's parameter for ethical conduct guides the manner in which the psychologist practices, trains, and educates others in the area of personality assessment, but does not focus per se on supervision. The Canadian Psychological Association (2009) provides this focus in its "Ethical Guidelines for Supervision in Psychology: Teaching, Research, Practice, and Administration." Pettifor, McCarron, Schoepp, Stark, and Stewart (2011, p. 198) reviewed the four ethical principles that comprise the 2000 Canadian Code of Ethics for Psychologists (i.e., "Respect for Dignity of Person, Responsible Caring, Integrity in Relationships, and Responsibility to Society") and discussed them in relation to clinical supervision. They also summarized a literature on supervisor and supervisee behaviors that supported ethical conduct. Supervisors are expected to (a) maintain a working alliance, (b) evaluate, observe, and serve as gatekeepers, (c) provide support and feedback, (d) facilitate self-evaluation, (e) instruct, model, mentor, and encourage collaborate problem solving. Supervisees are expected to (a) understand tasks, boundaries, purpose, and roles of supervision, (b) maintain a working alliance with the supervisor and prepare for supervision, and (c) be receptive to feedback and initiate discussion of "innovative ideas."

Multicultural Competencies

The importance of multicultural competency has become a focal point in training and education of psychologists. Rodolfa et al. (2013) noted that Interpersonal and Multicultural Competence was one of six central competency areas for education and training. Schaffer, Rodolfa, Hatcher, and Fouad (2013) found that diversity and assessment were the only core competencies included as part of the competency matrices of seven major professional training organizations. The importance of culture and diversity in education and training was highlighted by Rings, Genuchi, Hall, Angelo, and Cornish (2009), who reported that internship directors felt that supervisor competence should include knowledge of diversity. This finding fits with the importance of cultural and individual diversity as part of internship training. For example, Stedman, Schoenfeld, and O'Donnell (2013) reported that internship directors dedicated 13% of their time to issues of cultural and individual diversity, with only intervention (23%) and assessment/diagnosis (23%) garnering more time.

The development of supervisee competence in multiculturalism and diversity is influenced by the quality of the supervisory experience. When the supervisor is culturally competent, the supervisee is more apt to develop knowledge, skills, and attitudes that reflect this same area. Yabusaki's (2010) definition of supervision "as a process of communication embedded in cultural nuances" (p. 56) captured a supervisory process that entwines culture and diversity with the interpersonal and collaborative elements of supervision. Yet, despite the growing significance of multicultural and diversity competence in supervision, it was just a decade ago that Falender and Shafranske (2004) stated, "Notwithstanding that it is a core component of psychology training, diversity is one of the most neglected areas in supervision training and research" (p. 115). To redress this neglect, they included the following as cultural competency requisites for supervisors (also see López, 1997): (a) an understanding of factors that affect one's worldview; (b) self-identity awareness and competencies with respect to diversity (also see Ancis & Ladany, 2010; Singh & Chun, 2010); (c) modeling of multicultural and diversity conceptualizations (also see Inman & Kreider, 2013); (d) respect, openness, and curiosity about diversity; and (e) the willingness to initiate conversations with supervisees about diversity factors in supervision (also see Andrews et al., 2013; Aten & Hernandez, 2004; Jernigan, Green, Helms, Perez-Gualdron, & Henze, 2010; Nilsson & Anderson, 2004).

One might also incorporate and apply the work of Helms (1990) and Sue and Sue (1999) to the supervisory triad (i.e., client, supervisee, supervisor) to enhance competency through a deeper appreciation of how culture, race, and power each affect identity development and inform the supervisory process. Additionally, the concept of "diversity supervision" (Roysircar, Dobbins, & Malloy, 2010), with its emphasis on the supervisor's well-rounded integration of knowledge, skill, and attitudinal considerations, would appear to provide further direction to supervisors who incorporate diversity into their supervisory practice. Diversity supervision has "several facilitative components" that include the supervisor's "awareness of their own racial, cultural, sexuality, class, and ability values; openness, vulnerability and self-disclosure; sincere commitment to attending to and exploring cultural factors, and providing opportunities to their supervisees for diversity activities" (p. 192).

Developmental Benchmarks and Supervision Models

What are the developmental expectations for assessment students at different stages of training and how do they dovetail with cultural competency? Training models expect students to accumulate knowledge, skills, and attitudes consistent with the profession and to receive supervision appropriate to their progressive development. This holds for cultural and diversity learning and for assessment. Krishnamurthy and Yalof (2010) described benchmarking criteria for assessment education and training. During the *practicum* stage of training, expectations for assessment supervisees include basic knowledge of ethics, test and measurement theory, and a model or strategy for assessment. Foundation skills are expected in the areas of test administration and scoring, conveying results to clients, explaining decisions, constructive use of supervision, and the development of a respectful objectivity and inquiry about the assessment process. As supervisees advance to *predoctoral internship*, expectations shift. Supervisees on internship are expected to know constructs and theories that underlie tests, the strengths and limitations of intellectual and personality tests, norming methods with application to diverse populations, and how to identify and plan a course of action related to risk issues in assessment. Internship is also a time when supervisees move toward more openness in defining and addressing issues about the supervision process, integrative test interpretation, test selection that is specific to referrals, and providing test feedback in a way that includes a more sophisticated understanding of tests through the application of intervention skills. Interns are also expected to mature in their attitude about the value of psychological testing in clinical work. At the *postdoctoral* level, expectations include the ability to apply relevant legal and ethical principles to all aspects of the assessment process, seek consultation as needed, select and evaluate tests critically, and commit to an attitude of life-long learning in the area of assessment. This model covers multiculturalism, diversity, and ethics as part of the sequential assessment curriculum and expects assessment supervisors to support student development throughout their educational experience.

With this background in the areas of multiculturalism and diversity, supervisors are better equipped to help students move through their own growth and development in acquiring the knowledge, skills, and attitudes for assuming supervisory and management responsibilities in their roles as psychologists (Malloy, Dobbins, Ducheny, & Winfrey, 2010). The knowledge, skills, and attitudes that define different stages of education and training in supervision and management transverse several domains, including: (a) assuring client and organizational welfare, (b) training/mentoring, (c) evaluation/gatekeeping, (d) ethics, and (e) health care leadership and advocacy. Jones, Sander, and Booker (2013) added an "advocacy and action" dimension to the knowledge, skills, and attitude component of student learning about diversity and multiculturalism. They recommended several teaching tools (e.g., questionnaires, literature and film, case conceptualizations, and being mentored by someone who is "culturally different") to nurture the acquisition of these skills. Assessment-specific supervisory techniques that further support this identification might include specially designed cases that tap issues of multiculturalism and diversity, and other supervisory assessment techniques discussed later in this chapter (Krishnamurthy & Yalof, 2010; Yalof & Abraham, 2009).

While key markers in the supervisee's acquisition of knowledge, skills, and competencies are part of any assessment curriculum, models of assessment supervision that systematically benchmark supervisee progress through developmental stages are scarce. Allen's (2007) model of multicultural assessment is an exception because of its primary focus on assessment and movement toward the integration of racial identity, development of supervisor and supervisee, working alliance, multicultural assessment competence, assessment supervision, and evaluation methods reflective of multicultural assessment competence. According to Allen:

> *Multicultural assessment supervision* can refer to supervision of an assessment process in which the person assessed and the assessor are from different backgrounds, the supervisor and trainee are from different cultural backgrounds, or the assessment instrument used was developed with a cultural group different from the cultural background of the person assessed.
>
> (p. 248; italics in original)

Allen outlined the dimensions of culturally competent assessment: (a) measurement theory, (b) collaborative assessment, (c) culturally sensitive interviewing,

(d) assessment of acculturation status, (e) test interpretation that is based on cultural understanding, local norms, culture-sensitive tests, and ethics, and (f) report writing that reflects a multicultural awareness.

Allen's model was informed by Finkelstein and Tuckman's (1997) developmental stage model of assessment supervisee identity formation. Finkelstein and Tuckman discussed how the developmental level of the supervisor has to match the supervisee's developmental level to support the supervisee's integration of requisite skills and knowledge. The model has eight stages through which the supervisee achieves higher levels of autonomy. Although Finkelstein and Tuckman's model provided a general framework for tracking the internal shifts in supervisee identity as an assessor and speculated about supervisor development in relation to supervisee experience, it has not been tested empirically nor does it offer specific direction related to multiculturalism and cross-cultural assessment. Indeed, empirical models of supervisor development have been lacking in general, as noted by Barker and Hunsley (2013) in their systematic review of the literature. They found that Watkins' "Supervisor Complexity Model" (SCM; 1993) was the most frequently cited model and the only model that had a measurement instrument for evaluating supervisor development. In the SCM, supervisors move through various stages, which, according to Watkins, "each represent increasingly complex constellations of tasks, crises, and responsibilities with which supervisors must cope" (p. 65). The stages are (a) "role shock" (i.e., struggling with imposter feelings), (b) "role recovery and transition" (i.e., improved self-confidence and maturing identity as a supervisor), (c) "role consolidation" (i.e., increased consistency in self-assessment), and (d) "role mastery" (i.e., consistent use of theory, increased flexibility, more comfortable in the supervision"). More recently, Watkins and Scaturo (2013) described a supervisory model that engages affective, cognitive, and psychomotor learning corresponding to a "three-stage supervision structure": (a) Supervision Alliance Building and Maintenance/predominantly affective learning, (b) Educational Interventions/predominantly cognitive learning, and (c) Learning/Relearning/predominantly psychomotor learning or "putting it into practice" (p. 78). Thus, an integrative approach to the supervision of personality assessment might wish to incorporate some of these ideas.

Culturally Competent Personality Assessment

The Society for Personality Assessment (2006) advocated education and training standards for competent personality assessment practice. These standards included an understanding of psychometrics, and skills with a range of performance-based and self-report personality tests and measures (e.g., administration, integrative data analysis and report writing, feedback, assessment–treatment relationship). Other sources are needed to direct supervisors and students in their work with students in the area of culturally competent personality assessment. Krishnamurthy (2013), for example, recommended that students actively seek assessment experiences with diverse clients, read the literature on multicultural and cross-cultural assessment, and engage in non-clinical psychology diversity experiences; these are recommendations that supervisors can offer to students. Comas-Diaz (2012) described the importance of culturally sensitive diagnostic interviewing and presented an extensive listing of 32 categories to investigate during an interview. Included among these categories were ability and disability, acculturation, discrimination, ethnicity, folk beliefs, immigration and migration, language, socioeconomic status, sexual orientation, race, and religion and spirituality. Careful diagnostic interviewing safeguards against what López (as cited in Comas-Diaz, 2012) identified as bias sources; namely, pathologizing, minimizing, overdiagnosing, and underdiagnosing. Other ways to increase test score validity included engaging in emic (i.e., culture-specific) etiquette, exercising caution when using computerized interpretive narrative reports that are not attentive to cultural factors, and displaying sensitivity to cultural factors during feedback (see also Rosenberg, Almeida, & Macdonald, 2012).

Regarding instrumentation and application, and their relationship to multicultural personality assessment, Dana (2005) has been a pioneer in addressing many of the areas that are easily overlooked in the typical training curriculum. Dana stated, "Multicultural assessment distinguishes between what clinicians now understand about standard instruments and familiar populations and what remains to be known from research and experience that is relevant for high-stakes assessment practice with unfamiliar populations" (p. ix). Dana presented a checklist for multicultural assessment reports that included: (a) relationship to the examinee, (b) cultural information, (c) adequacy of test data and cultural information for clinical inferences, (d) assessment confounds, (e) summarizing the report, and (f) formal report characteristics, such as length and readability. Dana also described ethical multicultural assessment-intervention practice that included the importance of evaluating the presence or absence of language barriers, use of emic measures, cultural diagnostic formulation, and attention to cultural-racial identity. Dana offered suggestions for acculturation measures for different groups (pp. 85–89), and a listing of culture-specific and culture-general measures (p. 106). He commented on the need for additional measures related to the client's culture (p. 104), and offered several instructive examples integrating cultural factors with personality test findings.

Many of the more commonly taught personality assessment instruments have been studied for cross-cultural and international applications. Recent literature (Piotrowski, 2015) supports the continued usage of personality assessment across cultures. Personality assessment supervisors should have some familiarity with this literature. For example, international Rorschach norms have been developed (Shaffer, Erdberg, & Meyer, 2007), with a more confident recommendation for their application to adults than children or adolescents (Meyer, Erdberg, & Shaffer, 2007). Abraham (2003) offered a review of multicultural and diversity assessment with story-telling techniques and measures. Adaptation of the MMPI-2 has been studied cross-culturally (e.g., Butcher, 2011; Pace et al., 2006), internationally (e.g., Butcher & Williams, 2009) and for cross-racial implications (e.g., Hall, Bansal, & López, 1999). Between-group racial differences have been studied using the Beck Depression Inventory-II (Sashidharan, Pawlow, & Pettibone, 2012). The Revised

NEO Personality Inventory has been studied internationally (McCrae, Terracciano, & 79 Members of the Personality Profiles Project, 2005) as well and for cross-racial differences (Sutin, Costa, Evans, & Zonderman, 2013). Cross-cultural applications of the Personality Assessment Inventory have also been investigated (Correa & Rogers, 2010). Recently, Ponterotto et al. (2014) reported on the psychometric properties of a new Multicultural Personality Inventory. In sum, there exists a body of literature from which supervisors can draw when helping supervisees make decisions about personality assessment applications to a culturally diverse population.

Guidelines for Diversity-Sensitive Assessment Supervision and Training

Clinical applications of the literature summary provide supervisors and supervisees with illustrations for diversity-sensitive assessment. A hypothetical case illustration is presented, which provides instructional opportunities for supervisors and faculty members who teach clinical supervision. The illustration permits integration of the literature review, discussion of key learning points, and a model for developing other illustrations with different client–assessor–supervisor pairings related to multiculturalism and diversity that support student and supervisor professional development.

Illustration

Bill, a Latino, transgender, 33-year-old man (female to male) complained of anxiety and depression. He had been in two relationships post-gender transition, each of which were ungratifying. He sought help at a clinic that accepted his insurance, and met with Dr. James, a Caucasian, heterosexual 44-year-old senior-level male psychologist for an intake. Dr. James then referred Bill to Jane, a Caucasian, heterosexual, 28-year-old woman who was completing her first clinical practicum. Dr. James was Jane's supervisor and asked Jane to evaluate Bill prior to assigning a therapist.

Jane was aware that she would be evaluating a transgender individual; she thought this was an "exciting" opportunity, shared it with her classmates, and told her mother, with whom she was very close. Jane conducted a clinical interview as part of the assessment. During the clinical interview Jane felt anxious. She was writing down background information, but made little eye contact and was self-conscious about her desire to look directly at Bill. Bill, with somewhat of a flirtatious grin, told Jane that he sensed her nervousness, which made Jane blush. Jane also was aware that she found Bill attractive. She had the thought of asking Bill: "What was it *really* like to change from a woman to a man?" but this felt more like a personal curiosity that could embarrass Bill than a clinically based question, so Jane opted not to ask it. She also wanted to ask: "How accepted do you feel in the Latin community," but withheld this question for the same reason; that is, it felt too personal. As the interview concluded, Bill and Jane shook hands. Bill noticed that Jane's palms were sweaty and apologized if he made her nervous. Jane thanked him for his comment and told Bill that he would be assigned a therapist. Bill asked if Jane would work with him; again, she blushed, but said that the decision would be up to Dr. James.

Jane administered a self-report inventory and the Rorschach test. Jane then met with Dr. James for supervision. She was reluctant to share her personal reactions to Bill, but mentioned that she was not sure whether to identify Bill as male or female when entering Bill's identifying information into the computerized scoring programs. MMPI-2 T scores were elevated (range of 65–70) on scales of hypochondriasis, depression, and psychasthenia. When reviewing the Rorschach test, Jane noted several incongruous combination (Exner, 2003) responses (e.g., Card I: "A bat with hands;" Card VII: "A woman with what looks like a protruding Adam's Apple") as well as one fabulized combination (Card VIII: "A mountain lion climbing a stairway") response, each of which Jane attributed to Bill's transgender self-image.

In what follows, I offer some questions that might facilitate supervisory formulations about how to best help Bill.

1. Are Dr. James and Jane familiar with the transgender literature, especially female-to-male transition?
2. Are Dr. James and Jane familiar with the literature on how Latinos feel about transgender individuals?
3. What does the literature say about how to best utilize gendered, normative data for transgender individuals who are administered personality tests?
4. How might Dr. James facilitate discussion of Jane's concerns about entering information about Bill's gender into the computerized interpretive programs?
5. How might Dr. James help Jane think flexibly about the content of Bill's Rorschach responses such that all interpretive options are considered?
6. Are there other tests that Dr. James might have recommended? If so, which?
7. How might Dr. James invite Jane to talk about the client–assessor interaction, and about her excitement in talking to her mother about her assessment of a transgender individual, in a way that encourages discussion of transference-countertransference issues that could emerge in therapy?
8. How might Dr. James' developmental level as an experienced supervisor affect his understanding of Jane's developmental stage as a trainee, and how might it differ if Dr. James was a relatively inexperienced supervisor?
9. If you were Dr. James, would you assign Jane to be Bill's therapist and why/why not?

Evaluation of Supervisees

There are many items for the supervisor's reflection when deciding how to evaluate supervisee progress in the area of multicultural and diversity assessment.

The literature suggests that the following categories be considered when evaluating the supervisee, with awareness of the supervisee's developmental level: (a) ethics, test and measurement theory, and personality assessment in general and applied to multicultural psychology and human diversity in particular; (b) familiarity with different cultural groups and openness to discussing differences; (c) ability to establish rapport with the client; (d) ability to raise questions about the fit between test/measure and client background; (e) presence of a supervisory working alliance; (f) responsiveness to feedback about knowledge, skills, and attitudes, (g) ability to write reports that display sensitivity to culture and diversity; (h) ability to develop a cultural formulation from assessment findings; (i) ability to provide feedback in a culturally sensitive manner; and (j) cultural self-awareness. Tsong and Goodyear (2014) reported on the Supervision Outcome Scale as a psychometrically sensitive method for assessing how supervision impacts the supervisee in the areas of clinical and multicultural competence. There might be other categories that fit the supervisor's needs, and these categories have to be measured against the interests of the student's academic program, which conducts its own review of student competencies (e.g., Kaslow et al., 2009) that might or might not dovetail with the supervisor's preferences and methods. Of equal importance is the supervisor's competence in each of these areas, recognition of limits, and ability to take steps to strengthen weaker areas. Deficits in training, resistance to new learning, discomfort with the topics of race-ethnicity, or questions about the bases of multicultural and/or diversity research are among variables that can pose obstacles to achieving supervisory competence in the areas of multiculturalism and diversity (Falender & Shafranske, 2004), and compromise supervision outcomes. Learning about supervision and its roles (e.g., Majcher & Daniluk, 2009; Watkins, 2013) and about cultural self-awareness (Roysircar, 2004), might be the best way of staving off such resistance.

Conclusion

The roles and responsibilities of supervisors are defined by practice guidelines, ethics, and a comprehensive psychotherapy and counseling literature that provides essential information to the supervisor who strives to prepare supervisees for culturally competent assessment practice. There is much to absorb, assimilate, and organize, but the literature is both rich and ready for application. One such needed application is in the areas of personality assessment. Dana (2005) and Allen (2007) are among the few contributors with a primary assessment focus that integrates personality testing with multiculturalism. From their work it is easy to extend application to human diversity. Many of the core personality tests have been studied cross-culturally. More research on diversity applications and personality assessment supervision is needed. Integrating this knowledge into academic curricula is important as it provides a foundation for educating and training future supervisors who will oversee direct service to an increasingly multicultural and diverse clientele.

References

Abraham, P. (Summer, 2003). Multicultural/diversity assessment: An evolving process. *Society for Personality Assessment Exchange, 15*(2), 10–11, 22.

Allen, J. (2007). A multicultural assessment supervision model to guide research and practice. *Professional Psychology: Research & Practice, 38*(3), 248–258. doi: 10.1037/0735-7028.38.3.248.

American Educational Research Association, American Psychological Association, & National Council on Measurement in Education. (2014). *Standards for educational and psychological testing.* Washington, DC: American Educational Research Association.

American Psychological Association. (2003). Guidelines on multicultural education, training, research, practice, and organizational change for psychologists. *American Psychologist, 58*(5), 377–402. doi: 10.1037/0003-066X.58.5.377

American Psychological Association. (2010). *Ethical principles of psychologists and code of conduct.* (2002, Amended June 1, 2010). Retrieved from www.apa.org./ethics/code/index.aspx

American Psychological Association. (2012a). Guidelines for psychological practice with lesbian, gay and bisexual clients. *American Psychologist, 67*(1), 10–42. doi: 10.1027/a0024659

American Psychological Association. (2012b). Guidelines for assessment of and intervention with persons with disabilities. *American Psychologist, 67*(1), 43–62. doi: 10.1037/a0025892

American Psychological Association. (2015). Guidelines for clinical supervision in health service psychology. *American Psychologist, 70*(1), 33–48. http://dx.doi.org/10.1037/a0038112

Ancis, J. R., & Ladany, N. (2010). A multicultural framework for counselor supervision. In N. Ladany & L. J. Bradley (Eds.), *Counselor supervision* (pp. 53–94). New York: Routledge.

Andrews, E. E., Kuemmel, A., Williams, J. L., Pilarski, C. R., Dunn, M., & Lund, E. M. (2013). Providing culturally competent supervision to trainees with disabilities in rehabilitation settings. *Rehabilitation Psychology, 58*(3), 233–244. doi: 10.1037/a0033338

Aten, J. D., & Hernandez, B. C. (2004). Addressing religion in clinical supervision: A model. *Psychotherapy: Theory, Research, Training, 41*(2), 152–160. doi: 10.1037/0033-3204.41.2.152

Barker, K. K., & Hunsley, J. (2013). The use of theoretical models in psychology supervisor development research from 1994–2010: A systematic review. *Canadian Psychology, 54*(3), 176–185. doi: 10.1037/a0029694

Butcher, J. N. (2011). Fifty historical highlights in cross-cultural MMPI/MMPI-2/MMPI-A assessment. Retrieved from www.umn.edu/mmpi

Butcher, J. N., & Williams, C. W. (2009). Personality assessment with the MMPI-2: Historical roots, international adaptations, and current challenges. *Applied Psychology: Health and Well-Being, 1*(1), 105–135. doi: 10.1111/j.1758-0854.2008.01007.x

Byrne, B. M., Oakland, T., Leong, F. T. L., van deVijver, F. J. R., Hambleton, R. K., Cheung, F. M., & Barton, D. (2009). A critical analysis of cross-cultural research and testing practices: Implications for improved education and training in psychology. *Training and Education in Professional Psychology, 3*(2), 94–105. doi: 10.1037/a0014516

Canadian Psychological Association. (2000). *Canadian code for ethics for psychologists* (3rd ed.). Ottawa, ON: Author.

Canadian Psychological Association. (2009). *Ethical guidelines for supervision in psychology: Teaching, research, practice, and administration.* Ottawa, ON: Author.

Comas-Diaz, L. (2012). *Multicultural care: A clinician's guide to cultural competence.* Washington, DC: Author.

Correa, A. A., & Rodgers, R. (2010). Cross-cultural applications of the PAI. In M. A. Blais, M. R. Baity, & C. J. Hopwood (Eds.), *Clinical applications of the Personality Assessment Inventory* (pp. 135–148). New York: Routledge.

Dana, R. H. (2005). *Multicultural assessment: Principles, applications, and examples.* Mahwah, NJ. Erlbaum.

Exner, J. E. (2003). *The Rorschach: A comprehensive system, Vol. 1: Basic foundations and principles of interpretation* (4th ed.). New York: Wiley.

Falender, C. A., & Shafranske, E. P. (2004). *Clinical supervision: A competency-based approach.* Washington, DC: American Psychological Association.

Finkelstein, H., & Tuckman, A. (1997). Supervision of psychological assessment: A developmental model. *Professional Psychology: Research & Practice, 28*(1), 92–95.

Hall, G. C. N., Bansal, A., & López, I. R. (1999). Ethnicity and psychopathology: A meta-analytic review of 31 years of comparative MMPI/MMPI-2 research. *Psychological Assessment, 22*(2), 186–197.

Helms, J. E. (1990). *Black and White racial identity: Theory, research, and practice.* Westport, CT: Praeger.

Inman, I. G., & Kreider, E. D. (2013). Multicultural competences: Psychotherapy practice and supervision. *Psychotherapy, 50*(3), 346–350. doi: 10.1037a0032029

Jernigan, M. M., Green, C. E., Helms, J. E., Perez-Gualdron, L., & Henze, K. (2010). An examination of people of color supervision dyads: Racial identity matters as much as race. *Training and Education in Professional Psychology, 4*(1), 62–73. doi: 10.1037/a0018110

Jones, J., Sander, J. B., & Booker, K. (2013). Multicultural competency building: Practical solutions for training and evaluating student progress. *Training and Education in Psychology, 7*(1), 12–22. doi: 10.1037/a0030880

Kaslow, N. J., Grus, C. L., Campbell, L. F., Fouad, N. A., Hatcher, R. L., & Rodolfa, E. E. (2009). Competency assessment toolkit for professional psychology. *Training and Education in Professional Psychology, 3*(4, Suppl.), 527–545. doi: 10.1037/a0015833.

Krishnamurthy, R. (2013, March). Diversity-sensitive personality assessment: Considering cultural factors in determinations of maladjustment. In C. A. Denckla & K. M. Thomas (Chairs). *Current topics in personality assessment and diversity: Tips, insights, and guidelines for graduate students.* Symposium conducted at the Annual Meeting of the Society for Personality Assessment, San Diego, CA.

Krishnamurthy, R., & Yalof, J. A. (2010). The assessment competency. In M. B. Kenkel & R. L. Peterson (Eds.), *Competency-based education for professional psychology* (pp. 87–104). Washington, DC: American Psychological Association.

Ladany, N., Friedlander, M. L., & Nelson, M. L. (2005). *Critical events in psychotherapy supervision: An interpersonal approach.* Washington, DC: American Psychological Association.

Leong, F. T. L., Leung, K., & Cheung, F. M. (2010). Integrating cross-cultural psychology research methods into ethnic minority psychology. *Cultural Diversity and Ethnic Minority Psychology, 16*(4), 590–597. doi: 10.1037/a0020127

López, S. R. (1997). Cultural competence in supervision. In C. E. Watkins, Jr. (Ed.), *Handbook of psychotherapy supervision* (pp. 570–588). New York: Wiley.

Majcher, J. A., & Daniluk, J. C. (2009). The process of becoming a supervisor for students in a doctoral supervision training course. *Training and Education in Professional Psychology, 3*(2), 63–71. doi: 10.1037/a0014470

Malloy, K. A., Dobbins, J. E., Ducheny, K., & Winfrey, L. L. (2010). The management and supervision competency: Current and future directions. In M. B. Kenkel & R. L. Peterson (Eds.), *Competency-based education for professional psychology* (pp. 161–178). Washington, DC: American Psychological Association.

McCrae, R. R., & Terracciano, A., & 79 Members of the Personality Profiles of Cultures Project. (2005). Personality profiles of cultures: Aggregate personality traits. *Journal of Personality and Social Psychology, 89*(3), 407–425. doi: 10.1037/0022-3514.89.3.407

Meyer, G. J., Erdberg, P., & Shaffer, T. W. (2007). Toward the international normative reference data for the Comprehensive System. *Journal of Personality Assessment, 89*(S1), S201–S216. doi: 10.1080/00223890701629342

Nilsson, J. E., & Anderson, M. Z. (2004). Supervising international students: The role of acculturation, role ambiguity, and multicultural discussions. *Professional Psychology: Research & Practice, 35*(3), 306–312. doi:10.1037/0735-7028.35.3.306

Pace, T. M., Robbins, R. R., Choney, S. K., Hill, J. S., Lacey, K., & Blair, G. (2006). A cultural-contextual perspective on the validity of the MMPI-2 with American Indians. *Cultural Diversity and Ethnic Minority Psychology, 12*(2), 320–333. doi: 10.1037/1099-9809.12.2.320

Pettifor, J., McCarron, M. C. E., Schoepp, G., Stark, C., & Stewart, D. (2011). Ethical supervision in teaching research, practice, and administration. *Canadian Psychology, 52*(3), 198–205.

Piotrowski, C. (2015). Projective techniques usage worldwide: A review of applied settings 1995–2015. *Journal of the Indian Academy of Applied Psychology, 41*(3) (Special Issue), 9–19.

Ponterotto, J. G., Fietzer, J. W., Fingerhut, E. C., Woerner, S., Stack, L., Magaldi-Dopman, D., et al. (2014). Development and initial validation of the Multicultural Personality Inventory (MPI). *Journal of Personality Assessment, 96*(5), 544–558. doi: 10.1080/00223891.2013.843181

Rings, J. A., Genuchi, M. C., Hall, M. D., Angelo, M.-A., & Cornish, J. A. E. (2009). Is there consensus among predoctoral internship training direction regarding clinical supervision competencies? A descriptive analysis. *Training and Education in Professional Psychology, 3*(3), 140–147. doi: 10.1037/a0015054

Rodolfa, E., Greenberg, S., Hunsley, J., Smith-Zoeller, M., Cox, D., Sammons, M., et al. (2013). A competency model for the practice of psychology. *Training and Education in Professional Psychology, 7*(2), 71–83. doi: 10.1037/a0032415

Rosenberg, A., Almeida, A., & Macdonald, H. (2012). Crossing the cultural divide: Issues in translation, mistrust, and cocreation of meaning in cross-cultural therapeutic assessment. *Journal of Personality Assessment, 94*, 223–231. doi: 10.1080/00223891.2011.648293

Roysircar, G. (2004). Cultural self-awareness assessment: Practice examples from psychology training. *Professional Psychology: Research & Practice, 35*(6), 658–666. doi: 10.1037/0735-7028.35.6.658

Roysircar, G., Dobbins, J. E., & Malloy, K. A. (2010). Diversity competencies in training and clinical practice. In M. B. Kenkel & R. L. Peterson (Eds.), *Competency-based education for professional psychology* (pp. 179–197). Washington, DC: American Psychological Association.

Sashidharan, T., Pawlow, L. A., & Pettibone, J. C. (2012). An examination of racial bias in the Beck Depression Inventory-II. *Cultural Diversity and Ethnic Minority Psychology, 18*(2), 203–209. doi: 10.1037//a002/689

Schaffer, J. B., Rodolfa, E. B., Hatcher, R. L., & Fouad, N. A. (2013). Professional psychology competency initiatives: Reflections, contrasts, and recommendations. *Training and Education in Professional Psychology, 7*(2), 92–98. doi: 10.1027/a0032038

Shaffer, T. W., Erdberg, P., & Meyer, G. J. (2007). Introduction to the *JPA* special supplement on international reference samples for the Rorschach Comprehensive System. *Journal of Personality Assessment, 89*(S1), S2–S6. doi: 10.1080/00223890701629268

Singh, A., & Chun, K. Y. S. (2010). "From the margins to the center": Moving towards a resilience-based model of supervision for queer people of color supervisors. *Training and Education in Professional Psychology, 4*(1), 36–46. doi: 10.1037/a0017373

Society for Personality Assessment. (2006). Standards for education and training in psychological assessment: Position of the Society for Personality Assessment: An official statement of the Board of Trustees of the Society for Personality Assessment. *Journal of Personality Assessment, 87*(3), 355–367.

Stedman, J. M., Schoenfeld, L. S., & O'Donnell, L. (2013). An investigation of internship directors' perspectives on the learning and objectives required by the Commission on Accreditation. *Training and Education in Professionals Psychology, 7*(2), 134–138. doi: 10.1037/a0031660

Sue, D. W., & Sue, D. (1999). *Counseling the culturally different: Theory and practice* (3rd ed.). New York: Wiley.

Sutin, A. R., Costa, P. T. Jr., Evans, M. K., & Zonderman, A. B. (2013). Personality assessment in a diverse urban sample. *Psychological Assessment, 25*(3), 1007–1012. doi: 10.1037/a0032396.

Tsong, Y., & Goodyear, R. K. (2014). Assessing supervision's clinical and multicultural impacts: The Supervision Outcome Scale's psychometric properties. *Training and Education in Professional Psychology, 8*(3), 189–195. doi: 10.1037/tep0000049

Watkins, C. E. Jr. (1991). Psychodiagnostic assessment supervision: What do we really know about it? *Professional Psychology: Research & Practice, 22*(1), 3–4.

Watkins, C. E. Jr. (1993). Development of the psychotherapy supervisor: Concepts, assumptions, and hypotheses of the supervisor complexity. *American Journal of Psychotherapy, 47*(1), 58–74.

Watkins, C. E. Jr. (Ed.). (1997). *Handbook of psychotherapy supervision*. New York: Wiley.

Watkins, C. E. (2013). Being and becoming a psychotherapy supervisor: The crucial triad of learning difficulties. *American Journal of Psychotherapy, 67*(2), 135–151.

Watkins, C. E. Jr., & Scaturo, D. J. (2013). Toward an integrative, learning-based model of psychotherapy supervision: Supervisor alliance, educational interventions, and supervisee learning/relearning. *Journal of Psychotherapy Integration, 23*(1), 75–95. doi: 10.1037/a0031330

Yabusaki, A. S. (2010). Clinical supervision: Dialogues in diversity. *Training and Education in Professional Psychology, 4*(1), 55–61. doi: 10.1037/a0017378

Yalof, J., & Abraham, P. (2009). An integrative approach to assessment supervision. *Bulletin of the Menninger Clinic, 73*, 188–202.

CHAPTER 20

Evidence-Based Practice in Diversity-Sensitive Personality Assessment

Steven R. Smith and Radhika Krishnamurthy

In the preceding chapters, you have received extensive information on diversity-related topics, including assessment of diverse populations and best practices in diversity-sensitive personality assessment. There are, indeed, a number of ways that humans can differ from one another and the intersectionality of these identities can be head-dizzying. Do we need measures that are specifically designed, validated, and normed for *every possible* permutation and combination of diversity factors (e.g., socioeconomically disadvantaged and medically ill European-American women)? Given the overwhelming number of considerations presented in this text, we might begin to wonder what to *do* when it comes time to work with a particular client. How can we possibly begin to construct an appropriate test battery? Should we abandon the process of assessment completely?

Some might argue that psychological testing with non-majority populations should be abandoned due to the perception of bias. However, this is not feasible in light of the diverse clientele we assess in the current era. Others might potentially err in one of two directions in arriving at determinations of psychopathology: (a) not taking diversity factors into account, or (b) viewing diversity factors as wholly explanatory. We could think of these errors or oversights as somewhat analogous to Type I and Type II errors of signal detection theory and psychopathology diagnosis (e.g., Krishnamurthy, 2013). In the first "false positive" type of pathology-centered diagnostic error, we arrive at the conclusion that the client has significant psychopathology through bypassing or rejecting the role of diversity considerations. Such an oversight of diversity factors usually does not occur because of deliberate insensitivity. Rather, it likely arises from the typical psychopathology/symptomatology focus of clinical diagnostic assessment and/or the assessor's uncertainty about how to incorporate these alternative factors. In the second "false negative" type of pathology-centered diagnostic error, we dismiss the possibility of psychological maladjustment through attributing the client's presentation entirely to cultural variables. This might arise from a personal desire to be seen as benevolent, enlightened, and diversity-minded. Both types of errors, or biases, are problematic in terms of producing a faulty conclusion, and can be quite costly. Complicating these decisions is the fact that identifying the various sources of psychological difficulty is usually not a simple either/or proposition. In essence, one would need to consider both a pathology-centered hypothesis *and* a diversity-centered hypothesis (e.g., López, 2002), as well as the intersection of multiple variables within and across each domain.

Given the propensity to make one or the other of these errors, we need to engage in evidence-based practice. Luckily, most psychologists today are well-versed in the principles and concepts of evidence-based practice in psychology (EBPP Task Force, 2006).[1] Rather than a prescriptive list of treatment or assessment practices, EBPP describes a clinical approach that is grounded in research, informed by clinical experience, and guided by the needs, background, and desires of the patient. Although this is stated quite simply, the EBPP calculus is a complicated one, and the intersection of research, experience, and patient factors is not easily defined. However, as a guiding principle for assessment selection, it likely serves us well. Therefore, we have chosen to organize this chapter in three broad sections (i.e., research considerations, clinician considerations, and client considerations) prior to making some concluding recommendations and suggestions.

Research Considerations in Diversity-Sensitive Assessment Selection

The first component of EBPP is that psychologists should avail themselves of the best available research on personality constructs and specific assessment measures.

Research on Personality

Before a clinician can start a personality assessment, he or she should consider the universality of the constructs he or she wants to measure. Furthermore, what are the cultural variants in those constructs and how might they be expressed? McAdams and Pals (2006) outlined five broad principles for personality theory: (a) personality is a unique variant on evolution-derived human nature and is expressed as (b) a pattern of dispositional traits (e.g., the Big Five; Costa & McCrae, 1994), (c) characteristic adaptations (e.g., motivation and behavior related to social role and context), (d) in a larger life narrative that (e) takes place in a cultural and social context. They go on to state that

> Culture exerts different effects on different levels of personality: It exerts a modest effect on the phenotypic expression of traits; it shows a stronger impact on the content and timing of characteristic adaptations; and it reveals its deepest . . . influence on life stories, essentially providing a menu of themes, images, and plots for the psychosocial construction of narrative identity.
> (p. 211)

For example, they would argue that traits such as the Big Five might be consistent across cultures, but the expression of those traits is bounded by cultural norms. Therefore, extraversion might be common to both Asian and American cultures, but the expression of extraversion might be quite different, as would be the self-narrative around the trait. The same trait might lead to pride in one culture, but shame in another.

With this much complexity in the very science of personality theory, the assessment of personality in underrepresented groups requires substantial diligence. Given the principles of McAdams and Pals (2006), we must consider research on how different groups might tend to express personality traits and how those personality traits are responded to by the social and cultural groups in which they reside. A thorough review of the literature and diligent interviewing (particularly at the point of feedback) might help construct a general framework by which we can avoid either Type I or Type II errors and make full sense of the test results we obtain.

Research on Assessment Measures

In terms of the assessment measures themselves, research on diversity factors can be a challenging proposition given the general paucity of research using diverse samples. Furthermore, although things are changing in journal article publications, there has been a tendency for assessment researchers to neglect even adequately describing the demographics of their samples (Sumalpong, Cook, & Smith, 2011). However, as psychologists, we still have the burden of conducting psychological assessments using tests that are appropriate for a given question with a particular population.

According to classical test theory, there are three primary areas of consideration for evaluating a measure: the normative sample, score reliability, and score validity. First, the strength of conclusions about a given patient is often a function of the adequacy of a normative sample. For many patients from underrepresented groups, there is often little or no representation in normative samples or such groups are inadequately described. For example, the manual for the Personality Assessment Inventory (Morey, 2007) notes that the normative sample is comprised of about 79% European Americans, about 13% African Americans, and about 9% described as "other" (which presumably includes Latino/a, Native American, Asian American, and Pacific Islander individuals; Morey, 2007). Therefore, if a psychologist is grappling to interpret a PAI given by a Latino/a patient, how confident should she be that the patient is represented in that normative sample? What if the patient is biracial? What is the role of acculturation in determining appropriateness of a normative sample for a particular patient? Clearly, we cannot answer these questions here (and our goal is not to single out the PAI in this respect), but merely to highlight that we always need to be cognizant of the samples that help determine a measure's reflection of normative functioning.

Second, we need to consider the demonstrated score reliability for the measures we choose. Trochim (2000) notes that reliability is a function of the stability of a score, both internally (internal consistency) and across time (temporal stability). Although we might expect most aspects of score reliability to be unaffected by diversity factors, it might be that some populations generate scores that differ in consistency and stability from the majority (Dana, 2005). However, this inconsistency might be primarily related to the cross-cultural validity of the constructs in question. As a hypothetical example, if African American clients differed in their expression of depression relative to a measure's normative sample, then perhaps we might obtain scores that differed in terms of their temporal stability.

Third, and arguably the most important, are considerations of test score validity. As is true for all measures, validity is an indication of how adequately a test developer has translated a construct into a measureable form (Trochim, 2000). According to classical test theory, a test is an operationalized form of a latent variable that is thought to exist in some quantity in all people. For example, the Beck Depression Inventory, Second Edition (BDI-II; Beck, Steer, & Brown, 1996) is an operationalization of the variable of *depression*. An assumption of this measure is that *depression* is a variable that is more or less the same in all people, regardless of background. However, it might be that *depression* is fundamentally different across genders, age, ethnicity, religion, etc. Therefore, any operationalization of this latent construct will yield results that mean something different across different patient groups.

One way that researchers investigate the cross-cultural/diversity-related validity is to examine factor invariance. That is, if a factor analysis of a given measure is different across cultural groups, one can conclude that the measure is addressing a latent variable differently in different groups or that the latent variable itself is different across groups. Factor invariance analysis can be a powerful way to examine not only the measurement of a variable but also the consistency of a construct across groups. In fact, the BDI-II has consistently shown factor invariance across several samples of national and international samples (e.g., Dere et al., 2015) suggesting that its use with these groups is likely to be appropriate.

For any measure, validity is a function of the clinical question, prior research samples, and the presenting concerns of a client. We can never say that a measure is valid or invalid, only that its scores might be valid for a given question in a particular population. The validity of the measure's scores and their implications at a given time are a function of what we know from research. If a given clinical question with a particular population has not been adequately studied, we cannot be certain that a measure has validity for that population. For example, if a new measure seems to be a robust measure of anxiety in college students, we cannot know if it has validity for measuring anxiety in older people. We cannot say that this hypothetical measure is *not* valid, but merely that we do not have information about validity in another sample.

Given that assessment research has not adequately sampled underrepresented populations in the past, it might be that clinicians will be left with little robust data on the validity of their tools with some of their clients. In those cases, we urge clinicians to be cautious, consult when necessary, and acknowledge the limitations of the measures they have chosen. We also suggest that clinicians continue to remain abreast of the most updated literature on the populations they serve and the measures they choose. However, there will be times when all of the published research will still come up short and clinician experience will be an even more important component of the assessment process.

Clinician Experience-Related Considerations in Diversity-Sensitive Personality Assessment

When a skilled carpenter wields a hammer, he or she can craft marvelous things; when others of us wield hammers, we smash our thumbs and bend nails. Likewise, the relationship between a psychological assessor and a measure. When done right, experience with a particular tool can lead to increased efficiency, skill, and precision. However, research tells us that experience with a given tool can also result in overconfidence and drift from standardized procedures and best practices. This dichotomy is the double-edged sword of clinical experience with a particular measure or assessment question.

Measurement-related experience aside, clinician experience can have a vital role in the assessment of diverse populations. In EBPP, a clinician with good experience is the bridge between the controlled and group-oriented data from research and the individual patient struggling with a unique set of issues in a given context. In this perspective, the clinician acts as a translator between the nomothetic and the idiographic. And in cases where there are no research data to guide decision-making, clinicians must feel empowered to rely on their experience to do their best for the patient. As we note above, all patients have multiple intersecting identities and often present with multiple concerns; research simply cannot capture all of these intersections.

As a class exercise to teach students the importance of clinical experience in the face of limited research data, one of us (SRS) gives the students details derived from real-life cases from his practice and then asks the students to find what research literature would guide their choice of test and best practices for interpreting those tests, given the real-life assessment question. For example:

> The patient is a 12-year-old girl from the Middle East who, in an accident at home, was burned over 70% of her body. After brief emergency treatment in her home country, her parents decided to seek care in the United States. During the time in air travel, the girl's significant wounds became severely infected, resulting in significant brain damage. You are called in to the hospital to perform a baseline cognitive assessment of this girl who speaks no English, is on significant pain and antibiotic medication, and who has limited mobility due to bandages and skin grafts.

Clearly, there will be no research data on a case of this complexity and specificity, so if a clinician was hesitant to rely on experience, this girl might not receive services (even if those test results are questionable, at best). The complexity and multiple intersecting identities and contexts of our patients dictate that we often rely on our experiences, hunches, and best guesses (or the best guesses of supervisors). We expect psychologists to regularly consult the literature with the cases they see, but when coming up short, they often must make difficult decisions about how (or if) to proceed.

Clinician experience is particularly relevant when dealing with patients who are very different from us. As is noted in the first chapter of this text, clinician self-knowledge is a vital component to culturally competent care. If we want clinicians to be the translators between the nomothetic and idiographic realms, we expect them to be cautious and reflective about their assumptions, knowledge, and beliefs. In the absence of clear research data or recommendations, experience, consultation, and a cautious and informed use of hunches in the context of a larger hypothesis-testing approach are the best protections against clinical care that is either harmful or ineffective.

We recognize that there is a fine line between taking a clinical leap based on prior experience and acting outside of one's competency. There is a difference between a clinical stretch to a new problem and really being out of our clinical competency element. Our ethics code dictates that we maintain a strict adherence to our areas of competence (or that we seek supervision to "borrow" the competence of others) and competence is built by experience. Part of knowing one's competence is knowing when that competence has been exceeded and having the humility to refer the patient to another clinician. We assume, however, that clinicians will avail themselves of trainings, literature, and consultations that will continue to expand their cultural and assessment competence.

Another way that clinician experience is key in diversity-sensitive assessment is by understanding local context. All communities have a history that might be important for assessment. Is the community generally supportive of diversity? Has there been a community-wide trauma (such as a natural disaster)? Have there been conflicts around immigration? Has there been a general economic upheaval and loss of jobs? Are there idiosyncratic uses of language that might impact scores on cognitive or personality assessment measures? Understanding these sorts of contextual variables will not only help the clinician understand a particular patient, but also how a particular patient's identity variables are likely to be met in their given community at a particular point in time, and how those identity variables might evidence on a given test.

Client-Related Factors in Diversity-Sensitive Personality Assessment

According to EBPP, psychologists must adapt their work to meet the needs and wishes of the client, taking into account diversity factors. In a sense, client-related factors in diversity-sensitive personality assessment form the bulk of the focus of this book. The complexity of diversity is well covered in other chapters, but we wish to highlight the concept of *intersectionality*. Although definitions of intersectionality are somewhat controversial (Rosenthal, 2016), essentially the notion is that *identity* is a fluid construct wherein our various identifiers (e.g., African American, woman, Christian, homosexual) are more or less salient depending on context. Intersectionality arises from postmodernist and social constructive perspectives that suggest that there are multiple truths, and that those truths might be in flux given the demands of the greater system (Cole, 2009).

Recognizing the importance of our environments in shaping our self-narrative, an intersectional approach highlights the salience of various aspects of a patient's selfhood. An African American client in a region, occupation, or school system with few other African Americans will have a different way of thinking about themselves (and presenting themselves) than if they were in a system with more African Americans. In that sort of context, clients might grapple more with their own ethnic identity, face more racism, and be forced to reckon with their own racial development. As we see different aspects of our selfhood as discrepant from those in our surroundings, they become more salient and at the forefront of our minds.

Given that self-report measures assess a client's conscious self-representation and performance-based measures might capture themes related to personality dynamics, we must remember how each client's intersecting identity variables might impact assessment. Consider that personality assessment provides a snapshot of how a client presents in a particular sociocultural environment, so that interpreting a measure without awareness of context runs the risk of detrimental inaccuracy. Alternatively, over-interpreting a measure based on gender or ethnic variables when those variables might be less relevant can also lead to harm.

In this text, we have generally avoided narrow-band chapters on particular racial and/or ethnic groups, diagnoses, or other identifiers because such an approach runs the risk of stereotyping based on what the clinician might deem as most salient. By approaching diversity in a broad-band fashion, we encourage clinicians to have real conversations with their patients about what aspects of their identities are important and relevant given their setting, context, and current circumstances. Furthermore, in making interpretations, clinicians should consider the role of intersectionality in their attempts to have a genuine understanding of their patients and their lives. Under- and over-interpreting based on diversity factors is committing the same error.

Recommendations for Selecting Measures

Throughout this text and this chapter, we have consciously steered clear of providing a cookbook or template for different selecting or interpreting measures. We feel that such an approach negates the complexity of our clients and possibly leads to stereotyping. Not all diversity factors are salient for each individual, so there can be no simple algorithm for choosing measures for a particular purpose or type of client. Instead, we urge clinicians to avail themselves of the latest research and rely on their judgment and that of more experienced colleagues. In the spirit of honoring EBPP, we have a few suggestions for guiding principles.

Given the discussions of diversity-related factors in this text, how do we select measures for our patients that will be in keeping with EBPP? In most ways, diversity-sensitive assessment is just good patient-centered assessment. However, as we note above, greater humility and care are required the more different we are from our patients and their life experiences. In that spirit, we offer a number of recommendations for assessment selection:

1. Ultimately the assessor has to be better than the assessment measure, hence our emphasis in Chapter 1 on clinician self-appraisal. We should begin with a

thorough and honest appraisal of our biases, not only about patient factors (such as ethnicity, gender, etc.), but about assessment measures as well. If we believe that a particular measure is particularly robust, "insightful," or sensitive, we risk misinterpretation. In the same way we should be humble about our personal limitations, we need to be circumspect about our tools as well. This is particularly true when we have been using a particular measure for several years because it can make us prone to "interpretation drift."

2. In keeping with the spirit of therapeutic models of assessment (See Chapter 15), we need to actively involve patients in the assessment process. This includes comprehensive interviews that involve frank and honest appraisal of each patient's intersecting identities. Most importantly, patients (or their families), must be active and engaged in helping to shape and form the assessment question(s) to be answered. Finally, patients must be the final arbiters of the interpretation process, such that they feel they have a voice in shaping the clinician's interpretations.
3. Clinicians must avail themselves of the best psychometric data about the measures they choose. Evidence-based practice means that visiting the scientific literature should be a constant step in all of our clinical activities. How adequate are the norms? Is there research demonstrating equivalence with diverse populations? Is the assessment format appropriate for non-majority clients or those with physical disabilities?
4. Related to this, assessment clinicians need to continue to refine their interpretations based on available data and current nomenclature. Psychological assessment (particularly neuropsychological assessment) is a rapidly changing field with frequent updates to validity and interpretation information. Continuing to make interpretations based on habit or lessons from graduate school is not evidence-based practice and can lead to errors or mistakes that might have implications for the patients we serve. Consult and seek supervision when necessary.
5. We must always strike a balance between assessing diversity and assessing personality. Remember, the assessor does not have a binary choice between "personality" and "diversity." We must always remember the importance of context and diversity factors and how they impact our clients. On the other hand, we cannot get lost in the labyrinth of diversity facets and throw our hands up in the air, or opt for the easier option of eschewing use of psychological tests in favor of interview alone. Good clinical practice is, in fact, the melding of diverse expressions of personality variables that lead to rich and useful interpretations.
6. As is true for all forms of assessment, we should never rely on one measure in isolation. Psychological assessment involves the use of multiple measures interpreted in light of client history, presenting problem, and referral context. We urge clinicians to seek competence in a multimethod approach that captures both broad-band assessment of personality factors (e.g., MMPI-2) as well as specific symptom clusters (e.g., BDI-II) in different response formats. Incorporating performance-based measures (e.g., TAT, Rorschach) can also

provide data in a culture-rich and consistent manner. By incorporating both paper-and-pencil self-report with performance-based measurement, clinicians increase their perspectives and thus increase the likelihood that their data will be culturally sensitive and useful for the client.

Note

1 Although note that the phrase EBPP is frequently misused in the field as well (Shedler, 2015).

References

Beck, A. T., Steer, R. A., & Brown, G. K. (1996). *Manual for the Beck Depression Inventory-II.* San Antonio, TX: Psychological Corporation.

Cole, E. R. (2009). Intersectionality and research in psychology. *American Psychologist, 64*, 170–180. doi: 10.1037/a0014564

Costa, P. T. Jr., & McCrae, R. R. (1994). Stability and change in personality from adolescence through adulthood. In C. F. Halverson Jr., G. A. Kohnstamm, & R. P. Martin (Eds.), *The developing structure of temperament and personality from infancy to adulthood* (pp. 139–150). Hillsdale, NJ: Lawrence Erlbaum Associates.

Dana, R. H. (2005). *Multicultural assessment: Principles, applications, and examples.* Mahwah, NJ: Erlbaum.

Dere, J., Watters, C. A., Yu, S. C.-M., Bagby, R. M., Ryder, A. G., & Harkness, K. L. (2015). Cross-cultural examination of measurement invariance of the Beck Depression Inventory–II. *Psychological Assessment, 27*(1), 68–81. doi: 10.1037/pas0000026

EBPP Task Force. (2006). Evidence-based practice in psychology. *American Psychologist, 61*(4), 271–285.

Krishnamurthy, R. (2013, March). *Diversity-sensitive personality assessment: Considering cultural factors in determinations of maladjustment.* Paper presented at the Society for Personality Assessment annual convention, San Diego, CA.

López, S. R. (2002). Teaching culturally informed psychological assessment: Conceptual issues and demonstrations. *Journal of Personality Assessment, 79*, 226–234. doi: 10.1207/S15327752JPA7902_06

McAdams, D. P., & Pals, J. L. (2006). A new big five: Fundamental principles for an integrative science of personality. *American Psychologist, 61*, 204–217. doi: 10.1037/0003-066X.61.3.204

Morey, L. C. (2007). *Personality Assessment Inventory professional manual.* Odessa, FL: Psychological Assessment Resources.

Rosenthal, L. (2016). Incorporating intersectionality into psychology: An opportunity to promote social justice and equity. *American Psychologist, 71*, 474–485. doi: 10.1037/a0040323

Shedler, J. (2015). Where is the evidence for "evidence-based" therapy? *Journal of Psychological Therapies in Primary Care, 4*, 47–59.

Sumalpong, P., Cook, A., & Smith, S. R. (2011, March). *Ethnic and cultural diversity in psychological assessment literature: A preliminary content analysis.* Paper presented at the Society for Personality Assessment annual convention, Boston, MA.

Trochim, W. (2000). *The research methods knowledge base* (2nd ed.). Cincinnati, OH: Atomic Dog Publishing.

Index

Page numbers in *italics* indicate figures; page numbers in **bold** indicate tables.